cx/ɔ

Since 1947 Stephen M. Schwebel has written more than 100 articles, commentaries, and book reviews in legal and other periodicals and in the press. This volume republishes thirty-six of his legal articles and commentaries of continuing interest.

The first part treats aspects of the capacity and performance of the International Court of Justice. The second addresses aspects of international arbitration. The third examines problems of the United Nations, especially of the authority of the Secretary-General, the character of the Secretariat, and financial apportionment. The fourth deals with questions of international contracts and taking of foreign property interests. The fifth discusses diverse aspects of the development of international law and particularly considers the central problem of international law, the unlawful use of force.

This collection does not include Judge Schwebel's judicial opinions, nor (with one exception) papers written in his former official capacities as a legal officer of the US Department of State or as a special rapporteur of the International Law Commission of the United Nations. Together with his unofficial writings, his judicial opinions as of July 1993 are cataloged in the list of publications with which this volume concludes.

Justice
in
International Law

Stephen M. Schwebel

Justice
in
International Law

❧

Selected Writings of

STEPHEN M. SCHWEBEL

Judge of the International Court of Justice

GROTIUS PUBLICATIONS

CAMBRIDGE
UNIVERSITY PRESS

CAMBRIDGE UNIVERSITY PRESS
Cambridge, New York, Melbourne, Madrid, Cape Town, Singapore, São Paulo

Cambridge University Press
The Edinburgh Building, Cambridge CB2 8RU, UK

Published in the United States of America by Cambridge University Press, New York

www.cambridge.org
Information on this title: www.cambridge.org/9780521462846

First published 1994
This digitally printed version 2008

A catalogue record for this publication is available from the British Library

Library of Congress Cataloguing in Publication data

Schwebel, Stephen M. (Stephen Myron), 1929–
Justice in international law: selected writings of Judge Stephen M. Schwebel.
p.   cm.
Includes index.
ISBN 0 521 46284 3 (hardback)
1. International Court of Justice. 2. Arbitration, International.
3. United Nations. 4. International law. I. Title.
JX1971.6.S39   1994
341.5′2 – dc20   93–42341 CIP

ISBN 978-0-521-46284-6 hardback
ISBN 978-0-521-07299-1 paperback

To my brother Jack

CONTENTS

ॐ

PREFACE

૭

In taking up the invitation of Eli Lauterpacht, for which I am grateful, to compile a selection of my writings to be published by Grotius Publications in my sixty-fifth year, I have chosen a third of the legal articles and commentaries written since 1947 which may have a measure of continuing interest. They are republished as initially written. That is not to say that many of them would not benefit by revision, for hindsight is illuminating, particularly in a field which has developed as much as has international law in the last forty-five years. But to have brought these essays up to date would have been a time-consuming task inconsonant with more pressing demands. Thus whatever their limitations, these pieces are published essentially as they were. I do not today subscribe to all the views they express, but in the main, I do; it is chastening to acknowledge that neither the substance nor the style of my analyses has much improved over the years.

For their faithful typing onto a word processor of the considerable contents of this volume, my warm thanks to Jean van Hamel-Newall and Helen Jeffares. I wish to thank as well Robin Pirrie of Grotius Publications for able assistance in the planning of the publication of this compilation, and Mary Starkey of the Cambridge University Press and her colleagues for their exemplary editing and printing of it. The acquisition of Grotius Publications by the Cambridge University Press while this volume was in press has had the happy result that it is the first of what will be many books in the field to be published by the Cambridge University Press through its Grotius Publications division.

PART I
International Court of Justice

☙

Reflections on the Role of the International Court of Justice

ॐ

I greatly appreciate the privilege of giving the Jurisprudential Lecture this academic year at the University of Washington at the invitation of the *Washington Law Review*. It is a pleasure to return to this distinguished law school, which I visited years ago at the invitation of Professor Henderson. It is a particular pleasure for two reasons, apart from those of being at the University and revisiting Seattle. This occasion gives me the opportunity to see again one of my most valued former colleagues at the Office of the Legal Adviser of the Department of State, Professor Ted Stein. Professor Stein and I worked closely together in that great Office – perhaps the world's greatest office of the practice of public international law – in that happier day when the United States was plaintiff rather than defendant in the International Court of Justice – happier not of course for the imprisoned hostages; but I am sure you know what I mean when I use the word "happier."

Another reason why it is a particular pleasure to speak is that I do so under *Law Review* auspices. I wonder how many of you appreciate how uniquely and refreshingly American is the institution of the law review. I refer not to legal journals, which are widespread throughout much of the world; I speak of law reviews, produced at law schools not by faculty but by students. Law reviews are remarkable instruments of legal scholarship, of legal education, and healthily American irreverence. The law review editor does not hesitate to edit whatever and whomever he or she can get his or her hands on. It may irritate the contributor of an article or book review to have his principles and prose challenged by a youngster whom the contributor may see as more presumptuous than profound. But the process generally does both the contributor and the editor some good. In any event, it is an element in spurring the American lawyer to challenge authority, to ask questions, to demand citations, to seek the truth. I may add that I feel free to say these nice

Jurisprudential Lecture at the University of Washington, April 22, 1985. First published in *Washington Law Review*, 61, 3, p. 1061.

things about law review editors not having been one; I declined an invitation to compete for membership in the *Yale Law Journal*, for reasons that, subsequently, potential employers never found persuasive.

I would like this evening to share with you some reflections on the role of the International Court of Justice in an unjust world. You will appreciate that, while I shall try to speak the truth as I see it, I am not able to speak the whole truth: not only because I do not know it, but because of the constraints of my position and the confidentiality of aspects of the work of the Court. In particular, I shall not speak about matters which are *sub judice*, either in these remarks or in the answers to questions which some of you may wish to ask after them.

The Court is a body of high achievement and unused potential. But it is not a body of uniformly high achievement or unlimited potential. In the early years of this century, such a court was looked upon by the peace movement of that day as a means – if not *the* means – for avoiding resort to the use of force in international relations. It was thought that States should and even would submit to arbitration rather than the arbitrament of war. The Hague Peace Conferences of 1899 and 1907, which had a number of successes, particularly in codifying the law of war, succeeded in forming the Permanent Court of Arbitration. Actually, it was not a court which was permanently formed, and it arbitrated relatively infrequently. But arbitral panels drawn from the membership of the Permanent Court of Arbitration did dispose constructively of more than a score of international legal disputes, nearly all in the first three decades of this century. Nowadays, while the processes of international arbitration, and especially international commercial arbitration, go forward actively elsewhere, the main function of the Permanent Court of Arbitration lies in the role of its national groups of potential arbitrators who are the members of that Court in nominating candidates for election to the International Court of Justice. Each State Party to the Hague Convention of 1907 may nominate four persons as potential arbitrators, and these persons in turn nominate candidates of whatever nationality for election to the International Court. Where a State is not a party to the Hague Convention, it forms a comparable national group to make nominations. Judges of the Court are elected in concurrent elections of the Security Council and General Assembly.

It is interesting to recall that, in 1907, the United States took the lead at The Hague in pressing for the establishment of a true international court of justice. Agreement then proved elusive, especially on how the judges were to be elected. It was not practical to have a judge from every State, even though in 1907 there were less than fifty States, but the mechanism for selection or

4

election was not at hand. With the conclusion of the Covenant of the League of Nations, a mechanism was. Judges of the Permanent Court of International Justice were chosen by the concurrent election of the League Assembly and Council, thus mixing the predominant role of the smaller Powers in the Assembly with that of the larger in the Council.

In 1922, the first World Court in history came into operation, in the Peace Palace in The Hague, which a gift of Andrew Carnegie had built for the Permanent Court of Arbitration.

All too obviously, that Court did not succeed in preventing World War II or lesser wars. Nevertheless, it was regarded as a marked success, not only by international lawyers but by diplomats and politicians. For between 1922 and 1940, it successfully disposed of twenty-nine contentious cases between States, and rendered twenty-seven advisory opinions to the League of Nations (and, through it, several advisory opinions to the International Labor Organization [ILO] and a few to other international bodies). While those disputes almost invariably were not the stuff of war, they were often important, not only in the substance of the issues of which the Court's judgments disposed (many concerned the peace treaties), but because the Court's judgments, which were of high quality, contributed so significantly to the progressive development of international law. Consider the contributions of the courts in a common-law system to the development of the law. While the situation is not altogether the same in international law, there is ample room in that skeletal and primitive system of law for its development through the judicial decisions of a truly international court, representative of the principal legal systems of the world. As the late Judge Sir Hersch Lauterpacht so convincingly demonstrated in his classic study, *The Development of International Law by the International Court*,[1] that contribution has been significant indeed.

Thus, at the San Francisco Conference on International Organization at which the United Nations Charter was concluded, and in the preparatory meetings of the Committee of Jurists which prepared a revision of the Statute of the Permanent Court, there was not the slightest doubt about the utility of maintaining a world court. While it was found to be politically and legally desirable to create a new court, the International Court of Justice, its Statute was in fact a very modest revision of the Statute of the Permanent Court. Every effort was made to maintain continuity between the two Courts. It was recognized on all sides that the Permanent Court had created a heritage

---

[1] Sir Hersch Lauterpacht, *The Development of International Law by the International Court* (1958; repr. 1982).

worth preserving intact and nurturing. In this regard, attitudes towards the League of Nations and towards the World Court stood in striking contrast.

What has been the record of the International Court of Justice? In terms of cases dealt with, between the time it began functioning in April 1946 until the end of 1984, it gave forty-five judgments in contentious cases between States, and eighteen advisory opinions to the United Nations and certain of its Specialized Agencies. The number of contentious cases compares to that with which the Permanent Court dealt between the two World Wars, though the business of the Court since the mid-1960s has, until recently, been markedly less than earlier. In fact, in a world full of international legal disputes between States, too few are submitted to the Court, even if, for the moment, its docket is relatively full. Moreover, the United Nations and its Specialized Agencies have resorted to the Court for advisory opinions proportionately far less frequently than did the League and the ILO resort to the Permanent Court of International Justice in the eighteen years of its activity. It is widely agreed in the international legal community that the judgments and opinions of the Court have been sound and of high quality – though some maintain that there are a few extraordinary exceptions. The Court has been criticized for elliptical conclusions which at times are not sufficiently supported by reasons, and for insufficient citation of authority. Very recently, questions of observance of due process have been raised. But, as a whole and over the years, the Court's procedural and substantive record is very good.

A critical weakness of the World Court which has been manifest from 1922 persists. Its jurisdiction is at root optional and consensual. States must agree to bring their disputes to the Court, either when a dispute has arisen, or in advance of it. More often, after a dispute has arisen, the parties agree to bring it to the Court by concluding a special agreement to do so. This was the procedure in the *Gulf of Maine* case which Canada and the United States submitted to the Court, in which judgment was rendered last year. It is the procedure in the current case before the Court between Malta and Libya over the continental shelf boundary between them. There is nothing to stop States from submitting considerable numbers of cases in this way to the Court, apart from their apparent unwillingness to do so, about which I shall say something more in a moment.

But States may, if they wish, bind themselves in advance of when a particular dispute arises to submit disputes of that character to the Court. A large number of treaties – at the latest count, no less than 244 – provide that, if a dispute as to the treaty's interpretation or application arises, any party may submit the dispute to the International Court of Justice.

Such clauses have produced some cases: for example, the dispute between

Iran and the United States over the detention of American hostages was submitted to the Court under such treaties, and the Court sustained its jurisdiction under the multilateral Vienna Convention on Diplomatic Relations and the bilateral Treaty of Amity, Economic Relations, and Consular Rights between the United States and Iran. Iran did not appear, though it challenged the Court's jurisdiction. But the treaties in which the Imperial Government of Iran had submitted to the Court's jurisdiction remained in force, and they provided a valid basis for the Court to issue not only its order of provisional measures – an interim injunction – but its judgment.

In addition to agreeing in advance of a particular dispute to submit disputes arising under a particular treaty, States may generally and even comprehensively bind themselves to the Court's compulsory jurisdiction by making a declaration under the so-called "Optional Clause" of the Court's Statute.

There is a lot of history attached to the Optional Clause, and some of it is in the making. The Statute of the Permanent Court of International Justice was drafted in 1920 by a Committee of Jurists formed by the Council of the League. It was a distinguished committee, whose distinguished secretariat was composed primarily of League Under-Secretary-General Anzilotti (later President of the Court) and Ake Hammarskjöld, later the Court's first and longest-serving Registrar, and subsequently a judge (and the eldest brother of Dag Hammarskjöld). The draft Statute as prepared by that committee provided for general compulsory jurisdiction over legal disputes arising between the States Parties to the Statute.

It also provided, incidentally, that the sole official language of the Court should be French. Balfour, in a declaration for which he is not as well known as another, raised an objection, and English became one of the two official languages of the Court, which it remains.

As a result of discussion in the League Council, and subsequently in the League Assembly, the critical draft provision for the Court's mandatory, compulsory jurisdiction was deleted, a decision which was attributed to the influence of the Great Powers. In its place was put the "Optional Clause." By its terms, States Parties to the Statute may agree – and that is their option – to submit to the Court any legal dispute which may arise in the future between them and other States reciprocally so agreeing. It soon became the practice to attach reservations to the extent of such agreement.

The Optional Clause was regarded in 1920 as a sensible and promising compromise between, on the one hand, confining the Court to jurisdiction over such disputes as the parties could agree to submit to it after a dispute had arisen, and, on the other, endowing the Court with general compulsory jurisdiction over all legal disputes between parties to the Statute. If most

States were progressively to adhere to the Optional Clause, it was believed, then the Court would, step by step, achieve that general compulsory jurisdiction which the League thought premature in 1920. And, in fact, in the interwar years, the Optional Clause went a long way towards achieving that goal, since the very large majority of the States then in existence adhered to it. Forty-four States at one time or another deposited declarations accepting the jurisdiction of the Permanent Court of International Justice under the Optional Clause. They included Great Britain, France, and China. They did not include the United States, which, despite a good deal of effort in various quarters, never became a party to the Statute of the Permanent Court, and they did not include the Soviet Union.

Moreover, these forty-odd adherences did not contain crippling reservations. But today the situation is radically different – if one can apply the word "radical" to so regressive a tendency. Today, only 47 of the 162 States party to the Statute of the International Court of Justice are bound at all under the Optional Clause. Only 19 of those adherences are not expressly subject either to unilateral termination by the declarant State at any time, or to modification at any time. The Soviet Union has never adhered to the Court's compulsory jurisdiction under the Optional Clause; neither China nor France currently adhere. The only Permanent Member of the Security Council party to the Optional Clause other than the United States is the United Kingdom, which has reserved "the right at any time . . . and with effect from the moment of . . . notification, either to add to, amend or withdraw" any of its extensive reservations, and this in a declaration which has been made "until such time as notice may be given to terminate" it.[2] Many other leading States, including Algeria, Argentina, Brazil, the Federal Republic of Germany, Italy, Poland and the other States of Eastern Europe, Senegal, and Syria, do not adhere to the Optional Clause.

Furthermore, far-reaching reservations are not merely temporal. Most notably, some would say notoriously, are self-judging reservations, of which there are about a half-dozen. The United States was the pioneer with the Connally Reservation, which withholds from the Court's compulsory jurisdiction "disputes with regard to matters which are essentially within the domestic jurisdiction of the United States of America as determined by the United States of America."[3] While as a matter of legal principle self-judging reservations are most objectionable, conflicting as they do with the authority of the Court under its Statute to determine its jurisdiction, in practice other reservations may have more effect in withholding disputes from the Court.

---

[2] International Court of Justice, *Yearbook 1983–1984*, pp. 89, 90.   [3] *Ibid.*, p. 90.

These and other dolorous facts led a distinguished scholar who later became President of the Court, Sir Humphrey Waldock, to write a noted article entitled "The Decline of the Optional Clause."[4] Despite recent events on which I am not free to comment, it is not possible to conclude that that decline has been arrested. On the contrary, there are indications that it may accelerate. The Government of the United States has announced that it will examine reformulating the terms of its adherence to the Court's compulsory jurisdiction. That will be a matter of national concern, on which not only the Administration – and of course the Senate – but the bar, the academic community, and learned societies all have a contribution to make.

In sum, the Court's compulsory jurisdiction is not general, is not increasing, and is under attack insofar as it does exist. The blame for that deplorable situation lies in various quarters. The situation is not helped by the tendency of some of those who have refused to submit themselves to the Court's jurisdiction to cluck at the disadvantages and discomfiture of those who have. Moreover, some States, whose distrust of international adjudication is a matter of ideology, have strongly and rather successfully resisted writing the Court's compulsory jurisdiction into treaties concluded under the auspices of the United Nations.

The Court is confronted by another problem no less grave than the decline of the Optional Clause and resistance to other avenues of its jurisdiction: the refusal in some cases of certain States defendant to appear in Court even where the Court clearly or arguably has jurisdiction. This has happened five times in the history of the International Court of Justice. It is a development which contrasts painfully with the record of the Court between the two World Wars, when States regularly appeared to argue and invariably abided by the results. Whatever view one takes of recent developments, it may be noted that, of all the States which have been the object of a request for an order of provisional measures in the International Court of Justice, only the United States has appeared, and it has done so in two cases.

Still another, obviously fundamental, problem of the Court is that of conformity with its judgments. That too was not a problem of the Permanent Court. But it is a problem which has arisen so far no less than three times in the history of the International Court of Justice. I am speaking now not of conformity with orders of the Court for provisional measures, which are not binding upon the States to which they are addressed, but of final judgments of the Court. Again, this is a problem which shows no sign of amelioration, but rather of exacerbation.

---

[4] Sir Humphrey Waldock, "The Decline of the Optional Clause," *British Year Book of International Law 1955–1956* (1957), 32, p. 244.

Still another weakness of the current structure of international adjudication complements that of failure to comply with judgments of the Court. Even though under the United Nations Charter the Security Council is authorized to make recommendations or decide upon measures to be taken to give effect to a judgment of the Court, the Security Council does not appear to be seen as a reliable enforcer of the Court's judgments. Its voting to give effect to Court judgments would be subject to the limitations which govern voting upon its other substantive matters. In the event, the party in whose favor the Court has ruled has not generally had recourse to the Security Council, presumably because it has apprehended that the Council would not effectively support the Court's judgment.

Still another pervasive weakness of the structure of modern international adjudication is that States and international organizations freely resort to the Court less frequently than they did and certainly less frequently than they should. Why? That is not clear in the nature of things, but various explanations have been proffered:

- International relations are in large measure run by politicians and diplomats who like to keep their hands on the disposition or indisposition of problems; they do not want lawyers and the law telling them what they must do but prefer "to keep their options open."
- States are unwilling to lose cases. They too often are prepared to go to Court only when they believe that they will win. Thus they sacrifice their higher, long-term interest in a working system of peaceful settlement for the transient interests of a particular case.
- The content of international law is uncertain, that is to say, the law to be applied by the Court is uncertain.
- The Court is unpredictable in its application of the law.
- The United Nations (and too often its specialized agencies) act on the basis of political rather than legal considerations and wish to remain free to do so, unrestrained by the Court's advisory opinions.

All of these theories – and there are others as well – may have some basis in fact. Whatever the causes, the effects are clear. The processes of international adjudication, particularly those concentrated at its summit in the International Court of Justice, are under-used. At the same time, one must bear in mind that there are not thousands or millions of potential litigants before the Court. Only States may be parties to contentious cases, and there are some 170 States in the world.

Nevertheless, it could not be more obvious that peaceful settlement of international disputes is preferable to continuing conflict. It is equally obvious that peaceful settlement on the basis of law builds expectations of consistency and stability in international life, and that application of the law by an impartial international court both solves particular disputes and contributes to the development of the law.

At the same time, for the Court to be seen as impartial, it must be impartial, and act impartially. That requires the most scrupulous adherence to its Rules and the most careful regard for its precedents. The structure of international adjudication is fragile. The States which have a tradition and a practice of devotion to international arbitration and adjudication are in a minority. If the impression should be given and grow that the interests of such States are expendable, that, when it comes to them, or certain of them, the Court can take liberties not earlier taken, the Court risks losing the support of those States which have created and sustained it.

I am afraid that I have spoken so far in a predominantly pessimistic way. I am sorry to say that there are in fact grounds for pessimism. But there are more promising countervailing trends as well.

In the first place, the Court is a far busier place these days than it has been for some years; its docket has been fuller the last twelve months than it has been for some twenty-five years. Second, there appears to be an increasing tendency among some of the newer States to bring cases to the Court. Third, the Court has grappled, and is soon to grapple, with new problems, such as intervention by a third State in proceedings between two other States, or interpretation or revision of a judgment already handed down. There may be room for difference of opinion about how constructively the Court has dealt with these new problems, but the fact that it is being confronted with them is – or so I am determined to think – a sign of life and vitality. And finally, there is a new departure in the practice of the Court: the constitution of a chamber of judges out of the membership of the full Court which renders a judgment in the name of the Court.

More than a decade ago, the Court, faced with the paradox that, in a world full of international legal disputes, it had relatively little business, set about revising its Rules. A primary revision was to facilitate access by States to chambers of the Court – to a group of judges less than the whole court – for a particular case. The main change, a former President of the Court wrote, was "to accord to the Parties a decisive influence in the composition of *ad hoc* Chambers."[5] This was done by introducing into the Rules of Court the provision that, where the Parties to a case have agreed upon the formation of

---

[5] Eduardo Jiménez de Aréchaga, "The Amendments to the Rules of Procedure of the International Court of Justice," *American Journal of International Law* (1973), 67, pp. 1, 2.

a chamber to deal with a particular case, the President of the Court "shall ascertain their views regarding the composition of the Chamber, and shall report to the Court accordingly."[6] By the terms of the Court's Statute, a judgment given by a chamber "shall be considered as rendered by the Court."[7]

The first such chamber was constituted by the Court in response to a request of the United States and Canada in the *Gulf of Maine* case. It was not easily constituted, but constituted it was. Despite the differences in the Court about the composition of the chamber, it functioned extremely well. It rendered an important judgment determining a single, comprehensive maritime boundary, governing both the continental shelf and fishing above it, which Canada and the United States have accepted and implemented. And now a request from Mali and Upper Volta – renamed Burkina Faso – is pending before the Court for constitution of another chamber, to pass upon a land boundary dispute.

Chambers of the Court offer what could prove to be an attractive halfway house between international arbitration and adjudication. While recourse to the full court is closer to the ideal, in the real world chambers may sometimes afford States a likelier forum by permitting them a voice in the choice of judges. They thus provide that advantage of arbitration while at the same time having the advantages over arbitration of an accepted body of rules of procedure and the facilities of the Court in The Hague. Proceedings before a chamber of the Court should be less expensive for the parties than those which require forming and funding of an arbitral tribunal.

There will remain an important role for international arbitration, which the current Iran–United States Claims Tribunal, also at work in The Hague, demonstrates in dealing with some thousands of damage claims. But the chamber system may well mark a marriage between the processes of international arbitration and adjudication which holds some promise for a more effective rule of law in international life. It may offer the opportunity to States otherwise unwilling to submit disputes to the Court to make use of its facilities and possibilities. At the same time, the chamber system may perhaps present dangers of fractionalizing the Court and the development of international law. But, in my view, it presents markedly more opportunity for progress than dangers to that progress. Certainly there is nothing in the judgment of the Chamber in the *Gulf of Maine* case that suggests a regional or parochial view of international law.

---

[6] International Court of Justice, *Rules of Court*, Article 17, para. 2.
[7] Statute of the International Court of Justice, Article 27.

Human institutions rarely grow and prosper in an unbroken pattern of progress. It is not surprising that so frail an institution as international adjudication not only has congenital weaknesses but that it may have caught some of the diseases of its environment. We live in a world in which international law and international institutions, while enormously valuable, are nevertheless dangerously far from being as effective as they should be and need to be if this is to be a less troubled and precarious world. There is no use in pretending that we have the sort of international law we need simply because we need it. On the contrary, there is a need for realism, for sobriety, for a critical spirit – and for a constructive spirit. On the whole, the World Court has a distinguished record of achievement – even if that record is not as extensive or exemplary as one might wish. It is one of the principal tasks of the student and practitioner of international law, and, for that matter, of people the world over who are concerned with promoting a more peaceful and less lawless world, to give their critical but constructive support to the strengthening of the institutions of international adjudication, and especially the only universal such institution, the International Court of Justice.

2

Relations Between the International Court of Justice and the United Nations

❧

The principles governing relations between the International Court of Justice and the United Nations at first sight seem clear. On reflection, and in the light of practice, they are, in a few important respects, not quite so clear.

Let us begin at the beginning, with the pertinent provisions of the United Nations Charter. Chapter XIV of the Charter is devoted to the International Court of Justice. Article 92 provides:

> The International Court of Justice shall be the principal judicial organ of the United Nations. It shall function in accordance with the annexed Statute, which is based upon the Statute of the Permanent Court of International Justice and forms an integral part of the present Charter.

The first sentence of Article 92 complements Article 7 of the Charter, which establishes among "the principal organs of the United Nations ... an International Court of Justice."

What significance is to be attached to the status of the Court as the principal judicial organ of the United Nations? In particular, is the Court to be judicial, or is it to be an organ of the United Nations – two attributes which may not invariably be altogether consistent? To the extent that the Court is to be both judicial and an organ of the United Nations, how may and should these attributes be reconciled?

The second sentence of Article 92 provides a partial answer to that question in that it specifies that the Court "shall function" in accordance with its Statute which is "annexed" to the Charter, which Statute is "based upon" the Statute of the Permanent Court of International Justice and which "forms an integral part of the present Charter." The Permanent Court of International Justice (PCIJ), which, though intimately related to the League of Nations, was not an organ of it, operated as a judicial body; it did not act as an organ of

First published in *Le Droit International au Service de la Paix, de la Justice et du Développement, Mélanges Michel Virally* (1991), Paris, Editions Pedone.

an international organization responsive to its policies rather than to legal considerations. Thus that the International Court of Justice "shall" function in accordance with a Statute based upon – indeed, very closely based upon – the Statute of the Permanent Court may be read to mean that the Court shall function as a judicial organ. Yet, in contrast to the position of the PCIJ, the International Court of Justice is an organ of the United Nations; in contrast to the Covenant of the League, its Statute is part of the Charter. Thus what is of greater importance than the ambivalent precedent of the PCIJ and the Covenant is that the Court shall function in accordance with the Statute which is annexed to the Charter and which "forms an integral part" of it.

I have elsewhere maintained that "because of the meaning of the term 'integral', i.e., composed of constituent parts making a whole, it is clear" that two legal instruments which are described as integral "must be read together as the integral whole which they are proclaimed to be."[1] I there observed that my colleagues of a Chamber of the Court shared this conclusion, and indeed

> could hardly do otherwise. It [the Chamber] itself is a creature of a treaty, its Statute, which, the United Nations Charter provides, "forms an integral part of the present Charter." It would be hard to conceive of an argument that nevertheless the Statute and Charter are not to be interpreted together, as a single instrument forming an integral whole, and harder still to imagine that the Court could accept such an argument.[2]

In practice, as that eminent commentator on the Court, Shabtai Rosenne, has concluded:

> when the Charter uses the expression that the Statute is an integral part of the Charter, it intends that the Charter and the Statute are to be read as one instrument. That does not mean that there is any subordinate status in the Statute in relation to the Charter . . . What it does mean, however, is that those portions of the Charter which are of general application to the Organization as a whole, and to each one of its organs individually, are applicable also to the Court. In particular, the principles and purposes for which the Organization exists apply to the Court as much as to any other organ.[3]

Dr. Rosenne supports this conclusion with his customary careful examination of the Court's jurisprudence.[4]

But while the Charter and the Statute are to be read together as one

---

[1] *Elettronica Sicula S.p.A. (ELSI), Judgment, ICJ Reports 1989*, Dissenting Opinion of Judge Schwebel, p. 96.

[2] *Ibid.*, p. 96–97.   [3] S. Rosenne, *The Law and Practice of the International Court* 1965, Vol. I, p. 68.

[4] Two interpretations of Article 92 are possible. One interpretation, stressing, as the dominant principle, the intention of the founders of the United Nations to maintain the functional continuity of the two Courts, would place the emphasis upon the essential independence of the Statute from the

instrument, the provisions of the Statute are the provisions in accordance with which the Court "shall function" (as is reiterated by Article 1 of the Statute). Article 2 of the Statute provides that:

> The Court shall be composed of a body of independent judges, elected regardless of their nationality from among persons of high moral character, who possess the qualifications required in their respective countries for appointment to the highest judicial offices, or are jurisconsults of recognized competence in international law.

Article 9 is not inconsistent in adding that:

> not only that the persons to be elected should individually possess the qualifications required, but also in the body as a whole the representation of the main forms of civilization and of the principal legal systems of the world should be assured.

Article 16 provides that: "No Member of the Court may exercise any political ... function." Article 18 provides that: "No Member of the Court can be dismissed unless, in the unanimous opinion of the other Members, he

Charter in the same way that the old Statute was distinct from the Covenant. This point of view would regard the undoubted organic connection between the Court and the United Nations as having primarily an administrative or ministerial significance. This would mean that the governing principles of the Charter operate only to the extent that the relations of the United Nations to the Court are concerned; applying that is to say, to Chapter XIV of the Charter, but not to the working of the Court, so that the Court is not limited in its freedom of action by those provisions of the Charter which may limit the freedom of action of the other organs of the United Nations. Such an interpretation would attribute no more than formal value to the statement, appearing in the Charter but not in the Statute, that the annexed Statute forms an integral part of the Charter. It would also imply disregarding, or at least minimizing the importance of, the undoubted closer organic connection that now exists. Some support for this view can be seen in the *Corfu Channel* case (preliminary objection) where a joint separate opinion of seven out of the 15 judges of the Court declined to regard the Charter, particularly Article 36 (3), as affecting the jurisdiction of the Court according to the Statute.

This however, does not seem to be the interpretation placed on these words by the majority of the judges who, after stating that the working of the Court is governed by the Statute and not by the Charter, yet gave an interpretation to the Statute and Rules of Court which would render effective certain action which had been taken by the Security Council. Later, in the *Peace Treaties* case, the Court found it necessary to deal with a preliminary objection to its competence, based on the theory that the Court, as an organ of the United Nations, is bound to observe the provisions of the Charter, including Article 2 (7) (the so-called domestic jurisdiction clause). The fact that the Court dismissed the objection is immaterial. The important thing is that the Court did not deal with that objection *a priori* by summarily dismissing it, but disposed of it only after an examination of its merits. This suggests that the organic connection of the Court with the United Nations points to a societal relationship between the two, meaning, in this context, that the problems of interpretation are to be solved on the basis that the Court exists and functions in line with the general existence and functioning of the United Nations. In the *Aerial Incident of 27 July 1955* case the Court stated as a principle that in order to interpret a provision appearing in the Statute, it should consider it "in its context and bearing in mind the general scheme of the *Charter and the Statute*". This point of view may also be observed in the attitude of the General Assembly and the Security Council, which have been careful to preserve the functional independence of the Court and have hesitated to impose upon it tasks which would be incompatible with the judicial function.

(*Ibid.*, pp. 66–67; footnotes omitted.)

has ceased to fulfill the required conditions." Article 19 provides that: "The Members of the Court, when engaged on the business of the Court, shall enjoy diplomatic privileges and immunities." Article 20 provides that: "Every Member of the Court shall, before taking up his duties, make a solemn declaration in open court that he will exercise his powers impartially and conscientiously." Article 13 provides that the Members of the Court shall be elected for nine years and may be re-elected; and Article 32 provides that the salaries, allowances, and compensation of judges "may not be decreased" during their term of office and "shall be free of all taxation." Finally, Article 38 provides that the function of the Court is to decide "in accordance with international law" such disputes as are submitted to it and further provides that it shall in so doing apply specified sources of law (inferentially, not political or other sources of decision-making).

The foregoing provisions, taken together, establish that the International Court of Justice is – and certainly is intended to be – an independent, judicial organ, and no less a judicial organ because at the same time it is the principal judicial organ of the United Nations. In reaching its judgments and advisory opinions, it shall take account of the generally applicable provisions of the United Nations Charter, particularly its Purposes and Principles. That requirement does not detract from the Court's judicial character, not only because of the content of those Purposes and Principles (which speak, *inter alia*, of "conformity with the principles of justice and international law") but because the States and international organizations which plead before the Court in any event are obliged to take account of those Purposes and Principles. At the same time, the fact that the Court is a principal organ of the Organization may influence its readiness to participate in the work of the Organization particularly insofar as it is requested by other organs to render advisory opinions – a matter to be dealt with shortly.

Let us turn now to Article 93 of the Charter, which provides:

1. All Members of the United Nations are *ipso facto* parties to the Statute of the International Court of Justice.
2. A State which is not a member of the United Nations may become a party to the Statute of the International Court of Justice on conditions to be determined in each case by the General Assembly upon the recommendation of the Security Council.

These provisions are straightforward. They are no less significant, for, in contrast with the situation of the PCIJ, they assure the Court of a constituency, the membership of the United Nations, which today is virtually universal. The provisions for a non-member State becoming a party to the Court's Statute have worked smoothly.

The same cannot be said of Article 94 of the Charter, which provides:

1. Each Member of the United Nations undertakes to comply with the decision of the International Court of Justice in any case to which it is a party.
2. If any party to a case fails to perform the obligations incumbent upon it under a judgment rendered by the Court, the other party may have recourse to the Security Council, which may, if it deems necessary, make recommendations or decide upon measures to be taken to give effect to the judgment.

While compliance by Members of the United Nations with the Court's decisions has been general, it has not been invariable. In the two cases in which a party consequently has had recourse to the Security Council, the Council has not deemed it necessary to make recommendations or decide upon measures to be taken to give effect to the decision or judgment. In other cases in which there has been non-compliance with a judgment of the Court, the winning party has not had recourse to the Security Council, presumably in the belief that such recourse would not prove productive. In principle, Article 94 affords judgments of the Court possibilities of enforcement of great potential; in practice, that potential has yet to be realized. Given the uncertainties of international law and life, it would be unjustified to conclude that Article 94 may not assume greater practical importance than it has.

Article 95 of the Charter provides:

Nothing in the present Charter shall prevent Members of the United Nations from entrusting the solution of their differences to other tribunals by virtue of agreements already in existence or which may be concluded in the future.

This Article requires no comment in the current context except to observe that the United Nations, in providing in the Third United Nations Convention on the Law of the Sea for the establishment of a Law of the Sea Tribunal, may have made provision for a court to which eventually may be removed a large part of the traditional docket of the International Court of Justice.

Finally, Article 96 of the Charter provides:

1. The General Assembly or the Security Council may request the International Court of Justice to give an advisory opinion on any legal question.
2. Other organs of the United Nations and specialized agencies, which may at any time be so authorized by the General Assembly, may also request advisory opinions of the Court on legal questions arising within the scope of their activities.

Article 96 is central to relations between the Court and the United Nations. It authorizes the General Assembly and Security Council to request the Court to give advisory opinions "on any legal question" – a very broad authority indeed; so broad that it has been argued that this provision would entitle the General Assembly to serve as a conduit (though a conditional rather than a "mere" conduit) for requests to the Court from national courts to answer international legal questions arising in the course of national judicial proceedings.[5] While other organs of the United Nations and Specialized Agencies may request advisory opinions only on legal questions "arising within the scope of their activities," this limitation constrains no more than it should.

Some twenty advisory opinions have been requested of the Court by the General Assembly, the Security Council, the Economic and Social Council, and a few Specialized Agencies of the United Nations. The great majority of advisory opinions have been requested by the General Assembly, more frequently in the earlier years of the work of the Organization than in later years.

While in the era of the League of Nations, the League Council, acting under the Unanimity Rule, was the invariable source of requests for advisory opinions (or the immediate source, for it requested opinions not only on League questions, but on questions posed by the International Labor Organization (ILO) or sought on behalf of other international organizations or by States), the organs and organizations which have requested the opinion of the International Court of Justice have sometimes acted in more contentious circumstances. A majority, over the opposition not only of a minority viewpoint on the question at issue, but over the opposition of a minority to asking the Court for its opinion at all, has put a question or questions to the Court. The Court has acted independently in responding to those questions. A majority of the Court has not necessarily shared what may have appeared to be the view of a majority of the requesting organ (as is illustrated, for example, by the opinions rendered by the Court on the *Competence of the General Assembly for the Admission of a State to the United Nations*[6] and in proceedings brought to review certain judgments of the United Nations Administrative Tribunal[7]). At the same time, however clearly the position of the majority of the members of a United Nations organ on the answer to the question put might emerge from a reading of the dossier, the questions themselves have been posed in resolutions which were objectively cast. Those

---

[5] For an examination of the constitutionality and desirability of this proposal, see Stephen M. Schwebel, "Preliminary Rulings by the International Court of Justice at the Instance of National Courts," *Virginia Journal of International Law* (1988), 28, 2, p. 495; and Shabtai Rosenne, "Preliminary Rulings by the International Court of Justice at the Instance of National Courts: A Reply," *ibid.*, (1989) 29, 2 p. 401, as well as the sources there cited.

[6] *ICJ Reports 1950*, p. 4.

[7] E.g., *Application for Review of Judgement No. 273 of the United Nations Administrative Tribunal, ICJ Reports 1982*, p. 325.

resolutions do not presume to answer the question put to the Court. That seems elementary, not only because an answer to a legal question normally should not be sought by an organ that purports to know it but because the appearance of telling the Court what the answer is to the question put to the Court is not consonant with the judicial character and independence of the Court.

A striking departure from this practice is found in the advisory proceedings on the *Applicability of the Obligation to Arbitrate under Section 21 of the United Nations Headquarters Agreement of 26 June 1947*. The General Assembly, in requesting the Court's advisory opinion as to whether the United States was under an obligation to enter into arbitration in accordance with Section 21 of the Headquarters Agreement, affirmed the position of the Secretary-General "that a dispute exists between the United Nations and the host country concerning the interpretation or application of the Agreement" (resolution 42/229B). In its companion resolution 42/229A, also adopted on March 2, 1988, the General Assembly considered "that a dispute exists between the United Nations and the United States ... concerning the interpretation or application of the Headquarters Agreement, and that the dispute settlement procedure set out in section 21 of the Agreement should be set in operation." That is to say, the General Assembly, after appearing to answer the question on which it sought the advice of the Court, requested the Court's opinion on that very question. Thereafter, on March 23, 1988, while proceedings in the Court were pending, the General Assembly reaffirmed its answer by holding "that a dispute exists between the United Nations and the United States ... concerning the interpretation or application of the Headquarters Agreement, and that the dispute settlement procedure provided for under section 21 of the Agreement ... should be set in operation ..." (resolution 42/230).[8]

What is appropriate is the practice of the Court in holding that, as the principal judicial organ of the United Nations, its reply to a request for an advisory opinion represents the Court's participation in the activities of the Organization and, in principle, should not be refused, unless there are compelling reasons for such a refusal.[9] In fact, the Court has never declined to answer a question so put to it.

So much for Chapter XIV of the Charter. There are other articles as well of the Charter that concern the Court and other articles of the Statute that give rise to relations between the United Nations and the Court.

---

[8] *ICJ Reports 1988*, p. 12.

[9] *Interpretation of Peace Treaties with Bulgaria, Hungary and Romania, First Phase, ICJ Reports 1950*, p. 71. This position has been regularly reaffirmed in subsequent opinions.

Under Chapter VI of the Charter, on the Pacific Settlement of Disputes, the parties to any dispute, the continuance of which is likely to endanger the maintenance of international peace and security, shall seek a solution by various specified means, including judicial settlement. Article 36 empowers the Security Council to recommend appropriate procedures or methods of adjustment of disputes which may endanger international peace, and further provides:

> In making recommendations under this Article the Security Council should also take into consideration that legal disputes should as a general rule be referred by the parties to the International Court of Justice in accordance with the provisions of the Statute of the Court.

The Security Council has employed this authority only once, when it recommended to the Governments of the United Kingdom and Albania that they "should immediately refer the dispute to the International Court of Justice" which had arisen between them over the Corfu Channel incident.[10]

What if the Security Council does not refer a dispute to the Court but if, when a dispute is before the Council, a party to it at the same time has recourse to the Court?

In the jurisprudence of the Court, there is nothing

> irregular in the simultaneous exercise of their respective functions by the Court and the Security Council ... It is for the Court, the principal judicial organ of the United Nations, to resolve any legal question that may be in issue between parties to the dispute; and the resolution of such legal questions by the Court may be an important, and sometimes decisive, factor in promoting the peaceful settlement of the dispute.[11]

This position, which was foreshadowed in the Court's treatment of a request for the indication of interim measures of protection in the *Aegean Sea Continental Shelf* case,[12] and expounded in the "Hostages Case",[13] was confirmed by the Court in *Military and Paramilitary Activities in and against Nicaragua*. The Court there held that:

> The Council has functions of a political nature assigned to it, whereas the Court exercises purely judicial functions. Both organs can therefore perform their separate but complementary functions with respect to the same events.[14]

---

[10] *Corfu Channel case, Judgment on Preliminary Objection: ICJ Reports 1948*, p. 17.

[11] *United States Diplomatic and Consular Staff in Tehran, ICJ Reports 1980*, pp. 21–22.

[12] *ICJ Reports 1976*, pp. 11–13.   [13] Note 11 above.

[14] *Military and Paramilitary Activities in and against Nicaragua, Jurisdiction and Admissibility, ICJ Reports 1984*, p. 435.

In that case, the United States argued that, since Nicaragua charged the United States with acts of aggression in the Security Council, and charged the United States with the same acts of aggression in the Court, those charges could only be dealt with by the Security Council under Article 39 of the Charter, which provides that the Security Council shall determine the existence of any act of aggression. The Court dismissed that US contention by holding that the United States misconstrued Nicaragua's complaint as a case of armed conflict which could only be dealt with by the Security Council, whereas the Court construed Nicaragua's complaint as one demanding the peaceful settlement of a dispute: "Hence, it is properly brought before the principal judicial organ of the Organization for peaceful settlement."[15] In my view, this is one of the many unpersuasive holdings of the Court in this case, for it reconstructs a precise charge of Nicaragua both in the Security Council and before the Court, namely, that the United States was engaged in acts of aggression against Nicaragua. Nevertheless, I did not find persuasive the argument of the United States on this point (however vulnerable I believe was the Court's handling of it), for other reasons set out at length elsewhere.[16] The essence of my conclusion was that, however plausible is the US argument that it was the intent of the drafters of the Charter and Statute to vest exclusively in the Security Council and not concurrently in the Court the determination of acts of aggression, the terms and *travaux préparatoires* of the Charter and Statute do not sufficiently demonstrate that that was their purpose nor do those terms accomplish that purpose.[17]

Still another function of the Court which is intertwined with the functions of the United Nations is as an, or the, authoritative interpreter of legal questions to which the provisions of the United Nations Charter may give rise. It was accepted at the San Francisco Conference on International Organization that each organ of the United Nations would interpret its own powers, and that, while the Organization's structure did not embrace a process of constitutional, judicial, review, advisory opinions could be requested of the Court should differences about interpretations of Charter provisions arise. In fact, there has been recurrent recourse to the Court to interpret salient Charter provisions.

In the first opinion requested of the Court, on *Conditions of Admission of a State to Membership in the United Nations*, the Court affirmed that, as the

---

[15] *Ibid.*, p. 434.
[16] *Military and Paramilitary Activities in and against Nicaragua Merits, Dissenting Opinion of Judge Schwebel, ICJ Reports 1986*, pp. 287–293.
[17] *Ibid.*

principal judicial organ of the United Nations, it could exercise, in regard to the Charter, "a multilateral treaty, an interpretative function which falls within the normal exercise of its judicial powers."[18] In its opinion in *Certain Expenses of the United Nations*, the Court, while emphasizing its discretion to give or not to give an opinion, and its authority to answer only "a legal question," held that it cannot "attribute a political character to a request which invited it to undertake an essentially juridical task, namely, the interpretation of a treaty provision."[19] The provision in that case was an article of the Charter. In that opinion, as in *Competence of the General Assembly for the Admission of a State to the United Nations*,[20] the Court did not hesitate to consider the structure of the Charter and the relations established by it between the General Assembly and the Security Council. In its advisory opinion on the *Legal Consequences for States of the Continued Presence of South Africa in Namibia (South West Africa) notwithstanding Security Council resolution 276 (1970)*, the Court acknowledged that it "does not possess powers of judicial review or appeal in respect of the decisions taken by the United Nations organs concerned."[21] At the same time, "in the exercise of its judicial function" and since objections had been raised to the legality of certain resolutions of United Nations organs, the Court proceeded to consider those objections before "determining any legal consequences arising from those resolutions."[22] In the same opinion, the Court gave a broad, and most important, construction to Article 25 of the Charter, which provides that: "The Members of the United Nations agree to accept and carry out the decisions of the Security Council in accordance with the present Charter," holding that it is not confined to decisions in regard to enforcement action but applies to the decisions of the Security Council adopted in accordance with the Charter.[23] In this and in other respects, the Court has generally interpreted the Charter in ways which enhance its reach and effectiveness and the vitality of the Organization as a whole.

---

[18] *ICJ Reports 1947–1948*, p. 61.   [19] *ICJ Reports 1962*, p. 155.   [20] *ICJ Reports 1950*, pp. 8–9.

[21] *ICJ Reports 1971*, p. 45.

[22] *Ibid.* In this connection, Judge Onyeama, in a Separate Opinion, stated:

> In exercising its functions the Court is wholly independent of the other organs of the United Nations and is in no way obliged or concerned to render a judgment or opinion which would be "politically acceptable". Its function is, in the words of Article 38 of the Statute, "to decide in accordance with international law".
>
> The Court's powers are clearly defined by the Statute, and do not include powers to review decisions of other organs of the United Nations; but when, as in the present proceedings, such decisions bear upon a case properly before the Court, and a correct judgment or opinion could not be rendered without determining the validity of such decisions, the Court could not possibly avoid such a determination without abdicating its role of a judicial organ.
>
> (*Ibid.*, pp. 143–144.)

[23] *Ibid.*, p. 53.

But what has been the general rule has not been the invariable practice. While, in its opinion in *Reparation for Injuries Suffered in the Service of the United Nations*,[24] the Court in 1949 liberally construed Article 100 of the Charter,[25] in the "*Yakimetz*" case the Court in 1987 in my view otherwise treated Article 100 – and Article 101, paragraph 3 of the Charter as well – to the prejudice of the independence of the Secretariat and the Secretary-General.[26] In its contentious judgment on the merits in the contentious case of *Military and Paramilitary Activities in and against Nicaragua*,[27] the Court interpreted paramount provisions of the United Nations Charter, notably Article 2, paragraph 4, and Article 51, not, it maintained, with the purpose of construing those articles but rather in order to ascertain what is the content of customary international law governing the use of force in international relations and the exercise of self-defense. In my view, the construction of the concept and term of "armed attack" at which the Court so arrived narrowly and wrongly construes both customary international law and the content of Article 51 to the prejudice of international peace and security.[28]

> Far from contributing, as so many of the Court's judgments have, to the progressive development of the law, on this question the Court's Judgment implies a regressive development of the law which fails to take account of the realities of international relations ... the Court's Judgment on this profoundly important question may detract as much from the security of States as it does from the state of the law.[29]

At the same time, in respect of the obligation of States acting in self-defense to report to the Security Council under Article 51, the Court took an expansive view,[30] whose consistency with the Charter and customary international law may be open to question.[31]

Remaining articles of the Statute and Charter which underlie relations

---

[24] *ICJ Reports 1949*, pp. 183–184.

[25] The breadth of the Court's construction of Article 100 is instructive. The Court was prepared to hold, as in fact it did, that in the relatively unlikely event of an agent of the Organization being injured in the course of his duties in circumstances involving the responsibility of a State, or, rather, in the contingency of the agent's anticipating the possibility of the occurrence of such an event, his independence might be compromised unless he were able to rely upon the very limited protection afforded by the presentation of a monetary claim *post facto*, not by his State, but rather by the Organization. This attitude of the Court is of importance for its possible approach to a less indirect encroachment upon Article 100.
(S. M. Schwebel, "The International Character of the Secretariat of the United Nations," *The British Year Book of International Law*, [1953], 30, p. 82.)

[26] *Application for Review of Judgement No. 333 of the United Nations Administrative Tribunal, ICJ Reports 1987*, p. 18; *Dissenting Opinion of Judge Schwebel*, pp. 118–128.

[27] *ICJ Reports 1986*, p. 14.   [28] *Ibid.*, *Dissenting Opinion of Judge Schwebel*, pp. 331–347.

[29] *Ibid.*, p. 332.

[30] *Ibid.*, pp. 121–122.   [31] *Ibid.*, *Dissenting Opinion of Judge Schwebel*, pp. 373–377.

between the United Nations and the Court may be more summarily cited. Judges of the Court are elected by the General Assembly and Security Council.[32] That that process of election has its powerful political elements is undeniable and probably inescapable. (It may be observed that the selection of judges in national political systems is not always free of political factors.) It has, however, been proposed by the *Institut de Droit International* that, rather than judges of the Court being elected to a term of nine years and eligible for re-election,[33] judges should be elected to a single term of fifteen years, and not be eligible for re-election.[34] That would be a wise revision of the Statute, were the Statute to be revised – a process which, however, might risk more than it would be likely to gain.

The budget of the Court (including the salaries and pensions of judges) is part of the regular budget of the United Nations, adopted and apportioned by the General Assembly pursuant to Article 17 of the Charter. The power of the purse is the traditional lever which an assembly presses to exercise authority over other organs. Presumably in order to forestall any such possibility, Article 32 of the Statute provides that the salaries, allowances, and compensation of judges of the Court shall be fixed by the General Assembly and "may not be decreased during the term of office." While, after a judgment of the Court unpopular in the General Assembly, some unsuitable rumblings were heard, there has never been a political eruption affecting the compensation of the Court. (At the same time, the salary of judges, established in 1946 by the General Assembly on the recommendation of the Preparatory Commission to be equivalent to that of judges of the Permanent Court in the years 1936–9, has been permitted to erode, so that, in real terms, their current compensation is about one-third of that which PCIJ judges enjoyed.)

Article 15 of the Charter provides that the General Assembly "shall receive and consider" annual and special reports from the Security Council and "reports from the other organs of the United Nations." The Court has not treated itself as bound by this provision; for its first quarter of a century, it did not transmit an annual report to the General Assembly. Beginning with the Twenty-Sixth Session of the General Assembly, the Court submitted a report covering its activities during the period from August 1, 1970 to July 31, 1971 and, since that time, it has annually submitted such reports. The General Assembly has taken note of these reports, but has neither discussed nor

---

[32] Articles 4–15 of the Statute.   [33] Article 13 of the Statute.
[34] "With a view to reinforcing the independence of the judges, it is suggested that members of the Court should be elected for 15 years and should not be re-eligible. In this event an age-limit should be laid down; it might be fixed at 75 years." (*Annuaire de l'Institut de Droit International* [1954], p. 297.)

approved them – an appropriately restrained procedure in view of the independent judicial character of the Court.

It may further be recalled that, at a period when recourse to the Court was sparse, the General Assembly invited States and the Court to submit to the Secretary-General views and suggestions concerning the role of the Court on the basis of a questionnaire to be prepared by the Secretary-General. It requested the Secretary-General to prepare a comprehensive report in the light of the opinions so expressed, which he did.[35] The result was a valuable exploration of ways and means of reviving recourse to the Court. In subsequently revising the Rules of Court, the Court gave careful attention to the views and suggestions of States. One result was the revision of the Rules to provide for the President of the Court ascertaining the views of the parties regarding the composition of a chamber for a particular case, a revision which has been productive.[36]

It may furthermore be noted that Article 21 of the Statute provides that the Court shall appoint its Registrar and may provide for the appointment of such other officers as may be necessary. Thus the Registrar and Deputy-Registrar are elected by the Court, not elected by the General Assembly nor selected by the Secretary-General of the United Nations. The Registrar and the staff of the Registry are responsible to the Court, rather than to the Secretary-General or to the General Assembly. At the same time, the staff of the Registry are subject to Staff Regulations which conform as far as possible to the United Nations Staff Regulations and Rules.

The Court has played an important role in interpreting the provisions of the Charter, and of the Staff Regulations and Rules and related resolutions of the General Assembly, which govern the status and responsibilities of the Secretariat of the United Nations and of agents of the United Nations not members of the Secretariat. Such questions have arisen in the normal course of its advisory proceedings.[37] Moreover, there is a special procedure for what is, in effect, appeal on specified, restricted grounds from judgments of the United Nations Administrative Tribunal to the Court. The opinions – which have decisive force – rendered pursuant to this exceptional procedure have significantly borne on the authority of the Secretary-General and the status of the Secretariat.[38]

---

[35] *Review of the Role of the International Court of Justice, Report of the Secretary-General*, United Nations doc. A/8382 (September 15, 1971).

[36] Article 17 of the Rules of Court.

[37] E.g., in *Reparations for Injuries Suffered in the Service of the United Nations, ICJ Reports 1949*, p. 174. Of related significance is the Court's opinion in *Effect of Awards of Compensation made by the United Nations Administrative Tribunal, ICJ Reports 1954*, p. 47.

[38] See, e.g., note 26, above.

3

Was the Capacity to Request an Advisory Opinion Wider in the Permanent Court of International Justice than it is in the International Court of Justice?

ℰℐ

In the nineteen years of active life of the Permanent Court of International Justice (PCIJ), 1922–1940, the Court gave twenty-seven advisory opinions. By way of contrast, the International Court of Justice (ICJ), in the forty-four years 1946–1990, has given twenty advisory opinions. This is despite the fact that, *prima facie*, the capacity to request advisory opinions of the Court is wider under the United Nations Charter and the ICJ Statute than it was under the Covenant of the League of Nations and the PCIJ Statute. In point of fact, however, that appearance is misleading, because, in practice, the capacity to request an advisory opinion of the Permanent Court was more generously applied in important respects than is the capacity to request an advisory opinion of the International Court of Justice. It is the purpose of this paper to recall that this was so and to consider what light the PCIJ experience may shed upon the current potential of the International Court of Justice. It is appreciated, of course, that such light will not be defining, because the frequency of requests for the Court's advisory opinions depends on a number of factors, of which capacity to make a request is just one, and not the most important.

The Provisions of the Covenant, the Statute, and the Rules of Court

Article 14 of the Covenant of the League of Nations provided:

> The Council shall formulate and submit to the Members of the League for adoption plans for the establishment of a Permanent Court of International Justice. The Court shall be competent to hear and determine any dispute of an international character which the Parties thereto submit to it. The Court may also

The British Year Book of International Law 1991 (1992), 62.

give an advisory opinion upon any dispute or question referred to it by the Council or by the Assembly.[1]

The Statute, as the distinguished Advisory Committee of Jurists[2] which was appointed by the Council drafted it, duly contained an article governing the Court's advisory jurisdiction. It provided that, when the Court shall give an opinion on a question of an international nature which does not refer to a dispute that may have arisen, it shall appoint a special commission of three to five members, and when it shall give an opinion on a question which forms the subject of an existing dispute, it shall do so under the same conditions as if the case had been actually submitted to it for decision.[3] That is to say, what in effect would have been a chamber would have dealt with what were termed theoretical questions, but when a "practical case" came to the Court (which could involve the very question which had been the subject of a theoretical opinion) the full Court would sit and would not be bound by the opinion *in abstracto*. In advisory proceedings dealing with an existing dispute, the Court would deal with the case as if it were contentious; there could be *ad hoc* judges and the parties would be allowed to present arguments and proofs.

The draft Statute prepared by the Advisory Committee of Jurists was revised by the League Council in two notable and lasting respects: a provision for general compulsory jurisdiction was deleted and a provision to make English an official language (in addition to French) was added. When the draft Statute came to be considered by the first Assembly of the League of Nations, a truncated discussion in Committee ensued of the proposed provision concerning advisory opinions. In the course of it, an amendment by Argentina which would have authorized States Members of the League to request advisory opinions was rejected.[4] A proposal by the International Labor Organization (ILO) to give it the same right to request advisory

---

[1] The authority of the Court, as contained in the Covenant, to render advisory opinions principally derived from drafts of the Covenant prepared by Lord Cecil, Sir Cecil Hurst, and, most immediately, David Hunter Miller. See David Hunter Miller, *The Drafting of the Covenant* (1928), Vol. I, pp. 52, 391–393, 406.

[2] The Chairman of the Advisory Committee was Baron Descamps, the Rapporteur was Albert de Lapradelle, among the members were Elihu Root and Lord Phillimore, and its Secretary was Dionisio Anzilotti, then Under Secretary-General of the League of Nations, subsequently Judge and President of the Court.

[3] Permanent Court of International Justice, Advisory Committee of Jurists, *Procès-Verbaux of the Proceedings of the Committee*, June 16–July 24, 1920, pp. 730–731, 732. These proposals and their rationales are recounted in Dharma Pratap, *The Advisory Jurisdiction of the International Court of Justice* (1972), pp. 6–8, and Michla Pomerance, *The Advisory Function of the International Court in the League and United Nations Eras* (1973), pp. 10–14. See also Kenneth James Keith, *The Extent of the Advisory Jurisdiction of the International Court of Justice* (1971), pp. 13, 22.

[4] League of Nations, *The Records of the First Assembly, Meetings of the Committees*, 1920, pp. 519, 387, 401. See also League of Nations, *Documents concerning the Action Taken by the Council of the League of Nations*

opinions as was given to the Council and the Assembly was not seriously discussed.[5] It was unanimously recommended that the entire article proposed by the Advisory Committee of Jurists be deleted, on the ground, as Mr. Fromageot of France put it, that, in view of the terms of Article 14 of the Covenant, "the Court could not refuse to give advisory opinions. It was therefore unnecessary to include a rule to the same effect in the constitution of the Court."[6] At the same time, he regretted that the Court had been given an advisory jurisdiction at all.[7] In the report recommending the deletion of the article on advisory opinions proposed by the Advisory Committee of Jurists, it was stated that the Court should give advisory opinions, whether on a dispute or a question, with the same quorum; that the distinction made by the Advisory Committee between the two categories was unclear and could give rise to practical difficulties; and that, were the Argentinian and ILO proposals to have been adopted, such provisions "would involve a considerable extension of the duties of the members of the Court and might lead to consequences difficult to calculate in advance."[8] The resultant report sailed through the League Assembly, and the Statute as originally adopted contained no reference to advisory opinions. This was the more surprising in view of the fact that the Covenant and the PCIJ Statute, unlike the United Nations Charter and the ICJ Statute, were not integrally bound together; the PCIJ Statute was attached to and came into force pursuant to a separate and subsequent instrument of ratification; membership in the League did not entail being party to the Court's Statute and a State could be party to the Statute without becoming a Member of the League. Reliance for the Court's advisory authority upon a provision of the Covenant alone accordingly was questionable, and it gave rise to questions.

When the Court came to draft its Rules of Procedure, this singular history led Judge John Bassett Moore to submit in a comprehensive memorandum that:

> No subject connected with the organization of the Permanent Court of International Justice has caused so much confusion and proved to be so baffling as the question whether and under what conditions the Court shall undertake to give "advisory" opinions.
>
> This state of doubt and uncertainty may in large measure be ascribed to the nature of the proposal.[9]

---

under Article 14 of the Covenant and the Adoption by the Assembly of the Statute of the Permanent Court, 1921, pp. 68, 146, 195, 211.
[5] League of Nations, *Documents*, pp. 74, 79, 211; Note 5, *Records*, pp. 401, 563.   [6] *Ibid.*, p. 401.
[7] *Ibid.*, p. 389.   [8] *Ibid.*, p. 534.
[9] "*The Question of Advisory Opinions*," Memorandum by Mr. Moore, February 18, 1922, Permanent Court of International Justice, *Acts and Documents concerning the Organization of the Court*, Series D, No. 2, p. 383.

Judge Moore maintained that "to impose upon a court of justice the duty of giving advice, which those requesting it were wholly at liberty to reject, would reduce the Court to a position inferior to that of a tribunal of conciliation,"[10] and he proceeded to question whether the obligation to render advisory opinions had been imposed on the Court at all. He referred in raising this challenge to the fact that the Statute contained no specific provision on the subject, and he observed that the Covenant's terms properly interpreted left to the Court itself "the sole power to determine in each instance whether, and in what circumstances, and on what conditions, it would undertake to give advice."[11] He concluded that Article 14 of the Covenant "cannot be regarded as imposing upon the Court an obligation to render such opinions ..." and that "the giving of advisory opinions ... is not an appropriate function of a Court of Justice."[12] He finally submitted that it was preferable that there should be no special rule concerning advisory opinions but that the Court should deal with an application for an advisory opinion "according to what should be found to be the nature and merits of the case."[13]

In the event, the Court did treat advisory opinions in the Rules of Court. The Rules specified that advisory opinions should be rendered by the full Court, and provided for an orderly procedure for transmission of requests, for an exact statement of the question upon which an opinion is required, accompanied by all documents likely to throw light on the question, and for notice of the request to be sent to States Members of the Court and the League, as well as international organizations which are likely to be able to furnish information on the question.

Despite this uncertain beginning, the very large majority of cases brought to the Court in its earliest years turned out to be advisory. By 1927 a committee of the Court recorded:

> The Statute does not mention advisory opinions, but leaves to the Court the entire regulation of its procedure in the matter. The Court, in the exercise of this power, deliberately and advisedly assimilated its advisory procedure to its contentious procedure; and the results have abundantly justified its action. Such prestige as the Court today enjoys as a judicial tribunal is largely due to the amount of its

---

[10] *Ibid.*, p. 383. [11] *Ibid.*, p. 384. [12] *Ibid.*, p. 397.

[13] *Ibid.*, p. 398. For further indication of Judge Moore's attitude towards the Court's advisory jurisdiction, and for an analysis of the extraordinary role which the Court's advisory jurisdiction played in the question of United States adherence to the Court's Statute, see Michla Pomerance, "The United States and the Advisory Function of the Permanent Court of International Justice," in Y. Dinstein (ed.) and M. Tabory (assoc. ed.), *International Law at a Time of Perplexity: Essays in Honour of Shabtai Rosenne* (1989), pp. 567, 570–571, 575–576. See also Michael Dunne, *The United States and the World Court 1920–1935* (1988), pp. 86–121.

advisory business and the judicial way in which it has dealt with such business. In reality, where there are in fact contending parties, the difference between contentious cases and advisory cases is only nominal. The main difference is the way in which the case comes before the Court, and even this difference may virtually disappear, as it did in the Tunisian case. So the view that advisory opinions are not binding is more theoretical than real.[14]

In that year, the Court adopted on the proposal of Judge Anzilotti a further rule providing that, on a question relating to an existing dispute between two or more States, Article 31 of the Statute (relating to the maintenance of national judges and the appointment of judges *ad hoc*) shall apply.

By 1929, when revision of the Statute was undertaken, it was accepted that it should be amended to incorporate the substance of what the Rules of Court by then provided respecting advisory opinions, as well as an article providing that, in the exercise of its advisory functions, the Court shall be guided by the provisions of the Statute which apply in contentious cases to the extent which it recognized them to be applicable. The revised Statute entered into force in 1936, as did Revised Rules which brought the process of assimilation of the advisory to contentious procedure as close to completion as was possible.[15]

The Capacity to Request Advisory Opinions of the PCIJ in Practice

Not only did early recourse to the Court's advisory jurisdiction exceed by far the expectations of the drafters of the Statute, but a significant element of that extensive recourse proved to be the liberal practice followed by the League Council and the Court in entertaining requests for advisory opinions which in fact originated not in the League Council or Assembly but in other quarters. All requests for advisory opinions addressed to the PCIJ were transmitted by the Council; the Assembly considered but did not adopt such requests on a few occasions. But not all of the requests transmitted by the Council were, in substantial terms, requests of the Council; rather, the majority of them actually were submitted at the instance of States or of an international organization other than the League. Thus, the Fourteenth Annual Report of the Court could as of 1938 declare:

> The 28 requests for advisory opinion which the Council has submitted to the Court may be divided into two categories: those really originating with the Council itself and those – more numerous – submitted at the instigation or request of a State or international organization.

---

[14] *Fourth Annual Report of the Permanent Court of International Justice, PCIJ, Series E, No. 4,* p. 76.
[15] See Pratap, *Advisory Jurisdiction,* p. 35.

The following tables give a list of the cases submitted to the Court for advisory opinion, divided into these two categories.[16]

The Report then lists "Requests from the Council *proprio motu*"; under that rubric are 12 cases, listed by name, date and "Governments and international organizations directly interested." These cases are described as belonging "to the first category," i.e., cases "really originating with the Council itself." The table then proceeds to list the following cases which "belong to the second category," i.e., those more numerous cases submitted at the instigation or request of a State or international organization. The 16 cases then listed are also described by name, date, and "Governments and international organizations directly interested."[17]

As for that second category, six of the sixteen cases so instigated derived from the ILO (though it is of interest to note that the Court's Report lists among the international organizations interested in the case not only the ILO but various non-governmental organizations as well, both international and national, such as the International Confederation of Christian Trades Unions and the Netherlands General Confederation of Trade Unions). Thus while the ILO more than once in the history of the Permanent Court was denied the right it sought directly to request advisory opinions of the Court, in practice it, more than any international organization other than the League itself, effectively had recourse to the Court. Paradoxically, when, with the adoption of the United Nations Charter and its implementation by the United Nations General Assembly, the ILO finally won its long fight for direct access to the Court, it made no use of that right in the years in which it has possessed it (as of this writing, forty-four).

Of the remaining ten cases described in 1938 as submitted at the instigation of States or international organizations, the other international organizations involved were the Mixed Commission for the Exchange of Greek and Turkish Populations and the Greco-Bulgarian Mixed Emigration Commission (and, arguably, the Conference of Ambassadors which represented the Principal Allied Powers).

Exchange of Greek and Turkish Populations

Greece and Turkey concluded a Convention in 1923 concerning the exchange of Greek and Turkish populations. Article 11 of the Convention provided for

---

[16] *Fourteenth Annual Report of the Permanent Court of International Justice*, PCIJ, Series E, No. 14, pp. 72–73. As early as 1925, the *First Annual Report* was similarly framed: *Annual Report of the Permanent Court of International Justice*, PCIJ, Series E, No. 1, pp. 149–150.

[17] *Ibid.*, pp. 73–75.

the establishment of a Mixed Commission composed of four members representing Greece and four members representing Turkey, respectively, and three members chosen by the Council of the League from among nationals of States which did not take part in the First World War. The Mixed Commission's duties were to supervise and facilitate the emigration provided for in the Convention and to settle the methods to be followed. The principle governing emigration was, with certain exceptions, the compulsory exchange of Greek and Turkish nationals "established" in each other's territory.[18] The question of the meaning of that term and measures which had been taken relating to it had been raised by Greece, which requested the League Council to place the question on its agenda. The arrest and expulsion of some thousands of Greeks in Turkey were claimed to be at issue. Greece's action followed inconclusive consideration of the problem in the Mixed Commission. The Council, acting in the presence of the President of the Mixed Commission who addressed the Council on it, initially referred the matter back to the Mixed Commission. In so doing, the Council's Rapporteur on the question, Viscount Ishii, stated:

> Should the Members of the Commission feel, however, that there are in the Convention points of great legal difficulty, which they doubt whether they have sufficient juridical knowledge to interpret, it is always open to them to ask the two Governments signatories of the Convention to place the matter before the Court of International Justice, one of whose special duties it is to undertake the interpretation of treaties. The Council, too, would, I feel sure, be willing, should the Mixed Commission desire it, to ask the Court for an advisory opinion on such points.[19]

Following further exchanges in the Mixed Commission, the Commission unanimously agreed to request the Council of the League to seek an advisory opinion of the Court on the following question, which the Council did in these terms:

> The Council of the League of Nations, having been asked by the Mixed Commission for the Exchange of Greek and Turkish populations to obtain from the Permanent Court of International Justice an Advisory Opinion on the dispute regarding the interpretation of Article 2 of the Convention on the Exchange of Greek and Turkish populations ... has decided to ask the Permanent Court of International Justice to give an advisory opinion on the following question:
>
> What meaning and scope should be attributed to the word "established" in Article 2 of the Convention ... regarding the exchange of Greek and Turkish populations, in regard to which discussions have arisen and arguments have been put forward which are contained in the documents communicated by the Mixed

---

[18] *Exchange of Greek and Turkish Populations, Advisory Opinion, 1925, PCIJ,* Series B, No. 10, p. 6.

[19] *Ibid.,* p. 13. For the complete text, see *League of Nations Official Journal,* 1924, pp. 1669–1670.

Commission? And what conditions must the persons who are described in Article 2 ... under the name of "Greek inhabitants of Constantinople" fulfil in order that they may be considered as "established" under the terms of the Conventions and exempt from compulsory exchange?[20]

In so doing, the Council invited the Mixed Commission as well as the two Governments represented thereon to furnish the Court with any documents or explanations it might require. The President of the Mixed Commission transmitted a dossier to the Court.[21] As the matter was deemed to be urgent (involving as it did the alleged arbitrary arrest and expulsion of populations), the Court met in extraordinary session to deal with it. The Court's Opinion of February 21, 1925 was communicated by the League Council to the Mixed Commission with an expression of hope that it would facilitate the work of the Commission, which would doubtless attach to it "the same high value and authority which the Council always gave to the opinions" of the Court.[22] The matter was thereafter dealt with by the Commission and by the Governments concerned, finally by means of a convention which defined "established persons." The Mixed Commission ceased to exist pursuant to agreement in 1934.

Thus, while the League Council itself played more than the role of a mere conduit in requesting the Court's advisory opinion, it is clear that an international organization also played a considerable role. That international organization was neither universal nor permanent; it cannot be analogized to the ILO or to what today are termed the Specialized Agencies of the United Nations, nor even to a regional agency such as the OAS or OAU. Rather it was an evanescent international organization established by treaty and the agency of the League to resolve a passing though highly important dispute between two States.

Interpretation of the Greco-Turkish Agreement of December 1, 1926

Greece and Turkey in 1926 concluded an agreement which conferred further powers on the Mixed Commission for the Exchange of Greek and Turkish Populations. The agreement provided that any questions of principle which might arise in the Mixed Commission in connection with the new duties entrusted to it should be submitted to the President of the Greco-Turkish Arbitral Tribunal sitting at Constantinople for arbitration. That clause gave rise to differences of interpretation regarding the conditions of appeal to the arbitrator, whereupon the President of the Mixed Commission, citing the

---

[20] *Exchange of Greek and Turkish Populations, Advisory Opinion, 1925, PCIJ, Series B, No. 10*, p. 6.
[21] *Ibid.*, p. 9.
[22] *League of Nations Official Journal*, 1925, p. 155.

above-quoted 1924 statement of Viscount Ishii, wrote to the Secretary-General of the League recounting that the Commission had by a majority "decided ... to apply to the Permanent Court of International Justice ... through the agency of the League of Nations, for an advisory opinion as to the interpretation of the article in question so far as it concerns the conditions for appeals to the arbitrator."[23] He asked the Secretary-General to place the dispute before the Council. The Secretary-General questioned whether the item could be placed on the Council's agenda on the initiative of the Mixed Commission. The Council was advised by a committee of jurists that it could be but that, having regard to the *Eastern Carelia* precedent,[24] the Council probably would not be prepared to request the Court's opinion without Turkey's concurrence.[25] Both Turkey and Greece did agree to requesting an

---

[23] *Interpretation of the Greco-Turkish Agreement of 1 December 1926 (Final Protocol, Article IV), Advisory Opinion, 1928, PCIJ, Series B, No. 16*, p. 5.

[24] *Status of Eastern Carelia, Advisory Opinion, 1923, PCIJ, Series B, No. 5*.

[25] The Report of the Committee of Jurists appointed by the President of the Council in order to furnish it with an opinion on the preliminary question of including on the agenda the request of the Mixed Commission for an advisory opinion from the Court is of interest insofar as it shows the then limited authority of an international organization to request an advisory opinion of the Court. It reads as follows:

> The Committee finds that the Mixed Commission's request is based upon the following passage in the report submitted to the Council by Viscount Ishii on October 31st, 1924, and approved by the Council on the same day:
>
> > The Council, too, would, I feel sure, be willing, should the Mixed Commission desire it, to ask the Court for an advisory opinion on such points.
>
> The Committee considers that the only preliminary objections that can be raised to the inclusion of the Mixed Commission's request in the Council's agenda are the two following:
>
> 1. Viscount Ishii's suggestions, which were approved by the Council, referred to certain special points submitted to the Council on a request from the Greek Government under Article 11 of the Covenant.
>
> 2. Viscount Ishii's report referred only to the Convention between Greece and Turkey of January 30th, 1923, whereas the request now made to the Council by the Mixed Commission concerns an agreement concluded between Greece and Turkey subsequently to the Convention and the report.
>
> The Committee unanimously agree that the first objection is not decisive. While the origin of Viscount Ishii's report was a request made under Article 11 of the Covenant, the fact remains that the passage quoted has an entirely general signification and contemplates the future working of the Mixed Commission.
>
> The Committee considers that the second objection is of greater importance. Some doubt arose in the Committee as to the view to be taken of this objection. On the one hand, it may be urged that the objection accurately states actual facts of the case and that the authorization given to the Mixed Commission in regard to the application of the Convention of January 30th, 1923, cannot be interpreted as extending also to the application of the agreement of December 1st, 1926. It may, on the other hand, be observed that the Mixed Commission still exists in the form in which it was established under the Convention of 1923 and has merely acquired additional powers consonant with the object for which it was created.
>
> It appears from the above that the Council, acting according to the spirit of the decision of 1924, might decide to place the Mixed Commission's request on its agenda; but it is equally certain that,

advisory opinion while renouncing the right to appoint judges *ad hoc*. The Council, "referring to the letter addressed to the Secretary-General . . . by the President of the Mixed Commission for the Exchange of Greek and Turkish Populations," thereupon requested the Court to give an advisory opinion upon the question raised in the latter's letter regarding the conditions of reference to the arbitrator contemplated by the Greco-Turkish Agreement.[26] Greece and Turkey submitted written statements to the Court and took part in oral hearings.

The Court felt bound to reformulate the question put to it. It found that, by expressing in this revised form the question contemplated by the letter of the President of the Mixed Commission to the Secretary-General, the Court was in a position to reply, while it held that it could not deal with points of dispute between interested Governments which fell outside the scope of the question as the Court reformulated it to be. In the course of reaching its conclusions (which need not be set out for the purposes of the present paper), the Court made observations of interest for the international arbitral process. But what is of immediate interest is that, when the advisory opinion came before the League Council, the report placed before it re-stated the question put to the Court as reformulated by the Court and recounted the Court's unanimous answers thereto and recommended that, "as it was at the request and for the use of the Mixed Commission that the Court was requested by the Council to give an opinion," the Council take note of the opinion and transmit it to the Mixed Commission.[27]

It will be observed that, in this case as well, the League Council exerted no control over the drafting of the question put by the Mixed Commission, which was obscurely worded; in this respect it did act as a mere conduit. However, it was prepared to act at the request of the Mixed Commission only with the concurrence of the two States whose interests were affected (one of which, Turkey, was not then a League Member). As for the Court, it

---

even if it did so, the Council should respect the precedent established by the advisory opinion of the Permanent Court of International Justice dated July 23rd, 1923, on the question of Eastern Carelia between Finland and Russia. Having regard to this precedent, the Council would probably not be prepared to ask the Court's opinion without Turkey's concurrence.

In view of this circumstance, the Committee is unanimous in asking whether it might not be desirable for the President of the Council first of all to ask the two Governments concerned whether they are prepared to consent to the Council submitting to the Court the question raised by the Mixed Commission.

(*League of Nations Official Journal*, 1928, p. 404.)

[26] *Interpretation of the Greco-Turkish Agreement of 1 December 1926 (Final Protocol, Article IV), Advisory Opinion, 1928, PCIJ, Series B, No. 16*, pp. 6–7.

[27] *League of Nations Official Journal*, 1928, p. 1487.

was not prepared to deal with differences between Greece and Turkey which fell outside the terms of the Council's question.

Greco-Bulgarian "Communities" Case

The Greco-Bulgarian Mixed Emigration Commission was a similar body. It encountered difficulties in the interpretation of articles of the convention which established it, concerning the "communities" whose property was subject to liquidation. The President of the Mixed Commission proposed that an advisory opinion of the Court be sought. Greece and Bulgaria agreed but the members of the Commission as a whole could not agree on the terms of the questions to be submitted; accordingly, questions drawn up by the neutral members of the Commission, and by the Greek and Bulgarian members respectively, were transmitted by the President of the Commission to the League Council. In submitting a draft resolution for reference of the questions to the Court, the French representative, Mr. Briand, stated that, "since the request is submitted by the Mixed Commission on behalf of the two Governments, and since the Council has, in the past, acceded to similar applications made by the Mixed Commission for the Exchange of Greek and Turkish Populations ... the Council should comply with the Mixed Commission's request."[28] The Council, "having considered the letter addressed by the President of the Greco-Bulgarian Mixed Commission to the Secretary-General, in the name of the Bulgarian and Greek Governments, to submit to the Council of the League a request that an advisory opinion be obtained from the Permanent Court of International Justice, for the use of the Commission, with regard to the interpretation of those clauses of the Greco-Bulgarian Convention ... which relate to communities,"[29] requested the Court to give an advisory opinion covering the questions formulated in the annexes to the letter of the Commission's President. The Council also requested the Bulgarian and Greek Governments and the Mixed Commission to furnish the Court with the necessary documents and explanations. Greece and Bulgaria appointed judges *ad hoc* and the two Governments submitted written statements and oral arguments. The Commission submitted documentation to the Court, which put questions to the Commission's President. The Court gave its unanimous replies to the multiple questions submitted to it. When the advisory opinion came before the League Council, Briand, observing that it was "given at the Mixed Commission's request and for the Commission's use,"[30] proposed that the Council take note of it and transmit

[28] *League of Nations Official Journal*, 1930, p. 109.
[29] *Greco-Bulgarian "Communities," Advisory Opinion, 1930, PCIJ, Series B, No. 17,* pp. 4–5.
[30] *League of Nations Official Journal*, 1930, p. 1300.

it to the Commission. It was so agreed, amidst the plaudits of the representatives of Bulgaria and Greece, it being observed that the Court's unanimous opinion included that of the national judges. The President of the Mixed Commission, addressing the Council, stated that, thanks to the Court's advice, the Mixed Commission was now in possession of an "authoritative opinion which would be of great assistance in its work. It was to be hoped that the Commission would now be able to liquidate the question of the communities to the general satisfaction."[31] The Commission was wound up in 1932, having successfully completed the exchange between Bulgaria and Greece of more than 150,000 persons.[32]

It will be observed that the Council, relying upon the precedent of transmitting requests for advisory opinions made by the Mixed Commission for the Exchange of Greek and Turkish Populations, transmitted the request of the Greco-Bulgarian Mixed Emigration Commission, and again did so by passing along unchanged and apparently unscrutinized the multiple questions prepared by its neutral members and its Greek and Bulgarian members.

Advisory Opinions Sought by the ILO

The process by which the International Labor Organization sought advisory opinions of the Permanent Court through the agency of the League Council will not be examined in like detail, because today the ILO has unchallenged competence directly to request an advisory opinion on a legal question arising within the scope of its activities, having been so authorized by General Assembly resolution adopted pursuant to Article 96 of the Charter. Thus the capacity of the ILO and other Specialized Agencies to seek advisory opinions of the Court today is, if not wider, certainly more direct than the ILO enjoyed in the Permanent Court. Nevertheless some observations are in order.

The first three cases to be submitted to the Court, and the only cases before it in 1922, were three requests for advisory opinions which concerned the ILO. The first, *Designation of the Workers' Delegate for the Netherlands at the Third Session of the International Labor Conference*,[33] originated in the ILO Conference, which called upon the Governing Body to request the League Council to request an advisory opinion of the Court. Lord Balfour was the first to speak in the League Council and he expressed doubt, not about the propriety of the League Council requesting an advisory opinion at the

---

[31] *Ibid.*, p. 1301.   [32] *League of Nations Official Journal*, 1932, pp. 469–470.

[33] *Designation of the Workers' Delegate for the Netherlands at the Third Session of the International Labor Conference, Advisory Opinion, 1922, PCIJ, Series B, No. 1.*

instance of the ILO but about a challenge to "the undoubted discretion"[34] of a Government Member of the League to name a delegate. His doubt was dispelled by Albert Thomas, the ILO's Director-General, who appeared before the Council to explain that the Court's opinion would serve in the future for similar cases which might come before the Conference and that the Netherlands did not oppose the request. Lord Balfour at once agreed that there could be no further objection. The question put was precisely as posed by the ILO.[35]

The origins of the Court's proceedings in two other advisory cases were very different: *Competence of the ILO in Regard to International Regulation of the Conditions of Labor of Persons Employed in Agriculture*[36] and *Competence of the ILO to Examine Proposals for the Organization and Development of the Methods of Agricultural Production.*[37] France, which questioned whether the competence of the ILO extended to agricultural labor, proposed to the League Council that the Court be requested to give an advisory opinion on the question: "Does the competence of the International Labor Organization extend to international regulation of the conditions of labor of persons employed in agriculture?"[38] The Council had before it a letter from Mr. Thomas stating that it was the view of the ILO Governing Body that requests to the Court respecting the ILO should first be submitted to the Governing Body. The representative of France and some others did not find that necessary and, after a discussion in which Mr. Thomas suggested another rendering of the question to be put to the Court, the Council adopted that proposed by France.[39]

Thereafter, France proposed that a supplementary question be addressed to the Court, namely: "Does examination of proposals for the organization and development of methods of agricultural production, and of other questions of a like character, fall within the competence of the International Labor Organization?"[40] The first speaker invited to address the Council on this proposal was Albert Thomas, who maintained that the ILO had never

---

[34] *League of Nations Official Journal*, 1922, p. 529.

[35] *Ibid.* The Court held that the Workers' Delegate for the Netherlands was nominated in accordance with the provisions of the governing instrument. PCIJ, *Series B, No. 1*, p. 27.

[36] *Competence of the ILO in Regard to International Regulation of the Conditions of Labor of Persons Employed in Agriculture, Advisory Opinion, 1922, PCIJ, Series B, No. 2.*

[37] *Competence of the ILO to Examine Proposals for the Organization and Development of the Methods of Agricultural Production, Advisory Opinion, 1922, PCIJ, Series B, No. 3.*

[38] *PCIJ, Series B, No. 2,* p. 9.

[39] *League of Nations Official Journal*, 1922, pp. 527–528. The Court held that the competence of the ILO did extend to international regulation of the conditions of labor of persons employed in agriculture. *PCIJ, Series B, No. 2,* p. 43.

[40] *PCIJ, Series B, No. 3,* p. 49.

claimed competence in matters relating to agricultural production. He therefore failed to see why the Court should be consulted. The French representative replied that, if the ILO claimed no such competence, there was no objection to submitting a question to the Court and, in any event, the ILO might in future claim a competence as to which any question would best be resolved. Mr. Thomas replied:

> The International Labor Office did not concern itself with the technical problems of agriculture except in so far as these problems were bound up with problems affecting the protection of workers ... He would like to draw the attention of the Council to the risks involved in the procedure which it was proposed to adopt. Should the Council automatically transmit every request for an opinion submitted to it? There was a danger that such a method might weaken the authority both of the Council and of the Court itself. Moreover, it might do serious harm to the International Labor Office. To refer the question to the Permanent Court would suggest that the International Labor Office had claimed a competence which, as a matter of fact, it had never claimed, and so might cause the Office once more to be unjustly suspected of desiring to extend the range of its competence.[41]

But the French representative maintained that, if France were denied recourse to the Court, other Governments might be discouraged from resorting to the Court, whereas the Court's opinion would contribute to establishing a useful jurisprudence.[42] The Council unanimously agreed to put the above question to the Court.

Albert Thomas himself argued all three of ILO's cases before the Court, reportedly to great effect.[43] The cases are of high interest, arising as early in the history of the Court and of international organization as they did; as examples of a State's challenge to a claimed or perceived competence of an international organization which was submitted to the Court; as instances in which the chief administrative officer of an international organization personally argued before the Court; and as cases in which not only States and international governmental organizations, but non-governmental organizations, were heard by the Court. But only the first of the three ILO cases which so early came to the Court came at the instance of an international organization not authorized itself to seek an opinion.

---

[41] *League of Nations Official Journal*, 1922, p. 794.

[42] *Ibid.*, p. 794. The Court held that the functions of the ILO did not extend to the promotion of improvement in the processes to increase the amount of production, in agriculture or any other branch of industry. *PCIJ, Series B, No. 3*, pp. 59–60.

[43] The extended oral arguments of Mr. Thomas are reproduced in *PCIJ, Series C, No. 1*, pp. 123, 221, and 309. See also p. 269. Thomas's arguments make exceptional reading, and the manner of their composition and delivery is evocatively recounted in a fascinating memoir by one of his distinguished successors: E.J. Phelan, *Yes and Albert Thomas* (1936), pp. 136–142.

Three further advisory opinions were subsequently requested by the League Council at the instance of the Governing Body of the ILO: *Competence of the ILO to Regulate Incidentally the Personal Work of the Employer*,[44] *Free City of Danzig and ILO*,[45] and *Interpretation of the Convention of 1919 concerning Employment of Women during the Night*.[46] In all three cases, the League Council requested the opinions sought by the ILO in exactly the terms sought, and with minimal discussion.[47]

Opinion Sought by the League High Commissioner in Danzig

A dispute between Poland and the Free City of Danzig in regard to treatment of Polish nationals and persons of Polish origin in Danzig was submitted to the League of Nations High Commissioner for Danzig. He, in turn, with the agreement of the Parties, suggested the eminent desirability of obtaining an advisory opinion of the Court, a suggestion which was transmitted by the League Secretary-General to the Council. The Council requested the Court to give an advisory opinion.[48] Memorials were presented to the Court by Danzig and Poland and they took part in oral hearings. The opinion of the Court was accepted by the Parties in settlement of the dispute.[49] For present purposes, the case is of interest as an illustration of the League Council seeking an advisory opinion at the instance of what might be described as a subsidiary organ of the League. The Council concerned itself neither with the merits of the dispute nor with the wording of the questions put to the Court.

Advisory Opinions Requested at the Instance of States

The remaining advisory opinions of the Court which were sought neither by the Council of the League on its own initiative nor at the instance of international organizations were sought on behalf of States. Among this number were two opinions sought at the instance of the Council of Ambassadors constituted in pursuance of the Peace Treaties (however, these may

---

[44] *Competence of the ILO to Regulate Incidentally the Personal Work of the Employer, Advisory Opinion, 1926, PCIJ, Series B, No. 13*, p. 6. For Mr. Thomas's argument before the Court, as well as those of representatives of non-governmental organizations, see *PCIJ, Series C, No. 12*, pp. 53, 17, 19.

[45] *Free City of Danzig and ILO, Advisory Opinion, 1930, PCIJ, Series B, No. 18*, p. 4. For the argument to the Court of Mr. Thomas, see *PCIJ, Series C, No. 18*, p. 67.

[46] *Interpretation of the Convention of 1919 concerning Employment of Women during the Night, Advisory Opinion, 1932, PCIJ, Series A/B, No. 50*, p. 365. In this case, Mr. Phelan, then head of the Diplomatic Division of the International Labor Office, spoke for the ILO. *PCIJ, Series C, No. 60*, p. 207.

[47] *League of Nations Official Journal*, 1926, pp. 596, 857; *ibid.*, 1930, pp. 531, 1308; *ibid.*, 1932, p. 1169.

[48] *League of Nations Official Journal*, 1931, p. 1137; *Treatment of Polish Nationals and Other Persons of Polish Origin or Speech in the Danzig Territory, PCIJ, Series A/B, No. 44*, p. 5.

[49] *League of Nations Official Journal*, 1932, pp. 2288–2289.

alternatively be viewed as having been sought not by States but by an international body, the Conference of Ambassadors). It is striking that, although the first Assembly of the League declined to adopt a proposal which would have authorized States to request advisory opinions, in practice the League Council so often and easily agreed to act as the channel through which advisory opinions sought by States could be requested of the Court. The Court itself, however, treated this facility as one subject to the Council's authority, and it rebuffed any attempt by States to go beyond the questions which the Council had adopted.

Nationality Decrees Issued in Tunis and Morocco

As indicated above, the second and third advisory opinions requested of the Court were proposed by France through the medium of the Council. The fourth case to come before the Court, and the fourth advisory opinion to be issued by it, concerned *Nationality Decrees Issued in Tunis and Morocco*.[50] Decrees had been issued concerning the nationality of certain persons born in Tunis and in Morocco, and the British Government protested to the French Government about the application of these decrees to British nationals. The British Government proposed that the question of such application be referred to the Court or to arbitration, proposals which France did not accept. The British Government thereupon submitted the dispute to the Council of the League of Nations, pursuant to Article 15 of the Covenant. France in response invoked paragraph 8 of Article 15, which provided: "If the dispute between the parties is claimed by one of them, and is found by the Council, to arise out of a matter which by international law is solely within the domestic jurisdiction of that party, the Council shall so report and shall make no recommendation as to its settlement." Instead of leaving that preliminary question to the resolution of the Council, Great Britain and France agreed to submit it to the Court. The League Council accordingly adopted the following resolution:

> The Council has examined the proposals made by Lord Balfour and Mr. Léon Bourgeois on the subject of the following question, placed on its agenda of August 11th at the request of the Government of His Britannic Majesty:
> "Dispute between France and Great Britain as to the Nationality Decrees issued in Tunis and Morocco (French zone) on November 8th, 1921, and their application to British subjects, the French Government having refused to submit the legal questions involved to arbitration."
> The Council, noting that friendly conversations have taken place between the

[50] PCIJ, Series B, No. 4, p. 7.

representatives of the two Governments and that they have agreed on the proposals to be made to the Council;

Expresses its entire adhesion to the principles contained in these proposals, and has adopted the following resolution:

(a) The Council decides to refer to the Permanent Court of International Justice, for its opinion, the question whether the dispute referred to above is or is not by international law solely a matter of domestic jurisdiction (Article 15, paragraph 8, of the Covenant);

(b) And it requests the two Governments to bring this matter before the Permanent Court of International Justice, and to arrange with the Court with regard to the date on which the question can be heard and with regard to the procedure to be followed;

(c) Furthermore, the Council takes note that the two Governments have agreed that, if the opinion of the Court upon the above question is that it is not solely a matter of domestic jurisdiction, the whole dispute will be referred to arbitration or to judicial settlement under conditions to be agreed between the Governments.

(d) The Secretary-General of the League will communicate paragraphs (a) and (b) to the Court.[51]

Just before adoption of the resolution, the representative of Italy stated that it was "understood that this decision related simply to an arrangement between the French and British Governments, and that it did not in any way bind other Governments,"[52] a statement which elicited no comment.

The British and French Governments, pursuant to agreement between them, named agents for the case, transmitted to the Court Memorials and Counter-Memorials, and engaged in oral argument before the Court, which concluded with the deposit of their respective final conclusions, as if the proceedings were contentious. Oral hearings terminated on January 13, 1923, and the Court's advisory opinion was read out in Court on February 7, 1923,[53] i.e., about three weeks later. The Court reached its well-known conclusions in favor of Great Britain, essentially on the ground that the dispute entailed the construction of international agreements, which, by international law, is not solely a matter of domestic jurisdiction. The French agent immediately announced France's acceptance of what he termed "une

---

[51] *Nationality Decrees Issued in Tunis and Morocco*, PCIJ, Series B, No. 4, pp. 7–8 and PCIJ, Series C, No. 2, pp. 20–21. While the foregoing version of the Council's resolution was read out in Court, and incorporated in the Court's opinion, the League's *Official Journal* contains a slightly different version: *League of Nations Official Journal*, 1922, p. 1207.

[52] *League of Nations Official Journal*, 1922, p. 1207. Of this case, the *Annual Report* stated: "The Council merely transmitted the request and invited the Court to make direct arrangements with the two Governments concerned for the submission of the written documents" (PCIJ, Series E, No. 1, p. 150).

[53] PCIJ, Series C, No. 2, pp. 10, 12.

décision" and proposed to submit the merits of the case to the Court.[54] The opinion was transmitted to the League Council, which took no further action in the matter. The opinion enabled the British and French Governments to reach an agreement which definitely settled the dispute and to proceed no further in the Court.[55]

Status of Eastern Carelia

In 1922, Finland requested the League Council to deal with the dispute between Finland and the Soviet Government over the status of Eastern Carelia, particularly what Finland claimed were Soviet violations of an international agreement to accord autonomy to the Finnish-speaking population of Carelia, which had resulted in armed revolt.[56] The Council expressed its willingness to consider the question if the two Parties agreed.[57] The Soviet Government declined any intervention by the League, contending that the question of Carelian autonomy was a domestic one.[58] In 1923, Finland accordingly asked the Council to request an advisory opinion of the Court.[59] The Council voted to request the Court to give an opinion on the following question: "Do Articles 10 and 11 of the Treaty of Peace between Finland and Russia, signed at Dorpat on October 14th, 1920, and the annexed Declaration of the Russian Delegation regarding the autonomy of Eastern Carelia, constitute engagements of an international character which place Russia under an obligation to Finland as to the carrying out of the provisions contained therein?"[60] Finland participated in the Court's proceedings, but the Soviet Government confined itself to the dispatch of a telegram from People's Commissar for Foreign Affairs Tchitcherin, which stated:

> The Russian Government finds it impossible to take any part in the proceedings, without legal value either in substance or in form, which the Permanent Court intends to institute as regards the Carelian question. Whereas the Workers' Commune of Carelia is an autonomous portion of the Russian Federation without any right to independent international relations; whereas its autonomy is based on the decree of the Pan-Russian Central Executive Council, dated June 8th, 1920, which was enacted before the examination of this question by the Russo-Finnish Peace Conference at Dorpat; furthermore, whereas the Treaty of Dorpat, in connection with another matter, refers to the autonomous territory of Carelia

---

[54] *PCIJ, Series C, No. 2*, p. 13.   [55] *PCIJ, Series C, No. 3*, p. 55.

[56] *League of Nations Official Journal*, 1922, pp. 104, 165.

[57] *Ibid.*, p. 108.   [58] *League of Nations Official Journal*, 1923, p. 660.   [59] *Ibid.*

[60] *Status of Eastern Carelia, PCIJ, Series B, No. 5*, p. 7. The question as adopted by the Council was in substance, though not in terms, that which Finland proposed. The Finnish text is found in the *League of Nations Official Journal*, 1923, p. 661. See also the interesting Rapporteur's report and accompanying Finnish legal opinions, *ibid.*, pp. 659, 660, 661, 663.

as already existing without imposing any obligation in this respect upon Russia; whereas the Russian Delegation at Dorpat declared each time that this question was raised that it was an internal question affecting the Russian Federation; furthermore, whereas Berzine, the President of the Russian Delegation, at the meeting of October 14th, 1920, brought the fact that Carelia was autonomous to the knowledge of the Finnish Delegation solely for their information; further-more, whereas . . . Tchitcherin . . . protested categorically against the action taken by the Finnish Government in placing the Eastern Carelian question before the League of Nations, a course which in the view of the Russian Government constituted an act of hostility to the Russian Federation and an intervention in its domestic affairs; furthermore, whereas . . . the Commissary of the People for Foreign Affairs declared that the Russian Government absolutely repudiated the claim of the so-called League of Nations to intervene in the question of the internal situation of Carelja and stated that any attempt on the part of any power to apply to Russia the article of the Covenant of the League relating to disputes between one of its Members and a non-participating State would be regarded by the Russian Government as an act of hostility to the Russian State: the Russian Government categorically refuses to take any part in the examination of this question by the League of Nations or by the Permanent Court. Apart from considerations of law, according to which the question of the status of Carelia is a matter of Russian domestic jurisdiction, the Soviet Government is compelled to affirm that it cannot consider the so-called League of Nations and the Permanent Court as impartial in this matter, having regard to the fact that the majority of the Powers belonging to the League of Nations have not yet accorded the Soviet Government *de jure* recognition, and several of them refuse even to enter into *de facto* relations with it.[61]

The Court recounted the pertinent provisions of the Treaty of Dorpat and of a Declaration of the Russian Delegation on Carelian autonomy made on the day of its conclusion, which Declaration Finland claimed, and Russia denied, constituted part of the terms of the Treaty. The Court held that the question of whether the Declaration formed part of the obligations into which Russia entered, as Finland asserted, or was merely by way of information, as Russia contended, "is, in the very nature of things, a question of fact. The question is, was such an engagement made?"[62] The Court continued:

> There has been some discussion as to whether questions for an advisory opinion, if they relate to matters which form the subject of a pending dispute between nations, should be put to the Court without the consent of the parties. It is unnecessary in the present case to deal with the topic.
>
> It follows from the above that the opinion which the Court has been requested to give bears on an actual dispute between Finland and Russia. As Russia is not a

---

[61] *Ibid.*, pp. 12–14.   [62] *Ibid.*, p. 26.

Member of the League of Nations, the case is one under Article 17 of the Covenant. According to this article, in the event of a dispute between a Member of the League and a State which is not a Member of the League, the State not a Member of the League shall be invited to accept the obligations of membership in the League for the purposes of such dispute and, if this invitation is accepted, the provisions of Articles 12 to 16 inclusive shall be applied with such modifications as may be deemed necessary by the Council. This rule, moreover, only accepts and applies a principle which is a fundamental principle of international law, namely, the principle of the independence of States. It is well established in international law that no State can, without its consent, be compelled to submit its disputes with other States either to mediation or to arbitration, or to any other kind of pacific settlement. Such consent can be given once and for all in the form of an obligation freely undertaken, but it can, on the contrary, also be given in a special case apart from any existing obligation. The first alternative applies to the Members of the League who, having accepted the Covenant, are under the obligation resulting from the provisions of this pact dealing with the pacific settlement of international disputes. As concerns States not members of the League, the situation is quite different; they are not bound by the Covenant. The submission, therefore, of a dispute between them and a Member of the League for solution according to the methods provided for in the Covenant, could take place only by virtue of their consent. Such consent, however, has never been given by Russia. On the contrary, Russia has, on several occasions, clearly declared that it accepts no intervention by the League of Nations in the dispute with Finland. The refusals which Russia had already opposed to the steps suggested by the Council have been renewed upon the receipt by it of the notification of the request for an advisory opinion. The Court therefore finds it impossible to give its opinion on a dispute of this kind.[63]

The Court added that the question of whether Finland and Russia had contracted on the terms of the Declaration as to the nature of the autonomy of Eastern Carelia was "really one of fact,"[64] and that the Court would be at great disadvantage in inquiring about the facts in the absence of Russia. The question put to the Court concerned the main point of controversy between Finland and Russia and could only be decided by an investigation into the facts underlying the case. "Answering the question would be substantially equivalent to deciding the dispute between the parties. The Court, being a Court of Justice, cannot, even in giving advisory opinions, depart from the essential rules guiding their activity as a Court."[65]

Recalling the *Eastern Carelia* case in some detail is merited, even if it may

---

[63] *Ibid.*, p. 27. Relying particularly on the first paragraph of this quotation, Keith (*Advisory Jurisdiction*, pp. 90–97) argues that all the Court held in *Eastern Carelia* was that the *Council* (not the Court) lacked competence in the absence of Russia's consent.

[64] *Ibid.*, p. 28.   [65] *Ibid.*, p. 29.

be seen as an example not of the Council simply acting as the conduit for a request for an advisory opinion, but rather requesting an opinion on a dispute with which a State Member had earlier endeavored to seize the Council.[66] The case is important because – at least in predominant interpretation – it emphasizes a fundamental of States asking advisory opinions of the Court through the medium of an international organ: it must be the States concerned who so move the international organ, and not just one or some of the States concerned. If the States actually in dispute do not jointly move for an advisory opinion, or at any rate clearly manifest that they mutually desire an opinion, then, whatever the action of the international organ, it may be maintained that the Court should not give the opinion, for to do so would be to evade the basic jurisdictional constraints imposed upon the Court. The Court, in this view, is not entitled to pass upon the merits of a dispute between States without the consent of the real parties in interest. Where, as in *Eastern Carelia*, the facts are essentially at issue, there is an *a fortiori* case for the Court not responding to the question.

But whether this predominant interpretation of the meaning of the *Eastern Carelia* case is correct, or, more, whether, if it is, it is still the law, particularly in view of the advisory opinion of the International Court of Justice in the

---

[66] See the reception in the League Council of the Court's Opinion: *League of Nations Official Journal*, 1923, p. 1335. The case is among those listed by the Registry as submitted "at the instigation or request of a State or international organization" (*PCIJ, Series E, No. 14*, pp. 72, 74).

A request for another opinion from the Court may be cited as in accord with the *Eastern Carelia* approach. The League Council requested an advisory opinion in the case of the *Expulsion of the Oecumenical Patriarch*, *PCIJ, Series C, Nos. 9–11*. In that case, the Prime Minister of Greece appealed to the League Council to take up a dispute between Greece and Turkey concerning the forcible expulsion from Constantinople of the Patriarch (*ibid.*, p. 16). The Turkish Foreign Minister denied the competence of the Council to deal with the dispute, on the grounds that the status of the Patriarchate was a Turkish domestic matter and that "the exchange of Monseigneur Constantine Araboglou is properly a matter for the Mixed Commission" (*ibid.*, p. 19). The Council's Rapporteur recommended that the Council ask the Court to give an advisory opinion on whether the Council was empowered to deal with the dispute (*ibid.*, p. 89). The Council requested an advisory opinion on the question: "Do the objections to the competence of the Council raised by the Turkish Government ... preclude the Council from being competent in the matter brought before it by the Greek Government?" (*ibid.*, p. 14). The Court did not render an opinion, since the League Council withdrew the request on Greece's initiative (*ibid.*, p. 10). But the Council's entertaining such doubts about its competence in response to Turkey's challenge may suggest that, particularly in the light of the *Eastern Carelia* precedent, it would have been reluctant to request the Court for an advisory opinion on the merits of the dispute between Greece and Turkey without the consent of both States.

In its advisory opinion on *German Settlers in Poland*, 1923, *PCIJ, Series B, No. 6*, pp. 6, 19, 22, the Court observed that if "the subject matter of the controversy is not within the competency of the League, the Court would not be justified in rendering an opinion." It found that the subject matter had been placed by the terms of the Treaty of Versailles within the competence of the League and that those terms clearly made it "proper for the Council to exercise its power under Article 14 of the Covenant to request the advice of the Court on points of law, on the determination of which its action may depend."

Peace Treaties case,[67] is open to question.[68] It is not a question on which an answer is ventured in this essay.

Question of Jaworzina

The Conference of Ambassadors of the Principal Allied Powers was entrusted in 1920 with drawing a border between Czechoslovakia and Poland. A dispute arose between those two States as to whether that authority had been exhausted or whether the border question was still open. The Governments of France, Great Britain, Italy, and Japan, who were represented in the Conference of Ambassadors, brought the matter to the attention of the League Council, stating, *inter alia*, that they would have "no objection should the Council desire to ask the opinion" of the Court on the legal question which had arisen.[69] A Rapporteur of the Council reached agreement with representatives of Czechoslovakia and Poland on so doing and on the terms of the question.[70] The Council thereupon agreed to request an advisory opinion of the Court on the question:

> Is the question of the delimitation of the frontier between Poland and Czechoslovakia still open, and, if so, to what extent; or should it be considered as already settled by a final decision, (subject to the customary procedure of marking boundaries locally, with any modifications of detail which that procedure may entail)?[71]

In this case, the League Council acted as the conduit for requesting an opinion desired by all the States concerned. But it was not a mere conduit; it played a modest role in framing the question as well as in passing it to the Court for its opinion.

The Monastery of Saint-Naoum

As the Court stated in this advisory opinion, the question closely resembled that asked of it in the *Jaworzina* case.[72] The background of this opinion is intricate and (as others of the PCIJ considered in this essay) is usefully

---

[67] *Interpretation of Peace Treaties with Bulgaria, Hungary and Romania, ICJ Reports 1950*, pp. 65, 71–72.

[68] See Sir Hersch Lauterpacht, *The Development of International Law by the International Court* (1982), pp. 107–109, 248–250, 352–358; Keith, *Advisory Jurisdiction*, pp. 89–132; and Pomerance, *Advisory Function*, pp. 287–296. Among other relevant cases are *Interpretation of Article 3, Paragraph 2, of the Treaty of Lausanne, 1925, PCIJ, Series B, No. 12; Reservations to the Convention on the Prevention and Punishment of the Crime of Genocide, ICJ Reports 1951*; and *Legal Consequences for States of the Continued Presence of South Africa in Namibia (South West Africa) notwithstanding Security Council Resolution 276 (1970), ICJ Reports 1971.*

[69] *League of Nations Official Journal*, 1923, p. 1472.　　[70] *Ibid.*, p. 1474.

[71] *Ibid.*, p. 1332, and *PCIJ, Series B, No. 8*, p. 10.

[72] *PCIJ, Series B, No. 9*, pp. 6, 15.

summarized in a headnote found in *World Court Reports*.[73] For present purposes, what is pertinent is that the Conference of Ambassadors, acting on behalf of the Governments of the British Empire, France, Italy, and Japan, remitted the question of the border between Albania and Yugoslavia at the point of the monastery of Saint-Naoum to the League Council, which decided, with the agreement of Albania and Yugoslavia,[74] to put the following request for an advisory opinion to the Court:

> Have the Principal Allied Powers, by the decision of the Conference of Ambassadors of December 6th, 1922, exhausted, in regard to the frontier between Albania and the Kingdom of the Serbs, Croats and Slovenes at the Monastery of Saint-Naoum, the mission, such as it has been recognized by the interested Parties, which is contemplated by a unanimous Resolution of the Assembly of the League of Nations of October 2nd, 1921?[75]

This appears to be a case in which the Council exerted a measure of initiative, together with that of the Conference of Ambassadors. The Conference of Ambassadors put two questions to the Council; the Council's Rapporteur concluded that the first question was "purely legal" and "interlocutory" and, "in accordance with precedent," he proposed that it be referred to the Court for its advisory opinion; and this was done.[76]

Jurisdiction of the European Commission of the Danube

Differences arose between Romania, on the one hand, and Great Britain, France, and Italy, on the other, on the extent of the competence of the European Commission of the Danube. The British Government brought these differences to the Advisory and Technical Committee for Communications and Transit of the League of Nations, whose jurisdiction Romania challenged. As a result of discussions among the States concerned, the representatives in the European Commission of the Danube of France, Great Britain, Italy, and Romania concluded an agreement (which was registered as a treaty with the League) to request the Council of the League to submit three questions to the Court for its advisory opinion.[77] When that request came before the League Council, the British representative, while not opposing its adoption, placed on record that requesting an advisory opinion of the Court, "instead of referring the dispute for decision, must be regarded as an

---

[73] Manley O. Hudson, *World Court Reports* (1934), Vol. I, pp. 391–392. See also *League of Nations Official Journal*, 1924, p. 1006.

[74] *Ibid.*, p. 920.   [75] *PCIJ, Series B, No. 9*, p. 7.

[76] *League of Nations Official Journal*, 1924, p. 1006.

[77] *Jurisdiction of the European Commission of the Danube, PCIJ, Series B, No. 14*, p. 8, and *League of Nations Official Journal*, 1927, pp. 233–234.

exceptional case, and must not be thought to constitute a precedent for similar action in the future. Nor must it be deemed to constitute an abandonment of the view that, in virtue of treaties and arrangements in force, any party to this dispute would have been entitled to bring the question to the Permanent Court of International Justice for decision ... To abandon that contention would weaken the machinery which has been set up for the settlement of disputes as to the meaning and application of the Ports and Waterways Sections of the Treaties of Peace."[78] In response, the representative of Romania stressed the difference between an advisory opinion and a judgment of the Court and emphasized that negotiations in progress on the dispute would continue.[79] The Council then adopted a resolution requesting the Court to give an advisory opinion on the three questions precisely as they had been drafted by the representatives of the four States concerned. The resolution also invited the four Governments to afford the Court all the assistance it might require in the consideration of those questions.[80] Those Governments filed Memorials and Counter-Memorials and took part in oral argument.

The case is an interesting one, in that apparently there was a basis for bringing contentious proceedings but the parties nevertheless concluded a kind of special agreement, not for proceeding contentiously, but for requesting the League Council to ask for an advisory opinion. The Council did as asked.

Access to German Minority Schools in Upper Silesia

A last advisory opinion which is described by the Registry of the Permanent Court as sought not by the Council *proprio motu* but at the instance of States is *Access to German Minority Schools in Upper Silesia*.[81] However, as far as examination of the proceedings in the League Council,[82] as well as the Court's opinion,[83] indicates, while the question put to the Court was formulated by the Council's Rapporteur in agreement with the German and Polish Governments, it is not clear that this is an illustration of an opinion being requested at the instance of States rather than by the Council as an element of its consideration of an item with which it was dealing.

Constraints Imposed by the Court on Seeking Advisory Opinions

In its contentious proceedings over *German Interests in Polish Upper Silesia*, the Court had occasion to observe that whereas the Court may give advisory

---

[78] *League of Nations Official Journal*, 1927, p. 151.   [79] *Ibid.*, pp. 151–152.
[80] *PCIJ, Series B, No. 14*, p. 6.
[81] See *Fourteenth Annual Report of the Permanent Court of International Justice, PCIJ, Series E, No. 14*, p. 75.
[82] *League of Nations Official Journal*, 1931, pp. 228–229, 1151, 2263.   [83] *PCIJ, Series A/B, No. 40*, p. 4.

opinions at the request of the Council or Assembly of the League of Nations, "a request of this kind directly submitted by a State will not be considered."[84] Moreover, a request made by the Council or Assembly on behalf of States (or international organizations) will be held to the terms of the request made. Thus, in the *Interpretation of the Greco-Bulgarian Agreement of 9 December 1927*, the Council requested the Court to give an advisory opinion on two questions; however, its answering of the second question was conditional on an affirmative answer to the first question.[85] The Court held:

> As the Court has arrived at the conclusion that the answer to the first question is not in the affirmative, the second question does not arise ...
>
> In the course of the written pleadings and also in the course of the oral arguments before the Court, the Agents and Counsel of each of the Governments concerned stated that they were anxious that the Court should give an opinion upon the second question whether the first question was answered in the affirmative or not. The Court feels unable to comply with this desire.
>
> By the terms of Article 14 of the Covenant, the right to submit a question to the advisory jurisdiction of the Court is given only to the Assembly and to the Council of the League. The Court is therefore bound by the terms of the questions as formulated in this case by the Council. The second question is so worded as to be put to the Court conditionally upon an affirmative answer being given to the first question. To ignore this condition at the request of the Parties would be in effect to allow the two interested Governments to submit a question for the advisory opinion of the Court.[86]

Reconsideration of the Extent of Advisory Jurisdiction

It has been shown that, in the Permanent Court, while only the League Council and Assembly were authorized to request advisory opinions, in practice a large number of opinions were requested through the medium of the Council by States and international organizations. The Council retained a supervening authority, certainly in the eyes of the Court, but in most cases it actually exerted no such authority beyond being the conduit through which the request to the Court passed; that is, for the most part, the Council served

[84] *German Interests in Polish Upper Silesia (Jurisdiction)*, PCIJ, Series A, No. 6, p. 21. Notice the qualification "directly." The Court observed that the applicant State "could not have intended to obtain an advisory opinion, for which it was not entitled to ask" (*ibid.*).

[85] PCIJ, Series A/B, No. 45, p. 70. The questions put were:

In the case at issue, is there a dispute between Greece and Bulgaria within the meaning of Article 8 of the Caphandaris–Molloff Agreement concluded at Geneva on December 9th, 1927?

If so, what is the nature of the pecuniary obligations arising out of this Agreement?

[86] *Ibid.*, p. 87. See also *Exchange of Greek and Turkish Populations*, PCIJ, Series B, No. 10, p. 17, where the Court indicated that it could not take cognizance of a question not asked by the Council; and, to similar effect, *Interpretation of the Greco-Turkish Agreement of 1 December 1926*, PCIJ, Series B, No. 16, p. 16.

as a mere conduit. It might be said that this was so because the two leading Powers of the League, Great Britain and France, were the real movers behind the requests for opinions; but while this was true in some cases, it was not true in all (as in the requests concerning disputes among Turkey, Greece, and Bulgaria). When the provisions of the United Nations Charter and the Statute of the International Court of Justice relating to the Court's advisory jurisdiction came to be drafted, to what extent was account taken of this practice of the League Council and the Permanent Court?

Report of the Informal Inter-Allied Committee

The first stage of reconsideration of the Court's Statute took place in an Informal Inter-Allied Committee on the Future of the Permanent Court of International Justice (of which Gerald Fitzmaurice was the Secretary), which met in London 1943–4.

Its Report of February 10, 1944 contained these innovative passages about the scope of a projected advisory jurisdiction, which call for extended quotation:

65. Some of us were inclined to think at first that the Court's jurisdiction to give advisory opinions was anomalous and ought to be abolished, mainly on the ground that it was incompatible with the true function of a court of law, which was to hear and decide disputes. It was urged that the existence of this jurisdiction tended to encourage the use of the Court as an instrument for settling issues which were essentially of a political rather than of a legal character and that this was undesirable. Attention was drawn to instances of this which had occurred in the past. Subsidiary objections were that the existence of this jurisdiction might promote a tendency to avoid the final settlement of disputes by seeking opinions, and might lead to general pronouncements of law by the Court not (or not sufficiently) related to a particular issue or set of facts.

66. Despite these considerations we have come to the conclusion that the jurisdiction to give advisory opinions ought to be retained and ought even to be enlarged. In the first place it is not correct to say that a jurisdiction of an "advisory" nature is inconsistent with the proper function of a court of law. The legal systems of certain countries contain a procedure whereby certain matters can be referred to the courts for an opinion, or for a declaration of what the law is, or what the rights or status of the applicant are or would be under a given set of circumstances. The exercise of this jurisdiction by municipal courts has not, so far as we are aware, led to difficulty, and has proved of undoubted utility.

67. Secondly, it is clear that a General International Organization, if it possesses anything in the nature of a regular Constitution, will require authoritative

legal advice on points affecting the Constitution, the rights and obligations of Member States and the interpretation of the instrument setting up the Organization. There are distinct limits to the extent to which such matters can be dealt with internally (e.g., by the legal section of the Organization's Secretariat) or by such means as reference to an *ad hoc* committee of jurists. League experience has shown the necessity of having an authoritative standing tribunal to which, in suitable cases, questions of this kind can be referred for an opinion. On this ground alone, therefore, we think that the jurisdiction of the Court to give advisory opinions must be retained.

68. In the third place, there are reasons which make it desirable to allow two or more States, acting in concert, to obtain an advisory opinion. They are as follows:

(a) From an international point of view, it seems desirable to provide a procedure whereby the legal rights and position of parties can be determined or at any rate assessed, before any difference of opinion between them has ripened into an issue or definite dispute which can only be settled by actual litigation.

(b) It may be useful to countries to be able to ascertain their legal position without involving themselves in a judicial decision binding on them as such and requiring immediate execution.

(c) The faculty to ask for an advisory opinion may be very helpful to parties engaged in negotiations (e.g., for a treaty or for the settlement of some outstanding issue) where the requisite basis for negotiation does not exist until the legal rights of the parties, or the correct interpretation of some existing instrument, has been definitely ascertained.

(d) There may well be cases in which special relations between countries render them reluctant to appear before the Court as apparently hostile contending parties in a litigation, but where the existence of a "friendly dispute" between them nevertheless requires some form of disposal by legal means.

(e) Whereas an International Organization can to some extent meet its needs by referring questions to an *ad hoc* committee of jurists, this procedure is difficult, if not impossible, for States. Reference to some *ad hoc* tribunal is no doubt possible, but if the Court exists it is best that it should be used, and its pronouncements will carry greater weight than those of any such tribunal.

69. In the light of this conclusion, the subject of advisory opinions resolves itself mainly into two questions, whether the scope of the jurisdiction should remain as it is at present, or be enlarged; and what safeguards should be instituted to control it and to prevent its misuse. The first of these questions is, in essence, whether the faculty to request advisory opinions should be confined to the executive organs of any future General International Organization, or should be extended to other bodies, and to individual States. The second question concerns the steps to be taken to ensure what we are all agreed are most important requirements, namely, that only questions of law should be referred for an advisory opinion, and that such questions should not be of a merely general or abstract character, but should relate to some definite issue or circumstance, and be based on an agreed and stated set of facts. Failing some

such control, there is a risk that the Court may be used for making pronouncements on political issues, or in a semi-legislative capacity for making general statements or declarations of law, instead of giving advice as to what the law is in relation to a defined issue or set of facts.

70. Concerning the scope of the faculty to seek advisory opinions, we are agreed that there is no reason to confine it to the executive organs of the future General International Organization, and that it could usefully be extended to other associations of States such as the International Labor Office, the Universal Postal Union, etc. Unless the list of such Associations is settled for this purpose, either in the Statute of the Court or from time to time by the General International Organization, it would be for the Court itself to decide whether the body concerned had the international and intergovernmental character necessary to give it the capacity to ask the Court for an advisory opinion.

71. We are also agreed that, provided the necessary safeguards can be instituted, there would, for the reasons given in paragraph 68, be considerable advantage in permitting references on the part of two or more States acting in concert. Applications by an individual State *ex parte* could not be permitted, for, given the authoritative nature of the Court's pronouncements, *ex parte* applications would afford a means whereby the State concerned could indirectly impose a species of compulsory jurisdiction on the rest of the world. In addition, the Court must have an *agreed* basis of fact on which to give its opinion.

72. With regard to the question of how the necessary control can be secured over matters referred to the Court for an advisory opinion, so as to ensure that only questions proper to be put to the Court are heard by it, we have considered whether all applications should pass through and be required to receive the fiat of the appropriate organ of the General International Organization. The objections to this are, first, that the nature and functions of such an Organization are at present unsettled; secondly, that some control will require to be established over the Organization's own applications for advisory opinions.

73. On the whole therefore it seems to us desirable to leave the necessary control to be exercised by the Court itself . . . we attach the greatest importance to the Court's jurisdiction being confined to matters which are really "justiciable," and this applies equally to advisory opinions. It would, accordingly, be for the Court to decline to deal with an application directed to political and not legal issues, or to require a restatement of the case so as to confine it to pure questions of law or treaty interpretation. The Court would equally refuse to consider the application if the facts were not agreed, or were inadequately stated, or if the questions put were of too general a character, not involving concrete issues in which the parties were actively interested. In the same way the Court would refuse to allow the procedure by way of advisory opinions to be used as a means of reopening questions already judicially determined, or for pronouncing on questions of municipal law where these lay solely within the competence of domestic tribunals.

74. All these would be matters to be provided for in the Statute of the Court. In

addition, it would be necessary to ensure that it was not open to two States, acting in concert, to obtain a pronouncement from the Court on a matter of interest to other States (e.g., the interpretation of a multilateral convention) where the latter had had no opportunity of intervening. We consider that this point would be adequately met by maintaining the procedure of notification by the Registrar of the Court set out in the existing Statute.

75. If such a scheme be adopted, we see no objection to allowing two or more States, acting in concert, to apply direct to the Court for an advisory opinion.[87]

Revisions Proposed by the United States to the PCIJ Statute, and the Dumbarton Oaks Proposals

No representative of the United States took part in the work of the Inter-Allied Committee. The Statute of the Permanent Court of International Justice with Revisions Proposed by the United States, August 1944, would have amended the Statute to provide that: "Questions upon which the advisory opinion of the Court is asked shall be laid before the Court by means of a written request, signed by the chairman of the executive council of the general international organization."[88] That is to say, in this initial United States conception, only the council – which was shortly to be renamed the Security Council – would have been authorized to request advisory opinions of the Court. This regressive approach appears to have reflected the then current preoccupation of the United States with the exclusive role of the Council in the maintenance of international peace and security. Advisory opinions were viewed as adjunctive to that role.[89]

The Dumbarton Oaks Proposals for the Establishment of a General International Organization, prepared by the United States, the United Kingdom, and the Soviet Union, and then by the United States, the United Kingdom, and China, provided that there should be an international court of justice which should constitute the principal judicial organ of the Organization, and that all members of the Organization should *ipso facto* be parties to the Statute of the Court, but it did not decide whether that Statute should be that of the Permanent Court, suitably modified, or a new Statute. The Dumbarton Oaks Proposals further provided, in the Chapter on "Arrangements for the Maintenance of International Peace and Security ...," and in

---

[87] *Report of the Informal Inter-Allied Committee on the Future of the Permanent Court of International Justice,* 1944, Cmd. 6531, paras. 65–74.

[88] The text is reprinted in Ruth B. Russell and Jeanette E. Muther, *A History of the United Nations Charter* (1958), pp. 1017, 1023–1024.

[89] *Ibid.,* p. 873.

line with the foregoing US approach, that: "Justiciable disputes should normally be referred to the international court of justice. The Security Council should be empowered to refer to the court, for advice, legal questions connected with other disputes."[90] Refinement of the bare Dumbarton Oaks Proposals was left to the Washington Committee of Jurists, which convened under the chairmanship of Green H. Hackworth two weeks before the San Francisco Conference.

The Washington Committee of Jurists

When the Statute of the Permanent Court was re-examined at the session of the Washington Committee of Jurists, the United States maintained its proposal that advisory opinions may be requested only on the authority of the Security Council, "in conformity with the Dumbarton Oaks Proposals."[91] However, the United Kingdom made proposals which reflected the approach of the Inter-Allied Committee. It suggested:

> The jurisdiction to give advisory opinions is at present limited to those cases in which such an opinion is requested by the appropriate body of the International Organization. There does not appear to be any sufficient ground for this limitation and it is suggested that the faculty to give advisory opinions, which has proved in the past to be of great value, should be extended to two further classes of cases. In the first place, it should be open to any recognized and properly constituted International Organization to apply directly to the Court with a request for an advisory opinion. Secondly, it is suggested that it would also be of great value if States, *by agreement amongst themselves* (not, of course, unilaterally), were able to apply to the Court for an advisory opinion. They would thus, in many cases, obtain advice as to their legal position which would prevent an eventual dispute leading to litigation.
>
> If the foregoing suggestions concerning advisory opinions were adopted, it would of course, be necessary to introduce safeguards, with a view to ensuring that the requests addressed to the Court were confined to matters of a strictly justiciable nature, and, moreover, related to actual matters of fact which had arisen between the parties concerned. To achieve this, it would be desirable to confer on the Court a right to reject any request for an advisory opinion, if the Court considered that, in the circumstances, the request was not one to which it, as a court of law, ought to accede.[92]

A number of States, including China, Guatemala, Mexico, Norway, and Venezuela, proposed that the General Assembly as well as the Security

---

[90] *Documents of the United Nations Conference on International Organization (UNCIO)*, 1945, Vol. 14, p. 458. See also p. 455.

[91] *Ibid.*, pp. 325, 345.

[92] *Ibid.*, p. 319. Venezuela also proposed that States be authorized to seek advisory opinions (*ibid.*, p. 373).

Council be authorized to request advisory opinions.[93] A Chinese proposal to this effect was unanimously accepted, while, at the same time, the Committee of Jurists recognized that it was for the Charter and not the Statute to determine what organs of the United Nations should be qualified to request an advisory opinion.[94] However, the Report of the Washington Committee of Jurists submitted to the San Francisco Conference recorded that: "The suggestion has been made to allow international organizations and, even to a certain extent, States to ask for advisory opinions. The Commission did not believe that it should adopt it."[95]

The debate in the Committee of Jurists that led to these conclusions remains of interest. The British representative (Fitzmaurice) referred to the utility of advisory opinions as a means of avoiding actual litigation and resolving differences before they reached the stage of disputes.[96] The representative of Venezuela (Gomez-Ruiz) proposed that the right to request advisory opinions be granted directly to public international organizations and to individual states, subject to the right of the Court to decide whether it was competent in the matter.[97] He indicated that he had in mind organizations which today would be termed Specialized Agencies. The British representative seconded the Venezuelan proposal. The French representative (Basdevant) gave measured support to Venezuela's proposal, particularly in relation to the Specialized Agencies.[98] The representative of the Soviet Union (Novikov) objected to granting individual States the right to apply directly to the Court for an advisory opinion. The Court could be overloaded with minor matters. Its function was not to serve as general adviser. States could apply to the General Assembly to seek an advisory opinion, but if they were entitled directly to seek opinions of the Court, Charter procedures for dealing with international disputes might be endangered. Thus he favored doing no more than adding the right of the General Assembly to that of the Security Council to seek advisory opinions.[99] The Australian representative (Eggleston) also maintained that the United Nations should in each case pass on whether an advisory opinion was to be asked of the Court. If the right were to be accorded to international organizations, such organizations must be permanent ones which had States as members; temporary or *ad hoc* organizations should be excluded.[100] The Venezuelan representative agreed that, if international organizations were to be accorded the authority to request advisory opinions, they should be permanent organizations of States,

---

[93] *Ibid.*, pp. 177, 445–447.   [94] *Ibid.*, pp. 179, 850.   [95] *Ibid.*, p. 850.   [96] *Ibid.*, p. 179.

[97] *Ibid.* See also an earlier Belgian proposal which, in restricted circumstances, would have authorized a State to request an advisory opinion (*ibid.*, pp. 445–446).

[98] *Ibid.*, p. 180.   [99] *Ibid.*, p. 181.   [100] *Ibid.*, p. 182.

connected with the United Nations.[101] Judge Hudson, who was present as a representative of the PCIJ, declined to express a view on the policy questions involved, but observed that the Court several times had given advisory opinions to international organizations other than the League, such as the Danube River Commission, the Greco–Bulgarian Mixed Emigration Commission, and the ILO, "all on requests made through the League. All such requests had promptly been transmitted to the Court."[102] The Chairman (Hackworth) observed that it was not yet known what international organizations would be created. He contrasted the orderly procedure of going through the Assembly with the confusion and crowding of dockets which might result from direct requests to the Court. There was no reason now for creating such rights. One might arise in the future, but the Committee should not look too far ahead.[103] A vote was then taken on the question whether the right to ask for advisory opinions should be extended to international organizations generally, and the proposal was disapproved by sixteen votes to four.[104] Rejection of a proposal to permit States directly to request advisory opinions appears to have been tacit.

It will be observed that this record of discussion is consistent with the conclusion that there was no intention in the Committee of Jurists to narrow the capacity to request advisory opinions from that which obtained in League days. The majority against according any international organizations, and States, the right directly to request advisory opinions was large, and a few representatives maintained that any decision which might be made to accord international organizations direct access to the Court's advisory jurisdiction should be restricted to the Specialized Agencies. But there was no disposition to debar international organizations and States from requesting the General Assembly or Security Council to request advisory opinions on their behalf, in pursuance of the precedent of the League of which the Committee was informed: via requests "through" the Organization to be "promptly transmitted" to the Court.

The San Francisco Conference

At the San Francisco Conference on International Organization, the United Kingdom proposed that provision be made in the Charter to empower the General Assembly and Security Council to request advisory opinions from the Court and that "suitable provision be made to enable such international agencies as the General Assembly may authorize for the purpose to request

[101] *Ibid.*   [102] *Ibid.*, pp. 182–183.   [103] *Ibid.*, p. 183.   [104] *Ibid.*, p. 184.

advisory opinions on questions of a constitutional or judicial character arising within the scope of their activities."[105] It was readily agreed to add to the Charter the provision, now Article 96, paragraph 1, providing that: "The General Assembly or the Security Council may request the International Court of Justice to give an advisory opinion on any legal question."[106] It was likewise agreed to insert a complementary provision in the Statute (today Article 65).[107] It was also agreed to make provision for agencies authorized by the General Assembly to request advisory opinions, but this agreement was restricted to intergovernmental agencies brought into relationship with the United Nations (i.e., Specialized Agencies).[108] The United Kingdom explained that its draft to this effect was safeguarded against abuse by adding the requirement that the international agencies be ones closely connected with the United Nations. Subsequently this provision was revised to provide that other organs of the United Nations and Specialized Agencies at any time so authorized by the General Assembly may request advisory opinions of the Court on legal questions arising within the scope of their activities.[109] However, the proposal, renewed by Venezuela, that two or more States acting in agreement should be empowered to request advisory opinions of the Court failed for lack of a two-thirds majority.[110]

This drafting history at San Francisco of the Charter and the Statute is no less consonant than that of the Committee of Jurists with the maintenance of the authority of international organizations which are not Specialized Agencies, and of States, to ask the General Assembly or Security Council of the United Nations to request advisory opinions of the Court on their behalf. At San Francisco, the point was made that the General Assembly would have to authorize which agencies independently could request opinions; but nothing in the record suggests that other organizations (and States) could not request the General Assembly to transmit to the Court their requests for advisory opinions. The Charter as adopted articulated the authority of the General Assembly and Security Council to request the Court to give an advisory

---

[105] *Ibid.*, Vol. 9, p. 359. This proposal was described as designed "to enable certain international agencies which are to be brought into relationship with the United Nations Organization to request advisory opinions from the Court on questions relating to the interpretation of their constitutions or of conventions within their respective fields" (*ibid.*, pp. 358–359).

[106] *Ibid.*, Vol. 13, p. 241.

[107] *Ibid.*, p. 242, on the ground that, "while the Statute was part of the Charter, the Charter was not a part of the Statute." See also Vol. 9, pp. 161–162, 363–364.

[108] *Ibid.*, Vol. 9, pp. 161–162, and Vol. 13, p. 298.

[109] *Ibid.*, p. 247. A Soviet proposal to require General Assembly authorization "in each case" rather than "at any time" was not adopted, to avoid the inconvenience and delay which going to the General Assembly in each case might occasion. *Ibid.*, Vol. 13, pp. 298–299.

[110] *Ibid.*, Vol. 13, p. 235.

opinion "on any legal question" (a broader formulation than that of the Covenant, which apparently occasioned no analytical discussion in its drafting). It represented an advance on the Covenant, insofar as it provides that other organs of the Organization and the Specialized Agencies may be authorized to request advisory opinions of the Court on legal questions arising within the scope of their activities. That advance did not fully codify and progressively develop the practice that evolved in League days, for, if it had, two further innovations would have been introduced: the right of intergovernmental organizations to be authorized to request an advisory opinion even if such organizations were not Specialized Agencies; and the right of States by agreement in a particular case to request an advisory opinion. Shabtai Rosenne characterizes the restriction of Article 96, paragraph 2 of the Charter to organs and Specialized Agencies authorized by the General Assembly as "unduly limitative" and he rightly observes that, in this respect, "the practice of the United Nations compares unfavorably with that of the League, where, despite the formal centralization of the political control over requests in one of the two organs authorized to initiate advisory cases, several widely differing types of international organizations and organs, as well as groups of States, were in fact in a position to avail themselves of the Court's advice. It may therefore be hoped that it will be found possible to broaden the circle of public international organizations entitled to request advisory opinions, without impairing the general control of the General Assembly over those matters . . ."[111] He thus appears to recognize that, within the terms of the Charter and Statute, an evolution of practice comparable to that which existed in League days is possible.

United Nations Practice

Not only does the United Nations Charter provide for a broader capacity to request advisory opinions of the International Court of Justice than did the Covenant for requests of the Permanent Court, but there are other differences between the League and the United Nations which affect their readiness, if not their authority, to request advisory opinions, some cutting one way and some the other; among them are the following. The League of Nations operated largely on the unanimity rule,[112] whereas United Nations

---

[111] Shabtai Rosenne, *The Law and Practice of the International Court* (1965), Vol. II, p. 661.

[112] Whether, however, unanimity in the League Council (including the votes of States in dispute) was required for adoption of a request for an advisory opinion was an unsettled and vexed issue. See *Twelfth Report of the Permanent Court of International Justice*, PCIJ, Series E, No. 12, pp. 117–127; *Sixteenth Report of the Permanent Court of International Justice*, PCIJ, Series E, No. 16, pp. 63–64; *League*

organs operate by absolute or qualified majority vote.[113] The Covenant of the League, and the concerns of League organs, were more highly charged with considerations of international law than are those of the United Nations Charter and its organs. The League Council, at least initially, was a smaller and more homogeneous body than is the Security Council; it operated less formally and, in its early years, more congenially and effectively, than has the Security Council, and thus may have been a likelier organ to act as a conduit for requests to the Court for advisory opinions made by other international organizations and States. Moreover, unlike the League Council, the Security Council is not the executive committee of the Organization at large but an organ which rather has primary responsibility for the maintenance of international peace and security. It is not clear whether the Security Council is, and would regard itself as, a suitable organ to request advisory opinions which are not directly related to that charge. Yet Chapter VI of the Charter, "Pacific Settlement of Disputes," is a "Security Council" chapter of the Charter, and it embraces the settlement of disputes whose continuance "is likely to endanger the maintenance of international peace and security." In pursuance of such settlement, and its even wider authority under Article 34 to "investigate any dispute, or any situation which might lead to international friction or give rise to a dispute, in order to determine whether the continuance of the dispute or situation is likely to endanger the maintenance of international peace and security," the Security Council may call on the parties to settle their dispute by judicial means. It may accordingly be maintained that the Council's remit is wide enough to embrace requesting an advisory opinion on a dispute or situation which "might lead to international friction" which is in turn requested by States or an international organization, even if the maintenance of international peace and security is not immediately at stake. That conclusion may call in aid the authority of the Security Council under Article 96, paragraph 2, to request the Court to give an advisory opinion "on any legal question."[114] At the same time, it may be recalled that

---

of Nations Official Journal, 1937, pp. 77–79; Manley O. Hudson, *The Permanent Court of International Justice, 1920–1942* (1943), pp. 488–494; and Pomerance, *Advisory Function*, pp. 213–221. In practice, the League Council was generally prepared to request the Court's opinion only on the basis of a unanimous vote. There were at least two apparent exceptions to this rule: *Acquisition of Polish Nationality*, PCIJ, Series B, No. 7; and *Interpretation of Article 4, Paragraph 2, of the Treaty of Lausanne*, PCIJ, Series B, No. 13.

[113] See Rosenne, *Law and Practice*, Vol. II, p. 659.

[114] It is of interest to recall that, at San Francisco, the representative of the USSR, Professor Golunsky, stated that authorizing the Security Council to give effect to decisions of the Court would accord the Council authority to deal with matters which might have nothing to do with security. (*Documents of the United Nations Conference on International Organization*, Vol. 17, p. 97.) But see a restrictive British view of the Council's authority, *ibid.*, Vol. 9, p. 359.

the Security Council, in forty-five years, has asked the Court for an advisory opinion just once. The large majority of all advisory opinions have been sought by the General Assembly. While most advisory opinions requested by the League Council concerned specific disputes between States, the advisory opinions requested by the General Assembly largely have concerned questions of what may be termed international constitutional law.

Authorizing United Nations Organs to Request Advisory Opinions

In implementation of Article 96, paragraph 2 of the Charter, the General Assembly proceeded to authorize certain United Nations organs to request advisory opinions on legal questions arising within the scope of their activities. The organs so authorized are the Economic and Social Council, the Trusteeship Council, the Interim Committee of the General Assembly, and the Committee on Applications for Review of Judgments of the United Nations Administrative Tribunal. The Economic and Social Council has exercised that authority once. The Committee on Applications for Review of UNAT Judgments has exercised its authority three times. The General Assembly itself has requested the remaining advisory opinions, apart from three requested by Specialized Agencies (and the single opinion requested by the Security Council).

In connection with authorizing the Committee on Applications for Review of Judgments of the United Nations Administrative Tribunal to request advisory opinions, the question was raised whether it would be an organ entitled to request advisory opinions of the Court on legal questions arising within the scope of *its* activities, as contrasted with the legal activities of the Tribunal itself. When the first request for an advisory opinion brought by the Committee came before the Court, the Court dealt with that question in this way:

> 19. Article 96, paragraph 2, of the Charter, empowers the General Assembly to authorize organs of the United Nations to "request advisory opinions of the Court on legal questions arising within the scope of their activities". In the present instance ... the Statute of the Administrative Tribunal expressly states that the Committee "For the purpose of this article ... is ... authorized under paragraph 2 of Article 96 of the Charter to request advisory opinions of the Court". These two provisions, prima facie, suffice to establish the competence of the Committee to request advisory opinions of the Court. The point has been raised, however, as to whether under ... the Statute of the Administrative Tribunal the Committee has any activities of its own which enable it to be considered as requesting advisory opinions "on legal questions arising within the scope of [its] activities". Thus, the view has been expressed that the

Committee has no other activity than to request advisory opinions, and that the "legal questions" arise not within the scope of "its activities" but of those of another organ, the Administrative Tribunal.

20. The functions entrusted to the Committee ... are: to receive applications which formulate objections to judgments of the Administrative Tribunal on one or more of the grounds set out ... and which ask the Committee to request an advisory opinion; to decide within 30 days whether or not there is a substantial basis for the application; and, if it so decides, to request an advisory opinion of the Court. The scope of the activities of the Committee which result from these functions is, admittedly, a narrow one. But the Committee's activities ... have to be viewed in the larger context of the General Assembly's function in the regulation of staff relations of which they form a part. This is not a delegation by the General Assembly of its own power to request an advisory opinion; it is the creation of a subsidiary organ having a particular task and invested it with the power to request advisory opinions in the performance of that task. The mere fact that the Committee's activities serve a particular, limited, purpose in the General Assembly's performance of its function in the regulation of staff relations does not prevent the advisory jurisdiction of the Court from being exercised in regard to those activities; nor is there any indication in Article 96 of the Charter of any such restriction upon the General Assembly's power to authorize organs of the United Nations to request advisory opinions.

21. In fact, the primary function of the Committee is not the requesting of advisory opinions, but the examination of objections to judgments in order to decide in each case whether there is a substantial basis for the application so as to call for a request for an advisory opinion. If it finds that there is not such a substantial basis for the application the Committee rejects the application without requesting an opinion of the Court. When it does find that there is a substantial basis for the application, the legal questions which the Committee then submits to the Court clearly arise out of the performance of this primary function of screening the applications presented to it. They are therefore questions which, in the view of the Court, arise within the scope of the Committee's own activities; for they arise not out of the judgments of the Administrative Tribunal but out of objections to those judgments raised before the Committee itself.[115]

The only bodies which may, under Article 96, paragraph 2 of the Charter be authorized by the General Assembly to request advisory opinions are "organs of the United Nations and specialized agencies." In the foregoing case, the Court construed "organs" to include subsidiary as well as principal organs.[116] However, when it was contemplated that the Human Rights

---

[115] *Application for Review of Judgement No. 158 of the United Nations Administrative Tribunal, ICJ Reports 1973*, pp. 166, 172–175.

[116] *Ibid.*, pp. 172–173.

Committee to be constituted pursuant to the then proposed International Covenant on Civil and Political Rights should be authorized to request advisory opinions, the Secretary-General advised that, since the Committee was to be established under an instrument separate and distinct from the Charter and would be neither a principal nor subsidiary organ of the United Nations nor a Specialized Agency, it could not itself be authorized to request advisory opinions. Nor, the Secretary-General concluded, could the Committee be given the right to request advisory opinions through the simple intermediation of another organ (as the United Kingdom had proposed):

13. After careful consideration, it is our conclusion that it is not possible under the Charter to provide that an organ shall act solely as an intermediary in transmitting to the Court legal questions which the Human Rights Committee would request. The reasons for this conclusion can be stated briefly. If an organ were to act merely as a transmitting agent, it is evident that the Human Rights Committee would, in fact, be empowered to make the requests for advisory opinions. The organ would then be only performing a purely administrative or "ministerial" function, similar to that which the Secretary-General now performs in transmitting to the Court questions put by the General Assembly. It would, therefore, mean that a body which could not be authorized to request advisory opinions under the Charter was in fact being given that authority. This, in our view, would be contrary to Article 96.

14. We should also like to make it clear that this conclusion is not merely based on a technicality. The right to present requests for advisory opinions has been conferred by the Charter, or, in accordance with the Charter, by the General Assembly, only to [sic] certain organs which are expected to weigh the proposal in the light of the general interests of the United Nations as well as in regard to the particular question. During the drafting of the Charter at San Francisco, the policy was laid down that the right to make requests for advisory opinions should be restricted to public international organizations which are part of the United Nations or brought into relationship with it. The language of Article 96(2) was carefully drawn up to express this policy. It would be defeating the object of the provision if the authorized organs were to act merely as conduits for transmitting requests of a body which could not be authorized directly.

15. However, there seems to be no reason why an organ properly authorized to request advisory opinions may not be instructed to take into account suggestions or recommendations of another organization. As a precedent one might note that in the Covenant of the League it was considered proper for the Council to give consideration to suggestions of the ILO in regard to requests for advisory opinions concerning that organization, although it was not considered proper that the Council automatically transmit the requests of the ILO. Consequently, it would be permissible to provide in the Covenant that the proposed Human Rights Committee may recommend or suggest to a

competent organ of the United Nations that that organ request the Court to give an advisory opinion on a legal question arising out of the Committee's activities. It would be clearly understood that the responsibility would remain with the authorized organ, and, therefore, that the organ would have discretion with respect to presenting the legal question and with respect to framing the language of the question. In short, the Human Rights Committee would be in a position to make suggestions but the final responsibility would be placed in a competent organ of the United Nations.[117]

In the light of the tenor of the pertinent exchanges in the Washington Committee of Jurists and at San Francisco which have been described above, the Secretary-General's conclusion is certainly a possible and even plausible one, but it goes farther than required. The drafters of the Charter and Statute were on notice of the practice of the League Council in serving as a conduit for requests of other international organizations for advisory opinions. They certainly indicated no intention and drafted no text designed to debar that practice from being pursued in the United Nations. What they did do was to provide, after some debate on the question, that only organs of the United Nations and the Specialized Agencies – i.e., international organizations as defined in Article 57 of the Charter which are brought into relationship with the United Nations – could be authorized at any time to request advisory opinions of the Court on legal questions arising within the scope of their activities. But Article 96 of the Charter does not in terms or intent preclude other international organizations from requesting that particular questions be transmitted on their behalf by the General Assembly or the Security Council to the Court. The Secretary-General indeed accepts that conclusion, provided that the role of the transmitting organ is not that of a mere conduit – i.e., provided that it is prepared to exert a measure of supervision and control over questions put. Such a measure of supervision and control may be seen as inherent in the fact that the question cannot be directly put by the international organization immediately concerned but can be forwarded only through the medium of the General Assembly or Security Council. But in practice the General Assembly or Security Council may lawfully forgo such supervision and control, as, in practice, the League Council frequently did. Such abstinence itself would not, it is believed, invalidate the procedure. The General Assembly and Security Council may each act as conduit; either could

---

[117] United Nations Doc. E/1732 of June 26, 1950, pp. 4–6 (footnotes omitted). C. Wilfred Jenks commented that "the view that an organ established under an international agreement concluded under the auspices of the United Nations is not an organ of the United Nations for this purpose appears to be a somewhat narrow view which might well be reconsidered" (*The Prospects of International Adjudication* [1964], p. 197).

constitute a subsidiary organ to act on its behalf; but neither could surrender ultimate responsibility for questions transmitted to the Court on behalf of other organizations or of States. The originating organization or State would not be confined, as the Secretary-General argues, to making suggestions; as in the League, the precise questions could come from the source of origin and the transmitting organ in practice could confine itself to transmitting them to the Court, provided that it retains, as it must, an ultimate authority to transmit or not to transmit, and to revise or not to revise. Of course, the fact that (as in the practice of League organs) the General Assembly and Security Council do retain a residual competence to request or not to request the advisory opinion sought, or even to amend the terms of the question to be put, may inhibit international organizations and States from having recourse to the process.

Authorizing the Specialized Agencies

The International Labor Organization, the Food and Agriculture Organization, the United Nations Educational, Scientific and Cultural Organization (UNESCO), the World Health Organization (WHO), the International Bank for Reconstruction and Development, the World Bank's International Finance Corporation and International Development Association, the International Monetary Fund, the International Civil Aviation Organization, the International Telecommunication Union, the World Meteorological Organization, the International Maritime Organization (IMO), the World Intellectual Property Organization, the International Fund for Agricultural Development, the United Nations Industrial Development Organization, and the International Atomic Energy Agency (IAEA)[118] have all been

---

[118] The authorizing instruments are listed in *ICJ Yearbook 1989–1990*, pp. 56–61. The IAEA is not regarded, strictly speaking, as a Specialized Agency, and the relationship agreement between it and the United Nations, unlike others, does not expressly describe it as a Specialized Agency, apparently because that agreement was not entered into by the Economic and Social Council pursuant to Article 63 of the Charter. When the General Assembly approved the authorization of the IAEA to request advisory opinions, the British representative expressed some doubt on the point. See Keith, *Advisory Jurisdiction*, pp. 40–41.

There are a number of other agreements which bear on the Court's advisory jurisdiction, also listed in the Yearbooks of the Court. For example, the Convention on the Privileges and Immunities of the United Nations provides, in Section 30:

All differences arising out of the interpretation or application of the present convention shall be referred to the International Court of Justice unless in any case it is agreed by the parties to have recourse to another mode of settlement. If a difference arises between the United Nations on the one hand and a Member on the other hand, a request shall be made for an advisory opinion on any legal question involved in accordance with Article 96 of the Charter and Article 65 of the Statute of the Court. The opinion given by the Court shall be accepted as decisive by the parties.

(*United Nations Treaty Series*, Vol. I, p. 30)

authorized by the General Assembly to request advisory opinions of the Court on legal questions arising within the scope of their activities. These authorizations are largely contained in agreements between the United Nations and the various Agencies which have been approved by the General Assembly. These agreements exclude the authority to request advisory opinions on relationships of the Organization in question with the United Nations or other Specialized Agencies.

There was "some substantial initial hesitation" on the part of the United Nations about granting to the Specialized Agencies general authorization to request advisory opinions, stemming from the otherwise perspicacious Report of the Preparatory Commission of the United Nations.[119] It manifested itself in a claimed reservation by the General Assembly of a right to revoke the authorizations granted, a claim which Dr. Jenks sharply criticized as legally questionable and practically unnecessary.[120] But Jenks concluded that:

> The liberal policy in regard to authorizations which has been adopted by the General Assembly should progressively and ultimately enable the Court to play a major role in the development of international institutions; a more restrictive policy would inevitably have led to the creation of a multiplicity of special tribunals and would have tended to limit severely the opportunities open to the Court to exercise a unifying influence on the development of international law, and in particular on the law relating to international institutions.[121]

By 1991, three Specialized Agencies had sought advisory opinions of the Court: UNESCO;[122] IMCO (IMO);[123] and WHO.[124] This paucity of requests demonstrates that frequency of recourse to the Court's advisory jurisdiction is not simply a function of the extension of the capacity to request opinions.[125]

No other international organization, such as the Organization of American

---

[119] Jenks, *Prospects*, p. 197.

[120] *Ibid.*, pp. 197–206. See United Nations, *Repertory of Practice of United Nations Organs*, Vol. V, pp. 88–89.

[121] Jenks, *Prospects*, p. 203.

[122] UNESCO's Executive Board requested the advisory opinion, acting within the framework of Article XII of the Statute of the Administrative Tribunal of the ILO. *Judgments of the Administrative Tribunal of the ILO upon complaints made against the UNESCO, ICJ Reports 1956*, p. 77.

[123] *Constitution of the Maritime Safety Committee of the Inter-Governmental Maritime Consultative Organization, ICJ Reports 1960*, p. 150.

[124] *Interpretation of the Agreement of 25 March 1951 between the WHO and Egypt, ICJ Reports 1980*, p. 73.

[125] For speculations on why so few requests have been made, see Jenks, *Prospects*, pp. 204–208, and H.C.L. Merillat, *Legal Advisers and International Organizations* (1966), pp. 10–12. As pointed out in the exchanges among legal advisers of international organizations reported by Merillat, there may be very good practical reasons for not requesting the Court's advisory opinion in a given case.

States or INTELSAT, or any other of the many intergovernmental institutions in existence, has requested the General Assembly or Security Council to request an advisory opinion of the Court on its behalf. But, in view of the precedent of the League and the Permanent Court and the considerations set out in this essay, no persuasive legal reason is seen which debars that procedure. As for States requesting the General Assembly or Security Council to request opinions on their behalf, that remains an equal option. In the *Case Concerning the Northern Cameroons*, the Court observed that "The Court may, of course, give advisory opinions – not at the request of a State but at the request of a duly authorized organ or agency of the United Nations."[126] But that statement does not bear upon the ability of a State to seek an advisory opinion through the agency of the General Assembly[127] or the Security Council.

Diverse Views of States

In view of the shrunken docket of the Court in the 1960's, the General Assembly on December 15, 1970 invited States to submit their views and suggestions concerning the role of the Court to the Secretary-General who was requested to prepare a comprehensive report. That report remains an important compendium of conflicting perspectives on reviving recourse to the Court (a revival which has come about, apparently not for the most part in response to initiatives then generated – with the exception of the revision of the Rules of Court concerning chambers, which has succeeded in promoting the establishment of four *ad hoc* chambers). On the question of increasing resort to the Court's advisory jurisdiction, the United States proposed:

> Access to the advisory jurisdiction of the Court should be expanded concomitantly with access in contentious cases. Although at the present time the United Nations and its specialized agencies have the capacity to seek advisory opinions, there is a growing number of other international organizations, including regional organizations, whose activities are increasingly important to international law and yet who cannot obtain an advisory opinion from the International Court of

---

[126] *Case concerning the Northern Cameroons, Preliminary Objections, ICJ Reports 1963*, pp. 15, 30.

[127] On the proposal that national supreme courts should be enabled to request advisory opinions of the Court on questions of international law through the agency of a committee to be established by the General Assembly, see Stephen M. Schwebel, "Preliminary Rulings by the International Court of Justice at the Instance of National Courts," *Virginia Journal of International Law* (1988), 28, p. 495, and the sources there cited, and Shabtai Rosenne, "Preliminary Rulings by the International Court of Justice at the Instance of National Courts: A Reply," *Virginia Journal of International Law* (1989), 29, 2, p. 41.

Justice. Although the more important question is perhaps how to convince international organizations to request advisory opinions once they have that option, the essential first step is still to make that exercise possible.

Accordingly, the United States favors making the advisory procedures available to more intergovernmental organizations, including regional organizations. A procedure not requiring amendment of the Statute could at the present time be established by the General Assembly through creation of a new special committee similar to the committee used for review of decisions of the Administrative Tribunal of the United Nations. The new special committee could be given authority to request from the Court an advisory opinion on behalf of other international organizations.

In addition, the new committee could be given authority to seek an advisory opinion on behalf of two or more States who voluntarily agree to submit to the advisory jurisdiction of the Court with respect to a dispute between them. This would in effect permit States which would be reluctant to submit a dispute to the binding decision of a contentious case to obtain from the Court an authoritative statement of the relative [sic] principles of international law."[128]

Cyprus[129] and Canada[130] expressed interest in a like approach, while a number of other States declared that they favored international organizations in addition to Specialized Agencies, as well as States, being accorded access to the Court (some suggested amendment of the Statute to this end). Poland[131] and France[132] opposed authorizing more institutions to request advisory opinions or affording this possibility to States, while Switzerland expressed doubt about the desirability of permitting States to request advisory opinions, particularly in the case of current disputes.[133]

Conclusions

As stated above, no persuasive reason is seen for debarring international organizations which have not been authorized directly to request advisory opinions of the Court from seeking such opinions through the medium of the General Assembly or Security Council (or a standing committee of the General Assembly constituted for that purpose). Is the case for permitting States to request advisory opinions of the Court through the agency of the General Assembly or Security Council less compelling?

It may well be that, in practice, there would not be much demand among States for advisory opinions. As more than one special agreement which has

---

[128] *Review of the Role of the International Court of Justice, Report of the Secretary-General,* United Nations doc. A/8382 of September 15, 1971, pp. 92–93.

[129] *Ibid.,* pp. 90–91.   [130] *Ibid.,* p. 98.   [131] *Ibid.,* p. 90.   [132] *Ibid.,* pp. 99–100.

[133] *Ibid.,* pp. 94–97.

been the basis of jurisdiction in a contentious case illustrates, it is possible for States as it stands to bring a case to the Court in which the Court is requested not to decide the dispute between them but to determine what are the "principles and rules of international law"[134] which are applicable to its determination. This facility may be seen as approaching the freedom of action with which an advisory opinion leaves the States concerned; the legal principles are set forth by the Court but the disputing States may be left with the freedom to apply or not to apply them (or may not be left with that freedom: in the *North Sea Continental Shelf* cases, it was provided that the States concerned "*shall* delimit the continental shelf ... by agreement *in pursuance of the decision requested from the International Court of Justice*"[135]). Be that as it may, the possible advantages of permitting States to request advisory opinions of the Court were set out by the Informal Inter-Allied Committee in terms that remain persuasive (see paragraph 68 of its Report, quoted above). Of course, the States in dispute would have jointly to request the General Assembly or Security Council to seek an opinion on their behalf; an *ex parte* request would permit a State to escape the constraints of the Court's consensual jurisdiction. Might such a facility lead to a decline in the number of contentious cases? That is possible but altogether uncertain. It is just as possible that such a facility, when used, would enable the disputing States subsequently to engage in negotiations that take account of the law of the matter as clarified by the Court's advisory opinion, and, if those negotiations do not succeed in resolving the dispute, to submit the dispute to the Court for a judgment binding upon them.

This essay endeavors to interpret the relevant terms of the Charter and Statute as they stand, in the light of the precedent of the League and the Permanent Court, and in the light of the *travaux préparatoires* of the Charter and Statute which, it is significant to recall, make clear their intent to preserve the Statute of the Permanent Court to the maximum possible extent. As the Chairman of the Advisory Committee of Jurists pointed out to the San Francisco Conference, "the basic text" of the ICJ Statute "was essentially the same as that of the Statute of the International Court of Justice."[136] There is, in view of this history, reason to presume that it was the intent of the drafters of the Charter and ICJ Statute not only to preserve the words of the Permanent Court's Statute, but the living law of its interpretation as that Court had formed it. The advisory jurisdiction of the Permanent Court was largely created through practice, and there is equal reason to presume that it

---

[134] *North Sea Continental Shelf, ICJ Reports 1969*, p. 6.   [135] *Ibid.*, p. 6. (Emphasis supplied.)
[136] *Documents of the United Nations Conference on International Organization*, Vol. 17, p. 99.

was the intent at San Francisco to preserve that practice together with the text that underlay it, except insofar as that text was changed. A striking part of that practice was the pattern of States and international organizations seeking and receiving advisory opinions of the Court through the agency of the Council of the League.[137]

But the premise of the present terms of the Charter and Statute is not ineluctable; in this rapidly changing world, in which the verities of the Court's jurisdiction as well as so many other matters large and small are in process of reconsideration, the question of amendment of the Charter and Statute may well arise. In such a context, various possibilities meriting study may be open: not only giving international organizations in addition to the Specialized Agencies the independent authority to request advisory opinions; not only authorizing States to request advisory opinions; but more far-reaching innovations, such as authorizing international organizations to take part in contentious proceedings, and authorizing certain entities other than States and international organizations to have direct recourse to the Court.[138]

---

[137] It may be noted that the Vienna Convention on the Law of Treaties between States and International Organizations or between International Organizations provides, in Article 65, in respect of the procedure to be followed with respect to invalidity, termination, withdrawal from or suspension of the operation of a treaty, that the parties shall seek a solution through the means indicated in Article 33 of the United Nations Charter, and further provides, in Article 66, with respect to treaties conflicting with a peremptory norm of international law, that:

(b) if a State is a party to the dispute to which one or more international organizations are parties, the State may, through a Member State of the United Nations if necessary, request the General Assembly or the Security Council or, where appropriate, the competent organ of an international organization which is a party to the dispute and is authorized in accordance with Article 96 of the Charter of the United Nations, to request an advisory opinion of the International Court of Justice in accordance with article 65 of the Statute of the Court;

(c) if the United Nations or an international organization that is authorized in accordance with Article 96 of the Charter of the United Nations is a party to the dispute, it may request an advisory opinion of the International Court of Justice in accordance with article 65 of the Statute of the Court;

(d) if an international organization other than those referred to in sub-paragraph (c) is a party to the dispute, it may, through a Member State of the United Nations, follow the procedure specified in sub-paragraph (b);

[138] See Elihu Lauterpacht, *Aspects of the Administration of International Justice* (1991), pp. 60–75, and Jenks, *Prospects*, especially pp. 119–224.

4

Authorizing the Secretary-General of the United Nations to Request Advisory Opinions of the International Court of Justice

❧

Article 96 of the Charter of the United Nations provides:

1. The General Assembly or the Security Council may request the International Court of Justice to give an advisory opinion on any legal question.
2. Other organs of the United Nations and specialized agencies, which may at any time be so authorized by the General Assembly, may also request advisory opinions of the Court on legal questions arising within the scope of their activities.

Article 65(1) of the Statute of the Court correspondingly provides:

The Court may give an advisory opinion on any legal question at the request of whatever body may be authorized by or in accordance with the Charter of the United Nations to make such a request.

Pursuant to Article 96(2) of the Charter, the General Assembly has authorized the Economic and Social Council, the Trusteeship Council, the Interim Committee of the General Assembly, and the Committee on Applications for Review of Administrative Tribunal Judgments, as well as fourteen Specialized Agencies of the United Nations and the International Atomic Energy Agency, to request advisory opinions of the Court. Two of these United Nations organs are not principal organs of the Organization. Of the principal organs of the United Nations other than the Court itself, only the Secretariat has not been authorized to request advisory opinions. The questions this Note accordingly addresses are: Is the General Assembly legally entitled to authorize the Secretary-General, or the Secretariat (and by so doing, its chief administrative officer in whose name the Secretariat acts, the Secretary-General), to request advisory opinions of the Court? If it is legally so entitled, would it be desirable for the General Assembly to exercise its

Previously published in *American Journal of International Law* (1984), 78, 4. An earlier version of this paper was published in J. Makarczyk (ed.), *Essays in International Law in Honour of Judge Manfred Lachs* (1984).

authority so as to vest in the Secretary-General or Secretariat the right to request advisory opinions?

Legal Entitlement

Organs of the United Nations other than the General Assembly and the Security Council "may at any time be ... authorized by the General Assembly" to request advisory opinions of the Court. Article 96 does not qualify or restrict the organs of the United Nations which may be so authorized. Since the Secretariat is expressly denominated an organ – indeed, a "principal" organ – of the United Nations by the terms of Article 7(1) of the Charter, it is clear that the General Assembly may authorize the Secretariat to "request advisory opinions of the Court." The sole qualification laid down by Article 96(2) does not relate to the personality of the United Nations organs that may be authorized to request advisory opinions but to the scope of legal questions that they may put to the Court, a qualification which is considered below.

The Secretary-General of the United Nations himself has evidenced no doubt about the capacity of the General Assembly to authorize the Secretariat to request advisory opinions.

Thus, in 1950 a report by the Secretary-General to the Commission on Human Rights considered the question whether the Human Rights Committee to be constituted pursuant to the Human Rights Covenants would itself be entitled to request advisory opinions. The Secretary-General concluded that, since the Committee would not be a subsidiary organ of the United Nations, but a body established by an international instrument, separate and distinct from the Charter, the Committee would not be an organ that the General Assembly could authorize to request advisory opinions. Relying on the *travaux préparatoires* of the San Francisco Conference on International Organization, the Secretary-General further concluded that the object of Article 96(2) would be defeated if authorized organs were to act merely as conduits for transmitting requests of a body that could not be authorized directly. However, the Secretary-General saw no reason why an organ properly authorized to request advisory opinions could not be instructed to take into account suggestions or recommendations of another organization, provided that the responsibility for deciding whether any question should be presented to the Court, and its framing, remained with the authorized organ. The Secretary-General's report considered various possible organs that could appropriately receive the suggestions of the Human Rights Committee and then decide upon making requests to the Court, and concluded:

18. A fourth possibility would be the Secretariat, which can be authorized under Article 96 since it is a principal organ of the United Nations. In the case of the Secretariat, the question arises as to whether these questions may be considered to be within the scope of its activities, as required by Article 96(2). The answer to this may be found by reference to Article 98 which provides that the Secretary-General shall perform such other functions as are entrusted to him by the General Assembly and the Councils of the Organization. Accordingly, it would be necessary for the General Assembly to entrust the Secretary-General with the function of considering suggestions of the Human Rights Committee in regard to requests for advisory opinions on questions arising out of that Committee's work. Pursuant to this, the General Assembly could then extend an authorization to the Secretary-General under Article 96(2) in the same terms as those suggested in the preceding paragraph for the Commission on Human Rights.[1]

In 1955, another occasion arose for the Secretary-General to express a view on the question, this time in connection with modalities for review of judgments of the United Nations Administrative Tribunal by the International Court of Justice. In a report to the General Assembly that considered, *inter alia*, the possibility of the Court's serving as the reviewing body for judgments of the Administrative Tribunal, the Secretary-General observed:

67. Under Article 65 of its Statute, the International Court of Justice may give an advisory opinion on any legal question at the request of any organ of the United Nations or specialized agency authorized to make such a request. It would appear to be too cumbersome a procedure for the General Assembly, itself, to request advisory opinions in each case. Article 96, paragraph 2, of the Charter, however, provides that organs of the United Nations which may at any time be so authorized by the General Assembly may request advisory opinions of the Court on legal questions arising within the scope of their activities. The General Assembly could therefore authorize the Secretary-General, who is the head of a principal organ of the United Nations, to request advisory opinions on legal questions concerning Administrative Tribunal judgements, and conceivably it might be able to authorize him to do so, not only on his own initiative, but also at the request of some other body, such as, for example, a Member State or Member States, or possibly the applicant.[2]

If any Member State then or on another occasion objected to the conclusion of the Secretary-General that he may be authorized by the General Assembly to request advisory opinions of the Court, no such objections

[1] United Nations doc. E/1732, at p. 7 (June 26, 1950).

[2] Judicial Review of United Nations Administrative Tribunal Judgements, Working Paper submitted by the Secretary-General, 10 United Nations GAOR Annexes (Agenda Item 49) at pp. 17, 23, United Nations doc. A/AC.78/L.1 and Corr. 1 (1955).

appear to be reflected in United Nations documentation. Indeed, in the review of the role of the International Court of Justice that took place in the General Assembly in 1970 and 1971, Iraq maintained that "[t]he possibility of authorizing the Secretary-General of the United Nations to request the advisory opinion of the Court in certain cases is worth considering."[3] No other State made observations on this point.

It is true that, in the proceedings of the Special Committee on the Charter of the United Nations and on Strengthening the Role of the Organization, the Philippines in 1976 proposed amending Article 96 to authorize the Secretary-General to request advisory opinions, in these terms: "The General Assembly, the Security Council, or the Secretary-General may request the International Court of Justice to give an advisory opinion on any legal question."[4] But this proposal does not necessarily imply that, in the view of the Philippines, the General Assembly, acting under the present terms of Article 96, could not authorize the Secretary-General to seek advisory opinions, particularly because the proposal of the Philippines would have authorized the Secretary-General to request an advisory opinion "on any legal question" and not, as Article 96(2) now provides, "on legal questions arising within the scope of their [the Secretariat's or the Secretary-General's] activities." Nothing in the official summaries of the committee's discussions suggests that the Philippines or another member was of the view that the General Assembly could not now authorize the Secretary-General to request advisory opinions on legal questions arising within the scope of his activities.

The Scope of the Secretary-General's Activities

If the Secretariat or the Secretary-General as its chief were to be authorized by the General Assembly to request advisory opinions, those opinions could, as noted, by reason of the terms of Article 96(2), only be "on questions arising within the scope of their activities." That restriction raises two questions: What is its extent? Is that extent so broad as to be coextensive with all the Organization's activities and hence – it could be argued – no restriction at all, with the result that authorization of the Secretary-General would not conform to Article 96(2)?

The scope of the activities of the Secretary-General and of the Secretariat, which he directs, is defined primarily by Charter Articles 97–102.

---

[3] *Review of the Role of the International Court of Justice, Report of the Secretary-General*, United Nations doc. A/8382, para. 299 (September 15, 1971).

[4] *Report of the Special Committee on the Charter of the United Nations and on Strengthening the Role of the Organization*, United Nations doc. A/32/33, at p. 190 (1976).

Under Article 97, questions relating to the composition of the Secretariat and the Secretary-General's authority as chief administrative officer of the Organization would be legal questions arising within the scope of the Secretary-General's activities. Legal questions have arisen in the past with respect to Article 97 and could again. For example, there may be room for questioning whether the authority to appoint staff accorded by the General Assembly to the High Commissioner for Refugees and to the Administrator of the United Nations Development Program is consistent with the provisions of Article 97.

Article 98 provides that the Secretary-General shall act in that capacity in all meetings of the General Assembly, of the Security Council, of the Economic and Social Council, and of the Trusteeship Council "and shall perform such other functions as are entrusted to him by these organs." Those functions may well raise legal questions within the scope of the Secretary-General's activities. The Secretary-General gave such an illustration in connection with the Human Rights Committee, quoted above. Another example was the extent of the authority of the Secretary-General under the resolutions of the Security Council that, beginning in 1960, charged him with heavy responsibilities in the case of the Congo, a question which was in acute controversy in the last year of Dag Hammarskjöld's distinguished tenure. Still another example was the extent of the Secretary-General's authority in respect of the withdrawal from Egypt of the United Nations Emergency Force in 1967. This is not to say that any of these electric questions would necessarily have been suited, politically or temporally, to the Court's advisory processes. But they do illustrate that genuine and important legal questions do arise that are peculiarly or particularly within the scope of the Secretary-General's activities.

The provision of Article 99 that the Secretary-General may bring to the attention of the Security Council any matter that in his opinion may threaten the maintenance of international peace and security may also give rise to legal questions within the scope of his activities. For example, there have been at times differences in the Security Council over the authority the Secretary-General has more than once asserted to conduct field investigations, without the express authorization of the Security Council, in order independently to gather information on the basis of which he can make an informed decision as to whether or not he should invoke his powers under Article 99.

Article 100 enshrines the exclusively international character of the responsibilities of the Secretary-General and the staff. It has been the focus of disputes posing a variety of legal questions within the scope of the activities of the Secretariat and Secretary-General. Among the issues that may be recalled are those turning on loyalty investigations of members of the Secretariat of United States nationality by US legislative and executive authorities; proposals for replacing the office of the Secretary-General with a "troika" representative of the "East," the "West," and the "Third World" (proposals that implicated Article 97 and 101 as well); the arrest of officials of the United Nations by national authorities; and practices of some States respecting the salaries of Secretariat members of their nationality.

Article 101 concerns the appointment of staff. The application of the Charter criteria governing such appointment could give rise to legal questions, such as the relationship of considerations of geographical distribution to the highest standards of efficiency, competence, and integrity.

Article 102 provides for the registration with the Secretariat of treaties and international agreements, a process that has given rise to legal questions, for example, those which arose regarding the question of reservations to treaties, as to which the General Assembly requested an advisory opinion of the Court at the instance of the Secretary-General.

Finally, Article 105 provides that the Organization shall enjoy in the territory of each of its members such privileges and immunities as are necessary for the fulfillment of its purposes, and further provides that representatives of the members of the United Nations and officials of the Organization shall similarly enjoy such privileges and immunities as are necessary for the independent exercise of their functions in connection with the Organization. These provisions have give rise to differences, which may be linked to the Headquarters Agreement between the United States of America and the United Nations,[5] or to the General Convention on the Privileges and Immunities of the United Nations.[6] Under the Headquarters Agreement, disputes are subject to arbitration. Section 21(b) provides that either the Secretary-General or the United States may ask the General Assembly to request an advisory opinion on any legal question arising in the course of such arbitral proceedings. Presumably, that specific provision would pre-empt any more general authorization of the Secretary-General directly to request advisory opinions on legal questions arising within the scope of his activities. Under Section 30 of the General Convention, differences arising out of the interpretation or application of the Convention shall be referred to the International Court of Justice:

---

[5] March 23, 1948, 62 Stat. 3725, TIAS No. 1899, 19 UNTS 43; Supplemental Agreement, February 9, 1966, 17 UST 71, TIAS No. 5961, 554 UNTS 308; *amended* December 8, 1966, 17 UST 2319, TIAS No. 6176, 581 UNTS 362; Second Supplemental Agreement, August 28, 1969, 20 UST 2810, TIAS No. 6750, 687 UNTS 408.

[6] *Done* February 13, 1946, 21 UST 1418, TIAS No. 6900, 1 UNTS 16.

If a difference arises between the United Nations on the one hand and a Member on the other hand, a request shall be made for an advisory opinion on any legal question involved in accordance with Article 96 of the Charter and Article 65 of the Statute of the Court.

The General Convention does not further specify who may request such an advisory opinion. If the Secretary-General were to be authorized by the General Assembly to request advisory opinions, presumably he would thereby be authorized directly to request an opinion on a question arising under section 30 of the General Convention, provided that that question were within the scope of his activities.

In addition to the various illustrations of legal questions arising within the scope of the activities of the Secretariat and Secretary-General that have been given, it might be argued that, since the Secretary-General acts in that capacity in all meetings of the General Assembly, Security Council, Economic and Social Council, and Trusteeship Council, and their subsidiary organs, all the activities of such organs are *ipso facto* within the scope of the activities of the Secretary-General.[7] That is a possible interpretation but not a necessary or persuasive one, for the activities of an organ may be more reasonably seen as its activities and not the services of the Secretariat that are incidental to them. In so far as those services (or delegated powers under Article 98) are at issue, a question would be within the scope of the Secretary-General's activities. But that does not mean that the activities of those organs would of themselves pose questions on which the Secretary-General would be entitled to request advisory opinions. Thus, it is believed that any resolution of the General Assembly authorizing the Secretary-General to request advisory opinions of the Court should exclude, implicitly or perhaps expressly, the authority to request opinions on disputes between States that do not implicate the powers or functions of the Secretary-General. But if a contrary approach were, *arguendo*, to be accepted, would it follow that, because of the consequent breadth of the Secretary-General's activities, Article 96(2) would impose no effective restriction, with the result that authorizing the Secretary-General to ask advisory opinions would be to confer on an organ a degree of authority which, if in that respect consistent with Article 96(1), would not be consistent with the governing provision, Article 96(2)?

While the question itself is not, for the reason just given, a plausible one, it should in any event be noted that, even if the scope of the activities of the Secretary-General were to be so broadly interpreted as to encompass all of the

---

[7] See D. Pratap, *The Advisory Jurisdiction of the International Court of Justice* (1972), p. 73.

Organization's activities, Article 96(2) still would impose a restriction, albeit a loose one. For example, the Secretary-General would not be entitled to request an advisory opinion on a question solely within the scope of activities of the Organization of American States and not also within that of the United Nations.

It may be noted that Kelsen maintains that there is no difference between the scope of the authority afforded by the first and second paragraphs of Article 96:

> The competence of requesting advisory opinions as established by Article 96, paragraph 2, in contradistinction to that established by Article 96, paragraph 1, is restricted in so far as the organs authorised by the General Assembly are permitted to request advisory opinions only on legal questions "arising within the scope of their activities". No such restriction is imposed upon the analogous competence of the General Assembly and of the Security Council in paragraph 1 of Article 96. Nevertheless, these organs, too, are competent to request advisory opinions on legal questions only if such questions arise within the scope of their activities, that is to say, within their jurisdiction. The determination of any organ's jurisdiction implies the norm not to act beyond the scope of its activity as determined by the legal instrument instituting the organ. It is not very likely that it was intended to enlarge, by Article 96, paragraph 1, the scope of the activity of the General Assembly and the Security Council determined by other Articles of the Charter. Hence the words "arising within the scope of their activities" in paragraph 2 of Article 96 are redundant.[8]

Secretary-General or Secretariat?

Professor Kelsen makes another, less persuasive point bearing upon the question whether it is the Secretary-General or the Secretariat that may be authorized by the General Assembly to request advisory opinions:

> As to the question to whom advisory opinions may be given, Article 65 of the Statute is not quite in conformity with Article 96 of the Charter. Under Article 65 of the Statute the Court is authorised to give advisory opinions only to a "body", that is to say, to a collegiate organ, consequently not to the Secretary-General, who – under Article 96, paragraph 2, of the Charter – may be authorised by the General Assembly to request such advisory opinion of the Court.[9]

Paul Szasz, referring to Kelsen's "narrowly" construing the Statute, declares that "this objection, even if valid, could be overcome by simply vesting the authority in the Secretariat (the organ named in Charter Articles

---

[8] H. Kelsen, *The Law of the United Nations* (1950), p. 546.   [9] *Ibid.*, at p. 547.

7(1) and 97), whose political functions are embodied in the Secretary-General."[10]

Judge Jessup, in advocating authorizing the Secretary-General to request advisory opinions, observes:

> Technically, under Article 96 of the Charter, the authorization is to an organ of the United Nations, and under Article 7 it is the Secretariat and not the Secretary-General which is the "organ". This presents a simple question of the phraseology of a General Assembly resolution, since any power of the Secretariat would be exercised by or under the authority of the Secretary-General.[11]

K.J. Keith responds to Kelsen's point as follows:

> A second question of interpretation arises from Kelsen's allegation that paragraph 2 of Article 96 conflicts with Article 65(1) of the Statute. He contends that under the latter article the Court could not consider requests for opinions from the Secretary-General although he could be authorised to request them under Article 96(2). This argument is based on the fact that the Secretary-General is not a "body" and that under Article 65(1) the Court can answer requests from "bodies" only. In the first place, however, it is likely that this "difficulty" would be avoided in practice by authorising the Secretariat to make requests. If the Secretariat were so authorised the Secretary-General, as head of that organ, would be constitutionally and ultimately responsible for any requests. While, therefore, in form, the Secretary-General would not be authorised, in fact, he would be. Second, there is a general canon of construction that provisions of a treaty should be construed so as to read consistently with its other provisions. It was surely the intention of the draftsmen of the Charter and Statute that the word "body" in Article 65 of the Statute should be shorthand for "authorised organs of the United Nations (including the General Assembly and the Security Council) and of the specialised agencies" (cf. Article 96 of the Charter). The Secretary-General's authority to request an opinion and the Court's competence would then depend not directly on the Secretary-General coming within the genus "body" but on whether he was an organ of the United Nations. This he would appear quite clearly to be.[12]

In the light of these apt observations, it is concluded that a resolution of the General Assembly adopted under Article 96(2) could properly authorize the Secretary-General to request advisory opinions on legal questions arising within the scope of his activities. But, if there were any doubt on the point, it

---

[10] Szasz, "Enhancing the Advisory Competence of the World Court", in L. Gross (ed.), *The Future of the International Court of Justice* (1976), Vol. II, pp. 499, 541 n.88.

[11] Jessup, "To Form a More Perfect United Nations," *Columbia Journal of Transnational Law* (1970), 9, pp. 177, 187.

[12] K. J. Keith, *The Extent of the Advisory Jurisdiction of the International Court of Justice* (1971), p. 38 (footnotes omitted).

could be resolved by the resolution's authorizing "the Secretariat, acting through the Secretary-General," to make such requests.

Should the General Assembly so authorize the Secretary-General?

It is believed that it has been shown above that scope of the activities of the Secretary-General affords ample reason for the General Assembly's authorizing him to request advisory opinions of the Court. The issue is not whether there are questions that the Secretary-General could put to the Court, and not whether his doing so would increase recourse to the Court (obviously, it would). It is not whether such increased recourse would contribute to the clarification of concrete problems of international law and the development of international law by the Court. There is no reason why the Court's contribution in these spheres should be any less in response to questions put by the Secretary-General than it has been in response to the questions of others since the Permanent Court of International Justice began work in 1922.

The issue is rather whether the General Assembly may be willing to afford such authority to the Secretary-General and, if not, why not. In this regard, Shabtai Rosenne has written:

> It will be noted that the Secretariat – which is also a principal organ – is not authorized to request advisory opinions. Suggestions are occasionally heard that this ought to be changed. But it may be pointed out that there have been several cases in which the decision to request an opinion was taken after the item which gave rise to the request had been placed on the agenda of the General Assembly at the initiative of the Secretary-General – the *Reparation*, *Reservations* and *United Nations Administrative Tribunal* cases being important instances of this. The Secretariat differs from the other organs in that it is not composed of States, and for that reason there is room for doubt lest the grant to it of authorization to request advisory opinions would not constitute too radical a departure from what has hitherto been the fundamental postulate of all the Court's judicial activities.[13]

Szasz observes:

> Evidently one way of increasing the likelihood that requests for advisory opinions be addressed to the I.C.J. is to increase the number of entities empowered to approach the Court. In this connection, consideration should first be given to those entities that might be authorized directly under Charter Article 96(2).
> First of these is the Secretariat of the United Nations, or rather its Secretary-

---

[13] S. Rosenne, *The Law and Practice of the International Court* (1965), Vol. II, p. 673. *Accord*, Pratap, *Advisory Jurisdiction*, at pp. 72–73; M. Pomerance, *The Advisory Function of the International Court in the League and U.N. Eras* (1973), p. 38.

General, the only one of the principal organs (aside from the Court itself) that does not already have the requisite authority. From the point of view of increasing the business and utility of the Court, authority granted to the Secretary-General might be more fruitful than a similar grant to almost any political organ. The Secretariat, charged with the day-to-day task of administering the Organization and subject to contradictory pressures from political organs and from States, frequently needs authoritative legal opinions on which it might rely; moreover the Secretary-General has from time to time been charged with the execution of delicate and complicated assignments (such as the temporary trusteeship of West Irian in the course of its transfer from the Netherlands to Indonesia and the subsequent supervision of the plebiscite there; or the operation of truce observation and peace-keeping bodies) in connection with which legal questions and disputes inevitably arise. At the same time, the political status and responsibility of the Secretary-General is a fair guarantee against any abuse of such authority. Nevertheless, it would constitute a major departure from prevailing concepts to vest in a single person the authority to approach the Court and the consequent political objection is likely to make this innovation unacceptable to the General Assembly.[14]

Dubisson in this regard writes of an unjustified mistrust that States have displayed towards the Secretary-General.[15]

While it may be said that authorizing the Secretary-General to request advisory opinions of the Court would be a departure from precedent, the extent of that departure should not be magnified. After all, the Secretary-General enjoys by the terms of Article 99 of the Charter the authority to seize the Security Council, in dramatic circumstances that rarely are found in the proceedings of the Court, not merely of questions of international law within the scope of his activities, but of "any matter which in his opinion may threaten the maintenance of international peace and security." If the Secretary-General can be endowed with that politically delicate right in the area of international affairs which trenches upon the most vital interests of States, why should it be thought that the General Assembly would be unwilling to afford him the less sensitive authority to request advisory opinions of the Court? Indeed, experience of almost forty years shows that no Secretary-General has used his authority under Article 99 lightly or excessively or in any manner that has run counter to the interests of the United Nations. On the contrary, the Secretaries-General have demonstrated extreme, perhaps excessive, caution in invoking Article 99. There is no reason to believe that, if the Secretary-General were accorded the authority to request advisory opinions of the Court, he would exercise that authority

---

[14] Szasz, *Advisory Competence*, at p. 513 (footnotes omitted).
[15] M. Dubisson, *La Cour Internationale de Justice* (1964), pp. 281–282.

incautiously. It may of course be argued that, since recourse by the Secretary-General to the Court would be less vivid and visible than recourse to the Security Council, the Secretary-General would be likelier to request advisory opinions, some of which would raise delicate international questions. That may be. The question then comes to whether the advantages of authorizing the Secretary-General to request advisory opinions outweigh any risks. There may be room for difference of view over the answer to that question. But it is believed that, on balance, the undoubted advantages outweigh the questionable risks.

Statesmen and international lawyers of the distinction of Philip Jessup[16] and C. Wilfred Jenks[17] have supported authorizing the Secretary-General to request advisory opinions of the Court. The possibility has been aired in analyses of scholars and discussed in authoritative United Nations circles, but it has not been squarely addressed by the General Assembly. The time may have come for placing the question on the General Assembly's agenda.

---

[16] Jessup, "A More Perfect United Nations."
[17] C.W. Jenks, *The Prospects of International Adjudication* (1964), p. 195.

5

Preliminary Rulings by the International Court of Justice at the Instance of National Courts

∽

As long ago as 1929, Dr. H. Lauterpacht wrote:

One may consider the possibility of a development in which the highest national tribunals will prefer to ask competent international tribunals, preferably the Permanent Court of International Justice, sitting in its full strength, for an opinion on difficult or unsettled questions of international law which do not involve national interests. In a more integrated stage of international organization – which is still far off – this request for an opinion might assume the form of leave to appeal against the decision of the national court on a point of international law. It is not unusual for inferior municipal courts to invite an appeal from their own decision on questions of legal interest on which the opinion of the highest organs of the judiciary is felt to be desirable. However, a formal application, emanating from the highest judicial authorities of the country and addressed to the Permanent Court, for a ruling on any important question of international law pending before the municipal court would constitute a less radical step. Such a procedure, being a voluntary one in form and substance, would derogate neither from the sovereignty of States nor from the authority of their highest tribunals; it would testify that these tribunals regard themselves as the organs of the international community when administering international law, and it would give the Permanent Court, whose main work consists at present in interpreting treaty provisions, the opportunity of developing international law in much needed directions. A suggestion of a procedure of this kind naturally raises a number of questions, such as the right of the Court to deal under its present constitution with matters referred to it in this way, and the necessity of appropriate changes in the Statute; the desirability of reserving to the Court the right to decide whether the matter raised in the application for an opinion is important enough to put into motion the machinery of the Court; the definite obligation, moral rather than legal, on the part of the municipal court in question to give effect to the ruling of the Permanent Court. These are questions of detail which need not be discussed here. But it is believed that such an innovation would bring into relief the deep

Virginia Journal of International Law (1988), 28, 2, p. 495.

84

significance of the fact that international law is the only branch of law containing identical rules professedly administered as such by the courts of all nations.[1]

The success of reference procedures followed in pursuance of Article 177 of the European Community's Treaty of Rome has led to the revival of this idea. Whether, and how, it could be adapted to the International Court of Justice (ICJ) is a matter of some ingenuity and controversy.

Under the Treaty of Rome, the European Community's Court of Justice is competent to make a preliminary decision concerning the interpretation of that Treaty and the validity and interpretation of acts of the institutions of the Community and of bodies set up by it. Where any such question is raised in a case pending before a lower domestic court of a Member State, the Community Court may be requested to give a ruling on it if the domestic court considers that its judgment depends upon that preliminary decision. Where any such question is raised in a case before a court from whose decision no appeal lies, such a court must refer the matter to the Community Court. This procedure has been frequently and successfully employed. From 1953 to April 30, 1987, 1,592 preliminary questions were submitted to the Court of Justice of the European Community.[2]

Professor Leo Gross, taking up ideas of C. Wilfred Jenks, advanced a proposal in 1971,[3] which noted the difficulties national tribunals may face when called to interpret a treaty or principle of international law. He submitted that, "being national institutions, their impartiality may not be above suspicion."[4] Professor Gross suggested that the preliminary decision procedure of the EC, if adapted to the International Court of Justice, could apply to the interpretation of treaties and the validity and interpretation of acts of organs of the United Nations. A third category would embrace the interpretation of the principles of customary international law. The likeliest option, he indicated, would be with respect to treaties, whether bilateral or multilateral. "Once the Statute is revised so as to admit this procedure, it would be up to States to take advantage of it and include a suitably drafted jurisdictional clause."[5] He concluded that:

> A reform along these lines would not involve any curtailment of national sovereignty. Consent of the State or States concerned would be required in any

---

[1] "Decisions of Municipal Courts as a Source of International Law," *The British Year Book of International Law 1929*, 10, pp. 94–95.

[2] Pieter VerLoren van Themaat, "Preliminary Rulings by the International Court of Justice at the Request of National Courts: Lessons from the EEC-Experience," in *Mededelingen van de Nederlandse Vereniging voor Internationaal Recht* (October 1987), 95, p. 73.

[3] Leo Gross, "The International Court of Justice: Consideration of Requirements for Enhancing Its Role in the International Legal Order," *American Journal of International Law* (1971), 65, pp. 308–313.

[4] *Ibid.*, p. 311.   [5] *Ibid.*, p. 312.

event, and the application of the law would remain in the hands of national tribunals.[6]

In 1976, in response to a resolution of the United States Senate, the Department of State published a study on "Widening Access to the International Court of Justice," which endorsed, "in principle," amendment of the Court's Statute to incorporate an advisory "preliminary opinion" recourse from national appellate courts to the International Court of Justice on issues of international law.[7]

At the instance of a committee of which Professor Louis B. Sohn was Chairman and guiding spirit, the American Bar Association (ABA) was induced to lend its support to a particular procedure for such reference, namely, reference to the International Court of Justice by a committee of the General Assembly which would screen requests from national courts.[8] In 1982, the House of Representatives of the Congress of the United States followed with a resolution urging the President to:

> explore the appropriateness of the establishment of a special committee, under United Nations auspices, authorized to seek an advisory opinion of the International Court of Justice, upon request by a national court or tribunal which is duly authorized by national legislation to make such a request, regarding any question of international law of which such court or tribunal has jurisdiction.[9]

The ABA proposal contemplates referral to the International Court of Justice early in the national proceedings, "as soon as it has become evident that a complex issue of international law is involved."[10] Once the parties to the dispute have agreed to the referral, the national tribunal would formulate the question to the Court and forward it to the screening committee of the General Assembly, together with the briefs prepared by the litigants. The screening committee would submit the question to the Court only after deciding that it satisfied the criteria for referral established by the General Assembly. The screening committee might be authorized by the General Assembly to limit the cases to those which raise important issues, e.g., where there have already been "conflicting interpretations of a particular rule by

---

[6] *Ibid.*, p. 313. For criticism of the proposal, see Lucius Caflisch, "Reference Procedures and the International Court of Justice," in Leo Gross (ed.), *The Future of the International Court of Justice* (1976), Vol. II, p. 572.

[7] *Digest of United States Practice in International Law 1976*, p. 651.

[8] Louis B. Sohn, "Broadening the Advisory Jurisdiction of the International Court of Justice," *American Journal of International Law* (1983), 77, p. 124.

[9] H.R. Con. Res. 86, as revised, adopted December 17, 1982, quoted *ibid.*, p. 129, note 23.

[10] *Ibid.*, p. 127.

tribunals of different countries."[11] It could take account of the Court's workload. Professor Sohn maintained that this procedure might be instituted without amendment of the Statute of the Court.[12]

Nevertheless, American official and unofficial opinion is divided, as is illustrated by Jack M. Goldklang's note, "House Approves Proposal Permitting ICJ to Advise Domestic Courts."[13]

As far as I am aware, proposals in this vein have not advanced farther. They do not appear to have struck an official responsive note in other countries, at least as yet. However, in November 1987, the Netherlands Branch of the International Law Association held a meeting in the Peace Palace in which these proposals were debated in some depth, on the basis of papers prepared by the former Advocate General of the Court of Justice of the European Communities and myself. The informed opinions exchanged at that meeting were sharply divided.[14]

Is the Idea Good?

The idea is fundamentally appealing. Over the years, the International Court of Justice and its predecessor have not only settled a substantial number of international legal disputes; they have contributed significantly to the progressive development of international law. National courts have also made their contribution, as is demonstrated in the volumes of *International Law Reports* and *International Legal Materials*. Nevertheless, knowledgeability of national courts about international law is variable, and national and parochial perspectives may come into play. If there were provision for reference by national courts of questions of international law to the International Court of Justice for its opinion, a number of benefits would or should follow, including the following.

(1) The rendering of justice in the particular case presumably would be assisted by giving the national court the benefit of the opinion of the ICJ on a question of international law of importance to the disposition of the national case.

---

[11] *Ibid.*, p. 128.   [12] *Ibid.*, p. 129.

[13] *American Journal of International Law* (1983), 77, p. 338. For a vigorous attack on the idea, see William T. M. McLaughlin, "Allowing Federal Courts Access to International Court of Justice Advisory Opinions: Critique and Proposal," *Hastings International and Comparative Law Review* (1983), 6, p. 745.

[14] The excellent exchange of views is reproduced in *Mededelingen van de Nederlandse Vereniging voor Internationaal Recht* (March 1988), 96, p. 3 (in English), analyzing the paper referred to in note 2 above, as well as that of Stephen M. Schwebel, "Preliminary Rulings of the International Court of Justice at the Instance of National Courts," *ibid.*, p. 3.

(2) Uniformity and professionalism in the interpretation of international law by national courts should be promoted.

(3) Links would be established, in what has been described by C. Wilfred Jenks as a procedure "outflanking" the ICJ Statute's provision that "Only States may be parties in cases before the Court," between national courts (and the litigants before them) and the ICJ, which should strengthen the latter's "constituency" and support by influential opinion.

(4) While individuals would continue to have no direct access to the ICJ, such preliminary opinion procedures would afford "meaningful indirect rights and duties for individuals under international law."[15]

(5) The ICJ would in this fashion be given increased area in which to contribute to the resolution of disputes and to the development of international law, an area which embraces international legal disputes in which the actors are not just States but individuals, corporations, traders, etc.

(6) The ICJ might be more fully utilized than at times it has been.

At the same time, the proposal has its drawbacks and difficulties, some of which are the following.

(1) The problem of "uniformity of interpretation" of international law by national courts may be – in Professor Shabtai Rosenne's term – "exaggerated"; he submitted to The Hague debate to which reference has been made that: "I must say that in all my experience I have never yet encountered it as a serious problem."[16]

(2) It may be wondered whether the executive authorities of adhering States would permit their national courts to seek opinions of the ICJ – whether binding or advisory – without the clearance of those executive authorities in each case. One can imagine that certain subjects might be ones on which a State would not actually wish to have the opinion of the ICJ (even if a less politically aware national court might wish to have it): certain questions of human rights, sovereign immunity, and expropriation of alien property are among those that spring to mind. At the same time, such questions are among the questions of international law which may most frequently arise in national courts.

(3) In view of the history of submission to the Court's compulsory jurisdiction, there is no reason to expect that States generally would adhere to

---

[15] Verloren van Themaat, "Preliminary Rulings," p. 59.

[16] See the first source cited in note 14 above, at p. 16, as well as Rosenne, "Preliminary Rulings by the International Court of Justice at the Instance of National Courts: A Reply," *Virginia Journal of International Law* (1989), 29, p. 401.

reference procedures, were they to be opened. On the contrary, it is to be expected that a relatively small number of States would adhere, mostly drawn from societies in which the independence of the judiciary is entrenched. Would these States, however, actually adhere – and would their courts actually invoke reference procedures – in the knowledge that referred questions would be passed upon by a Court composed as an international court cannot but be composed in the present-day world? Judge Petrén drew attention to the effect of an analogous lack of symmetry in submission of cases to the Court; it could carry over into the sphere of reference procedures.[17]

(4) Reference by a national court of a question to the ICJ for the latter's opinion before the national court adjudicates the case would necessarily substantially delay the latter's rendering of judgment and increase the expense of the proceedings.

If the Court were to render binding judgments on questions referred to it by national courts, this would require amendment of the Statute. As the Statute stands, "Only States may be parties in cases before the Court."[18] National courts, and the parties to cases before it, could have *locus standi* only if the Statute were amended to provide for it.

Amendment of the Statute, an integral part of the Charter of the United Nations, is subject to the exigent requirements of Charter amendment set out in Article 108 of the Charter, which provides:

Amendments to the present Charter shall come into force for all Members of the United Nations when they have been adopted by a vote of two thirds of the members of the General Assembly and ratified in accordance with their respective constitutional processes by two thirds of the Members of the United Nations, including all the permanent members of the Security Council.

Even if two-thirds of the members of the United Nations were to support and ratify the requisite amendments (a consummation by no means to be assumed), can it be supposed that all the permanent members of the Security Council would ratify such amendments? Moreover, if the Statute were to be opened to such amendments, it – and the United Nations Charter – would be opened to a flood of other amendments, many of which might be undesirable, regressive, or unworkable.

---

[17] B. A. S. Petrén, "Some Thoughts on the Future of the International Court of Justice," *Netherlands Yearbook of International Law* (1975), 6, pp. 61–62.

[18] Statute of the Court, Article 34, paragraph 1.

May Amendment of the Statute be Circumvented?

Essentially to avoid what may be the insuperable difficulties of amendment of the Statute, it has been proposed that the reference procedure be confined to the seeking of advisory opinions of the International Court of Justice. Article 96 of the Charter of the United Nations provides:

1. The General Assembly or the Security Council may request the International Court of Justice to give an advisory opinion on any legal question.
2. Other organs of the United Nations and specialized agencies, which may at any time be so authorized by the General Assembly, may also request advisory opinions of the Court on legal questions arising within the scope of their activities.

Article 65, paragraph 1, of the Statute correspondingly provides:

The Court may give an advisory opinion on any legal question at the request of whatever body may be authorized by or in accordance with the Charter of the United Nations to make such a request.

The ABA and Professor Sohn maintain that the General Assembly might establish a committee whose function would be *(a)* to screen requests from national courts for advisory opinions of the International Court of Justice and *(b)* to forward to the Court such requests as it finds appropriate.[19] In this vein, Dr. C. Wilfred Jenks earlier had written:

The precedent of the Administrative Tribunal Judgment Review Committee suggests that the General Assembly could also create an organ of the United Nations specially for the purpose of requesting advisory opinions in defined circumstances, instruct such an organ to request an opinion whenever satisfied that certain conditions exist, and make such an opinion binding on the parties substantively interested in the matter.

By combining these devices advisory proceedings may be used as a method of introducing innovations not possible in the form of contentious proceedings without an amendment of the Statute. In this manner both the provision that only States may be parties in cases before the Court and any limitation of the procedures and remedies available in the Court which may result from a restrictive interpretation of the provisions of the Statute can to a significant extent be outflanked. Nor is such outflanking in any way illegitimate as a method of legal and institutional progress. It is a normal incident of the growth of any vigorous and flourishing legal system.

The advisory procedure as developed by these various devices can be used in this manner in a wide range of cases ...

An instrument the provisions of which are designed to be incorporated in the

---

[19] See Sohn, "Advisory Jurisdiction," pp. 128–129.

municipal law of the parties might provide that when a municipal court is called upon to give a decision involving the interpretation of the instrument it may, through an organ of the United Nations created for the purpose, submit the question for an advisory opinion on undertaking to attribute to the advisory opinion the effect of a declaratory judgment.[20]

Would this scheme work, if the General Assembly could be persuaded to adopt it and States could be persuaded to adopt the requisite implementing legislation?

That would ultimately depend on the decision of the International Court of Justice. If a screening committee of the General Assembly were given that function of screening, if that were "the scope of" its activity (Article 96, paragraph 2 of the Charter), the Court might well find valid a process of such a screening committee selecting and forwarding for the Court's advisory opinion certain requests from national courts. A clear analogy can be drawn to the Court's upholding in 1973 of the functioning of the General Assembly's Committee on Applications for Review of Administrative Tribunal Judgements.[21]

At the same time, it should be recognized that the Court has indicated its unease and even dissatisfaction with aspects of the functioning of that Committee. As the Court's advisory opinion of May 27, 1987 in the "*Yakimetz*" case indicates, there is sentiment in the Court for the restructuring or even jettisoning of this process.[22] Whether the Court would be prepared to adopt so expansive a construction of advisory opinion authority in respect of preliminary opinions is unpredictable.

Moreover, it might be argued that Article 96 of the Charter is meant to embrace not "any legal question" however unrelated to the problems or processes of the United Nations, but any legal question of concern to the General Assembly or the Security Council; and that other organs of the United Nations authorized by the General Assembly may be authorized to request advisory opinions of the Court on legal questions "arising within the scope of their activities," which activities must in turn be of United Nations concern. Would questions of international law arising in national courts necessarily fall within this ambit? Arguably they would, having regard to the provision of Article 13 of the Charter providing that the General Assembly "shall initiate studies and make recommendations for the purpose of ...

---

[20] C. Wilfred Jenks, *The Prospects of International Adjudication* (1964), pp. 160–161.

[21] See *Application for Review of Judgement No. 158 of the United Nations Administrative Tribunal, Advisory Opinion, ICJ Reports 1973*, pp. 166, 171–175.

[22] *Application for Review of Judgement No. 333 of the United Nations Administrative Tribunal, ICJ Reports 1987*, pp. 32–33, 74–75, 76–80, 107–109.

encouraging the progressive development of international law and its codification." Yet that is far from clear. The question does not admit of a confident answer.

Furthermore, it should be recalled that, when the Statute of the Permanent Court of International Justice was being redrafted as the Statute of the International Court of Justice, proposals of the United Kingdom and Venezuela to authorize States to request advisory opinions of the Court were not accepted.[23]

In short, it would be left to the International Court of Justice to uphold or not uphold the consistency of such a scheme with the Charter and Statute. What can be said is that the 1973 advisory opinion referred to above furnishes support for sustaining the consistency of such a scheme. But that support is not necessarily conclusive.

A screening committee of the General Assembly would present not only the compelling advantage of furnishing an avenue of approach which might avoid the necessity of Charter amendment, but it would also furnish a mechanism to screen out excessive numbers of, or unsuitable requests for, advisory opinions. It could thus keep the Court from being inundated with questions, some inappropriate, from national courts, should that unlikely eventuality ever threaten.

At the same time, a screening committee could interpose a body which might make political, rather than legal, decisions as to which requests from national courts for advisory opinions should be forwarded to the Court. That difficulty might be mitigated if the screening committee itself were not politically composed (as is the General Assembly's Committee on Applications for Review of Administrative Tribunal Judgments). But that may be a counsel of perfection rather than practicality.

It should be noted that, even though the Court's advisory opinion were to be requested, there would be nothing to prevent the national court concerned from giving binding effect to the Court's answer to the questions submitted to it, either by the terms of the governing instruments or *proprio motu*. There is precedent for an instrument giving binding effect to prospective advisory opinions of the Court.

---

[23] *Documents of the United Conference on International Organisation (UNCIO)*, 1945, Vol. 14, pp. 319, 373, 850, and Vol. 3, pp. 209, 225, 230.

6

Chambers of the International Court of Justice Formed for Particular Cases

◌ↄ

Among the many aspects of the International Court of Justice (ICJ) which have been uniquely illuminated by Shabtai Rosenne is that of the Court's formation of a chamber for dealing with a particular case, in pursuance of its authority under Article 26, paragraph 2 of its Statute. With characteristic specificity and subtlety of analysis, Rosenne's treatment brings out – or anticipates – the problems such chambers may pose and the possibilities they may offer. In this as in other of his dissections of the *corpus* of the Court's anatomy and jurisprudence, Rosenne has made an exceptional contribution to the understanding of how the Court works and to the prospects of its working more effectively.[1]

This essay examines *ad hoc* chambers of the Court as provided for in the Court's Statute and Rules and as they have developed in practice. In the light of that exposition, it identifies what appear to be the principal questions such chambers pose, and suggests answers to those questions.

The Statute of the Permanent Court

The Statute of the Permanent Court of International Justice (PCIJ) contained detailed provisions regarding chambers for specified categories of cases.[2] It provided that, at the request of the parties, labor cases shall be heard and determined by a special chamber of five judges appointed every three years by the Court and "selected so far as possible with due regard to the provisions

First published in Y. Dinstein (ed.), M. Tabory (assoc. ed.), *International Law at a Time of Perplexity: Essays in Honour of Shabtai Rosenne* (1989), Dordrecht, Martinus Nijhoff. Reprinted by permission of Kluwer Academic Publishers.

[1] See, in particular, Shabtai Rosenne, "The 1972 Revision of the Rules of the International Court of Justice," *Israel Law Review* (1973), 8, pp. 197, 211–213, and his *Procedure in the International Court: A Commentary on the 1978 Rules of the International Court of Justice* (1983), pp. 40–47.

[2] Articles 26–28.

of Article 9." (Article 9 of that Statute provided, as Article 9 of today's Statute continues to provide, that in the body of the Court as a whole the representation of the main forms of civilization and of the principal legal systems of the world should be assured.) The Permanent Court's Statute also made provision for appointment of a special chamber of five judges to hear cases concerning transit and communications, equally to be selected with due regard to the provisions of Article 9. It was further provided that these chambers could sit elsewhere than at The Hague.

In the event, they never sat anywhere. The chambers were regularly appointed but never used, despite the fact that the Court dealt with cases in the areas of their concern. There was a further provision for the annual formation of a chamber of three judges for determination of cases by summary procedure. That procedure was employed in just one case in the history of the Permanent Court.[3] A similar summary procedure has never been employed by the ICJ.

The Revision of the Statute

The Washington Committee of Jurists which revised the Statute of the Permanent Court adopted an American proposal to eliminate the detailed provisions on chambers for specified categories of cases in favor of a general power of the Court to form from time to time one or more chambers, composed of three or more judges as the Court may determine, for dealing with particular categories of cases, for example, labor cases and cases relating to transit and communications (Article 26, paragraph 1). In fact, this general power of the Court has yet to be applied. (Provision for formation of a chamber of summary procedure was also maintained, in Article 29; while that chamber has regularly been elected by the Court, it has yet to be used.)

What is especially interesting in the light of subsequent history is not the foregoing generalization of dormant specifics but other changes made by the Washington Committee of Jurists and ratified at San Francisco. There was added to the Statute a proposal of the United States[4] for the new provision, now found in Article 26, paragraph 2, which reads:

---

[3] Or, more precisely, two linked cases: *Treaty of Neuilly, Article 179, Annex, Paragraph 4 (Interpretation), Judgment No. 3, 1924, PCIJ, Series A, No. 3*, and *Interpretation of Judgment No. 3, Judgment No. 4, PCIJ, Series A, No. 4*.

[4] Initially drafted to read: "The Court may from time to time form one or more chambers for dealing with particular cases or with particular categories of cases." The United Kingdom proposed to replace the chamber provisions of the PCIJ Statute with "a general faculty ... to constitute special chambers in such cases as may seem appropriate." (*The International Court of Justice, Selected Documents Relating to the Drafting of the Statute*, Department of State Publication 2491 (1946), pp. 63–78.) For a still earlier draft in

The Court may at any time form a chamber for dealing with a particular case. The number of judges to constitute such a chamber shall be determined by the Court with the approval of the parties.

It was further provided in Article 26, paragraph 3, as it was in substance in the PCIJ Statute, that: "Cases shall be heard and determined by the chambers provided for in this article if the parties so request." Moreover, the new Statute made explicit the intention of the PCIJ Statute (embodied in that Court's Rules) by providing, in Article 27: "A judgment given by any of the chambers provided for in Articles 26 and 29 shall be considered as rendered by the Court." (Thus there can be no question of appeals from a chamber to the full Court.) The Statute maintains the fundamental provision of Article 25, paragraph 1 that: "The full Court shall sit except when it is expressly provided otherwise in the present Statute." The drafters of the current Statute deleted the provision of the PCIJ Statute that chambers shall be selected so far as possible with due regard to the provisions of Article 9.

The *travaux préparatoires*

What was intended by these changes? The records of the San Francisco Conference are cryptic. The principal report states that, since the chambers provided for in the Permanent Court's Statute were established but never functioned, "it appears henceforth superfluous to retain the provisions concerning them."[5] The relevant report continues:

> But it has appeared advisable to authorize the Court to establish, if necessary, on the one hand, Chambers dealing with particular categories of cases, and the cases relating to labor, transit and communications have been kept as examples in this connection, and on the other hand, at the request of the parties, to establish a special Chamber to deal with a particular case. The Committee has believed that this change might facilitate, under certain circumstances, recourse to that jurisdiction.[6]

The records of the discussion in subcommittee and committee which led to these changes are also abbreviated. Yet they are of high interest in three respects. First, they concentrate on the authority of the Court to fix the

---

the State Department of provisions respecting chambers, which would have accorded the Court's President particular powers in their constitution, and which would have permitted appeal of chamber decisions to the full Court, see *Postwar Foreign Policy Preparation 1939–1945*, Department of State Publication 3580 (1949), pp. 487–488. See also Ruth B. Russell and Jeannette E. Muther, *A History of the United Nations Charter* (1958), pp. 381–384, 872–873, 1011–1012.

[5] *Documents of the United Nations Conference on International Organization (UNCIO)*, 1945, Vol. 14, p. 834.
[6] *Ibid.*

number of judges who compose either chambers formed for particular categories of cases or a chamber formed for dealing with a particular case.[7] Second, these records admit the possibility – strikingly supported by the representative of the Soviet Union – of forming "a chamber consisting of only one judge," provided that "the parties agree."[8] Third, there is indication that, in introducing into the Statute the provision for formation of a chamber for a particular case, a decided departure was intended from the system of the Statute of the Permanent Court – a departure apparently designed to permit the parties to the case to influence both the size and the composition of the chamber. Judge Manley O. Hudson, who represented the Permanent Court in the meetings of the Committee of Jurists, is reported to have said the following in this suggestive passage of the summary record:

> The next question, the Chairman said, was the number of judges on chambers. Sir Frederic Eggleston (Australia) asked whether the chamber of summary procedure could sit at the same time as the full Court. Judge Hudson pointed out that there had been little use of chambers and that the question had never arisen. He pointed out that under the present Statute the Court elected members to chambers for a given term of years and that the parties did not decide the number or the composition of the chambers. He thought the subcommittee was proposing a wholly different system when it provided for *ad hoc* appointment of chambers with the approval of the parties.[9]

It will be observed that Judge Hudson specified that, whereas under the Statute of the Permanent Court, the parties did not decide "the number or the composition of the chambers," he understood the subcommittee which proposed what is now Article 26, paragraph 2 of the Statute to be "proposing a wholly different system when it provided for *ad hoc* appointment of chambers with the approval of the parties." That is to say, Judge Hudson's contemporaneous interpretation of the intention of the drafters of Article 26, paragraph 2 of the Statute appears to have been that the parties shall be involved in the decisions determining both the number of judges composing an *ad hoc* chamber and the choice of the judges who compose an *ad hoc* chamber. There was no dissent from Judge Hudson's understanding.[10] The

---

[7] *Ibid.*, pp. 199–202, 271–273, 278–279, 282–283.

[8] *Ibid.*, p. 273. See also pp. 199–200, and p. 222. However, the use of the word "judges" in Article 26, paragraph 2 imports a chamber of more than one judge.

[9] *Ibid.*, p. 199. See also Judge Hudson's emphasis on the "considerable change" introduced into the Statute in respect of special chambers (*ibid.*, p. 234).

[10] At the same time, in interpretation of the same provision, Ambassador Cordova (Mexico) "pointed out that the Court was to be given the power to fix the number to sit in the Chambers and the parties given the opportunity to approve this arrangement" (*ibid.*, p. 199). (See also, to the same effect, Mr. Fitzmaurice (United Kingdom), at p. 202.)

system which he – and, as far as it appears, the drafters of the Statute – seem to have understood to be incorporating by the terms and intent of Article 26, paragraph 2 was indeed "wholly different" in this respect from that of the Statute of the Permanent Court, with which Judge Hudson was pre-eminently familiar. The essential difference is that the Statute of the Permanent Court contained no provision for *ad hoc* chambers. It is worth recalling, moreover, that a proposal was made to the Advisory Committee of Jurists which, in 1920, drafted the Statute, which would have authorized the parties to a case to submit it to "three judges nominated by them from among the members of the Court; or . . . to the decision of a single judge also named by them."[11] That proposal was rejected on the ground that "this method would too much resemble that proper to arbitration."[12] While Article 26, paragraph 2 of the Statute by no means accords the parties to a case so determinative a voice in the choice of the judges comprising an *ad hoc* chamber, Judge Hudson clearly saw it as, in the least, affording the parties a voice in the choice – a "wholly different system" from that of the Permanent Court. It may also be suggestive that, when the chairman of the drafting committee introduced the text of Article 26, he stated that the draft "provided that when the Court set up chambers to decide particular cases the approval of the parties should be obtained"[13] – an approval which he did not limit to the fact of the chamber's formation or the number of judges comprising the chamber. Paragraph 3 of Article 26 of the Statute as adopted provides that: "Cases shall be heard and determined by the chambers provided for in this article if the parties so request."

While these constructions of cryptic *travaux préparatoires* are necessarily somewhat speculative, it is striking that there is not a word in the records of the Washington Committee of Jurists or the San Francisco Conference which explains why there was deleted from the new Statute the provision of the PCIJ Statute that chambers shall be "selected so far as possible with due regard to the provisions of Article 9." Nevertheless, that deletion allows but one inference: the new Court could, at the request of the parties, form a special chamber to deal with a particular case which might not be representa-

---

[11] PCIJ, Advisory Committee of Jurists, *Procès-Verbaux of the Proceedings of the Committee, June 16th–July 24th 1920 with Annexes* (1920), pp. 184, 524. See also pp. 111, 171, 173, 175–181, 183–184, 186, 516–517, 524–526. (See also, League of Nations, *Comité de Juristes chargé de l'étude du Statut de la Cour Permanente de Justice Internationale, Procès-Verbal de la Session tenue à Genève du 11 au 19 mars 1929*, pp. 47–50.)

[12] Advisory Committee of Jurists, *Procèc-Verbaux*, p. 526.

[13] *UNCIO*, Vol. 14, p. 221. While the view was expressed by Judge Delgado (Philippine Commonwealth) that "the composition of chambers" should not be "determined by political agencies" (i.e., presumably, by States parties), his proposal to conform paragraph 2 of Article 26 to paragraph 1 was not accepted (*ibid.*, p. 222.)

tive of the Court as a whole in the sense that it need not reflect in its composition the main forms of civilization and the principal legal systems of the world. That inference, strong as it is of itself, is supported by the cited indication in records of the Committee of Jurists that the formation of an *ad hoc* chamber consisting of one judge was not excluded, since a single judge of the Court is hardly capable of representing the main forms of civilization and the principal legal systems of the world.

Proposals for the Activation of *Ad Hoc* Chambers

In the first thirty-five years of the life of the current Court, these provisions lay dormant. What may have been the first small sound of life is to be found in 1968 in the pages of the *American Journal of International Law*, in an innovative note by James Nevins Hyde.[14] Hyde later indicated, in the October 1986 issue of the *Journal*, that he was stimulated to write that note by discussions with Judge Jessup, to whose idea reference is made below.[15] About the same time, at the Vienna Conference on the Law of Treaties (1968–9), the United States proposed that a Commission on Treaty Disputes to be established pursuant to an Annex to the Vienna Convention on the Law of Treaties be authorized under specified circumstances to:

> request an advisory opinion from the International Court of Justice. If the parties agree, the Commission shall request the Court to form a chamber under Article 26 of its Statute to deal with the questions.[16]

At the time that Mr. Hyde's note appeared, the Court as a whole lay relatively dormant. The poverty of its docket, in a world bursting with international legal disputes, was a cause of increasing concern. That concern was constructively addressed in 1970 at the Annual Dinner of the American Society of International Law by Secretary of State William P. Rogers. He suggested that:

> Greater use might be made of the chambers of the Court in an effort to relieve apprehensions about submitting disputes to the 15–judge tribunal sitting *en banc*.[17]

---

[14] "A Special Chamber of the International Court of Justice – an Alternative to Ad Hoc Arbitration," *American Journal of International Law* (1968), 62, p. 439. (See also Nicholas M. Poulantzas, "The Chambers of the International Court of Justice and the Judicial Settlement of Disputes: The Delimitation of the Maritime Boundary in the Gulf of Maine Area Case," *Revue de Droit International* [1985], 63, p. 323.)

[15] James N. Hyde, "Jessup: Memorials and Reminiscences," *American Journal of International Law* (1986), 80, p. 905.

[16] United Nations Conference on the Law of Treaties, *Official Records*, p. 190.

[17] William P. Rogers, "The Rule of Law and the Settlement of International Disputes," *Proceedings of the American Society of International Law at its Sixty-Fourth Annual Meeting (1970)*, p. 288.

A few months later, Judge Jessup, speaking to The Hague Academy of International Law in commemoration of the twenty-fifth anniversary of the United Nations, made the following comment which clearly referred to Hyde's note:

> It has been suggested elsewhere that if the difficulty of resort to the International Court of Justice lies in a State's preference for a tribunal in whose composition it will have a say, this result can be achieved by the use of "a Chamber for dealing with a particular case", as is authorized by Article 26 (2) of the Statute. Under Article 31 of the Statute, the provisions about national judges are applicable to such a Chamber so that the Chamber could be composed of a judge of the nationality of each one of the parties, with a third judge elected by the Court very much as the President of the Court now often is authorized to appoint presiding arbitrators.[18]

The United States and a number of like-minded States at the same time took their concern at the increasing inactivity of the Court to the United Nations General Assembly. For its part, the American Society of International Law constituted a distinguished panel on the future of the ICJ, under the leadership of Judge Jessup and Ambassador Edvard Hambro, in which Ambassador Rosenne played a leading part. The Society produced a substantial book on that subject, to which Rosenne contributed an essay on "The Composition of the Court."[19] The General Assembly did not produce all that was hoped. It declined to set up a special committee to consider the dearth of the Court's business and make recommendations to deal with it. But it did agree to request the Secretary-General to prepare a report, and it invited States to submit to the Secretary-General their views and suggestions concerning the role of the Court in response to a questionnaire prepared by the Secretary-General.[20] To that short questionnaire, a relatively short list of States replied, some thirty in all.

A small number of those replies made mention of the authority of the Court to form a chamber for a particular case. Cyprus observed that the Court possessed that authority which, if used, might lessen the length of proceedings and the great costs and delays characteristic of the full Court.[21]

---

[18] Philip C. Jessup, "To Form a More Perfect United Nations," Hague Academy of International Law, *Collected Courses* (1970–1), 129, p. 21. This proposal of Judge Jessup resembles that supported by Professor Golunsky (adviser of the Soviet Union) at the Washington Conference of Jurists. (*UNCIO*, Vol. 14, p. 273.)

[19] Leo Gross (ed.), *The Future of the International Court of Justice* (1976).

[20] *Review of the Role of the International Court of Justice, Report of the Secretary-General*, United Nations doc. A/8382 (September 15, 1971), p. 6. See also *Review of the Role of the International Court of Justice, Report of the Sixth Committee*, United Nations doc. A/8568, p. 6.

[21] United Nations doc. 8382, p. 46.

The United States supported "the establishment and wide use of *ad hoc* chambers of the Court for legal problems requiring expertise in technical areas, and for peculiarly regional problems, for whose solution all parties prefer to address a regionally oriented bench."[22] The United States continued:

> The Court has adequate authority to create such chambers under the present Statute; liberal exercise of that authority could make the forum of the International Court of Justice considerably more flexible and mobile, and its use less costly and less formal.
>
> To encourage use of such chambers, States might write into future treaties provisions referring disputes to a special chamber rather than to the full Court, if appropriate. The prospect that different chambers might arrive at different conclusions on similar issues could be dealt with by providing for appeal to the full Court but such appeal should be limited to cases of conflicts between chambers.[23]

Finland[24] and France[25] made like if more elliptical references. In the most innovative of the comments made on the matter, Sweden said the following:

> No State has ever made use of the possibility of having a dispute adjudicated on by ... a special chamber as provided for in Article 26 of the Statute. By virtue of Article 26, paragraph 2 of the Statute, it is in the hands of the parties to a dispute to request that a special chamber be formed for dealing with their case. In determining the number of judges constituting the chamber, the Court shall have the approval of the parties. On the other hand, the parties are without any influence when it comes to the election of the individual judges of such a chamber. The President of the special chamber as well as its members shall, according to Article 24, paragraph 2 of the Rules of Court, be elected by the Court, by secret ballot, and by an absolute majority of votes. The Swedish Government is of the view that the use of a special chamber could in certain circumstances be of great advantage to the parties.
>
> The Swedish Government believes that the procedure envisaged in paragraph 2 of Article 26 of the Statute would prove more attractive to potential litigants if the Rules of Court were modified to the effect that also the election of the individual members of a chamber should be based on a consensus between the Court and the parties. In this way the parties will have the opportunity of submitting their case to a chamber of their choice, thereby avoiding *ab initio* also the delicate question of disqualification of a particular chamber member on account of incompatibility ... In this way, that is with the consent of the parties, a special chamber could be constituted either as a regional chamber or as a chamber composed of judges possessing expert knowledge of the particular subject to be dealt with.[26]

---

[22] *Ibid.*, pp. 46–47.   [23] *Ibid.*, p. 47.   [24] *Ibid.*   [25] *Ibid.*, p. 50.

[26] *Ibid.*, pp. 48–49. (It may be presumed that these prescient lines were prepared by a distinguished former student of Judge Jessup and colleague of Ambassador Rosenne who was to occupy the highest national and international offices.) See also the comments of Canada, *ibid.*, pp. 49–50.

The United Kingdom in a like vein observed:

> One reason why more use has not been made of the possibility of establishing *ad hoc* chambers under Article 26, paragraph 2, may be that Article 24, paragraph 2, of the Court's Rules provides for the election of members of the chamber of the Court by secret ballot. In some cases the parties might wish to have a chamber composed of judges chosen by them and it is suggested that ways of making this possible should be considered.[27]

All this did not escape the attention of the judges of the Court in The Hague, who indeed at that time had little else to attend to. The Court not only took account of the foregoing views of States and scholars, it also took the initiative in securing the advice of former judges and of leading counsel before the Court. In the light of their observations and its own deliberations, the Court undertook a revision of its Rules. It first considered making a comprehensive revision; in the end, it concentrated on three areas: facilitation of recourse to chambers; simplification of written and oral proceedings; and preliminary objections.

But before describing the changes in its Rules which the Court made, it may be remarked that there was one more occurrence, in 1971, which may have influenced the Court: the *Beagle Channel* case. In that case, one party wished to go to the Court, the other required arbitration. They compromised by selecting an arbitration tribunal, all five members of which, however, were judges of the Court.[28] They did not sit as a chamber of the Court, because, under the governing arbitration treaty, the British Crown was the Arbitrator. It fell to the Crown, not the Court, to appoint the arbitrators, and their decision was subject to the Crown's confirmation, so clearly the Court of Arbitration in the *Beagle Channel* case could not have been a chamber of the Court – unless the parties had been prepared to entertain judicial recourse outside the terms of their arbitration treaty. But it is of interest to note that the Crown acted much as the Court presumably would have acted, consulting the parties on the tribunal's composition and accepting the parties' proposals for it. Thus, in the *Beagle Channel* case, five judges of the Court were chosen and were constructively occupied; in addition to their Court salaries, they were paid arbitral fees. The parties not only had that unnecessary burden, they were also deprived of the free services of the Registry of the Court and of the Peace Palace; they did not have the benefit of the Rules of Court; and – perhaps most

---

[27] United Nations doc. A/8383/Add.1 of September 30, 1971, p. 5.
[28] International Court of Justice, *Yearbook 1970–1971*, p. 114.

significantly as things turned out – the judgment in the *Beagle Channel* case, not being a judgment of a chamber of the Court, was not embraced by the terms of Article 94 of the Charter of the United Nations, which in part provides that,

> Each Member of the United Nations undertakes to comply with the decision of the International Court of Justice in any case to which it is a party.

The Court's Revision of its Rules

The final product of the process of revising the Rules in respect of chambers which the Court undertook in the light of these considerations is encapsulated in Article 17, which provides:

1. A request for the formation of a Chamber to deal with a particular case, ... may be filed at any time until the closure of the written proceedings. Upon receipt of a request made by one party, the President shall ascertain whether the other party assents.
2. When the parties have agreed, the President shall ascertain their views regarding the composition of the Chamber, and shall report to the Court accordingly ...
3. When the Court has determined, with the approval of the parties, the number of its Members who are to constitute the Chamber, it shall proceed to their election, in accordance with the provisions of Article 18 ... of these Rules ...
4. Members of a chamber formed under this Article who have been replaced ... following the expiration of their terms of office, shall continue to sit in all phases of the case, whatever the stage it has then reached.

Article 18 of the Rules continued to provide that:

1. Elections to all Chambers shall take place by secret ballot.

The revised Rules introduced two especially significant changes respecting chambers. First, they provide for consultation by the Court's President with the parties to a case in order to ascertain their views regarding the composition of the chamber. Second, they provide that, once a judge is elected to a chamber, he shall continue to sit on that case even if his term on the Court has expired, regardless of the phase of the case which has been reached when his term does expire. The latter proviso is an exception to the general rule that a judge who has been replaced on the Court only continues to sit in a case if oral argument in the pending phase of the case has taken place while he was a member of the Court.

The Constitutionality and Desirability of the Revised Rules

The constitutionality and desirability of consulting the parties on the composition of the chamber were challenged when the Court was in the process of revising its Rules[29] and have been challenged since.[30] The immutability in the chamber's composition proved hardly less controversial in the *Gulf of Maine* case.[31]

The essential ground for attacking the constitutionality of the revised Rule is the following. Article 26 of the Statute provides that the Court may at any time form a chamber for dealing with a particular case, and that the *number* of judges constituting such a chamber shall be determined by the Court with the approval of the parties. Since the Statute provides for the approval by the parties of the number of the chamber's judges, it is argued that, inferentially, it excludes requiring the approval by the parties of its composition. Thus the provision of the revised Rules requiring the President of the Court to ascertain the views of the parties regarding the composition of the chamber, it is claimed, is inconsistent with the Statute, which, of course, governs the Rules.

The ground for attacking the desirability of revising the Rules in this way was that it would give the parties to a case a voice, practically a determinative voice, in the composition of the chamber. In itself, a chamber, by including only some judges, excludes others. To permit the parties to influence the choice of whom to include and whom to exclude would be to divide the Court invidiously, perhaps along ideological or regional lines. It would permit the parties to choose judges as if they were choosing arbitrators, and to exclude some judges, perhaps invariably exclude some judges, on political or other unmentionable grounds. The dangers of such a process would be accentuated by the provision of Article 27 of the Statute that a judgment given by a chamber "shall be considered as rendered by the Court."

---

[29] Edvard Hambro, "Will the Revised Rules of Court Lead to Greater Willingness on the Part of Prospective Clients?," in Leo Gross (ed.), *The Future of the International Court of Justice* (1976), Vol. 1, p. 369. See also Edvard Hambro, "Quelques Observations sur la Révision du Règlement de la Cour Internationale de Justice," in *Mélanges offerts à Charles Rousseau* (1974), pp. 128–131.

[30] *Delimitation of the Maritime Boundary in the Gulf of Maine Area, Constitution of Chamber, Order of 20 January 1982, ICJ Reports 1982*, pp. 11–13. See also Mohammed Bedjaoui, "Universalisme et Regionalisme au sein de la Cour Internationale de Justice: La Constitution de Chambres 'Ad hoc'," *Liber Amicorum, Colección de Estudios Jurídicos en Homenaje al Prof. Dr. D. José Perez Montero* (1988), p. 155. The most searching criticism is found in the dissenting opinion of Judge Shahabuddeen in *Land, Island and Maritime Frontier Dispute (El Salvador/Honduras), Application to Intervene, Order of 28 February 1990, ICJ Reports 1990*, p. 18; see also the dissenting opinion of Judge Tarassov, p. 11. For a commentary on Judge Shahabuddeen's dissent, see Elihu Lauterpacht, *Aspects of the Administration of International Justice* (1991), p. 90. See also, Rosenne, "1972 Revision," pp. 210, 212–213, and in *Procedure in the International Court*, pp. 42–45.

[31] *ICJ Reports 1982*, pp. 11–13.

While these objections to the revisions of the Rules of Court were not publicly voiced by the objectors at the time, they subsequently were. They were known at the time of the revision of the Rules and were addressed by an exceptionally distinguished and knowledgeable triumvirate: two sitting Members of the Court, Judge Eduardo Jiménez de Aréchaga and Judge Sture Petrén, and Ambassador and former Registrar Edvard Hambro.

Writing in 1973 in the *American Journal of International Law* on "The Amendments to the Rules of Procedure of the International Court of Justice," Judge Jiménez de Aréchaga stated:

> The main change introduced on this subject is to accord to the parties a decisive influence in the composition of *ad hoc* Chambers. One of the most frequent suggestions made in this respect, particularly by Judge Jessup, was that recourse to *ad hoc* Chambers would prove more attractive to potential litigants if the election of their members were to be based on a consensus between the Court and the parties.
>
> The idea of giving effect to the wishes of the parties in the selection of the members of an *ad hoc* Chamber as a means of breathing new life into this dormant institution has, however, encountered some objections. It has been objected that this would constitute an unwarranted extension of the Statute, since Article 26, paragraph 2, requires the approval of the parties for "the number of judges to constitute such a Chamber" but not for the determination of who are to serve. Along this same line, it has also been observed that such a proposal would constitute a derogation from the requirement of a secret ballot for the designation of members of a Chamber and might affect the unity of the Court, transforming Chambers into privately selected bodies.
>
> In 1945 two changes with respect to Chambers had been introduced in the Statute of the Permanent Court. The first was to allow the constitution of *ad hoc* Chambers to deal, at the request of the parties, with a particular case. The second was to delete from the Statute a requirement that Chambers should be selected so far as possible with due regard to the provisions of Article 9 of the Statute, prescribing that Members of the Court should represent the principal legal systems of the world.
>
> It must be further pointed out that, while under the Statute the approval of the parties is required for the determination of the number of judges to compose an *ad hoc* Chamber, the Statute does not restrict the scope of the consultations that may be carried out by the President with the parties. It would be in order for the President to consult the parties and to inform the Court of their views as to the Chamber's composition, and this is precisely what the new Rules envisage.
>
> After the President reports on these consultations, the Court must always proceed to an election of the members of the Chamber by secret ballot, thus retaining ultimate control over the composition of any Chamber. However, from a practical point of view, it is difficult to conceive that in normal circumstances those Members who have been suggested by the parties would not be elected. For

that it would be necessary for a majority of the Members of the Court to decide to disregard the expressed wishes of the parties. This would be highly unlikely since it would simply result in compelling the parties to resort to an outside arbitral tribunal or even to abandon their intention to seek a judicial settlement of the dispute.[32]

Judge Jiménez de Aréchaga went on to point out that the revision of the Rules providing that a member of an *ad hoc* chamber shall continue to sit in all phases of the case after the expiry of his term of office as a member of the Court reinforced the influence of the parties in definitively determining the chamber's composition.[33]

Ambassador Hambro made a like analysis in the Society's volumes on *The Future of the International Court of Justice*.[34] As to the objection that the Statute, by requiring the assent of the parties to the number of judges forming a chamber excluded taking account of their views on its composition, Hambro observed that: "This objection is not of a very important character since nothing in the Statute would forbid the President to consult."[35] The objection that such consultations render meaningless the secret ballot for election of the judges of the chamber "is not very serious" since "the ultimate decision must belong to the Court."[36] As to splitting the Court into two categories, those asked to participate in chambers and those not, while that was true, it would not be "more true than that some judges are more often elected than others to be members of the drafting committee set up to formulate judgments or advisory opinions."[37]

Judge Petrén's analysis has particular interest for current events. He maintained that:

> There can be no denying that the actual presence on the bench of judges from States which do not themselves recognize the jurisdiction of the Court is bound to have a negative effect on the readiness of States which do recognize its jurisdiction to submit cases to the Court . . . their Governments would certainly hesitate before having questions of national interest decided by judges from States who cannot be relied upon to allow international adjudication of disputes in which they are themselves involved.[38]

---

[32] Eduardo Jiménez de Aréchaga, "The Amendments to the Rules of Procedure of the International Court of Justice," *American Journal of International Law* (1973), 67, pp. 2–3. Rosenne has voiced his doubts about Judge Jiménez de Aréchaga's conclusion as "too optimistic" (*Procedure in the International Court*, p. 44).

[33] Jiménez de Aréchaga, "Amendments," p. 4. [34] Hambro, "Revised Rules," Vol. I, p. 365.

[35] *Ibid.*, p. 369. [36] *Ibid.* [37] *Ibid.*

[38] B. A. S. Petrén, "Some Thoughts on the Future of the International Court of Justice," *Netherlands Yearbook of International Law* (1975), 6, pp. 61–62. (See also Richard R. Baxter, "Two Cheers for International Adjudication," *American Bar Association Journal* [1979], 65, p. 1189.)

The Court, he maintained, had accordingly taken an initiative,

> which is that States who hesitate to address themselves to the plenary Court now have the possibility of submitting a dispute to a Chamber *ad hoc*, composed in conformity with their own wishes regarding not only the number, but also the names, of its members.[39]

There is room for difference of opinion on the constitutionality of the modalities of forming *ad hoc* chambers and, more, on their desirability. The objections are not frivolous; Ambassador Hambro revealed no secret in stating that they clearly divided the Court;[40] and the replies to those objections are not unarguable. For the reasons which are set out in the conclusions of this essay, it is believed that the better of the argument lies with the exponents of the Rules of Court as revised. At this juncture, it should be observed that the United Nations General Assembly lent its support to the Rules as revised, explicitly in order to allow the parties an influence on the chamber's composition. In resolution 3232 (XXIX) on a "Review of the role of the International Court of Justice,"[41] the General Assembly in 1974 declared:

> *Considering* that the International Court of Justice has recently amended the Rules of Court with a view to facilitating recourse to it for the judicial settlement of disputes, *inter alia* by simplifying the procedure, reducing the likelihood of undue delays and costs and allowing for greater influence of parties on the composition of *ad hoc* chambers, . . .
>
> *Draws the attention* of States to the possibility of making use of chambers as provided in Articles 26 and 29 of the Statute of the International Court of Justice and in the Rules of Court, including those which would deal with particular categories of cases.

Another question is the compatibility with the Statute of Article 17, paragraph 4 of the Rules of Court, which provides:

> Members of a Chamber formed under this Article who have been replaced, in accordance with Article 13 of the Statute following the expiration of their terms

---

[39] Petrén, "Some Thoughts," p. 63.

[40] Hambro, "Revised Rules," p. 369. For a close analysis of the Court's revision of its Rules in respect of chambers, see Rosenne, *Procedure in the International Court*, pp. 39–47. See also Shabtai Rosenne, "Some Reflections on the 1978 Revised Rules of the International Court of Justice," *Columbia Journal of Transnational Law* (1981), 19, pp. 248–249; Rosenne in the Israel Law Review as cited, above, note 1; Geneviève Guyomar, *Commentaire du Règlement de la Cour Internationale de Justice* (1983), pp. 67–71; René Jean Dupuy, "La Réforme du Règlement de la Cour Internationale de Justice," *Annuaire Français de Droit International* 1972, 18, pp. 270–274; and Alain Pillepich, "Les Chambres (avec particulière référence à la Cour Internationale de Justice)," Société française de droit international, *La Jurisdiction Internationale Permanente* (1986), p. 45.

[41] *Resolutions adopted by the General Assembly during its Twenty-Ninth Session*, Vol. I, pp. 141–142.

of office, shall continue to sit in all phases of the case, whatever the stage it has then reached.

By way of contrast, Article 33 of the Rules provides:

> Except as provided in Article 17 of these Rules, Members of the Court who have been replaced, in accordance with Article 13, paragraph 3, of the Statute following the expiration of their terms of office, shall discharge the duty imposed upon them by that paragraph by continuing to sit until the completion of any phase of a case in respect of which the Court convenes for the oral proceedings prior to the date of such replacement.

Article 13, paragraph 3 of the Statute – the governing provision – provides:

> The Members of the Court shall continue to discharge their duties until their places have been filled. Though replaced, they shall finish any cases which they may have begun.

What is a case which a judge of the Court has "begun"? Article 33 of the Rules takes an exigent view, interpreting such a case as "any phase ... in respect of which the Court convenes for oral proceedings ..." Thus a retiring judge, over a period of years, may have spent months studying massive pleadings, but, if oral hearings have not convened in the particular phase of the case then current, he does not continue to sit on the case. This is not a necessary interpretation of the Statute but surely it is a possible, and perhaps a desirable, interpretation.

In respect of an *ad hoc* chamber, however, the parties characteristically attach particular importance to the chamber's particular composition and do not or may not wish it to change. Thus the thrust of Article 17, paragraph 4 of the Rules is politic; it increases the attractions of an *ad hoc* chamber for the States who must request its formation if it is to be formed at all. The terms of Article 17, paragraph 4 of the Rules are no less consistent with Article 13 of the Statute than are the terms of Article 33 (except, arguably, in a respect set out in the next paragraph). It is true that Article 17, paragraph 4 and Article 33 of the Rules arrive at divergent interpretations of the same governing provision, namely, Article 13, paragraph 3 of the Statute. But both interpretations are legally tenable, and, it is believed, neither is undermined by the fact that the Rules do not opt only for one of two plausible interpretations.

However, it should be observed that Article 13 refers to cases which a judge has "begun." Article 17, paragraph 4 of the Rules is more broadly cast. Thus, in the *Gulf of Maine* case, in conformity with that provision of the Rules, Judge Gros was elected a member of the chamber when his term was about to expire, though it could be argued that he had hardly "begun" on a case in which no pleadings had been filed.[42]

The *Gulf of Maine* Chamber

The next development was well described after the fact, once more in the pages of the *American Journal of International Law*, by the then Legal Adviser of the State Department, Davis Robinson, and two of his senior colleagues:

> In the negotiations that took place during the Carter administration, the United States and Canada chose to take the boundary case to a five-member Chamber of the International Court of Justice rather than to the full 15-member Court or to an independent ad hoc arbitral tribunal. The United States was first attracted to the Chamber procedure for the reasons set out by Eduardo Jiménez de Aréchaga in a 1973 article in the *American Journal of International Law* on the 1972 amendments to the Rules of Court.
>
> In that article, the then judge (and later President) of the International Court of Justice indicated that the Rules of Court had been modified to attract States to use the Chamber procedure that had been available for many years but never utilized. He suggested that the Chamber procedure combined the attractive elements of an international arbitration, where the parties can influence court procedure and the make-up of the tribunal, with the convenience of an established institution, where such matters as judges' salaries, courtrooms, registry, translation and interpretation and reproduction facilities are independently provided and funded.
>
> This previously untested procedure proved appealing. The case was expected to raise a host of novel issues of law and fact and to require a degree of procedural innovation, especially since two nations from the common law tradition were involved. It was believed that the Chamber procedure would provide the parties the opportunity to submit the complex of historical, geographical, biological, environmental and other issues to a small group of judges with special experience in the area. We furthermore wanted to make good and appropriate use of the International Court of Justice as an institution and hoped that the first Chamber process would set a positive precedent for other nations in the peaceful resolution of their disputes.
>
> Cost was also a factor in not resorting to an independently created ad hoc arbitral tribunal. The United States and Canada already were substantial contributors to the budget of the Court through their United Nations dues. Not only would the establishment of a separate ad hoc tribunal be expensive, but it would be time-consuming as well.
>
> Throughout the negotiating process, there was a consensus that any boundary judgment resulting from a binding adjudication between the United States and Canada must be fair not only in substance, as a matter of law, but in perception as well. The decision could also affect broader interests because of its precedential

[42] *ICJ Reports 1982*, pp. 11, 12–13.

value. Thus, the Chamber procedure had the advantage of utilizing the institutional significance and established facilities of the International Court of Justice, while seeking convenience and innovation in presenting the case to a limited number of specially qualified jurists.[43]

The Court elected as members of the chamber in the *Gulf of Maine* case the five persons precisely prescribed by the parties (Judges Ago, Gros, Mosler, Schwebel, and Judge *ad hoc* Cohen). Their choice proved controversial. Of this, Messrs. Robinson, Colson, and Rashkow wrote:

> The fact that the Chamber consisted only of judges from North America and Western Europe was criticized by some. However, the parties did not in any way preordain that result, which occurred in the process of reaching a balance of experienced jurists that both sides could propose. Moreover, in our view, the parties should be free to select members of a Chamber within the Court's rules and prerogatives. The requirement that members of a Chamber should represent the "principal legal systems of the world," which appeared in the Statute of the Permanent Court, was deleted in 1945 when the ICJ Statute was drafted. We believe that the make-up of a Chamber should be based upon the views of the parties as to its ability to settle the dispute between them in an acceptable manner – not upon some abstract notion of geographic balance or blending of various legal systems.[44]

The order of the Court establishing the first *ad hoc* chamber in the history of the Court is of high interest. It adverts to the fact that the United States and Canada initially concluded a Special Agreement on March 29, 1979, which was later modified.[45] It may be interpellated that that Agreement was modified essentially because the composition of the chamber initially agreed upon by the parties was rendered impossible by three deaths.[46] That initial composition, not wholly confined to judges of the North Atlantic, for that and other reasons would not have attracted the criticism that was levelled at the composition of the chamber as finally formed by the Court.[47]

The Court's order records that, when the Acting President of the Court

---

[43] Davis R. Robinson, David A. Colson, and Bruce C. Rashkow, "Some Perspectives on Adjudicating before the World Court: The Gulf of Maine Case," *American Journal of International Law* (1985), 79, pp. 581–582.

[44] *Ibid.*, p. 583.

[45] *Delimitation of the Maritime Boundary in the Gulf of Maine Area, Order of 20 January 1982, ICJ Reports 1982*, p. 3.

[46] Those of Judge Richard R. Baxter, Professor Max Sorensen, and Judge Sir Humphrey Waldock.

[47] For examples of such criticism (in addition to that of Judges Morozov and El-Khani referred to below), see L. C. Green, "Is There a Universal International Law Today?," *Canadian Yearbook of International Law* (1985), 23, p. 27; Edward McWhinney, "Special Chambers Within the International Court of Justice: The Preliminary, Procedural Aspect of the Gulf of Maine Case," *Syracuse Journal of International Law and Commerce* (1985), 12, pp. 1–13; and Brigitte Stern, "Chronique de jurisprudence de la Cour internationale de Justice (1975–1983)," *Journal du Droit International* (1984), 111, pp. 652–654.

reported to the Court the results of his consultations with the parties, "some" of the Members of the Court saw "problems . . . because of possible incompatibilities with the Statute and the Rules of Court."[48] Questions were accordingly put to the parties. The focus of this essay does not require examination of those questions and of the answers to them;[49] they have been acutely analyzed by commentators, particularly by Professor Elisabeth Zoller.[50] The Court, to the extent that the Court as a whole shared the problems which some of its Members saw, apparently was sufficiently satisfied, since, by a vote of eleven to two, it decided "to accede to the request of the Governments of Canada and the United States . . . to form a special Chamber" and elected to the chamber judges who met the expressed wishes of the parties.[51]

Judges Morozov and El-Khani vigorously dissented. Judge Morozov explained that he had voted against the Court's order because the parties had incorrectly presumed that "they may dictate to the Court who should be elected" to the chamber.[52] He also appeared to have an *ad hominem* objection, directed to the person of a judge whose term on the Court was about to expire but who, having been elected to the chamber while still a member of the Court, would continue to sit on the chamber for its life.

Judge El-Khani observed that the parties had transmitted to the Court not only their Special Agreement submitting the case to a chamber but an additional agreement to submit the same question to arbitration in the event that the Court did not form the chamber "within the specified time and in the desired manner."[53] He pointed out that the parties "further insisted" on the identity of any replacements elected in case of vacancy being subject to their approval, failing which they would withdraw the case and discontinue proceedings before the Court in favor of arbitration.[54] Judge El-Khani concluded that all this deprived the Court of "its freedom of choice" and

[48] *ICJ Reports 1982*, pp. 3, 4.   [49] *Ibid.*, pp. 5–8.

[50] Elisabeth Zoller, "La Première Constitution d'une Chambre Spéciale par la Cour Internationale de Justice: Observations sur l'Ordonnance du 20 Janvier 1982," *Révue Générale de Droit International Public* (1982), 86, p. 305. See also Baxter, "Two Cheers"; Heribert Golsong, "Report" in Max Planck Institute, *Judicial Settlement of International Disputes* (1974), pp. 109–111; Francis Rigaldies, "Le Canada et les Etats-Unis soumettent à une chambre spéciale de la Cour Internationale de Justice la délimitation de la Frontière Maritime dans la golfe du Maine," *La Revue Juridique Thémis* (1981–2), 16, p. 544; Robert H. Brauer, "International Conflict Resolution: ICJ Chambers and the Gulf of Maine Dispute," *Virginia Journal of International Law* (1983), 23, p. 462; D. M. McRae, "Adjudication of the Maritime Boundary in the Gulf of Maine," *Canadian Yearbook of International Law* (1979), 18, pp. 294–297; Geneviève Guyomar, "La Constitution au sein de la Cour Internationale de Justice d'une Chambre Chargée de Régler le Différend Frontières Maritimes entre les Etats-Unis et le Canada," *Annuaire Français de Droit International* (1981), 27, p. 213; and René-Jean Dupuy, "Réforme du Reglement."

[51] *ICJ Reports 1982*, pp. 8–9.   [52] *Ibid.*, p. 11.   [53] *Ibid.*, p. 13.   [54] *Ibid.*

resulted "in its regionalization by depriving it of its basic and essential characteristic of universality."[55]

While the author of this essay did not and does not share the views which Judges Morozov and El-Khani expressed, he shares the opinion which Professor Zoller offered that the United States and Canada manifested not so much wariness of the Court as of each other.[56] As so often in the process of international adjudication and arbitration, each party was intent on the other's gaining no advantage, actual or imaginary. This preoccupation also may have led the parties to tell the Court more than it needed or wanted to know. The parties' conclusion of an alternative agreement to arbitrate, and their notification of its terms to the Court, made their concerns unnecessarily clear. Thus the parties went so far as not only to provide that the chamber would not be constituted until the name or names of the *ad hoc* judge or judges had been notified to the Registrar, thereby preserving an explicit recourse against the Court's election of an unacceptable chamber. They also provided for either party withdrawing the case in the event that a replacement elected by the Court to fill a vacancy were not to be acceptable to the parties.

This is not the place to appraise the judgment in the *Gulf of Maine* case. Clearly there is room for difference of opinion about its merits, as Judge Gros,[57] a member of the chamber, and Judge Oda, not a member of the chamber,[58] have emphasized.

Three observations on the *Gulf of Maine* judgment may be made. The first is that the judgment, accepted and applied by the parties, has settled the dispute – a dispute which was exceptionally knotty and difficult. The second is that this first judgment of an *ad hoc* chamber figured in the arguments to and the judgment of the full Court in the succeeding continental shelf case (that between Libya and Malta) no less than comparable earlier judgments of the full Court; it was not discounted because it was a chamber judgment. The third observation is that, despite the criticism of the alleged regional character of the chamber, the judgment of the chamber shows no signs of regional particularity. It does not manifest a peculiarly "Western" or "Atlantic" outlook. It could as easily have been a judgment of the Court as it was a judgment of a chamber. The substance of the criticism by Judges Gros and Oda – which relates the *Gulf of Maine* judgment of 1984 to that of the Court in the *Continental Shelf (Tunisia/Libya)* case of 1982 – confirms that very point.

---

[55] *Ibid.*   [56] Zoller, "Première Constitution," p. 311. See also, Pillepich, "Chambres," p. 69.
[57] *Delimitation of the Maritime Boundary in the Gulf of Maine Area, Judgment, ICJ Reports 1984*, p. 360.
[58] *Continental Shelf (Libyan Arab Jamahiriya/Malta), Judgment, ICJ Reports 1985*, pp. 165–169.

The most that could be said about the singularity of a chamber judgment is that this judgment of a chamber – or any judgment of any chamber – may perhaps give more room for the play of influence of a single, influential judge than does a judgment of the full Court. In the Court, the particular perceptions of the single judge tend to be watered down by the cascade of comments of his fourteen or fifteen colleagues. In a five-judge chamber, less water flows and the flavor of individual views may be stronger.

A tangential element of the procedure followed by the Court in electing a chamber in the *Gulf of Maine* case merits mention; it concerns the institution of the *ad hoc* judge. The Court initially elected five judges of the Court as members of the chamber, including Judge Ruda. Then the Acting President of the Court, the Court's Order records,

> in the exercise of his powers under Article 31, paragraph 4, of the Statute of the Court, ... requested Judge Ruda to give place in due course to the judge *ad hoc* to be chosen by the Government of Canada, and ... Judge Ruda ... indicated his readiness to do so.[59]

Article 31, paragraph 4 of the Statute provides:

> The provisions of this Article shall apply to the case of Articles 26 and 29. In such cases, the President shall request one or, if necessary, two of the Members of the Court forming the chamber to give place to the Members of the Court of the nationality of the parties concerned, and, failing such, or if they are unable to be present, to the judges specially chosen by the parties.

Was the application of the foregoing provision respecting *ad hoc* judges to the formation of the *ad hoc* chamber in the *Gulf of Maine* case necessary or desirable? The Court employed an artificial and useless procedure which it would have been preferable to avoid, if legally possible. It may be argued that the Court would have been on defensible ground, under the Statute, if it had avoided the application of Article 31, paragraph 4 to the *Gulf of Maine* case by robustly holding that that provision need apply only to standing (and not to *ad hoc*) chambers. The Statute admits such an interpretation. However, the terms of Article 17, paragraph 2 of the Rules of Court do provide for application of the provision of Article 31, paragraph 4 of the Statute to *ad hoc* chambers. Thus its application in the *Gulf of Maine* case was seen by the Court as necessary. Nevertheless in the establishment of subsequent chambers, the Court adopted the former, more forthright interpretation and directly installed *ad hoc* judges.

---

[59] *ICJ Reports 1982*, pp. 8–9. See also *ibid.*, p. 16.

Three more *Ad Hoc* Chambers

What of the three chambers which have followed that of the *Gulf of Maine?* The chamber in the *Case Concerning the Frontier Dispute (Burkina Faso/ Republic of Mali)* was easily elected by the Court in full conformity with the clearly expressed wishes of the parties. As the Court's order indicates, the Court acted unanimously.[60] The chamber was composed of judges from three continents (Judges Bedjaoui, Lachs, and Ruda). Unlike the chamber in the *Gulf of Maine* case, which dealt with massive pleadings and extended oral argument, the *Frontier Dispute* chamber arrived at a judgment in December 1986 more quickly than the full Court characteristically does, thus realizing one of the possible advantages of resort to a chamber. (The Rules of Court provide that written proceedings in a case before a chamber may consist of only a single pleading by each side, and, in fact, the parties each filed only a single pleading. Oral argument did take place.[61]) Again, this judgment of a chamber shows no parochial peculiarities. It was warmly praised and readily accepted by the parties, who earlier had complied with an indication of provisional measures by the chamber in circumstances in which a measure of hostilities had broken out.

While the first two chambers were constituted in response to special agreements of the parties, the *Elettronica Sicula ("ELSI")* chamber was formed after the United States so requested in a letter which accompanied its application and Italy accepted that proposal. The parties were duly consulted on the composition of the proposed chamber, which was elected by the Court in full consonance with the indications given in the course of those consultations. It consists of judges from three continents, and includes the President of the Court, Nagendra Singh, who, in accordance with Article 18, paragraph 2 of the Rules of Court, shall preside over that chamber.[62] (The other members are Judges Ago, Jennings, Oda, and Schwebel.)

The fourth *ad hoc* chamber formed by the Court is in the *Case concerning the*

---

[60] *Frontier Dispute, Constitution of Chamber, Order of 3 April 1985, ICJ Reports 1985,* p. 6.

[61] Article 92 provides that:

> Written proceedings in a case before a Chamber shall consist of a single pleading by each side ... The Chamber may authorize or direct that further pleadings be filed if the parties are so agreed, or if the Chamber decides, *proprio motu* or at the request of one of the parties, that such pleadings are necessary. Oral proceedings shall take place unless the parties agree to dispense with them, and the Chamber consents.

[62] *Case Concerning Elettronica Sicula S.p.A. (ELSI), Constitution of Chamber, Order of 2 March 1987, ICJ Reports 1987,* p. 3. (After the death of Judge Singh, his successor as President of the Court, Judge Ruda, was elected in his place.)

Land, Island and Maritime Frontier Dispute (El Salvador/Honduras).[63] This case arose out of the "soccer war" between El Salvador and Honduras, who committed themselves to submit their dispute to the Court in the event that it was not otherwise settled by pacific means. Ultimately, they agreed upon formation of a chamber of five judges (including two *ad hoc* judges). They were consulted by the President of the Court regarding the composition of the chamber, and subsequently submitted a joint letter specifying the composition contemplated by them. By its order of May 8, 1987, the Court observed, *inter alia*, that:

> 6. Whereas the Special Agreement ... defines ... the questions submitted for decision, and provides ... that the Parties submit those questions to a Chamber of the Court composed of three members, and further that in addition, the Chamber shall comprise two judges *ad hoc* ... and whereas the Court understands the Special Agreement as requesting the Court to form a Chamber to deal with the case in accordance with Article 26, paragraph 2, of its Statute;
> 7. Whereas the Parties were duly consulted, on 17 February 1987, as to the composition of the proposed Chamber of the Court in accordance with Article 26, paragraph 2, of the Statute and Article 17, paragraph 2, of the Rules of Court;
> 8. Whereas the Parties in the course of such consultation confirmed the indication, given in the Special Agreement, that as regards the number of judges to constitute such chamber, they approve, pursuant to Article 26 of the Statute, that number being fixed at five judges, including two judges *ad hoc* chosen by the Parties pursuant to Article 31, paragraph 3, of the Statute.[64]

The Court's order makes no reference to the parties' letter regarding the chamber's composition, and refers to their approval as relating only to the number of judges constituting the chamber. At the same time, the order describes consultations with the parties on composition of the chamber as "in accordance with Article 26, paragraph 2, of the Statute ..." as well as Article 17, paragraph 2 of the Rules of Court (as, in identical terms, does the Court's order of March 2, 1987 in the *ELSI* case). The Court thereby held in those two orders that consulting the parties on the composition of an *ad hoc* chamber *is* in accordance with the Statute. The Court, having earlier elected the chamber, "unanimously" decided to accede to the request to form a special chamber of five judges, composed of one judge from Asia, one from Latin America, and one from Western Europe (Judges Oda, Sette-Camara, and Jennings), as well as the two *ad hoc* judges designated by the parties (both European), in accordance with the views of the parties.

---

[63] *Case Concerning the Land, Island and Maritime Frontier Dispute (El Salvador/Honduras), Constitution of Chamber, Order of 8 May 1987, ICJ Reports 1987*, p. 10.
[64] *Ibid.*, pp. 11–12.

One member of the chamber so elected, Judge Oda, made the following declaration:

> In the case of a chamber provided for in Article 26, paragraph 2, of the Statute of the Court, the consent of the two parties is essential and, as that provision clearly states, the number of judges to constitute such a chamber shall be determined by the Court with the approval of the parties. At the same time, regarding the composition of the chamber, the views of the parties shall be ascertained by the President in accordance with Article 17, paragraph 2, of the Rules of Court. The Court, being sovereign in judicial proceedings, is free to choose any composition it likes; yet the possibility must also be borne in mind that sovereign States have the legal right to withdraw a case if they prefer a composition different from that determined by the Court. In practical terms, therefore, it is inevitable, if a chamber is to be viable, that its composition must result from a consensus between the parties and the Court. To ensure that viability, it accordingly behoves the Court to take account of the views of the parties when proceeding to the election. Nevertheless, the chamber is a component of the Court, bound by its Statute and Rules; and the process of election whereby it comes into being should be as judicially impartial as its subsequent functioning.[65]

Judge Oda thus economically expressed the essence of the matter. His last sentence is suggestive of an additional element; his saying that "the process of election" of a chamber "should be as judicially impartial as its subsequent functioning" may perhaps imply that, in this case, that process, in Judge Oda's view, was not. By the terms of Article 18 of the Rules of Court, "Elections to all Chambers shall take place by secret ballot." Accordingly, it is not possible to expand upon Judge Oda's intimation.

The Report of the AALCC

Since the filing in 1981 of the first case to be referred to an *ad hoc* chamber, the Court has had eleven contentious cases on its docket. Thus more than a third of the contentious cases brought to the Court in the last six years has involved *ad hoc* chambers. The importance of this development is clear. Whether what appears to be a trend towards chambers will persist is unpredictable. But there are substantial signs of interest in recourse to chambers of the Court.

How substantial that interest is is illustrated by a report of the Asian–African Legal Consultative Committee on the "Role of the International Court of Justice" which was circulated as a United Nations document in 1985.[66] The Committee brings together a very large number of the international legal advisers of Asian and African countries. Its report concentrates

---

[65] *Ibid.*, p. 13.   [66] A/40/682 of September 26, 1985.

115

on chambers of the Court and the revisions in the Court's Rules of 1972 and 1978. The report compares the relative merits of States resorting to *ad hoc* procedures of arbitration and *ad hoc* chambers of the Court.

The Committee's report observes that one of the principal reasons why Governments have favored *ad hoc* arbitral procedures is the desire to have their disputes settled by tribunals of their own choice. This desire can be met by the Court's chamber procedure which, the report states, affords the parties "a clear voice in the constitution of the Chamber."[67] The report concludes:

> The submission of a dispute to a chamber of the Court has the following merits *vis-à-vis* seeking settlement by *ad hoc* arbitration. The parties are afforded as much, if not more, recognition in the constitution of the Chamber as they are in the composition of an arbitral tribunal or court of arbitration. Secondly, the specific rules of procedure to be applied are clear and distinct and are not left to be determined by the arbitral tribunal. The parties can save the enormous expenses involved in the fees of the arbiters and experts and in the establishment and maintenance of a Secretariat. The Registry of the Court ensures custody of records. The place of proceedings may be elsewhere than at the Hague and finally the judgment is final and binding on the parties.[68]

Conclusions

Over the years, the Court has been afforded insufficient opportunity to contribute to the solution of international legal disputes. Its jurisdiction has always been severely limited. Those limitations give no sign of lifting. The very fact that some States have had a State policy antipathetic, if not to the Court, then to the Court's jurisdiction, has not encouraged other States to submit disputes to a Court on which nationals of the former States sit. That is the reality, or, rather, part of the reality. It reflects larger realities which inhibit recourse to the full Court.

Faced with these and other realities, and, in particular, with a dearth of cases, the Court revised its Rules so as, among other things, to afford States a voice in the composition of *ad hoc* chambers. In reliance upon the Court's revision of its Rules, and the authoritative interpretation of that revision which was placed on the public record, the United States and Canada submitted a case to a chamber of the Court and made it crystal clear exactly which judges they wished to sit on the chamber. The Court wisely proceeded to elect a chamber in accordance with the wishes of the parties. If it had not, the possibility of activating the Court by recourse to chambers would have been stillborn. That chamber functioned well and produced a judgment

---

[67] *Ibid.*, p. 27.   [68] *Ibid.*, pp. 31–32.

which has been accepted and applied. Since that time, three other chambers have been formed. Equally, nothing in their procedures to date lends substance to the fears which have been expressed about recourse to *ad hoc* chambers.

The workings of this process to date show that it affords the Court the opportunity to settle international disputes in a fashion which meets the needs of the parties and the international community and does not detract from the integrity of the Court. It has not "fractionalized" or "regionalized" international law in any degree. It has not thrown into question the universal character of international law. It may be that sometimes the parties may wish, or settle upon, a chamber that appears relatively regional; other times they will not. That happens in *ad hoc* arbitration as well. In the *Beagle Channel* case, the Latin American parties chose five judges of the Court, none of whom were from Latin America. Too much should not be made of such choices. The process of recourse to chambers is not a process free of risk in this or other respects, but neither is resort to the Court.

It is believed that the questions raised by the formation of a chamber for dealing with a particular case boil down essentially to five issues:

- What is the subject matter which such a chamber may properly dispose of?
- May such a chamber give an advisory opinion?
- Must such a chamber be representative of the main forms of civilization and of the principal legal systems of the world?
- How many judges shall constitute an *ad hoc* chamber?
- Shall the parties to the case have a voice in the determination of the composition of the chamber as well as in the number of judges comprising it?

In answering the first question, it is important to bear in mind that a chamber formed for dealing with a particular case is not the equivalent of a chamber which the Court from time to time may form for dealing with a particular category of cases. The thrust of Article 26, paragraph 2 of the Statute is not to be confused with that of Article 26, paragraph 1. The Court may (or may not) form one or more chambers for dealing with particular categories of cases. In addition to the examples which the Statute provides (labor cases and cases relating to transit and communications), others have been suggested, such as a chamber for the law of the sea, or a chamber for cases concerning the environment. No such chambers have in fact been formed to date. By definition, a chamber formed for dealing with a particular category of case is categorized. Equally, by definition, a chamber which the Court "may at any time form ... for dealing with a particular case" is not categorized. Such a chamber may be entrusted with a case which is particularly technical in character (as in the *Gulf of Maine*) or which has peculiarly regional aspects (as in the *Case Concerning the Frontier Dispute*). But the terms of the Statute afford no warrant for the contention that a chamber formed for a particular case *must* be so confined or otherwise confined; they afford no warrant for the contention that a case which is suitable for judgment by the Court as a whole is not suitable for judgment by an *ad hoc* chamber. It is one thing to recognize that an *ad hoc* chamber may be especially equipped to deal with a technical, a specialized, a regional – or a minor – case. It is another to conclude that, under the Statute, an *ad hoc* chamber can have no broader charge. It may well be that, as a matter of principle, it is preferable that cases which involve universal principles and problems of international law be submitted to the plenary Court. But States are legally entitled to request that such a case be submitted to a chamber, and the Court is entitled to refer such a case to a chamber. In the *Gulf of Maine* case, it did precisely that. The *Gulf of Maine* case, like other law–of–the–sea disputes, had its technical aspects and regional aspects, but so have the several maritime and continental shelf boundary cases which the Court as a whole has adjudged.

As to the second question, it is believed that the better – but certainly not the only – view is that a chamber of the Court may not give an advisory opinion. The latest version of the Rules of Court takes no position on this question, which may be taken as a reflection of the fact that the Statute is open to alternative constructions on the issue. The current rendering of the Rules contrasts with pre-1972 versions (at any rate, in one of the Court's two official languages), which indicated in Rule 84 that advisory opinions were to be delivered "par la Cour en séance plénière."

Article 26, paragraph 2 of the Statute provides that the number of judges to constitute an *ad hoc* chamber shall be determined by the Court "with the approval of the parties." Article 28, which refers comprehensively to chambers, likewise specifies that they may sit and exercise their functions elsewhere than at The Hague, with the consent "of the parties." In advisory proceedings, there are no "parties." The following exchanges in the Washington Committee of Jurists are instructive:

> Professor Basdevant (France) called attention to a change in the French text from "arrêts" to "jugements". He suggested that this might limit the role of chambers and would, for example, make it impossible for chambers to deliver advisory opinions. Judge Hudson explained that as a chamber could function only with the consent of the parties a chamber could not deliver an advisory opinion. It was agreed, however, to substitute "arrêts" for "jugements" in the French text ...
>
> Dr. Moneim-Riad Bey (Egypt) pointed out [in respect of Article 28] that

exercise of functions would cover advisory opinions, but though the chambers did not give advisory opinions he thought the phraseology was satisfactory. Judge Hudson agreed that chambers might give orders and that therefore the term "judgment" [in Article 27] might not be adequate.[69]

Nevertheless, Dr. C. Wilfred Jenks (without referring to the foregoing) later concluded:

> There is nothing in the Statute to prevent advisory proceedings before a Chamber of the Court, and the Rules of Court without envisaging the possibility of advisory proceedings in a chamber no longer contain the requirement of Article 84 (I) of the Rules of Court of the Permanent Court that "advisory opinions shall be given after deliberation by the full Court". There is therefore no reason why a request for an advisory opinion should not indicate a desire that the matter be heard by an appropriate Chamber of the Court; on receiving such a request the Court could rely on Article 68 of the Statute to refer the matter to a Chamber.[70]

Dr. Jenks's opinion is entitled to great weight. Apparently the United States, in making the proposal described above to the Vienna Conference on the Law of Treaties,[71] shared the view of Dr. Jenks, which has otherwise attracted much authoritative support.[72]

However, while recognizing that a number of arguments of law – particularly those deriving from the force of Article 68 of the Statute – and of policy may be adduced to the contrary, and appreciating that the text of the Statute is inconclusive, the terms of Article 26, paragraph 2 of the Statute and the uncontradicted interpretation placed upon them, particularly by Judge Hudson, when they were adopted, import that chambers may not render advisory opinions. Furthermore, Article 25 of the Statute provides that: "The full Court shall sit except when it is expressly provided otherwise in the present Statute." There is no express provision for referral of an advisory opinion to a chamber. In addition, Article 27 of the Statute provides that "a judgment" given by a chamber shall be considered as rendered by the Court; it does not refer to an advisory opinion. As the quoted exchange in the

---

[69] *UNCIO*, Vol. 14, p. 223.

[70] C. Wilfred Jenks, *The Prospects of International Adjudication* (1964), p. 160. Article 68 of the Statute provides: "In the exercise of its advisory functions the Court shall further be guided by the provisions of the present Statute which apply in contentious cases to the extent to which it recognizes them to be applicable." It is clear that Article 68 does grant the Court wide powers. Its basic effect is to empower the Court to apply, by analogy or *mutatis mutandis*, any of the provisions of the Statute to the exercise of its advisory functions. This is so regardless of the fact that these provisions may use words not directly intended for advisory proceedings, such as "judgment," "party," "case," "contentious case," "hear and determine," etc.

[71] Note 16 above and the text to which that note appertains.

[72] Elihu Lauterpacht concludes that chambers may deal with requests for advisory opinions, *Aspects of Administration*, pp. 95–98.

Washington Committee of Jurists suggests, while it was understood that chambers might issue orders, the term "judgment" (despite its French rendering as "*arrêt*") was not thought to encompass "advisory opinion."

In any event, on prudential grounds, the idea of referring questions to an *ad hoc* chamber – or any chamber – of the Court for an advisory opinion is unappealing. Moreover, in practice, if two or more States wish to have the benefit of the Court's judgment on governing legal principles while withholding its determination of their dispute, the approach taken in the Court in three continental shelf cases presents a path less circuitous and complex than that of inducing the United Nations Security Council or the General Assembly, or a body authorized by the latter, to seek an advisory opinion. Finally, it should be recalled that both the United Kingdom and Venezuela proposed that the revised Statute should authorize States to request advisory opinions of the Court.[73] These proposals were not accepted by the Washington Committee of Jurists.[74] In view of that fact as well, it may be asked whether it would be appropriate to amend the Rules of Court to permit States in effect to secure advisory opinions which would be requested on their behalf by a United Nations organ. Nevertheless, Article 102 of the Rules recognizes that a request for an advisory opinion may relate "to a legal question actually pending between two or more States." Both the Permanent Court and the ICJ have given opinions on such questions.

Need a chamber formed for dealing with a particular case be representative of the main forms of civilization and of the principal legal systems of the world? The deletion of that desideratum – it was never a requirement – from the Statute of the Permanent Court in the course of the adoption of the provisions of the Statute of the ICJ respecting chambers demonstrates that a chamber need not be representative. If the parties wish it and if the Court decides it, a chamber may – or may not – be "representative." In the *Gulf of Maine* case, it happened that the judges selected by the parties and elected by the Court were "Atlantic" or "Western" in their geographic and legal derivation. All had had experience in law-of-the-sea questions, some much more experience than others. The parties' selection may, in practice, not have fallen upon judges of such diversity as to minimize criticism, but to suggest that it – and the election by the Court – on this ground transgressed the letter or spirit of the Statute has no foundation in either the terms of the Statute or the apparent intention of its drafters.

As to the number of judges to constitute an *ad hoc* chamber, it "shall be determined by the Court with the approval of the parties." The question of

---

[73] *UNCIO*, Vol. 14, pp. 319, 373; Vol. 3, pp. 209, 225, 230.   [74] *UNCIO*, Vol. 14, p. 850.

whether the Statute should determine the number of judges or set limits to that determination was discussed in the Washington Committee of Jurists; a proposal to set such limits was not accepted.[75] The possibility of a chamber being composed of one judge alone apparently was admitted.[76] There accordingly appears to be no legal barrier to the suggestion of Judge Jessup and James N. Hyde that a chamber could be made up of a judge and two *ad hoc* judges. At the same time, in practice, such composition of a chamber appears neither probable nor prudent.

Finally, there is the most contentious question of all: whether the parties to a case shall have a voice in the choice of the particular judges who compose the *ad hoc* chamber to which they wish to have recourse.

The terms of the Statute give no conclusive answer to this question. It can be argued that, since Article 26, paragraph 2 specifies that the number of judges constituting an *ad hoc* chamber shall be determined by the Court "with the approval of the parties," their approval does not extend to their persons. It can alternatively be argued that the Statute does not in terms debar consultation by the Court with the parties as to which judges shall form the chamber, and that there is no necessary implication of any such preclusion. A body may be given certain express powers; it does not follow that it lacks all other powers. Such sparse indication as there is in the *travaux préparatoires* – the seasoned interpretation of Judge Hudson which has been quoted above[77] – supports participation by the parties in the choice of the judges composing the chamber. The revised Rules of Court expressly contemplate that participation, providing as they do that "the President shall ascertain their [the parties'] views regarding the composition of the Chamber, and shall report to the Court accordingly."[78] The Court deliberately crafted that provision, after mature consideration. Its obvious intention to give full weight to the views of the parties on which judges shall compose the chamber was accurately and authoritatively confirmed by Judge Jiménez de Aréchaga, who was a member of the Rules Committee which drafted the revised Rules in their 1972 version (and who was President of the Court when definitive revisions were adopted in 1978). Can it be persuasively maintained that this provision of the Rules is inconsistent with the Statute? Clearly the General Assembly, in considering that the "recently amended ... Rules of Court" allow "for greater influence of parties on the composition of *ad hoc* chambers," accepted the revised Rules as in accord with the Statute, as did the Court when it adopted the Rules. Moreover, as pointed out above, the orders of the Court

---

[75] See above, note 7.   [76] See above, note 8.
[77] *UNCIO*, Vol. 14, p. 199, and the text to which that note appertains.
[78] Article 17, paragraph 2 of the Rules of Court, in force since 1978.

in the *ELSI* and *El Salvador/Honduras* chamber cases explicitly treat consultation with the parties "as to the composition of the proposed chamber" as "in accordance with Article 26, paragraph 2 of the Statute."[79]

If the Rules of Court provided that the parties to a case were entitled to name the judges composing an *ad hoc* chamber and if the Court were bound by the Rules to act in accordance with the parties' designation, there would be an inconsistency with the Statute. By the terms of the Statute, it is the Court which "may" form the chamber which "shall" hear and determine a case only "if the parties so request"; the number of its judges "shall be determined by the Court with the approval of the parties."[80] The Court accordingly has the authority to form a chamber and to determine its size and composition. But the parties must approve the number of the chamber's judges and, more fundamentally, determination of their case by the chamber. Thus responsibility for the activation – and hence, at bottom, composition as well as size – of an *ad hoc* chamber is shared by the Court and the parties.

The Rules provide that the parties shall agree as to whether an *ad hoc* chamber shall be formed for the particular case (as required by Article 26, paragraph 3 of the Statute), whereupon "the President shall ascertain their views regarding the composition of the Chamber." Those views shall be reported to the Court, which, after determining, "with the approval of the parties, the number of its Members who are to constitute the Chamber, ... shall proceed to their election." Since the Rules provide that there is to be an election (which is not required by the terms of the Statute), that process need not, as a matter of law, coincide with the parties' selection; that is to say, while the Court shall take account of the parties' "views regarding the composition of the Chamber," the Court retains the authority to elect whom it decides to elect. That being so, there is no inconsistency with the Statute.

As a matter of practice, it is unlikely that the Court will vote in disregard of the views of the parties regarding the composition of the chamber. To do so not only may offend one or more of the parties; it also may offend one or more judges, who may regard such a vote as a vote of non-confidence. Such a vote may well lead the parties to withdraw the case from the Court in favor of arbitration – as the United States and Canada made so plain in the *Gulf of Maine* dispute[81] – or even to abandon third-party settlement altogether. Paragraph 2 of Article 26 of the Statute provides that the Court may form a chamber for dealing with a particular case; paragraph 3 prescribes that it shall hear and determine the case "if the parties so request." The sequence may be

[79] *ICJ Reports 1987*, pp. 4, 12.　　[80] Statute of the Court, Article 26, paragraph 2.
[81] *Delimitation of the Maritime Boundary in the Gulf of Maine Area, Constitution of the Chamber, Order of 20 January 1982, ICJ Reports 1982*, pp. 3, 6.

said to imply that, if a chamber's size or composition is uncongenial to the parties, they remain free not to so request or to withdraw a request already made – which, as Judge Oda pointed out, in any event is their legal right.[82] For its part, the Court retains final discretion, whose exercise cannot be excluded. But "In practical terms ... it is inevitable, if a chamber is to be viable, that its composition must result from a consensus between the parties and the Court."[83] Such a consensus is fully in accord not only with practicalities but legalities; it follows from the freedom of the parties, recognized by the Statute, to request or not to request determination of their case by a chamber.

The system of recourse to a chamber constituted for a particular case, as it is now provided for in the Rules of Court and as it has been developed in practice, may be seen as a halfway house between adjudication and arbitration. It may be seen as an advanced and effective form of the "judicial arbitration" which the International Law Commission sought under the idealistic and pertinacious guidance of the late Professor Georges Scelle.[84] Yet by no means may an *ad hoc* chamber be equated with an arbitral tribunal, however impregnable that tribunal's processes of constitution and operation may be.

Unlike arbitration, the parties before the Court are not altogether free to determine the composition and rules of a chamber. The chamber is an arm of the Court; its judgment, as Article 27 of the Statute provides, "shall be considered as rendered by the Court." Accordingly, an *ad hoc* chamber may operate only within the Court's Statute and Rules, served by the Court's Registry, and in consonance with the Court's agenda and proceedings.

The Court sets the chamber's timetable. When provisional measures were sought by Nicaragua in the midst of oral hearings before the *Gulf of Maine* chamber, the Court interrupted those hearings to consider and indicate provisional measures, in accordance with Article 74 of the Rules of Court which provides that a request for provisional measures shall have priority over all other cases. In contrast, the Court's rendering of its advisory opinion in the *Application for Review of Judgement No. 333 of the United Nations Administrative Tribunal* (the "*Yakimetz*" case) was delayed by the Court's decision to give priority to the work of the chamber in the *Case Concerning*

---

[82] *ICJ Reports 1987*, p. 13.   [83] *Ibid.*

[84] See "Arbitral Procedure," Rapport par Georges Scelle, rapporteur spécial, *Yearbook of the International Law Commission (1950)*, 2, p. 114, and Stephen M. Schwebel, *International Arbitration: Three Salient Problems* (1987), pp. 149–151, 154–177. The Agent of Canada in the *Gulf of Maine* case, L. H. Legault, later wrote that the parties "were fortunate to have available to them a mechanism combining some of the flexibility of an ad hoc tribunal with the authority and prestige of the World Court" ("A Line for All Uses: The Gulf of Maine Boundary Revisited," *International Journal* (1985), 40, pp. 461, 477).

the Frontier Dispute (Burkina Faso/Republic of Mali) – in the circumstances, an appropriate decision.

In the chamber cases, the pleadings of the parties were circulated to all judges of the Court for their information before public circulation. This courtesy did not imply that judges not members of the chamber had a judicial role to play in it. Since, for the case in question, the chamber is the Court, judges not members of the chamber, including the President and Vice-President of the Court, are not entitled as of right to the pleadings, still less to a place in the work of the chamber (though in subsequent cases, judges may of course comment on chamber judgments). At the same time, circulation of the pleadings to the full Court permits judges who are not members of a chamber to inform themselves on the problems with which colleagues are dealing. Such information may be helpful to the Court in deciding upon competing priorities between cases and otherwise.

Perhaps the institution of the *ad hoc* chamber may be said not to represent the full ideal of international judicial settlement at which the founders of the Permanent Court aimed in 1920. Its inherently selective – and hence exclusionary – character does not invariably lubricate relations among the Members of the Court. The further revision of the Court's relevant Rules may not be inconceivable. However, as the Rules stand, the *ad hoc* chamber embodies a practical and productive option, an option which the drafters of the Statute of the ICJ introduced – wisely, it is believed. As so often in international law and life, it illustrates the case in which the best should not be allowed to become the enemy of the good.

7

Three Cases of Fact-Finding by the International Court of Justice

⳩

The editor of this volume, Professor Richard B. Lillich, has written a Preface to it which he is particularly qualified to write, as the chairman of the Sokol Colloquia at the University of Virginia, the editor of the distinguished *Procedural Aspects of International Law Series*, and a leading scholar and practitioner in the field of international litigation. He has invited me to prepare an Introduction, containing such observations on the topic and papers of this volume as I may have been stimulated to make by them and by my participation in the Eleventh Sokol Colloquium. While I found all of the papers stimulating, I shall confine these comments to aspects of fact-finding in the International Court of Justice. In taking up Professor Lillich's invitation, I have been guided by the forthright Foreword written by Judge Philip C. Jessup to Volume 13 of the *Procedural Aspects of International Law Series*, the revised edition of D. Sandifer's *Evidence before International Tribunals* (1975). My concerns may be illustrated by the Court's fact-finding in three cases in which I have participated: the *ELSI* case, the *Yakimetz* case, and the *Nicaragua* case. In my discussion of these cases, I am constrained to say no more than I have already set out in my dissenting opinions.

Case Concerning Elettronica Sicula S.P.A. (ELSI) – and Chamber Advantages

The *ELSI* case turned on allegations by the United States that the requisition by Italian authorities of a factory in Sicily operated by an Italian company whose stock was wholly owned by two American companies was in breach of provisions of a 1948 Treaty of Friendship, Commerce, and Navigation between the United States and Italy.

In his chapter in this volume on "Evidence, the Chamber and the ELSI

First published in Richard B. Lillich (ed.), *Fact-Finding before International Tribunals* (1991), Irvington-on-Hudson, N.Y., Transnational Publishers, Inc.

Case," Keith Highet subjects the fact-finding processes of the Chamber of the International Court of Justice in the *ELSI* case to incisive and congratulatory scrutiny. I believe that he is right in many respects in concluding that that case was a model of fact-finding. The parties presented the facts rather fully; further facts were elicited through the processes of advocacy and cross-examination of witnesses; and what was especially notable was that all the members of the Chamber took an active part in posing a plenitude of probing questions to witnesses and counsel. At the same time, Italy chose not to present any witnesses on the facts of its own actions, which hardly conduced to an informed judgment by the Chamber as to whether actions or inactions of Italian authorities which the United States contended were arbitrary actually were arbitrary. The Chamber's lack of authority to compel the attendance of witnesses, and the absence of established procedures for discovery, did not strengthen the possibilities of the United States proving its contentions concerning Italy's breach of its treaty obligations including the obligation to refrain from the taking of arbitrary measures against investments by US corporations.

Quite apart from these weaknesses in the fact-finding procedures of the International Court of Justice, there remains room for questioning the Judgment of the Chamber in the *ELSI* case on the facts as well as the law. Not that the Chamber failed to elicit the facts (within the Court's limited powers), or that it failed to weigh the facts which were before it. But there are facts and facts, and whether the Chamber demonstrated commercial sophistication in the selection of the facts on which it chose to base its Judgment is open to more than one view.[1]

What is not open to dispute is that the Chamber, within its limitations, functioned in the process of fact-finding as a court should, and this, in my view, is in contrast with the Court as a whole in the other two cases which I shall discuss, and possibly in a measure of contrast with the Court in general. When fifteen or more judges of the full Court sit (and *ad hoc* judges can bring the total to sixteen or seventeen), that formidable phalanx may not always establish the optimum rapport with counsel. In the Great Courtroom of the Peace Palace, with all those judges up high and counsel well below, a reluctance of the Court, or at any rate of many of its members, to ask questions governs. Whether or not questions of fact are at issue (and even though the Court is a court of first as well as last instance, issues of fact are not always centrally at issue), whether or not witnesses are presented (more often

---

[1] My view, which did not coincide with that of the Chamber's majority, is to be found in *ICJ Reports 1989*, pp. 94, 100–108 (judgment of July 20).

they are not), whether or not both parties to the case are present (too often in recent decades they have not been), questions from the bench tend to be relatively few. The Court too often fails to probe. Counsel read out their arguments, copies of which usually have been supplied beforehand to the translators; the judges listen; some appear not to enlighten counsel on what they do not know or fully understand, on what counsel might do well to argue or elucidate. There is some, but not much, give-and-take between the Court and counsel. Counsel may ably rebut opposing counsel on the facts as well as the law, but the role of the full Court, in my experience, has tended to be predominantly passive.

This is not invariably so. There have been some cases in the full Court in which there have been many questions from the bench: the *South West Africa* cases and the case concerning *Military and Paramilitary Activities in and against Nicaragua* are two notable examples. However, Judge Jessup did not find the former experience satisfactory;[2] I did not find the latter experience satisfactory. While in the *Nicaragua* case, some Members of the Court at the outset of oral proceedings on the merits asked some questions which did not probe what was probative, virtually all the rest of the extensive individual questioning was left by every other Member of the Court to the only national judge who was sitting. The impression might have arisen that it was only he who saw reason to question the factual affirmations of Nicaragua, an impression which the Court's Judgment on the Merits (though not the dissenting opinions) was largely to sustain. This would have been unfortunate in any case. In that case, it was peculiarly unfortunate, for reasons which will be alluded to below.

To some extent, the reluctance of some members of the Court sitting *en banc* to ask questions perhaps may be a function of language and of professional formation. Questioning in English and French, especially when questions have not been written out beforehand but are spontaneous, may come to some judges whose native language is an official language of the Court more easily than to some judges whose language is not; and, more than this, it may be a matter of tradition in some legal systems, notably the common law, to ask questions, whereas in some others, it may not equally be. My impression is that common-law judges tend to ask questions about what is bothering them, about where they find the facts or law obscure, while some others may be less prone to do so, perhaps in the apprehension that any such questions could give the impression that the judge has formed or is forming a particular line of thought, and possibly a prejudicial one.

---

[2] See Judge Jessup's Foreword to D. Sandifer, *Evidence before International Tribunals* (rev. ed. 1975).

Yet the contrast with proceedings in Chamber is striking. The five judges are no nearer to counsel, but they are fewer. In a Chamber, the atmosphere is less constraining, both for judges and for counsel. Questions flow, whether from judges whose professional origins are those of the common law or of another legal system. Facts are elicited. This was so at any rate in the two Chamber cases in which I have participated, the *Delimitation of the Maritime Boundary in the Gulf of Maine*, and *ELSI*.

At the same time, the International Court of Justice cannot be expected to operate as do English courts or as the Supreme Court of the United States does. A judge in London or New York may, by questions, comments, witticisms, gestures of impatience, and the like, steer the argument in the direction in which he needs help and away from the areas where he has read or heard sufficient argument. He may interrupt the argument of counsel, cut off argument, interject questions. The Justices of the Supreme Court of the United States may pre-empt counsel with a cascade of questions which reflect their preoccupations with the case more than counsels' argument of it. The fifteen Judges of the International Court of Justice, or even the five of a Chamber of the Court, can hardly proceed in those ways. They are dealing not with supplicants but with sovereigns, with the representatives of States which have consented to appear and, as events have shown, may disappear. A State must be permitted to make its arguments to an international court as it chooses to make them. This reality conditions the operations of the Court. It explains why cases may move slowly, why written pleadings may be exceptionally extended, why oral argument may be long and at times long-winded, and why, in real though not full measure, questioning from the Court may not be as frequent or as incisive or as influential as it may be in other judicial proceedings.

Mr. Highet's chapter suggests that the *ELSI* case presents a new path for the production of evidence, a kind of "discovery," which may be suitable for recurrent use. He also suggests that the use of depositions (affidavits figured in the *Nicaragua* case) and interrogatories (which unfortunately did not figure in that case) may well merit consideration, suggestions with which I agree. He rightly points out that the Statute and Rules of Court contain provisions for the exercise of the Court's power to obtain evidence, to call for additional evidence, and to seek an expert inquiry, provisions which the Court has invoked sparingly, perhaps too sparingly (as at any rate the *Nicaragua* case illustrates).

The *Yakimetz* Case

Since the *Yakimetz* case – officially entitled *Application for Review of Judgement No. 333 of the United Nations Administrative Tribunal*[3] – may not be as familiar as others, and is not treated by the chapters of this volume, a summary of the relevant aspects of it may be appropriate.

Mr. Vladimir Victorovich Yakimetz, a national of the USSR who had been employed by the United Nations between 1969 and 1974, in 1977 was offered a five-year, fixed-term appointment, on secondment from the USSR Government, in the United Nations Secretariat. In 1982, his appointment was extended for one year, also on secondment. On February 8, 1983, the Assistant Secretary-General for Program Planning and Coordination, who was Yakimetz's superior, informed him that it was his intention to request an extension of Yakimetz's contract after its expiration on December 26, 1983, since Yakimetz's continued services would be in the interests of the Office. On February 9, 1983, Yakimetz, who had been unofficially informed that he was to be replaced by another Soviet national already selected by Soviet authorities, whom he was to return to the Soviet Union to train, applied for asylum in the United States. He notified the Secretary-General of his resignation from all official positions held in the Soviet Government, and of his intention to acquire permanent resident status in the United States, and assured the Secretary-General of his wish and intention to continue to perform all his obligations under his employment contract.

On February 28, 1983, he was informed that the Secretary-General had decided to place him on special leave with full pay. On March 11, 1983, he was informed that the Secretary-General had also determined that "it is in the best interests of the Organization" that he did "not enter the premises of the United Nations,"[4] with immediate effect and until further notice. On October 25, 1983, Yakimetz requested that, on the basis of his performance, his contract be extended or that, "even better," he be given "a career appointment."[5] On November 8, 1983, the Assistant Secretary-General for Program Planning and Coordination wrote that he found no difficulty in recommending a further extension of his contract. On November 23, 1983, however, Yakimetz was informed by the Office of the Secretary-General that his fixed-term appointment would not be extended beyond its expiration date of December 26, 1983. Yakimetz on November 29, 1983 protested this decision, invoking his acquired rights under General Assembly

---

[3] *Application for Review of Judgement No. 333 of the United Nations Administrative Tribunal, Advisory Opinion, ICJ Reports 1987*, p. 18.

[4] *Ibid.*, p. 22.   [5] *Ibid.*, pp. 22, 146.

resolution 37/126 by which the General Assembly: "*Decides* that staff members on fixed-term appointments upon completion of five years of continuing good service shall be given every reasonable consideration for a career appointment."[6]

On December 2, 1983, the Assistant Secretary-General for Program Planning and Coordination wrote that he found it "extraordinary" that the decision not to extend Yakimetz's contract "should be taken without consulting the head of the Office concerned," "especially in the case of an officer with eleven years of excellent service to the Organization" who "is in some ways uniquely well qualified."[7] On December 13, 1983, Yakimetz requested a review of the decision. After referring to the quoted terms of General Assembly resolution 37/126, recounting his excellent performance reports, and recalling assurances to him that his contract would be extended or converted to a career position, Yakimetz concluded:

> Given this service record and these assurances, and after six years of continuous service, most staff members would have an expectancy that their candidacy for a career appointment would be "given every reasonable consideration", as General Assembly resolution 37/126 IV requires. The contested administrative decision appears to preclude such reasonable consideration. The interests of good administration cannot be served by the interruption of the work with which I have been entrusted by my Department. I can think of no impediment to the forwarding of my name to the Appointment and Promotion Board except factors extraneous to my performance. The quoted General Assembly resolution places no restrictions as to eligibility ... Extraneous factors may not be used as a consideration in promotion, extension, transfer or in any of the areas where the paramount consideration must be the necessity of securing the highest standards of efficiency, competence or integrity. Extraneous factors may not be used to deny a candidate for a post fair and reasonable consideration ...
>
> To deny me the right to reasonable consideration for a career appointment for any reason unrelated to merit – efficiency, competence, integrity – would, I believe, be a violation of Article 100 of the Charter.
>
> Therefore, I respectfully request that the Administrative decision be withdrawn and my name forwarded to the appropriate Appointment and Promotion body for reasonable consideration.[8]

The official reply of December 21, 1983 to Yakimetz's letter was as follows:

> The Secretary-General has given careful consideration to the issues raised in your request for administrative review dated 13 December 1983 as well as in your earlier letter dated 29 November 1983, in connection with the communication, dated 23 November 1983, that "it is not the intention of the Organization to

---

[6] *Ibid.*, p. 23.   [7] *Ibid.*, pp. 146–147.   [8] *Ibid.*, p. 148.

extend your fixed-term appointment beyond its expiration date, i.e., 26 December 1983". In your letters, after referring to your service record and the evaluations of your supervisors, you state that under such conditions "most staff members would have an expectancy that their candidacy for a career appointment would be 'given every reasonable consideration,' as General Assembly resolution 37/126 IV requires".

Your situation, however, is not similar to that of "most staff members" with comparable service records, because your present contract was concluded on the basis of a secondment from your national civil service. At the time your present appointment was made your Government agreed to release you for service under a one-year contract, the Organization agreed so to limit the duration of your United Nations service, and you yourself were aware of that arrangement which, therefore, cannot give you any expectancy of renewal without the involvement of all the parties originally concerned.

Furthermore, you are serving under a fixed-term appointment, which, as expressly provided in staff rule 104.12 (b) and reiterated in your letter of appointment, "does not carry any expectancy of renewal or of conversion to any other type of appointment".

In view of the foregoing, the reasons advanced by you in your memorandum of 13 December do not require the Secretary-General to alter the decision communicated to you by letter of 23 November 1983. That decision is maintained and, therefore, the Secretary-General is not in a position to agree to your request "that the Administrative decision be withdrawn and [your] name forwarded to the appropriate Appointment and Promotion body for reasonable consideration" for career appointment.[9]

On January 6, 1984, Yakimetz filed an application with the United Nations Administrative Tribunal in respect of which Judgement No. 333 was given. On January 9, 1984, Yakimetz filed a new job application with the United Nations, which was never acknowledged.

By a vote of two to one, the Administrative Tribunal held, on the decisive question of whether Yakimetz had been given every reasonable consideration for a career appointment as required by resolution 37/126, that, while the Secretary-General was bound by that resolution, the resolution did not state who should give "every reasonable consideration" and by what procedure. The Tribunal considered that the letter addressed to Yakimetz on December 21, 1983 contained "the plain and simple inference" that the Secretary-General had given the required consideration of a career appointment of Yakimetz and that the Secretary-General had the sole authority to decide what constituted "reasonable consideration."[10] The Tribunal concluded that the Secretary-General, "in the background" of Yakimetz's secondment, had

---

[9] *Ibid.*, pp. 149–150.   [10] *Ibid.*, p. 38.

"exercised his discretion properly, but he should have stated explicitly before 26 December 1983 that he had given 'every reasonable consideration'" to Yakimetz's career appointment. His not having done so led the Tribunal to express "its dissatisfaction with the failure" of the Secretary-General "to record sufficiently early and in specific terms the fact that he had given the question of the Applicant's career appointment 'every reasonable consideration' as enjoined by the General Assembly resolution."[11]

Thereafter, Yakimetz presented an application for review of the Tribunal's judgment to the General Assembly's Committee on Applications for Review of Administrative Tribunal Judgments. The Committee decided that there was a substantial basis for the application and referred the following two questions to the Court:

1. In its Judgement No. 333 of 8 June 1984, did the United Nations Administrative Tribunal fail to exercise jurisdiction vested in it by not responding to the question whether a legal impediment existed to the further employment in the United Nations of the Applicant after the expiry of his contract on 26 December 1983?
2. Did the United Nations Administrative Tribunal, in the same Judgement No. 333, err on questions of law relating to provisions of the Charter of the United Nations?[12]

In answering these questions, the Court acknowledged – as had the Secretary-General – that the essential issue of fact was, had the Secretary-General given "every reasonable consideration" to Yakimetz as a candidate for career appointment as he was required to do by the terms of General Assembly resolution 37/126? The Court considered that it was clear from the judgment of the Administrative Tribunal that, for the Tribunal, the Secretary-General did give "every reasonable consideration" to the possibility of a career appointment for Yakimetz and thus complied with the requirements of General Assembly resolution 37/126. The Court recognized that the Tribunal accepted as sufficient a statement by the Secretary-General that the "reasonable consideration" required by resolution 37/126 had been given, and did not require him to furnish any details of when and how it was given, let alone calling for evidence to that effect. For its part, the Court found that it was not in a position to reconsider the Tribunal's critical holding of fact, namely, that the Secretary-General had given reasonable consideration to a career appointment for Yakimetz, essentially because that holding did not, in the Court's view, give rise to an error of law of the Tribunal relating to a provision of the United Nations Charter.

[11] *Ibid.*, pp. 39, 40. [12] *Ibid.*, p. 19.

Three Members of the Court (including myself) dissented from the Court's answer to the second question put to it by the General Assembly; they found precisely such errors of law. The differences in the Court on questions of law were complex and need not be set out for present purposes. But the essential difference in the Court between the majority and the minority – as between Yakimetz and the Secretary-General – remained over the issue of fact: had or had not the Secretary-General given Yakimetz's career appointment every reasonable consideration?

As noted, the majority concluded that, since the Administrative Tribunal's holding that the Secretary-General had given Yakimetz such consideration was not a holding which entailed an error of law relating to a provision of the Charter, it could not review that holding. The minority – which held a broader view of the Court's authority and which in any event found such error – maintained that it was obvious that the Secretary-General had not given a career appointment of Yakimetz every or indeed any reasonable consideration, essentially because:

- The letter of December 21, 1983 written on behalf of the Secretary-General stated that Yakimetz's candidacy for a career appointment could not be given consideration because "Your situation" was "not similar to that of 'most staff members' with comparable service records, because your present contract was concluded on the basis of a secondment" having no "expectancy ... of conversion to any other type of appointment"; hence Yakimetz's name could not be sent forward for consideration for a "career appointment."[13]
- The Tribunal's finding of "fact" that such consideration had been given, which the Tribunal acknowledged to be no more than an inference, was unsupported by a particle of evidence, none having been pleaded by the Secretary-General at any stage of the case.
- The Secretary-General's debarring Yakimetz from even entering the premises of United Nations Headquarters was hardly consistent with a then existing, contemporaneous disposition on the part of the Secretary-General to give to Yakimetz every reasonable consideration for a career appointment.
- The failure of the Secretary-General even to acknowledge, let alone act upon, the application for a permanent appointment submitted by Yakimetz on January 9, 1984 suggests not that "every reasonable consideration" was given to a career appointment, but rather that no consideration was given to it.

[13] *Ibid.*, pp. 149–150.

Space does not permit a fuller exposition of and commentary upon the Court's processes of fact-finding – or fact-avoidance – in the *Yakimetz* case. I leave it to the interested readers to read the Court's Opinion and the dissents thereto and decide for themselves how they would categorize the Court's conclusions and whether they would find those conclusions persuasive. In the process, they will also evaluate the adequacy, or absence, of fact-finding in the Yakimetz case by the United Nations Administrative Tribunal.

The *Nicaragua* Case

In his exceptionally stimulating chapter in this volume on "Fact-Finding in the ICJ," Professor Thomas M. Franck considers, among other cases in which questions of fact-finding were of importance in determining the legal outcome of the case, the Court's Judgment on the Merits in the case concerning *Military and Paramilitary Activities in and against Nicaragua*.[14] He concludes that the fact-finding processes of the Court in that case produced "incredible facts which, when they are proven wrong, undermine the credibility not only of the facts found by the Court, or the specific decision in which those facts play a role, but even the very institution of the Court itself." He refers in that regard to "a Nicaraguan cargo plane full of highly sophisticated rocketry equipment" which in 1989 was forced to land in El Salvador, an incident which he states "was not so much to embarrass the Sandinista regime as the ICJ, which had made what was now clearly the wrong guess as to the facts, and had made the facts seem unimportant."[15] Professor Franck's evaluation of the Court's handling of the facts in the case is very different from that of Mr. Highet in his article, "Evidence, the Court, and the Nicaragua Case," which was published in the *American Journal of International Law* in 1987 and which was distributed to the participants in the Eleventh Sokol Colloquium.[16]

At this writing, the reparations phase of the case concerning *Military and Paramilitary Activities in and against Nicaragua* remains on the docket of the Court. It would accordingly be inappropriate for me to comment outside the Court's proceedings on contemporaneous events which may bear upon the accuracy of the Court's factual conclusions in its 1986 Judgment in that case. I shall therefore not express a view on the incident to which Professor Franck refers or comment directly on his conclusions. Nor am I able to comment on other incidents which have taken place or come to light since the Court's

---

[14] See Note 17 below.   [15] *Ibid.*, p. 31.

[16] Keith Highet, "*Evidence, the Court, and the Nicaragua Case*," *American Journal of International Law* (1987), 81.

1986 Judgment, some of which gave rise to legal proceedings in the United States.

At the same time, it is appropriate that I summarize on the question of fact-finding in the case concerning *Military and Paramilitary Activities in and against Nicaragua* elements of what I very much more fully maintained in my dissent to the Merits of the Court's Judgment in that case. What follows is no more, but necessarily far less, than I set out in that dissent.

I suggest earlier in this Introduction that the Court might have manifested a greater willingness than it did in that case to use its power to obtain evidence, to call for additional evidence, and to seek an expert inquiry. For example, one of the several questions of fact at issue was whether El Salvador had ever requested the United States to assist it in the exercise of collective measures of self-defense. In the phases of the case in which it participated, the United States maintained that El Salvador had. In the phase of the case in which El Salvador sought to intervene, El Salvador declared that it had made precisely that request of the United States. It specified two periods in which such requests had been made of the United States and which Governments of El Salvador had made those requests, but it did not supply the precise dates or texts of those requests. The Court concluded that there was "no evidence"[17] that El Salvador had declared itself the victim of an armed attack and had asked the United States to exercise its right of collective self-defense at the time when the United States undertook the actions claimed to be so justified. The Court held that it was only in its Declaration of Intervention of 1984 that El Salvador referred to requests addressed at various dates to the United States for it to exercise its right of collective self-defense.[18] But the Court gave no weight to these references; on the contrary, the Court concluded that there was "no evidence" that in fact El Salvador had requested United States measures of collective self-defense when these measures were launched and the Court attributed importance to this finding, holding that it tended to show that neither the United States nor El Salvador at the critical time believed that they were acting in collective self-defense.[19]

But since El Salvador officially maintained in a communication to the Court that it had made requests to the United States at the critical time, why did not the Court invite El Salvador to submit its evidence? Indeed, on the much more fundamental question of whether the Nicaraguan Government was providing arms and other material support to the insurgents in El Salvador, President Duarte had affirmed, in a public statement which was

---

[17] Case concerning *Military and Paramilitary Activities in and against Nicaragua*, Merits, Judgment, *ICJ Reports 1986*, p. 120.
[18] *Ibid.*, p. 121.   [19] *Ibid.*, pp. 120–121.

before the Court, that he had ample evidence so proving which he was prepared to furnish to the Court. The Court concluded that there was insufficient evidence before it to attribute any responsibility to Nicaragua for providing arms to the Salvadoran insurgents at any time.[20] In this regard as well, why did the Court fail to ask El Salvador for its evidence? Or why did it fail to send a commission of inquiry to El Salvador as well as to other States concerned in an effort to establish or disestablish controverted facts centrally at issue in the case?

One may say, of course, that El Salvador could have intervened at the stage of the Merits and submitted its evidence. But, as Mr. Highet points out in his *Journal* article, such intervention was implausible once the United States had withdrawn from the case.[21] I would add that intervention was more unlikely in view of the fact that, when El Salvador sought to exercise its right under the Statute to intervene in the case at the jurisdictional stage, the Court not only peremptorily denied its intervention for an unprecedented and unpersuasive reason which it does not expound[22] and no analyst appears to have understood or approved; it even denied El Salvador a hearing on its request to intervene, in violation of the governing provision of the Rules of Court.[23]

This and what it saw as other departures from due process of law in the early phases of the case were cited by the United States as leading to its withdrawal from the proceedings, in addition to its fundamental conviction that the Court lacked jurisdiction and that the case was inadmissible. Mr. Highet, Professor Franck, and others understandably tax the United States for its withdrawal and rightly stress the difficult position in which the Court consequently found itself, particularly in fact-finding. But it is also right to take account of the consideration that, where the Court or its President fail fully to observe the Court's Rules and judicial proprieties, any fault may not lie with the withdrawing party alone. I am not referring to the Court's reaching out to assert dubious titles of jurisdiction in contravention of its tradition of judicial caution in finding jurisdiction, particularly to its going so far as to find to be "still in force" a declaration made under Article 36 of the Statute of the PCIJ which had never come into force. The incidents to which I refer are specifically set out in my Dissenting Opinion.[24]

The nub of my dissent on the facts was that the processes and results of fact-finding in which the Court engaged in that case were patently if only

---

[20] *Ibid.*, pp. 86, 119.   [21] Highet, "Evidence," p. 4.

[22] Case concerning *Military and Paramilitary Activities in and against Nicaragua* (Declaration of Intervention), *ICJ Reports 1984*, pp. 215–216.

[23] *Ibid.*, and see my Dissenting Opinion.

[24] *ICJ Reports 1986*, pp. 313, 314, 315, and 320–321 (Dissenting Opinion).

partially unconvincing. Its finding of the facts in respect of the activities of the United States at issue was largely sound and was easy enough. Its finding of the facts in respect of the activities of Nicaragua at issue, while far from easy, was unsound; indeed, in my view, as I stated in my dissent, it was "incredible."[25]

The essential issue was whether or not Nicaragua had been providing arms and other material support – command-and-control facilities, sanctuary, training, and so forth – to the Salvadoran insurgents. The Court concluded that no supply of arms could be attributed to the Government of Nicaragua at any time. As to whether the Government of Nicaragua had been giving the Salvadoran insurgents sanctuary, training, and transit and had permitted Nicaraguan territory to serve as the situs for the Salvadoran insurgents' command-and-control apparatus, the Court disposed of those charges essentially by ignoring them. It never confronted the paramount question of whether Nicaragua's provision of arms to the Salvadoran insurgents, *together with* provision of training and transit facilities for those insurgents; *together with* its serving as the physical and military headquarters of the leadership of the Salvadoran insurgent operations; and *together with* its permitting that leadership to broadcast from and continuously travel from Nicaragua to El Salvador and back, was tantamount to "substantial involvement" in aggression against El Salvador (to use the formula of the United Nations Definition of Aggression).[26] Its Judgment does not pass upon the considerable evidence to these effects; it makes no holding on these issues at all. The Court rather chose to deal only with the charge of provision of arms, a choice that suited its legal conclusion that, even if Nicaragua had supplied arms to the Salvadoran insurgency, such supply of itself was not tantamount to an armed attack. That is to say, by sidestepping key elements of the factual allegations of the United States, and by not weighing substantial evidence supporting those allegations, the Court was able to confine the critical question of whether Nicaragua was substantially involved in acts of aggression against El Salvador to whether the Nicaraguan Government was responsible for providing arms to the Salvadoran insurgents. With respect of the supply of arms, the Court held that no responsibility could be attributed "at any time" to the Government of Nicaragua and it did so despite the following examples in a record before it which is much too detailed to recount comprehensively:

---

[25] *Ibid.*, p. 330.

[26] The Court agreed that the description, contained in the Definition of Aggression – "the sending by or on behalf of a State of armed bands, groups, irregulars or mercenaries, which carry out acts of armed force against another State of such gravity as to amount to" an armed attack "or its substantial

- The Court acknowledged that an airfield had operated in Nicaragua from which arms were flown to Salvadoran insurgents. But it held that it was not proved that the Government of Nicaragua knew about the airfield before the United States made representations concerning it.[27]
- The chief witness on the issue of arms supply presented by Nicaragua, when questioned from the bench, admitted that "it could be taken as a fact that at least in late 1980/early 1981 the Nicaraguan Government was involved in the supply of arms to the Salvadoran insurgents."[28] He acknowledged that, when Secretary of State Muskie declared in January 1981 that the arms being flown into El Salvador for the use of the insurgents were sent with the knowledge and support of the Nicaraguan Government, Mr. Muskie spoke the truth.[29] Yet the Court held that no responsibility for such supply could be attributed to the Government of Nicaragua at any time.
- One of the nine then governing comandantes of Nicaragua, Commander Carrion, swore before the Court that Nicaragua "never" had a policy of sending arms to foreign insurgents, while at the same time he submitted a sworn affidavit to the Court in which he stated that Nicaragua had not sent arms to the Salvadoran insurgents "in a good long time."[30]
- President Ortega was quoted as declaring, in an interview published in Spanish in *ABC* and in English in *The New York Times*, that: "We're willing to stop the movement of military aid, or any other kind of aid, through Nicaragua to El Salvador . . . In return, we're asking for only one thing: that they don't attack us."[31] This statement, cited officially by El Salvador in the United Nations General Assembly as an "eloquent confession,"[32] was never corrected, withdrawn, or denied by the Government of Nicaragua. For its part, the Court in setting out evidential rules for the case, said it would discount statements of officials in the interest of the party making them but would give weight to admissions against interest. What did the Court do with this remarkable admission against interest? It said that it could not regard the quoted statement as an admission, essentially because it ran counter to the reiterated official denials of Nicaragua.[33]

In my view there is, in any consideration of the Court's processes of fact-finding, ground for profound concern that, in a case as important and as delicate as that of the case concerning *Military and Paramilitary Activities in and*

involvement therein" may "be taken to reflect customary international law" (*ibid.*, p. 103). But, on the facts, it failed to find Nicaragua so involved.
[27] *Ibid.*, p. 82. See my dissent, *ibid.*, at pp. 330–331.   [28] *Ibid.*, pp. 436–437.   [29] *Ibid.*
[30] *Ibid.*, p. 328.
[31] *Ibid.*, pp. 278, 328–329, 412–414.   [32] *Ibid.*, pp. 79–80.   [33] *Ibid.*

against Nicaragua, the Court failed to use its fact-finding capacities to the full. Moreover, it made a critical factual holding contrary to the weight of evidence before it and in doing so failed to apply the very evidentiary criterion it had laid down, as the foregoing example indicates.

Nor can the question of fact-finding in the case of *Military and Paramilitary Activities in and against Nicaragua* be dismissed as actually unimportant to the results in that case, on the ground that the Court held that, even if Nicaragua had been providing arms to the Salvadoran insurgents, such supply could not have amounted to an armed attack which could have justified United States reaction in collective self-defense. On the contrary, if the Court had found what was the fact, it should have found, on the basis of the evidence before it in 1986, that Nicaragua had provided arms to the Salvadoran insurgents and otherwise assisted them by provision of command-and-control facilities, training, sanctuary, and transit which was tantamount to the "substantial involvement" in acts of aggression interdicted by the General Assembly's Definition of Aggression and customary international law, that these acts were tantamount to armed attack, and that consequently the United States reaction was – or might have been – legally justified. Indeed, it is significant that both Nicaragua and the United States agreed with such a construction of the law, i.e., that the cumulation of such actions was tantamount to an armed attack; they essentially disagreed not on the law but the facts.[34] In real measure, then, the case turned on the facts, and the Court's treatment of the facts had a profound influence on the Court's conclusions of law. But even if I am wrong in so believing, even if a correct appraisal of the facts would not have materially altered the Court's conclusions of law, the Court's handling of the cited aspects of the facts in the *Nicaragua* case must remain profoundly puzzling and disquieting to students of fact-finding by international tribunals.

[34] *Ibid.*, pp. 332–336.

8

Indirect Aggression in the International Court

❧

We are living through dramatic days of the direct use of force by one State against another across an internationally recognized frontier. Today's issue is not one of indirect aggression but of direct conquest. Apart from the failed but bloody and destructive attempt to conquer the Republic of Korea in the early 1950s, this use of force is largely without parallel in the 45 years in which the United Nations Charter has been in force. As has been widely appreciated, current events rather evoke events of the 1930s.

Equally unparalleled is the unity and trenchancy of the resultant resolutions of the Security Council. Those resolutions are replete with invocations of international law and the authority of the Security Council to bind States – to bind both the object of the sanctions and the States enjoined to apply sanctions. Current concerns thus focus on a direct use of force which the Security Council has authoritatively condemned and is seeking vigorously to deal with by applying the panoply of powers accorded it by the terms of the Charter.

I cannot speculate on whether the International Court of Justice may play a part in these portentous proceedings, nor can I address events bearing on cases pending before the Court; I am obliged to confine my remarks to the substance of what I have earlier expressed in Court opinions. Within those confines, I do wish to make some observations on what part the Court can play in dealing with the legal aspects of the use of force in international relations, and what role it has played.

In a recent case of exceptional notoriety, the Court rejected the contention that it was only for the Security Council and not for the Court to adjudge an allegation of the continuing use of force internationally. The permanent

Address to the USSR–USA Conference of Scholars of the American Society of International Law and the Carnegie Endowment for International Peace, 1990. Reprinted from *Law and Force in the New World Order* (1991), edited by Lori Fisler Damrosch and David J. Scheffer, by permission of Westview Press, Boulder, Colorado.

member of the Security Council which was respondent in that case, the United States, argued that the scheme of the Charter and the Statute of the Court was one in which it fell to the Security Council to adjudge and deal with ongoing uses of international force, whereas the Court's authority fell, so to speak, not under Chapter VII of the Charter but under Chapter VI. Article 36 of Chapter VI provides that the Security Council should take into consideration that legal disputes as a general rule should be referred by the parties to the International Court of Justice. Chapter VII makes no reference to the Court at all. It entrusts to the Security Council alone the determination of a threat to the peace, breach of the peace, or an act of aggression. It was argued that it made little sense to read the Charter and the Statute as empowering the permanent members of the Security Council to veto such a determination in the Council while permitting the Court to make precisely that determination by a veto-free decision in the very same case and on the very same facts.

The Court as a whole did not accept this argument, nor did I, though I found it more plausible than did most of my colleagues. A difficulty with the argument, in my view, is that it requires reading the provisions of the Charter and the Statute as implicitly withholding from the Court the authority to render judgment respecting allegations of acts of aggression, while nothing explicit in the Charter or the Statute so prescribes. On the contrary, the language of the Statute cuts the other way. The Statute provides that the jurisdiction of the Court comprises "all cases" which the parties refer to it and "all matters" specially provided for in treaties in force,[1] and it further provides that the States Parties to the Statute may recognize the compulsory jurisdiction of the Court "in all legal disputes" concerning the interpretation of a treaty, any question of international law, the existence of any fact which, if established, would constitute a breach of an international obligation, and the nature or extent of the reparation to be made for such breach.[2] These are capacious terms, which may embrace disputes over the use of force in international relations, whether that use be past, present, or threatened. Cases before the Court in which issues of the current use of force have been posed have been rare, but it does not follow that such a case is beyond the authority of the Court, if jurisdiction in the particular case has been accorded to it. The relevant practice of the Court and the argumentation of parties before it, while not extensive, support this conclusion.

In addition to the argument of admissibility, a prudential argument of justiciability was made, namely that the Court was not in a position to find

---

[1] Statute of the International Court of Justice, Article 36, para. 1.   [2] *Ibid.*, Article 36, para. 2.

the facts of the ongoing use of force, where the situation was inherently fluid and where the facts at issue were in controversy and were indeed covertly rather than overtly treated. While I was not impressed with the argument of fluidity, I must say that the judgment of the Court was to impress – and depress – me with the inability which the Court then displayed to get at facts which were concealed rather than acknowledged.

I believe that it is increasingly recognized, as it should have been recognized at the time, that while the Court was essentially correct in finding the facts of the actions of the respondent State – the United States – it was essentially incorrect in its fact-finding in respect to the applicant State, Nicaragua. That miscarriage of justice was not to be attributed to the Court alone, since the applicant State purposefully and emphatically misled the Court about the truth of its actions while the respondent State was not present to refute those misrepresentations. The result was that the Court's judgment turned essential facts on their head, and found that no responsibility could be attributed to Nicaragua for acts in blatant violation of international law for which it indubitably was responsible.

A second divisive issue was not factual but legal. Even if Nicaragua had done what was charged, were such acts tantamount to an armed attack in response to which action in individual and collective self-defense could lawfully be undertaken? Here the Court moved from its inadequacies of fact-finding to innovations of legal doctrine, which, in my view, do not correspond to customary international law or the law of the Charter as they were before the Court's judgment and as they are today.

The United States charged that it was Nicaragua which was the aggressor, because, before (and after) the United States responded, Nicaragua had extended material support to an insurgency in a neighboring State, El Salvador, which was tantamount to an armed attack, consisting as it did of the provision of arms, a command-and-control apparatus for the continuing direction of the insurgency, sanctuary, and training for the insurgents, and ceaseless transit of the leadership of the insurgency between the territory of Nicaragua and the territory of El Salvador. The Court dealt with these allegations in two ways. It ignored critical elements of them, essentially reducing the multiple charges to the single charge of whether "the provision of arms to the opposition in another State constitutes an armed attack on that State."[3] Then, while refusing to attribute responsibility to the Government of Nicaragua for the undeniable and undenied transfer of arms through its

---

[3] *Case Concerning Military and Paramilitary Activities In and Against Nicaragua (Nicaragua v. United States), ICJ Reports 1986*, para. 14, p. 119.

territory to the Salvadoran insurgents, it held that in any event the provision of arms could not be tantamount to an armed attack. Since there was no armed attack, there could be no self-defense, individual or collective.

I found difficulties with this disposition and still do. In the first place, customary international law, reflected on this issue by the Definition of Aggression adopted by the General Assembly of the United Nations after half a century of intense though intermittent negotiation, treats as an act of aggression the "substantial involvement" of a State in the sending of armed bands, groups, irregulars, or mercenaries which carry out acts of armed force against another State of such gravity as to amount to an actual armed attack conducted by regular forces.[4] There was in this case compelling evidence of such substantial involvement of Nicaragua (acting together with Cuba), since the flow of insurgents trained and armed by it, and of the leadership of those insurgents, from its territory to that of El Salvador was very substantial indeed and since those insurgents carried out armed attacks in the course of their insurgency equivalent to the armed attacks of regular forces. Such substantial involvement, as Professor Julius Stone put it in his critical analysis of the Definition of Aggression, gave rise "like any other direct aggression to response by self-defense under general international law and under Article 51 of the Charter."[5] While the Court for its part held that the Definition of Aggression reflects customary international law, in effect it dismissed the import of the Definition on this paramount point by failing to deal seriously with Nicaragua's "substantial involvement." It addressed only the question of the provision of arms and on this question arrived at an answer at odds with the weight of the evidence before it.

In the second place, not only is the Court's judgment inconsistent with customary international law as expressed in the Definition of Aggression, it is also inconsistent with the law applied by the inter-American system in the very area at issue. The Organization of American States had earlier interpreted and applied the Inter-American Treaty of Reciprocal Assistance, the Rio Treaty, precisely to characterize acts very similar to those at issue in this case as "acts that possess characteristics of aggression and intervention" which could justify the essential rights of member States to "the use of self-defense in either individual or collective form, which could go so far as resort to armed force ..."[6] The Court ignored this precedent.

In the third place, the Court's interpretation of the meaning of armed attack was inconsistent with the shared interpretation of the applicant and the

---

[4] General Assembly resolution 3314 (XXIX), Appendix, quoted *ibid.*, at pp. 103, 343.
[5] J. Stone, *Conflict Through Consensus* 75 (1977), quoted in *ICJ Reports 1986*, p. 343.
[6] Quoted in *ICJ Reports 1986*, p. 360.

respondent States in the case. They did not essentially differ on the law of self-defense but on the facts. Nicaragua admitted and indeed expounded the very law pleaded by the United States. Nicaragua set out in its pleading the extensive practice of the United Nations and the considerable commentaries of scholars which tend to equate acts of direct and indirect aggression. But Nicaragua maintained that the armed bands at issue in the case were organized and provisioned only by the United States and not by Nicaragua. The problem with the Nicaraguan argument on the facts was that it was untrue. But it remains remarkable that the Court should have arrived at conclusions of law so hard to reconcile with the shared interpretation of the parties.

Finally, there is the question that if the Court's construction of what is armed attack is not consistent with customary international law, the Definition of Aggression, the practice of the United Nations and the Organization of American States, and the shared interpretation of the parties to the case, is it nevertheless a sound view of the law *de lege ferenda*?

The argument for the Court's position is that a narrow construction of the meaning of "armed attack" produces a narrow ambit for the use of measures of self-defense, individual and collective. In the Charter era, States resorting to the use of force characteristically invoke self-defense, whether justifiably or not. If States cannot be heard to invoke measures of self-defense in response to actions by other States which, summarily speaking, constitute indirect rather than direct aggression, then there will be a desirable constraint on what in some cases will be unjustified resort to allegedly defensive measures.

In my view, this argument is superficially appealing but unpersuasive. The Court's judgment demonstrates just how unpersuasive it is.

Assuming for the sake of argument the charges against Nicaragua to be true (at any rate in the provision of arms to the Salvadoran insurgents), the Court treated its actions not as tantamount to armed attack but as acts of intervention. It then held that, while an armed attack would give rise to an entitlement to collective self-defense, a use of force of a lesser degree of gravity cannot produce any entitlement to take collective counter-measures involving the use of force. The acts of which the applicant State was accused "even assuming them to have been established and imputable to the State," could only have justified proportionate counter-measures on the part of the State which had been the victim of these acts. "They could not justify counter-measures taken by a third State ... and particularly could not justify intervention involving the use of force."[7]

[7] *Ibid.*, p. 127.

One wonders from what source the Court derived this construction. It provides no foundation whatsoever for it in treaty law, customary international law, State practice, general principles of law, judicial decisions, or the writings of scholars. Presumably, it did not derive this construction from the provisions of the United Nations Charter, since it maintained that it was debarred from applying the Charter by reason of the invocation by the United States of the "Vandenberg" reservation; and the Charter does not require such a construction in any event. But quite apart from these infirmities and the obvious infirmities of application of this theory to the facts of the case then before it, let us consider the worrisome questions of principle which this innovative *dictum* imports.

Let us suppose that State A's support of the armed subversion of State B, while serious and effective enough to place the independence of State B in jeopardy, does not amount to an armed attack upon State B as the Court narrowly defines armed attack. Let us further suppose that State A acts against State B not only on its own behalf but together with a Great Power and with other significant international actors. If the Court's *obiter dictum* were to be treated as the law to which States deferred, other Great Powers and other States would be or could be essentially powerless to intervene effectively to preserve the independence of State B and other similarly situated States, most of which will be small. According to the Court, State B could take counter-measures against State A, but whether they would include measures of force is not said. What is said is that third States could not use force, whether or not the preservation of the territorial integrity or political independence of State B depended on the exertion of such measures. In short, the Court appears to offer, quite gratuitously, a prescription for the overthrow of weaker Governments while denying potential victims what in some cases may be their only hope for survival.

There is more which is no less critical which could be said about the judgment of the Court in question – a judgment which in my view must remain just that, very much in question. While in principle the Court is a judicial organ which may adjudicate cases turning upon the continuing use of force, in practice the record to date is not wholly reassuring. What that may suggest for the future, however, is difficult to say.

9

Human Rights in the World Court

☙

The International Court of Justice is not a human rights court in the contemporary sense of that term. The Statute of the Court provides, in Article 34, that: "Only States may be parties in cases before the Court."[1] It follows that individuals, corporations, non-governmental organizations, even international governmental organizations, may not be parties to contentious cases before the Court. Moreover, the focus of the large majority of contentious cases between States, and advisory opinions given by the Court in answer to questions of international governmental organizations (the United Nations and its Specialized Agencies) has not been on human rights questions.[2]

Of course, the fact that, since the drafting of the Statute of the Permanent

First published in R.S. Pathak, D.P. Dhokalia (eds.), *International Law in Transition, Essays in Memory of Judge Nagendra Singh* (1992), New Delhi, Lancers Books. An abbreviated version appears in *Vanderbilt Journal of Transnational Law* (Winter 1992).

[1] Statute of the International Court of Justice, Art. 34, para. 1.

[2] What may be viewed as a regressive development of judicial possibilities is that the PCIJ dealt with some requests for advisory opinions which the League Council put to it not on its own behalf or on behalf of what today would be called a "Specialized Agency," i.e., the International Labor Organization, but on behalf of States (e.g., in *Nationality Decrees Issued in Tunis and Morocco*, PCIJ, Series C, No. 2) and other international organizations (e.g., *Jurisdiction of the European Commission of the Danube*, PCIJ, Series C, No. 13 (IV)), whereas the United Nations Charter provides, in Article 96:

1. The General Assembly or the Security Council may request the International Court of Justice to give an advisory opinion on any legal question.

2. Other organs of the United Nations and specialized agencies, which may at any time be so authorized by the General Assembly, may also request advisory opinions of the Court on legal questions arising within the scope of their activities.

That is to say, the effective advisory jurisdiction of the ICJ appears to be narrower than was that of the PCIJ. A question which nevertheless remains is, could the General Assembly or Security Council construe their authority to ask for an advisory opinion "on any legal question" to embrace questions originating in States (or their national courts), or in international organizations other than Specialized Agencies, governmental (regional or otherwise), or, even, non-governmental? The answer to that question is unclear. It might be argued that the expansive approach taken by the League Council and PCIJ supports a positive answer to that question. But the *travaux préparatoires* of the San Francisco Conference on International Organization are open to more than one interpretation. For a diversity of

Court of International Justice by a distinguished Advisory Committee of Jurists in 1920, it has provided that only States may be parties to contentious cases in no way signifies that the Statute could not provide otherwise, as indeed the constituent instruments of the European Court of Human Rights, the Inter-American Court of Human Rights, and some other international judicial bodies do. The principle that only States have standing before international tribunals[3] has long since been modified. But that principle continues to govern the World Court and will unless and until its Statute is amended.

In his seminal book on *International Law and Human Rights* published in 1950, the then professor and later Judge Sir Hersch Lauterpacht proposed to amend Article 34 to provide that:

> The Court shall have jurisdiction:
> (1) in disputes between States;
> (2) in disputes between States and private and public bodies or private individuals in cases in which States have consented, in advance or by special agreement, to appear as defendants before the Court.[4]

But there is no sign of a disposition among the States of the world to consider, still less amend, the Statute of the Court to make such provision.

All this said, it nevertheless is the fact that questions of human rights have arisen in a number of cases before the World Court, and that in some of those cases the Court has rendered judgments or given advisory opinions which have significantly influenced international law bearing on human rights. The principal cases in which the Court has treated human rights questions, and a sense of how it has disposed of them, will now be given.

---

views, see C. Wilfred Jenks, *The Prospects of International Adjudication* (1964), pp. 160–161; Stephen M. Schwebel, "Preliminary Rulings by the International Court of Justice at the Instance of National Courts," *Virginia Journal of International Law* (1988), 28, p. 495 and Shabtai Rosenne, "Preliminary Rulings by the International Court of Justice at the Instance of National Courts: A Reply," *Virginia Journal of International Law* (1989), 29, p. 401, as well as Schwebel, "Was the Capacity to Request an Advisory Opinion Wider in the Permanent Court of International Justice than it is in the International Court of Justice?," *British Yearbook of International Law 1991* (1992), 62. If it were to be accepted by the General Assembly and the Court that international bodies other than Specialized Agencies (e.g., the United Nations Committee that monitors implementation of the International Covenant on Civil and Political Rights) and, *a fortiori*, national courts, could ask for advisory opinions on questions transmitted to the Court in the form of General Assembly resolutions, the possibilities of the Court acting in the sphere of human rights could be transformed.

[3] The PCIJ referred to "the general character of an international tribunal which, in principle, has cognizance only of inter-state relations," in the case of the *Factory at Chorzow (Indemnity), PCIJ, Series A, No. 17*, p. 27.

[4] Sir Hersch Lauterpacht, *International Law and Human Rights* (1950), p. 58.

German Settlers in Poland

In the second year of its functioning, 1923, the Permanent Court of International Justice, in an advisory opinion on *German Settlers in Poland*, dealt with one of the "Minorities Treaties" which were a favored instrument of the maintenance of human rights in post-World War I years. By a Minorities Treaty which Poland concluded in pursuance of the Treaty of Versailles, Poland undertook "to assure full and complete protection of life and liberty to all inhabitants of Poland without distinction of birth, nationality, language, race or religion." The Treaty provided that: "All Polish nationals shall be equal before the law and shall enjoy the same civil and political rights without distinction as to race, language or religion."[5] It further provided that: "Polish nationals who belong to racial, religious or linguistic minorities shall enjoy the same treatment and security in law and in fact as the other Polish nationals."[6]

Beginning in 1886, Imperial Germany had pursued a policy of implanting German farmers in areas of the German Empire in which much of the population was Polish in order to counter what German law characterized as "efforts to Polonize the provinces,"[7] through legal enactment and purchase of lands which were delivered to settlers on concessionary terms. Under a Polish law of July 14, 1920, German settlers in territories which had been transferred from Germany to Poland were notified that they would be required to leave their farms. Germany maintained that such notifications were in contravention of the quoted provisions of the Minorities Treaty. The Court held that:

> As has been seen, Article 7 of the treaty provides that all Polish nationals shall be equal before the law and shall enjoy the same civil and political rights without distinction as to race, language or religion. The expression "civil rights" in the Treaty must include rights acquired under a contract for the possession or use of property, whether such property be immovable or moveable.
>
> Article 8 of the Treaty guarantees to racial minorities the same treatment and security "in law and in fact" as to other Polish nationals. The facts that no racial discrimination appears in the text of the law of July 14th, 1920, and that in a few instances the law applies to non-German Polish nationals who took as purchasers from original holders of German race, make no substantial difference. Article 8 is designed to meet precisely such complaints as are made in the present case. There must be equality in fact as well as ostensible legal equality in the sense of the absence of discrimination in the words of the law.
>
> Article 5 of the law of July 14th, 1920, provides for the expulsion from the lands

<hr>

[5] *German Settlers in Poland*, Advisory Opinion of September 10, 1923, *PCIJ*, Series B, No. 6, p. 20.
[6] *Ibid.*
[7] *Ibid.*, p. 16.

in question of any persons who may occupy them under an agreement with any of the proprietors for whom the Polish Treasury has been substituted under Article I of the law, and by Article I it appears that those for whom the Polish Treasury has been substituted include the German States. The outstanding, fundamental point in the present case is the fact that the persons whose rights are now in question are as a class persons of the German race who settled on the lands in question under the Prussian law of 1886 and subsequent legislative acts, under contracts made with the Prussian State. Indeed, it is for this very reason that Poland contends that the contracts now under consideration are to be held invalid. Hence, although the law does not expressly declare that the persons who are to be ousted from the lands are persons of the German race, the inference that they are so is to be drawn even from the terms of the law. This is also clearly established as a fact by the proofs before the Court. It undoubtedly is true, as Poland has stated, that the persons whose rights are involved were settled upon the lands in pursuance of a policy of Germanization which appears upon the face of the legislation under which the contracts were made. The effect of the enforcement of the law of July 14th, 1920, would be to eradicate what had previously been done, so far as de-Germanization would result from requiring the settlers in question to abandon their homes. But, although such a measure may be comprehensible, it is precisely what the Minorities Treaty was intended to prevent. The intention of this Treaty was no doubt to eliminate a dangerous source of oppression, recrimination and dispute, to prevent racial and religious hatreds from having free play and to protect the situations established upon its conclusion, by placing existing minorities under the impartial protection of the League of Nations.[8]

The Court consequently concluded that the eviction of German settlers by Poland would be in violation of Poland's international obligations.

The Court's opinion in *German Settlers in Poland* today is striking in several respects. The language of Article 55 of the United Nations Charter providing that the United Nations shall promote "universal respect for, and observance of, human rights and fundamental freedoms for all without distinction as to race, sex, language or religion" mirrors, in its "without distinction" clause, the terms of the Minorities Treaties. The opinion holds that discrimination in fact is debarred even if discrimination in form is absent. And the Court defines "civil rights" to include property rights, a holding supportive of the conclusion that human rights in international law include property rights.

Treatment of Polish Nationals in Danzig

In its advisory opinion on the *Treatment of Polish Nationals and Other Persons of Polish Origin or Speech in the Danzig Territory*, the Court held

[8] *Ibid.*, pp. 23–24.

that the prohibition against discrimination, in order to be effective, must ensure the absence of discrimination in fact as well as in law. A measure which in terms is of general application, but in fact is directed against Polish nationals and other persons of Polish origin or speech, constitutes a violation of the prohibition. A similar view has already been expressed by the Court in its Advisory Opinion No. 6 relating to German settlers in Poland. Whether a measure is or is not in fact directed against these persons is a question to be decided on the merits of each particular case. No hard and fast rule can be laid down.[9]

Minority Schools in Albania

Very similar international obligations were at issue in 1935 in the Court's advisory proceedings in the case of *Minority Schools in Albania*. Albania entered into undertakings in 1921 which embodied provisions like those described in the previous cases and which included the right of minorities to maintain or establish their own schools. In 1933, Albanian legislation provided for the abolition of all private schools in Albania. The Albanian Government contended that the measure was not discriminatory, since it was applicable alike to the majority and the minority. The Court held:

> The idea underlying the treaties for the protection of minorities is to secure for certain elements incorporated in a State, the population of which differs from them in race, language or religion, the possibility of living peaceably alongside that population and cooperating amicably with it, while at the same time preserving the characteristics which distinguish them from the majority, and satisfying the ensuing special needs.
>
> In order to attain this object, two things were regarded as particularly necessary, and have formed the subject of provisions in these treaties.
>
> The first is to ensure that nationals belonging to racial, religious or linguistic minorities shall be placed in every respect on a footing of perfect equality with the other nationals of the State.
>
> The second is to ensure for the minority elements suitable means for the preservation of their racial peculiarities, their traditions and their national characteristics.
>
> These two requirements are indeed closely interlocked, for there would be no true equality between a majority and a minority if the latter were deprived of its own institutions, and were consequently compelled to renounce that which constitutes the very essence of its being as a minority.[10]

It further held that Albania's international obligation to ensure that "Albanian nationals who belong to racial, linguistic or religious minorities, will enjoy the same treatment and security in law and in fact as other Albanian nationals" meant more than equality before the law. It held:

[9] *Treatment of Polish Nationals in Danzig*, Advisory Opinion of February 4, 1932, *PCIJ*, Series A/B, No. 44, p. 28.

[10] *Minority Schools in Albania*, Advisory Opinion of April 6, 1935, *PCIJ*, Series A/B, No. 64, p. 17.

Equality in law precludes discrimination of any kind; whereas equality in fact may involve the necessity of different treatment in order to attain a result which establishes an equilibrium between different situations.

It is easy to imagine cases in which equality of treatment of the majority and of the minority, whose situation and requirements are different, would result in inequality in fact; treatment of this description would run counter to . . .[11]

Albania's international obligations. It thus concluded that the plea of Albania that, since the abolition of private schools constituted a general measure applicable to the majority as well as the minority, it was in accordance with Albania's international obligations, was unfounded.

The modern student of human rights will surely find in this opinion an early and incisive precursor of what today would be called "affirmative action."

Consistency of Danzig Legislative Decrees

In its advisory proceedings on the *Consistency of Certain Danzig Legislative Decrees with the Constitution of the Free City*, the Court was confronted with a very different and no less fundamental question of human rights: whether two legislative decrees amending the Penal Code of the Free City of Danzig, following like legislation previously adopted by the German Reich, were consistent with the Danzig Constitution in providing that:

ARTICLE 1 – *Creation of law by the application of penal laws by analogy.*
Articles 2 and 2*a* of the Penal Code are amended as follows:
ARTICLE 2 – Any person who commits an act which the law declares to be punishable or which is deserving of penalty according to the fundamental conceptions of a penal law and sound popular feeling, shall be punished. If there is no penal law directly covering an act, it shall be punished under the law of which the fundamental conception applies most nearly to the said act.[12]
(*a*) The following provisions shall be inserted in the Code of Criminal Procedure and shall constitute Article 170*a* and Article 267*a*.
ARTICLE 170*a* – If an act which, according to sound popular feeling, is deserving of penalty is not made punishable by law, the Public Prosecutor shall consider whether the fundamental conception of any penal law covers the said act and whether it is possible to cause justice to prevail by the application of such law by analogy (Art. 2 of the Penal Code).
ARTICLE 267*a* – If, in the course of the trial, it appears that the accused has committed an act which, according to sound popular feeling, is deserving of penalty but which is not made punishable by law, the Court must satisfy itself that

---

[11] *Ibid.*, p. 19.
[12] *Consistency of Certain Danzig Legislative Decrees with the Constitution of the Free City*, Advisory Opinion of December 4, 1935, *PCIJ, Series A/B, No. 65*, p. 45.

the fundamental conception of a penal law applies to the act and that it is possible to cause justice to prevail by the application of such law by analogy (Penal Code, Art. 2).[13]

Prior to the foregoing amendments adopted in 1935, the Penal Code provided that:

ARTICLE 2. An act is only punishable if the penalty applicable to it has been prescribed by a law in force before the commission of the act.[14]

The foregoing provision, the Court held,

gives expression to the well-known twofold maxim: *Nullum crimen sine lege*, and *Nulla poena sine lege*. The law alone determines and defines an offence. The law alone decrees the penalty. A penalty cannot be inflicted in a given case if it is not decreed by the law in respect of that case. A penalty decreed by the law for a particular case cannot be inflicted in another case. In other words, criminal laws may not be applied by analogy.[15]

The Court continued:

The Agent for the Free City contends that, according to the new conception of penal law, real justice will take the place of formal justice, and that henceforth the rule will be *Nullum crimen sine poena* instead of *Nullum crimen sine lege* and *Nulla poena sine lege*. Detailed explanations have been given on behalf of the Senate of the Free City concerning the advantages of the new penological idea over the old. With this the Court was not concerned. The sole question for it is whether the two decrees violate any of the provisions or principles of the Constitution.

Under the two decrees a person may be prosecuted and punished not only in virtue of an express provision of the law, as heretofore, but also in accordance with the fundamental idea of a law and in accordance with sound popular feeling.

Whatever may be the relation between the two elements – whether it be, as suggested by the wording of the first decree, that the act to be punished must in any case fall within the fundamental idea of the law and yet escape punishment unless condemned by sound popular feeling, or whether it be, as suggested by the wording of the second decree, that attention is first to be paid to the question of what is condemned by sound popular feeling but no prosecution initiated or punishment imposed unless the act falls within the fundamental idea of some penal law – it is clear that the decision whether an act does or does not fall within the fundamental idea of a penal law, and also whether or not that act is condemned by sound popular feeling, is left to the individual judge or to the Public Prosecutor to determine. It is not a question of applying the text of the law itself – which presumably will be in terms equally clear both to the judge and to the person who is accused. It is a question of applying what the judge (or the Public Prosecutor) believes to be in accordance with the fundamental idea of the law, and what the

---

[13] *Ibid.*, p. 46.   [14] *Ibid.*, p. 45.   [15] *Ibid.*, p. 51.

judge (or the Public Prosecutor) believes to be condemned by sound popular feeling. A judge's belief as to what was the intention which underlay a law is essentially a matter of individual appreciation of the facts, so is his opinion as to what is condemned by sound popular feeling. Instead of applying a penal law equally clear to both the judge and the party accused, as was the case under the criminal law previously in force at Danzig, there is the possibility under the new decrees that a man may find himself placed on trial and punished for an act which the law did not enable him to know was an offence, because its criminality depends entirely upon the appreciation of the situation by the Public Prosecutor and by the judge. Accordingly, a system in which the criminal character of an act and the penalty attached to it will be known to the judge alone replaces a system in which this knowledge was equally open to both the judge and the accused.

Nor should it be overlooked that an individual opinion as to what was the intention which underlay a law, or an individual opinion as to what is condemned by sound popular feeling, will vary from man to man. Sound popular feeling is a very elusive standard. It was defined by the Agent of the Free City as "une conviction correspondant aux strictes exigences de la morale". This definition covers the whole extra-legal field of what is right and what is wrong according to one's ethical code or religious sentiments. Hence it follows that sound popular feeling may mean different rules of conduct in the minds of those who are to act in accordance therewith. It is for this reason that legislation is necessary in order to lay down the precise limits between *morale* and law. An alleged test of sound popular feeling, even when coupled with the condition providing for the application of the fundamental idea of a penal law, could not afford to individuals any sufficient indication of the limits beyond which their acts are punishable.[16]

After recounting that Constitution of the Free City of Danzig, which was guaranteed by the League of Nations, provided for a State governed by the rule of law – a *Rechtsstaat*, and that the Constitution assured the inhabitants of Danzig of fundamental rights and individual liberties, the Court held:

> The rule that a law is required in order to restrict the liberties provided for in the Constitution therefore involves the consequence that the law itself must define the conditions in which such restrictions of liberties are imposed. If this were not so, i.e., if a law could simply give a judge power to deprive a person of his liberty, without defining the circumstances in which his liberty might be forfeited, it could render [Constitutional liberties] entirely nugatory. But, as the Court has already explained, the decrees of August 29th, 1935, so far from supplying any such definition, empower a judge to deprive a person of his liberty even for an act not prohibited by the law, provided that he relies on the fundamental idea of a penal law and on sound popular feeling. These decrees therefore transfer to the judge an important function which, owing to its intrinsic character, the Constitution intended to reserve to the law so as to safeguard individual liberty from any arbitrary encroachment on the part of the authorities of the State.

[16] *Ibid.*, pp. 52–53.

It is true that a criminal law does not always regulate all details. By employing a system of general definition, it sometimes leaves the judge not only to interpret it, but also to determine how to apply it. The question as to the point beyond which this method comes in conflict with the principle that fundamental rights may not be restricted except by law may not be easy to solve. But there are some cases in which the discretionary power left to the judge is too wide to allow of any doubt but that it exceeds these limits. It is such a case which confronts the Court in the present proceedings.

The problem of the repression of crime may be approached from two different standpoints, that of the individual and that of the community. From the former standpoint, the object is to protect the individual against the State: this object finds its expression in the maxim *Nulla poena sine lege*. From the second standpoint, the object is to protect the community against the criminal, the basic principle being the notion *Nullum crimen sine poena*. The decrees of August 29th, 1935, are based on the second of these conceptions; the Danzig Constitution is based upon the former. For this Constitution takes as its starting-point the fundamental rights of the individual; these rights may indeed be restricted, as already pointed out, in the general public interest, but only in virtue of a law which must itself specify the conditions of such restriction, and, in particular, determine the limit beyond which an act can no longer be justified as an exercise of a fundamental liberty and becomes a punishable offence. It must be possible for the individual to know, beforehand, whether his acts are lawful or liable to punishment.[17]

The Court thus concluded that the decrees of the Danzig Senate were not consistent with the guarantees which the Danzig Constitution provided for the fundamental rights of the individual.

In this case as well, the Permanent Court of International Justice took an approach worthy of the most progressive of modern human rights courts, in terms which can hardly be improved upon. The issue of crimes by analogy has bedevilled the post-World War II years as it did the Nazi years. The Court's condemnation of criminal liability by analogy is vigorous and persuasive, as is its analysis of the centrality of a constitutional rule of law to the fundamental rights of the individual. But it is important to bear in mind that the Court was interpreting not customary international law but a constitutional law which gave individuals rights which were internationally guaranteed by a treaty-like instrument.

Jurisdiction of the Courts of Danzig

The Court earlier laid the groundwork for international concern with individual human rights when it confronted and surmounted the doctrine that States only and exclusively are the subjects of international law, the

---

[17] *Ibid.*, pp. 56–57.

doctrine dominant at the time of the Court's establishment. The claim that an individual could be and was a subject of international law was radical in the 1920s. It bore squarely on the question of whether human rights could be international rights as contrasted with rights established and maintained by domestic law alone.

In its advisory opinion concerning the *Jurisdiction of the Courts of Danzig*,[18] the issue, in respect of financial claims of Danzig railway officials who had passed into Polish service, was whether treaties can confer rights directly on individuals. Poland argued that the agreement between it and Danzig conferred no right of action on the railway officials. Poland maintained that the agreement, being a treaty which had not been incorporated into Polish municipal law, created rights and obligations only between the parties, and that Poland's failure, if any, to carry out the agreement made her responsible not to the interested private individuals but only to the Danzig Free State. That was a position fully in accordance with orthodox international law. But the Court rejected that position "in what was in effect a revolutionary pronouncement" (to use Lauterpacht's words in *The Development of International Law by the International Court*[19]).

The Court acknowledged that, "according to a well-established principle of international law," the agreement, being "an international agreement, cannot, as such, create direct rights and obligations for private individuals."[20] But, it continued, the actual answer must depend upon the intention of the contracting parties. It held that:

> It cannot be disputed that the very object of an international agreement, according to the intention of the contracting parties, may be the adoption by the parties of some definite rules creating individual rights and obligations and enforceable by national courts.[21]

It then found that this was in fact the intention of the parties in this case, with the result that Danzig railway officials had a right of action against the Polish Railway Administration based on the treaty. Thus the Court, as Lauterpacht pointed out,[22] ignored the postulated insurmountable barrier between the individual and international law and denied the exclusiveness of States as the beneficiaries of international rights – holdings which are fundamental to the modern international law of human rights.

---

[18] *Jurisdiction of the Courts of Danzig*, Advisory Opinion of 3 March 1928, *PCIJ*, Series B, No. 15, p. 4.
[19] Sir Hersch Lauterpacht, *The Development of International Law by the International Court* (1958), p. 174.
[20] *Jurisdiction of the Courts of Danzig* (note 18 above), p. 17.   [21] *Ibid.*
[22] Lauterpacht, *Development of International Law*, p. 175.

Nationality Decrees Issued in Tunis and Morocco

A final case in the Permanent Court which merits recalling is the advisory opinion on *Nationality Decrees Issued in Tunis and Morocco*. Procedurally it is a singular case, since the League Council, at the request of the disputing parties, Great Britain and France, requested an advisory opinion of the Court, in which proceedings, however, those two States argued before the Court, with the presentation of a Memorial and Counter-Memorial and oral argument, as if it were a contentious proceeding between them. It suggests that, in the early days of the Court, the distinction between contentious and advisory jurisdiction may not have been fully established, which was understandable since the Statute of the Permanent Court at that stage did not provide for advisory opinions.[23] In any event, the case did not directly deal with questions of human rights apart from the fact that the subject of dispute ultimately related to matters of nationality. But the case did and does have great significance for human rights questions, because it is the established authority on the scope of domestic jurisdiction. The question put to the Court was whether a dispute between France and Great Britain as to nationality decrees issued in Tunis and Morocco and their application to British subjects "is or is not by international law solely a matter of domestic jurisdiction (Art. 15, para. 8, of the Covenant)."[24] The Court dealt with that question in terms which have become the classic arbiter of what is within and without the domestic jurisdiction of a State:

> The question whether a certain matter is or is not solely within the jurisdiction of a State is an essentially relative question; it depends upon the development of international relations. Thus, in the present state of international law, questions of nationality are, in the opinion of the Court, in principle within this reserved domain.
>
> For the purpose of the present opinion, it is enough to observe that it may well happen that, in a matter which, like that of nationality, is not, in principle, regulated by international law, the right of a State to use its discretion is nevertheless restricted by obligations which it may have undertaken towards other States. In such a case, jurisdiction which, in principle, belongs solely to the State, is limited by rules of international law. Article 15, paragraph 8, then ceases to apply as regards those States which are entitled to invoke such rules, and the dispute as to the question whether a State has or has not the right to take certain

---

[23] See, however, Article 68 of the Statute, as well as the Rules of Court of the ICJ, Article 102, paras. 2 and 3, published in International Court of Justice, *Acts and Documents concerning the Organization of the Court*, No. 4, pp. 87, 157–158 (1978).

[24] *Nationality Decrees Issued in Tunis and Morocco*, Advisory Opinion of February 7, 1923, *PCIJ, Series B, No. 4*, p. 21.

measures becomes in these circumstances a dispute of an international character and falls outside the scope of the exception contained in this paragraph.[25]

Accordingly, as Professors McDougal, Lasswell and Chen put it:

> The choice between "international concern" and "domestic jurisdiction" was thus made to depend not only upon fact, but upon changing fact, permitting a continuing readjustment of inclusive and exclusive competences as conditions might require.[26]

And they relate this fundamental holding to human rights considerations by pointing out that:

> How a State treats its own nationals was long regarded as an internal affair of the particular State, beyond the reach of international law. The very essence of the contemporary international law of human rights is, however, precisely to shatter this traditional insulation of competence.[27]

Once a State has undertaken obligations towards another State or towards the international community in a specified sphere of human rights, it is no longer entitled to maintain, *vis-à-vis* the other State or the international community, that matters in that sphere are exclusively or essentially within its domestic jurisdiction and outside the range of international concern.

Reservations to the Genocide Convention

To turn to the International Court of Justice, one of its earlier advisory opinions concerned the making of reservations to treaties, an opinion which had a determinative influence on the content of the subsequent Vienna Convention on the Law of Treaties in respect of reservations. In the course of its opinion, the Court declared:

> The solution of these problems must be found in the special characteristics of the Genocide Convention. The origins and character of that Convention, the objects pursued by the General Assembly and the contracting parties, the relations which exist between the provisions of the Convention, *inter se*, and between those provisions and these objects, furnish elements of interpretation of the will of the General Assembly and the parties. The origins of the Convention show that it was the intention of the United Nations to condemn and punish genocide as "a crime under international law" involving a denial of the right of existence of entire human groups, a denial which shocks the conscience of mankind and results in great losses to humanity, and which is contrary to moral law and to the spirit and aims of the United Nations (resolution 96 (I) of the General Assembly, December

---

[25] *Ibid.*, p. 24.
[26] Myres S. McDougal, Harold D. Lasswell, and Lung-Chu Chen, *Human Rights and World Public Order* (1980), p. 211.
[27] *Ibid.*

11th, 1946). The first consequence arising from this conception is that the principles underlying the Convention are principles which are recognized by civilized nations as binding on States, even without any conventional obligation. A second consequence is the universal character both of the condemnation of genocide and of the cooperation required "in order to liberate mankind from such an odious scourge" (Preamble to the Convention). The Genocide Convention was therefore intended by the General Assembly and by the contracting parties to be definitely universal in scope. It was in fact approved on December 9th, 1948, by a resolution which was unanimously adopted by fifty-six States.

The objects of such a convention must also be considered. The Convention was manifestly adopted for a purely humanitarian and civilizing purpose. It is indeed difficult to imagine a convention that might have this dual character to a greater degree, since its object on the one hand is to safeguard the very existence of certain human groups and on the other to confirm and endorse the most elementary principles of morality. In such a convention the contracting States do not have any interests of their own; they merely have, one and all, a common interest, namely, the accomplishment of those high purposes which are the *raison d'être* of the convention. Consequently, in a convention of this type one cannot speak of individual advantages or disadvantages to States, or of the maintenance of a perfect contractual balance between rights and duties. The high ideals which inspired the Convention provide, by virtue of the common will of the parties, the foundation and measure of all its provisions.[28]

The Court thus recognized that genocide is supremely unlawful under international law, customary as well as conventional, and foreshadowed its later holdings on international obligations *erga omnes*.

International Status of South West Africa

In its advisory opinion on the International Status of South West Africa,[29] the International Court of Justice carried the conclusion described above of the PCIJ in *Jurisdiction of the Courts of Danzig* further, by holding that, as a result of resolutions adopted by the Council of the League of Nations in 1923, the inhabitants of the mandated territories acquired the international right of petition, a right maintained by Article 80, paragraph 1 of the United Nations Charter, which safeguards "not only the rights of States, but also the rights of the peoples of mandated territories."[30] Once again, individuals are treated by the World Court as invested by an international instrument with an international right.

Reparation for Injuries Case

In its advisory opinion on *Reparation for Injuries Suffered in the Service of the United Nations*, the Court held that: "The subjects of law in any legal system

[28] *ICJ Reports 1951*, pp. 15, 23.　　[29] *ICJ Reports 1950*, pp. 133, 136, 137–138.　　[30] *Ibid.*, p. 136.

are not necessarily identical in their nature or in the extent of their rights"[31] and concluded that the United Nations possessed a large measure of international personality, including the right to bring an international claim – a holding which reinforced the principle that international rights do not belong only to States.

Corfu Channel Case

In its first contentious case, the *Corfu Channel* case, the Court held that Albania had an obligation under international law to notify international shipping of the existence of a minefield in Albanian territorial waters, an obligation which derived from "certain general and well-recognized principles, namely, elementary considerations of humanity, even more exacting in peace than in war"[32] as well as other principles such as the freedom of maritime communication and the obligation of a State not knowingly to allow its territory to be used for acts contrary to the rights of other States. The Court, as will be shown, has had cause to return to the "elementary considerations of humanity, even more exacting in peace than in war." The relation of such considerations to the substance and application of human rights requires no elaboration.

Asylum Case

In the *Asylum* case between Colombia and Peru, to which Colombia's grant of diplomatic asylum to Sr. Haya de la Torre gave rise, the Court concluded that regular prosecution by judicial authorities, even if such prosecution relates to revolutionary activities, does not constitute an "urgent case" within the terms of the Havana Convention, for "in principle ... asylum cannot be opposed to the operation of justice." But the Court significantly qualified this holding by stating that:

> An exception to this rule can occur only if, in the guise of justice, arbitrary action is substituted for the rule of law. Such would be the case if the administration of justice were corrupted by measures clearly prompted by political aims. Asylum protects the political offender against any measures of a manifestly extra-legal character which a Government might take against its political opponents.[33]

Peace Treaties Case

In its advisory proceedings concerning the *Interpretation of Peace Treaties with Bulgaria, Hungary and Romania*, the General Assembly put questions to the

---

[31] *ICJ Reports 1949*, p. 178.   [32] *Ibid.*, p. 22.

[33] *ICJ Reports 1950*, p. 284. See also the definition of an arbitrary act in the *ELSI* case: "To identify arbitrariness with mere unlawfulness would be to deprive it of any useful meaning in its own right ...

Court concerning the obligations of those States to implement dispute settlement procedures of the Peace Treaties. The disputes turned on allegations of failure of the three States to

> take all measures necessary to secure to all persons under [their] jurisdiction, without distinction as to race, sex, language or religion, the enjoyment of human rights and fundamental freedoms, including freedom of expression, of press and publication, of religious worship, of political opinion and of public meeting.[34]

It was contended that the request for an advisory opinion was an act *ultra vires* the General Assembly because, in dealing with the question of the observance of human rights and fundamental freedoms in these three States, the Assembly was "interfering" or "intervening" in matters essentially within the domestic jurisdiction of States. This alleged incompetence of the Assembly was deduced from the terms of Article 2, paragraph 7 of the United Nations Charter.[35]

The Court held this argument to be based on a misunderstanding. The Court itself was not called upon to deal with the charges of the violation of the human rights provisions of the Peace Treaties but only the procedure for dispute settlement under the Treaties. It held that the interpretation of the terms of a treaty for this purpose could not be considered a question essentially within the domestic jurisdiction of a State. "It is a question of international law which, by its very nature, lies within the competence of the Court."[36] The Court held that these considerations sufficed also to dispose of the argument based on Article 2, paragraph 7.

The United Nations Charter, hardly less a treaty than the Peace Treaties, proclaims the purpose of achievement of international cooperation in "promoting and encouraging respect for human rights and for fundamental freedoms for all without distinction as to race, sex, language or religion" (Article 1, paragraph 3). It provides, in Article 55, that the United Nations shall promote universal respect for and observance of human rights and fundamental freedoms for all, without distinction as to race, sex, language or religion, and further provides, in Article 56, that the Members of the United Nations pledge to take joint and separate action in cooperation with the

---

Arbitrariness is not so much something opposed to a rule of law, as something opposed to the rule of law." *Elettronica Sicula S.p.A. (ELSI), ICJ Reports 1989*, pp. 74, 76.

[34] *ICJ Reports 1950*, p. 73.

[35] Article 2, paragraph 7 provides:

Nothing contained in the present Charter shall authorize the United Nations to intervene in matters which are essentially within the domestic jurisdiction of any state or shall require the Members to submit such matters to settlement under the present Charter; but this principle shall not prejudice the application of enforcement measures under Chapter VII.

[36] *ICJ Reports 1950*, pp. 70–71.

Organization to achieve these purposes. It appears to follow (see the discussion above in *Nationality Decrees Issued in Tunis and Morocco*) that any question of the breach of these treaty obligations – if they be obligations – equally would not be matters essentially within the domestic jurisdiction of a State. The importance of that conclusion to the contemporary international law of human rights is fundamental in view of the fact, discussed below, that the Court was later to hold that these Charter provisions do give rise to international obligations.

South West Africa Cases

There has been repeated involvement of the Court with the governance of, and the promotion of the independence of, *South West Africa*, today the independent State of Namibia. One such involvement is referred to above. Another was the South West Africa Cases brought by Ethiopia and Liberia against South Africa, alleging, among other things, that the practice of apartheid in South West Africa constituted a violation of South Africa's mandatory obligation to promote to the utmost the well-being of the inhabitants of the territory. South Africa lodged a number of preliminary objections to the standing of Ethiopia and Liberia and the jurisdiction of the Court. The Court, by a vote of eight to seven, held in 1962 that it had jurisdiction to adjudicate upon the merits of the dispute.[37] But four years later, it held, by the casting vote of the President, that the applicants had not established any legal right or interest appertaining to them in the subject matter of the dispute.[38] The Court held that the argument of Ethiopia and Liberia

> amounts to a plea that the Court should allow the equivalent of an "*actio popularis*", or right resident in any member of a community to take legal action in vindication of a public interest. But although a right of this kind may be known to certain municipal systems of law, it is not known to international law as it stands at present: nor is the Court able to regard it as imported by the "general principles of law" referred to in Article 38, paragraph 1 *(c)*, of its Statute.[39]

Accordingly the Court never reached the Merits, which had given rise to exceptionally extended and detailed argument over human rights issues posed by the practice of an overt and acute form of racial discrimination.

Continued Presence of South Africa in Namibia

The Court's 1966 Judgment in the *South West Africa Cases* was widely and trenchantly criticized, not least in the United Nations General Assembly,

---

[37] *ICJ Reports 1962*, p. 319.   [38] *ICJ Reports 1966*, pp. 6, 51.   [39] *Ibid.*, p. 47.

which proceeded to find that "South Africa has failed to fulfil its obligations ... to ensure the moral and material well-being and security of the indigenous inhabitants of South West Africa and has, in fact, disavowed the Mandate." The General Assembly accordingly decided that the Mandate conferred upon South Africa to administer the territory "is therefore terminated" and "that South Africa has no other right to administer the Territory."[40]

In 1970, the Security Council requested an advisory opinion of the Court on the legal consequences for States of the continued presence of South Africa in Namibia despite a Security Council resolution holding, as a consequence of General Assembly resolution 2145 (XXI), that presence to be illegal. The Court found that "the continued presence of South Africa in Namibia being illegal, South Africa is under obligation to withdraw its administration from Namibia immediately and thus to put an end to the occupation of the Territory."[41] The Court held that the General Assembly had acted within the framework of its competence in terminating the Mandate. Among the several objections to the validity of General Assembly resolution 2145 (XXI) which South Africa maintained before the Court was its claim that the resolution's holding that South Africa had failed to fulfil its obligations in respect of the administration of the Mandated Territory required detailed factual investigation, which had not been made. The Court responded:

128. In its oral statement and in written communications to the Court, the Government of South Africa expressed the desire to supply the Court with further factual information concerning the purposes and objectives of South Africa's policy of separate development or *apartheid*, contending that to establish a breach of South Africa's substantive international obligations under the Mandate it would be necessary to prove that a particular exercise of South Africa's legislative or administrative powers was not directed in good faith towards the purpose of promoting to the utmost the well-being and progress of the inhabitants. It is claimed by the Government of South Africa that no act or omission on its part would constitute a violation of its international obligations unless it is shown that such act or omission was actuated by a motive, or directed towards a purpose other than one to promote the interests of the inhabitants of the Territory.

129. The Government of South Africa having made this request, the Court finds that no factual evidence is needed for the purpose of determining whether the policy of *apartheid* as applied by South Africa in Namibia *is in conformity with the international obligations assumed by South Africa under the Charter of the United Nations*. In order to determine whether the laws and decrees applied by South Africa in Namibia, which are a matter of public record, *constitute a violation of the purposes and principles of the Charter of the United Nations*, the question of intent or

---

[40] General Assembly resolution 2145 (XXI).   [41] *ICJ Reports 1971*, para. 58.

governmental discretion is not relevant; nor is it necessary to investigate or determine the effects of those measures upon the welfare of the inhabitants.

130. It is undisputed, and is amply supported by documents annexed to South Africa's written statement in these proceedings, that the official governmental policy pursued by South Africa in Namibia is to achieve a complete physical separation of races and ethnic groups in separate areas within the Territory. The application of this policy has required, as has been conceded by South Africa, restrictive measures of control officially adopted and enforced in the Territory by the coercive power of the former Mandatory. These measures establish limitations, exclusions or restrictions for the members of the indigenous population groups in respect of their participation in certain types of activities, fields of study or of training, labor or employment and also submit them to restrictions or exclusions of residence and movement in large parts of the Territory.

131. Under the Charter of the United Nations, the former Mandatory had pledged itself to observe and respect, in a territory having an international status, human rights and fundamental freedoms for all without distinction as to race. *To establish instead, and to enforce, distinctions, exclusions, restrictions and limitations exclusively based on grounds of race, color, descent or national or ethnic origin which constitute a denial of fundamental human rights is a flagrant violation of the purposes and principles of the Charter*[42] [Emphasis added].

These holdings are of fundamental importance to the contemporary character of international law governing human rights. As Egon Schwelb put it:

> When the Court speaks of "conformity with the international obligations assumed . . . under the Charter," of "a violation of the purposes and principles of the Charter," of the pledge to observe and respect human rights and fundamental freedoms for all, when it finds that certain actions "constitute a denial of fundamental human rights" and classifies them as "a flagrant violation of the purposes and principles of the Charter", it leaves no doubt that, in its view, the Charter does impose on the Members of the United Nations legal obligations in the human rights field.[43]

It is true that the Court specified that South Africa had pledged itself to observe and respect, "in a territory having an international status," human rights and fundamental freedoms for all without distinction as to race. But that clause imports an aggravating, not a necessary, circumstance. Schwelb was right to maintain, in commenting upon this passage, that: "What is a flagrant violation of the purposes and principles of the Charter when com-

---

[42] *Ibid.*, pp. 56–57.
[43] Egon Schwelb, "The International Court of Justice and the Human Rights Clauses of the Charter," *American Journal of International Law* (1972), 66, pp. 337, 348.

mitted in Namibia, is also such a violation when committed in South Africa proper or, for that matter, in any sovereign Member State ..."[44]

Barcelona Traction

In 1970 the Court rendered its Judgment in the second phase of the proceedings in the case concerning *The Barcelona Traction, Light and Power Company, Limited.* In the course of holding the Applicant's claims inadmissible, the Court made a distinction

> between the obligations of a State towards the international community as a whole, and those arising vis-à-vis another State in the field of diplomatic protection. By their very nature the former are the concern of all States. In view of the importance of the rights involved, all States can be held to have a legal interest in their protection; they are obligations *erga omnes*.
>
> 34. Such obligations derive, for example, in contemporary international law, from the outlawing of acts of aggression, and of genocide, as also from the principles and rules concerning the basic rights of the human person, including protection from slavery and racial discrimination.[45]

This is another holding of paramount importance for international law concerning human rights. By it, the Court has found that the rules concerning the basic rights of the human person are the concern of all States; that obligations flowing from these rights run *erga omnes*, that is, towards all States. Thus it follows that, when one State protests that another is violating the basic human rights of the latter's own citizens, the former State is not intervening in the latter's internal affairs; it rather is seeking to vindicate international obligations which run towards it as well as all other States.

At the same time, in *Barcelona Traction*, the Court held that "obligations the performance of which is the subject of diplomatic protection are not of the same category" as obligations *erga omnes*. "It cannot be held, when one such obligation in particular is in question, in a specific case, that all States have a legal interest in its observance."[46] The Court found that Belgium lacked standing to maintain a claim against Spain before the Court, on the ground that, while Belgians might be the principal shareholders of Barcelona Traction, the company was of Canadian nationality. Professors McDougal, Lasswell, and Chen accordingly conclude: "In contemporary international law it is thus apparent that the individual human being is almost completely dependent upon a state of nationality for securing a hearing upon the merits upon injuries done to him by other States."[47]

---

[44] *Ibid.*, p. 349.   [45] *ICJ Reports 1970*, p. 32.   [46] *Ibid.*

[47] McDougal *et al.*, *Human Rights*, p. 878.

Nottebohm Case

The issue in the *Nottebohm* case was whether Liechtenstein could exercise diplomatic protection *vis-à-vis* Guatemala on behalf of Nottebohm, who had been granted, under the law of Liechtenstein, its nationality shortly after the outbreak of the Second World War. Nottebohm, a German national, had been a resident of Guatemala since 1905 and continued to reside there after the grant of Liechtenstein nationality. The Court held that, in view of the absence of any bond of attachment between Nottebohm and Liechtenstein, the latter was not entitled to extend its protection to Nottebohm *vis-à-vis* Guatemala and that, accordingly, its claim was inadmissible.[48] While this decision was widely criticized,[49] the "genuine link" concept which it embodied has been sustained. The principle may have the result that no State is in a position to maintain a claim on behalf of an individual, a result which may foreclose the realization of that individual's human rights. Nevertheless, the law of international claims has traditionally been replete with limitations on the exercise of diplomatic protection which may have precisely such a result. But the question arises, if fundamental human rights do complement obligations which exist *erga omnes*, and if those rights indeed are of fundamental importance, should their pursuance on the international plane be so limited by the traditional rules of diplomatic protection?

Western Sahara

In the course of rendering its advisory opinion on the *Western Sahara*, the Court spoke of "the right of that population [of the Western Sahara] to self-determination"[50] in terms that demonstrate its conviction that peoples have the right "to determine their future political status by their own freely expressed will."[51] It supported the application "of the principle of self-determination through the free and genuine expression of the will of the peoples of the Territory."[52]

Hostages Case

In the case concerning *United States Diplomatic and Consular Staff in Tehran*, the Court, in holding unlawful the detention of the hostages, occupation of the Embassy of the United States and rifling of the Embassy archives, also held that:

> Wrongfully to deprive human beings of their freedom and to subject them to physical constraint in conditions of hardship is in itself manifestly incompatible

---

[48] *ICJ Reports 1955*, pp. 4, 26.
[49] See McDougal *et al.*, *Human Rights*, p. 872, and the sources there cited.
[50] *ICJ Reports 1975*, pp. 12, 36.   [51] *Ibid.*   [52] *Ibid.*, p. 68.

with the principles of the Charter of the United Nations, as well as with the fundamental principles enunciated in the Universal Declaration of Human Rights.[53]

Subsequent grave and prolonged international incidents were to show the continuing relevance of that holding to the contemporary world.

Military and Paramilitary Activities in and against Nicaragua

In the case of *Military and Paramilitary Activities in and against Nicaragua*, the Court made several holdings of interest – and controversy – in the sphere of human rights. In respect of mine-laying in Nicaraguan waters by United States agencies without US notice to international shipping, the Court, citing the above quotation from the *Corfu Channel* case, held that "a breach of the principles of humanitarian law"[54] had been committed. It also concluded that the United States did not exercise operational control over the *contras* and thus could not be held responsible for violations of the law of war which might have been committed by the *contras*.

The Court did consider the lawfulness of the production and dissemination by United States officials of a war manual which had been provided to the *contras*. In so doing, the Court held that the Geneva Conventions of 1949, in their common Article 3, define rules which reflect "elementary considerations of humanity" which are applicable as customary international law.[55] Doubt was expressed at the time,[56] and there has been question raised since, about whether the Court was correct in holding that the rules set out in the common Article 3 of the Geneva Conventions have the status of customary international law,[57] a conclusion for which the Court supplied scant support. The Court held that the United States was bound to, and had failed to, ensure respect for these rules, in their character as rules of customary international law: rules which provide for humane treatment without any adverse distinction founded on race, color, religion, sex, birth, or wealth or other similar criteria, and which prohibit in respect of persons taking no part in hostilities violence to life and person, taking of hostages, humiliating and degrading treatment, and arbitrary sentencing and execution. The Court held the production and dissemination of a manual which advocated some acts incompatible with these standards to have encouraged the commission by the *contras* of acts contrary to general principles of humanitarian law.

---

[53] *ICJ Reports 1980*, p. 42.   [54] *ICJ Reports 1986*, p. 112.   [55] *Ibid.*, pp. 113–114.

[56] *Ibid.*, Separate Opinion of Judge Ago, p. 184, and Dissenting Opinion of Judge Jennings, p. 537.

[57] See Theodor Meron, *Human Rights and Humanitarian Norms as Customary Law* (1989), pp. 7–36; and Rosemary Abi-Saab, "The 'General Principles' of Humanitarian Law According to the International Court of Justice," *International Review of the Red Cross* (1987), No. 256, p. 367.

As one justification of its activities towards Nicaragua, the United States had publicly maintained (though it did not plead this position before the Court) that Nicaragua, upon the assumption of power by its revolutionary Government, had undertaken commitments to the Organization of American States and its Members to respect human rights, and in particular to hold free elections, which commitments it had failed to observe. The Court held that, even in the absence of such commitments, Nicaragua could not with impunity violate human rights. But it continued:

> However, where human rights are protected by international conventions, that protection takes the form of such arrangements for monitoring or ensuring respect for human rights as are provided for in the conventions themselves.[58]

The implication was that the United States was not entitled to take other measures to uphold human rights in Nicaragua (and not being party to the conventions in question, it could not invoke them) – a position which may not be wholly consistent with the *erga omnes* character of human rights obligations elsewhere affirmed by the Court. This holding has been strongly attacked as evidencing a regressive approach by the Court to questions of standing in the maintenance of human rights akin to the approach taken in the *South West Africa Cases*.[59] It has been argued that the logic of the position taken by the Court in the *Nicaragua* case is, if a Government abuses human rights, but is nevertheless a party to a human rights convention, other States are confined to seeking redress by the means provided by that convention, however limited in scope is the convention, however few the parties to it, and however inadequate those means may be. The Court's holding that, in law, Nicaragua had assumed only a political, not a legal, obligation through its assurances to the OAS, and that those assurances ran only to the Organization and not to its Members, have also been criticized as factually and legally erroneous, inconsistent with the Court's jurisprudence, and conceptually regressive.[60]

The Court also held that: "While the United States might form its own appraisal of the situation as to respect for human rights in Nicaragua, the use of force could not be the appropriate method to monitor or ensure such respect."[61] The Court concluded that the protection of human rights cannot be compatible with the mining of ports, the destruction of oil installations,

[58] *ICJ Reports 1986*, p. 134.
[59] Fernando R. Tesén, "Le Peuple, C'est Moi! The World Court and Human Rights," *American Journal of International Law* (1987), 81, 173.
[60] *Ibid.* See also my Dissent, *ICJ Reports 1986*, pp. 274, 382–385, 398–402, and the Separate Opinion of Judge Ago, pp. 186–187.
[61] *ICJ Reports 1986*, p. 134.

and support for the *contras*. It therefore held that any argument derived from the protection of human rights in Nicaragua could not afford a legal justification for the conduct of the United States: a holding, which, however, did not of itself exclude that that conduct was justified by considerations of collective self-defense. Whether the Court's extraordinary holdings of fact and law respecting issues of collective self-defense are persuasive poses issues beyond the scope of this paper.

ELSI Case

Two recent cases merit a final mention. The case concerning *Elettronica Sicula S.p.A. (ELSI)*,[62] is the most recent illustration in the Court of a State taking up the claim of its national and espousing it in an area of human rights, i.e., property rights (albeit, rights of a corporation, whose shares, however, are ultimately owned by human beings). In that case, the Court found no violation of such rights as established by treaty, and it also found to be absent a claimed arbitrary act, which, as noted above, it defined as an act contrary not to "a rule of law" but "to the rule of law."[63]

Mazilu Case

Finally, in its advisory proceedings in the "Mazilu case" (*Applicability of Article VI, Section 22, of the Convention on the Privileges and Immunities of the United Nations*),[64] the Court held that a special rapporteur of a subcommission of the United Nations Human Rights Commission was entitled to the privileges and immunities of a United Nations expert on mission, even in circumstances in which he had not been permitted to leave Romania to perform his functions.

Conclusion

It is apparent from this survey of the cases in which the Permanent Court of International Justice and the International Court of Justice have treated questions of human rights, and allied questions, that the influence of the Court on the evolution of the international law of human rights has been considerable and constructive. While there may be little prospect in the near term that the Court will become a court of human rights, there is ground for the expectation that the Court will continue to contribute to the progressive development of the international law of human rights.

[62] *ICJ Reports 1989*, p. 15.   [63] *Ibid.*, p. 76. (But see my Dissent, at pp. 108–121.)
[64] *ICJ Reports 1989*, p. 177.

PART II
International Arbitration

ॐ

10

Arbitration and the Exhaustion of Local Remedies

ひつ

Where a State and an alien agree in a contract to arbitrate disputes relating to the contract, in terms which indicate that arbitration is to be the exclusive remedy, need the alien exhaust any other remedy before an international claim may be presented relating to a dispute which falls within the scope of the arbitration clause?

New light has been shed on this unresolved question by the Convention on the Settlement of Investment Disputes between States and Nationals of Other States which has been submitted to governments by the Executive Directors of the International Bank for Reconstruction and Development.[1] Article 26 of the Convention provides:

> Consent of the parties to arbitration under this Convention shall, unless otherwise stated, be deemed consent to such arbitration to the exclusion of any other remedy. A Contracting State may require the exhaustion of local administrative or judicial remedies as a condition of its consent to arbitration under this Convention.[2]

The Report of the Executive Directors on the Convention states with regard to "Arbitration as exclusive remedy" that:

> 32. It may be presumed that when a State and an investor agree to have recourse to arbitration, and do not reserve the right to have recourse to other remedies or require the prior exhaustion of other remedies, the intention of the parties is to have recourse to arbitration to the exclusion of any other remedy. This rule of interpretation is embodied in the first sentence of Article 26. In order to make

---

Written with Dr. J. Gillis Wetter. First published in the *American Journal of International Law* (1966), 60.

[1] Convention on the Settlement of Investment Disputes between States and Nationals of Other States Submitted to Governments by the Executive Directors of the International Bank for Reconstruction and Development and Accompanying Report of the Executive Directors, March 18, 1965; *International Legal Materials* (1965), 4, 532, 524. The Convention will come into force thirty days after the date of deposit of the twentieth instrument of ratification, acceptance, or approval.

[2] Convention on the Settlement of Investment Disputes, p. 536.

clear that it was not intended thereby to modify the rules of international law regarding the exhaustion of local remedies, the second sentence explicitly recognizes the right of a State to require the prior exhaustion of local remedies.[3]

An earlier draft of the Convention and its commentary came to the same conclusion in somewhat differing terms. Section 16 of the Preliminary Draft provided:

> Consent to have recourse to arbitration pursuant to this Convention shall, unless otherwise stated, be deemed consent to have recourse to such proceedings in lieu of any other remedy.[4]

The commentary to the Preliminary Draft indicates that a requirement of the exhaustion of local remedies which the State may impose must be a term of its agreement to arbitrate, or otherwise be stipulated (a reservation to the Convention presumably would be effective). The requirement will not be deemed to operate by reason of municipal law. As the commentary concludes:

> If a State were to include an unqualified arbitration clause in an agreement with a foreign investor, it would seem to run counter to normal rules of interpretation to read into that clause a requirement of the prior exhaustion of local remedies.[5]

While the focus of the Convention is not upon State responsibility, it would seem that the presumption which the Convention embodies – that consent of the parties to arbitration shall be deemed consent to such arbitration to the exclusion of any other remedy – should, if well founded, apply equally to the sphere of State responsibility.

This article will consider whether or not the presumption of Article 26 of the Convention is well founded. It will be submitted that, essentially, it is, in terms both of principle and precedent.

Article 26 is believed to constitute the first conventional expression of what appears to be the trend of customary international law: that, where a State and an alien agree in a contract to arbitrate disputes relating to that contract, in terms indicating that arbitration is the exclusive remedy, then that remedy only must be exhausted before an international claim may be maintained. This trend is a plausible one, whose principle would appear, *prima facie*, to be sound. However, both the principle and the practice have their refinements – refinements which indicate that the exclusion of other remedies is and ought

---

[3] Report of the Executive Directors, pp. 528–529.

[4] International Bank for Reconstruction and Development, Preliminary Draft of a Convention on the Settlement of Investment Disputes between States and Nationals of Other States, October 15, 1963, p. 33.

[5] *Ibid.*, p. 34.

not to be absolute. In particular, the alien may be obligated to exhaust certain local remedies which pertain to the enforcement of the arbitration agreement or the arbitral award itself. Arguably these remedies may not be only those of the contracting State.

After illustration of a typical arbitration clause of a contract between a State and an alien, there will be considered, first, the related practice, notably the cases in which the question at issue has been argued before the Permanent Court of International Justice and the International Court of Justice. Then the considerations of principle which the cases canvass will be discussed. Finally, the relationship of the question under discussion to that posed by an agreement between States to arbitrate will be noted.

A Characteristic Arbitration Clause

The number of contracts between States (and State agencies) and aliens which provide for arbitration of disputes arising thereunder is large. The arbitral clauses vary considerably in their provisions, but apparently are constant in their comprehensive description of the scope of the obligation to arbitrate; typically, they provide that "any dispute" or "any and every dispute" relating to the contract which is not otherwise settled shall be settled by arbitration in accordance with the specifications of the agreement. A recent example is the Joint Structure Agreement between the National Iranian Oil Company, an Iranian governmental agency, and Bataafse Petroleum Maatschappij NV. Article 38 of the Agreement provides for the optional conciliation of differences, prescribing that, if the dispute is not settled by conciliation, "the sole method of determining it shall be arbitration in accordance with Article 39." Article 39 in part provides that:

> 1. Any dispute arising from the execution or interpretation of the provisions of this Agreement shall be settled by an Arbitration Board consisting of three arbitrators.[6]

The article then proceeds, in thirteen detailed paragraphs, to specify the mode of appointment and operation of the tribunal, and to demonstrate amply the intention of the parties that arbitration shall be the comprehensive and exclusive remedy, which is not to be permitted to fail for any of a variety of reasons (such as the incapacity of an arbitrator or the termination of the Agreement). While some arbitration provisions are more complex still – for

---

[6] The Agreement, dated January 16, 1965, is reprinted in *Platt's Oilgram News Service*, Spec. Suppl., May 4, 1965, Vol. 43 No. 85–Y, p. 10.

example, that of the Iranian Consortium Agreement of 1954[7] – and most others are simpler, it appears justified to conclude that normally their terms indicate that arbitration is to be the exclusive remedy.

The Practice

Before considering those cases in which the question under analysis has been the focus of international controversy, it is worth recalling that a large number of arbitrations between States and aliens have taken place pursuant to the arbitration clauses of contracts between them. The authors have reviewed thirty-eight of these awards (many of them unpublished), which, it is believed, include a high proportion of all the instances in which arbitrations between States and aliens have taken place.[8] In all of the cases examined, except as noted below,[9] the State and the alien concerned treated the arbitral remedy as exclusive. The State concerned did not contend that other remedies were available and should be pursued, before or after arbitration. Such a contention quite understandably was not made, not only because of the exclusive import of the contractual obligation to arbitrate but also because of the fact that arbitration actually was undertaken. Nevertheless, it may reasonably be said to follow from this pattern of State–alien arbitration that it is the view of the States concerned that arbitration as prescribed by the contract is the exclusive remedy and the only one to be exhausted. While the States Parties to these arbitrations did not, as far as is known, explicitly address themselves to the question of whether the exclusive character of the arbitral remedy means that, upon resort to that remedy, the international legal rule of exhaustion of local remedies is satisfied, the fact that they did engage in arbitration without raising the possibility of resort to other remedies suggests that they would have acknowledged this conclusion had there been occasion to do so.

Correspondingly, those instances in which arbitration, though demanded, has been refused, and the Contracting State has contended that local remedies have not been exhausted indicate that States do not uniformly treat arbitra-

---

[7] The Agreement is reprinted in *Platt's Oilgram News Service*, Spec. Supp., October 5, 1954, Vol. 32, No. 192–A, p. 1; and in Hurewitz, *Diplomacy in the Near and Middle East* (1956), Vol. II, pp. 348–383.

[8] The cases examined do not include the significant number of unpublished awards of the Court of Arbitration of the International Chamber of Commerce. See Böckstiegel, "Arbitration of Disputes between States and Private Enterprises in the International Chamber of Commerce," *American Journal of International Law* (1965), 59, pp. 579–586.

[9] To the four cases discussed below, there should be added the award in *Société Européenne d'Etudes et d'Entreprises v. the Government of Yugoslavia* (1956), [1957] ILR 761, which was attacked by Yugoslavia.

tion as an exclusive remedy which alone must be invoked to satisfy the rule of exhaustion of local remedies. There are only a few such instances; by far they are lesser, and the less persuasive element in the pattern of State practice. Moreover, the State of which the alien is a national has characteristically contested any claim of the Contracting State that local remedies had not been exhausted.[10] These cases will now be set forth and discussed.

The *Losinger & Co.* Case

The Losinger case is the first of four cases before the Permanent Court of International Justice and the International Court of Justice in which the precise issue under analysis was joined by the parties and left unresolved by the Court, since, in each case, a settlement supervened. Nevertheless, the character of the arguments and the consequence of the cases is such as to merit their exposition. As will appear, much of the heart of the matter was laid bare by the advocacy of Switzerland and Yugoslavia in the *Losinger* case.

Losinger & Co. was the assignee of a railway construction contract entered into in 1929 by an American company with a then autonomous district of Yugoslavia (for which the State of Yugoslavia was substituted when Losinger replaced the American firm in 1931). Article XVI of the contract contained the following arbitration clause:

> Any differences of opinion or disputes which may arise between the Contracting Parties in connection with the carrying out or interpretation of the clauses and conditions of this contract shall be settled by compulsory arbitration, if a friendly settlement cannot be reached by the Contracting Parties.
>
> Within 30 days of a demand made by either of the Contracting Parties, each Party shall appoint an arbitrator for the joint settlement of the disputes. If these two arbitrators fail to agree, or if one of the Parties fails to appoint an arbitrator within the time specified, the case shall be referred either to the President of the Swiss Federal Court or a neutral person who shall be appointed by the latter and who shall in the capacity of umpire give his decision alone upon the dispute. The award of the arbitrators or of the umpire shall be rendered in Yugoslavia. There shall be no appeal from this decision.[11]

In 1934, the Yugoslav Government declared the contract canceled. A dispute arose as a result of the cancellation, which led Losinger & Co. to institute arbitral proceedings pursuant to Article XVI. Yugoslavia failed to

---

[10] Apart from the cases analyzed below, there are instances of a State refusing arbitration which have not been the source of subsequent international proceedings, for lack of international jurisdiction or otherwise. For example, Iraq is known to have declined to arbitrate a certain dispute with the Iraq Petroleum Company, and Lebanon reportedly failed to name an arbitrator in another case to which the Iraq Petroleum Company was party.

[11] *PCIJ, Series C, No. 78*, pp. 7–8.

appoint an arbitrator within the time specified, and, in accordance with Article XVI, the case was referred to the President of the Swiss Federal Court for decision. In the course of the proceedings, the Yugoslav Government claimed that the umpire lacked jurisdiction by reason, *inter alia*, of the fact that a Yugoslav law of July 19, 1934, which came into effect shortly before the company requested arbitration, provided that any dispute with the State could only be brought before the ordinary courts of the State. The umpire, in an interlocutory judgment, ruled that he was not competent to adjudicate upon this plea since it related to the validity of the arbitration clause[12] and, while retaining the case, "left the Parties to submit this question to the competent authority."[13]

At the request of Losinger & Co., the Swiss Government then intervened, and asked the Permanent Court to give judgment to the effect that the Yugoslav Government could not claim release from the terms of a clause of its contract with Losinger & Co. by adducing a law concerning the conduct of State litigation which was of more recent date than the contract. Yugoslavia responded that "the application of the Swiss Government cannot be entertained because the rule which requires the previous exhaustion of the remedies available under Yugoslav municipal law was not observed by the firm of Losinger & Co."[14]

The Swiss Memorial contended that the Court's jurisdiction could not be denied on the ground of failure to exhaust local remedies. The rule of exhaustion of local remedies did not apply in situations where no remedies existed or the results which could be obtained through their pursuit were illusory. Moreover, the arbitration clause of the contract demonstrated that "it was the will of all the Contracting Parties to withdraw their disputes from any of the Yugoslav courts, for recourse to the courts was entirely excluded, and the arbitrators or the umpire were empowered to give a definitive decision."[15] Switzerland further argued that the Court's decision in the *Chorzow Factory (Indemnity)* case[16] showed that no State could plead that its local remedies had not been exhausted when it itself, because of its failure to observe its contractual obligations, prevented the other Contracting Party from seeking the vindication of its rights before the truly competent jurisdiction.[17]

---

[12] *Ibid.*, p. 116.   [13] *Ibid.*, p. 117 [authors' translation].   [14] *Ibid.*, p. 214.   [15] *Ibid.*, p. 40.
[16] *PCIJ, Series A, No. 9.*
[17] The Swiss Memorial quoted the Chorzow holding that "one party cannot avail himself of the fact that the other has not fulfilled some obligation or has not had recourse to some means of redress, if the former party has, by some illegal act, prevented the latter from fulfilling the obligation in question, or from having recourse to the tribunal which would have been open to him" (*ibid.*, p. 31).

For its part, Yugoslavia argued that the Swiss Government's assertion that the object of the arbitration clause was to withdraw possible disputes entirely from the Yugoslav courts was

> absolutely without foundation. No civilized State, in which there is a regular administration of justice, with independent courts, could accept it ... The object of the arbitration clause was to submit possible disputes to arbitration. It contains no provision which excludes the jurisdiction of the Yugoslav courts. And the arbitration clause, in the same way as any other contract, is subject to the laws which determine its conditions of validity, define its mechanism, and govern its operation."[18]

The Yugoslav Government contended that it was "beyond question" that the relations between Losinger & Co. and the Yugoslav Government were governed by the laws of Yugoslavia. Thus "everything connected with the arbitration clause" was governed by Yugoslav law. An arbitral award could be annulled by a Yugoslav court, and Losinger & Co. could have asked the Yugoslav courts

> to adjudicate upon the soundness of the plea to the jurisdiction that had been raised by the Yugoslav State in the proceedings before the umpire. It is not, therefore, correct to say that Yugoslav law provides no remedies for this situation. Nor is it possible to anticipate what would be the decision of the Yugoslav courts, seeing that these courts have not hitherto had any opportunity of deciding as to the period of time covered by the provisions of Article 24 of the Yugoslav law of July 19th, 1934. The fact that this law prohibits the conclusion of arbitration agreements on behalf of the State, in the future, does not prejudge the question whether it is retrospective in character. The law itself contains no provision stating that it operates retrospectively. In regard to that point, the character of the law remains to be determined by the courts; so that if ordinary Yugoslav courts had ruled that the plea to the jurisdiction submitted by the State was not well-founded, the Yugoslav Government would have abandoned that argument. In any case, Losinger & Co. S.A. were able, and were obliged, to exhaust these municipal judicial remedies before applying through their Government to the Permanent Court."[19]

Switzerland responded that the arbitration clause itself excluded the possibility of any recourse against an award rendered pursuant to it, citing the provision that: "There shall be no appeal from this decision."[20] It argued that Yugoslavia as well as Losinger & Co. had thus agreed to accept the definitive character of the award and to renounce the submission of any question to any Yugoslav tribunal.

In the oral argument, Yugoslavia maintained and elaborated its contention

---

[18] *PCIJ, Series C, No. 78*, p. 132.   [19] *Ibid.*, pp. 133–134.   [20] *Ibid.*, p. 160.

that "arbitration in private law does not constitute a kind of judicial autarchy,"[21] and accordingly was subject to the intervention of the regular courts. It could not be claimed that the arbitration clause barred access to the Yugoslav courts, for the reason that it was these courts and not the Arbitral Tribunal which could resolve any difficulties which might impede the functioning of the Arbitral Tribunal.[22] Switzerland contended that it was "absolutely inconceivable" that Yugoslavia could hold Losinger & Co. responsible for not having applied to Yugoslav courts to vindicate the validity of an arbitration clause which Yugoslavia challenged and the company upheld; if there were to have been an action in the Yugoslav courts to set aside the arbitration clause, it was up to Yugoslavia to have brought it.[23]

The *Losinger* case will be commented upon in conjunction with the three remaining cases.

The *Anglo-Iranian Oil Company* Case

In the *Anglo-Iranian Oil Company* case,[24] the Iranian Government claimed to have annulled the concession of the company through enactment of the Iranian Oil Nationalization Act of May 1, 1951.[25] Article 22 of the Convention concluded between the Government and the company on April 29, 1933 provided for arbitration of "any differences between the parties of any nature whatever," in the following terms:

(A) Any differences between the parties of any nature whatever and in particular any differences arising out of the interpretation of this Agreement and of the rights and obligations therein contained as well as any differences of opinion which may arise relative to questions for the settlement of which, by the terms of this Agreement, the agreement of both parties is necessary, shall be settled by arbitration.

The article proceeded to specify the manner of constituting the tribunal, even in an instance where a party defaulted in the process. It further provided:

(E) The procedure of arbitration shall be that followed, at the time of arbitration, by the Permanent Court of International Justice. The place and time of arbitration shall be fixed by the umpire or by the sole arbitrator provided for in clause (D), as the case may be.

(F) The award shall be based on the juridical principles contained in Article 38 of the Statute of the Permanent Court of International Justice. There shall be no appeal against the award.[26]

---

[21] *Ibid.*, p. 193 [authors' translation].   [22] *Ibid.*, p. 346.   [23] *Ibid.*, pp. 311–312.
[24] *ICJ Pleadings*, Anglo-Iranian Oil Co. case (United Kingdom v. Iran).
[25] *Ibid.*, pp. 279–280.   [26] *Ibid.*, p. 268. The original French text is reproduced at pp. 256–257.

Article 26 of the Convention provided in part:

> Before the date of the 31st December 1993, this Concession can only come to an end in the case that the *Company* should surrender the Concession (Art. 25) or in the case that the Arbitration Court should declare the Concession annulled as a consequence of default of the *Company* in the performance of the present Agreement.
>
> The following cases only shall be regarded as default in that sense:
>
> (a) if any sum awarded to Persia by the Arbitration Court has not been paid within one month of the date of the award;
>
> (b) if the voluntary or compulsory liquidation of the *Company* be decided upon.
>
> In any other cases of breach of the present Agreement by one party or the other, the Arbitration Court shall establish the responsibilities and determine their consequences.[27]

The United Kingdom contended before the International Court of Justice that the termination of the concession was internationally unlawful on multiple grounds and that, if it otherwise were lawful to nationalize the enterprise, the amount of compensation due must be decided by the Arbitration Tribunal provided for in the concession.[28] The United Kingdom further claimed that a measure of confiscation or nationalization of a concession which is contrary to international law engages directly the international responsibility of a State "if it is the result of legislation or other action admitting of no recourse against the measure to local courts or the tribunals provided for in the concession agreement." It submitted that, in addition, the international responsibility of the State is directly engaged on the further ground of denial of justice if the right to cancel the concession is not established "to the satisfaction of the appropriate judicial tribunal (in particular to the satisfaction of the judicial tribunal provided for in the concession, if one is so specified)."[29]

Noting that there were no local remedies to exhaust in any event, since the law of Iran afforded no remedies against a law passed by the Iranian legislature, the British Memorial continued:

> Moreover, the legal remedies for a breach of the Convention of 1933 are the remedies provided for in Article 22 of the convention, namely, recourse to the Arbitration Court provided for in that Article. That legal remedy the Government of Iran has repudiated expressly and repeatedly – a repudiation which in itself constitutes the international delinquency of denial of justice. Further, Iran has

---

[27] *Ibid.*, p. 269. Article 21 of the Convention also provided in part:
   This Concession shall not be annulled by the Government and the terms therein contained shall not be altered either by general or special legislation in the future, or by administrative measures or any other acts whatever of the executive authorities.

[28] *Ibid.*, pp. 81–82.   [29] *Ibid.*, p. 122.

not only excluded arbitration as a remedy for the Company to use if the Company disputes, as it does, the legality of the expropriation. The expropriation has itself been justified in part by allegations of default or misconduct on the part of the Company, yet Iran has not called upon the Arbitration Court provided for in the Convention to examine these allegations, although this Arbitration Court certainly had exclusive jurisdiction to pronounce upon allegations of default. Instead Iran has made herself the judge in her own cause on this issue also."[30]

The United Kingdom in conclusion asked the Court to declare that Iran was under a duty to submit to arbitration within the terms of the Convention, and, alternatively, to declare, *inter alia*, that, by denying to the company "the exclusive legal remedy provided," Iran had committed "a denial of justice contrary to international law."[31]

In its Preliminary Observations, the Government of Iran replied that the concession, which, it alleged, was invalid, in any event automatically "disappeared ... in all its articles" by virtue of the nationalization, with the consequence that Articles 21 and 22 were a "dead letter."[32] It contested the alleged denial of justice, contending that a denial of justice could not arise without the "prior exhaustion of local remedies" and did not arise because of the refusal to arbitrate pursuant to Article 22.[33] Iran alternatively contended that, were Article 22 considered to remain in force, it would, because of its exclusive reliance on arbitration, oust any jurisdiction of the International Court of Justice.[34]

The United Kingdom responded that "the implication that in the present case the Anglo-Iranian Oil Company should have had recourse to the Iranian municipal courts ... is quite obviously untenable ... the Convention of 1933 provided for arbitration and ... on any view, therefore, the Company was not obliged or even permitted to have recourse to the Iranian municipal courts ..."[35] As to the alternative Iranian contention, the United Kingdom submitted that:

> It is hardly credible that, after its total rejection of arbitration, and its repudiation of the articles of the Concession Convention which provide for it, the Iranian Government should now suggest that those articles constitute a bar to the jurisdiction of the Court ... It is a novel answer to an accusation of denial of justice to say that the jurisdiction of the International Court to hear the accusation at the

---

[30] *Ibid.*, pp. 122–123 (footnotes omitted).   [31] *Ibid.*, pp. 18–19.

[32] *Ibid.*, p. 288 [authors' translation].

[33] *Ibid.*, p. 291 [authors' translation].   [34] *Ibid.*, pp. 304–305.

[35] Observations and Submissions presented by the Government of the United Kingdom of Great Britain and Northern Ireland to the Preliminary Objection lodged by the Imperial Government of Iran, *ibid.*, p. 365.

suit of a Government is ousted by the exclusive jurisdiction of that very tribunal to which access to the national has been wrongfully and unjustly denied.[36]

In oral argument, Professor Rolin, as agent for Iran, submitted that Article 22 established the competence of the arbitrators to pass upon the interpretation or application of the Convention but that it was not relevant in the type of case which was at bar. Moreover, Professor Rolin contended, Article 22 had had the same fate as the concession contract as a whole: it was annulled by the nationalization law. In these circumstances, arbitration "was not that procedure which one could consider to be the normal recourse which must be open and which was "open to the Company."[37] Rather, recourse must be had to the Iranian courts, which were entitled to pass upon the question of any compensation due to the company.[38] The agent of the United Kingdom, Sir Eric Beckett, while denying that the Iranian courts were competent to deal with that question, contended that Professor Rolin had further failed to deal with the British contention that, even if the concession had ceased to operate in its principal provisions, nevertheless the tribunal specified in Article 22 of the Convention ought to assess the compensation.[39] The remaining discussion in the course of oral argument with respect to the exhaustion of local remedies did not relate to the effect of the arbitral remedy, nor, of course, did the Court's judgment holding that it lacked jurisdiction in the case advert to this question.

Electricité de Beyrouth Company Case

In the *Electricité de Beyrouth Company* case differences arose between the Government of Lebanon and the French concessionaire. The company requested arbitration pursuant to a clause of its contract[40] which provided that

> Disputes which arise between the concessionaire and the Government concerning the execution or interpretation of the clauses of this contract shall be brought before the competent administrative jurisdiction, unless the concessionaire makes use of the right which it nevertheless reserves to submit the dispute to an Arbitral Tribunal composed of three arbitrators, one named by the Government, the other

---

[36] *Ibid.*, p. 367.   [37] *Ibid.*, p. 501 [authors' translation].

[38] The Court quoted this limited Iranian reliance on the rule of exhaustion of local remedies in these terms: "That the claim concerning the amount of the compensation due to the Anglo-Iranian Oil Company is also inadmissible, because that company has not yet exhausted the local remedies provided by Iranian Law" (*Anglo-Iranian Oil Co. case [jurisdiction]*, Judgment of July 22, 1952, *ICJ Reports 1952*, pp. 93, 99).

[39] *Ibid.*, pp. 555–556, 642.

[40] The company was the holder of five concessions in Lebanon, whose *Cahiers des Charges* (General Conditions) provided for arbitration in the terms quoted.

by the concessionaire, and the third by the two arbitrators or, failing their agreement, the Vice-President of the Conseil d'Etat of the French Republic.[41]

The Lebanese Government took no action under the arbitration clause, but sequestered the concessionary enterprises. The company renewed its request for arbitration, but the Government did not reply.

France thereupon instituted proceedings before the International Court of Justice. It noted that, in a treaty of January 24, 1948 between France and Lebanon, Lebanon had given certain relevant undertakings concerning concessions of French companies operating in Lebanon and had agreed to submit any disputes arising under the treaty to the International Court. "The refusal of the Lebanese Government to accept arbitration, as it is bound to do under the General Conditions, constitutes a further violation of the obligations it had assumed" under the treaty, "and this violation constitutes a culminating point of all the measures which it has taken in contravention of the Instruments of Concession ... The Company is now denied recourse to the tribunal to which it is entitled under its contract." France claimed that the breach of the concessionary contract and "the denial of justice involved in the Lebanese Government's refusal to accept arbitration provided for" by the contract are "by reason of the treaty obligations cited ... violations of international law for which the Government of the Lebanese Republic must bear responsibility."[42] Even absent the treaty, it amounted to an internationally illegal act:

> in refusing arbitration, the Lebanese Government violated ... the contract and consequently the treaty ...; the denial of justice thus committed, was, moreover, of itself, an internationally illegal act, even in the absence of such a treaty.[43]

The only indication of the position taken by Lebanon is a reference in the French Memorial to the fact that, in the course of diplomatic correspondence, the Lebanese Government had maintained that arbitration could not take place since there was no justiciable dispute, and this for the reason that the granting authority could by virtue of its sovereign powers unilaterally alter concessionary provisions.[44]

After the submission of the French Application and Memorial, and before the Lebanese Government had replied, the dispute was settled by agreement between the two Governments, and the case was removed from the Court's list.[45]

---

[41] *ICJ Pleadings*, "Electricité de Beyrouth" Company case (France v. Lebanon), p. 57 [authors' translation].

[42] *Ibid.*, p. 14.   [43] *Ibid.*, p. 58 [authors' translation].   [44] *Ibid.*, p. 48.

[45] "Electricité de Beyrouth" Company case, Order of July 29, 1954, *ICJ Reports 1954*, pp. 107–108.

Case Concerning the Compagnie du Port, des Quais et des Entrepôts de Beyrouth and the Société Radio-Orient

The facts in the *Compagnie du Port* case resemble those in the *Electricité de Beyrouth Company* case. The Compagnie du Port and the Société Radio-Orient were parties to concession contracts with the Lebanese Government, the concession of the former containing the following provision for arbitration:

> Any disputes that may arise between the *Compagnie du Port de Beyrouth* and the Administration concerning the execution or interpretation of the clause of the Company's concessionary instruments shall be submitted to the competent administrative jurisdictions, unless the concessionary Company exercises the right which it reserves to itself, nevertheless, to submit the dispute to an arbitration commission composed of three arbitrators, one appointed by the Government, another by the concessionaire and the third by the former two or failing agreement between them, by the Vice-President of the *Conseil d'Etat* of the French Republic.[46]

The Franco-Lebanese Treaty of January 24, 1948 covered these concessions. In 1956, the Lebanese Government adopted a law providing that companies which had enjoyed certain tax exemptions should, as from January 1, 1952, be subject to income and other taxes. The Compagnie du Port and the Société Radio-Orient were among such companies. After unproductive negotiations, the Compagnie du Port requested arbitration. The Lebanese Government gave no positive reply, leading the French Government to institute proceedings before the International Court of Justice.

France claimed that the infringements of the concessionary contracts of the two companies and, so far as the Compagnie du Port was concerned, the failure of the Lebanese Government to accept arbitration were, by reason of the Treaty of 1948, violations of international law for which the Lebanese Government was responsible.[47] It further argued that Lebanon, by refusing to settle its differences with the Compagnie du Port by arbitration as prescribed by the concession contract, was "guilty of a denial of justice, thus engaging its international responsibility."[48]

Lebanon responded that the French application should be rejected on the ground that there had been a failure to exhaust local remedies.[49] Lebanon contended that, under Lebanese law, recourse existed in an instance in which one contracting party refused to go to arbitration. The Compagnie du Port,

---

[46] *ICJ Pleadings*, Case Concerning the *Compagnie du Port, des Quais et des Entrepôts de Beyrouth and the Société Radio-Orient (France v. Lebanon)*, p. 7.
[47] *Ibid.*, p. 9.   [48] *Ibid.*, p. 39 [authors' translation].   [49] *Ibid.*, p. 67.

it maintained, accordingly should have taken the case to the Lebanese courts in accordance with the Lebanese Code of Civil Procedure. But the company had neither sought a remedy against the refusal to arbitrate nor had it exhausted the remedies open to it for contesting the taxes. Lebanon concluded that: "One could not conceive of a case in which the rule of exhaustion of local remedies was more completely and more deliberately ignored" than the present.[50]

France rejected the Lebanese contentions on two main grounds. First, it contended that the rule of exhaustion of local remedies could have no application to a claim by France that Lebanon was in breach of treaty obligations it owed to France.[51] Second, it maintained that arbitration was an incontestable right of the Compagnie du Port, and a vital element of the contract. The result of the company's opting for arbitration, it argued, citing the Swiss argument in the *Losinger* case, was "to withdraw the dispute definitively from any Lebanese jurisdiction. In according the Company this right, the Lebanese Government had renounced in advance requiring the Company to apply to its courts ... As soon as the Company ... requested arbitration of any dispute whatsoever, it had fulfilled the conditions necessary to prevent application of the rule of exhaustion of local remedies." Thus, "once the Company had chosen arbitration, at no point nor on any pretext could the dispute be submitted to the ordinary courts."[52] The question was not whether Lebanese law allowed the State to be compelled to arbitrate against its will, although, in any event, the law did not. Rather, the point was that recourse to arbitration withdrew the dispute from Lebanese jurisdiction; and it would be an impairment of the company's contractual rights to allow the Lebanese courts to pass upon issues which the company had declined to submit to them because of Lebanon's failure to abide by the arbitration clause.[53]

The case was settled by the two Governments before the stage of oral argument.[54]

Commentary

The foregoing cases are of great interest in a number of respects. Three of the leading Western trading and capital-exporting States, whose contributions to the growth of customary and conventional law are notable, took the position

---

[50] *Ibid.*, p. 70 [authors' translation].   [51] *Ibid.*, p. 89.   [52] *Ibid.*, pp. 91–92 [authors' translation].
[53] *Ibid.*, p. 93.
[54] Case concerning the *Compagnie du Port, des Quais et des Entrepôts de Beyrouth and the Société Radio-Orient (France v. Lebanon)*, Order of August 31, 1960, *ICJ Reports* 1960, p. 5.

that arbitration was the exclusive remedy, pursuance of which within the terms of the arbitration clause satisfied the rule of exhaustion of local remedies. Three States which, in current international parlance, at any rate, tend in matters economic and legal to align themselves with the non-aligned, took the position that the rule of exhaustion of local remedies was not discharged by the concessionaire's request for arbitration.

The *Losinger* case is of particular interest in its exposition of a key problem: whether the exhaustion of the arbitral remedy itself entails recourse to the courts of the contracting State. Switzerland maintained that the arbitration clause was designed to exclude entirely recourse to Yugoslav courts. Switzerland so claimed despite the fact that the arbitration clause provided that: "The award of the arbitrators or of the umpire shall be rendered in Yugoslavia" – a provision which it might be argued subjects procedural aspects of the arbitration to Yugoslav law. The alleged intention of the parties to withdraw their disputes wholly from the cognizance of Yugoslav courts found support in the provisions for selection of the umpire and for the definitive character of the award,[55] but was weakened by the provision that the arbitration should take place in Yugoslavia.

Yugoslavia argued strongly that, since the contract was governed by Yugoslav law, exhaustion of the arbitral remedy required pursuit of those Yugoslav remedies which pertained to enforcement of an agreement to arbitrate. While, in the circumstances, this argument had a disingenuous ring, it nevertheless has considerable theoretical cogency. It is of equal interest that Yugoslavia did not argue either that cancellation of the1 contract of itself rendered the arbitral remedy nugatory,[56] or that Losinger & Co. was bound to exhaust those local remedies which did not pertain to invocation of the arbitral process itself.

---

[55] In the case of the *Société Commerciale de Belgique*, PCIJ, Series A/B, No. 78, Belgium sought the Court's declaration that all the provisions of two arbitral awards rendered in proceedings between the Société Commerciale and Greece were binding upon the Greek Government without reservation. The awards were rendered pursuant to an arbitration clause which provided for arbitration of "all disputes of every kind," for ultimate appointment of an umpire by "the President of the International Court of Arbitration at The Hague," and for the final character of the award. (At p. 166.) The Court held that, "since the arbitral awards ... are, according to the arbitration clause under which they were made, 'final and without appeal,' and since the Court has received no mandate from the Parties in regard to them, it can neither confirm nor annul them either wholly or in part." (At p. 174.) In speaking of "definitive and obligatory character of the arbitral awards," it further held that: "If the awards are definitive and obligatory, it is certain that the Greek Government is bound to execute them and to do so as they stand." (At p. 176.)

[56] Yugoslavia did maintain before the umpire that "the cancellation of the contract resulted in cancellation of the arbitration clause and thus did away with the right to have recourse to arbitration"; this submission was rejected by the umpire. Interlocutory Award of the Umpire, the *Losinger & Co.* case,

The Swiss argument that, since it was Yugoslavia which claimed that the arbitration clause was invalid, the burden of bringing an action in the Yugoslav courts to establish this contention rested on Yugoslavia, was a singular attempt to shift the burden of exhausting local remedies from the alien to the contracting State. Losinger & Co. sought to rely on the validity of the agreement to arbitrate and, if any action in the Yugoslav courts to establish the validity of the arbitral agreement was maintainable, the burden of bringing it clearly was Losinger's.

The *Anglo-Iranian Oil Company* case in some respects presents fewer difficulties. Here the comprehensiveness of the obligation to arbitrate and the clear divorce of the arbitral remedy from Iranian municipal law, substantive and procedural, would have made much less persuasive any claim that recourse must be had to Iranian procedures to enforce the obligation to arbitrate. In fact, Iran made no such claim, while the United Kingdom maintained that "the Company was not obliged or even permitted to have recourse to the Iranian municipal courts . . ."[57] Iran rather took the position that annulment of the concession entailed abrogation of any obligation to arbitrate under the concession. This contention at any rate had the virtue of simplicity. Such legal merit as it might have had was dependent on the answer given to what Professors Sohn and Baxter describe as "the larger question of the extent to which a State may, without engaging its responsibility, alter the law applicable to contracts or concessions."[58] In the authors' view, on the facts of the Anglo-Iranian Oil Company case (where "the law applicable" to the contract would not seem to have been Iranian law), the obligation to arbitrate disputes arising under the concession remained valid. If so, it is submitted that, in view both of the comprehensive character of the obligation to arbitrate and the explicit subjection of the arbitral process to international law, procedural and substantive,[59] exhaustion of the arbitral remedy, without any reference to Iranian procedures, would have been sufficient to satisfy the rule of exhaustion of local remedies.

Iran did not contend that the British claim as a whole could not be maintained because of the failure of the Anglo-Iranian Oil Company to

---

PCIJ, Series C, No. 78, pp. 109–111. Yugoslavia did not, however, rely on this argument before the Permanent Court of International Justice.

[57] See the quotation at note 36 above. The Comment on the Preliminary Draft of a Convention on the Settlement of Investment Disputes between States and Nationals of Other States, referred to above at note 6, is to the effect that a mutual intent to exclude remedies other than arbitration would oblige a municipal court to dismiss a claim brought before it.

[58] Sohn and Baxter, *Convention on the International Responsibility of States for Injuries to Aliens,* Draft No. 12 with Explanatory Notes, 1961, p. 165.

[59] See Art. 22 of the Convention, Secs. (E) and (F), quoted above.

exhaust local remedies. The case was plainly one in which there were no local remedies to exhaust; Iran, far from suggesting that there were local remedies against nationalization, confined itself to the claim that the company should have had recourse to Iranian courts only on the question of any compensation due to the company in respect of its claims and the counter-claims of the Government. For its part, the United Kingdom, while contending that the Convention as a whole could not be legally annulled, maintained that in any event "the exclusive legal remedy" provided for in Article 22 of the Convention remained in force and that Iran "committed a denial of justice contrary to international law" in denying the company that remedy, which, in any event, was the only legal procedure for determining the compensation due to the company.[60]

The *Electricité de Beyrouth Company* case is of interest insofar as France maintained that, even apart from treaty obligations, the refusal of the Lebanese Government to arbitrate its dispute with the company constituted a "denial of justice ... an internationally illegal act." By bringing an international claim against Lebanon for what it alleged to be an act in violation of international law, France by necessary implication took the position that the rule of exhaustion of local remedies had been satisfied, presumably by the company's demand for arbitration. Lebanon apparently took a position resembling that of Iran in the *Anglo-Iranian Oil Company* case, namely that, by virtue of its sovereign powers, it could rid itself of any obligation to arbitrate.[61] That contention once more raised "the larger question of the extent to which a State may, without engaging its responsibility, alter the law applicable to contracts or concessions,"[62] in an instance where the law applicable might be claimed to have been Lebanese. The international references which characterize the arbitration clause of the Anglo-Iranian Convention of 1933 were not to be found in the concession of the Electricité de Beyrouth Company. The sole proviso which tended to withdraw the contract from Lebanese jurisdiction was that for the appointment of the umpire by the Vice-President of the French *Conseil d'Etat* (that is, appointment by an official of the country of which the concessionaire was a national).

The *Compagnie du Port* case recalls the *Losinger* case. France alleged a denial of justice because of Lebanon's refusal to arbitrate; Lebanon claimed a failure to exhaust local remedies pertaining both to enforcement of the arbitral process and to the validity of the taxes imposed. Like Switzerland, France maintained that the arbitration agreement withdrew the dispute definitively

---

[60] See above.   [61] See note 44 above.
[62] Sohn and Baxter, *Convention on International Responsibility*.

from the jurisdiction of the contracting State. Like Yugoslavia, Lebanon maintained that the alien contractor should have litigated the State's refusal to arbitrate in the State's municipal courts. It so claimed in a case where, as in the *Electricité de Beyrouth Company* case, the obligation to arbitrate was not clearly subjected to a law other than that of the contracting State.

Conclusions

What conclusions are suggested by the Bank's analysis and the considerations which State practice brings to light?

As the Report of the Executive Directors states:

> It may be presumed that when a State and an investor agree to have recourse to arbitration, and do not reserve the right to have recourse to other remedies or require the prior exhaustion of other remedies, the intention of the parties is to have recourse to arbitration to the exclusion of any other remedy.[63]

However, as the argumentation in the *Losinger* and *Compagnie du Port* case suggests, the decisive factor may be not simply the intention of the parties to have recourse to arbitration only; it may and probably should be whether the arbitration proceedings are or are not subject to the law of the contracting State. While proceedings pursuant to an arbitration clause such as the characteristic clause summarized above[64] would not seem to be subject to the contracting State's municipal law, the arbitration clauses of certain agreements between States and aliens stipulate that any arbitration shall be governed by the arbitration law of the contracting State,[65] and in other agreements the same intention may be implied. In such a case, the reasonable rule would seem to be that the alien must exhaust those remedies which pertain to the enforcement of the obligation to arbitrate or, where an award has been rendered, to enforcement or interpretation of the award itself. Other remedies unrelated to the arbitral process, however, need not be exhausted.

Conversely, where the arbitral process is not governed by the municipal law of the contracting State, then no municipal remedies of the contracting

---

[63] Note 4 above.   [64] See "A Characteristic Arbitration Clause" above.

[65] For example, a contract of October 23, 1964, between the Government of the Bahama Islands and Home Lines, Inc., a Panamanian corporation, provides for arbitration of disputes, the sole arbitrator, who shall hold or have held high judicial office in the United Kingdom or Canada, being named by the parties or ultimately by the Supreme Court of the Bahama Islands. Art. 26 (2) provides that:

> Either party may demand that a dispute or claim as set forth in the preceding paragraph be made the subject of arbitration in accordance with the provisions of the Arbitration Act of the Bahama Islands or any statutory modification or re-enactment thereof for the time being in force. (unpublished).

State need be exhausted;[66] arbitration within the four corners of the agreement to arbitrate is the sole remedy which the alien must exhaust.

It is further submitted that, while arbitral proceedings between the contracting State and the alien are in progress, an international claim based on violation of the rights of the alien is not maintainable by the State of which the alien is a national, on the ground that the arbitral remedy has not been exhausted, it being the equivalent of local remedies for this purpose.[67]

In referring to the "well-established rule of customary international law" that local remedies must be exhausted before international proceedings may be instituted, the International Court of Justice noted that "it has been considered necessary that the State where the violation occurred should have an opportunity to redress it by its own means, within the framework of its own domestic legal system."[68] The rule thus has no application to the question of whether an alien is required to exhaust the remedies of a forum other than that of the contracting State before the State of which he is a

---

[66] Professors Sohn and Baxter contend, however, that:

> If a procedure exists under the law of the responsible State whereby the alien may through action before the courts either compel resort to the arbitral machinery provided under the agreement, or secure judicial enforcement of the decision of the Arbitral Tribunal against a State not complying with the award, or seek review of the propriety of the decision of the Arbitral Tribunal, there can be little doubt that the alien must exhaust his judicial as well as arbitral remedy. The obligation of seeking judicial redress may thus exist even though the contract or concession states that the special form of arbitration provided is the exclusive remedy as to all disputes arising under the agreement. If, however, the procedure stipulated in the contract or concession does not under the law of the responsible State lend itself to judicial enforcement or review, it may constitute the sole available remedy, especially if the contract or concession itself has the status of a law of the respondent State as well as that of an agreement to which that State is a party. (*Convention on International Responsibility*, pp. 164–165).

It is submitted that Professors Sohn and Baxter, in this passage, fail to distinguish between arbitral remedies governed by municipal law and those governed by a law other than the municipal law of the contracting State. As noted above, it is believed that the latter type of arbitral process does not require the exhaustion of any remedies of the contracting State. See in support of this conclusion, Bourquin, "Arbitration and Economic Development Agreements," *The Business Lawyer* (1960), 15, pp. 860–872, at pp. 870–871. See also Hyde, "Economic Development Agreements," Hague Academy *Recueil des Cours* (1962), 105, pp. 271–374, at p. 352; Young, "Remedies of Private Claimants Against Foreign States," *Proceedings of the 1961 Institute on Private Investments Abroad* (1961), pp. 45–100, at p. 57; and American Branch of the International Law Association, Report of the Committee on Nationalization of Property, *Proceedings and Committee Reports 1957–1958*, pp. 61–85, at p. 75, note 25.

[67] Professors Sohn and Baxter (*Convention on International Responsibility*) describe arbitration, including that under a contract such as the Iranian Consortium Agreement, as a "local remedy," a description which appears accurate when applied to an arbitration whose procedure is governed by the law of the contracting State. It may be questioned whether an arbitration in which the umpire is foreign and internationally appointed, which takes place abroad, and applies another law, substantively or procedurally, or both, is a "local remedy."

[68] *Interhandel Case, Judgment of March 21, 1959, ICJ Reports 1959*, pp. 6, 27. See also Bagge, "Intervention on the Ground of Damage Caused to Nationals, with Particular Reference to Exhaustion of Local Remedies and the Rights of Shareholders," *British Year Book of International Law* (1958), 34, p. 169.

national may maintain an international claim on his behalf. However, as noted above, the law governing the procedure of an arbitration may well be that of another jurisdiction, for example, Switzerland.[69] The law of that forum will typically contain remedies pertaining to the arbitral process. A question which possibly may merit consideration is whether, in such a case, the alien should be required to exhaust those remedies before an international claim may be maintained on his behalf.[70]

It may finally be noted that the case in which two States agree to arbitrate is distinct from the subject of this article. The rule applicable to such treaties seems to be that, where States agree in a claims convention that the rule of exhaustion of local remedies shall not bar any claim, their agreement is effective to waive the rule. In the absence of a clear provision in the treaty, such waiver may sometimes be inferred. However, where there is not a claims convention but rather a general agreement to arbitrate disputes which may arise in the future, such an agreement is not normally viewed as waiving the rule.[71]

---

[69] Cf. *Sapphire International Petroleums Limited v. National Iranian Oil Company* (1963). The whole of the award in this arbitration is unpublished, but extracts from it – unrelated to the issue discussed here – have been quoted, *inter alia*, by Lalive, "Contracts between a State or a State Agency and a Foreign Company," *International and Comparative Law Quarterly* (1964), 13, pp. 987–1021, at pp. 1011–1021. The umpire in the Sapphire case held that the arbitration proceedings were governed by the procedural law of the Canton of Vaud and were "subject to the judicial sovereignty of Vaud" [authors' translation]. For a critique of the umpire's holding, see Suratgar, "The Sapphire Arbitration Award, The Procedural Aspects: A Report and a Critique," *Columbia Journal of Transnational Law* (1965), 3, pp. 153, 184–185, 198–203.

[70] A negative answer to that question is suggested by the award in *Saudi Arabia v. Arabian American Oil Company (Aramco)* (1958) 27 *ILR* 117, 155–156, where the tribunal held that the law of Geneva, the tribunal's seat, could not be applied as the procedural law of the arbitration, on the ground of the jurisdictional immunity of States. See to the same effect Bourquin, "Economic Development Aagreements" at 870–871. In contrast with the Sapphire case, the tribunal in the Aramco case held that the law governing the procedure of the arbitration was international law. Whether the law of another State, or international law, is held to govern the procedure of the arbitration, the result is the same for the question under analysis: in neither case need any local remedies, pertaining to arbitration or otherwise, be exhausted if the contracting State fails to arbitrate in accordance with its contractual obligation.

[71] Cf. Law, *The Local Remedies Rule in International Law* (Geneva and Paris, 1961), pp. 93–98 and the sources there cited. See also Garcia Amador, "International Responsibility, Third Report by F. V. Garcia Amador, Special Rapporteur," *ILC Yearbook* (II) (1958), pp. 59–60, 72.

11

Arbitration and the Exhaustion of Local Remedies Revisited

ϾϽ

Some twenty years ago, Dr. J. Gillis Wetter and the author wrote an article analyzing, particularly in the light of litigation before the International Court of Justice, whether:

> Where a State and an alien agree in a contract to arbitrate disputes relating to the contract, in terms which indicate that arbitration is to be the exclusive remedy, need the alien exhaust any other remedy before an international claim may be presented relating to a dispute which falls within the scope of the arbitration clause?[1]

After extended analysis of the arguments of the parties in *The Losinger & Co.* case,[2] the *Anglo-Iranian Oil Company* case,[3] the *Electricité de Beyrouth Company* case,[4] and the case concerning the *Compagnie du Port, des Quais et des Entrepôts de Beyrouth and the Société Radio-Orient*,[5] as well as the pertinent provision and preparatory work of the World Bank's Convention on the Settlement of Investment Disputes between States and Nationals of Other States,[6] it was concluded that, as the Report of the Bank's Executive Directors on the ICSID Convention stated:

> It may be presumed that when a State and an investor agree to have recourse to arbitration, and do not reserve the right to have recourse to other remedies or require the prior exhaustion of other remedies, the intention of the parties is to have recourse to arbitration to the exclusion of any other remedy.[7]

First published in *The International Lawyer* (Winter, 1989), 23, 4. Copyright 1989 American Bar Association, reprinted by permission.

[1] S.M. Schwebel and J.G. Wetter, "Arbitration and the Exhaustion of Local Remedies," *American Journal of International Law* (1966), 60, p. 484, and Chapter 10, this volume.

[2] *PCIJ*, Series C, No. 78, p. 7 (1935).

[3] *ICJ Pleadings, Anglo-Iranian Oil Co. Case (United Kingdom v. Iran)*, p. 8 (1951).

[4] *ICJ Pleadings, "Electricité de Beyrouth" Company Case (France v. Lebanon)*, p. 9 (1953).

[5] *ICJ Pleadings, Case Concerning the Compagnie du Port, des Quais et des Entrepôts de Beyrouth and the Société Radio-Orient (France v. Lebanon)*, p. 4 (1959).

[6] Convention on the Settlement of Investment Disputes between States and Nationals of Other States, 17 UST 1270, TIAS No. 6090, 575 UNTS 159 (1965).

[7] Schwebel and Wetter, "Arbitration and Local Remedies," p. 499.

It was further concluded by the authors that:

> However, as the argumentation in the *Losinger* and *Compagnie du Port* cases suggests, the decisive factor may be not simply the intention of the parties to have recourse to arbitration only; it may and probably should be whether the arbitration proceedings are or are not subject to the law of the contracting State. While proceedings pursuant to [a typical international] arbitration clause ... would not seem to be subject to the contracting State's municipal law, the arbitration clauses of certain agreements between States and aliens stipulate that any arbitration shall be governed by the arbitration law of the contracting State, and in other agreements the same intention may be implied. In such a case, the reasonable rule would seem to be that the alien must exhaust those remedies which pertain to the enforcement of the obligation to arbitrate or, where an award has been rendered, to enforcement or interpretation of the award itself. Other remedies unrelated to the arbitral process, however, need not be exhausted.
>
> Conversely, where the arbitral process is not governed by the municipal law of the contracting State, then no municipal remedies of the contracting State need be exhausted; arbitration within the four corners of the agreement to arbitrate is the sole remedy which the alien must exhaust.[8]

In none of the four cases before the Permanent Court of International Justice and the International Court of Justice just referred to, in which the issue under discussion was extensively argued, was a judgment rendered; all four cases were settled.

However, in 1988 the International Court of Justice rendered an advisory opinion on the *Applicability of the Obligation to Arbitrate under Section 21 of the United Nations Headquarters Agreement of 26 June 1947.*[9] That opinion was essentially concerned with whether there existed a dispute between the United Nations and the United States giving rise to an obligation of the United States, as party to the Headquarters Agreement with the United Nations,[10] to enter into arbitration in accordance with Section 21 of that Agreement. Section 21 provides:

> Any dispute between the United Nations and the United States concerning the interpretation or application of this agreement or of any supplemental agreement, which is not settled by negotiation or other agreed mode of settlement, shall be referred for final decision to a tribunal of three arbitrators, one to be named by the Secretary-General, one to be named by the Secretary of State of the United States, and the third to be chosen by the two, or, if they should fail to agree upon a third, then by the President of the International Court of Justice.[11]

---

[8] *Ibid.*   [9] *ICJ Reports 1988*, p. 12
[10] 61 Stat. 3416, TIAS No. 1676; 12 Bevans 956; 11 UNTS 11 (1947).
[11] *Ibid.*

The Secretary-General of the United Nations maintained that a dispute did exist between the United Nations and the United States, in view of the enactment into the law of the United States of the "Anti-Terrorism Act of 1987," which provides that:

It shall be unlawful ... notwithstanding any provision of law to the contrary, to establish or maintain an office, headquarters, premises, or other facilities or establishments within the jurisdiction of the United States at the behest or direction of, or with funds provided by the Palestine Liberation Organization ...[12]

The Secretary-General further invoked as evidencing the existence of a dispute the initiation by the Attorney-General of the United States of legal action in pursuance of the Act to close the office of the PLO Observer Mission to the United Nations.

The United States maintained that a dispute requiring arbitration did not then exist, since the issue of whether the office of the PLO Observer Mission was to be closed in pursuance of the Anti-Terrorism Act had been submitted to the United States District Court for the Southern District of New York. The United States had informed the Secretary-General that

The United States will take no action to close the Mission pending a decision in that litigation. Since the matter is still pending in our courts, we do not believe arbitration would be appropriate or timely.[13]

In substance, the United States appeared to argue that the enactment of legislation providing for closure of PLO offices within the jurisdiction of the United States, and action by the Attorney-General to implement his reading of the Anti-Terrorism Act which required the closure of the office of the PLO Observer Mission to the United Nations, and his consequent seeking of an injunction to that end, were not sufficient of themselves to trigger obligations under the dispute settlement mechanism of the Headquarters Agreement. The inference of the United States position was that a holding by the competent United States court that the Act did require closure would activate the United States obligation to arbitrate.

In the event, Judge Edmund Palmieri of the United States District Court for the Southern District of New York held that the Act was not to be interpreted as embracing the office of the PLO Observer Mission to the United Nations, since such application of the Act would place the United States in breach of its treaty obligations under the Headquarters Agreement, a

---

[12] Title X of the Foreign Relations Authorization Act, Fiscal Years 1988 and 1989.
[13] *ICJ Reports 1988*, p. 29.

position which could not be sustained in the absence of demonstration of a clear intention of the Congress to override the international obligations of the United States.[14]

The International Court of Justice earlier had unanimously expressed the opinion:

> that the United States of America, as a party to the Agreement between the United Nations and the United States of America regarding the Headquarters of the United Nations of 26 June 1947, is under an obligation, in accordance with section 21 of that Agreement, to enter into arbitration for the settlement of the dispute between itself and the United Nations.[15]

In the course of so concluding, the Court declared:

> The Court must further point out that the alleged dispute relates solely to what the United Nations considers to be its rights under the Headquarters Agreement. The purpose of the arbitration procedure envisaged by that Agreement is precisely the settlement of such disputes as may arise between the Organization and the host country without any prior recourse to municipal courts, and it would be against both the letter and the spirit of the Agreement for the implementation of that procedure to be subjected to such prior recourse. It is evident that a provision of the nature of section 21 of the Headquarters Agreement cannot require the exhaustion of local remedies as a condition of its implementation.[16]

In a Separate Opinion, the author stated that among the "restatements of legal principle" made by the Court with which he agreed was that: "It is accepted that a provision of a treaty (or a contract) prescribing the international arbitration of any dispute arising thereunder does not require, as a prerequisite for its implementation, the exhaustion of local remedies."[17]

While an international treaty provision for arbitration such as that contained in the Headquarters Agreement is not to be equated with an arbitral clause of a contract between a State or State agency and an alien, and still less with that of an international commercial contract between two private parties, nevertheless it is believed that – in the Court's words – "it would be against both the letter and the spirit" of such arbitral agreements for the implementation of their arbitral obligations "to be subjected to such prior recourse" as that entailed by the exhaustion of local remedies (at any rate, if the particular arbitral process is not governed by the law of the contracting State which requires such exhaustion). The Court's conclusion that "it is evident that a provision of the nature of section 21 of the Headquarters

---

[14] *United States of America v. the Palestine Liberation Organization, et. al., International Legal Materials,* Volume XXVII, No. 4 (July, 1988), p. 1056.

[15] *ICJ Reports 1988,* p. 35.   [16] *Ibid.,* p. 29.   [17] *Ibid.,* pp. 42–43.

Agreement cannot require the exhaustion of local remedies as a condition of its implementation"[18] is not only sound but susceptible of wider application. When parties provide for international arbitration, they may not be presumed or assumed to contract for or to contemplate the prior exhaustion of local remedies in a contracting State or in the State of the nationality of one of the parties, for to require such exhaustion generally would or could mean defeating the purpose, or a purpose, of provision for international arbitration. Accordingly, it is believed that it is correct to state that: "It is accepted that a provision of a treaty (or contract) prescribing the international arbitration of any dispute arising thereunder does not require, as a prerequisite for its implementation, the exhaustion of local remedies."[19]

The Court's advisory opinion in the *Obligation to Arbitrate* case thus may be viewed as going some way towards answering the question raised at the outset of this article. While that question was left unanswered by four previous cases in the Court, which did not reach judgments on the merits, and while the circumstances of the *Obligation to Arbitrate* case are distinguishable from that addressed in that question and those four cases, nevertheless in substance a significant measure of extrapolation is warranted.

It may be added that there also sits in The Hague these days as there has since 1981 the Iran–United States Claims Tribunal, which has made its distinctive contribution to resolution of the question under discussion. From the outset of its work, the Tribunal has interpreted the Declaration of the Government of the Democratic and Popular Republic of Algeria concerning the Settlement of Claims by the Government of the United States of America and the Islamic Republic of Iran of January 19, 1981 as not conditioning the jurisdiction of that arbitral Tribunal on the exhaustion of local remedies.[20] It also has held that: "The mere availability of a local remedy, whether judicial or otherwise, cannot preclude the Tribunal from jurisdiction."[21]

It should finally be noted that, at its September 1989 session in Santiago de Compostela, Spain, the Institut de Droit International adopted a resolution on "Arbitration between States, State Enterprises, or State entities, and foreign enterprises," Article 8 of which provides: "A requirement of exhaustion of local remedies as a condition of implementation of an obligation to arbitrate is not admissible unless the arbitration agreement provides otherwise."[22]

---

[18] *Ibid.*, p. 29.   [19] *Ibid.*, pp. 42–43.

[20] See *Amoco Iran Oil Company v. Islamic Republic of Iran*, 1 Iran–US CTR 493, and *Amoco International Finance Corporation v. Islamic Republic of Iran*, 15 Iran–US CTR 189.

[21] *Rexnord Inc. v. Islamic Republic of Iran*, 2 Iran–US CTR 10.

[22] The text of the resolution is published in Institut de Droit International, *Annuaire*, 63, Part II (1989), p. 330.

12

Some Aspects of International Law in Arbitration Between States and Aliens

ოვ

Introduction

As an international lawyer who has had the good fortune to grapple with the body of international law in a number of its extensions – as a student, teacher, lawyer at the bar and in the State Department, member of the United Nations International Law Commission, and most lately, in a judicial and an arbitral capacity – I have been recurrently struck over some thirty-five years by the interplay between principles of public international law and the practice of international arbitration. Naturally international law is intertwined with arbitration between States, for that is so much of the stuff it is made of. But it is also involved in international commercial arbitration – not, typically, in arbitration between two private parties, but in arbitration between States and aliens.

That measure of involvement is important in a field which is important. How important is the field is indicated by the number of arbitration cases on the docket at any one time of the Court of the International Chamber of Commerce (ICC). The ICC these years has a few hundred cases in progress at any one time, and, of those, a strikingly large percentage – on the order of a quarter, I understand – is between States or State agencies on the one hand, and aliens on the other. These cases are among the largest and most complex of those which the ICC handles. Moreover, there are not infrequent, and important, *ad hoc* arbitrations between States and aliens. Furthermore, there are the very large numbers of arbitrations between States and aliens which in form or fact – more often form than fact – take place under intergovernmental auspices, pursuant to treaty or diplomatic espousal. Such cases in the nineteenth and twentieth centuries cumulatively run into thousands, indeed some tens of thousands. Their current exemplar is the Iran–United States Claims Tribunal, which sits in The Hague, a center for the pursuit of the arbitral settlement of international disputes since 1899.

I propose to illustrate the influence of principles of international law in arbitration between States and aliens in seven of its aspects, with examples which are illustrative rather than exhaustive. I shall consider (1) the authority of an Arbitral Tribunal to decide upon its jurisdiction; (2) the severability of an arbitration clause from the agreement which contains it; (3) whether the failure to exhaust local remedies may be persuasively pleaded as a bar to the invocation of arbitration; (4) whether a plea of sovereign immunity as a bar to arbitration is tenable; (5) whether a State that refuses to carry out a commitment to arbitrate thereby commits a denial of justice under international law; (6) whether a truncated Arbitral Tribunal possesses the authority to render a binding arbitral award; and (7) whether the parties may plead international law in such an arbitration and whether the tribunal may apply international law.

The Authority of an Arbitral Tribunal to Decide upon its Jurisdiction

The authority of an international court to decide upon its jurisdiction is a matter – not a question – which has attracted exceptional interest of late. It is the subject not only of learned articles and notes in legal journals but less learned articles in the press. In any event, it is an established principle of international law.

Thus the International Court of Justice in the *Nottebohm* case[1] held that:

> Since the *Alabama* case, it has been generally recognized, following the earlier precedents, that, in the absence of any agreement to the contrary, an international tribunal has the right to decide as to its own jurisdiction and has the power to interpret for this purpose the instruments which govern that jurisdiction.[2]

The Court referred to the recognition of that principle in The Hague Convention of 1899. The Convention's rapporteur described that principle as being "of the very essence of the arbitral function and one of the inherent requirements for the exercise of this function." The Court added that this "principle ... is accepted by general international law in the matter of arbitration."[3]

The International Court of Justice has made a number of other holdings in this vein. What is instructive for our purposes is, so have Arbitral Tribunals

---

[1] *ICJ Reports 1953*, p. 111.   [2] *Ibid.*, p. 119.   [3] *Ibid.*

sitting between States and aliens. Thus, the Tribunal in *Saudi Arabia v. Arabian American Oil Company* (Aramco)[4] held:

> The Arbitration Tribunal fully accepts the rule which authorizes it to be the judge of its own competence and to interpret the *compromis*, as expressed in Article 11 of the Draft Convention on Arbitral Procedure adopted by the International Law Commission at its fifth session.[5]

It will be observed that this Arbitral Tribunal, in fully accepting the rule that an international tribunal has the right to decide upon its own jurisdiction, had recourse to a Draft Convention on Arbitral Procedure designed to regulate arbitrations between States, which had been prepared by a body of experts nominated by States and elected by the United Nations General Assembly. The mass of the authorities on which that Draft Convention relies is very largely that of arbitrations between States. Nevertheless, the Aramco Tribunal had no difficulty in resorting to this source of public international law as the source of its authority. Similarly, in *Topco v. Libya*,[6] the sole arbitrator confirmed his entitlement to rule upon his jurisdiction by the authority of "a traditional rule followed by international case law and unanimously recognized by the writings of legal scholars."[7]

This public international law on competence to decide upon competence is reflected in legislation, international and national. The Convention on the Settlement of Investment Disputes between States and Nationals of Other States (the ICSID Convention) provides that: "The tribunal shall be the judge of its own competence."[8]

The Rules of the Court of Arbitration of the International Chamber of Commerce provide that "any decision as to the arbitrator's jurisdiction shall be taken by the arbitrator himself."[9]

The United Nations Commission on International Trade Law (UNCITRAL) Rules similarly provide that: "The Arbitral Tribunal shall have the power to rule on objections that it has no jurisdiction."[10]

The European Convention on International Commercial Arbitration articulates the principle in the following terms:

> Subject to any subsequent judicial control provided for under the *lex fori*, the arbitrator whose jurisdiction is called in question shall be entitled to proceed with the arbitration, to rule on his own jurisdiction and to decide upon the existence or the validity of the Arbitration Agreement or of the contract of which the Agreement forms part.[11]

---

[4] *International Law Reports* (1963), Volume 27, p. 146. [5] *Ibid.*
[6] *International Law Reports* (1979), Volume 53, p. 404.
[7] *Ibid.*, p. 404. [8] Article 41. [9] Article 8.3. [10] Article 21 (1). [11] Article 5 (3).

Thus, the possibility of judicial control of the arbitrator is reserved, a possibility which may reflect the common-law rule that, while the arbitrator could pass upon his jurisdiction, that issue could finally be decided by a court. On the whole, however, national legislation, even in common-law countries, today generally accepts the international legal rule that an arbitrator is competent to determine his jurisdiction. The fact that the decision of the arbitrator as to his jurisdiction is subject to review by courts where enforcement of the award may be sought, and sometimes by the courts of the place of arbitration under their domestic law, does not deprive the arbitrator of his authority to decide on his jurisdiction, any more than the fact that a decision of a lower court is subject to review by a higher court denies the competence of the lower court to pass upon its own jurisdiction.

The Severability of the Arbitration Clause

It is not unusual for the defendant in an arbitration proceeding to contend that, since the contract or agreement in which the obligation to arbitrate is void, the obligation to arbitrate has vanished with the voided contract. The rule in modern arbitration, international and national, is that of the severability – or separability or autonomy – of the arbitration clause. Far from the termination or even nullification of a contract which contains an arbitration clause entailing the end of the obligation to arbitrate disputes arising under that contract, the rule is the opposite: the obligation to arbitrate survives, not least to determine the validity and consequences of the termination or nullification.

This rule is codified in rules of arbitration. Thus the UNCITRAL Rules provide:

> The arbitral tribunal shall have the power to determine the existence or the validity of the contract of which an arbitration clause forms a part. For the purposes of article 21, an arbitration clause which forms part of a contract and which provides for arbitration under these Rules shall be treated as an agreement independent of the other terms of the contract. A decision by the Arbitral Tribunal that the contract is null and void shall not entail *ipso jure* the invalidity of the arbitration clause.[12]

Article 8 (4) of the ICC Rules has a similar thrust.

The severability of an obligation to arbitrate from the fate of a contract containing the arbitral obligation has been uniformly upheld in all arbitra-

---

[12] Article 21 (2).

tions between States and aliens which are known to have considered the question.

Thus in the *Losinger & Co.* case[13] – an arbitral award which formed part of a complex larger, classic case before the Permanent Court of International Justice between Switzerland and Yugoslavia – the umpire, a former President of the Swiss Federal Tribunal, held that Yugoslavia's annulment of a contract containing an obligation to arbitrate could "not affect in any way the intention of the parties to decide whether the annulment of the contract was justified or not."[14]

Again, in the *Lena Goldfields* case[15] in which the defendant was the Union of Soviet Socialist Republics, the Soviet Government maintained that the jurisdiction of an Arbitral Tribunal had been vitiated by dissolution of the contract which provided for arbitration. The tribunal held that it retained the capacity to render a valid arbitral award.[16]

More recently, the sole arbitrator in *Topco v. Libya* considered the question of whether measures of nationalization could have the effect of voiding deeds of concession which would extend to the provisions of those deeds relating to arbitration. He relied on the *Losinger* and *Lena Goldfields* cases and a good deal of municipal and doctrinal authority to sustain the principle of the autonomy of the arbitration clause.[17]

Similarly, the sole arbitrator in *Liamco v. Libya*[18] held:

> It is widely accepted in international law and practice that an arbitration clause survives the unilateral termination by the State of the contract in which it is inserted and continues in force even after that termination.[19]

In an analogous holding, the International Court of Justice concluded in the *ICAO Council* case that a party to a treaty cannot defeat recourse to arbitration or adjudication for which the treaty provides by maintaining that it has unilaterally terminated the underlying agreement which contains the obligation to arbitrate or adjudicate. "Such a result, destructive of the whole object of adjudicability, would be unacceptable." Indeed, acceptance of such a contention would make all arbitral clauses "potentially a dead letter."[20]

More recently, in 1978, the then President of the International Court of Justice, Judge Jiménez de Aréchaga wrote that:

---

[13] *PCIJ, Series C*, No.78, p. 54 (1936).   [14] *Ibid.*, p. 105.
[15] *The Times* (London), September 3, 1930, p. 7.
[16] *Ibid.*   [17] *International Law Reports* (1979), Volume 53, p. 408.
[18] *International Law Reports* (1982), Volume 62, p. 140.
[19] *Ibid.*, p. 178.
[20] *Appeal Relating to the Jurisdiction of the ICAO Council, ICJ Reports 1972*, pp. 46, 53–54, 64–65.

an arbitration clause in a contract would not be affected by the cancellation of the contract. The arbitration clause stands on its own and is separable from the contract: otherwise the purpose of having such a clause in a contract is defeated."[21]

Whether the rule of severability has entered into the law of arbitration from international law, or into international law from the law of arbitration, is not clear. What is clear is that the one influences the other.

The Exhaustion of Local Remedies

It has sometimes been argued that, where a contract between a State and an alien contains an arbitration clause, the alien must exhaust local remedies – such as judicial remedies – before the State may be obliged to arbitrate. However, the rule of international law appears to be that, where a State and an alien agree in a contract to arbitrate disputes relating to that contract, in terms indicating that arbitration is the exclusive remedy, then that remedy only must be exhausted – and that that is the only remedy which must be exhausted before an international claim relating to the contract can be maintained.

This interesting issue was engaged in four cases before the Permanent Court of International Justice and the International Court of Justice. Regrettably none of those cases came to judgment on the merits. Since a colleague and I have examined those cases in this respect in some detail elsewhere, I shall spare you an exposition of them.[22] What is more instructive is that the Executive Directors of the World Bank, in a report accompanying the ICSID Convention, concluded that:

> It may be presumed that when a State and an investor agree to have recourse to arbitration, and do not reserve the right to have recourse to other remedies or require the prior exhaustion of other remedies, the intention of the parties is to have recourse to arbitration to the exclusion of any other remedy.[23]

Article 26 of the ICSID Convention accordingly provides:

> Consent of the parties to arbitration under this Convention shall, unless otherwise stated, be deemed consent to such arbitration to the exclusion of any other remedy. A Contracting State may require the exhaustion of local administrative

---

[21] "State Responsibility for the Nationalization of Foreign Property," *New York University Journal of International Law and Politics* (1978), 11, pp. 179, 191.

[22] S.M. Schwebel and J.G. Wetter, "Arbitration and the Exhaustion of Local Remedies," *American Journal of International Law* (1966), 60, p. 484, and Chapter 10, this volume.

[23] Convention on the Settlement of Investment Disputes between States and Nationals of Other States Submitted to Governments by the Executive Directors ... and Accompanying Report of the Executive Directors, March 18, 1985, *International Legal Materials* (1955), 4, pp. 532, 524.

or judicial remedies as a condition of its consent to arbitration under this Convention.

A Plea of Sovereign Immunity

As noted, I believe that, where a State has entered into a contract with an alien providing for arbitration of disputes arising thereunder, it is not free to require him to exhaust alternative remedies (though the alien may be required to seek to enforce the obligation to arbitrate under local law if such a remedy of enforcement exists). Can the State resort to another plea of which so much is heard in international practice, that of sovereign immunity? That is to say, may a State, in an arbitration with an alien which it is resisting, plead before the Arbitral Tribunal its sovereign immunity from suit as a bar to the proceeding?

Based on the principle of *par in parem imperium non habet*, a State is entitled, in certain circumstances which today have become notably restricted, to plead immunity from suit against it which is maintained in the courts of another State. However, the principle that one sovereign shall not judge another without the latter's consent has no application to proceedings before an Arbitral Tribunal sitting between a State and an alien. Such a tribunal is not a sovereign tribunal. It derives its jurisdiction from an arbitration agreement concluded between the State and the alien in question. Accordingly, the tribunal is the instrument of the sovereignty of no State. Thus the question of sovereign immunity, or jurisdictional immunity from suit, cannot properly be pleaded before such an Arbitral Tribunal.

It may be added that, in any event, it is accepted that agreement by a State to arbitration constitutes a waiver by the State of any immunity which it might otherwise be entitled to assert. At any rate, there is a substantial weight of authority in favor of this conclusion. The question is of practical importance not before the Arbitral Tribunal itself, but when an action is brought in the courts of another State to enforce the arbitral award.

Denial of Justice by a Refusal to Arbitrate

Is there a rule of international law establishing that, where a State denies to an alien access to the exclusive arbitral remedy provided for in a contract between that State and the alien, the State commits, and incurs responsibility under international law for having committed, a denial of justice?

While there is dispute about the outer bounds of the concept of denial of justice, there is agreement that, at its core, a denial of justice consists of the failure of a State to accord aliens access to its courts and to its system for the administration of justice. There is also some authority for the proposition that, where a State denies to an alien the exclusive remedy of arbitration which a contract between that State and the alien prescribes for settlement of disputes arising under the contract, it commits a denial of justice. Dr. F. A. Mann in 1967 observed that:

> Denial of justice in the strict and narrow sense of the term implied the failure to afford access to the tribunals of the respondent State itself. But there is no reason of logic or justice why the doctrine of denial of justice should not be interpreted so as to comprise the relatively modern case of the repudiation of an arbitration clause.[24]

Very recently, the American Law Institute agreed. The commentary to the *Foreign Relations Law of the United States (Revised)* declares that:

> A State may be responsible for a denial of justice under international law ... if, having committed itself to a special forum for dispute settlement, such as arbitration, it fails to honor such commitment.[25]

In the *Losinger & Co.* case,[26] Switzerland claimed that Yugoslavia was guilty of a denial of justice in undermining the exclusive arbitral remedy assured to Losinger. The pleadings were subtle, but, as I read them, they suggest an implicit recognition by Yugoslavia that definitive repudiation by it of the arbitral remedy contained in the contract would have constituted a denial of justice. A judgment of the Permanent Court did not ensue, since the case was settled.

In the *Anglo-Iranian Oil Co.* case,[27] the United Kingdom maintained that Iran, in purporting to annul the company's concession contract and in denying the company the exclusive legal remedy expressly provided for, was guilty of a denial of justice. Iran denied the denial. The Court held that it lacked jurisdiction to pass upon the merits of the case. It did not pass upon the question of denial of justice. But one of the dissenting judges agreed with the British contention that the refusal of Iran to set up the Arbitral Tribunal provided for in the contract "constitutes a denial of justice on the part of the Iranian Government" and held that this was "a grave violation of international law."[28]

In two cases before the International Court of Justice brought by France

---

[24] F.A. Mann, "State Contracts and International Arbitration," *British Year Book of International Law* (1967), 42, pp. 1, 27–28.

[25] American Law Institute, *Restatement of the Law, Foreign Relations Law of the United States (Revised)*, Section 712.

[26] *PCIJ, Series C, No. 78*, p. 54 (1936).   [27] *ICJ Reports 1952*, p. 93.   [28] *Ibid.*, p. 165.

against Lebanon, France also maintained that a denial of justice sprang from Lebanon's refusal to carry out arbitral commitments it had made to French companies. Nowhere in its extensive responsive pleadings did Lebanon directly challenge the French contention that a refusal to arbitrate was a denial of justice under international law. But these two cases also were settled before judgment.

In the case of *Turriff Construction (Sudan) Limited v. The Sudan*,[29] Sudan withdrew from the proceedings in their midst, pleading that a non-commercial consideration beyond the competence of the tribunal had come to light. The tribunal concluded that: "The withdrawal not being justified, it would have been a denial of justice had they refused to exercise the power to proceed in the absence of the Government."[30] This case appears to be a holding that, where a Government without cause absents itself from an arbitral proceeding to which it is bound, a "denial of justice" would ensue if the tribunal refused to proceed. This would seem to be an inferential support for the position that repudiation by a State of the arbitral remedy to which it had committed itself would likewise constitute a denial of justice.

There are three other, older cases which I have analyzed elsewhere which also constitute a measure of authority for the proposition that refusal to arbitrate constitutes a denial of justice.[31] The *Yearbook Commercial Arbitration 1983* also summarizes a case, without revealing the names of its parties, which likewise provides support for the proposition, though by way of an *obiter dictum* since the State in question had not repudiated its obligation to arbitrate.[32] There also is substantial scholarly analysis by a number of commentators in addition to Dr. Mann in support of this conclusion, by, among others, F. V. Garcia Amador, Charles de Visscher, Alfred Verdross, Kenneth S. Carlston, and Prosper Weil.

Finally, many of the cases and other authorities to which I have made reference in connection with the question of a denial of justice have been examined by a contemporary Arbitral Tribunal sitting in a case between a State and an alien. In an unpublished award on jurisdiction, the tribunal squarely and decisively held that a State's refusal to carry out an obligation to arbitrate contained in a contract with an alien constitutes a denial of justice, even in circumstances where that State maintains that the contract is void *ab initio*.[33]

---

[29] T. Erades, "The Sudan Arbitration," *Nederlands Tijdschrift voor International Recht* (1970), 17, p. 200.
[30] *Ibid.*, p. 217.
[31] Stephen M. Schwebel, *International Arbitration: Three Salient Problems* (1987), pp. 89–95.
[32] Volume 8, pp. 108–109.
[33] See C. Reymond, "Souveraineté de l'Etat et Participation a l'Arbitrage," *Revue de l'Arbitrage* (1985), No. 4, p. 523.

The Authority of a Truncated Arbitral Tribunal to Render a Binding Award

A problem on which there is a large amount of precedent is whether an international Arbitral Tribunal from which a nationally or otherwise appointed arbitrator withdraws retains the power to proceed and to render a binding award. That problem has repeatedly arisen in inter-State arbitration; it has arisen in arbitrations between States and aliens; it has indeed arisen in the Iran–United States Claims Tribunal.

But while there is a large amount of precedent, and much discussion of this problem in the writings of scholars, it does not all cut one way. The cases and the comments are divided. Having examined those cases, which go back a few hundred years to the beginnings of modern international arbitration, or at any rate all of the cases I could find, I have concluded that the weight of the law supports the authority of a truncated Arbitral Tribunal to render a binding award.

Of course, if the arbitration agreement or treaty in question provides that, in the event of withdrawal of an arbitrator, the remaining members of the tribunal, being a majority, shall have the power to render an award, the problem is resolved. But often arbitral agreements or the governing rules do not. They may contain provision, in case of withdrawal, for the making of a fresh appointment in the manner of the original appointment, and in principle the problem may be overcome if third-party appointment of the nationally or party-appointed arbitrator is authorized. But even this may in practice result in undue and perhaps even unacceptable delay. Moreover, provisions for third-party appointment may not be sufficient to meet the situation of a claims tribunal hearing a multiplicity of claims in which arbitrators appointed by one of the parties repeatedly withdraw at critical stages of the proceedings.

The problem arises in an acute form when the withdrawal of an arbitrator purports to block the issuance of a valid award, and when the party which appointed that arbitrator either is the source of his withdrawal or adopts that withdrawal. Cases in which this has occurred are not as rare as one might suppose.

My broad view of the matter is that, once the parties have entered into a treaty to arbitrate, or into a contract providing for arbitration of disputes arising thereunder, which they implement by establishment of an Arbitral Tribunal designed to hear and resolve a particular dispute, and that tribunal receives pleadings and hears part or all of a case which the parties present at considerable cost to themselves, one party cannot lawfully render all this nugatory by the expedient of withdrawing its arbitrator. The International Court of Justice has more than once held that the parties to a treaty provision for arbitration are under an obligation to participate in constituting the tribunal.[34] It follows that such a party breaches an allied international obligation by withdrawing its arbitrator from the tribunal to which it was bound to appoint him. From this it follows, in my view, that the withdrawing State cannot be heard to challenge the tribunal's right to proceed and to render an award. The doctrine that no legal right may spring from a wrong is embedded alike in the jurisprudence of international arbitration and in the general principles of law recognized by civilized nations. On the plane of legal principle, it may be argued to resolve the problem under discussion in favor of the binding character of awards rendered by truncated international tribunals.

Let me assure you that, on the plane of practice, the problem has by no means been easily or consistently resolved. It was debated at length in the course of the preparation by the United Nations International Law Commission of its Draft Code of Arbitral Procedure. The Special Rapporteur, Professor Scelle, was clear in his view that a tribunal from which an arbitrator withdraws is authorized to continue the proceedings and render an award which shall be binding. But the Commission itself manifested no such certainty; views were divided. In the end, Professor Scelle carried the Commission with him. But when the Commission's draft was circulated to Governments for comment, it found a very mixed reception. Accordingly, on a re-reading of the draft, the Commission deleted its proposal that a truncated tribunal be authorized to continue the proceedings and render a binding award, in favor of a provision for the filling of the vacancy caused by withdrawal in the same way as the original appointment was made.

I will not in this paper review the many relevant cases, which go back to the Jay Treaties at the end of the eighteenth century. Some of the cases cut one way, some the other, still others are inconclusive. I would note that Mr. Justice Holmes, in *Republic of Colombia v. Cauca Co.*,[35] squarely held that a truncated international Arbitral Tribunal may render a binding award. While the *French–Mexican Claims Commission* cases[36] also furnish support for that principle, that support was beclouded by complexities beyond the scope of this evening's recounting. Another supportive precedent is the *Lena Goldfields* case,[37] to which I have earlier referred. More supportive still are the so-called

---

[34] *Ambatielos Case (Merits: Obligation to Arbitrate), ICJ Reports 1953, pp. 10, 23*; and *Interpretation of Peace Treaties with Bulgaria, Hungary and Romania, ICJ Reports 1950*, pp. 65, 70.

[35] 190 US 524 (1903).

[36] United Nations *Reports of International Arbitral Awards* (1952), Volume 4, pp. 309–560.

[37] Note 15, above.

Sabotage[38] cases decided by the United States–Germany Mixed Claims Commission. There the "retirement" of the German Commissioner was held not to oust the jurisdiction of the Commission. Despite the bitter, sharply reasoned German protests of 1939, the Commission proceeded to hand down 153 awards. In 1953, the United States and the Federal Republic of Germany concluded an agreement which treats those awards as valid awards. Thus in their entirety the *Sabotage* cases furnish persuasive authority for the conclusion that a truncated international Arbitral Tribunal is empowered to act and give valid judgment. Of course, it is not irrelevant to note that, in between these years, Germany launched and lost a war.

It may be added that the International Court of Justice, in its advisory opinion on the *Interpretation of Peace Treaties with Bulgaria, Hungary, and Romania*, stated, by way of what may be seen as *obiter dictum*, that:

> It has been pointed out that an arbitration commission may make a valid decision although the original number of its members, as fixed by the arbitration agreement, is later reduced by such circumstances as the withdrawal of one of the commissioners.[39]

This conclusion was positively elaborated in opinions of dissenters. Indeed, it is clear that both the majority and minority of the Court, in the light of the extensive argument presented to it on the authority of truncated international Arbitral Tribunals, was of the view that a truncated Arbitral Tribunal can render a binding award.

Finally, let me advert to the Iran–United States Claims Tribunal. The Tribunal has by no means been free of problems of this nature, since, on several occasions in 1983, more than one of the arbitrators appointed by Iran absented themselves from arbitral proceedings and refused to sign awards to which a majority had agreed. The judges appointed by Iran argued at length that, by reason of their absence and the absence of their signatures, the awards in question were invalid. Judges appointed by the United States argued no less fully that the absences of their Iranian colleagues and of their signatures was unjustified and that the awards were duly rendered. They carried the majority with them. The awards were issued and paid. Thereafter, Iran initiated suit in Dutch courts challenging the validity of those awards, but those suits were later discontinued. No fresh incidents of this kind have arisen during the last few years. There the matter rests. It is difficult to conclude

---

[38] Mixed Claims Commission, United States and Germany, *Opinions and Decisions in the Sabotage Claims handed down June 15, 1939, and October 30, 1939* and Appendix.

[39] *Interpretation of Peace Treaties with Bulgaria, Hungary and Romania (Second Phase), ICJ Reports 1950*, pp. 221, 229.

otherwise than that the experience to date of the Iran–United States Claims Commission reinforces what I believe is the correct view of the question: that a truncated Arbitral Tribunal can render a valid award.

A Plea of International Law before an Arbitral Tribunal Sitting Between a State and an Alien

Let us suppose that an arbitration takes place between a State and an alien over their rights under a contract between them, which contract is stated by the contract to be governed by the law of that State. Let us suppose that the arbitration itself has international elements, apart from the company's alienage, e.g., that the tribunal is composed of three persons, one appointed by the State, one by the company, and a third agreed upon by the two and, failing that, by the President of the International Court of Justice or the President of the International Chamber of Commerce, and that the tribunal sits in one of the customary favored places of international arbitrators abroad.

Let us further suppose that the issue is the conformity with the contract and the rights of the parties thereunder of certain actions taken by the State of which the alien complains. In these circumstances, may the alien be heard to invoke international law?

You may ask, why not? As indeed do I. But let me say why some argue to the contrary. Bear in mind that we do not posit the situation in which the tribunal is expressly empowered to apply international law, as is the Iran–United States Claims Tribunal. And we do not posit the situation in which the, or a, law of the contract is international law or some facsimile thereof. There is no reference in the authority granted the Arbitral Tribunal, or in the terms of the governing law of the contract, to international law. There is provision to the effect that if a dispute arises under the contract not otherwise resolved, it shall be settled by arbitration, etc.

In such a situation, it can be argued, and, I can assure you, has been argued, that the alien is not entitled to plead international law. Of course, for the alien to raise a plea under international law, he would have to have something to plead about. Let us then further posit that, in the view of the alien, the measures taken by the State in alleged violation of the contract are in violation of customary international law. The alien argues that the "non-commercial" use of sovereign authority by a State to violate a contract with an alien gives rise to a violation of customary international law. He also argues that it violates the standards of treatment and of compensation set out in a treaty of friendship, commerce, and navigation to which the State of which the company is a national and the contracting State are parties.

However, the contracting State maintains that the alien is not entitled to plead international law. It argues that a plea of international law – whether customary law or treaty law – may be made by the State of which the company is a national, in the event that it espouses the company's claim. It may be made by that State on the plane of inter-State arbitration or otherwise. But no mere company is entitled to proceed as if it were a State and to make pleas of international law before an Arbitral Tribunal in circumstances where that tribunal has not been expressly empowered to give judgment on the basis of international law and where the contract in question makes no reference to international law. On the contrary, since the contract is governed by the law of the contracting State, all argument must be within the framework of that law alone.

In my view, the answer to this line of argument, which can hardly be dismissed, runs along these lines. In modern international law, it is clear that individuals and companies they form may have rights under international law. A multiplicity of treaties, such as those on commerce, labor, tax, transit, road traffic, extradition, the conduct of hostilities, social security payments, copyrights, etc., give individuals rights under treaties. Whether, in a national court, a person may maintain suit on the basis of such rights depends on whether the treaty is self-executing and, if so, applies in a jurisdiction in which treaties are the law of the land. As you know, in some States, internal effect may be given to treaties only upon the enactment of enabling legislation, though that is not true in the United States. It is certainly clear that modern international law does not prevent States from endowing individuals with actionable rights under a treaty which they may invoke without the prior enactment of national legislation. As the Permanent Court of International Justice held in its advisory opinion on the *Jurisdiction of the Courts of Danzig*,[40] the question of whether individuals may maintain suit on the basis of a treaty depends upon the intention of the contracting parties.

Equally, individuals may have rights under customary international law. While court holdings vary from one State to another, it is the position in many States, including the United States, that individuals not only have rights under customary international law but may enforce those rights in national courts. A substantial number of countries permit the individual to benefit by and assert international legal rights against the State if the treaty provision at issue manifests that intention of the parties or if the rule of customary international law invests the individual with such rights.

Moving now to the plane of arbitration between a State and an alien, is it

---

[40] *Jurisdiction of the Courts of Danzig, 1928, PCIJ, Series B, No.15.*

open to the individual claimant to make a claim of right deriving from international law and is it open to the tribunal to entertain that claim?

In my view, it is. In addition to the holding of the World Court in the *Danzig* case to which I have referred, there are two facts of positive law which tend to sustain the general right of an alien in an arbitration with a State to plead international law. The first is that a number of arbitration treaties authorize the alien to do so. The second, which is more probative, is that, even in the absence of treaty or contractual authorization, international law on occasion has been invoked in such arbitral proceedings and been applied by such Arbitral Tribunals.

The ICSID Convention authorizes Arbitral Tribunals constituted pursuant to it to apply international law, and some ICSID tribunals have. The Iran–United States Claims Tribunal is so authorized, and it has applied international law. I recognize that one may argue that, where a tribunal lacks such authorization, it is not entitled to apply international law. But I believe that the better view is that such instruments confer not exceptional rights but rather are expressive of what is accepted in contemporary international law and arbitral practice.

I so conclude because awards of tribunals sitting between States and aliens not infrequently refer to and base elements of their decisions on international law. This is true even in cases in which the contract at issue and the terms of reference of the tribunal make no reference to international law. This was the case in the *Aramco* arbitration,[41] to which I earlier referred. It was so in *Petroleum Development Ltd. v. Sheikh of Abu Dhabi*,[42] and in the *Aminoil*,[43] case, as well as in the *Lena Goldfields* case.[44]

In its judgment in the *Barcelona Traction Company* case,[45] the International Court of Justice, in addressing the question of whether a State was entitled to exercise diplomatic protection of its nationals who were shareholders of a company of another nationality, observed that:

> Thus, in the present state of the law, the protection of shareholders requires that recourse be had to treaty stipulations or special agreements directly concluded between the private investor and the State in which the investment is placed. States ever more frequently provide for such protection, in both bilateral and multilateral relations, either by means of special instruments or within the framework of wider economic arrangements. Indeed, whether in the form of multilateral or bilateral treaties between States, or in that of agreements between

[41] Note 4, above. [42] *International Law Reports* (1951), Volume 18, p. 144.
[43] *International Law Reports* (1982), Volume 66, p. 519.
[44] *Ibid.*, section 12.03, note 4 above.
[45] *Barcelona Traction, Light & Power Co. Judgment, ICJ Reports 1970*, pp. 3, 47.

States and companies, there has since the Second World War been considerable development in the protection of foreign investments. The instruments in question contain provisions as to jurisdiction and procedure in case of disputes concerning the treatment of investing companies by the States in which they invest capital. Sometimes companies are themselves vested with a direct right to defend their interests against States through prescribed procedures.[46]

It seems to me that one may read the foregoing as meaning that, when a company is "vested with a direct right" to defend its interests against a State "through prescribed procedures," those procedures embrace the direct right of the company to invoke international law in defense of its interests. Certainly it is hard to maintain the contrary. How odd it would be if States were to conclude treaties such as the ICSID Convention or the Algiers Declaration providing for the Iran–United States Claims Tribunal, and were to conclude contracts with aliens providing for exclusive arbitration of disputes arising thereunder, and at the same time were to be deemed to have debarred the alien claimants and companies which are central to these processes from direct reliance upon international law to sustain their claims.

I must say that I agree with the conclusion of Pierre-Yves Tschanz that:

> In the transnational arbitral context, the standing of the foreign investor to assert claims under international law is generally recognized, even when international law is not the *lex contractus*.[47]

Conclusion

I have not discussed the substantive rules of international law which a party to an arbitral proceeding may invoke. Naturally that will depend upon the issues of the case and on whether there are governing treaties in point. But that there are principles of international law that may at times be relevant is obvious, such as those relating to expropriation and nationalization, and to a State's obligation not to employ its sovereign authority to rupture the expectations of the parties. In practice, principles such as these have been brought to bear recurrently in international arbitration.

It would be as misleading to overstate the place and influence of public international law in arbitration between States and aliens as to understate it. Its role, if any, generally may be secondary. But it may nevertheless be important. One of the more encouraging signs of international cooperation in a world which manifests too few such signs is the growth of international

---

[46] *Ibid.*, p. 47.

[47] Tschanz, "The Contribution of the Aminoil Award to the Law of State Contracts," *The International Lawyer* (1984), 18, pp. 245, 264.

commercial arbitration. Just as international commercial arbitration can make its contribution to the rational settlement of disputes upon the basis of law, so international law can make a certain contribution to the principles and practice of international commercial arbitration.

13

The Majority Vote of an International Arbitral Tribunal

❧

Is a majority vote in an international Arbitral Tribunal, the *compromis* or governing rules of which provide for decisions by majority vote, dispositive, or may the effectiveness of that vote be challenged on the ground that one of the two arbitrators constituting the ostensible majority stated a position which shows that he did not support, or fully support, the award which was carried by his vote?

This question was one of two questions of interest to the international arbitration community on which the International Court of Justice ruled in 1991 in its judgment in the *Case Concerning the Arbitral Award of 31 July 1989.*[1] On this question, the Court was unanimous.

How the issue came to be posed

In 1960, the predecessor States of Senegal and Guinea-Bissau, France and Portugal, exchanged letters for the purpose of defining the maritime boundary between Senegal (then an autonomous State in the French Community) and the then Portuguese province of Guinea. After the accession to independence of Senegal and Guinea-Bissau, a dispute arose between them concerning the delimitation of their maritime territories. In 1985, they concluded an Arbitration Agreement for submission of that dispute to arbitration, which in part provided:

> The Government of the Republic of Senegal and the Government of the Republic of Guinea-Bissau,

First published in C. Dominicé, C. Reymond, and R. Patry (eds.), *Etudes de droit international en l'honneur de Pierre Lalive* (1993), Basle, Editions Helbing & Lichtenhahn and reprinted in *The American Review of International Arbitration 1991* (1993), 2, 4, p. 402.

[1] *Case concerning the Arbitral Award of 31 July 1989* (Guinea-Bissau v. Senegal), *ICJ Reports 1991*, p. 40. The second question was whether the Arbitral Tribunal had fulfilled its mandate even though it did not proceed to answer the second, conditional question put to it in Article 2 of the *compromis*.

Recognizing that they have been unable to settle by means of diplomatic negotiations the dispute relating to the determination of their maritime boundary,

Desirous, in view of their friendly relations, to reach a settlement of that dispute as soon as possible and, to that end, having decided to resort to arbitration,

Have agreed as follows:

Article 1

1. The Arbitration Tribunal (hereinafter called "the Tribunal") shall consist of three members designated in the following manner:

    Each Party shall appoint one arbitrator of its choice;

    The third arbitrator, who shall function as President of the Tribunal, shall be appointed by mutual agreement of the two Parties ...

2. ...

3. ...

Article 2

The Tribunal is requested to decide in accordance with the norms of international law on the following questions:

1. Does the Agreement concluded by an exchange of letters on 26 April 1960, and which relates to the maritime boundary, have the force of law in the relations between the Republic of Guinea-Bissau and the Republic of Senegal?

2. In the event of a negative answer to the first question, what is the course of the line delimiting the maritime territories appertaining to the Republic of Guinea-Bissau and the Republic of Senegal respectively? ...

Article 4

1. The Tribunal shall take its decisions only in its full composition.

2. The decisions of the Tribunal relating to all questions of substance or procedure, including all questions relating to the jurisdiction of the Tribunal and the interpretation of the Agreement, shall be taken by a majority of its members ...

Article 10

1. The Arbitral Award shall be signed by the President of the Tribunal and by the Registrar. The latter shall hand to the Agents of the two Parties a certified copy in the two languages.

2. The Award shall be final and binding upon the two States which shall be under a duty to take all necessary steps for its implementation.

3. ...[2]

An Arbitration Tribunal was constituted by the appointment of Mohammed Bedjaoui, judge of the International Court of Justice, and André Gros, former judge of the International Court of Justice, as Arbitrators and Julio A. Barberis, Ambassador of Argentina, as President. On July 31, 1989, the Tribunal handed down the Award whose existence and validity came to be challenged by Guinea-Bissau before the Court. The Award was adopted by

---

[2] *Ibid.*, para. 14.

the votes of the President and Judge Gros, over the negative vote of Judge Bedjaoui.

For present purposes, the pertinent findings of the Tribunal were these. The Tribunal concluded that the 1960 exchange of letters gave rise to a valid Agreement which could be opposed to Senegal and Guinea-Bissau, and that that Agreement "does not delimit those maritime spaces which did not exist at that date, whether they be termed exclusive economic zone, fishery zone, or whatever ..." but that "the territorial sea, the contiguous zone and the continental shelf ... are expressly mentioned in the 1960 Agreement and they existed at the time of its conclusion ..."[3] The Tribunal declared that:

> Bearing in mind the above conclusions reached by the Tribunal and the actual wording of Article 2 of the Arbitration Agreement, in the opinion of the Tribunal it is not called upon to reply to the second question.[4]

The operative clause of the Award provides:

> For the reasons stated above, the Tribunal decides by two votes to one:
> To reply as follows to the first question formulated in Article 2 of the Arbitration Agreement: The Agreement concluded by an exchange of letters of 26 April 1960, and relating to the maritime boundary, has the force of law in the relations between the Republic of Guinea-Bissau and the Republic of Senegal with regard solely to the areas mentioned in that Agreement, namely the territorial sea, the contiguous zone and the continental shelf. The "straight line drawn at 240°" is a loxodromic line.[5]

The President of the Tribunal appended a Declaration to the Award which in pertinent part read as follows:

> I feel that the reply given by the Tribunal to the first question put by the Arbitration Agreement could have been more precise. I would have replied to that question as follows:

> > The Agreement concluded by an exchange of letters of 26 April 1960, and relating to the maritime boundary, has the force of law in the relations between the Republic of Guinea-Bissau and the Republic of Senegal with respect to the territorial sea, the contiguous zone and the continental shelf, but does not have the force of law with respect to the waters of the exclusive economic zone or the fishery zone. The "straight line drawn at 240°" mentioned in the Agreement of 26 April 1960 is a loxodromic line.

> This partially affirmative and partially negative reply is, in my view, the correct description of the legal position existing between the Parties. As suggested by Guinea-Bissau in the course of the present arbitration ... a reply of this kind would have enabled the Tribunal to deal in its Award with the second question

---

[3] *Ibid.*, para. 16.   [4] *Ibid.*, para. 17.   [5] *Ibid.*, para. 18.

put by the Arbitration Agreement. The *partially* negative reply to the first question would have conferred on the Tribunal a *partial* competence to reply to the second, i.e., to do so to the extent that the reply to the first question would have been negative.

In that case, the Tribunal would have been competent to delimit the waters of the exclusive economic zone or the fishery zone between the two countries. The Tribunal thus could have settled the whole of the dispute, because, by virtue of the reply to the first question of the Arbitration Agreement, it would have determined the boundaries for the territorial sea, contiguous zone and the continental shelf, as the Award has just done and, by its answer to the second question, the Tribunal could have determined the boundary for the waters of the exclusive economic zone or the fishery zone, a boundary which might or might not have coincided with the line drawn by the 1960 Agreement.[6]

In his Dissenting Opinion, Judge Bedjaoui referred to the President's Declaration which, he maintained,

> shows to what an extent the Award is incomplete and inconsistent with the letter and spirit of the Arbitration Agreement with regard to the single line desired by the Parties. Since it emanates from the President of the Tribunal himself, that Declaration, by its very existence as well as by its contents, justifies more fundamental doubts as to the existence of a majority and the reality of the Award.[7]

The Contentions of Guinea-Bissau

In the proceedings in the International Court of Justice, Guinea-Bissau maintained that the Arbitral Award was inexistent, on the ground that it was not supported by a real majority. It did not dispute the fact that the Award itself was framed to declare that the Tribunal, by two votes to one, decided as it decided; it acknowledged that "purely formal appearances have been preserved."[8] However, Guinea-Bissau contended that the Declaration of President Barberis rendered "the so-called 'award'" of July 31, 1989 inexistent "in view of the fact that one of the two arbitrators making up the appearance of the majority in favor of the text of the 'award', has, by a declaration appended to it, expressed a view in contradiction with the one apparently adopted by the vote."[9] Guinea-Bissau argued that the Declaration of President Barberis, "by its very presence and content, destroys appearances and indicates the obvious disagreement which had existed within the ficti-

---

[6] *Ibid.*, para. 19.   [7] *Ibid.*, para. 20.

[8] *Case concerning the Arbitral Award of 31 July 1989, Memorial Submitted by the Government of the Republic of Guinea-Bissau*, Vol. I, p. 76.

[9] *Case concerning the Arbitral Award of 31 July 1989, Application Instituting Proceedings*, p. 13.

tious majority itself."[10] It emphasized that the President would have recast the operative terms of the Award in a way which would have altered the Tribunal's competence and thus permitted settlement of the whole dispute, a change which "undermines the decision."[11] The President, Guinea-Bissau maintained, thereby showed that he did not share the view of the other Arbitrator (Judge Gros) "who was responsible for the operative provisions."[12] Indeed, by expressing his readiness to deal with the whole of the disputed maritime boundary, the President showed that he broke with the decision of the Award and expressed a view "irreconcilable" with it.[13] The content of President Barberis's Declaration, Guinea-Bissau concluded, showed that it constituted "a declaration of dissent"[14] and evidenced the inability of President Barberis to rally a majority for his position.[15] Thus the "award" lacked "the necessary foundation based on the existence of a majority having agreed to uphold it on all the essential points ... the 'award' is inexistent owing to the lack of a genuine majority."[16]

The Contentions of Senegal

Senegal rejected the foregoing arguments of Guinea-Bissau. It argued, on the basis of a number of judgments of the International Court of Justice, that a vote by a judge in favor of a judgment does not necessarily indicate his agreement on all points. A judge may vote in favor of a judgment even without supporting the whole of its operative part.[17] In international arbitral practice, Senegal maintained, "because of the majority rule applicable to the adoption of arbitral decisions, an arbitrator's vote must prevail over his separate opinion or declaration."[18] Senegal argued:

> 157. The primacy of the decision adopted by a majority vote, as specified in the relevant texts and as confirmed by practice, is moreover an expression of the very nature of the international adjudicating mechanism. The operative provisions adopted by a majority constitute in fact the sole common denominator of the majority judges, although they may not necessarily attract on all points the support of all these judges. This phenomenon of diversity is rendered more marked by the fact that Members of the Court are not allowed to abstain.
>
> 158. One is thus placed before a dilemma: either priority is granted to every nuance expressed by each judge, with the result that no decision can be reached

---

[10] Note 8 above, at p. 76. [11] *Ibid.*, p. 79. [12] *Ibid.*, p. 80. [13] *Ibid.*, pp. 80, 81.
[14] *Ibid.*, p. 83.
[15] *Ibid.*, p. 84. [16] *Ibid.*
[17] *Case concerning the Arbitral Award of 31 July 1989, Counter-Memorial Submitted by the Government of the Republic of Senegal*, p. 61.
[18] *Ibid.*, p. 63.

and the dispute cannot be settled; or else there is only a majority decision, without any room being left for separate views. These two extreme positions have had to be reconciled. In order to do so, absolute primacy has on the one hand been recognized for the operative provisions voted by a majority but, on the other hand, all the members of the adjudicating body have been authorized to express their separate views with the desirable precision and nuances.

159. These considerations must be supplemented with an argument connected with legal security. If there were no rule to ensure the primacy of decisions adopted by a majority vote, the defeated party could, at the end of every litigation, carry out a detailed analysis to identify any contradictions between the vote of the majority judges and the separate opinions or declarations made by them, with the aim of detecting some defect in the majority opinion on which to base an allegation that the decision is null or inexistent. The party concerned could carry out that analysis at any time since no precise time-limit has been laid down in the matter, on the sole condition of not having first accepted the decision. Obviously, many States would refuse to submit their disputes to judicial settlement in a system in which the result of the litigation – which is reputedly binding and final – could be questioned at any time.

160. Everything thus leads to the conclusion that the decision adopted by a majority prevails over any opinions or declarations which may have been issued by the majority of judges ...[19]

Senegal further contended that:

In reality, it is inherent in the nature of an international judgment or award rendered by a collegiate body that the decision cannot have the precision which each member of that body would have separately desired. The drafting of the decision is always the result of a compromise, so that the final text reflects the agreement of the majority rather than the precise text desired by any one of the members. Besides, if it is alleged that the award is in any way imprecise, the correct procedure is to apply for interpretation (or clarification) and not for annulment.[20]

The judgment of the Court

In disposing of these conflicting contentions, the Court, after finding that there was in fact no contradiction between the position adopted by the Tribunal and that preferred by President Barberis in his Declaration, held:

Furthermore, even if there had been any contradiction ... between the view expressed by President Barberis and that stated in the Award, such contradiction could not prevail over the position which President Barberis had taken when voting for the Award. In agreeing to the Award, he definitively agreed to the decisions, which it incorporated, as to the extent of the maritime areas governed

[19] *Ibid.*, p. 64.   [20] *Ibid.*, p. 65.

by the 1960 Agreement, and as to the Tribunal not being required to answer the second question in view of its answer to the first. As the practice of international tribunals shows, it sometimes happens that a member of a tribunal votes in favor of a decision of the tribunal even though he might individually have been inclined to prefer another solution. The validity of his vote remains unaffected by the expression of any such differences in a declaration or separate opinion of the member concerned, which are therefore without consequence for the decision of the Tribunal.[21]

Practice in support of the Court's conclusion

While the Court does not specify "the practice of international tribunals" to which it refers, such practice is not difficult to find. The practice of the Court itself to which Senegal made extended reference may not have been wholly relevant, since the Court decisions cited did not depend for their adoption on the vote of the judge who expressed a difference in a declaration or separate opinion. However, it may be recalled that the Court had occasion, in the "*Yakimetz*" case, to consider what was a relevant judgment of the United Nations Administrative Tribunal. In its judgment in *Yakimetz v. The Secretary-General of the United Nations*, Case No. 322 of June 8, 1984, three members of the Administrative Tribunal heard and ruled upon a politically delicate controversy, the critical legal issue of which was, had the applicant, Mr. V. V. Yakimetz, received "every reasonable consideration" for a career appointment, such consideration being acknowledged to be required by the governing resolution of the United Nations General Assembly. The Tribunal's majority, composed of two members of the Tribunal, President Ustor being one of them, held that Mr. Yakimetz had received such consideration, essentially because the Secretary-General said that he had. President Ustor, while voting for this majority holding, nevertheless appended a Statement to the Tribunal's judgment holding that Mr. Yakimetz was "not eligible for a career appointment" because, having been seconded from Government service of the USSR to the Secretariat, he was ineligible "not only" for the extension of a seconded fixed-term appointment "but also its conversion to any other type of appointment without the consent of the Government concerned."[22] Vice President Kean took a different view:

> Far from there being a generally accepted rule that in the absence of the Government's consent a seconded staff member must always be refused, in limine, a career appointment at the end of his period of secondment, this paragraph [of an

---

[21] Note 1 above, para. 33.
[22] *Application for Review of Judgement No. 333 of the United Nations Administrative Tribunal, ICJ Reports 1987*, pp. 18, 45–46.

International Civil Service Commission Report] makes it quite clear that the Government's view was not to be decisive but was to be fully taken into account together with all other relevant factors.[23]

In evaluating this state of affairs, the Court stated:

It is evident that if the remaining member of the Tribunal, who did not make any separate statement of his views, had shared the view of Mr. Ustor, the Judgement would have been drafted to convey the view of the two-member majority that the Applicant's secondment was an absolute bar to his obtaining a career appointment, so that the question of "reasonable consideration" would not arise. The Judgement of the Tribunal thus occupied the middle ground between Mr. Ustor and Mr. Kean, differing from the individual view of the former to the extent solely that it held that there was no "legal impediment" barring a career appointment; and differing from the latter in holding that "every reasonable consideration" had in fact been given. Mr. Ustor did not express any disagreement on this second point; he thought that "reasonable consideration" need not have been given, in view of the factor of secondment, but that on the facts it was given.[24]

The analogy between the Declaration of President Barberis and the Statement of President Ustor is plain. In both cases, the Tribunal Presidents made clear that they would have preferred a decidedly different judgment than the one rendered. In both cases, they nevertheless voted for the less preferable judgment which, only by their vote, was adopted. It is worth noting that, while the *Yakimetz* judgment of the Tribunal was challenged in the Court on multiple grounds, it was not alleged by counsel for the applicant nor imagined by the International Court of Justice to be "inexistent," or a nullity, on the ground that there was lack of a genuine majority for the judgment adopted.

Still other contemporaneous practice may be found in the judgments of the Iran–United States Claims Tribunal. There are numerous judgments of that Tribunal in which an arbitrator candidly recorded that he voted for an award not because he wholly agreed with it but because he thought it right to provide a majority for the decision.

---

[23] *Ibid.*, p. 46.

[24] *Ibid.*, p. 45. The Court earlier declared:

In order to interpret or elucidate a judgement it is both permissible and advisable to take into account any dissenting or other opinions appended to the judgement. Declarations or opinions drafted by members of a tribunal at the time of a decision, and appended thereto, may contribute to the clarification of the decision. Accordingly the wise practice of the Tribunal, following the example of the Court itself, has been not only to permit such expressions of opinion but to publish them appended to the judgement. It is therefore proper in the present case, in order better to grasp the position of the Tribunal on the point now under examination, to refer not only to the Judgement itself, but also to the "Statement" of Mr. Endre Ustor and the dissenting opinion of Mr. Arnold Kean.

In *Granite State Machine Co., Inc. v. The Islamic Republic of Iran, Bank Markazi Iran, and Bank Saderat Iran*,[25] Richard M. Mosk, concurring, stated that he did so because he thought it right to bring protracted deliberations to an end, deliberations otherwise "which must continue ... until a majority, and probably a compromise solution, has been reached ... I concurred in the decision as to the amount of costs specified in the award so as to provide a majority for the award." In *Ultrasystems Inc. v. The Islamic Republic of Iran, Information Systems Iran*,[26] Judge Mosk declared: "I concur in the Tribunal's Partial Award. I do so in order to form a majority so that an award can be rendered." Judge Mosk appended the following footnote to this statement: "As Professor Pieter Sanders has written, arbitrators are 'forced to continue their deliberations until a majority, and probably a compromise solution, has been reached.' Sanders, *Commentary on UNCITRAL Arbitration Rules*, 1977 II *Yearbook of Commercial Arbitration* 172, 208. If no majority can be reached, no award can be rendered, thus creating great injustice to the parties."

In *Economy Forms Corp. v. The Government of the Islamic Republic of Iran, et al.*, Howard M. Holtzmann declared:

I concur in the Award in this Case. The Award correctly holds that contracts of sale were formed, that the Respondents breached those contracts and that they are liable to pay damages. Unfortunately, however, the damages awarded are only about half of what the governing law requires.

Why then do I concur in this inadequate Award, rather than dissenting from it? The answer is based on the realistic old saying that there are circumstances in which "something is better than nothing". The operative circumstances here are that under Article 31, paragraph 1 of the Tribunal Rules (as well as under the UNCITRAL Arbitration Rules), "When there are three arbitrators, any award or other decision of the Arbitral Tribunal shall be made by a majority of the arbitrators." Thus, in a three-member Chamber a majority of two members must join, or there can be no Award. My colleague Dr. Kashani having dissented, I am faced with the choice of either joining in the present Award or accepting the prospect of an indefinite postponement of any Award in this case. For, as Professor Sanders has explained in his Commentary on UNCITRAL Arbitration Rules, arbitrators must continue their deliberations until a majority has been reached. II Yearbook Commercial Arbitration (1977) 208. The deliberations in this case have

[25] 1 *Iran–US CTR* 442, 450, 451.

[26] 2 *Iran–US CTR* 100. For other such statements of Judge Mosk, see *Chas. T. Main International Inc. v. Mahab Consulting Engineers, Inc. and the Ministry of Energy of the Islamic Republic of Iran*, 3 *Iran–US CTR* 270, 277, 278; *R.N. Pomeroy v. The Government of the Islamic Republic of Iran*, 2 *Iran–US CTR* 372, 390; *Alan Craig v. Ministry of Energy of Iran et al.*, 3 *Iran–US CTR* 280, 293; *American International Group, Inc. and American Life Insurance Co. v. The Islamic Republic of Iran et al.*, 4 *Iran–US CTR* 96, 111; *William L. Pereira Associates, Iran v. The Islamic Republic of Iran*, 5 *Iran–US CTR* 198, 230; *Ammann & Whitney v. Ministry of Housing and Urban Development*, 12 *Iran–US CTR* 94; and *Litton Systems, Inc. v. The Islamic Republic of Iran*, 12 *Iran–US CTR* 126.

continued long enough; the hearing was closed on February 15, 1983, four months ago. Neither the parties nor the Tribunal will, in my view, benefit from further delay.[27]

In Iran–United States, Case A/1, Judges Aldrich, Holtzmann, and Mosk declared:

> While we consider that crediting the interest directly to the Security Account rather than placing it in a separate account would have been more consistent with the language, object and purpose of the Algiers Declarations and more in keeping with banking practice, we nevertheless join the majority in order to enable this question to be resolved in an acceptable manner.*
>
> * Such a majority is required by Article 31, paragraph 1 of the Tribunal Rules. See Sanders, Commentary on UNCITRAL Arbitration Rules, II, (1977), Yearbook – Commercial Arbitration 172, 208.[28]

The unanimous confirmation by the International Court of Justice of a practice of international Arbitral Tribunals (of which the foregoing are contemporary examples) – a practice which is a characteristic of majority decision-making in judicial bodies – is not surprising. It nevertheless is to be welcomed.

---

[27] 3 *Iran–US CTR* 42, 55. For other such holdings by Judge Holtzmann, see *Starrett Housing Corp. et al.* v. *The Government of the Islamic Republic of Iran et al.*, 4 *Iran–US CTR* 122, 159 and 16 *Iran–US CTR* 112, 238; *Touche Ross* v. *The Islamic Republic of Iran*, 9 *Iran–US CTR* 284; *Housing and Urban Services International, Inc.* v. *The Government of the Islamic Republic of Iran*, 9 *Iran–US CTR* 313, and *First Travel Corp.* v. *The Government of the Islamic Republic of Iran*, 9 *Iran–US CTR* 360.

[28] 1 *Iran–US CTR* 189

14

The Prospects for International Arbitration: Inter-State Disputes

Comments on a Paper by Ambassador M. C. W. Pinto

℘

Introduction

I wish to congratulate Ambassador Pinto on his excellent paper on The Prospects for International Arbitration of Inter-State Disputes. His survey is scholarly, graceful, and enlightening; his analysis is stimulating; and his prescriptions, if modest and measured, make sense.

Before proceeding to comment further on Ambassador Pinto's paper, I should like to say a word about the remark of a previous speaker about the inflexibility of Professor Verzijl. I would rather emphasize his adherence to legal principle. His principled approach is illustrated by his performance as President of the French–Mexican Claims Commission. As President, Professor Verzijl declined to indulge endless delaying tactics. He rightly and courageously asserted the cardinal principles of international arbitration and international law that "the unilateral refusal of a State to recognize a regularly appointed umpire in the regular performance of his functions is contrary to international law" and that "yielding" to such "an illegal attitude would amount to disregarding the general principle of law according to which no one may take advantage, in his own favor, of the non-fulfilment of his engagements."[1]

I understand Ambassador Pinto's essential thesis to be this. International arbitration between States was in its origins a diplomatic as well as a judicial process. The critical component of its diplomatic character was the authority of the Arbitral Tribunal to adjudge not only on the basis of law but of equity. The Arbitral Tribunal was entitled not only to decide between a winner and a loser but to arrive at a judgment in which both parties were winners or both

---

First published in A.H.A. Soons (ed.), *International Arbitration: Past and Prospects* (1990). Reprinted by permission of Kluwer Academic Publishers; Dordrecht, Martinus Nijhoff Publishers.
[1] *Annual Digest and Reports of Public International Law Cases 1929–1930*, pp. 425–426.

losers but in any event in which a measure of compromise between conflicting interests was struck.

However, Ambassador Pinto maintains, for the last century or so international arbitration has rather tended to realize a judicial model. It has tended to assimilate itself to an international judicial procedure. To be sure it is more flexible than a court in that the parties choose the Arbitrators and maintain a measure of control over the Tribunal. But it is essentially a judicial process, particularly because the modern inter-State Arbitral Tribunal decides on the basis of law rather than equity.

Ambassador Pinto suggests that the widespread indisposition of many States to resort to international arbitration stems from this trend towards judicial arbitration. He indicates that judicial arbitration is acceptable only among like-minded and culturally similar parties, though he observes that the United Nations Convention on the Law of the Sea might run counter to that conclusion, should it receive sufficient ratifications to bring it into force. Since judicial arbitration generally is not acceptable to parties which do not share a close sense of community, Ambassador Pinto concludes that, in the greatly enlarged international community of today, there is and will be reluctance to accord international arbitration general acceptance as a reliable aid in the maintenance of constructive international relations. He suggests that efforts to close the constitutional and procedural "loopholes" of the diplomatic mode of arbitration may have the effect of inhibiting the willingness "of all but those culturally similar States, architects of the process and most familiar with it, to submit to arbitration," the implication being that States not of the West understandably shy away from it. He concludes that, today, arbitration stands alongside judicial settlement, creating "a distinction without a difference." He finally proposes that the arbitral process be subjected to inter-disciplinary study, with a view towards formulating rules on arbitration, founded on a common, worldwide perception of the arbitral process, which might actually attract worldwide support.

There is a good deal more in Ambassador Pinto's paper, on which time does not now permit comment. I shall accordingly largely confine my observations to what appears to be the essence of his analysis.

Commentary

I should first like to ask whether his historical summary and analysis are sound, and immediately reply that, in the main, they impress me as quite sound. I am not sure that Ambassador Pinto's sense of the decline of contemporary inter-State arbitration and what strikes me as Professor Sohn's evaluation of its modern rise are consistent. But, apart from what are the statistics and how one evaluates them, I should like to make the following comments.

The dichotomy which Ambassador Pinto makes between diplomatic arbitration and judicial arbitration is of course well established and rooted in the historical development of arbitration. However, for him, the essential difference between the two seems to be that diplomatic arbitration admits considerations of equity, that it indeed allows decisions to be made *ex aequo et bono*, whereas judicial arbitration is a process of application of legal rules to the case in hand.

In my view, that is not the whole or even the essential difference. An arbitration tribunal whether in the diplomatic or the judicial mode can be, and sometimes has been, seen as empowered to apply equitable considerations or even, exceptionally, to decide *ex aequo et bono*. The essential difference lies rather in whether an inter-State Arbitral Tribunal, at each stage of its establishment and its operation and in the conclusion of its mission, is subject to the autonomous will of its sovereign sponsors, or whether it is not.

The question is not so much one of applicable law as of applicable loopholes. I am reminded of the story of the late actor and humorist, W.C. Fields. Fields was not known for his religious devotion. So his family was surprised to see him, on his deathbed, intently studying the Bible, at which he had not been seen to look for some sixty years. "What are you doing?" they gently inquired. Fields replied: "Looking for loopholes."

Well, in the mode of diplomatic arbitration, States did not and do not have far to look. Loopholes abound. The State which had agreed to arbitrate with another disputes arising out of the interpretation of a particular treaty or another class of dispute could, once a dispute had arisen, maintain that there was no dispute. Or it could maintain that, if there were a dispute, it did not fall within the compromissory clause. Or it could fail to agree upon a *compromis* or to appoint its Arbitrator. Or it could fail to agree upon a neutral Arbitrator. Or, if it did all these things and if the tribunal were launched, it could withdraw its arbitrator once it saw that the award was coming out the other way. Or, if the award did come out, it could claim that it was void on the ground that the Arbitrators exceeded their competence. These are only traditional, well-tried illustrations of such loopholes; there are still others.

In contrast to diplomatic arbitration stands judicial arbitration, in which the loopholes are closed or almost so. The archetype of judicial arbitration is the "Draft on Arbitral Procedure" prepared by the International Law Commission of the United Nations in its early, especially distinguished days. Under the leadership of its eminent Special Rapporteur, Professor Georges

Scelle, the Commission produced a draft which was superb in its technical craftsmanship and in its fidelity to the principle that "While the free will of the parties is essential as a condition of the creation of the common obligation to arbitrate, the will of one party cannot, in the view of the Commission, be regarded as a condition of the continued validity and effectiveness of the obligation freely undertaken."[2]

The Commission's Draft embodied judicial arbitration in the most literal sense, since, at every point in which the arbitral process might be avoided or evaded, the International Court of Justice was to step in to block out the loophole.

A paramount deficiency of the Draft was that States were not generally prepared to accept it. It turned out, when States came to comment on the provisions of the Draft and to debate them in the Sixth Committee of the General Assembly, that many of them, too many, liked loopholes. The Committee split, and the majority did not favor the Commission's Draft.

But, contrary to what I believe Ambassador Pinto tends to imply, the division was not East–West or North–South; it apparently was not an expression of cultural differences. To be sure, the majority these days in the United Nations is overwhelmingly composed of Third World States, but that was not the case in the General Assembly in 1955. Rather, the Draft encountered a mixed reception in more than one quarter.

Thus, while the United Kingdom found itself "in very general agreement with the provisions of the draft code,"[3] the Netherlands, as Ambassador Pinto himself shows, maintained with characteristic bluntness that a "special characteristic of arbitration" is that "it is rather easy for an unwilling party to find an excuse for shirking its engagements" and that if such loopholes were to be closed then arbitration might lose its attractiveness for States.[4]

For its part, Uruguay transmitted comments on the Draft of the then Professor Eduardo Jiménez de Aréchaga, who unreservedly supported "the magnificent draft of the International Law Commission" and who supplied specific reasons for his view, concluding that:

> A State which has entered into an undertaking to submit disputes to arbitration cannot evade that undertaking by the simple expedient of refusing to perform the acts stipulated which are necessary for the fulfilment of the main obligation. It is a rule of good faith between individuals as between States, that anyone who has undertaken to follow a certain line of conduct is also bound to carry out the subsidiary acts essential for that purpose.[5]

---

[2] *Yearbook of the International Commission (1953)*, 2, p. 204.   [3] *Ibid.*, p. 237.   [4] *Ibid.*, p. 235.
[5] *Ibid.*, pp. 230–240.

While Norway supported the principles on which the Draft was based, as distinguished a pillar of the international legal establishment as Professor Charles de Visscher opposed them on the ground that the Draft, "by endeavoring . . . to plug up all the openings and to foresee every loophole, . . . runs the risk of hindering its [arbitration's] development."[6] Another Western expert in the field, Professor Kenneth S. Carlston, took a similar approach.[7]

There accordingly may be room for wondering whether cultural factors actually are the cause of any reluctance of newly independent States to employ arbitration. Perhaps they are, but an opposition to judicial arbitration is found in the West as elsewhere, and has been articulated with special acuity by leading Western commentators.

I may interpose that I am more favorable to judicial arbitration than I gather is Ambassador Pinto. I do not believe that it is a distortion of the true or desirable nature of international arbitration. In my view, many elements of the judicial mode of arbitration are rooted not only in international legal principle but in State practice. Moreover,

> some States, even at this nationalistic juncture in world affairs, may prefer resort to a process that gives promise of a higher degree of efficacy in the resolution of their disputes. While, for other States, the appeal, or an appeal, of arbitration may lie in the opportunities which the process traditionally has presented for the evasion of obligations, for some States the appeal of arbitration may be heightened by a process that affords the parties genuine equality under law.[8]

At the same time, it must be recognized that the Draft proposed by the International Law Commission went well beyond codification, as it was entitled to do, and into the sphere of progressive development. I use the word "progressive" not routinely but purposefully; I believe that the Draft was not regressive but progressive. But it should have been obvious that the generality of States was not at that time, as they are not at this time, prepared to accept it. The Commission's Draft repeatedly would have endowed the International Court of Justice with compulsory jurisdiction over crucial questions of the arbitral process. If States generally were then and are today unwilling to accord the Court compulsory jurisdiction, why should it be supposed that they would be disposed to grant it such pervasive compulsory jurisdiction in the processes of international arbitration?

Of course, it may be that the outlook of States in respect of the Optional

---

[6] Charles de Visscher, "Reflections on the Present Prospects of International Adjudication," *American Journal of International Law* (1956), 50, p. 469.

[7] Kenneth S. Carlston, "Codification of International Arbitral Procedure," *American Journal of International Law* (1953), 47, p. 218.

[8] Stephen M. Schwebel, *International Arbitration: Three Salient Problems* (1987), p. 151.

Clause, after what Sir Humphrey Waldock aptly characterized as a decline, is on a rise. There are at any rate promising signs of a turn for the better. It remains to be seen whether those signs actually signal very much. If it turns out that they do, such a development might have beneficent results for arbitral processes as well.

As it is, the work of the International Law Commission in this sphere has not rusted entirely unused. While no treaty or code was adopted, the model rules and commentary which the Commission in the end produced have been valuable not only in scholarly but in practical terms, as is illustrated by reliance upon them in the arbitral awards in the *Aramco*[9] and *Liamco*[10] cases.

Conclusions

Now let me return to Ambassador Pinto's statement that when judicial arbitration is placed alongside judicial settlement, there is "a distinction without a difference." This is not so, and actually Ambassador Pinto elsewhere evidences appreciation of that fact. In arbitration, however judicially inspired or shaped, the parties choose the arbitrators, but in the International Court of Justice, the United Nations elects the judges. In arbitration, the parties may prescribe the governing law, which in the Court is prescribed by the Statute. In arbitration, the parties or the tribunal may decide upon the rules of procedure, but in the Court, the Rules of Court govern. In arbitration, the proceedings and sometimes the award are secret but in the Court, the oral argument is public and judgments are published.

At the same time, chambers of the Court formed to deal with a particular case are a kind of halfway house between arbitration and adjudication. While the Court elects the chamber, the parties have a voice which has been decisive in the particular choice of the judges composing the chamber. They may appoint *ad hoc* judges as well. Nevertheless, the chamber is the Court, governed by its Rules, traditions, and docket.

Permit me to conclude with a few further points. As I suggested earlier, I do not think that the principal distinction between judicial and diplomatic arbitration is the law, or lack of law, applied. That is to say, the leavening of equity is not a characteristic of diplomatic arbitration alone. One finds it in some arbitrations of the last 100 years as well as earlier. It is not entirely absent from the judgments of the International Court of Justice, as decisions in

---

[9] *Saudi Arabia v. Aramco, International Law Reports,* (1963), Volume 27, p. 117.

[10] *Libyan American Oil Co. (LIAMCO) v. the Government of the Libyan Arab Republic, International Law Reports,* (1982), Volume 62, p. 140.

respect of maritime delimitation show. As the Netherlands put it in its comments on the Draft of the International Law Commission:

> Arbitration ranks among the oldest means of peacefully settling international disputes. In order to maintain its place beside more recent judicial means, arbitration should retain definite characteristics of its own by which to distinguish itself from judicial settlement. These special qualities should induce Governments to keep arbitration in store as a helpful instrument. Amongst these characteristics the somewhat mediatory quality of the award should be first in our mind. Though arbitration must be kept on the "basis of respect for law" according to the First Convention of The Hague of 1899, the award, however, will always show a predisposition towards mediation and arbitrations are prone to adhere to the law in a less orthodox way than a judge is apt to do . . .[11]

At the same time, in the arbitral process, there typically is a winner and a loser. Whether the loser wins something is often not so much a matter of the law specified to be dispositive as it is a matter of the merits of its case and the propensities of the particular arbitrators. Some arbitrators see their mission as strictly judicial but others do not.

What is the outlook for arbitration between States? The simple and safe answer is, it is unknown. But what is clear is that arbitration cannot flourish when international tensions are extreme and the use of force is rampant. If the nineteenth century was the apogee of arbitration, it may be that it was because war was at a relative perigee. Contrary to the expectations at the turn of this century, arbitration is not the way to prevent war; it is rather a product of peace. If in fact the signs of peaceful settlement, the signs of a reviving United Nations prove to be substantial and lasting, then we may expect a fuller flowering of the processes of international arbitration.

[11] *Yearbook of the International Commission* (1953), 2, p. 235

PART III
United Nations

෴

15

The Origins and Development of Article 99 of the Charter

The Powers of the Secretary-General of the United Nations

ᘓ

Article 99 of the Charter of the United Nations, which provides that "the Secretary-General may bring to the attention of the Security Council any matter which in his opinion may threaten the maintenance of international peace and security," was described by the Preparatory Commission of the United Nations as endowing the Secretary-General with "a quite special right which goes beyond any power previously accorded to the head of an international organization."[1] This description is perhaps slightly exaggerated as it fails to take account of resolutions of the First and Second Assemblies of the League of Nations which entrusted the League Secretary-General with powers of a nature remarkably similar to those with which the United Nations Secretary-General is invested by Article 99.[2] But the words of the

---

The British Year Book of International Law 1951 (1952), 28.

[1] Preparatory Commission, *Report*, doc. PC/20, p. 87.

[2] The First Assembly adopted on December 10, 1920 a Report on the Implementation of Article XVI of the Covenant which in part read:

> It shall be the duty of the Secretary-General to call to the attention of the Council any facts which in his opinion show that a member of the League has become a Covenant-breaking State within the meaning of Article XVI;
>
> Upon receiving such an intimation, the Council shall, on the request of any of its members, hold a meeting with the least possible delay to consider it.

The Second Assembly adopted on October 4, 1921 Interpretive Resolutions regarding Article XVI, one of which prescribed that

> if a breach of the Covenant be committed, or if there arise a danger of such breach being committed, the Secretary-General shall at once give notice thereof to all members of the Council. Upon receipt ... of such notice by the Secretary-General, the Council will meet as soon as possible (quoted in Rappard, *The Quest for Peace* [1940], pp. 227, 237. Professor Rappard discusses the origin of these Resolutions, pp. 220 ff.).

These Resolutions were not of course equal in weight to provisions of the Covenant. Moreover, inasmuch as they referred to Article XVI alone, their activation may be said to have depended upon the prior fulfillment of the first clause of that article: "Should any member of the League resort to war in disregard of its covenants ..." The late Earl of Perth explains his failure to implement the Resolutions by reference to this latter consideration (see S. M. Schwebel, *The Secretary-General of the United Nations: His Political Powers and Practice* [1952], p. 231).

Preparatory Commission aptly emphasize that, with respect to the express constitutional position of the Secretary-General of the international political organization, Article 99 represents a departure of consequence.

The substance of Article 99 is not to be found in the Covenant. While in the early drafts of the Covenant powers were to have been allotted to the Secretary-General which may be said to have approached those later given to the Secretary-General of the United Nations,[3] the text of the treaty which finally emerged from the Paris negotiations provided in its analogous article merely that, in case of war or threat of war, "the Secretary-General shall on the request of any Member of the League forthwith summon a meeting of the Council."[4] The Secretary-General's lack of express political authority in the Covenant, in that and in other articles,[5] was given emphasis by the attitude of the holders of the post, who confined their political initiative to private, "behind-the-scenes" activity.[6]

The desirability of a provision in the constitution of the organization which would succeed the League on the lines expressed in Article 99 was agreed upon in essence as early as 1940 by the Advisory Committee on Foreign Relations of the Department of State.[7] In 1943 the then Viscount Cranborne suggested, in a similar vein, that "it will be necessary in the new organization, that the chief permanent official ... who will be an international official and therefore not open to the same embarrassment as the Ministers of individual States, should be empowered to bring before its members, on his own initiative, any potentially dangerous development at an

---

[3] See Howard Ellis, *The Origin, Structure and Working of the League of Nations* (1928), p. 163, No. 2; Schwebel, *Secretary-General*, p. 227, notes 3 and 4; Viscount Cecil, *A Great Experiment* (1941), p. 89; Hunter Miller, *The Drafting of the Covenant* (1928), Vol. II, pp. 108, 110, 120–121, 142.

[4] Article XI.

[5] Those relating to the Secretary-General's powers are Articles VI, VII, XI, XV, and XVIII. For analyses which accent the political authority latent in these articles see Morley, *The Society of Nations* (1932), pp. 309–314, 264–265, 486, 566; and Cagne, *Le Secrétariat Général de la Société des Nations* (1936), pp. 54–66, 81–128.

[6] See Walters, *A History of the League of Nations* (1952), Vol. I, pp. 75–80, Vol. II, pp. 556–560; and Schwebel, *Secretary-General*, pp. 3, 6–10, 216–221, 253.

[7] See "Memorandum of May 1, 1940, by Hugh R. Wilson, Vice-Chairman of the Committee Arising from Conversations in Mr. Welles' Office, April 19 and 26," as reproduced in Department of State, *Postwar Foreign Policy Preparation, 1939–1945* (1949), Pub. 3580 (hereinafter cited as *Policy Preparation*), Appendix 5, p. 459: "There should be established a permanent group whose duty it would be to watch over events in the various countries and to announce to the Political Body any situation, together with recommendations for its treatment, which in the judgement of the group is likely to become acute and to lead to disturbance. The group should consist of selected individuals rather than government appointees, recognized for their wisdom, character and experience. The group should have wide powers for travel and investigation and perhaps for the maintenance of representatives in the various countries to furnish periodic reports of conditions."

early stage before the aggressor has time to gird himself for war ..."[8] In the same year, the State Department's planning group produced the first of the series of constitutional drafts, the last of which was to be placed before the Powers at Dumbarton Oaks. While this "Draft Constitution of International Organization" did not contain the substance of an Article 99 in terms, the Secretary-General was designated as permanent Chairman of the proposed Executive Committee and of the Council, and was empowered, in the event of a breach or threatened breach of the peace, to request the parties "to desist from any action which would further aggravate the situation" and to "forthwith summon a meeting of the Council."[9] His powers thus were to embrace and surpass those ultimately to be allotted to him by Article 99.

The Department's second draft went farther. The Director-General (as the Secretary-General was called at this stage) would preside over the Council and participate in its deliberations without the right to vote as well.[10] Moreover, it was provided that States failing to comply with the Director-General's request to desist from any action which might prejudice a peaceful settlement of a breach or threat of breach of the peace "shall be regarded as intending a breach of the peace," and that "the Council shall forthwith institute such measures, including measures of force, as it deems appropriate."[11]

The third draft proposal in Washington, the "Possible Plan for a General International Organization," went farthest in that direction.[12] According to that plan there would be two permanent international officials, the President and the Director-General. The latter would confine himself to administrative functions.[13] The President, "a person of widely recognized eminence,"[14] would preside over the Executive Council,[15] and perform such other duties

---

[8] "If the noble Earl, Lord Perth, had enjoyed this power as Secretary-General of the League," Lord Cranborne continued, "the history of the League might have been a very different one" (House of Lords, *Parliamentary Debates*, Official Report, 5th Series, Vol. CXXVII, April 15, 1943, p. 249). In the same debate, Viscount Cecil of Chelwood, who proposed the procedure upon which Lord Cranborne comments, twice emphasized the desirability of something in the nature of an Article 99 (*ibid.*, April 14, p. 182; April 15, pp. 255–256).

[9] Draft of July 14, 1943, reproduced in *Policy Preparation*, Appendix 13, pp. 475, 476, 478.

[10] "The Charter of the United Nations" (Draft), August 14, 1943, *ibid.*, Appendix 23, p. 528.

[11] *Ibid.*, Appendix 35, p. 590.   [12] Of April 29, 1944; *ibid.*, Appendix 35, pp. 582–591.

[13] *Ibid.*, p. 590.

[14] *Ibid.*

[15] *Ibid.*, p. 586. The International Civil Aviation Organization follows this pattern of two permanent officers. There is a President of the Council, who presides over ICAO's executive organ, and a Secretary-General, who acts as the Organization's chief executive officer (*Convention on International Civil Aviation*, Articles 51, 54, 59, 60). The desirability of entrusting the chairmanship of the main political organ of the world organization to either the Secretary-General or to an officer analagous to the President who would serve with the Secretary-General is discussed in Royal Institute of International Affairs, *The International Secretariat of the Future* (1944), pp. 32–33.

of a "general political character" as were entrusted to him by the General Assembly or by the Executive Council.[16] In the event that a threat to the peace or breach of the peace should occur, the council "should immediately be convened by the Chairman [President] who should be empowered also to initiate such emergency measures as may be necessary, subject to review by the council when it resumes session."[17]

However, the "Tentative Proposals for a General International Organization" which the United States evolved on the eve of the Dumbarton Oaks conversations reduced the proposed political authority of the Secretary-General to its nadir.[18] There would be no President, and the Director-General, far from presiding over the Council or having emergency powers to act in the Council's name, was to be denied the right to bring to the Council's attention matters which in his opinion threatened the peace.[19] Finally, the United States appears to have revised its views concerning the powers of the Secretary-General a fifth time, by accepting[20] the addition of what later came to be designated as Article 99.[21] The right of the Secretary-General to bring to the attention of the Security Council any matter which in his opinion may threaten international peace and security was in fact agreed upon without much difficulty by those participating in the Dumbarton Oaks Conference.[22]

These American drafts, being in the nature of *travaux préparatoires* twice

---

The Secretary-General of the United Nations, in the person of the Director of the Political Division of the Department of Security Council Affairs, has presided over governmental sub-committees of the Interim Committee of the General Assembly. The contribution of the Secretariat to the work of these subcommittees was acknowledged by the Interim Committee (see Parry, "The Secretariat of the United Nations," *World Affairs* [July 1950], 4, p. 362).

The *Articles of Agreement of the International Bank for Reconstruction and Development* (Article V, section 5) and the *Articles of Agreement of the International Monetary Fund* (Article XII, section 4) provide that the chiefs of their operating staffs shall be respectively President and Managing Director of their executive bodies.

[16] *Policy Preparation*, p. 590.

[17] *Ibid.*, p. 588. These emergency measures seem to have included the employment of armed forces which earlier would have been placed at the Council's disposition (*ibid.*).

[18] Of July 18, 1944; *ibid.*, Appendix 38, pp. 595–606.

[19] *Ibid.*, p. 605. See the summary and interpretation of these successive drafts contained in Russell and Muther, *A History of the United Nations Charter* (1958), pp. 371–377.

[20] Article 99 was "proposed by both China and Great Britain, evidently as a result of widespread criticism of the League system, which had allowed only a Member State to bring an alleged threat before the Council and thus had hampered its speedy convening to deal with a threat to the peace. The United States and the Soviet Union had no objections, and the provision was agreed to provide 'a very useful procedure when no Member of the Organization wished to take the initiative'. The American idea that the chief officer might also bring matters before the Assembly was apparently not discussed." Russell and Muther, *Charter*, p. 432 (the inner quotation is from Great Britain, *A Commentary on the Dumbarton Oaks Proposals for the Establishment of a General International Organization*, p. 11).

[21] Dumbarton Oaks, "Proposals for the Establishment of a General International Organization," reproduced in *Policy Preparation*, October 7, 1944, Appendix 43, p. 619.

[22] See Russell and Muther, *Charter*, p. 432.

removed from the Charter, would seem to have tenuous legal force, but they are instructive insofar as they shed light upon the intent of the prime drafter of the treaty from which the powers of the Secretary-General flow. They are of especial interest because the record of the Dumbarton Oaks discussions, to the limited extent that one exists,[23] is unpublished, and because the consideration of Article 99 at San Francisco did not come to grips with the essentials of the Article. The express political powers of the Secretary-General, as envisaged in these early statements and drafts, would seem to be of alternative classes, the second of which encompassed the first. The purpose of Article 99 first conceived is not to create in the Secretary-General an officer who will preside over and lead the discussions of the Council, but rather to secure an impartial watchdog, an agent who will bring to the attention of the organization threats to the peace which Member States, because of political considerations, will tend to be hesitant in raising. Alternatively, three of the State Department drafts enable, in varying degrees, the chief permanent international official not only to summon purposeful meetings of the council on his own initiative (the essence of Article 99), but empower him to preside over the Council, to admonish States threatening the peace, and to perform duties of a general political character – duties which may extend so far as to an emergency activation of the processes of collective security in the Council's name. Either to give to the Secretary-General these latter imposing powers, or no express political powers at all – these appear to have been the conflicting tendencies within the State Department. The conflict apparently was resolved by accepting the intermediate solution of an Article 99. While the inaccessibility of the Dumbarton Oaks records precludes a confident estimate, the pattern of pre-Dumbarton Oaks thinking, together with the interpretation of Article 99 later advanced by the United States representative in the course of the discussions of the Committee of Experts of the Security Council,[24] would perhaps seem to indicate that the United States foresaw the application of Article 99 in terms, and did not intend the article to invest the Secretary-General either with a broad participatory role in Security Council proceedings or with general political authority. The role of the Secretary-General in practice has developed in a manner precisely contrary to this seeming intention.[25]

---

[23] *Policy Preparation*, pp. 306, 309, 311, 331. (Since the writing of this article, the cited work of Russell and Muther was published in 1958. Those authors had access to the Dumbarton Oaks records as well as earlier unpublished files. Their summary of those records and of successive drafts of what came to be the Charter articles on the power of the Secretary-General is the fullest available. *Charter*, pp. 371–377.)

[24] Below, and Schwebel, *Secretary-General*, pp. 21–23, 84–87, 253. The United States representative in the Committee of Experts in these discussions, Mr. Joseph E. Johnson, participated in the Dumbarton Oaks negotiations (*Policy Preparation*, p. 303).

[25] See Schwebel, *Secretary-General*, pp. 85–117.

The debate at San Francisco over Article 99 was confined to three questions: whether its invocation should be a matter of the Secretary-General's right or a prescription of duty; whether its application should extend to the General Assembly or be restricted to the Security Council; and whether, in addition to matters threatening international peace and security, the Secretary-General should be empowered to draw the Organization's attention to "any matters which constitute an infringement or violation of the principles of the Charter."[26]

There was some sentiment in favour of imposing upon the Secretary-General as a duty the implementation of Article 99. A motion was offered which would have changed the article to read: "The Secretary-General shall bring to the attention of the Security Council," instead of "may bring." The majority, however, preferred that the exercise of Article 99 be a matter of the Secretary-General's discretion, and the motion was then withdrawn.[27] There may be said to flow from the discretionary nature of the article which was thus affirmed not only the evident option either to invoke or not to invoke Article 99, but, further, the Secretary-General's right to choose the precise means of implementing the article. As a matter of strategy, the Secretary-General may exert his influence so that it will not be necessary for him formally to bring the matter in question to the attention of the Security Council. Article 99, in other words, may be interpreted as providing a specific legal authorization for that extensive, informal, behind-the-scenes political activity of the Secretary-General for which the propensities of his position, and the precedent of the League, provide a non-textual basis. The option of attributing certain of that activity more or less directly to the text of the Charter may prove valuable to a Secretary-General in some contingencies.

It was further proposed that Article 99 be broadened to give to the Secretary-General the right to bring matters within its compass before either the General Assembly or the Security Council or both.[28] An amendment to this effect was voted down for a variety of slight reasons.[29] Its defeat has turned out to be of little consequence, however, for the Secretary-General was subsequently accorded by the rules of the General Assembly the right to add to the provisional agenda "all items which [he] deems it necessary to put before the General Assembly."[30] The Secretary-General has, not unreason-

---

[26] United Nations Conference on International Organization (UNCIO), *Documents*, Vol. 7, pp. 162–163, Committee I/2, 17th meeting.

[27] *Ibid.*, p. 556, draft report of Sub-committee I/2/D.   [28] *Ibid.*, p. 162, Committee I/2, 17th meeting.

[29] See *ibid.*, pp. 168–169, Committee I/2, 18th meeting; Goodrich and Hambro, *The Charter of the United Nations* (1949), p. 502; and Schwebel, *Secretary-General*, p. 20.

[30] General Assembly, *Rules of Procedure*, doc. A/520, Rule 12.

ably, interpreted "all items" to include political and security items.[31] This interpretation places the Secretary-General in a position *vis-à-vis* the Assembly comparable to that which he enjoys in relation to the Security Council by virtue of Article 99. For apparently the Secretary-General may add to the Assembly's provisional agenda any matter which he might, by the terms of that article, draw to the Council's attention. The Secretary-General's Assembly agenda rights would not seem to equate wholly with those he enjoys under Article 99, however. For the Security Council has, at least according to the Charter, "primary responsibility"[32] in security matters. It is, moreover, more likely that the General Assembly might decline to take up a security item submitted by the Secretary-General than that the Security Council would so decline; for the Secretary-General's raising of a matter before the Security Council is rooted in an explicit Charter authorization to which the Security Council must pay due respect. Furthermore, a matter raised under Article 99 would tend to draw more attention than another political item submitted for the Assembly's crowded schedule.[33]

Lastly, it was proposed that Article 99 be amended so as to endow the Secretary-General with authority to raise matters which would not necessarily threaten the peace, but which would constitute violations of the principles of the Charter. Iran and Egypt were prominent in backing this Uruguayan amendment, which viewed the Secretary-General as the agent who would bring to the Organization's attention domestic infringements of the Charter's principles. The United Kingdom, Canada, and New Zealand led the majority opposition to this proposal: it would, they held, give to the Secretary-General a wider authority than had been given to the Members in this respect, and, the more so in view of the "very heavy burdens" already placed upon him, would put the Secretary-General in a "very difficult position."[34] The Uruguayan amendment, which, had it been adopted, would have profoundly modified the Charter, failed by only three votes.[35] The significant degree of support which such an extreme proposal mustered illus-

---

[31] For example, the Secretary-General offered for the agenda of the Fifth Session his "Memorandum of Points for Consideration in the Development of a Twenty-Year Program for Achieving Peace through the United Nations" – a highly political item which included such matters as atomic control and periodic meetings of Foreign Ministers.

[32] Article 24, paragraph 1.

[33] The provision of Article 98 that "the Secretary-General shall make an annual report to the General Assembly on the work of the Organization" puts at the disposal of the Secretary-General another medium for bringing matters threatening international peace and security to the attention of the General Assembly.

[34] UNCIO, *Documents*, Vol. 7, p. 163, Committee I/2, 17th meeting.

[35] *Ibid.*, pp. 168–169, Committee I/2, 18th meeting.

trates the desire widespread at San Francisco to invest the Secretary-General with substantial political authority.

The Preparatory Commission moderately extended the official exegesis of Article 99. It was pointed out, in its Executive Committee discussions, that, as regards political disputes, the cases in which the Secretary-General would find it necessary to invoke the Article in terms might well be rare. Article 99 was seen to be of "very great political importance from a broader point of view. The Secretary-General's function encompassed the reporting of any developments – for example, in the economic and social field – which in his view could have serious political implications remediable only by political action. In holding this responsibility, the Secretary-General formed a vital link between the various units of the Organization."[36] Professor Lauterpacht similarly has drawn attention to the "considerable potentialities"[37] which Article 99 presents for bringing before the Security Council violations of human rights so grave that they threaten the maintenance of international peace and security.[38] Moreover, he notes: "The clause of domestic jurisdic-

---

[36] Executive Committee of the Preparatory Commission, Committee 6, 4th meeting, doc. PC/EX/SEC/ 9.

[37] Lauterpacht, *International Law and Human Rights* (1950), p. 187.

[38] Professor Lauterpacht's restriction of human rights matters which may be raised under Article 99 to those so grave that they may threaten international peace and security is more accurate than the looser characterization of the Preparatory Commission: developments which, in the Secretary-General's view, "could have serious political implications remediable only by political action." It should be noted, however, that the matters referred to in Article 99 are matters of the Secretary-General's appreciation ("The Secretary-General may bring ... any matter which in his opinion ..."); and that the norm to which he must conform is flexible. The determination of what is a threat to international peace and security is one susceptible of a considerable variance in judgement. And the Secretary-General's discretion is the broader in that he may raise matters which not only threaten but those which "may threaten" international peace and security. The wide area of appreciation thus accorded the Secretary-General is further emphasized by the stress upon the value of a procedure like that of Article 99 lying in its affording the means of bringing questions which may threaten the peace to the attention of the organization in their incipiency. "The great thing," Lord Cecil observed, in proposing that the successor to the Secretary-General of the League "should have a special duty to call the attention of the new authority to any dangers ... which might exist," "is to interfere at an early stage; if you wait until war has actually broken out, you will be faced with all kinds of difficulties which may prove overwhelming" (House of Lords, *Parliamentary Debates*, April 15, 1943, p. 256. See also the remarks of Lord Cranborne [note 8] and the State Department memorandum of May 1, 1940 [note 7], p. 372). Evidently, situations in their incipiency may take a variety of paths, which in the end do not threaten the peace; such paths are not open to a full-blown dispute which, if it is to be a threat, would probably be one at the outset.

Nevertheless, while the Secretary-General necessarily would seem to have broad latitude in his appreciation of which matters, in his opinion, may threaten international peace and security, the Security Council may decline to pursue a question which the Secretary-General brings to its attention under Article 99, whether or not his action in raising it objectively is consonant with the strictest interpretation of the terms of Article 99. The Secretary-General may do no more than place the matter on the Council's provisional agenda (Security Council, *Rules of Procedure*, doc. S/96/Rev.3, Rules 22, 6; Rule 3 provides that the President of the Council must call a meeting of the Council if the

tion of Article 2, paragraph 7, presents no impediment in the way of the exercise of this particular function of the Secretary-General. The matters referred to in Article 99 are not, by definition, essentially within the domestic jurisdiction of any State."[39]

A last source of early governmental commentary upon Article 99 is the meetings of the Committee of Experts of the Security Council which were held in May 1946 to consider, *inter alia*, the rights of intervention, on the part of the Secretary-General, in the Council's proceedings. In proposing an unrestricted right of intervention by the Secretary-General, the Soviet representative "pointed out the difference in the conception of the powers accorded the Secretary-General of the United Nations as opposed to those accorded the Secretary-General of the League ... Specifically, he noted the additional powers given the Secretary-General under Article 99."[40] In reply, the representative of the United States doubted "whether the Secretary-General had the right to draft specific resolutions and proposals under Article 99."[41] But he emphasized his "Government's interest in building up the strength of the Secretary-General within the provisions of Article 98"[42] (which speaks of the "capacity" in which the Secretary-General shall act in his relations with the Security Council). The American suggestion that the Committee's discussions did no more than establish "the minimum rules on the basis of which the Secretary-General's role could be developed in practice" and did not constitute a "definitive definition" of his rights under Article 99 was agreed to without difficulty.[43]

A number of interlocking powers flowing from Article 99 and its official exposition may at this point be distinguished. First of all, there is the evident

Secretary-General wishes to invoke Article 99). The Security Council remains the master of its working agenda. However, its members would in law be required to consider their response to the Secretary-General's action in the light of their obligations under Articles 2, paragraph 2, and 24, paragraph 2.

The discretionary aspects of Article 99, insofar as they concern the Secretary-General's appreciation of which matters may threaten international peace and security, are not to be confused with that discretionary element which comes into play after the Secretary-General has decided that a matter may constitute a threat under Article 99. At this latter point, it is still for the Secretary-General to decide whether he will formally invoke the article, or take other or no action.

[39] Lauterpacht, *International Law*, p. 187. The rejection at San Francisco of the Uruguayan amendment does not derogate from Professor Lauterpacht's conclusion, for the domestic infringements of the Charter's principles which the Uruguayan amendment would have empowered the Secretary-General to bring to the Organization's attention were those which would not threaten the peace.

[40] Summary Record of the 47th meeting of the Committee of Experts, doc. S/Procedure/100.

[41] The United States delegate was "not at all sure that the Charter can be construed as authorizing the Secretary-General to make comments on political and substantive matters" (doc. S/Procedure/103).

[42] Doc. S/Procedure/103.

[43] The Secretary-General, as a result of these discussions, was accorded broad rights of intervention in the proceedings of the Security Council (*Rules of Procedure*, doc. S/96/Rev.3, Rule 22).

authority of the Secretary-General to bring to the attention of the Security Council any matter which in his opinion may threaten the maintenance of international peace and security. In this, when taken together with Article 98, the position of the Secretary-General may be said to approximate to that of a twelfth member of the Security Council, without veto or vote. Or his situation may be likened to that of a Member State under Article 35, which may similarly have placed on the provisional agenda of the Security Council (or of the General Assembly) any dispute, or any situation which might lead to international friction or give rise to a dispute. In fact, the Secretary-General's prerogative here extends farther, for he may place "any matter" on the provisional agenda of the Security Council,[44] not just any dispute or situation. And, though the Secretary-General, like a State, can place a question on the Council's provisional agenda only, it seems improbable that the Security Council would refuse to take up an item submitted by the Secretary-General under Article 99. But the Council has been known to reject items placed on its provisional agenda by a Member State. The Secretary-General's authority may be further compared with that of the General Assembly, which "may call the attention of the Security Council to situations which are likely to endanger international peace and security."[45]

The parallels notwithstanding, the formal application of the Secretary-General's literal rights under Article 99 would seem to be of limited importance. In United Nations practice (as contrasted, perhaps, with that of the League), States have been far from hesitant in haling other States before the Security Council (though the authority of the Secretary-General to raise matters which States might be reluctant to raise appears to have been a factor in impelling the submission of certain matters to the Council).[46] The occasions upon which the Secretary-General will be led formally to exercise his powers under Article 99 promise to be few. So far, Article 99 has been expressly invoked but once (on the occasion of the outbreak of hostilities in Korea). And in this case it was in fact the United States rather than the Secretary-General that initially drew the crisis to the attention of the Security Council. Moreover, the influence which the Secretary-General may exert by invoking the Article evidently is severely restricted by the fact that his authority is of a moral rather than a political nature. Yet, in some circumstances, an appeal by the Secretary-General to the Security Council might well have considerable effect upon world public opinion, and, indeed, his

---

[44] And upon the provisional agenda of the General Assembly as well, by virtue of its *Rules of Procedure*.
[45] Article 11, paragraph 3.   [46] See Schwebel, *Secretary-General*, pp. 87–88.

action in the Korean case may have influenced the members in their disposition of it.[47]

Article 99 perhaps is more important as the prime and unmistakable affirmation of the true character of the office of Secretary-General. The power it confers, taken together with the Secretary-General's position as the chief permanent officer of the United Nations and as the individual who "more than anyone else ... stand[s] for the United Nations as a whole,"[48] constitutes, particularly when blended with Article 98, the legal basis for the Secretary-General's political authority. The discretionary nature of Article 99, as has been pointed out, allows the Secretary-General to attribute much of his extensive diplomatic activity to the implications of the Charter's text.

It may be argued that Article 99, furthermore, may be called into play as the authorizing clause of declarations, opinions, proposals, and resolutions which the Secretary-General may wish to offer in connection with the Security Council's work. Of the large number of interventions by the Secretary-General to date, the proposal implied in his statement to the Council of June 25, 1950 on the Korean question is clearly within the ambit of Article 99. The express citation of Article 99 as the basis of the more boldly political participation of the Secretary-General in the proceedings of the Security Council, with regard to his submitting opinions,[49] proposing resolutions, and the like, is largely a virgin field of influence which the Secretary-General might, if the need arises, find himself capable of exploiting. The range of such activity, moreover, would embrace those economic, social, and human rights areas which have been seen to fall within the compass of Article 99.

Lastly, it may be assumed that the Secretary-General will choose to exercise his powers under Article 99 only upon the basis of full and impartial data concerning the matter in point. From this assumption it follows that the Secretary-General has the right to make such inquiries and investigations as he may think necessary in order to determine whether or not to invoke his

---

[47] It has been suggested that the Secretary-General's statement to the Security Council of June 25, 1950 "probably resulted in winning the votes of India and his native Norway for the cease-fire resolution" (Hamilton, "The United Nations and Trygve Lie," *Foreign Affairs* (1950) 29, No. 1, p. 68).

[48] Preparatory Commission, *Report*, doc. PC/20, p. 87.

[49] The Secretary-General submitted a legal opinion on the purported withdrawal of the Iranian question from the Security Council's agenda in April 1946, which was in effect deprecated by the President of the Security Council. In reply, the delegate of the USSR stated that the functions of the Secretary-General "are more serious and more responsible than has been suggested just now. It is sufficient to refer to one article of the Charter in order to come precisely to this conclusion regarding the very great responsibility incumbent upon the Secretary-General. Article 99 ... The Secretary-General has all the more the right, and moreover the duty, to submit reports on the various aspects of questions that are being considered by the Security Council" (Security Council, 33rd Meeting, doc. S/PV/33).

powers; in fact, his assertion of this right in the course of Security Council proceedings has been unchallenged and generally acknowledged. In September 1946, in the course of the Council's consideration of the Greek question, the United States proposed "that the Security Council . . . establish a commission of three individuals to be nominated by the Secretary-General, to represent the Security Council on the basis of their competence and impartiality, and to be confirmed by the Security Council" to investigate the facts of the Greek frontier situation. The discussion, a moment later, proceeded as follows:

> *The Secretary-General:* Just a few words to make clear my own position as Secretary-General and the rights of this office under the Charter. Should the proposal of the United States not be carried, I hope that the Council will understand that the Secretary-General must reserve his right to make such inquiries or investigations as he may think necessary, in order to determine whether or not he should consider bringing any aspect of this matter to the attention of the Council under the provisions of the Charter.

> *The President:* As the representative of the Union of Soviet Socialist Republics . . . I think that Mr. Lie was right in raising the question of his rights. It seems to me that in this case, as in all other cases, the Secretary-General must act . . .[50]

There was no challenge of the Secretary-General's statement from any quarter, although his affirmation of his investigatory authority was particularly far reaching in that it claimed not merely the right to make inquiries or investigations without authorization from United Nations organs, but the right to initiate such investigations even in a case where the Security Council has decided not to look into the matter. The importance of this possibility is increased by the fact that a proposal to the Council to investigate a dispute or a situation seems to be subject to the veto.[51]

---

[50] Security Council, 70th Meeting, doc. S/PV/70, September 20, 1946.

[51] Professor Kelsen declares: "It might be doubted whether this interpretation [the affirmation of the Secretary-General's authority to make an investigation under Article 99 after the Security Council has refused to investigate the matter under Article 34] corresponds to the intention of the framers of the Charter" (Kelsen, *The Law of the United Nations* (1950), p. 304). The Charter would appear to bear out Professor Kelsen to the extent that Article 34 endows the Security Council with investigatory powers, while the Secretary-General, who likewise must decide for his purposes whether a matter may threaten international peace and security, is nowhere explicitly granted any investigatory authority. However, the *travaux préparatoires* of the pre-Dumbarton Oaks period pointedly envisage that the Secretary-General be endowed with wide investigatory rights; and later preparatory work of greater legal relevance appears to throw no light upon the question (Professor Kelsen gives no citation of the source of his impression of the intention of the framers of the Charter). On the face of it, it is not unreasonable to suppose that, on the contrary, the framers foresaw that the Secretary-General would wish to take so profound a step as invoking Article 99 only upon the basis of complete and objective data gathered, if need be, through his own investigations. It is difficult to see why the Secretary-General's investigatory

Of the greatest consequence to the development of the Secretary-General's powers is his statement to the Security Council of June 25, 1950 on the Korean question, when "for the first time," Mr. Lie later formally affirmed: "I invoked Article 99 of the Charter."[52] When the Council met in emergency session, the President called upon the Secretary-General, first of all, for the purpose of his delivering any "interim reports on the present situation" which he might have received from the United Nations Commission in Korea.[53] Mr. Lie took this opportunity to declare, before the members had stated the policies of their Governments, that:

> It [is] plain that military actions have been undertaken by North Korean Forces. These actions are a direct violation of the Resolution of the General Assembly [reaffirming the South Korean Government as the country's lawful régime and extending the life of the Korean Commission] ... as well as a violation of the principles of the Charter.
>
> The present situation is a serious one and is a threat to international peace. The Security Council is, in my opinion, the competent organ to deal with it.
>
> I consider it the clear duty of the Security Council to take steps necessary to re-establish peace in that area.[54]

The Secretary-General apparently considered this statement to be an invocation of Article 99 despite the fact that the emergency session of the Council was called not upon his initiative, but upon that of the United States.[55] It would seem that the United States, by requesting the meeting of the Council expressly to consider the Korean breach of the peace, first drew the Korean crisis to the Council's attention. It is submitted that the Secretary General's declaration was clearly in the spirit of Article 99. Mr. Lie appeared to regard it as also having been in accordance with the letter of Article 99,

authority would not extend to a matter which the Security Council had declined to investigate; for the essence of Article 99 lies in its providing an agent of the Organization as a whole who will raise those matters which, though they may constitute a threat to the peace, States find it impolitic to raise or to pursue; and particularly in such delicate cases the Secretary-General may not wish to take the initiative without full and impartial data at his disposal. The Soviet endorsement of the Secretary-General's assertion of such powers seems unqualified. The United States, in speaking of the "unprecedented political responsibilities" entrusted to the Secretary-General by Article 99, may also be said to have subscribed in some degree to the investigatory authority of the Secretary-General: "We need not await its [Article 99's] full implementation to recognize that the power of the Secretary-General to study conditions which in his opinion threaten the peaceful relations of the United Nations, and to make recommendations based on these findings, represents a significant departure from the usual concepts of international organization and national sovereignty" (Warren Austin, in an address to the General Assembly, *Official Records of the Second Part of the First Session of the General Assembly*, Plenary Meetings, p. 902).

[52] Address to the General Assembly of September 28, 1950, *Official Records of the Fifth Session of the General Assembly*, Plenary Meetings, p. 176.

[53] Proceedings of June 25, 1950, 43rd Meeting of the 5th Year, Security Council, *Official Records*, No. 15.

[54] *Ibid.*   [55] *Ibid.*, and doc. S/1495.

245

apparently on the ground that his drawing the Council's attention to a matter may constitute an appeal to that article, even if his action supplements the earlier raising of the same issue by a Member State. In describing his declaration of June 25 as relying on Article 99, the Secretary-General thus seems to define the article as admitting supplementary, and perhaps joint, as well as exclusive, action. While this interpretation is not unreasonable, it does not appear to be the one anticipated by the Preparatory Commission,[56] nor does it find support in the *travaux préparatoires*. However, the distinction is of limited practical importance, while the Secretary-General's statement, whether invoking that article or not, seems to have been of considerable practical effect.

The circumstances of the Secretary-General's Korean intervention illustrate a paradoxical quality inherent in the entrusting of political prerogative to the international secretariat. The Secretary-General, who is responsible to and representative of the Organization as a whole, and who must avoid identification with interests more limited than those of the Organization as a whole, is at the same time given a power the exercise of which may tend to bring him into conflict with those policies of Member States which constitute (directly or through their support of non-member States) a threat to the peace. Thus while the Secretary-General may be in a higher sense impartial in the carrying out of his political duties, he cannot be neutral. Neutrality implies political abstinence, not political action, and, in certain circumstances, such as the Korean, might well keep the Secretary-General from conscientious fulfillment of his Charter obligations. There is, indeed, an "un-neutral" predisposition about the Secretary-General's calling the attention of the Security Council to a matter threatening the peace, since it is unlikely that it can ever be in the equal interests of the parties to a dispute, in an exact, strictly "neutral" degree, that a situation in which they are involved be brought before the Council. The unequivocal character of the Secretary-General's intervention in the Korean case emphasizes this at least superficially partisan potentiality of Article 99.

The implementation of Article 99 has not been confined to the Korean question. Insofar as the article comprises the greater part of the express affirmation of the Secretary-General's political authority, the article may be said to be in fact "self-operating": even when not formally invoked, its presence provides the likeliest legal source for the continuing political initiative of the Secretary-General, which takes forms other than the implementation of Article 99 in terms.

[56] Doc. PC/EX/SEC/9.

Thus Article 99 has been invoked publicly on one occasion, apparently with effect (though in a fashion ancillary to the action of a Member State); and it has acted as a reserve force inducing States which otherwise might not have submitted questions to the Security Council to raise them. But the influence of Article 99 may be said to have extended farther than that. For that article has flavored and fortified the whole of the Secretary-General's political endeavor. Article 99 has set the tone of the office of Secretary-General; it has provided the constitutional base for a structure of varied and significant political activity. In this, Article 99 is of considerable, and may prove to be of very great, importance. Perhaps it is not too much to suggest that, as the development of the great national civil services profoundly affected the national histories of the nineteenth and twentieth centuries, so the growth of the powers of the international executive may in time influence the future course of world affairs.

16

The International Character of the Secretariat of the United Nations

ᘓᘐ

THE LEAGUE OF NATIONS AND THE CHARTER OF THE UNITED NATIONS

The Secretariat of the United Nations was established as a body exclusively international in its responsibilities as a matter of course. Article 100 of the Charter is couched in emphatic language admitting of no qualification:

1. In the performance of their duties the Secretary-General and the staff shall not seek or receive instructions from any government or from any other authority external to the Organization. They shall refrain from any action which might reflect on their position as international officials responsible only to the Organization.

2. Each Member of the United Nations undertakes to respect the exclusively international character of the responsibilities of the Secretary-General and the staff and not to seek to influence them in the discharge of their responsibilities.[1]

The concept of a Secretariat which, as the Charter prescribes, shall be of "exclusively international character" is relatively new. The authors of the Covenant of the League of Nations did not specify that the League Secretariat was to consist of anything more than a permanent grouping of national contingents. It was Sir Eric Drummond, the first Secretary-General, who made the epochal decision that the League Secretariat should be genuinely international.[2] However, the part of the Secretariat in the United Nations as

---

First published in *The British Year Book of International Law* 1953 (1954), 30.

[1] This is a classic provision, which is substantially duplicated in the constitutions of the Specialized Agencies. See the Constitution of the International Labor Organization (Article 9, paragraphs 4 and 5), the Articles of Agreement of the International Monetary Fund (Article 12, paragraph 4 (*c*)), the Constitution of the World Health Organization (Article 37), the Constitution of the Food and Agriculture Organization of the United Nations (Article VIII, paragraph 2), the Constitution of the International Trade Organization (Article 88, paragraphs 1, 2, and 3), and others.

[2] See Walters, *A History of the League of Nations* (1952), Vol. I, pp. 75–76 (hereinafter cited as *History*); the same, *Administrative Problems of International Organization* (1941), p. 16 (hereinafter cited as *Administrative Problems*).

the expression of an international outlook surpasses in significance the part which it played in the League. For the Secretary-General of the United Nations is endowed with political powers which were withheld from his League predecessors.[3]

The League Experience

The experiment of the League of Nations in international administration was, on the whole, notably successful.[4] The initiative of Sir Eric Drummond in creating the Secretariat as an international organism was readily accepted by the States Members as natural and sound. In 1920 the League Council adopted the Balfour Report which declared that "the members of the Secretariat once appointed are no longer the servants of the country of which they are citizens, but become for the time being the servants only of the League of Nations ... The members of the staff carry out ... not national but international duties."[5] The Noblemaire Report, adopted by the Assembly in the following year, likewise approved the Secretary-General's concept of the international civil

---

[3] Walters, *History*, Vol. I, p. 76. See also Schwebel, *The Secretary-General of the United Nations: His Political Powers and Practice* (1952), pp. 10–11, 230–231; the same, "The Origins and Development of Article 99 of the Charter," *British Year Book of International Law* (1951) 28, pp. 371–372.

[4] "The Secretariat," writes Lord Cecil, "was a creation very largely of Drummond's and, as far as I can tell, it was an extremely able body. It consisted of individuals who gave up positions in their own country of often considerable value because of their great interest in the work of the League. They were extraordinarily non-national in the sense that they were quite impartial and in that respect Drummond gave a most excellent example. I often found on discussing with colleagues who represented other countries in the League that if there was any difficulty they were always ready to accept the advice of Drummond as being both able and impartial. Drummond always regarded himself as the assistant and servant of the League and was quite ready to assist with his experience and knowledge any national representative who asked for it. It would, of course, be absurd to suggest that all the members of the Secretariat were equal in ability but I do think, as far as my knowledge is concerned, that they were all perfectly impartial and that they did not allow the fact of their nationality to influence unduly their action in the League" (letter to the author of May 6, 1953).

See Ranshofen-Wertheimer, *The International Secretariat: A Great Experiment in International Administration* (1945), *passim*; Walters, *History*, Vol. I, pp. 75–80, Vol. II, pp. 556–560; the same, *Administrative Problems, passim*; Royal Institute of International Affairs, *The International Secretariat of the Future: Lessons from Experience by a Group of Former Officials of the League of Nations* (1944), *passim*; Drummond, "The Secretariat of the League of Nations," in *Public Administration* (1931) 9, *passim*; Phelan, *Yes and Albert Thomas* (1936), *passim*; the same, "The New International Civil Service," in *Foreign Affairs* (1932–1933), *passim*; Boudreau, "International Civil Service – The Secretariat of the League of Nations," in Davis (ed.), *Pioneers in World Order* (1944), *passim*; Carnegie Endowment for International Peace, *Proceedings of the Exploratory Conference on the Experience of the League of Nations Secretariat, 1942,* and *Proceedings of the Conference on Experience in International Administration, 1943, passim.*

[5] "Staff of the Secretariat: Report Presented by the British Representative, Mr. A. J. Balfour," in *Official Journal*, 1920, Vol. I, pp. 137–139. See Krabbe, "Le Secrétariat Général de la Société des Nations et son activité," in Rask-Orstedfonden, *Les Origines et l'oeuvre de la Société des Nations* (1924), Vol. II, p. 268; Ranshofen-Wertheimer, *International Secretariat*, pp. 26–27, 81; and Calderwood, "The Higher Direction of the League Secretariat," *Arnold Foundation Studies in Public Affairs*, 5, 3, pp. 6–7.

service.[6] That concept was challenged, cautiously, in 1930 by the Minority Report of the Committee of Thirteen, but the majority upheld it,[7] while conceding the value of the Secretary-General engaging a small proportion of the staff whose task it would be to interpret, though not to represent, the policies of their respective States.[8] The Staff Regulations were at that time amended to read:

> The officials of the Secretariat of the League of Nations are exclusively international officials and their duties are not national, but international. By accepting appointment, they pledge themselves to discharge their functions and to regulate their conduct with the interests of the League alone in view. They are subject to the authority of the Secretary-General, and are responsible to him in the exercise of their functions ... They may not seek or receive instructions from any Government or other authority external to the Secretariat of the League of Nations.[9]

While, however, both official policy and dominant practice conformed to the concept of the Secretariat as being exclusively international in its responsibilities, there were exceptions which derogated from the rule. The Under-Secretaries-General created with some the impression of national representatives rather than international officials.[10] At the Secretariat's lowest ebb, in 1940, the second Secretary-General went so far as to pledge privately his allegiance to Marshal Pétain, expressing willingness to demonstrate that allegiance by resigning if the Marshal so wished.[11]

---

[6] *Organisation of the Secretariat and of the International Labor Office*, LN docs. C. 424, M. 305, 1921, X. and A. 140 (a), 1921. See Calderwood, "Higher Direction," pp. 8–14, and Ranshofen-Wertheimer, *International Secretariat*, p. 27.

[7] Committee of Enquiry on the Organisation of the Secretariat ..., *Report of the Committee*, LN doc. A. 16, 1930.

[8] The staff, the majority proposed, should consist "of two elements – one stable and tending towards that type of 'international man' ... committed to the strictest and most scrupulous impartiality in examining and solving all problems submitted to it; while the other would be temporary and specialized, freer in judgement and able so to modify solutions as to make them acceptable to the various nations." *Official Journal*, Special Supplement No. 84, p. 220. See Ranshofen-Wertheimer, *International Secretariat*, pp. 28–31; and Calderwood, "Higher Direction," pp. 16–21.

[9] *Staff Regulations*, 1933, Article 1. A committee of which the first Secretary-General was chairman later described this provision as one of "strict international loyalty," and affirmed that "the staff regulations were based on this premise throughout" (Royal Institute of International Affairs, *The International Secretariat of the Future*, p. 19).

[10] See Ranshofen-Wertheimer, *International Secretariat*, pp. 56–60. *The International Secretariat of the Future* concedes that "the existence of Under-Secretaries-General was a frank compromise between political necessity and administrative efficiency," and indicates that the compromise may have been in the interests of the Secretariat's influence (at pp. 28, 30). In support of this latter view see Salter, "The International Character of the League Secretariat," in *The United States of Europe and Other Papers* (1933), pp. 127–136. For a comparison of the status of the Assistant Secretaries-General of the United Nations see Schwebel, *Secretary-General*, pp. 56–59, 131–132, 166, and 246, n. 9.

[11] See Schwebel, *Secretary-General*, p. 221.

Italy appears to have been the first Member to break *de facto* with the principle, to which it had earlier subscribed, of the international responsibility of the Secretariat, and probably is the only State which may be said to have withdrawn support from that principle as a matter of law. An Italian law of June 16, 1927 required Italian nationals who enter the service of another Government or of a public international institution to obtain the authorization of the Ministry of Foreign Affairs or of a competent diplomatic authority, and to relinquish such service upon the order of the Government.[12] It was suggested that this regulation was contrary to the obligations of Italy under Article 6 of the Covenant.[13] It violated the Council and Assembly resolutions approving the Balfour and Noblemaire Reports, as well as the Staff Regulations. An Italian national who resigned from the Secretariat pursuant to orders issued thereunder, at least after the amendment of the Staff Regulations by the Eleventh Assembly, was acting contrary to Article 1 of the Regulations, in particular the clause which prescribed that officials of the Secretariat "may not seek or receive instructions from any Government ..." The Italian answer to the criticisms of the law was that it was within the area of Italian sovereignty and was designed to prevent elements disloyal to the régime from joining the Secretariat.[14]

The League experience has a further relevance to the personnel problems facing the Secretary-General. By an early League resolution, members of the staff were given the right to appeal against their dismissal to the Council.[15] In 1925 a former member of the Secretariat invoked this procedure,[16] and this led the Council to appoint a Commission of Jurists, whose conclusions it resolved in advance to adopt. The Commission took the view that a contract between a person and the Secretary-General "must be considered mainly in the light of the principles of public law and administrative legislation ... Relations connected with public employment are always governed by the exigencies of the public interest, to which the private and personal interests of

---

[12] *Raccolta delle Leggi d'Italia*, 1927, Vol. 6, p. 5932, as cited by Hudson, *The Permanent Court of International Justice, 1920–1942* (1943), p. 319, n. 22. The sanctions which the law prescribed for its violation are severe: a fine of not more than 5,000 lire (it should be recalled that this law was adopted in 1927), a prison sentence of not more than one year, and loss of civic prerogatives and rights of citizenship.

[13] See Basdevant, *Les Fonctionnaires internationaux* (1931), p. 154, presumably referring to paragraph 3 of that article: "The secretaries and staff of the Secretariat shall be appointed by the Council with the approval of the majority of the Assembly."

[14] See Basdevant, *Les Fonctionnaires*, p. 154.

[15] "All Members of the Secretariat and of the International Labor Office appointed for a period of five years or more by the Secretary-General or the Director of the International Labor Office shall, in case of dismissal, have the right of appeal to the Council or to the Governing Body ... as the case may be" (*Records of the First Assembly, Plenary Meetings*, 1920, pp. 663–664).

[16] See Ranshofen-Wertheimer, *International Secretariat*, pp. 256–262.

the officials must necessarily give way." Thus, "the administration must always retain discretionary powers, as otherwise it could not ensure the development of these relations with due regard for the recognized public requirements for the satisfaction of which they were constituted." Officials have their rights, especially economic, but these are "subject to the rights of the administration."

> The same principles [the Commission held] must undoubtedly be applied to the legal relations between the Secretary-General of the League of Nations and the officials of the Secretariat. If the relations connected with employment in individual States must be subject to the requirements of the public interest, to which they owe their existence, the same must *a fortiori* be true in the case of the League of Nations, which is called upon to satisfy requirements which are much more complicated in that they are international, and which, in consequence, must exercise a still wider discretionary power in respect of the engagement, retention and dismissal of officials.[17]

The League Administration was not unaware that a mechanism which was either arbitrary or harsh in its personnel policies could not expect to attract the devotion and energies of qualified officials. "Ability cannot be enlisted, nor loyalty and morale maintained, unless the usual civil service principles of permanence, promotion for merit and pension upon retirement are adopted."[18] Indeed, members of the Secretariat were recognized by the Staff Regulations to have certain "acquired rights,"[19] which, while not assuring tenure, did strengthen their claims to material compensation for dismissal or lesser impairments of their status. The very existence of the Administrative

---

[17] *Official Journal*, 1925, p. 1443. The Commission's report, which awarded an indemnity to the claimant, was adopted by the Council without discussion. For a critical view of the report see Kelsen, *The Law of the United Nations* (1950), p. 318. The prospect of officials appealing regularly to the Council led to the creation of the Administrative Tribunal (for the Statute and Rules of which see Hudson, *International Legislation* [1931], Vol. I, pp. 212–223). The Tribunal had rendered twenty-one judgements by 1939, granting affirmative relief in eight cases. Hudson, writing of these, declares that the Tribunal's "jurisprudence did not establish an extensive body of case-law" (Hudson, *International Tribunals, Past and Future* (1944), pp. 220–222). In 1946 the Tribunal gave sixteen judgements, upholding the claims of twelve former members of the League Secretariat and one former member of the International Labor Office who maintained that their "acquired rights" had been violated by the Secretary-General's and Director-General's interpretation of the resolution of the League Assembly of 1939 which amended the Staff Regulations so as to reduce the period of notice of termination of employment from six months to one month and to spread the payment of termination indemnities over four years. The Acting Secretary-General, who had contested the Tribunal's jurisdiction in these cases, declined to execute the judgements. The Assembly supported him on grounds of jurisdiction and substance, in a discussion which is of great interest for the questions of the relations between the Assembly and the Tribunal, of acquired rights, and of the nature of the law governing the international civil servant. (See *Records of the 20th (Conclusion) and 21st Session of the Assembly, Official Journal*, 1946, pp. 245–249, 130–133, 162, 123, and *Mayras v. The Secretary General of the League of Nations: Annual Digest*, 1946, Case No. 91.)

[18] *The International Secretariat of the Future*, p. 24.   [19] See Articles 78 and 80.

Tribunal imposed a check upon the Secretary-General. Moreover, the Secretary-General's ultimate authority was qualified by his responsibility to the League Assembly and Council. But, essentially, the limit to the Secretary-General's discretion in his staff policies was his own sense of propriety. The rules governing the organization of the service, as contrasted with the material rights of the officials, kept the actual power in his hands.[20] That power does not seem to have been ordinarily abused.[21]

The League experiment "worked well," a group of former Secretariat officials under the chairmanship of the first Secretary-General concluded, "until the League became the direct object first of subtle, then of open, sabotage. Whatever their final judgement of the League, observers agree that the concept of international loyalty is practicable, and we can affirm on empirical evidence that an administration based on international loyalty – to the organization in general and its secretariat in particular – can be highly efficient. Experience shows that a spirit of international loyalty among public servants can be maintained in practice. It shows also that maintenance of such a spirit is an essential factor in the activity of an international service, since this alone can ensure to it that confidence without which it cannot function as it ought."[22]

What is this spirit of international loyalty? "[It] is the conviction that the highest interests of one's own country are served best by the promotion of security and welfare everywhere, and the steadfast maintenance of that conviction without regard to changing circumstances. It is breadth of international outlook ..."[23] Sir Eric Drummond and his colleagues cite a characteristically perceptive definition of "the distinctively international outlook" by a writer of authority:

> A lack of attachment to any one country does not constitute an international outlook. A superior indifference to the emotions and prejudices of those whose world is bounded by the frontiers of a single State does not constitute an international outlook. A blurred indistinctness of attitude towards all questions, proceeding from a freedom of prejudice born of lack of vitality, does not constitute an international outlook. The international outlook required of the international civil servant is an awareness made instinctive by habit of the needs, emotions, and prejudices of the peoples of differently-circumstanced countries, as

---

[20] See Cagne, *Le Secrétariat Général de la Société des Nations* (1936), p. 43.

[21] The second Secretary-General was in 1939 entrusted by the Assembly with extraordinary powers, which he wielded in a manner provocative of severe criticism. It has been suggested that when staff, inevitably, had to be reduced, he was influenced by political motives. See Ranshofen-Wertheimer, *International Secretariat*, pp. 37–81, and Schwebel, *Secretary-General*, pp. 215–224.

[22] *The International Secretariat of the Future*, pp. 19–20.

[23] *The International Secretariat of the Future*, p. 18.

they are felt and expressed by the peoples concerned, accompanied by a capacity for weighing those frequently imponderable elements in a judicial manner before reaching any decision to which they are relevant.[24]

Thus from the League experience the founders of the United Nations were able to draw a formula for international loyalty which had been tested in practice. That test at one and the same time had demonstrated the validity of the concept of the internationally-responsible secretariat, and the difficulties of applying that concept in a world where the values of national loyalty remain predominant and assertive.

The Charter of the United Nations

The present Article 100 of the Charter was not included in the Dumbarton Oaks draft. It was inserted at San Francisco at the instance of four Sponsoring Powers[25] – as well as Canada,[26] New Zealand,[27] and Uruguay[28] – and was adopted unanimously. It would, it was agreed, "strengthen the position of the Secretariat."[29] While the discussion of Article 100 was of a cursory nature, it sufficed to make clear that no restrictive interpretation of the international allegiance which would be required thereunder was anticipated by the signatories of the treaty at San Francisco. On the contrary, it was foreseen that the national and international loyalties of the members of the Secretariat might clash. Nothing in the record of the discussions of the Conference gives the impression that it was intended, in such an event, that the international responsibilities of Secretariat officials should give way.

Two questions were considered: whether Article 100 "covered the risk which might be faced by a member of the Secretariat as a result of taking the oath of allegiance to the Organization"; and whether it was adequate to protect a Secretariat member "who participated in the preparation of military plans for possible use against his own State."[30] With respect to the latter problem, it was pointed out that if the official were to become aware of such military plans, he might be liable to heavy penalties under the law of his own State for failure to reveal them to his Government. In response to the first question, it was stated that "the experience of the League of Nations

---

[24] Jenks, "Some Problems of an International Civil Service," *Public Administration Review* (1943) 3, 2, p. 95. See also Aghnides, "Standards of Conduct of the International Civil Servant," *Revue internationale des sciences administratives* (1953) 19, 1, p. 182, and Langrod, "Les Problèmes fondamentaux de la fonction publique internationale," *ibid.*, pp. 33–40.

[25] The United States, the United Kingdom, the Soviet Union, and China. See United Nations Conference on International Organization (UNCIO), *Documents* (1945), Vol. 3, pp. 627–628.

[26] *Ibid.*, pp. 594–595.   [27] *Ibid.*, pp. 490–491.   [28] *Ibid.*, p. 37.   [29] *Ibid.*, Vol. 7, p. 393.

[30] *Ibid.*, p. 394.

demonstrated that there was no practical difficulty in this matter, except in the case of the Fascist States."[31] The second question, while seen as "highly important," could not, it was felt, be properly treated in Chapter XV of the Charter, but was referred to another committee of the Conference for such action as it might deem necessary – in order, apparently, to obviate the suggested danger to Secretariat members.[32]

The San Francisco Conference further provided, in Article 105 of the Charter, that: "Officials of the Organization shall ... enjoy such privileges and immunities as are necessary for the independent exercise of their functions in connection with the Organization."[33] (The Covenant was more liberal in this respect, Article 7, paragraph 4 providing that: "Officials of the League when engaged in the business of the League shall enjoy diplomatic privileges and immunities.")[34] Pursuant to paragraph 3 of Article 105, the

---

[31] *Ibid.* The Committee appears to have assumed that Fascist States would not be Members of the Organization, and that their nationals would not be employed in the Secretariat. It may be noted that the Preparatory Committee recommended, and the General Assembly agreed, that "the Secretary-General should take the necessary steps to ensure that no persons who have discredited themselves by their activities or connections with Fascism or Nazism shall be appointed to the Secretariat" (*Report of the Preparatory Commission*, p. 92; *Resolutions Adopted by the General Assembly during the First Part of its First Session from January 10, to 14 February 1946*, p. 15). This ban apparently was meant to apply to persons of the proscribed associations irrespective of their nationality. A rule expressive of the Assembly's injunction was included at first in the Staff Rules which the Secretary-General issued in implementation of the Staff Regulations adopted by the Assembly, but this rule was subsequently deleted.

[32] UNCIO, *Documents*, Vol. 7, p. 394. There is no recorded indication that the Committee to which this (and also the first question) was referred considered or took further action. But in support of the above interpretation see Kelsen, *Law of the United Nations*, pp. 307–308, and Goodrich and Hambro, *The Charter of the United Nations* (1949), p. 505.

[33] 1. The Organization shall enjoy in the territory of each of its Members such privileges and immunities as are necessary for the fulfillment of its purposes.
2. Representatives of Members of the United Nations and officials of the Organization shall similarly enjoy such privileges and immunities as are necessary for the independent exercise of their functions in connection with the Organization.
3. The General Assembly may make recommendations with a view to determining the details of the application of paragraphs 1 and 2 of this Article or may propose conventions to the Members of the United Nations for this purpose." (See also Article 104.)
See Hill, *Immunities and Privileges of International Officials* (1947), pp. 101–119; Preuss, "Immunity of Officers and Employees of the United Nations for Official Acts: The Ranallo Case," *American Journal of International Law* (1947), 41; Parry, "International Government and Diplomatic Privileges," *Modern Law Review* (1947), 10; King, *The Privileges and Immunities of the Personnel of International Organizations* (1949); and Kelsen, *Law of the United Nations*, pp. 314–319, 337–338.

[34] The literature relating to the privileges and immunities of the League and its officials is extensive. See, *inter alia*, Hammarskjöld, "Les Immunités des personnes investies de fonctions internationales," *The Hague Academy, Recueil des Cours*, 1936 (ii), especially pp. 117, 119, 161–162, 167–168, 200–201; the same, "Les Immunités des personnes investies de fonctions d'intérêt international," *Revue de droit international et de législation comparée* (1935), No. 1, pp. 6 ff.; Secrétan, *Les Immunités diplomatiques des représentants des états membres et des agents de la Société des Nations* (1928); the same, "Les Privilèges et immunités diplomatiques des agents de la Société des Nations," *Revue de droit international privé et de droit*

General Assembly adopted the General Convention on the Privileges and Immunities of the United Nations,[35] and the Convention on the Privileges and Immunities of the Specialized Agencies was subsequently adopted by the Assembly as a measure for coordinating the privileges and immunities of the Agencies with those of the Organization.[36] The United States has ratified neither Convention. Its International Organizations Immunities Act, as applied to the United Nations, accords the Organization and its officials some, but not all, of the privileges set forth in the General Convention.[37] The Headquarters Agreement between the United Nations and the United States, which is complementary to the Convention, assures the United Nations further privileges.[38] The effect of Article 105 and its ancillary treaties is evidently to reinforce the independence of the Secretariat.

pénal international (1925), 20, pp. 1 ff.; and "The Independence Granted to Agents of the International Community in their Relations with National Public Authorities," *British Year Book of International Law* (1935), 16, pp. 56 ff.; Preuss, "Diplomatic Privileges and Immunities of Agents Invested with Functions of an International Interest," *American Journal of International Law* (1931), 25, pp. 694 ff.; Rey, "Les Immunités des fonctionnaires internationaux," *Revue de droit international privé et de droit pénal international* (1928), 23, pp. 432 ff.; Gascon y Marin, "Les Fonctionnaires internationaux," *Recueil des Cours*, 1932 (iii); Hurst, "Diplomatic Immunities – Modern Developments," *British Year Book of International Law* (1929), 9; Martin, *La Situation juridique des agents internationaux* (1926); Secrétan, "Les Privilèges et immunités diplomatiques des agents de la S.D.N.," *Revue de droit international privé* (1925); Basdevant, *Les Fonctionnaires*, pp. 292–320; and Hill, *Immunities and Privileges*.

[35] See *Resolutions Adopted by the General Assembly during the First Part of its First Session from January 10, to 14 February 1946*, pp. 25 ff. See also Kunz, "Privileges and Immunities of International Organizations," in *American Journal of International Law* (1947), 41; Brandon, "United Nations Laissez Passer," *British Year Book of International Law* (1950), 27; and Crosswell, *Protection of International Personnel Abroad* (1952).

[36] See *Convention on the Privileges and Immunities of the Specialized Agencies* (adopted by the General Assembly on November 21, 1947) and *Final Texts of The Annexes* (as approved by the Specialized Agencies by December 29, 1951), United Nations doc. ST/LEG/4, March 1953. See also Jessup, "Status of the ILO: Privileges and Immunities of their Officials," in *American Journal of International Law* (1944), 38; and Chen, "The Legal Status, Privileges and Immunities of the Specialized Agencies," *ibid.* (1948), 42.

[37] (1945) 39 Stat. 669, 22 USCA, s. 288. See Preuss, "The International Organizations Immunities Act," *American Journal of International Law* (1946), 40, pp. 332–345; and *Report of the Secretary-General on Personnel Policy*, United Nations doc. A/2364, January 30, 1953, p. 14. The Act is based on the principle of nationality discrimination, its benefits being extended to aliens only, except in the case of immunity for official acts. It reflects an early concern for United States security (see Preuss, "Immunities Act," pp. 335, 337, 339). See also Liang, "The Legal Status of the United Nations in the United States," *International Law Quarterly* (1948), 2; Preuss in *American Journal of International Law*, 41 (1947); *Westchester County v. Ranallo*, 67 NYS (2nd) 31, noted in *Virginia Law Review* (1947), 33, and in *New York Law School Quarterly Review* (1947), 22; *United States v. Coplon et al.*, 84 F. Supp. 472; Spence, "Jurisdictional Immunity of United Nations Employees: The Gubitchev Case," *Michigan Law Review* (1949), 47; *United States v. Keeney*, 111 F. Supp. 233; "Privileges and Immunities Accorded by the United States to the United Nations," *Minnesota Law Review* (1950), 34; and Crosswell, *International Personnel Abroad*.

[38] Agreement between the United Nations and the United States of America regarding the Headquarters of the United Nations, *United Nations Treaty Series*, Vol. 11, p. 11. See Brandon, "The Legal Status of the Premises of the United Nations," *British Year Book of International Law* (1951), 28, pp. 90 ff., and Liang, "Legal Status." The United States affirmed on April 9, 1953 that the Joint Resolution of

The exclusively international responsibilities of the Secretariat which are prescribed in Article 100 and buttressed by Article 105 are rooted in the exclusively international process of appointment of its members. Article 101 makes it clear that the choice of staff is solely the province of "the Secretary-General under regulations established by the General Assembly."[39] Governments have no part in the choice of personnel, and the factors which Article 101 lists as governing the employment of the staff do not include governmental approbation. "The intent ... at San Francisco," the Secretary of State concluded in his Report to the President, "was to make it perfectly clear that the nationals of Member States serving on the staff of the Secretariat could not, in any sense of the word, be considered as agents of their governments."[40] The Preparatory Commission was careful to uphold this view. The Yugoslav Delegation proposed that the appointment of officials of the Secretariat "should be made with the consent of the Member Government of which the candidate is a national."[41] The Governments concerned, the Yugoslav Delegate maintained, were in the best position to assess the qualifications and capacities of prospective candidates. The United Nations was "an intergovernmental Organization"; persons appointed to the Secretariat "must command the confidence of their governments if they were to be of real value to it." Yet once the officials were appointed, "the exclusively international character of their responsibilities would naturally be respected and no government would seek to influence them" in their discharge.[42]

A "large majority"[43] opposed the Yugoslav proposal. In their view, it

Congress which authorized the President to bring the Headquarters Agreement into effect on the part of the United States, and the note of its Representative of November 21, 1947 bringing the Agreement into effect, were subject to a reservation respecting an American "right to safeguard its security." The Secretary-General of the United Nations declined to accept the contention of the United States that in fact a reservation to the Agreement exists (see the Memorandum by the Legal Department on the Admission of Representatives of Non-Governmental Organizations Enjoying Consultative Status, United Nations doc. E/2397, April 10, 1953). The dispute is being negotiated pursuant to Section 21 of the Agreement (see United Nations docs. E/2492 and E/2501).

[39] Article 101 reads as follows:
1. The staff shall be appointed by the Secretary-General under regulations established by the General Assembly.
2. Appropriate staffs shall be permanently assigned to ... organs of the United Nations ...
3. The paramount consideration in the employment of the staff and in the determination of the conditions of service shall be the necessity of securing the highest standards of efficiency, competence, and integrity. Due regard shall be paid to the importance of recruiting the staff on as wide a geographical basis as possible.

[40] *Report to the President on the Results of the San Francisco Conference by the Chairman of the United States Delegation, the Secretary of State*: Department of State Publication 2349, 1945, p. 150.

[41] United Nations doc. PC/AC/54, December 18, 1945.

[42] Preparatory Commission, Committee 6: Administrative and Budgetary, *Summary Record of Meetings*, December 19 and 20, 1945, 22nd and 23rd meetings, United Nations doc. PC/AB/66.

[43] *Ibid.*

impaired the exclusive responsibility of the Secretary-General for the appointment of staff under Article 101 of the Charter. It would, they held, "threaten the freedom, independence and truly international character of the Secretariat" and "defeat the spirit as well as infringe the letter of Article 100."[44] There was a problem to be faced, but the Yugoslav plan would accentuate rather than remedy it. It was "common sense that the staff should, as far as possible, be acceptable to the Member Governments, and also that the Secretary-General would often require information regarding candidates from governments or private bodies, but it would be extremely undesirable to write into the text anything which would give national governments particular rights in this respect, or permit political pressure upon the Secretary-General." The Yugoslav proposal was therefore defeated, the Committee deciding rather to "rely on the Secretary-General's discretion and good sense."[45] The Secretary-General was later to commend the Preparatory Commission for this "fundamental decision affirming the international character and independence of the Secretariat,"[46] which, it should be noted, the General Assembly adopted as its own.[47]

The Case of Reparation for Injuries to Officials of the United Nations

Perhaps the most significant affirmation of the principle of the independence of officials of the United Nations has come from the International Court of Justice, which had occasion to construe Article 100 in the course of its advisory opinion on *Reparation for Injuries Suffered in the Service of the United Nations*. The Court unanimously decided that the United Nations as an Organization has international legal personality, with the result that, in the event of an agent of the United Nations suffering injury in the performance of his duties in circumstances involving the responsibility of a State, the Organization enjoys the capacity to bring an international claim against the responsible State with a view to obtaining the reparation due in respect of the damage caused to the United Nations. The Court further decided, by eleven votes to four, that the United Nations has the capacity to bring an international claim against the State responsible with a view to obtaining the reparation due in respect of the damage caused to the victim or to his successors in interest. Lastly, it held that

---

[44] *Ibid.*   [45] *Ibid.*

[46] *Report of the Secretary-General on Personnel Policy*, United Nations doc. A/2364, January 30, 1953, p. 14.

[47] *Resolutions Adopted by the General Assembly during the First Part of its First Session*, etc., p. 14. By this resolution the Assembly confirmed the Secretary-General's exclusive power of appointment and assigned no qualifying role to the States Members.

such a claim could be brought by the Organization even against the State of which the victim was a national.[48]

In order to be able to reach these decisions the Court felt impelled to undertake a re-examination of the traditional rule of nationality of claims. That rule, the Court pointed out, rests on two bases. The first is that the defendant State has broken an obligation towards the plaintiff State in respect of its nationals. The second is that only the party to whom the international obligation is due can bring a claim in respect of the breach. "This is precisely what happens," the Court held, "when the Organization, in bringing a claim for damage suffered by its agent, does so by invoking the breach of an obligation towards itself. Thus, the rule of the nationality of claims affords no reason against recognizing that the Organization has the right to bring a claim for the damage [to the victim or to his successors in interest.] On the contrary, the principle underlying this rule leads to the recognition of this capacity as belonging to the Organization, when the Organization invokes, as the ground of its claim, a breach of an obligation towards itself."[49] The Court attached importance to uttering a warning against undue generalization of its reasoning: "It is not possible, by a strained use of the concept of allegiance, to assimilate the legal bond which exists, under Article 100 of the Charter, between the Organization on the one hand, and the Secretary-General and the staff on the other, to the bond of nationality existing between a State and its nationals."[50] Here the Court would seem to have taken a step backward, in the classic tradition,[51] *pour mieux sauter.*[52] It pointed out that the functions of the Organization necessitate entrusting agents with hazardous missions in

---

[48] *ICJ Reports 1949*, pp. 174, 187. The latter decision, with respect to the reconciliation of the claims of the Organization with those of the State of which the victim is a national, was made by ten votes to five.

[49] *Ibid.*, p. 182.   [50] *Ibid.*

[51] The Court usually made "courteous obeisance to the tradition of State sovereignty" while actually giving a "restrictive interpretation" of its claims (Lauterpacht, *The Development of International Law by the Permanent Court of International Justice* [1934], p. 89).

[52] An interpretation which finds support in the Dissenting Opinion of Judge Hackworth: "International law on this subject is well settled, and any attempt to engraft upon it, save by international compact, a theory, based upon supposed analogy, that organizations, not States and hence having no nationals, may act as if they were States and had nationals, is, in my opinion, unwarranted" (*ICJ Reports 1949*, p. 203; see also pp. 198–199).

   This is not to say, of course, that an unreserved equation between the bond of Article 100 and the bond of nationality is juridically valid, and the Court's care in this matter seems fully justified. The Court, moreover, could not put itself in the position of relying upon Article 100 alone, since its definition of "agent" is considerably broader than that of a member of the Secretariat (*ibid.*, p. 177). One may say, however, that thereby the Court's emphasis upon the independent status of the Organization's agents applies *a fortiori* to members of the Secretariat, for the latter's international ties clearly are stronger than those of a national delegate or an expert serving as the Organization's agent *ad hoc* (see the individual Opinion of Judge Azevedo, *ibid.*, pp. 194–195).

disturbed parts of the world. Both to ensure the efficient and "independent"[53] performance of these missions and to afford support to its agents, the Organization must provide them with adequate protection.

> In order that the agent may perform his duties satisfactorily, he must feel that this protection is assured to him by the Organization, and that he may count on it. To ensure the independence of the agent, and, consequently, the independent action of the Organization itself, it is essential that in performing his duties he need not have to rely on any other protection than that of the Organization (save of course for the more direct and immediate protection due from the State in whose territory he may be). In particular, he should not have to rely on the protection of his own State. If he had to rely on that State, his independence might well be compromised, contrary to the principle applied to Article 100 of the Charter. And lastly, it is essential that – whether the agent belongs to a powerful or to a weak State; to one more affected or less affected by the complications of international life; to one in sympathy or not in sympathy with the mission of the agent – he should know that in the performance of his duties he is under the protection of the Organization. This assurance is even more necessary when the agent is stateless.[54]

The breadth of the Court's construction of Article 100 is instructive. The Court was prepared to hold, as in fact it did, that in the relatively unlikely event of an agent of the Organization being injured in the course of his duties in circumstances involving the responsibility of a State, or, rather, in the contingency of the agent's anticipating the possibility of the occurrence of such an event, his independence might be compromised unless he were able to rely upon the very limited protection afforded by the presentation of a monetary claim *post facto*, not by his State, but rather by the Organization. This attitude of the Court is of importance for its possible approach to a less indirect encroachment upon Article 100.[55]

---

[53] *ICJ Reports 1949*, p. 183.   [54] *Ibid.*, pp. 183–184.

[55] See the Dissenting Opinions of Judge Hackworth (*ibid.*, pp. 199–201) and Judge Badawi Pasha (pp. 209–211). Judge Hackworth stated that the Court's view that, if the employee had to rely on the protection of his own State, his independence might be compromised, contrary to the intention of Article 100 of the Charter, is a "strange argument."

But, in support of the Court's broad construction of Article 100, see the interventions before the Court by Counsel for the Secretary-General and by the Second Legal Adviser to the British Foreign Office, as reported in Liang, "Reparations for Injuries Suffered in the Service of the United Nations," *American Journal of International Law* (1949), 43, pp. 460–467 (and see Wright, "The Jural Personality of the United Nations," *ibid.*, pp. 509 ff.).

Mr. Feller and Mr. Fitzmaurice may be said to have gone beyond the position of the Court. The former suggested that, in the situation at bar, the nexus of nationality had been replaced by the nexus of official status and official duties. If the needs of the international community require the rule that a State may demand reparation for its injured national, they equally demand, the late Counsel for the Secretary-General argued, that the United Nations may require reparation for its injured agent. The British representative took the view that the Organization would have a right to protect its servants as does a State its nationals, if a relationship between the former analagous to nationality were found to

THE PRACTICE OF THE UNITED NATIONS

Subversive Activities in the United States of America and Cognate Problems

The principle of the exclusively international responsibility of the Secretariat has been more troubled in its application than in its conception. The first Secretary-General stated on one occasion that he successfully resisted "strong pressures . . . from many quarters to appoint or replace Secretariat officials."[56] Procedures for the international recruitment of staff, the Secretary-General reported to the General Assembly in March 1953, were "working fairly well in most Member countries, with the notable exception of the Soviet Union."[57] These procedures as a rule have involved governmental assistance in scrutinizing the character and record of applicants and members of the staff. Indeed, most Governments have, at the Secretary-General's request and otherwise, given such assistance, since "the United Nations does not – and clearly cannot – have all the necessary facilities for personnel selection that are at the disposal of national governments."[58]

exist. The United Kingdom found such a relationship by reference to Article 100. Its representative stressed the importance of the Organization and its servants being free from any limitations deriving from considerations of nationality.

[56] United Nations, General Assembly, Seventh Session, *Official Records*, 413th Plenary Meeting, March 10, 1953, A/PV.413, p. 534.

[57] *Ibid.*, p. 533.

[58] *Ibid.*, p. 534. Mr. Hammarskjöld has likewise acknowledged that Governments have transmitted information to him concerning staff members (*Report of the Secretary-General on Personnel Policy*, November 2, 1953, United Nations doc. A/2533, p. 7, and General Assembly, Eighth Session, Official Records, Fifth Committee, United Nations docs. A/C.5/SR. 413, p. 9, A/C.5/SR. 414, p. 14).

The French Government, it may be noted, has created a board which recommends French nationals for appointment to posts in the international secretariats. It has gone so far as to remonstrate with the Secretary-General after he appointed certain French nationals not among those so recommended, though it did not question his legal right to do so. The *Conseil d'État*, in an Order of February 20, 1953 concerning the case of a former official of the Institute of Intellectual Cooperation whose application for employment with Unesco had not been supported by the French Government, ruled that the equity of French Governmental evaluations are not subject to judicial inquiry (see Rolin, *Advisory Opinion on the Rights and Obligations of International Civil Servants*, prepared for the Federation of International Civil Servants Associations, 1953, p. 19). Security evaluations by the United States Government, since 1953, have been subject to challenge by the United States nationals concerned before the International Organizations Employees Loyalty Board (see below, note 79, p. 87, n. 1). The French Government has expressed its view that: "[Every] Member of State, not only every host State, has the indisputable right to establish the conditions under which it authorizes its nationals to become staff members of the United Nations. However, whatever measures of this kind a State may take are a matter between it and its nationals; as far as the United Nations is concerned, such measures are *res inter alios acta*; the Organization is not called upon to sanction them and they cannot limit the right of the Secretary-General to employ or to continue to employ in the Organization any person he considers qualified for such service, even if that person is not authorized by his Government to accept or continue employment" (General Assembly, Seventh Session, *Official Records*, 418th Plenary Meeting, March 30, 1953,

The United States at first declined to provide aid of this kind, on the ground that it did not wish to appear in any way to influence the Secretary-General in his choice of personnel.[59] In 1949 the United States authorities modified their position, and, while not commenting upon the professional qualifications of applicants, commenced to take decisions on the question "whether any information of a derogatory character is of sufficient substance to warrant the conclusion that the individual would appear to be so predisposed, through political affiliation or sentiment, as to be a poor risk in terms of adherence to his oath as an international civil servant."[60] In practice, the relevant Department supplied the Secretary-General, confidentially and orally, with conclusions on the subject. It did not submit the facts upon which those conclusions were based. The Department's evaluations subsequently were extended from applicants to members of the staff of United States nationality.[61] The Department from the beginning acknowledged that "the decision of appointment or retention, as the case may be, rests as always with the Secretary-General."[62]

The Secretary-General stated that he "could not act on the basis of a mere adverse comment – usually expressed in a single word – without, in effect, accepting instructions from the United States Government."[63] The opinions of the Department served only to stimulate further investigation by the Secretary-General. The limitations of his resources in the matter of investigation were such that he was able in but few cases to reach conclusions which made action possible.[64]

In 1950 the Secretary-General terminated the appointment of several members of the staff, some apparently on "security" grounds, against whom he felt he had "convincing evidence."[65] It seems probable that this evidence was not of subversive acts, except insofar as affiliation of the United States nationals in question with the Communist Party of the United States might,

A/PV.418, p. 607). For comment on this French approach, which perhaps is more consistent rationally than practically, see Cohen, "The United States and the United Nations Secretariat: A Preliminary Appraisal," *McGill Law Journal* (1953) 1, 3, pp. 189–190.

[59] See Letter of the then Secretary of State, James F. Byrnes, to Congressman Karl Mundt in the United States Senate, Committee on the Judiciary, *Activities of United States Citizens Employed by the United Nations. Hearings before the Sub-Committee to Investigate the Administration of the Internal Security Act and Other Security Laws,* 1952 (hereinafter referred to as *Hearings*), p. 414.

[60] Memorandum of the Department of State on Arrangements with the United Nations for Provision of Information on United States Nationals, *Hearings,* p. 415.

[61] For details of the arrangement see *Report of the Secretary-General on Personnel Policy,* January 30, 1953, United Nations doc. A/2364, Annex 1, p. 15, and *Hearings,* p. 415.

[62] *Ibid.,* p. 416.

[63] United Nations doc. A/PV.413, p. 536. See also United Nations doc. A/2364, p. 16. It is interesting to note that "in at least four cases" adverse comments were later "completely withdrawn" (*ibid.*).

[64] United Nations doc. A/2364, p. 16; *Hearings,* p. 417.   [65] United Nations doc. A/2364, p. 16.

under a theory of conspiracy, be deemed to be such. In this connection the Secretary-General later stated as follows:

> In view of the present laws and regulations of the United States toward the American Communist Party and verdicts of the courts on the leadership of that party, no United States national who is a member of the American Communist Party and who is, thereby, barred from employment in the service of his own government, should, as a matter of policy, be employed in the Secretariat. A major consideration for such a policy is, of course, the fact that the United States is the host country to the permanent Headquarters.[66]

Those officials who were discharged in 1950 on account of membership of the Communist Party held temporary or fixed-term, as contrasted with permanent, contracts. The Secretary-General argued before the Administrative Tribunal,[67] to which the discharged employees appealed, that he had the power to terminate temporary contracts "without showing cause."[68] The Tribunal, in a controversial set of judgments,[69] rejected this contention. Accordingly, at the General Assembly Session in 1951, the Secretary-General sought and obtained an amendment to the Staff Regulations which permit him "at any time" to terminate the appointment of temporary staff "if, in his opinion, such action would be in the interest of the United Nations."[70]

The Assembly's definition of the Secretary-General's discretionary authority did not cover members of the staff holding permanent or fixed-term contracts. The Staff Regulations provide that such staff, who enjoy a tenure

---

[66] United Nations doc. A/PV.413, p. 536.

[67] A body established by the General Assembly in 1949 with competence to hear and pass judgement upon applications alleging non-observance of contracts of employment or of the terms of appointment of members of the Secretariat of the United Nations. The International Labor Organization has its own Administrative Tribunal, the jurisdiction of which has been accepted by the World Health Organization, Unesco, and the International Telecommunications Union. (See the Statute of the Tribunal and comments upon its establishment in *United Nations Yearbook, 1948/49*, pp. 919–922; *Reports of the Secretary-General*, October 16, 1946 and September 27, 1949, United Nations docs. A/91, A/986; Huet, "The Administrative Tribunals of International Organizations," *Journal de droit international* (1950) 77; Langrod, "Le Tribunal Administratif des Nations Unies," *Revue de droit public et de la science politique* (1951) 67; and Puget, "Le Tribunal Administratif des Nations Unies, ses décisions récentes en matière de licenciements et leur inexécution," *Jurisclasseur périodique, La semaine juridique* (April 10, 1952), 26, pp. 994 ff.)

[68] *Howrani and 4 Others v. The Secretary-General of the United Nations*, Judgment No. 4, September 14, 1951, p. 2. "[The] Secretary-General could not give such reasons in many instances without breach of confidence with the source" (United Nations doc. A/2364, p. 17).

[69] Sources as disparate as James P. Richards, United States Delegate to the General Assembly, and Senator Henri Rolin appear to agree that the Tribunal's rulings did not conform to the intentions of the General Assembly with respect to the clauses of the Provisional Staff Regulations upon which the rulings purported to be based (see United Nations doc. A/C.5/SR.407, pp. 13–14, and Rolin, *Advisory Opinion*, p. 57).

[70] *Staff Regulations and Staff Rules of the United Nations*, United Nations doc. ST/AFS/SGB/94, Regulation 9. 1 (*c*), p. 43.

status similar to that possessed by the civil servants of many national Governments, may be discharged "if the necessities of the service require abolition of the post or reduction of the staff, if the services of the individual concerned prove unsatisfactory, or if he is, for reasons of health, incapacitated for further service";[71] and, as a "disciplinary measure," the Secretary-General may "summarily dismiss a member of the staff for serious misconduct."[72]

In 1952 a Federal Grand Jury sitting in New York began to call United States nationals who were members of the Secretariat for questioning as to possible violations of laws of the United States, "including those directed against subversive activities and espionage."[73] In the same year, a Sub-Committee on Internal Security of the United States Senate began to take testimony in order "to determine whether United States citizens who, even though they are United Nations employees, have been engaged in subversive activities which are clearly beyond the scope of their employment."[74] Neither body informed the Secretary-General in advance of their intention to call members of the Secretariat. Eighteen of those summoned by the Senate Sub-Committee declined to answer questions concerning past or present membership in the American Communist Party, and, in some cases, with regard to espionage or subversive activities, on the ground of possible self-incrimination. For the most part, only those were called to testify in open, public session who had invoked the privilege in closed session. "Over a score" of staff members declined to answer questions of the Grand Jury concerning communist activities, "including in some instances past and present espionage activity against the United States."[75]

In December 1952 the Grand Jury advised the Court that "startling evidence has disclosed infiltration into the United Nations of an overwhelmingly large group of disloyal United States citizens," and declared it to be "self-evident" that this situation constituted "a menace" to the Government of the United States.[76] The Grand Jury did not return any indictment

---

[71] *Ibid.*, Regulation 9. 1 (*a*), pp. 42–43. Additional grounds for discharge were added in December 1953 (see below, "Action Taken upon the Decisions of the Administrative Tribunal.")

[72] *Ibid.*, Regulation 10. 2, p. 48. For "misconduct," as opposed to "serious misconduct," the Secretary-General may dismiss a staff member, but not in a summary fashion. He may invoke this disciplinary measure only after the matter has been referred for advice to the Joint Disciplinary Committee, unless the staff member agrees with the Secretary-General to waive this procedure (*ibid.*, Rule 110. 3, p. 49).

[73] The presentment of the Federal Grand Jury is reprinted in *Hearings*, pp. 407–411.

[74] *Activities of United States Citizens Employed by the United Nations, Report of the Sub-Committee to Investigate the Administration of the Internal Security Act and Other Internal Security Laws*, 1953, p. 1. See also *Hearings*.

[75] Presentment of the Federal Grand Jury on Disloyalty of Certain United States Citizens at the United Nations, in *Hearings*, pp. 407–411.

[76] *Ibid.* In June 1954, however, a successor Grand Jury found the situation greatly improved.

containing a charge of subversive activity or violation of the law by any member of the Secretariat, nor did it specify how many "disloyal" citizens had "infiltrated" the United Nations. The Senate Sub-Committee, for its part, issued an interim report which recommended, *inter alia*, that "legislative safeguards be established to prevent future employment by international organizations, located in this country, of American nationals of questionable loyalty to the United States."[77] In accordance with this recommendation the Senate, in June 1953, adopted without a dissenting vote a Bill introduced by Senator McCarran which, were it to become law, would prohibit a citizen of the United States from accepting employment in the United Nations without "security clearance" from the Attorney General, and would require citizens employed by the United Nations at the time of its enactment likewise to seek clearance. The penalty for violation of the proposed Act by a citizen of the United States is a fine of not more than $10,000, imprisonment for not more than five years, or both.[78]

Earlier in January 1953, the President issued an Executive Order prescribing procedures for making available to the Secretary-General information concerning United States citizens employed or being considered for employment in the Secretariat. The Order provides for the investigation of such persons, and the submission to the Secretary-General of any derogatory information, "in as much detail as ... security considerations will permit," for his use in exercising his responsibilities. The Order is applicable also to citizens who are employees of other public international organizations of which the United States is a member. The investigations prescribed by the Order involved the filling out of questionnaires by staff members of United States nationality, their fingerprinting, and their interview by agents of the United States Government. The Secretary-General advised such staff members to cooperate with their Government in these procedures, and, in order to expedite the conclusion of the investigations, permitted the distribution of the questionnaires and the fingerprinting and interviewing to take place on United Nations premises.[79]

---

[77] *Report of the Sub-Committee*, note 74, p. 18.

[78] See 83rd Congress, 1st Session, *A Bill to Prevent Citizens of the United States of Questionable Loyalty to the United States Government from Accepting any Office or Employment in or under the United Nations, and for Other Purposes*. Calendar No. 224, S. 3, and *Report No. 223* thereon. And see below, "Receipt by the Secretary-General of Information" etc., para. 3.

[79] See Executive Order No. 10422, 18 F.R. 239, as reprinted in United Nations doc. A/2364, pp. 35–36. The Order was amended in June 1953 by Executive Order No. 10459, 18 F.R. 3183, reproduced in United Nations doc. A/2533, Appendix to Annex I, pp. 5–11. The Order as amended affords persons investigated the opportunity of challenging alleged derogatory information in writing and in a hearing before an International Organizations Employees Loyalty Board, in which they may be represented by

Opinion of the Commission of Jurists

With regard to members of the staff who refused to testify, the Secretary-General expressed himself as "deeply disturbed" by their attitude in relation to an organization which had been "declared subversive by the United States Attorney General, an organization whose leaders had been convicted of teaching and advocating the overthrow of the United States Government by force and violence."[80] He invoked Article 9 (1) (c) of the Staff Regulations,[81] and, in the course of 1952, discharged those who held temporary contracts. Those having permanent appointments were put on compulsory leave, and an opinion was sought from an international Commission of three distinguished jurists as to what further action, if any, could properly be taken. The Commission submitted its Opinion on November 29.[82] It viewed the problem before it in terms of the "mutual tolerances" which it saw as necessary if the relationship between the Organization and its Secretariat, on the one hand, and their host country or countries, on the other, were to be satisfactory. Membership in the Secretariat, the Commission states, "in no way abrogates, limits or qualifies the loyalty a person owes to the State of which he is a citizen."[83] The Secretary-General, in exercising his exclusively international responsibility in the selection of staff, "should regard it as of the first importance to refrain from engaging or to remove from the staff any person whom he has reasonable grounds for believing to be engaged or to have been engaged, or to be likely to be engaged in any subversive activities against the host country."[84] If a member of the staff of United States

counsel, present witnesses and other evidence in their behalf, and cross-examine witnesses offered in support of the derogatory information. The standard the Board uses in making its determinations is "whether or not on all the evidence there is a reasonable doubt as to the loyalty of the person involved to the Government of the United States." The Board transmits its findings "as advisory opinions, together with the reasons therefor in as much detail as ... security considerations permit," to the Secretary of State for transmission to the Secretary-General. The Unesco Executive Board agreed, as a temporary measure, to circulate the questionnaire prescribed under the Executive Order to applicants for employment of United States nationality, while making it clear that Unesco assumes no responsibility for its contents (see Unesco docs. 33 EX/32, 33 EX/SR. 4 and 5). The General Conference subsequently defeated a move to reverse this policy.

[80] United Nations doc. A/PV.413, p. 536.   [81] See above.

[82] The Opinion is printed in United Nations doc. A/2364, Annex III, pp. 21–33. For critical comment on the Opinion see Cohen, "Preliminary Appraisal," pp. 180–191. See also Langrod, "La Crise de la fonction publique internationale," *Annales Universitatis Saraviensis* (1953), 6, and Boitel, "Situation et problèmes actuels de la fonction publique internationale," *Politique Étrangère* (March–April 1953), Vol. 18.

[83] United Nations doc. A/2364, p. 25.

[84] Where there has been a conviction of a staff member for a crime involving subversive activities by the courts of his own country or the courts of any country having jurisdiction over him by reason of his residence, the fact of the crime, the Commission held, is *ipso facto* established. "It is *res judicata* and should be accepted as such by the Secretary-General ... [We] are of the opinion that the Secretary-General

nationality declines to answer questions relating to past or present espionage or other subversive activities or to past or present membership in the American Communist Party or another organization declared to be subversive, by invoking the privilege against self-incrimination, that fact gives the Secretary-General cause to dismiss him, in that, in the Commission's view, "either his answers would have incriminated him or he had no right to claim the privilege."[85] Persons against whom the Secretary-General reaches the foregoing reasonable belief, or who pleaded the privilege in the foregoing circumstances, as well as those convicted of a crime involving subversion, may, if the particular circumstances warrant, be dismissed for serious misconduct under Staff Regulation 10.[86] Such persons may in any case be dismissed by the Secretary-General "on his own responsibility" for fundamental breach of their obligations under Articles 1 (4) and 1 (8) of the Staff Regulations, while those holding temporary contracts would be liable to discharge under Article 9 (1) (*c*) as well.[87] Article 1 (4) of the Regulations then provided:

> Members of the Secretariat shall conduct themselves at all times in a manner befitting their status as international civil servants. They shall not engage in any activity that is incompatible with the proper discharge of their duties with the United Nations. They shall avoid any action and in particular any kind of public pronouncement which may adversely reflect on their status. While they are not expected to give up their national sentiments or their political and religious convictions, they shall at all times bear in mind the reserve and tact incumbent upon them by reason of their international status."[88]

The Secretary-General announced on December 5 that he had decided to "use the conclusions and recommendations of this opinion as the basis of my personnel policy." However, he later added that this did not mean that he

should regard the conviction as an absolute bar to the employment or the continuation of the employment of the officer concerned in the State in question," whether the crime was committed before or after his joining the Secretariat. "In our opinion there should be no differentiation in this respect between a citizen of the United States and a citizen of some other State resident in the United States" (*ibid.*, p. 26).

[85] *Ibid.*, p. 27.   [86] See above, note 72.   [87] *Ibid.*

[88] *Staff Regulations*, as note 70, p. 4. Regulation 1.8 reads: "The immunities and privileges attached to the United Nations by virtue of Article 105 of the Charter are conferred in the interests of the Organization. These privileges and immunities furnish no excuse to the staff members who enjoy them for non-performance of their private obligations or failure to observe laws and police regulations. In any case where these privileges and immunities arise, the staff member shall immediately report to the Secretary-General, with whom it alone rests to decide whether they shall be waived" (*ibid.*, pp. 5–6). The Commission further suggested that the Secretary-General should establish a panel, composed of senior members of the Secretariat under independent chairmanship, which would afford staff members with permanent or fixed-term contracts the opportunity for a full hearing in private, and which would submit advisory opinions to the Secretary-General on what action, if any, he should take. Mr. Lie acted

"accepted all the arguments in the opinion or all the implications that might be drawn from it."[89] He requested staff members whom he had placed on compulsory leave after pleading the privilege to withdraw their plea. When they refused to do so, he terminated their employment on the ground that they were in breach of Regulation 1.4.[90] Shortly afterwards the Secretary-General, prompted by concern among the delegations about the course of events, requested the General Assembly to place the item of personnel policy on the agenda of its Seventh Session.[91] The report which the Secretary-General submitted to the General Assembly made it clear that the Secretary-General essentially accepted the recommendations of the Commission of Jurists with respect to discharging staff members who pleaded the privilege in response to questions involving subversive activities or against whom he had reasonable belief that they had been, were, or were likely to be, engaged in subversive activities. He defined such activities as those directed toward the overthrow of a Government by force, including conspiracy toward such overthrow and incitement of it. He would act, the Secretary-General pledged, only upon the basis of "tangible and convincing evidence." He quoted with approval the declaration of the Assistant Secretary-General for Administrative and Financial Services that "no organization dedicated to law and order in world affairs can hope to survive if its own administrative actions are arbitrary and precipitate, based on mere suspicion and devoid of the due process to

upon this suggestion, but, subsequently, the panel so constituted appears to have been dissolved (see United Nations doc. A/C.5/566, pp. 11–12).

[89] United Nations doc. A/2364, p. 9. In March 1953, in introducing the debate of the General Assembly upon his personnel policy, the Secretary-General pointed out that he had "by no means accepted everything" in the opinion of the Jurists. "Indeed, it was because of reservations about some aspects of the jurists' opinion that I did not place it before you for discussion and have instead submitted my own report" (United Nations doc. A/PV.313, p. 537).

The Director-General of the Food and Agriculture Organization of the United Nations announced that he regarded the opinion of the Jurists as a "valuable guide," which, he indicated, he would substantially apply to the FAO (see FAO Administrative Memorandum No. 472, December 19, 1952). The other Specialized Agencies have not publicly defined their policies. However, in accordance with the General Assembly's resolution of April 1, 1953, the Secretary-General consulted with the administrative heads of the Specialized Agencies concerning the substance of his Report of November 2, 1953 (United Nations doc. A/2533), which, it should be noted, represents a considerable modification of the approach recommended by the Jurists and of the policies initially adopted by the Secretary-General. He indicated that the representatives of the Specialized Agencies were in "general agreement" with him (ibid., p. 5). The Agreements between the United Nations and the Specialized Agencies, which provide for the development of common personnel standards, supply a continuing basis for such consultations.

[90] "Their refusal of my request constituted, in my opinion, a clear case for dismissal for misconduct under Article X of the Staff Regulations. Nevertheless, I chose a less severe method of termination, one that would entitle them to the normal indemnities and severance pay ..." (United Nations doc. A/PV.413, p. 537.)

[91] See United Nations docs. A/2327 and A/2330.

which all civilized peoples are dedicated."[92] And, "to place the problem in its proper setting," Mr. Lie stated as follows:

> It should be kept in mind that the Secretariat of the United Nations works in a glass house not only physically, but in every respect. It is not a profitable place for spies and saboteurs. Almost all meetings and documentation of the United Nations are open for all to see and hear. No military secrets are ever handled by the Secretariat. Furthermore, the policies and programmes of the United Nations in all fields ... are determined by the governments of Member States, not by the Secretariat. The work of the Secretariat in carrying out these policies and programmes is subject to the constant scrutiny of the governments."[93]

The Assembly's discussion of the Secretary-General's Report[94] concluded with the adoption of a resolution which neither approved nor disapproved the Secretary-General's personnel policy,[95] while rejecting a proposed resolution which might have been interpreted as impliedly critical of it.[96] There was a widespread disposition in the Assembly, before taking substantive action, to await the outcome of the appeals against their discharge which twenty former members of the staff had filed with the Administrative Tribunal.

The Decisions of the Administrative Tribunal

The principal contentions of the applicants to the Tribunal were that the contested decisions were illegal in that: (*a*) they were the result of improper pressure exercised by agencies of a Member State upon the Secretary-General in violation of Article 100; (*b*) they were based upon arbitrary political considerations, particularly suspected communist affiliations, in disregard of their rights to independent political convictions; (*c*) the plea of privilege does not constitute a breach of the Staff Regulations, in that United States staff

---

[92] United Nations doc. A/2364, p. 3. See also the statement on personnel policy with special reference to the Secretary-General's report of the Staff Council of the Secretariat, United Nations doc. A/2367, and a letter to the Secretary-General from certain representatives and alternates on the Staff Council, United Nations doc. A/2366.

[93] United Nations doc. A/PV.413, p. 537.

[94] See United Nations, General Assembly, Seventh Session, *Official Records*, 416th–422nd Plenary Meetings, March 28 and 30–31, April 1, 1953, A/PV.416–22.

[95] See the remarks of the Delegates of New Zealand (A/PV.422, p. 667), Lebanon (*ibid.*, p. 668), and France (A/PV.418 p. 606). The resolution noted the Secretary-General's Report, expressed confidence that the Secretary-General would conduct his personnel policy in accordance with Articles 100 and 101, and requested him to submit a further report to the Eighth Session (after consulting with the administrative heads of the Specialized Agencies), with his recommendations and with the comments of the Advisory Committee on Administrative and Budgetary Questions thereon. It was adopted by a vote of forty-one to thirteen, with four abstentions.

[96] The resolution proposed by certain Arab and Asian Delegations was rejected by a vote of twenty-nine to twenty-one, with eight abstentions.

members, as a condition of employment, had not surrendered their constitutional rights, and in that the exercise of the privilege, under American law, does not create a presumption of guilt; (d) in the case of permanent staff, discharge may be effected only for the reasons set forth in Regulations 9.1 and 10.2,[97] which do not apply here; and e) in the case of temporary staff, Regulation 9.1 (c)[98] cannot be regarded as granting the Secretary-General absolute discretion, and, were it so regarded, the applicants would none the less be entitled to benefit from the legal position existing prior to the amendment of the Regulations.[99]

The respondent Secretary-General[100] replied that: (a) he had confined himself to receiving information from the State Department, and at no time had surrendered his power of decision with respect to the retention or appointment of staff; (b) he discharged the applicants not because of their political opinions, but on account of their failure to conduct themselves in a manner befitting their status of international civil servants; (c) their claim of privilege gave rise to the presumption that they were or had been engaged in activities directed toward the violent overthrow of a Member State, and constituted a public pronouncement which reflected adversely upon the international civil service and rendered the applicants unworthy of trust and confidence; (d) this violation of duty constituted serious misconduct (Regulation 10.2) and failure to render satisfactory service (Regulation 9.1) and rendered void the subsisting contracts between the applicants and the United Nations; and e) in the case of temporary staff, the Secretary-General is not required to state reasons for termination, and, no evidence of bad faith having been produced and no acquired rights having been disturbed, his action was proper.[101]

The Administrative Tribunal upheld the action of the Secretary-General in nine cases involving temporary appointments.[102] It decided in favour of the applicants in one case involving a temporary appointment,[103] and in eleven cases involving permanent appointments.[104] In the four cases in which the

---

[97] See notes 70–72.　　[98] Ibid.

[99] See Crawford and Nineteen Others v. the Secretary-General of the United Nations, Brief on Behalf of Nineteen Appellants, 1953.

[100] It should be noted that on April 10, 1953 Mr. Dag Hammarskjöld succeeded Mr. Trygve Lie as Secretary-General. Mr. Lie had submitted his resignation six months earlier, for reasons unconnected with personnel problems.

[101] See Crawford and Nineteen Others v. The Secretary-General of the United Nations, Statement and Briefs for the Respondent, 1953.

[102] Judgments Nos. 19–27, August 21, 1953.

[103] Crawford v. The Secretary-General of the United Nations, Judgment No. 18, August 21, 1953.

[104] Judgments Nos. 28–37, August 21, 1953, Judgment No. 38, August 26, 1953 (Glaser v. The Secretary-General of the United Nations, the only case of an applicant being dismissed since Mr. Hammarskjöld's assumption of office).

Tribunal ordered reinstatement, the Secretary-General exercised his right to call upon the Tribunal to decree compensation instead.[105] In the cases where the applicants were successful the Tribunal awarded salaries up to the date of judgement, less termination indemnities, compensation in lieu of reinstatement, and costs.

With respect to the applicants' initial contention, the Tribunal ruled that it was "not competent to pass judgement on the validity, in relation to the Charter, of an agreement between the Secretary-General and a Member State, whatever influence this agreement might actually have had on the decision taken."[106] It emphasized that, since Article 1 (4) of the Staff Regulations recognizes the right of staff members not to give up political opinions, "membership of any particular party would not, of itself, be a justification, in the absence of other cause, for dismissal ... A decision based on such premises is a violation of an inalienable right of staff members and represents a misuse of power."[107] As to the third and fourth of the principal contentions of the applicant bearing on the provisions of the Constitution of the United States, the Tribunal held that: "Whatever view may be held as to the conduct of the Applicant, that conduct could not be described as serious misconduct, which alone under Staff Regulation 10.2 ... justifies the Secretary-General in dismissing a staff member summarily."[108] Nor could the plea of privilege justify discharge on the ground of "unsatisfactory services," since the word "services" is used in the Staff Regulations and Rules solely to designate professional behavior within the Organization. "If it is admitted that the plea of constitutional privilege in respect of acts outside a staff member's professional duties constitutes a breach of Staff Regulation 1.4,[109] this fact cannot be considered as unsatisfactory services and cannot fall within the purview of Staff Regulation 9.1."[110] The Tribunal thus found the Secretary-General's reliance upon Regulations 10.2 and 9.1 to be unfounded.

It likewise rejected his third submission, namely that, "under general principles of contract law if one party fails to carry out its obligations, the other party is justified in considering the contract at an end and in refusing to carry out its part."[111] The Staff Regulations, the Tribunal maintained, exhaustively list the grounds on which appointments may be terminated. The Opinion of the three jurists to the effect that the Secretary-General may terminate an appointment because of the contractual relationship between a

---

[105] See Judgments Nos. 39–42, October 13, 1953.   [106] See, e.g., Judgment No. 19, p. 4.
[107] Judgment No. 18, p. 6.
[108] Judgment No. 29, pp. 8–9, and some others.   [109] See above.
[110] Judgment No. 29 and some others; in particular Judgment No. 38 (*Glaser v. The Secretary-General of the United Nations*), pp. 5–8.
[111] *Statement and Briefs for Respondent* (see note 101), p. 28.

staff member and the Secretary-General disregarded the nature of permanent contracts and the character of the regulations established by the General Assembly. Accordingly, the Tribunal found the decisions terminating the appointments of permanent staff to be illegal. However, in the case of those holding temporary appointments, the Tribunal recognized that the intention of the General Assembly was to invest the Secretary-General with discretionary powers. "Such discretionary powers must be exercised without improper motive so that there shall be no misuse of power, since any such misuse of power would call for rescinding of the decision."[112] While thus reserving to itself the right to inquire into the Secretary-General's motives, the Tribunal placed the burden of proof of establishing their impropriety upon the applicant. In ten cases, it found no evidence of improper motivation, and decided in favour of the Secretary-General; in the eleventh, it reached a contrary conclusion, and decided against him.[113] The contention of the applicants that their "acquired rights" were invaded by the application to

---

[112] Judgment No. 19, p. 6, and some others. See also Judgments No. 18, p. 4; No. 21, p. 7; and No. 24, p. 6.

[113] The Tribunal's assertion of its competence to judge the motives of the Secretary-General in exercising his discretion under Regulation 9.1 (c) to "at any time terminate the appointment, if, in his opinion, such action would be in the interest of the United Nations" raises a difficult question. The Secretary-General had conceded, in discussing the scope of review in cases of termination where no reason is stated, that there "remain appealable questions of good faith, etc. Of course, it is up to the Applicant to produce evidence of bad faith if it is available" (*Statement and Briefs for Respondent* [see note 101], p. 66). On the other hand, the Regulation itself explicitly places the interpretation of the interest of the United Nations in the matter of termination in the hands of the Secretary-General alone; it is "his opinion" which governs, and not that of the Administrative Tribunal. The Tribunal held, in effect, in Judgments Nos. 11 and 12, that the opinion of the Secretary-General, in pursuance of Article 9 of the Statute of the Administrative Tribunal, that reinstatement of a staff member would be impossible or inadvisable – the Tribunal accordingly being charged with fixing compensation in lieu of reinstatement – was not subject to review. More than this, the Secretary-General's recommendations for the adoption of Article 9.1, and the Advisory Committee's comments thereon (United Nations doc. A/1912/Add. 1), together with the Secretary-General's explanation to the Fifth Committee that the interpretation to be placed upon the phrase "in his opinion" in his proposed text, would be the same as that which the Tribunal had given to that phrase in the cited judgments, reinforces the conclusion that his discretion thereunder was meant to be unreviewable. The relevant discussion of the Fifth Committee (General Assembly, Sixth Session, Fifth Committee, *Official Records*, 330th, 332nd, and 33rd Meetings) and its report to the Assembly (United Nations doc. A/2108) support this view. Moreover, the phrase "in his opinion," as it occurs in Article 99 of the Charter with regard to the Secretary-General's right to bring any matter to the attention of the Security Council which, in his opinion, may threaten the maintenance of international peace and security, appears, both in its obvious purport and in the interpretation given to the Article in the *travaux préparatoires*, to invest the Secretary-General with unreviewable discretion in appreciating such matters. (See Schwebel *British Year Book of International Law* [1951] 28, pp. 375 and 377, n. 7. On the other hand, it may be argued that the independence of the Secretary-General in the exercise of his powers under Article 99 is not duplicated in the exercise of his powers under Article 101, which empowers him to appoint staff "under regulations established by the General Assembly.") It was further understood that the Secretary-General would be able to invoke Article 9.1 (c) without providing the staff member concerned or the Tribunal with a statement of specific reasons for his action, but, if the applicant is free

them of a discretionary power with which the Secretary-General was invested after their appointment was rejected by the Tribunal.[114]

Action Taken upon the Decisions of the Administrative Tribunal

Following upon the award of the Tribunal, the Secretary-General requested the General Assembly to fill what he considered to be a gap in his powers, as found by the Administrative Tribunal. Considering himself bound by its rulings,[115] he proposed that the Assembly amend the law upon which those rulings had been based. The Assembly, of course, could not amend the

to present evidence of the Secretary-General's allegedly improper motives, this would seemingly tend to compel the Secretary-General to elucidate his allegedly proper ones (though the Secretary-General may choose to rest on the advantage he enjoys in his opponent having to bear the burden of proof). It may be argued that to strip the temporary staff member of this right would be to leave him wholly without a substantive right of appeal. Yet the General Assembly's intention in adopting Regulation 9.1 (c) would seem to admit this result, on the theory that safeguards afforded to permanent staff should not necessarily be extended to the temporary staff, because of the need for freedom of action in choosing a permanent Secretariat. The power of the Tribunal to review the Secretary-General's motives in cases involving permanent contracts is unquestioned. (See United Nations doc. A/C.5/566, p. 13.)

[114] It may be noted that, in contending for "acquired rights," the applicants argued that the relations between the United Nations and its staff are contractual in nature, a view which the Secretary-General urged, but which the Tribunal did not unqualifiedly accept, in contending that breach of Regulation 1.4 by a staff member of itself justified the Secretary-General in considering the contract voidable. With respect to the legal position of the staff, the Tribunal declared:

> Relations between staff members and the United Nations involve various elements and are consequently not solely contractual in nature. Article 101 of the Charter gives the General Assembly the right to establish regulations for the appointment of the staff, and consequently the right to change them ...
>
> In determining the legal position of staff members a distinction should be made between contractual elements and statutory elements: all matters being contractual which affect the personal status of each staff member e.g., general rules that have no personal reference.
>
> While the contractual elements cannot be changed without the agreement of the two parties, the statutory elements on the other hand may always be changed at any time through regulations established by the General Assembly, and these changes are binding on staff members.
>
> With regard to the case under consideration, the Tribunal decides that a statutory element is involved and that in fact the question of the termination of temporary appointments is one of a general rule subject to amendment by the General Assembly and against which acquired rights cannot be invoked.

See Judgments No. 19; No. 27, pp. 4–5; and No. 20, p. 4. See also Staff Regulations 12.1 (United Nations doc. ST/AFS/SGB/94, p. 53), and compare the Tribunal's views with those of the League Commission of Jurists of 1925 (above), of the League Committee of Jurists of 1932 (*Official Journal*, 1932, Special Supplement 107, p. 208), of the League Administrative Tribunal, and of the Assembly (*Official Journal*, 1946 citations above, note 17. And see United Nations doc. A/C.5/566, p. 12).

[115] As chief executive officer of the United Nations, Mr. Hammarskjöld declared: "I consider myself bound by the findings and decisions of the Administrative Tribunal which the General Assembly itself established. Thus, I have to submit to the Assembly a request for such supplementary appropriations as are required for compensations decided upon by the Tribunal" (United Nations doc. A/C.5/544, p. 6. See also United Nations doc. A/2534, Annex A, pp. 4–5).

Charter; it was a matter of revising the Staff Regulations "in the light of the Charter."[116] The Secretary-General proposed, in the first instance, that there should be added to the Staff Regulations an explicit statement that staff members shall not engage in any political activities outside the scope of their official duties, other than voting, unless otherwise authorized in accordance with the Staff Rules issued by the Secretary-General. In the course of the debate in the Fifth Committee, it was made clear that such a regulation would not preclude "passive membership" in a political party.[117] "The Secretary-General . . . should have the right to exercise his judgement in these matters . . . free from arbitrariness and discrimination . . . A staff member may consider his political activities appropriate to and consistent with his international status, and may, for that reason, be unwilling to accept the judgement of the Secretary-General to the contrary . . . The sound operation of the Organization requires that such a staff member choose between continuing his political activities or remaining an employee of the United Nations."[118] This provision, the Secretary-General added, would have "no retroactive implications. Previous activities are of significance only if they should reflect unfavourably on the staff member's present integrity or administrative suitability under the standards established by the Charter."[119] Moreover, "in

---

[116] United Nations doc. A/2533, p. 10. See also the comments of the Advisory Committee on the proposals set forth in this document (United Nations doc. A/2555), as well as those of the Staff Council (doc. A/C.5/561), and the observations of the Secretary-General on their commentaries (doc. A/C.5/563), together with the following documents which appeared in the course of the Fifth Committee's debate on the Secretary-General's proposals: A/C.5/L. 255–62; A/C.5/564–74; A/2534, A/2580–1, A/2591–2; and the summary records of the proceedings of the Committee, A/C.5/SR.406–22.

[117] The Secretary-General declared that he intended to implement the regulation prohibiting political activities by a staff rule which, with respect to party membership, would in substance run as follows: "Membership of a legal political party is permitted, provided that such membership, in the case of the staff member concerned, does not entail subjection to party discipline or action in favour of the party, other than the payment of normal financial contributions." The Fifth Committee suggested that the Secretary-General should consider the alternative text proposed by the United Kingdom: "Membership of a political party is permitted, provided that such membership does not entail any positive action, current or potential, other than voting or payment of normal financial contributions, contrary to the provisions of Staff Regulation 1.7. In any case of doubt, the staff member should consult the Secretary-General." The Secretary-General explained that his reference to a legal political party did not imply that membership in a party which was illegal under the laws of the country of the staff member concerned would in all cases be considered a violation of the regulation, but that each such case would have to be considered individually. The representative of the United Kingdom explained that his proposal deliberately omitted the word "legal," as membership of illegal parties would be debarred under Staff Regulation 1.4 (General Assembly, Eighth Session, *Report of the Fifth Committee on Personnel Policy*, December 7, 1953, United Nations doc. A/2615, pp. 6–7. See also United Nations doc. A/C.5/566, pp. 1–3, as well as the other documentation cited below, note 121.)

[118] United Nations doc. A/2533, p. 11. See also United Nations docs. A/C.5/566, pp. 1–3, and A/C.5/SR.414, p. 13.

[119] United Nations doc. A/2533, p. 25.

the implementation of the provision the staff member's rights to his religious or political convictions should be fully respected."[120] The Advisory Committee, the Staff Council, and the Delegations supported the essence of the Secretary-General's proposal, which was adopted by the Fifth Committee of the General Assembly without a dissenting vote.[121] There was even wider support for the Secretary-General's proposal to add a clarifying phrase to Staff Regulation 1.4, which is of interest more because of the remarks with which it was annotated than for its substance.[122]

In addition, the Secretary-General proposed to broaden his powers by adding a clause to Regulation 9.1 (*a*)[123] which would permit him to discharge a permanent employee if the latter's conduct indicates that he does "not meet the high standards of integrity required by Article 101, paragraph 3, of the Charter."[124] The phrases "unsatisfactory services" and "misconduct," as employed by the Staff Regulations and interpreted by the Administrative Tribunal, did not, the Secretary-General explained, adequately cover the requirements of integrity set forth in the Charter. An example of lack of integrity, the Secretary-General suggested, might be the case in which a member of the staff seeks to safeguard his purely personal interests despite his knowledge that by so doing he causes real and substantial harm to the

---

[120] *Ibid.*

[121] There was a diversity of views as to the precise extent of the prohibition against political activities, which was not clearly reflected in the vote, however. The text adopted, which was proposed by the United Kingdom, was as follows: "Staff members may exercise the right to vote but shall not engage in any political activity which is inconsistent with or might reflect upon the independence and impartiality required by their status as international civil servants" (United Nations doc. A/2615, p. 26. See also docs. A/C.5/561, p. 3, A/C.5/564, pp. 2–3, A/C.5/566, pp. 1–3, A/C.5/SR.408, p. 17, A/C.5/SR.412, pp. 6–7, A/C.5/SR.413, p. 8, A/C.5/SR.414, p. 13, A/C.5/SR.417, p. 15).

[122] The Secretary-General proposed that Article 1.4 be amended to read: "Members of the Secretariat ... shall avoid any action and in particular any kind of public pronouncement which may adversely reflect on their status, or on their integrity, independence and impartiality which are required by that status." The Secretary-General noted:

One problem in this connexion is the use by a staff member of the privilege against self-incrimination in an official national inquiry concerning subversive activities and related matters ... Under certain conditions, it may be considered as incompatible with the status of an international civil servant. But a conclusion to the effect that the staff member should cease to serve in the Secretariat because of his invoking the privilege cannot be drawn without further investigation. If this investigation gives an explanation of the action which removes its unfavourable implications, termination is not justified on the basis of the standards proper to the United Nations ...

And acts which are generally recognized as offences by national criminal laws normally will be violations also for the independent standard of integrity developed by, and proper to, the United Nations. However, the Organization must remain free to take no account of convictions of staff members for trivial offences or for offences which are generally held not to reflect on integrity, or of convictions made without observance of the generally recognized requirements of due process of law.

(United Nations doc. A/2533, p. 24.)

[123] See notes 70–71.   [124] United Nations doc. A/2533, p. 20.

Organization.[125] He continued: "On the other hand, the term integrity and the term loyalty, as often applied in the political sphere, do not cover the same set of considerations, although, of course, in a case of contested 'loyalty', acts might come to light which indicate a lack of integrity as an independent fact."[126] This proposal of the Secretary-General likewise gained wide support.[127]

The Secretary-General affirmed that his exercise of his new powers would be subject to review by the Administrative Tribunal to the full extent of its legal authority, an assurance which the Fifth Committee took pains to note. At the same time the Secretary-General submitted that the Tribunal might be expected to accept his views as to what constitutes "lack of integrity" or "political activity," to the extent that they obviously involve considerations of administrative policy not open to a review of a strictly legal nature.[128] Yet he did not thereby appear to intend to suggest that the Tribunal's previous opinion as to what constitutes another ground for dismissal, namely, serious misconduct, exceeded its legal authority. On the one hand, the Secretary-General took the initiative in stating that he would be required to give reasons for action taken under his new powers; on the other hand, he declared that the

---

[125] "It is not very clear what is meant here, and the Council doubts whether integrity, in its accepted meaning, is likely to be involved in such conduct" (*Statement by the Staff Council*, United Nations doc. A/C.5/561, p. 7). One might gather from his arguments before the Administrative Tribunal that the Secretary-General believed the case of a staff member who pleads the privilege in an inquiry regarding subversive activity, to be in point (*Statement and Briefs for Respondent* [see note 101], p. 28). But see note 124 above.

[126] United Nations doc. A/2533, p. 21.

[127] The additional provisions of Staff Regulation 9.1 (*a*) which the Assembly adopted, with the exception of a last paragraph discussed below, are as follows:

The Secretary-General may also, giving his reasons therefor, terminate the appointment of a staff member who holds a permanent appointment:

(i) If the conduct of the staff member indicates that the staff member does not meet the highest standards of integrity required by Article 101, paragraph 3, of the Charter;

(ii) If the facts anterior to the appointment of the staff member and relevant to his suitability come to light which, if they had been known at the time of his appointment should, under the standards established in the Charter, have precluded his appointment.

No termination under sub-paragraphs (i) and (ii) shall take place until the matter has been considered and reported on by a special advisory board appointed for that purpose by the Secretary-General.

After considerable discussion, the Fifth Committee approved the suggestion of the Secretary-General that the special advisory board shall be composed of a chairman, appointed by the Secretary-General on the nomination of the President of the International Court of Justice, and four members appointed by the Secretary-General in agreement with the Staff Council (see United Nations doc. A/2615, pp. 13–15).

With respect to sub-paragraph (ii), see the decision of the Administrative Tribunal in *Wallach v. The Secretary-General of the United Nations*, Judgement No. 28, August 21, 1953, and the arguments of the Secretary-General in this case in *Statement and Briefs for the Respondent* (see note 101), pp. 33–56.

[128] See United Nations doc. A/2533, pp. 14, 16.

widening of his responsibilities would be "in a sphere which cannot appropriately, to its full extent, be subject to review by a tribunal confined to strictly legal criteria ..."[129] He thus seemed to accept the form of the Tribunal's power of review, while restricting its substance. This proposal he combined with an affirmation of "the right of the Tribunal to decide on its own competence."[130]

To balance these extensions of his powers, the Secretary-General suggested, in addition to the establishment of an advisory panel which would consider instances of their proposed exercise, a measure of review by the General Assembly of the principles developed in his implementation of the Staff Regulations. He was willing to undertake that the standards on which he intended to base his decisions would be announced as fully as possible for the guidance of the staff. The Secretary-General further declared that he would establish procedures whereby staff members could place on record any statements, evidence, or information they considered relevant to charges made against them. Lastly, he gave assurances that the staff would be enabled to secure qualified legal counsel for their applications to the Administrative Tribunal more easily than in the past, through procedures which would be instituted under its aegis. These suggestions met with general support, and the General Assembly resolved to review the Staff Regulations and the principles and standards progressively developed and applied by the Secretary-General thereunder at its Tenth Session in 1955.

The Secretary-General's request for appropriations to pay the indemnities awarded by the Administrative Tribunal did not meet with equal success. After a prolonged debate the General Assembly decided to request an Advisory Opinion of the International Court of Justice on the following questions:

1. Having regard to the Statute of the United Nations Administrative Tribunal and to any other relevant instruments and to the relevant records, has the General Assembly the right on any grounds, to refuse to give effect to an award of compensation made by that Tribunal in favour of a staff member of the United Nations whose contract of service has been terminated without his assent?

2. If the answer given by the Court to question (1) is in the affirmative, what are

---

[129] *Ibid.*, p. 14.

[130] United Nations doc. A/C.5/563, p. 3. See also United Nations docs. A/C.5/L.259, A/C.5/574, and A/C.5/566, p. 13. In the last-cited document the Secretary-General clarified his approach with an illustration: "In a case of lack of integrity it is for the Administrative Tribunal to decide whether the action referred to by the Secretary-General is *capable* of being labelled as 'lack of integrity', while it is for the Secretary-General to say whether it *should* be labelled as 'lack of integrity'. The Tribunal sets the limits, so to speak, for the interpretation. The real implementation inside those limits, the setting of the standard, will primarily be the duty of the Secretary-General."

the principal grounds upon which the General Assembly could lawfully exercise such a right?[131]

THE PRINCIPAL LEGAL ISSUES

The Allegiance of Members of the Secretariat

It is convenient to take as a starting point for the consideration of the principal legal issues involved a significant passage from the Report of the Commission of Jurists referred to above:[132]

> The United Nations is an entity separate and distinct from its Member States. It has its own policy-forming organs ... its own judicial organization ... and ... the Secretary-General is given a large measure of independence and certain powers of initiation ... It is equally clear that the United Nations is in no sense a super State. It has no sovereignty and can claim no allegiance from its own officers or employees. Membership of its staff in our opinion in no way abrogates, limits or qualifies the loyalty a person owes to the State of which he is a citizen ... We can find nothing in the constitution of the United Nations or the provisions governing the employment of its staff which gives the least ground for supposing that there is or should be any conflict whatever between the loyalty owed by every citizen by virtue of his allegiance to his own State and the responsibility of such a citizen to the United Nations in respect to work done by him as an officer or employee of the United Nations ... In our opinion the immunities and privileges granted to members of the staff of the United Nations in no way qualify or limit the principle of the undivided loyalty to his own State of a member of the United Nations staff.[133]

On the face of it, the Commission's emphasis – if not its argument – is significant and calls for reflection. Membership of the staff of the United Nations qualifies the loyalty of a person to the State of which he is a citizen insofar as the policies of that State and of the Organization do not coincide. In this and all other cases, with respect to his official duties the member of the staff owes his entire responsibility to the Organization; this exclusively international responsibility, whether or not it is described as "loyalty" or "allegiance," takes precedence over national obligations. The authors of the constitution of the United Nations explicitly considered the possibility of a conflict between the two loyalties. They appear to have intended that, in such

---

[131] United Nations doc. A/Res./194. See also United Nations docs. A/C.5/SR.420–4, A/2534, Annex A, pp. 4–5, A/2580, p. 6, and A/C.5/544, p. 6. And see above, note 17, and the references there given to the League's *Official Journal*, 1946.

[132] See above, "Opinion of the Commission of Jurists."

[133] United Nations doc. A/2364, pp. 24–25.

an eventuality, the international obligations of the staff member would prevail.[134] It may be maintained that there can be no essential conflict of loyalties in that international loyalty is no more than "the conviction that the highest interests of one's own country are served best by the promotion of security and welfare everywhere."[135] It might further be suggested that loyalty to the State would be upheld by adherence of the staff member to its treaty obligations under Articles 100, 101, and 105, Article 2, paragraph 2,[136] and Article 103[137] of the Charter, which, insofar as treaties among States bind the individuals who are the nationals thereof, would constitute law to which the staff member is subject. These possibilities need not be pursued here. For the authors of the Charter approached the problem in a more practical vein. They foresaw the possibility of a conflict between loyalties and apparently resolved such conflict in favor of the Organization. The interpretation of Article 100 by the International Court of Justice tends strikingly to reinforce

[134] See above, "The Charter of the United Nations." The Staff Regulations have, from the outset, provided that the responsibilities of the staff "are not national but exclusively international. By accepting appointment, they pledge themselves to discharge their functions and to regulate their conduct with the interests of the United Nations only in view" (*Provisional Staff Regulations*, Regulation 1, United Nations doc. ST/AFS/SGB/94, p. 3). The clause governing the regulation of the conduct of the staff member, which is elaborated in Regulation 1.4, does not indicate that, in his private life, the staff member must act "with the interests of the United Nations only in view." Yet it would seem to indicate that, insofar as his status as an international civil servant is affected by his private life, he must so act – an interpretation which tends further to subordinate his national obligations. Regulation 1.9 restates the link between conduct and official functions, and employs the word "loyalty" with respect to the latter:
"Members of the Secretariat shall subscribe to the following oath or declaration:
'I solemnly swear (undertake, affirm, promise) to exercise in all loyalty, discretion and conscience the functions entrusted to me as an international civil servant of the United Nations, to discharge these functions and regulate my conduct with the interests of the United Nations only in view, and not to seek or accept instructions in regard to the performance of my duties from any government or other authority external to the Organization.'" It should be added that Article 100, in providing that the staff shall not receive instructions from "any government or from any other authority external to the Organization," makes clear that instructions from a government other than that of the staff member, or from a body such as an international political party, are equally inadmissible – considerations which seem particularly germane to the situation of the staff member, of whatever nationality, who is under Communist discipline.

[135] See above, "The League Experience." See also Scott, "The World's Civil Service," *International Conciliation* (January 1954), 496, p. 287.

[136] "All Members, in order to ensure to all of them the rights and benefits resulting from membership, shall fulfill in good faith the obligations assumed by them in accordance with the present Charter."

[137] "In the event of a conflict between the obligations of the Members of the United Nations under the present Charter and their obligations under any other international agreement, their obligations under the present Charter shall prevail." Article 103 might be said to have an additional relevance, for if it "is true of a State, it must also, *mutatis mutandis*, be true for individual Staff members who serve one of the principal organs of the United Nations" (*per* the Representative of the Netherlands in a speech to the Fifth Committee on November 23, 1953, summarized in United Nations doc. A/C.5/SR.408, pp. 17–18). If States are so obliged by Article 103, "so should individual staff members be expected to place their obligations to the Secretariat above their national political life" (*Ibid*).

the pre-eminence which the Organization enjoys.[138] The Secretary-General appears to have excluded the above-quoted observations of the Commission of Jurists from those portions of their opinion which he accepted.[139] The Delegations of Member States were explicitly or impliedly critical of them,[140] with the possible exception of Argentina.[141] On the level of formal recognition, it may be said that the exclusively international character of the official responsibilities of the members of the United Nations Secretariat has received increased emphasis in the course of the United Nations debate. However, while the importance of such formal recognition is not to be discounted, it is not sufficient to resolve the problems with which the Organization has been and continues to be confronted.[142]

Receipt by the Secretary-General of Information from Governments Concerning Members of the Staff and Applicants

It is believed that the submission by Governments to the Secretary-General of information regarding the qualifications of applicants for employment and of members of the staff is legally unobjectionable, provided that the Secretary-General remains free to evaluate and act or not act upon such data, and provided that he actually exercises that freedom. The Preparatory Commission foresaw that the Secretary-General might require information from Governments concerning candidates for employment,[143] and various delegations to the General Assembly maintained that view also with regard to

---

[138] *ICJ Reports 1949*, pp. 183–184.

[139] See United Nations doc. A/PV.421, p. 660, together with United Nations doc. A/2364.

[140] See the statement of the Delegate of the United Kingdom: "We also felt that the report was perhaps rather too emphatic about the allegiance of international civil servants to their own governments and made too little allowance for their allegiance to international civil organizations in which they worked" (United Nations doc. A/PV.421, p. 651). See also the statements of the Delegates of New Zealand (A/PV.417, p. 583), France (A/PV.418, p. 606), Canada (*ibid.*, pp. 603–604), and Yugoslavia (A/PV.421, p. 660).

[141] See United Nations docs. A/PV.418, p. 612, and A/C.5/SR.408, p. 8. See also the statement by the Delegate of Australia, United Nations doc. A/PV.417, pp. 592, 593.

[142] The statement of the Delegate of France aptly summarizes the theory and adumbrates the pitfalls of practice:

> When an official enters the service of the Organization, he does not of course lose his nationality; but he pledges loyalty, in all matters relating to his work, towards the international body alone ... If, in connexion with his work, a conflict arises between his obligations as an international civil servant and his duties as a citizen, his only choice is either to remain faithful to the Organization or to submit his resignation ...
>
> In the exercise of his duties, the international civil servant is, as it were, denationalized; outside his duties, he remains the citizen of a particular State, subject to the obligations which rest upon the citizens of that State.

(United Nations doc. A/PV.418, p. 606.)

[143] See above, "The Charter of the United Nations."

members of the staff.[144] The Administrative Tribunal found that it was not competent to rule on the validity of the specific arrangements for the receipt of information which were agreed upon by the first Secretary-General and the United States Department of State.[145] However, a substantial majority of the Governments which expressed themselves on the matter regarded the arrangements as admissible.[146] Mr. Lie made it clear that he did not act solely on the basis of the terse evaluations of the Department, which did not include the evidence on which they were based,[147] and the record would seem to bear him out.[148] This is not to say that the arrangements approached the optimum in either their procedure or substance. While the communication by Governments of information to the Secretary-General is evidently not a matter for deliberate publicity, the question was asked whether the atmosphere of secrecy surrounding the procedures arrived at by the Department and the Secretary-General in 1949 was such as to induce confidence, and to afford the applicant or staff member in question the opportunity of contesting charges made against him.

While, as a matter of law, the procedures which the United States, the French, and other Governments have introduced for transmitting information concerning their nationals to the Secretary-General would appear to respect the discretion in the selection of staff of which the Secretary-General – as "the chief administrative officer of the Organization"[149] – is assured by Articles 100 and 101 of the Charter, the question arises whether, as a matter of practice, they actually do not tend to impair that discretion, at least in recruiting staff. For there may be a likelihood that the Secretary-General may not wish to appoint persons who had received their Government's disapproval. Although the Secretary-General may in law consider, *inter alia*, the facts and recommendations submitted to him by Governments, the political inducement to give those facts and recommendations predominant, even if not conclusive, weight, is apparent. It may be said that, as long as the Secretary-General reserves to himself the actual decision, this is not only legal

---

144 See the statements by the Delegates of the Philippines (United Nations doc. A/PV.430, pp. 636–637), Egypt (A/PV.417, p. 581), the Netherlands (*ibid.*, p. 584), Ecuador (*ibid.*, p. 590), Australia (*ibid.*, p. 593), France (A/PV.418, p. 607), the United Kingdom (A/PV.421, p. 652), Iraq (*ibid.*, p. 655), and Yugoslavia (*ibid.*, p. 659). The Delegate of Guatemala dissented, however (A/C.5/SR.414, p. 10).

145 See above, "The Decisions of the Administrative Tribunal."

146 The Delegations of Syria (United Nations doc. A/PV.418, p. 611), the Byelorussian SSR (*ibid.*, pp. 598–600), and Poland (A/PV.420, p. 635) were not among the majority.

147 See above, "The League Experience."

148 *Statement and Briefs for the Respondent* (see note 101), p. 68. For a more critical interpretation of the 1949 arrangements see Rolin, *Advisory Opinion*, pp. 16–18.

149 Article 97 of the Charter. See Carnegie Endowment for International Peace, "The United Nations Secretariat," *United Nations Studies* (1950) 4, pp. 63–69.

but desirable, because of the relevance which governmentally supplied data may have to the applicants' qualifications, because the United Nations lacks the facilities to gather such data itself, and because the effect of appointing governmentally approved staff will be likely to promote the international confidence which the Secretariat must enjoy. There is force in these considerations – though the latter suggestion is perhaps open to challenge on the ground that the greater the confidence shown by a Government in its nationals appointed to the Secretariat, the more will the objectivity of such nationals be distrusted by other Member States. While this would not necessarily be the fact in all cases, it is a consideration which must be borne in mind.

It may be observed that if the McCarran Bill[150] had become law, the question would have arisen whether the United States as a result acted in breach of Articles 100 and 101 and Article 2, paragraph 2. The Committee on the Judiciary, in its Report to the United States Senate on the proposed Bill, stated as follows: "Enactment of s.3 does not attempt to interfere with the discretion of employing officials of the United Nations. It does not tell them who they may employ or who they must employ. It only says to American nationals that they may not accept employment in or under the United Nations or any organ or agency thereof unless they have received security clearance."[151] This argument is perhaps not fully persuasive. Under the Bill if enacted, if the Secretary-General exercises his discretion and appoints a United States citizen who has not received security clearance, and if such person accepts appointment, he thereupon "shall be fined not more than $10,000 or imprisoned for not more than five years, or both."[152] The consequent limitations upon his usefulness as a member of the United Nations staff must be far-reaching.[153]

Use of United Nations Facilities and Premises to Facilitate the Submission by Governments of Information concerning Staff Members

In order to expedite the processes of investigation under the Executive Order issued by the United States, the prompt conclusion of which the Secretary-

---

[150] See above, "Subversive Activities in the United States of America and Cognate Problems."

[151] United States Senate, *Report No. 223* (see note 78), p. 6.

[152] United States Senate Bill, s.3 (see note 78), p. 5.

[153] The Department of State opposed the enactment of the Bill for a variety of reasons, without considering whether it would put the United States in breach of its treaty obligations under the Charter (see *Report No. 223* [see note 78], pp. 7–9.)

The Bill prescribes the same penalties for United States citizens who are employed by the United

General believed to be in the interests of the public credit of the Organization and the alleviation of the personnel crisis, the Secretary-General assisted in the distribution to staff members of United States nationality of the questionnaires prescribed under the Order. He also permitted the fingerprinting required by the Order to take place within the Permanent Headquarters, and authorized staff members of United States nationality who might be interviewed by United States Government agents to invite the latter to their offices, if they so wished. The Secretary-General made it clear that, while advising such staff members to cooperate in these procedures, he did not order them to do so.[154] He further emphasized that the authorization to be interviewed at Headquarters was of a limited nature and did not constitute a general waiver of the inviolability of the premises assured by the Headquarters Agreement.[155]

The actions of the Secretary-General gave rise to varying degrees of criticism among a number of the Delegations,[156] the staff associations,[157] and others.[158] The Secretary-General defended his attitude by reference to the interests of the Organization, which, in his view, lay in expediting the completion of the investigations.[159] The Secretary-General acted within his rights under the Headquarters Agreement[160] and the General Convention on

Nations on the day of its enactment if they do not, within sixty days, file with the Attorney General of the United States registration statements in such form as the latter shall determine. "Of course," the Report states, "no country can absolutely require that an employee of the United Nations be dismissed ... With regard to persons already employed, s. 3 merely requires that each such person shall file a registration statement ... If the disclosure of such information should reveal that some of these employees are subversives, that would be a matter to be dealt with by negotiation between the State Department and the United Nations" (*ibid.*, p. 6; see also Aghnides, "Standards of Conduct," p. 186).

Compare the proposed Bill with the Italian law of 1927; see above, "The League Experience."

154 See Mr. Trygve Lie's address to the General Assembly, United Nations doc. A/PV.413, p. 538. See also the decision of the Administrative Tribunal in *Glaser v. The Secretary-General of the United Nations*, Judgment No. 38, August 26, 1953, pp. 2, 4–5.

155 United Nations doc. A/PV.413, pp. 538–539. See also Brandon, "Laissez Passer," pp. 101–106.

156 The Netherlands (United Nations doc. A/PV.417, p. 586), the Byelorussian SSR (A/PV.418, p. 599), France (*ibid.*, p. 607), Indonesia (A/PV.419, pp. 620–621), the United Kingdom (A/PV.421, p. 652), and Iraq (*ibid.*, p. 655).

157 Federation of International Civil Servants' Associations, *Investigations into the Political Activities of International Civil Servants by National Agents* (FICSA/EX/4), and *Fingerprinting of United Nations & Specialized Agencies Personnel by National Agents* (FICSA/EX/7).

158 See, particularly, Rolin, *Advisory Opinion*, pp. 19–21, on the distribution of United States questionnaires.

159 United Nations doc. A/PV.412, p. 661.

160 "The Headquarters district shall be inviolable. Federal ... officials of the United States ... shall not enter the headquarters district to perform any official duties therein except with the consent of and under conditions agreed to by the Secretary-General." (Section 9 (*a*)). Section 7 (*a*) provides: "The headquarters district shall be under the control and authority of the United Nations as provided in this agreement." It would thus seem to follow that admission of national officials is a matter within the discretion of the Secretary-General, but that, in the exercise of his discretion, he is accountable to the Organization.

Privileges and Immunities.[161] This is so although there is room for the view that the extension of facilities of the Secretariat and the Headquarters to further the enforcement of the internal laws of a State is not altogether consonant with the international character of the Organization, even if such enforcement is reasonably deemed to be in the interests of the Organization.

The Concept of the "Host Country"

The Commission of Jurists, influenced perhaps by the wording of the questions submitted to it by the Secretary-General,[162] approached its task in terms of what it saw as the "peculiar relationship which must exist between an international body such as the United Nations and the Member State within whose borders that international body works . . ."[163] It accordingly advanced the theory that the "host country" (or countries) enjoys certain special rights *vis-à-vis* its own nationals in the Secretariat, and, to a lesser degree, with respect to staff members of other nationalities.

The distinction between the rights of host and other Member States does not follow from the Charter or the Staff Regulations. In a sense it may be said to derogate from "the principle of the sovereign equality of all its Members" on which the Organization is based.[164] The question also arises as to its

---

[161] See Sections 20 and 21. The privileges and immunities of United States staff members under Article 105 and the United States International Organizations Immunities Act were not directly in point, however, in that they were not questioned about their official acts. When it was announced that Senate hearings would be held at which members of the Secretariat would be questioned, the Secretary-General on October 13, 1952 issued a memorandum to staff members of United States nationality recalling that "staff members of the United Nations called before the Senate Committee are not authorized to testify with regard to official activities of the United Nations and do not have the right to waive the immunity conferred by law. They are authorized to answer questions which are matters of public record regarding their position as staff members, such as title, job description, compensation, date of appointment and the like" (United Nations doc. A/2364, p. 14. See also *Report of the Sub-Committee* [see note 78], pp. 2–3, and *United States v. Keeney*, III F. Supp. 233, noted in *International Law and Comparative Law Quarterly* [1953], 2, pp. 482–483. With respect to the action of Unesco regarding Executive Order No. 10422 see above, note 76).

[162] See United Nations doc. A/2364, p. 21.

[163] *Ibid.*

[164] Article 2, paragraph 1 of the Charter. Nor does the General Convention on Privileges and Immunities make any distinction between the treatment it requires an adhering State to accord to members of the Secretariat who are its nationals and to those who are not. The United States International Organizations Immunities Act does discriminate against American nationals, however.

The Headquarters Agreement, as interpreted by the United States, might be said to constitute support for the Jurists, since, in the view of the United States, it is subject to a reservation respecting the right to safeguard the nation's security. The concept of special privilege inuring to the host country finds support in the headquarters agreements which host countries other than the United States have signed with certain of the Specialized Agencies. The Agreement between the International Civil Aviation Organization and the Government of Canada regarding the Headquarters of ICAO goes

conformity with the requirements of the independence and exclusively international character of the Secretariat in accordance with Articles 100 and 105. It may lead to some difficulties of an administrative nature. The conception of "host country" in this connection met with a varied reception on the part of the Member States.[165] The United States itself appeared to discard it by extending the application of Executive Order No. 10422 to United States citizens who are employees or applicants for employment in public international organizations of which the United States is a member other than the United Nations, many of which have their headquarters in countries other than the United States.[166] The Secretary-General stated that

beyond incorporating provisions of differentiation in respect of Canadian nationals (see Section 24). It assures the Canadian Government of far-reaching security guarantees. See Sections 10 and 29, and, in particular, Section 40, which provides: "Nothing in this Agreement shall be construed as in any way diminishing, abridging, or weakening the right of the Canadian authorities to safeguard the security of Canada, provided the Organization shall be immediately informed in the event that the Canadian Government shall find it necessary to take any action against any person enumerated in the Agreement." The Agreement between the Swiss Federal Council and the World Health Organization concerning the Legal Status of WHO likewise discriminates against Swiss nationals (see Article 18), and Article 25 in part provides: "Nothing in the present agreement shall affect the right of the Swiss Federal Council to take the precautions necessary for the security of Switzerland . . . The World Health Organization shall collaborate with the Swiss authorities to avoid any prejudice to the security of Switzerland resulting from its activity." The Agreement between the World Health Organization and the Government of India concerning the Privileges, Immunities, and Facilities to be Granted by the Government of India to WHO provides, in Section 30, that "Nothing in the present agreements shall be construed to preclude the adoption of appropriate security precautions in the interests of the Government of India which shall be determined by agreement between the Government of India and the Director-General." The Headquarters Agreement between the Food and Agriculture Organization and Italy has a limited security clause (Section R34 (c)). While, however, the Headquarters Agreement itself contains no such provisions, the Joint Resolution of the United States Congress authorizing the President to bring the Agreement into effect on the part of the United States in part provides, in Section 6 (listed in 61 Stat. 767 [1947] under Annex 2, inappositely entitled "Maintenance of Utilities and Underground Construction") as follows: "Nothing in the agreement shall be construed as in any way diminishing, abridging, or weakening the right of the United States to safeguard its own security and completely to control the entrance of aliens into any territory of the United States other than the headquarters district and its immediate vicinity." The Secretary-General has not accepted the contention of the United States that this in fact constitutes a legally valid reservation to the Agreement. See also "Subversives in the United Nations: The World Organization as an Employer," *Stanford Law Review*, 5, 4, pp. 769–782.

165 The Representatives of India (United Nations doc. A/PV.416, p. 566), Belgium (*ibid.*, p. 569), Syria (A/PV.418, p. 611), Indonesia (A/PV.419, p. 620), Liberia (A/PV.421, p. 649), the United Kingdom (*ibid.*, p. 651), and Yugoslavia (*ibid.*, p. 660) criticized the concept, while the Delegations of Canada (A/PV.418, pp. 602, 604), the Philippines (A/PV.420, pp. 637–638), Iraq (A/PV.421, pp. 4–5), and, to some extent, France (A/PV.418, p. 607) spoke substantially in favor of it. See, in particular, the Filipino statement.

166 See United Nations doc. A/2364, p. 36, and United States Senate, *Report No. 223* [see note 78], pp. 7–8. The State Department undertook to establish arrangements pursuant to the Order with forty-six international organizations other than the United Nations.

the Jurists' recommendation for a special régime for host countries was one which he did not accept.[167]

Conviction and Suspicion of Members of the Secretariat on account of Subversive Activities

A member of the Secretariat who engages in subversive activities against his own or any other Government violates the standards of conduct incumbent upon him and should be discharged. What weight is to be given by the Secretary-General in his finding that a member of the staff has so acted to the fact that the latter has been convicted by a national court of a crime involving subversion?[168] The Commission of Jurists advised that "where there has been such a conviction the fact of the crime is *ipso facto* established," that "it is *res judicata*," and that it "should be accepted as such by the Secretary-General."[169] The first Secretary-General, in affirming that there must be "reasonable ground" for believing accusations of subversive activities – that charges "must be supported by a preponderance of evidence" – stated that the Secretary-General "should give proper weight" to national laws and legislative findings and to the findings of fact of national courts and tribunals, in addition to the evidence of the facts of each case.[170] He thus seemed to modify the Jurists' view that the decision of a national court *ipso facto* establishes the fact of the crime by allotting to that decision "proper" rather than conclusive weight. His successor stated that "the conclusions of national authorities concerning activities by staff members, are, of course, not binding on the United Nations, which must apply its own standards," but that "national findings of fact, arrived at in accordance with generally recognized requirements of due process of law, are entitled to weight."[171]

---

[167] See United Nations doc. A/PV.421, p. 661.

[168] A member of the staff of Soviet nationality, Valentin Gubitchev, was convicted of espionage in the United States, and allowed by American authorities to leave the country (see *United States v. Coplon et al.*, 84 f. Supp. 472, and Spence, "Jurisdictional Immunity").

[169] United Nations doc. A/2364, p. 26.

[170] See United Nations doc. A/2364, p. 13. "This standard," Mr. Lie later added, "should, I believe, be applied ... in complete independence of any national proceeding. The standard is a United Nations standard and would be applied by United Nations organs" (United Nations doc. A/PV.421, p. 661).

[171] United Nations doc. A/2533, p. 22. "A conviction by a national court," the Secretary-General added, "will usually be persuasive evidence of the commission of the act for which the defendant was prosecuted ... However, the Organization must remain free to take no account of convictions ... made without observance of the generally recognized requirements of due process of law" (*ibid.*, p. 24. See above, note 119.). A number of delegations counselled caution against the automatic acceptance of national criteria in this respect. See the statement of the Delegates of New Zealand (A/PV.416, p. 561), India (*ibid.*, p. 567), Belgium (*ibid.*, p. 571), Sweden (*ibid.*, p. 573), Norway (*ibid.*, p. 576), the Netherlands (A/PV.417, p. 584), Indonesia (A/PV.419, p. 620), and Yugoslavia (A/PV.421, p. 660). See

The Secretary-General may perhaps be expected to seek to avoid occasions for implementing these theories which he rightly affirms. His concern for the confidence which the Secretariat must enjoy, for the public standing of the Organization as a whole, and for his political responsibilities under Articles 98 and 99 of the Charter,[172] will impel him, as a matter of policy, to defer to the laws and judgments of courts of Member States. He may hesitate to exercise his discretion against the views of a complainant Government, except in cases in which the member of the staff is patently the victim of unreasonable or arbitrary process. Whatever the defects of the concept of the "host country," it is evident that the difficulties are much greater in cases where the staff member is resident in the State which finds him guilty of a crime involving subversive activities,[173] or, for that matter, of any other crime,[174] whether it is the country of his nationality or not. As with the submission of information by Governments, the actual degree of independence enjoyed by the Secretariat may be limited unless the Member States join the Secretary-General in mutual support of their obligations under Article 100.

There may be instances of charges or conviction of members of the staff for subversive activities which the Secretary-General clearly would have to receive with especial caution. The Charter and the Staff Regulations may not normally be interpreted to justify the dismissal of a staff member who is found guilty by a successor Government of "subversive activities" against it while that Government had not yet "succeeded"; a succession or a change of Government hardly entitles a State to request dismissal of its nationals who preferred or prefer the former Government. It would be for the Secretary-

also Friedmann, "The United Nations and National Loyalties," *International Journal (1952–1953)*, 8, 1, pp. 22–25, and Friedmann and others, "Loyalty Tests and the United Nations Secretariat," *Canadian Bar Review* (December 1952), pp. 1080–1083. For a point of view close to that of the Commission of Jurists, see the statements of the Delegates of France (A/PV.418, p. 607) and China (*ibid.*, p. 615); and see Cohen, "Preliminary Appraisal," on the French view.

[172] See Schwebel, *Secretary-General*, pp. 19–30.

[173] A possibility of evidently limited application would be the transfer of such a staff member to a post in another country (for comment on this point see the Opinion of the Commission of Jurists, United Nations doc. A/2364, p. 26).

If the member of the staff is convicted by the organs of the State in which he is resident, he may of course be subject to immediate imprisonment; indeed, he might be detained before trial. A host country has the power to enforce its jurisdiction and execute its judgments which other Member States lack, barring voluntary submission to that jurisdiction or extradition (which would not apply to political offenses), or the assertion of jurisdiction over their nationals when on home leave. The jurisdiction of all Member States is limited by the immunity of staff members from legal process in respect of all acts performed by them in their official capacity. It would appear to be limited further by Article 100, insofar as prosecution for unofficial acts must be in good faith and not designed to exert pressure upon the staff member *qua* staff member.

[174] Conviction of a member of the staff by any Government for crimes other than those related to subversive activities might so reflect upon his integrity and the conduct incumbent upon him as to call for his dismissal.

General to judge whether the political activities for which the staff member is charged or convicted were in breach of his obligations as an international civil servant. Counter-revolutionary activities might well be so judged, not because the revolution was successful, but because the staff member is required to abstain from political action, whatever its direction. An accusation or conviction of a member of the staff for subversive activities carried on before his appointment would be weighed by the Secretary-General with particular circumspection. The staff member could not have been guilty of a breach of the Staff Regulations prior to his appointment; however, his subversive activities in the past, if proven, may ordinarily be reasonably judged to reflect on his present integrity.[175] If the Secretary-General confines his definition of past subversive activities normally reflecting on the present integrity of the staff member concerned to "serious and generally recognized offences such as espionage or sabotage," as the Secretary-General suggested, there should be no difficulty.[176] It may be suggested that allegations by Governments of past subversive activities, viewed through the limits of that definition, would lead to few, if any, dismissals of staff members.

A particularly delicate question turns upon the alleged likelihood of a member of the staff engaging in subversive activities. The Commission of Jurists advised, and the first Secretary-General agreed, that the Secretary-General should not retain a staff member if he has "reasonable ground for believing that the staff member ... is likely to engage in subversive activities against the government of any Member State."[177] According to the first Secretary-General, for a finding that a staff member is likely to engage in such activities, "something more than a remote possibility of his doing so must be shown. Of necessity, such a finding must be largely based upon the staff member's past conduct. However, convincing evidence that in the past an official had engaged in subversive activities would not necessarily lead to a finding that he was likely to be engaged in such activities either at present or in the future. Later conduct and attitudes might show there was no likelihood of his engaging in such activities again."[178]

---

[175] That this will not necessarily be the case is shown by Rolin, *Advisory Opinion*, pp. 33, 54–55. See the comments of the Secretary-General, United Nations doc. A/2533, pp. 12, 21, 22, and of the Commission of Jurists, United Nations doc. A/2364, p. 28.

[176] See above, note 113. Elsewhere in the report there cited, however, the Secretary-General declared that subversive activities may be "properly defined as was done in the last report of the Secretary-General on personnel policy, that is, '[as] activities directed towards the overthrow of a government by force, including conspiracy towards such overthrow and incitement and advocacy of it'" (United Nations doc. A/2533, p. 21). This definition would appear to go beyond espionage and sabotage. Conspiracy, in particular, is a legal concept of considerable elasticity.

[177] United Nations doc. A/2364, p. 13. The Commission of Jurists restricted its reference to the Government of any host State.

[178] United Nations doc. A/2364, p. 13.

This appreciation of likelihood aroused considerable controversy, the Delegates of the United States[179] and the United Kingdom[180] speaking in favor of it, while some others vigorously opposed it.[181] The second Secretary-General announced that he would discard it: "The only sense in which the assumed likelihood may be of relevance should be covered by the standard of integrity required by Article 101 of the Charter and thus considered in the light of the rules concerning present suitability generally applied."[182]

The criterion of likelihood is, at first glance, open to the criticism that it involves the application of a sanction – dismissal – for an act which the Secretary-General suspects the staff member is performing or may in the future perform, but which actually the staff member may not now or ever commit. Article 100 enjoins members of the staff to refrain from any "action" which may reflect upon their status as international officials. It may be difficult to bring mere suspicion within the orbit of that duty.

The admissibility of the criterion of likelihood seems to depend upon the interpretation of what is "reasonable ground" for arriving at a belief that a likelihood exists. The standards advanced by the first Secretary-General would seem to have been satisfactory.[183] His successor's shift in emphasis, however, has the psychological advantage of dispensing with the notion of likelihood. Insofar as the Secretary-General interprets narrowly the scope of past activities reflecting on present integrity, the staff may be assured of an increased degree of security. Moreover, the more explicit prohibition of political activities which has been introduced into the amended Staff Regulations may tend to reduce the incidence of actions giving rise to the suspicion that the staff member is likely to engage in subversive activity. Particularly under the amended Regulations, such actions might in themselves give cause for dismissal. It may be assumed, finally, that, in engaging an applicant, the likelihood of his engaging in subversive activities will inevitably be con-

---

179 United Nations doc. A/PV.416, p. 559.   180 United Nations doc. A/PV.421, p. 652.

181 The Delegates of New Zealand (United Nations doc. A/PV.416, p. 561), the Netherlands (A/PV.417, p. 585), France (A/PV.418, p. 606), Indonesia (*ibid.*, p. 619), Mexico (A/PV.419, p. 628), and Yugoslavia (A/PV.421, p. 660).

182 United Nations doc. A/2533, p. 21.

183 See United Nations doc. A/2364, p. 13. Professor Cohen has pointed out that there is a gap between the standard enunciated by the Secretary-General (a "preponderance of evidence" in favor of the accusation) and that announced by the United States ("reasonable doubt as to the loyalty of the person"), and suggests that these differing criteria may give rise to friction between the United States and the Secretary-General ("Preliminary Appraisal," pp. 187, 194–195. See also above, note 76). The Delegate of the United Kingdom found the standards which the Secretary-General set out to be "perfectly satisfactory" (United Nations doc. A/PV.421, p. 652).

sidered, even if, in matters of termination of appointment, the criterion as such is discarded.

The suspicions aroused by members of the staff invoking the privilege against self-incrimination in inquiries by United States organs concerning subversive activities against the Government of the United States have been among the main difficulties which have beset the Secretary-General's personnel policy.[184] The Commission of Jurists, in a somewhat disputed interpretation of the privilege,[185] concluded that a member of the Secretariat who, under the protection of the Fifth Amendment to the Federal Constitution of the United States, declined to answer questions as to whether he is or has been engaged in subversive activities, "is just as unsuitable for continued employment by the United Nations in the United States as one who had actually been convicted."[186] A plea of the privilege in response to questions relating to membership in the Communist Party of the United States or some other organization declared to be subversive led the Commission, more hesitantly, to the same conclusion.

The first Secretary-General, in substantially accepting these views, stated as follows:

> Especially at a time of serious political tension and concern over national security, the United Nations staff member has a positive obligation to refrain from conduct which will draw upon himself grave suspicion of being a danger to the security of a particular State. When he has refused to answer official interrogations relating to crimes involving subversive activities, he has by his own free choice violated that obligation; he has thereby contributed substantially to undermining the confidence which the international official is required to maintain.[187]

[184] See above, "Subversive Activities in the United States of America and Cognate Problems" and "Opinion of the Commission of Jurists."

[185] "If in reliance upon this privilege a person refuses to answer a question, he is only justified in doing so if he believes or is advised that in answering he would become a witness against himself ... It follows from this, in our opinion, that a person claiming this privilege cannot thereafter be heard to say that his answer if it had been given would not have been self-incriminatory. He is in the dilemma that either his answer would have been self-incriminatory or if not he has invoked his constitutional privilege without just cause. As, in our opinion, he cannot be heard to allege the latter, he must by claiming the privilege be held to have admitted the former. Moreover, the exercise of this privilege creates so strong a suspicion of guilt that the fact of its exercise must be withheld from a jury in a criminal trial. It is clear also that in addition to arousing a suspicion of guilt, the plea of privilege may well affect prospects of employment" (United Nations doc. A/2364, pp. 26–27).

[186] United Nations doc. A/2364, p. 27.

[187] *Ibid.*, p. 12. The Secretary-General added: "I can conceive of circumstances when to plead the privilege would not necessarily be incompatible with the conduct required of international civil servants. But in these circumstances, for a United Nations staff member thus to draw upon himself grave suspicion of being a danger to the security of a Member State was, I felt, a grave breach of the staff regulations concerning the conduct required of staff members. Furthermore, the attitude taken by these witnesses tended to discredit and cause unjustified suspicion upon their fellow staff members and even to imperil the position of the whole Organization in the host country" (A/PV.413, p. 536). With regard to the

Mr. Lie accordingly dismissed the staff members concerned. His successor took similar action in the single case which arose after he took office.[188] On the other hand, the Administrative Tribunal, in the decisions examined above, declared:

> Whatever view may be held as to the conduct of the Applicant, that conduct would not be described as serious misconduct, which alone under Staff Regulation 10.2 and the pertinent Rules justifies the Secretary-General in dismissing a staff member summarily without the safeguard afforded by the disciplinary procedure.[189]

Subsequently, the Secretary-General announced that, while invocation of the privilege in an official inquiry concerning subversive activities might be considered "as incompatible with the status of an international civil servant ... the staff member should be given an opportunity to present his side of the case and to inform the Secretary-General of the reasons why he invoked the privilege." He added: "If this investigation gives an explanation of the action which removes its unfavourable implications, termination [of employment] is not justified on the basis of the standards proper to the United Nations."[190]

In dismissing the staff members who pleaded the privilege, the Secretary-General relied largely on the ground that the plea constituted a public pronouncement which, whatever the inferences that might legally be drawn therefrom, in fact drew grave popular suspicion upon the members of the staff concerned and ill will upon the Organization as such. The Tribunal did not directly dispute this, nor could it reasonably have done so. On what may be persuasive technical grounds the Tribunal confined the sources of power of dismissal upon which the Secretaries-General might have drawn under the Staff Regulations in these circumstances, to the clause relating to disciplinary measures.[191] Among the disciplinary measures for which Regulation 10.2 provides is dismissal for misconduct. This sanction is not, as a rule, to be invoked without prior consideration by the Joint Disciplinary Committee,

---

policy pursued towards a staff member who invoked the privilege in response to questions about Communist Party affiliations (rather than espionage), see below.

[188] The *Glaser* case, Judgment No. 38 of August 26, 1953.

[189] See above, "The Decisions of the Administrative Tribunal."

[190] United Nations doc. A/2533. It should be noted that the Secretary-General introduced a procedure of this kind in the *Glaser* case, before the Tribunal rendered its judgments. He appointed a committee to "ascertain and report to the Secretary-General on the facts, circumstances and reasons" that had led Mrs. Glaser to invoke the privilege. Mrs. Glaser appeared before the Committee, but apparently failed to dispel the unfavourable implications of her plea for, a week later, she was dismissed on the ground that she had violated her obligations under Staff Regulation 1.4 and under her oath to the United Nations, thereby rendering "unsatisfactory services" (see *Glaser v. The Secretary-General of the United Nations*, Administrative Tribunal, Judgment No. 38, pp. 2–3).

[191] See above, "The Decisions of the Administrative Tribunals."

which has merely advisory powers, except in cases of "serious misconduct," where the Secretary-General may "summarily dismiss" a staff member.[192] It was upon this latter exception that Mr. Lie relied. Was the conduct of the staff members who pleaded the privilege so "serious" as to merit summary dismissal? The Tribunal, stressing the complexity of the law surrounding the privilege and the apparent uncertainty of the Secretary-General himself as to the seriousness of the alleged misconduct, decided that it was not. While its emphasis upon what it saw as the procedural anomalies was plausible, it thereby substituted its judgment for that of the Secretary-General in a question which, it may be argued, is more properly the subject of political than legal appreciation. It did this despite the fact that there appears to be considerable support for the view that the Tribunal is not competent to override the Secretary-General's judgment in disciplinary matters – that the assessment of the gravity of an offence is the prerogative of the Secretary-General, except, perhaps, insofar as the Tribunal may consider whether his action was arbitrary or taken in bad faith.[193] The Tribunal did not consider the question whether the applicants could be found to have been properly dismissed on the ground of "unsatisfactory conduct."

The restatement of policy on the part of the Secretary-General has some advantages. It does not commit him to dismissing a staff member who pleads the privilege in an official inquiry relating to subversive activities, regardless of the equities of the case – an aspect of the question which was responsible for some criticism of the Report of the Commission of Jurists in this respect.[194]

---

[192] See above, note 69.

[193] Except for his ultimate responsibility to the General Assembly, the Secretary-General, before the establishment of the Administrative Tribunal in 1949, alone had the power to assess the gravity of the conduct of a member of the staff. During the debate of the Fifth Committee on the proposed Statute of the Tribunal, the Secretary-General, in supporting the creation of a Tribunal, declared: "There are three areas of decision in which the Secretary-General's judgement should be final – namely, a decision as to whether a particular staff member's services are satisfactory or unsatisfactory, the decision of fact in disciplinary cases where non-observance of the terms of the staff member's appointment cannot reasonably be alleged, and decisions of fact in cases of serious misconduct ... His responsibility under the Charter as Chief Administrative Officer of the Organization can be satisfactorily discharged only if his judgement on the facts in the cases indicated above is considered final. This responsibility could not be effectively discharged if an independent administrative tribunal were given authority to reconsider the facts in such cases, in the absence of any reasonable allegation that the terms of an appointment had been violated, and to reverse the decision of the Secretary-General" (General Assembly, Fourth Session, *Official Records*, Fifth Committee, Annex, Vol. 1, p. 146). The Committee appears to have upheld the Secretary-General's point of view (*ibid., Summary Record*, pp. 13–16, 21–25, 180, and the Annex thereto cited, pp. 153–154). It did not accept a suggestion by the Staff Committee that the jurisdiction of the Tribunal be extended to disciplinary cases. See also above, note 64.

[194] See, in the following United Nations documents, the statements of the delegates of Belgium (A/PV.415, p. 571), Sweden (*ibid.*, p. 573), Norway (*ibid.*, p. 577), the Netherlands (A/PV.417, p. 588), Australia (*ibid.*, p. 594), Canada (A/PV.418, p. 604), France (*ibid.*, p. 607), Indonesia (A/PV.419, pp. 619–620), Mexico (*ibid.*, p. 628), the Philippines (A/PV.420, p. 637), the United Kingdom (A/PV.421,

It affords the staff member an opportunity to remove the "unfavorable implications" of his plea, at least in the eyes of the Secretary-General.

Membership of the Staff in Political Parties

Passive membership in political parties is permitted to Secretariat officials under the Staff Regulations, subject to qualifications which have been noted above.[195] There remains the question of membership in parties which are illegal or "subversive" under the national laws of the countries of the staff members concerned. It is evident that the conduct incumbent upon a staff member will not normally be compatible with membership in an illegal political party.[196] Yet an absolute rule to this effect might be subject to the objection of being too automatic in its operation. The Secretary-General has accordingly made it clear that each case of membership in an illegal political party would be considered individually, and that such membership would not necessarily be held incompatible with employment in the United Nations.[197] This principle is scarcely capable of practical implementation if the staff member concerned is stationed in his own country. If he was a member of an illegal party before joining the Secretariat, but not during the course of his service with the United Nations, there might apply the considerations set forth above with regard to subversive activities carried on prior to employment with the United Nations.[198]

The attitude of the first Secretary-General on the subject was that, "in view of the present laws and regulations of the United States toward the American Communist Party and verdicts of the courts on the leadership of that party," no United States national who is a member of the Party should, "as a matter of policy," be employed in the Secretariat.[199] The Administrative Tribunal apparently took a sharply differing view: "Staff Regulation 1.4 recognizes the right of staff members not to give up their political opinions. So that membership of any particular party would not, of itself, be a justification, in the absence of other cause, for dismissal ... A decision based on such premises is a violation of an inalienable right of staff members and represents a misuse

pp. 651–652), and Yugoslavia (*ibid.*, p. 660). The United States Delegate, in supporting the Secretary-General's view, stressed that he did not propose to act automatically upon the plea of privilege, but would consider other information as to the staff member concerned (A/PV.416, p. 559); and the United Kingdom similarly emphasized this point.

[195] See notes 114 and 118.

[196] See the documentation cited note 118, and Rolin, *Advisory Opinion*, pp. 32–33.

[197] See United Nations doc. A/C.5/SR. 413, p. 8.

[198] See above, "Conviction and Suspicion of Members of the Secretariat."

[199] United Nations doc. A/PV.413, p. 536.

of power."²⁰⁰ It appears from the statements of the second Secretary-General that he will not apply a generalized ban on the employment of United States nationals who are members of the Communist Party, though such employees might be peculiarly liable to dismissal on other grounds.²⁰¹

The ruling of the Administrative Tribunal, if it is to be taken literally, would appear to involve a substantial *non sequitur*. Admittedly, the Staff Regulations recognize the right of staff members not to give up their political opinions. It hardly follows that membership of any particular party would not, of itself, be a justification for dismissal, for membership in a political party is not integrally related to the holding of political opinions, but to the expression of them. But the expression of political opinion is a right which in the case of Secretariat members was restricted at the time when the Tribunal made its ruling. It has been more restricted since.²⁰² The "inalienable right" referred to by the Tribunal is not the right of members of the staff to belong to a political party, but the right to hold to their political and religious convictions. This was made clearer by the debate at the Eighth Session of the General Assembly.²⁰³

²⁰⁰ *Crawford v. The Secretary-General of the United Nations*, Judgment No. 18, p. 6. It should be noted that the Secretary-General explicitly denied that his decision to dismiss Miss Crawford was based on the fact of her past or present party membership (see note 110).

²⁰¹ The following statement of the Secretary-General merits quotation: "Passive party-membership ... in a democratic society is somewhat in the nature of a civic right which should be restricted only for the most imperative reasons. On the other hand, such party membership, in some cases, I think should obviously be considered as covered by a general prohibition of political activities. I have in mind, for example, the case where a party is declared illegal. I do not think there is any difficulty for any delegation on that point. I have also in mind another case where party membership cannot be permitted in the individual case because it would entail an obligation to action in favour of the party or subjection to party discipline which amounts very much to the same. The practical difficulties of implementation arise obviously when you have to decide whether in a specific case party membership, which is not in a party which is declared illegal, on the basis of this very approach should be considered as admissible or not. I feel that the Secretary-General should not be in a position where he has to investigate and decide upon the obligations following from party membership. I think the responsi-bility should rest with the staff member who should himself judge about his position, his obligations and his rights ... The rule would make it clear to the staff member that he is perfectly entitled to all kinds of passive party membership but that he breaks his obligations towards the organization if the membership imposes upon him personally the duty to take action in spite of the prohibition in the staff regulations. As I said, on this basis, the Secretary-General would not have to go into the matter unless and until the staff member engages in activities which call for an investigation" (United Nations doc. A/C.5/566, pp. 1–3).

²⁰² See Staff Regulations 1.4 and 1.7, United Nations doc. ST/AFS/SGB/94, pp. 4, 5, and the same Regulations as amended (see notes 114 and 118, and United Nations doc. A/Res./191).

²⁰³ See, in particular, the statement of the delegate of Lebanon, United Nations doc. A/C.5/SR.412, pp. 6–8. The delegate of the Netherlands, together with the delegate of France, took the lead in pressing the contrary view: "Surrender of the basic political right of free association would constitute an infringement of one of the fundamental human and democratic rights; such a right should not be sacrificed to the administrative needs of the Organization" (A/C.5/SR.408, p. 17). That even he did not see the right as inalienable, however, may be gathered from the statement which this very delegate

The policy enunciated by the first Secretary-General provoked varying reactions. It was defended as a realistic recognition of the fact that the American Communist Party, if it had not been declared illegal in terms, had none the less been officially declared subversive.[204] It was criticized as constituting the incorporation into the law of the United Nations of a domestic standard of employment – a standard not consonant with the universal character of the Organization, which includes States with Communist Governments.[205]

It is possible that an arguable case could be made out for excluding from the Secretariat Communists of any nationality.[206] For Article 101 places the highest standards of integrity as a paramount consideration superior to that of geographical distribution. The question arises whether the members of a totalitarian party, subject to party discipline, can be reasonably deemed to lack the requisite integrity for honoring the injunction of Article 100 "not to seek or receive instructions . . . from any other authority external to the Organization." This seems to have been assumed by the Preparatory Commission and the General Assembly with respect to the members of two totalitarian parties other than the Communist (the Fascist and Nazi).[207] The League experience seems to lend support to that view.[208] The approach of the

of the Netherlands had made to the Assembly some eight months earlier: "The question might even be raised whether it would not be advisable, in the interest of our Organization, to stipulate that members of the Secretariat, for the duration of their service, shall not be members of any political party. This, I believe, would not be contrary to Staff Regulation 1.4 . . . Such a provision would avoid discrimination and might protect the Secretariat and its international character and forestall certain difficulties and criticisms, from any side whatever. A provision of this kind would follow from the same principle and from the same considerations as, for instance, Regulation 1.7, which stipulates: 'Any member of the Secretariat who becomes a candidate for a public office of a political character shall resign from the Secretariat'" (A/PV.417, pp. 584–585).

[204] See, in particular, the legislative findings of the Internal Security Act of 1950 (59 Stat. 669–73, cited in United Nations doc. A/2364, pp. 37–38), and the decision of the United States Supreme Court upholding the conviction of the leaders of the Communist Party under the Smith Act (*Dennis v. United States* (1951), 341 US 497). It should be noted, however, that membership in the United States Communist Party does not of itself constitute a violation of any criminal statute.

"Considering the climate of US opinion and the decisions of the US Supreme Court upholding the Smith Act – which virtually outlaws communist activity if not the Party itself – this proposition [not employing United States nationals who are Communist Party members] would seem to be one that the Secretary-General must accept." There are difficulties of principle involved, Professor Cohen suggests, but "whatever the theoretical variations, it would be very indiscreet today for the Secretary-General to retain in employment at home or abroad a member of the United States Communist Party who is a United States national" ("Preliminary Appraisal," p. 183). See also the statement of the Delegate of the United States, United Nations doc. A/PV.416, p. 558.

[205] See the statement of the Delegate of Norway (A/PV.416, p. 577). Senator Rolin found additional reasons (*Advisory Opinion*, pp. 53–54).

[206] See note 131.   [207] See note 28.

[208] On the other hand, similar charges of disloyalty to their oath to the League do not seem to have been made against the handful of Communists who were members of the League Secretariat. The policies of

Secretary-General to the question of passive staff membership in political parties emphasizes freedom from party discipline. So does that of the Fifth Committee of the General Assembly.[209] The standard thus jointly evolved at the Eighth Session of the General Assembly may, if it proves workable, be preferable to the rigid barring of employment of the members of any political party.[210] It is a standard which seems consonant with the principles of the international civil service. Should that standard not prove to be practicable, the question will arise of the prohibition of even passive membership in any political party by members of the Secretariat.

Solutions of that nature, it may be stated by way of conclusion, are implicit in the unavoidable combination of two principles, namely, the international character of the Secretariat and the confidence which the Secretariat enjoys. That confidence is, in the last analysis, complementary to the international character of the Secretariat. It flows from the integrity with which the Secretariat upholds its exclusively international responsibilities. Perhaps, paradoxically, that confidence may to some extent depend upon the success with which the principle of the independence of the Secretariat is reasonably accommodated to national sensibilities – and legitimate national interests – in periods of international tension.

the Soviet Union towards the League during the brief period of its membership, however, were not such as to put the allegiance of Communist members of the Secretariat to the test.

[209] See notes 114 and 118.

[210] It has been suggested that the chances of its workability have been enhanced by the terminations and resignations which took place before Mr. Hammarskjöld took office.

17

Secretary-General and Secretariat

ভৃ৩

Introduction

The concept of a Secretariat which, as the Charter prescribes, shall be of "exclusively international character," is relatively new; it might, in fact, in the context of modern nationalism, be viewed as revolutionary. The drafters of the Covenant of the League of Nations did not specify that the League Secretariat was to consist of anything more than a permanent grouping of national contingents, and it was actually Sir Eric Drummond who, as the first Secretary-General, made the epochal decision that the League Secretariat would be genuinely international. This "creation of a secretariat international alike in its structure, its spirit and its personnel, was without doubt one of the most important events in the history of international politics – important not only in itself, but as the indisputable proof of possibilities which had hitherto been confidently denied."[1] The role of the Secretariat in the United Nations as the avant-garde of the international outlook and structure has surpassed in significance that which it played in the League, for the Secretary-General of the United Nations is endowed with political powers which were withheld from his League predecessors. Yet the setting in which the Secretariat operates still emphasizes its unique international quality; fundamentally, the progress of international machinery since 1919 has not been great. The integrity of the international character, and the effectiveness of the United Nations Secretariat, thus remain of the most crucial consequence, not only because "the degree in which the objects of the Charter can be realized will be largely determined by the manner in which the Secretariat performs its task,"[2] but because the Secretary-General and his staff represent an advance in

First published in Commission to Study the Organization of Peace, *Charter Review Conference* (1955), p. 198.

[1] F. P. Walters, *A History of The League of Nations* (1952), Vol. I, p. 76.
[2] *Report of the Preparatory Commission of the United Nations*, 1946, p. 81.

internationalism with which the forward movement of the Organization is indissolubly bound.

Our attention will be centered upon that international character and, more, upon its political implementation by the Secretary-General. The essential criterion for judging the work of the Secretariat, it may be ventured, is its success in representing the unifying, international element in an Organization and world which are disparate and national. The Secretary-General's political activity in essence is, or should be, the process of applying to the actual world scene of conflicting nationalisms and ideologies an element of exclusively international responsibility whose ideology is that of the United Nations Charter. The text of the Charter affords considerable base for such activity, and, of course, an ideal Charter could provide one still broader.

Those Articles of the Charter which principally concern the Secretariat deal with the Secretary-General's appointment, his administrative and executive functions, his political powers, the international character of his staff, and the considerations which shall govern the staff's selection. They do not consider in detail the internal structure of the Secretariat, nor will this paper. A few remarks in this regard may suffice.

Events have proved the drafters of the Charter wise in declining to prescribe the pattern of the Secretariat's high-level organization. The effort of the Sponsoring Powers at San Francisco to amend the Charter's draft to provide for the election of four or five Deputy Secretaries-General, in the same manner as the Secretary-General, was fortunately defeated, not only because such a procedure might have compromised the Secretary-General's administrative authority and corroded the Secretariat's international character, but, as experience has shown, because it would have endowed the Secretariat with a structural rigidity ill suited to its changing needs. As it has turned out, the first Secretary-General relied upon eight (and, at one time, nine) Assistant Secretaries-General during the seven years of his service. Towards the end of his tenure, Mr. Lie proposed to exchange these for three or four Deputy Secretaries, a reconstruction which was forestalled by his resignation. Mr. Hammarskjöld, as his successor, has taken a third path, replacing the Assistant Secretaries-General and the Principal Directors who ranked below them with fifteen officers of the equal rank, if not title, of Under Secretary.

The ingathering of administrative authority which this and other of Mr. Hammarskjöld's alterations import has led some to wonder whether the Secretary-General's increased administrative concern may not impair the fullness of his political activity. The Secretary-General has assured the General Assembly that this in fact will not be the case.

Appointing the Secretary-General

The Charter provides that the Secretary-General shall be appointed by the General Assembly on the recommendation of the Security Council. When, over considerable opposition at San Francisco, it was decided that the veto would apply to that recommendation, it was agreed that no term of office would be specified in the Charter. A need for some room within which to maneuver was presciently anticipated. Trygve Lie was chosen without great difficulty in 1946, and his terms of appointment, laid down by the General Assembly, prescribed a tenure of five years. When, in 1950, the Soviet Union vetoed the renomination of Mr. Lie, and the United States threatened to veto the nomination of anyone but Mr. Lie, the Assembly exercised the modicum of latitude which the Charter, most flexibly interpreted, could be said to afford it, and extended Mr. Lie's term for three years. With Mr. Lie's resignation before the expiration of his extended term, much difficulty was found in selecting a successor. But the elective process of the Charter may be said to have "worked" two out of three times, in that the Security Council did ultimately reach agreement upon the appointment of Dag Hammarskjöld. Mr. Hammarskjöld took office for five years under the same terms of appointment which initially governed the first Secretary-General.

These developments may be said to demonstrate the desirability of the Charter's prescribing no term and the undesirability of the present elective process. Nothing would be gained by inserting a provision in the Charter setting the length of the Secretary-General's term, while a useful freedom to adjust it to experience, if not very occasional events, would be lost. It is of course clear that the General Assembly, as the most representative organ, must participate in electing the Secretary-General. To give to the Security Council the exclusive power to nominate is evidently to accord the permanent Members, as well as six transient States, a vote additional – indeed, prerequisite – to that which they exercise in the General Assembly. Shall that weight be further increased by subjecting the Council's nomination to the veto? It is unquestionably a matter of central importance that the Secretary-General be acceptable to the Great Powers, for he must exert his political influence in the world arena which they dominate. Trygve Lie has testified to the contraction of his political role after his breach with the Soviet Union in 1950.[3] The fault, of course, lay with Moscow, and Mr. Lie's experience may

---

[3] Trygve Lie, *In the Cause of Peace* (1954), p. 385. See also p. 411. Mr. Lie, at p. 428, writes that the "election of the Secretary-General of the United Nations should also be a matter not requiring five 'concurring votes'; in fact, the General Assembly should have the main responsibility for selecting the Secretary-General, on the recommendation of any seven members of the Security Council."

be said to indicate that too high a price should not be paid for Great Power unanimity in the Secretary-General's appointment, since a Secretary-General who fulfills his Charter responsibilities may not in any case be able to remain on good terms with a State which violates its. Yet the fact remains that Great Power sponsorship is profoundly desirable. Veto over the Secretary-General's nomination is the obvious way of initially insuring such sponsorship. But the drawback of this veto is peculiarly great. For while the Organization may (well or badly) survive the exercise of a veto of Council action on other issues, it cannot continue without a Secretary-General. If, for reasons of desirability or inevitability, the veto over the Secretary-General's appointment is to persist, some means of overcoming the prolonged failure of the permanent Members to reach agreement should be provided. Extension of the term of the incumbent is an inadequate palliative, if for no other reasons than that he may be unable or unwilling to continue to serve. Perhaps the Charter might be amended to provide that, absent a recommendation by the Security Council, the General Assembly shall appoint a Secretary-General *pro tempore*, who shall serve until a nomination is forthcoming from the Council and approved by the Assembly. Among other possibilities would be empowering the International Court of Justice to submit one or more nominations to the General Assembly, should the Security Council, by a vetoless seven-vote majority, call upon it to do so.

Aspects of the Secretariat's International Character

That the advanced international position of the Secretariat is correspondingly exposed has been most sensitively demonstrated in matters of hiring and firing. The Charter assigns to the Secretary-General the power to appoint the staff, under regulations established by the General Assembly. The Secretary-General is to seek "the highest standards of efficiency, competence, and integrity" while paying "due regard ... to recruiting the staff on as wide a geographical basis as possible." The Secretariat, "as international officials," are "responsible only to the Organization." Nothing is said of securing governmental nomination or approval of candidates or appointees. None the less, in practice, many Governments have submitted nominations. Indeed, the Secretary-General has found it necessary to seek them, the Organization's procedures of "direct recruiting" apparently being inadequately developed. Other Governments, and most notably the United States, have established procedures for "clearing" nominees and appointees who are their nationals. These arrangements, legally unobjectionable in so far as they recognize that it lies with the Secretary-General alone to evaluate the facts which Governments submit, may be argued to be practically inconsonant with the international character of the Secretariat to the extent that they in fact tend to determine the Secretary-General's decisions. Still other Governments, among them the Czech, have clearly breached their Charter obligations by demanding the discharge of certain of their nationals from Secretariat positions. The Secretaries-General have resisted these varying pressures with considerable success. Efforts such as the Czech, directed at firing, and other efforts directed at hiring, have had little effectual result. The Secretaries-General, against a background of pressures generated within the United States, did discharge certain American nationals, in actions which, on the balance, seem defensible.[4] But the pressures were far less so, whether viewed from the standpoint of international responsibility or national security. India's demand for the withdrawal of United Nations observers of United States nationality from Kashmir is perhaps open to similar criticism. Moscow's appointment of Arkady Sobolev to a high post in the Soviet Foreign Office immediately upon his resignation as Assistant Secretary-General, followed by his return to Headquarters as a Soviet delegate, may have been of doubtful propriety, and a like policy has not been adopted by Moscow alone.

"By far the most serious violation of Article 100 of the Charter that has occurred," Trygve Lie has pointed out, were the attacks upon the Secretary-General which the Soviet Government and its allies leveled after his stand against armed aggression in Korea and the failure even to recognize him as Secretary-General after the extension of his term. This Soviet policy, Mr. Lie protested, was a "policy of the crudest form of pressure, not only against me but against any future Secretary-General who may incur the displeasure of the Soviet Union for doing his duty as he sees it under the Charter."[5] The USSR's frontal assault upon the international responsibility of the Secretariat places the delinquencies of other Members, in matters of personnel policy, in subdued context.

It may perhaps be concluded that – as with some other articles of the Charter – the fault lies not with the text but with the Members' adherence to it. The relevant articles are among the more ably drafted sections of the Charter. While the Secretary-General has been criticized for doing too much and for doing too little in insuring the widest possible geographical representation in the Secretariat, the Charter's text in this respect does not require amending. It might be useful to lend emphasis to the meaning of Article 101 by providing that the staff shall be appointed "exclusively" by the Secretary-

---

[4] Schwebel, "The International Character of the Secretariat of the United Nations," *The British Year Book of International Law* (1953), 30, p. 71 ff.

[5] United Nations, General Assembly, Seventh Session, *Official Records*, March 10, 1953, A/PV.413, p. 535.

General. Possibly "the spirit as well as the letter of Article 100 should be clearly confirmed, perhaps by express reference to the 'general principles of law recognized by civilized nations' (Article 38, Statute of the International Court of Justice) as the standard applicable to United Nations employees accused of conduct incompatible with their duties."[6] The suggestion advanced by Messrs. Clark and Sohn of appending the General Convention on Privileges and Immunities to the Charter, and thus effecting the Convention's ratification with acceptance of an amended Charter, may merit particular consideration. Essentially, however, a thoroughgoing acceptance by the States Members of the exclusively international character of the personnel and practice of the Secretariat is not a matter susceptible of textual treatment.

Political Activity

Article 99 of the Charter provides that: "The Secretary-General may bring to the attention of the Security Council any matter which in his opinion may threaten the maintenance of international peace and security." Article 98 provides that the Secretary-General shall act in that capacity at all meetings of the General Assembly, and the Security, Economic and Social, and Trusteeship Councils, and "shall perform such other functions as are entrusted to him by these organs." Blended together, these articles supply the Secretary-General's constitutional authorization for a significant range of political activity.

Article 99 has been most prominently brought to bear against the aggression of North Korea. With his statement to the Security Council at the very opening of its meeting of June 25, 1950, Mr. Lie anticipated and associated himself and his office with the most determined effort the world has yet seen to give reality to the principle of collective security. In the development of the Organization's Korean effort, the Secretary-General exercised an element of leadership of the highest importance, both for the Organization and for the shaping of his political powers. Absent the Secretary-General's initiative, it appears that the United Nations action initially might well have been deprived of important governmental support – of votes in the Security Council – and might never have gained the degree of international participation which it did (limited as it was). Apart from this express invocation of Article 99, the Secretary-General has implemented the political powers with which it endows him in many questions, among them the Palestine, the Berlin blockade, and the Chinese representation. The reach

[6] W. Friedmann, "Strengthening the Secretariat," *Annals of the American Academy of Political and Social Science* (November, 1954), 296, p. 135.

of Article 99 has been extended to embrace the General Assembly. It has supported the Secretary-General's interventions in public and private, in matters such as those of the presence of Soviet troops in Iran, the powers of the Security Council with reference to Trieste and Palestine, and the practicality and procedures of East–West negotiation. The Secretary-General has attempted to influence the policies of the States Members on questions as broad as some of those enumerated in his Twenty Year Program for Achieving Peace through the United Nations, and as specific as the disposition of the former Italian colonies. He has won the rights to place items on the provisional agendas of United Nations organs, and to submit comments, and, apparently, resolutions and amendments, to them. His right to conduct such investigations of international situations as he may desire with a view towards determining the need for invoking Article 99 has been acknowledged by leading Powers. The Secretary-General has employed the annual report which he is obliged to make to the General Assembly not only to review the Organization's work, but to interpret and constructively criticize it. When, pursuant to Article 98, the Secretary-General was requested by the Assembly to use his best efforts to secure the release of United Nations fliers imprisoned by the Peking régime, Mr. Hammarskjöld boldly flew to China to urge the United Nations stand. The Secretary-General's execution of many other resolutions of United Nations organs, if less dramatic, is no less resourceful. The diplomatic, behind-the-scenes activity of the Secretary-General is continuous, and vital to the Organization's constructive functioning.

The manner, if not the character, of the Secretary-General's political activity has naturally altered somewhat with the change in the office's incumbents. The personality of the man who occupies even a well-defined and precedent-illuminated position gives a special quality to that office as long as he holds it and perhaps afterwards. This is the more true where a post is defined only in general terms and for which precedent exists only by analogy. Trygve Lie and Dag Hammarskjöld are not merely different people, but very different personages. Moreover, they were confronted with different events. Trygve Lie, as first Secretary-General, was confronted with problems his successor had been spared, and, at the same time, Dag Hammarskjöld has had to cope with difficulties which are both old and new, and the harder to overcome in some instances either because of their history or their novelty. World affairs evidently have not stood still, and a pattern of behavior of the Secretary-General of 1946 or 1950 is not necessarily appropriate to 1955.

Mr. Lie carried on extensive and intensive diplomatic activity of a private and not-so-private kind. If the main thrust of his political initiative was behind the scenes, an important auxiliary effort was that exerted publicly, in attempts to influence world opinion and give guidance to the policies of Governments and the actions of their representatives in United Nations organs. While Mr. Lie's open participation in the public workings of United Nations bodies was not so sustained as to give a consistent direction to their labors – perhaps a task beyond the powers of the Secretary-General and the forbearance of the States Members, as these have so far developed – the first Secretary-General did introduce upon the international scene a new force in international politics: the United Nations voice. National representatives spoke for their national interests; the Secretary-General spoke, in public and more often in private, for the higher, United Nations interest of the international community as a whole, which is more than the sum of the national parts. The results with which the Secretary-General spoke were varying, but not inconsequential, and, on occasion, they were crucial.

Mr. Hammarskjöld has likewise broadly interpreted the powers which the essential nature of his position, and the text of the Charter, afford him. His private diplomatic activity appears to have been no less full than that carried on by Mr. Lie. In fact, there are indications that Mr. Hammarskjöld's non-literal and non-limitative interpretation of the ambit of Article 99 possibly has extended farther still. The character of the Secretary-General's public role, however, has changed markedly. On the one hand, Mr. Hammarskjöld is more "accessible." He makes speeches more often than did Mr. Lie, but on the other hand, he says less. The Secretary-General confines his public addresses to the enunciation of principles which he applies in his private diplomacy. This policy does not win publicity, nor does the Secretary-General seek it. Moreover, apart from refraining to attempt to influence world public opinion on political issues, Mr. Hammarskjöld has been most cautious in trying to give public guidance to Governments, within United Nations meetings or without. While Mr. Hammarskjöld is evidently more the diplomat than the politician, his flight to Peking indicates that the dramatic move is not beyond his reach, that his emphasis on diplomacy is a matter of calculation as well as disposition, and one which the Secretary-General is prepared to adjust to events. Mr. Hammarskjöld has devoted more of his energies to internal administration than did Mr. Lie, and his leadership of the Directors General of the Specialized Agencies, in the Administrative Committee on Coordination, is said to be especially effective. Some informed observers believe that Mr. Hammarskjöld's present relatively exclusive reliance upon diplomacy, as the medium of exerting and developing the Secretary-General's influence, is in the best interests of his office and the Organization. But perhaps a confident assessment of his tactical innovations is as yet premature.

Political Amendments

It is questionable whether an effort at a General Conference for Charter review to add to the Secretary-General's political powers would be wise. The difficulties of amending the Charter need not be stressed; and should such proposals fail of adoption, the result, rather than expanding the Secretary-General's constitutional authority, might tend to delimit negatively the sphere of his initiative. Moreover, the comparative success of the Secretariat as a political as well as a ministerial organ, and its demonstrated capacity to develop its prerogatives through practice, indicate that there is no pressing need for revising the Articles of the Charter which concern it.

This is not to say that possible amendments are beyond suggestion. An acute commentator has ventured that "the main road toward strengthening the Secretariat would seem to be to remove the ambiguities, in the Charter and in the precedents, concerning the political leadership responsibilities of the Secretary-General and to make such responsibilities unequivocal and of first priority."[7] Article 97 describes the Secretary-General as merely "the chief administrative officer of the Organization." Conceivably it might be desirable to add words to the effect of: "and he shall have such political powers as are hereafter specified." The right of the Secretary-General to submit resolutions to United Nations organs, which finds a certain support in their rules of procedure and in precedent, might be set forth in the Charter's text. Even so entrenched a right as to speak on his own initiative in United Nations meetings might possibly be usefully inserted.

A plan which merits re-examination would be that of designating the Secretary-General as permanent President of the Security Council.[8] At present, the President of the Security Council changes monthly, rotating among the Council's eleven Delegations. The results have left much to be desired, in terms of responsibility of the President to the Council and to the Organization as a whole, rather than to his Delegation, and in terms of continuity and expertise. On occasion, the powers of the President have been

---

[7] Wallace W. Sayre, "The Future of the United Nations, Issues of Charter Revision," *Annals of the American Academy of Political and Social Science* (November, 1954), 296, p. 139. See also the thoughts of Trygve Lie, as informally expressed in 1950, quoted in Schwebel, *The Secretary-General of the United Nations: His Political Powers and Practice* (1952), p. 205.

[8] A committee of former high League officials, under the chairmanship of Sir Eric Drummond, considered and rejected such a plan (Royal Institute of International Affairs, *The International Secretariat of the Future*, 1944, pp. 32–33).

unabashedly abused. Were the Secretary-General to be the Council's President, a healthy element of international responsibility would be introduced into the Council's proceedings from a strategic vantage point, which could do much to enhance the procedures, if not the substance, of the Council's work. As President, the Secretary-General would naturally cast no vote. He would act much as the Speaker does in the House of Commons. An Under Secretary might act as Secretary-General of the Council. Were it felt that this plan would demand too much of the Secretary-General's energies (and it well might, especially were the Council's role in the Organization to revive), the Organization might elect a Council President, distinct from the Secretary-General.[9] If it were decided that an elected President might tend to compete with the Secretary-General as the representative of the Organization as a whole, or that he would be the product of partisanship, the Secretary-General might be entrusted with the power of choosing the President, possibly to serve at the Secretary-General's pleasure, or for a short term of office, such as one year. Or, perhaps, the President of the General Assembly might automatically serve as the President of the Security Council for the year following the Assembly's adjournment. Such a solution would not entirely deprive the Secretary-General of a role, for it is a fact of United Nations practice that the Secretary-General is an important influence in the annual choice of the President of the General Assembly. None of these suggestions, it should be noted, would necessitate Charter amendment, for the method of electing the Council's President is not prescribed by the Charter but rather left to the Council's rules of procedure.

It has been suggested that the Secretary-General's discretionary power to bring to the attention of the Security Council any matter which may threaten international peace should be made mandatory, and extend to embrace the General Assembly.[10] While there may be no harm in the latter proposal, amending the Charter to incorporate it is unnecessary in that the Secretary-General now in fact enjoys the right to call the Assembly's attention to such matters. It would probably be undesirable to require the Secretary-General to bring to the Organization's attention matters which in his opinion may threaten the peace, for to do so might be to deprive him of a valuable discretion in invoking the procedure, and in construing the substantive implications of Article 99.

---

[9] The Convention on International Civil Aviation (Articles 51, 54, 59, 60), and the Articles of Agreement of the International Bank for Reconstruction and Development (Article V, section 5), and of the International Monetary Fund (Article XII, section iv), embrace not dissimilar arrangements, which appear to have worked well.

[10] Grenville Clark and Louis B. Sohn, *A Digest of Peace Through Disarmament and Charter Revision* (1954), p. 67.

It has further been suggested that "consideration might well be given to the creation of an intelligence service which could provide him [the Secretary-General] with the type of information needed to exercise the immense responsibility conferred by Article 99."[11] General MacArthur proposed to the Secretary-General a somewhat related plan, perhaps more far-reaching still:

It is my personal view confirmed by many thoughtful men who have conferred with me that you should now proceed vigorously to provide within the structure of the United Nations a permanent supreme military command adequately staffed to develop and maintain current, on a global basis, strategical and logistical plans designed to effect the immediate deployment of the available military force to meet any emergency situation and to keep the United Nations constantly informed on the military aspects concerning any area of actual or threatened trouble. Stand-by forces earmarked for United Nations service within the political boundaries of members nations will do no good unless through detailed prior planning their deployment in time of need is strategically sound and immediate.[12]

The value of the first of these suggestions is open to question. The second may perhaps merit further consideration, if not in 1956, then at some later stage in the development of the executive arm of international organization.

---

[11] Waldo Chamberlin, "Strengthening the Secretariat," *Annals of the American Academy of Political and Social Science* (November, 1954), 296, p. 132. See the negative comments upon this proposal by Awni Khalidy, *ibid.*, p. 136. For an examination of the Secretary-General's right to make such investigations as he may deem necessary in order to exercise his powers under Article 99, see Schwebel, "The Origins and Development of Article 99 of the Charter," *The British Year Book of International Law* (1951), 28, pp. 379–380.

[12] As quoted by Trygve Lie, *In the Cause of Peace*, pp. 347–348.

18

A United Nations "Guard" and a United Nations "Legion"

༒

A United Nations "Guard": Introduction

In the introduction to his Annual Report for 1947–1948, the Secretary-General of the United Nations, Mr. Trygve Lie, described a plan he had announced during the Harvard University Commencement exercises a month earlier.[1]

> I have under study proposals for the creation of a small United Nations Guard Force which could be recruited by the Secretary-General and placed at the disposal of the Security Council and the General Assembly. Such a force would not be used as a substitute for the forces contemplated in Articles 42 and 43. It would not be a striking force, but purely a guard force. It could be used for guard duty with United Nations missions, in the conduct of plebiscites under the supervision of the United Nations and in the administration of truce terms. It could be used as a constabulary under the Security Council or the Trusteeship Council in cities like Jerusalem and Trieste during the establishment of international regimes. It might also be called upon by the Security Council under Article 40 of the Charter, which provides for provisional measures to prevent the aggravation of a situation threatening the peace.
>
> There are many uses for such a force. If it had existed during the past year it would, I believe, have greatly increased the effectiveness of the work of the Security Council, and have saved many lives, particularly in Indonesia and Palestine. It should not be a large force – from one thousand to five thousand men would be sufficient – because it would have behind it all the authority of the United Nations.[2]

First published in William R. Frye (ed.), *A United Nations Peace Force* (1957), New York, Oceana Publications.

[1] United Nations Press Release M/446, June 10, 1948, p. 4.
[2] United Nations doc. A/565, *Annual Report of the Secretary-General on the Work of the Organization, 1 July 1947 to 30 June 1948*, pp. xvii–xviii.

The Plan

On September 28, 1948, eleven days after the assassination of Count Bernadotte, the Secretary-General formally suggested to the General Assembly that "the formation of a United Nations Guard several thousand strong" should be "closely studied and reported upon" by the appropriate committees of the General Assembly.[3] As an immediate measure, the Secretary-General proposed the formation of an 800-man Guard, 500 of whom would be held in reserve in their national homes. He described the "primary positive purpose" of the Guard "to be representative of United Nations authority in support of United Nations Missions in the field and to provide a limited protection to United Nations personnel and property."[4] The Guard would afford security to a Field Mission's members, secretariat, premises, archives, and other property; furnish such transportation, communications, and supply as might be necessary to supplement services available to a Mission in the field; maintain order during hearings and investigations of United Nations Missions; "patrol points or guard objectives neutralized under truce or cease-fire order of the United Nations"; and "exercise supervisory and observation functions at polling points during the conduct of referendums conducted under United Nations auspices." "Availability of international protective personnel," the Secretary-General wrote, "is a *sine qua non* of a Mission's ability to proceed with the necessary confidence and authority ... without the suspicion of partiality which the use of local police or national foreign militia engenders. Absence of an independent international body representative of the authority of the United Nations and capable of offering minimum personal protection to United Nations staff has seriously embarrassed the work of the United Nations Missions both in the course of hearings and inquiries as well as in the operation of truce arrangements and the rendering of good offices."[5] The experience of United Nations Missions in the field, the Secretary-General submitted, had demonstrated that "there must be available at their disposal adequate representative and protective authority to give effect to their decisions as well as technical service assistance to enable them to function with speed and efficiency."[6]

He was not, Mr. Lie said, suggesting an international army. Both "on practical as well as on legal grounds such a Guard could not be used for enforcement purposes ... nor for the purpose of maintaining law and order in an area." But the Guard would "immeasurably strengthen" the hands of

---

[3] United Nations doc. A/656, September 28, 1948.   [4] *Ibid.*, p. 7.   [5] *Ibid.*, pp. 1, 8.
[6] *Ibid.*, p. 2.

United Nations Missions established "for the express purpose of assuring pacific settlements without recourse to the use of force."[7]

The Secretary-General submitted that "adequate constitutional authority"[8] existed under the Charter, notably in Articles 97 and 98, for his establishment of the Guard, provided that the General Assembly gave budgetary approval. For, he contended, he possessed the power to establish units of the Secretariat, if they were required to meet the needs of United Nations organs; and the Guard would be recruited as part of the Secretariat, pursuant to Articles 97, 98, 100, and 101, to fulfill the undoubted needs of United Nations field Missions. It would function in a territory "only with the consent, express or implied, of the territorial sovereign."[9]

The Secretary-General described the character, functions, and organization of the proposed Guard in some detail.[10] It would, he emphasized, be "entirely non-military"[11] in character. The Guard would be made available by the Secretary-General at the request of United Nations organs. Its equipment would be limited to "personal emergency defence weapons" (side-arms and light automatic weapons) and transport and communications material (including four armored staff cars); it would "not be organizationally of such a size or character as to be of possible use as an aggressive force." The Guard would "not have the powers, as such, of either a civilian or military police force (such as powers of arrest, quelling of insurrections or, generally, functions implying the use of force for other than personal protective reasons)." But it would be charged with protecting United Nations Observers from "undisciplined" attack, and with the guarding of neutralized objectives. A preliminary estimate of the cost of an 800-man force was four million dollars a year.

The Debate at the Assembly's Third Session

The *Ad Hoc* Political Committee did not consider the Secretary-General's proposal until the second part of its Third Session, in April 1949. The late Abraham Feller, who, as general counsel and the Secretary-General's intimate adviser, was prominent in the drafting of the Secretary-General's plan, opened the discussion with an exposition of it. He noted that the amelioration

---

[7] *Ibid.*   [8] *Ibid.*, p. 3.

[9] *Ibid.*, p. 5. These words have a ring which is familiar. The phraseology of Mr. Lie's plan does not specify that the Guard would function only with the "continued" consent of the territorial sovereign, but there is nothing in his proposals or the discussions upon them which lends support to a contrary view. Whether a sovereign which once consented to the entry of the Guard would have the right to compel its withdrawal apparently was not discussed.

[10] *Ibid.*, Appendices B and C, pp. 7–11.   [11] *Ibid.*, p. 7.

of the Palestine situation placed the creation of the Guard in a less urgent light than it had appeared the previous September. Meanwhile, he stated, "The Secretary-General had been approached ... by several delegations which had suggested the desirability of further study."[12] The Secretary-General accordingly proposed that the Committee recommend to the Assembly the creation of a small Special Committee of ten or twelve members, including the five Permanent Members of the Security Council, to study all aspects of the problem and report to the Fourth Session. This diplomatic indication that Mr. Lie's plan had met with a mixed reception was more than borne out by the debate which followed.

Speaking first, the Delegate of the Philippines noted that the death of Count Bernadotte might have been averted had there been a Guard. He warmly endorsed the Secretary-General's plan, and promptly submitted a resolution embodying his suggestion for the creation of a Special Committee to study it. The reasons advanced in support of the plan by the Philippine Delegate, and by the very few other representatives who unqualifiedly appeared to favour it (namely, Sweden, Haiti, and Peru), did not significantly differ from those of Mr. Lie.[13]

The opposition was more original. Its core was the Soviet bloc; their objections, if not the most influential, were the most fundamental. France, while not contesting the Guard's legality, did challenge its practicality; and a number of States, which gave qualified approval to the principle of the Secretary-General's plan, and unqualified approval to its study, expressed serious doubts on a number of points. The criticism of the plan may be summarized as follows:

In the view of the Soviet bloc, the Secretary-General's proposal was one more step in the progression of Anglo-American perversion of United Nations machinery to imperialist ends. The Observer and Guard force which had been improvised by the Secretary-General in Palestine, nine-tenths of whom were United States personnel, was a violation of the Charter; the Secretary-General's idea now was to legalize the unlawful.[14] In the last analysis, the Guard was intended to replace the forces envisaged by Articles 42 and 43, "to allow the United States and the United Kingdom to continue

---

[12] General Assembly, *Official Records*, Third Session, Pt. 2, *Ad Hoc Political Committee Summary Records of Meetings 6 April–10 May, 1949*, p. 24.

[13] *Ibid.*, pp. 35–36. Haiti, however, declaring that "right must be supported by strength," stressed the role of an international force "in maintaining law and restoring international justice."

[14] *Ibid.*, pp. 29, 30–33, 40, 43–44. (The Observers, who during the second truce period reached 500 strong, were officers drawn from the countries represented on the Security Council's Truce Commission, the United States, Belgium, and France. The Guards were volunteers from the United Nations Headquarters Guard Unit, and were of various nationalities.)

without restraint their political and military interference in the domestic affairs of other States." The Commissions on Greece and Korea were illegal; a Guard designed to assist such commissions could be no less.

Articles 97 and 98, or other provisions of the Charter bearing upon the Secretary-General's powers, the Soviet bloc argued, hardly authorized him to recruit an (however lightly) armed force, however small. And if the Guard had no connection with the provisions for enforcement laid down in Chapter VII, it was the more contrary to the Charter, since the latter prohibited any resort to force except by application of that Chapter's provisions. The Guard would be distinguished from the forces foreseen by Article 43 only by its size (which could increase), its international (as contrasted with national unit) character, and its illegality.

The Soviet bloc further objected that equipping the force with automatic weapons and with vehicles such as armored cars confirmed their view that the Guard was to be a real armed force.

The less extreme doubts expressed by other Delegations emphasized budgetary considerations. "Only when the entire question of the size of a United Nations Guard had been thoroughly examined in the light of what the Organization could afford," the Delegate of the Union of South Africa cautioned, "could any decision be taken on the principle of creating such a force."[15] Four millions were proposed for 800 men, the Soviet delegate noted; if the force were expanded as was proposed, the costs could exceed the annual budget of the United Nations.[16] Even the Guard's 800 men, France declared, "would obviously be an expensive and useless luxury."[17]

In all, the French delegation was "unenthusiastic" about the Secretary-General's plan, not on legal grounds – for the legal objections raised did not apply to an 800-man force, and need be considered only were its enlargement to be proposed – but on practical ones. A limited force of 800 men could not effectively protect United Nations Missions; past losses of personnel were not due to the absence of such protection; no police force ever had been able to prevent deliberate political assassination. The spirit which should animate the United Nations, the French Delegate contended, forbade connecting its prestige with a Guard's éclat.[18]

The South African Delegate raised other practical considerations, some of which China, India, and the United Kingdom reiterated. The 300-man active force would have to be recruited with great care to achieve adequate homogeneity "in language, religion and training." Inability to keep the active force constantly occupied would present morale problems. The pres-

---

[15] Ibid., p. 27.   [16] Ibid., p. 31.   [17] Ibid., p. 37.   [18] Ibid., pp. 36–37.

ence of a reserve cadre of 500 men domiciled in various States presented "the dangers of divided loyalty, differing standards of efficiency and language difficulties." These difficulties, and ones of training, would be heightened with the ultimate expansion of the force to 5,000 men (this was the figure the South African Delegate gave). He ventured that the principal source of recruits would be the five great Powers, yet ill will among their nationals might disrupt the Guard's unity.

Perhaps the most profound objection advanced by South Africa was that of

> the dangers inherent in the exercise of patrol duties in neutralized zones and supervision of elections conducted under United Nations auspices. The exercise of those two functions might encourage a tendency to regard the United Nations Guard as a body which bore the responsibility for the execution of the recommendations of the Organization. In practice, the Guard might thus acquire a paramilitary character which would be utterly incompatible with the avowed purposes for which it had been created.[19]

The paramilitary functions might draw the Organization into controversy with various States, the South African Delegate maintained, and, apart from that, might require a much larger force than had been contemplated or than the United Nations could afford. For example, a whole battalion might be needed to insure free movement of observers in an area as large as Indonesia. The Special Committee to study the Secretary-General's plan accordingly should consider the feasibility of employing the national police of the countries concerned for guard duties, as an alternative to the creation of the Guard.

The danger of the Guard's clashing with local forces, and the advantages of utilizing national police, struck a responsive note with the Indian and Chinese delegations, as well as the Soviet bloc. Yet the Indian Delegate suggested that, if care were taken to construct a non-military United Nations Guard, recruited with full regard to geographical distribution, it should be able to cooperate with local security forces.[20]

The British Delegation agreed that "further elucidation" on the status of the Guard in relation to local forces was needed. At the same time, while the Secretary-General had stressed that the Guard would function in a territory only with the express or implied consent of the territorial sovereign, the British Delegate pointed out that "the Guard might be most needed precisely where such consent was not available."[21]

The United States joined a number of other Delegations in reserving its

---

[19] *Ibid.*, p. 27.　　[20] *Ibid.*, p. 41.　　[21] *Ibid.*, pp. 31–32.

position on the substance of the Secretary-General's plan, while declaring in favour of the Philippine resolution for the study of it. Particular consideration, the United States Delegate said, should be given to the distinction between Guard functions and military functions. The United States rejected charges that the plan was contrary to the Charter or improperly motivated or supported. But, it declared, admittedly "some of the proposals of the Secretary-General went too far."[22]

Before the *Ad Hoc* Political Committee voted upon the Philippine resolution, Mr. Feller assured it that the Secretary-General, in proposing his plan, had acted on his own initiative, without pressure or suggestion from any Government. The Committee, by a vote of forty-one to six, with three abstentions, adopted the resolution proposed by the Philippines. "Realizing the need for a thorough study of the matter before concrete action can be taken," the Assembly thus resolved to establish a Special Committee of "specially qualified representatives" of Australia, Brazil, China, Colombia, Czechoslovakia, France, Greece, Haiti, Pakistan, Poland, Sweden, the USSR, the United Kingdom, and the United States, to study the Secretary-General's proposal "in all its relevant aspects, including the technical, budgetary and legal problems involved," as well as any other proposals by the Secretary-General and Member States for "increasing the effectiveness of the services provided to the United Nations missions by the Secretary-General."[23]

The Field Service and Panel

In the face of opposition by two great Powers, the doubts of three others, and the mixed response of lesser States, the Secretary-General retreated. The United States had suggested his plan "went too far"; the Secretary-General not unwisely replaced it with a proposal which was less far reaching.

"After careful consideration" of the observations made at the Third Session, the Secretary-General submitted "a substantial revision" of his original proposal.[24] Under his revised plan, two new units would be set up, a Field Service and a Field Reserve Panel. The Service, consisting of 300 men, would be part of the Secretariat, but recruited by secondment from national Governments. This uniformed force would provide transport and communications for Missions; guard United Nations premises, at Headquarters and abroad; and maintain order during meetings, hearings, and investigations. The Service would not have any truce or plebiscite functions. It would not

---

[22] *Ibid.*, p. 35.   [23] General Assembly resolution 270 (III), April 29, 1949.

[24] GAOR, Fourth Session, Supplement No. 13, *Report of the Special Committee on a United Nations Guard,* October 10, 1949, p. 6.

regularly be supplied with arms of any kind; in isolated instances, and when permitted by local authority, individual members might be authorized to carry side-arms.

Truce and plebiscite functions would be left to the Field Reserve Panel. The Panel would consist simply of a list of names of men in national service recommended by Governments, which would be compiled, reviewed, and kept current by the Secretariat. The members of the Panel would be called into service only in response to a special decision of the General Assembly or the Security Council, or an organ authorized by them. Membership in the Panel would establish eligibility, not obligation, to serve if called upon. Thus the Panel would need to be large enough to take account of the fact that not all of its members could or would serve at a given moment; and the Secretary-General suggested a list of 2,000. The Panel would, the Secretary-General maintained, enable him to dispense with emergency recruitment of personnel for observation and supervision tasks, and to secure a broader geographical distribution in their selection.

The Field Service, the Secretary-General noted, was designed to render precisely the same services as the Secretariat was already rendering in a less systematic way. The legal basis for its creation would be the same as that of any other Secretariat unit; legal objections made to the former Guard proposal, the Secretary-General ventured, accordingly did not seem relevant. The question of the legality of use of members of the Panel would be the responsibility of the United Nations organ drawing upon it. The cost of the Field Service was estimated at about one million dollars a year.[25]

The Report of the Special Committee

The majority of the Special Committee approved the Secretary-General's new plan. With respect to the Field Service, the Committee suggested that it be recruited in the normal Secretariat manner, rather than by secondment; and it proposed that the Secretary-General consider merging the existing Headquarters Guard Force into the Service. The Service should, the Committee recommended, be employed "only where the use of local services is not practicable."[26] When the costs of maintaining present field personnel were deducted from the cost of the Service, the Committee noted, it was found that the net additional expense was modest: no more than $233,000 a year, and perhaps less. The majority of the Special Committee saw no legal difficulties. The Service could not be considered an armed force; it would

[25] *Ibid.*, pp. 6–9.   [26] *Ibid.*, p. 2.

stand on the same legal basis as any other unit of the Secretariat. Equally, the Panel would be created for the sole purpose of assisting Missions; its members would not constitute an armed force; and the competence of United Nations organs to draw upon the Panel could not be considered by the Special Committee. The Committee accordingly recommended, by a vote of ten to two (two members being absent), that the Assembly adopt a resolution recognizing the authority of the Secretary-General "to establish the United Nations Field Service, subject to budgetary limitations and the normal administrative controls of the General Assembly."[27] It similarly recommended, by a vote of nine to two with one abstention (two members being absent), the establishment of a "United Nations Panel of Field Observers" to "assist United Nations missions in the functions of observation and supervision." The Delegations of the USSR, Poland, and Czechoslovakia, equating the Field Force and Panel with the Secretary-General's earlier proposal for a United Nations Guard, attached a vigorous dissent.[28]

The Debate at the Assembly's Fourth Session

At the Assembly's Fourth Session, the Secretary-General himself opened the discussion of the *Ad Hoc* Political Committee on the Special Committee's report. In formulating his revised plan, he said, three considerations had been paramount: the necessity for more system and strength in serving field missions; provision of such servicing efficiently and economically; and "the need to remove any elements of political controversy, a need that was all the more cogent" in view of the Secretary-General's determination that "no proposal of his should serve as a further cause of division among the Members of the United Nations."[29] The recommendations of the Special Committee were wholly acceptable.

The discussion which followed sheds but limited light on problems of an international police force, for most Members were convinced that that was hardly what was under discussion. The Soviet bloc differed, and it renewed and recapitulated all the arguments which had been made against the proposal for the Guard,[30] together with the fresh one that, if the Secretary-General

---

[27] *Ibid.*, pp. 3–4.

[28] *Ibid.*, pp. 4–5. For an enumeration of the issues raised in the discussions of the Special Committee, see United Nations doc. A/AC.29.W.I, July 13, 1949.

[29] *Summary Records of Meetings 6 April–10 May, 1949* (see note 12), p. 94.

[30] *Ibid.*, p. 106. Lumping the Field Force and Panel together, the Soviet bloc saw the sum as equal to the Guard. The Polish delegate added this interesting argument: "The United Nations was created as an association of sovereign and equal States and not as a new State ... still less a super-State ... The Member States had agreed to grant certain rights to the Organization, but they had never given it the

actually had the authority to set up the Field Force, why had he applied to the General Assembly for authorization to do so.

The Secretary-General's new plan met with widespread support. It was considered an improvement over his earlier proposal. The need for economy was still stressed; the importance of securing the guard services of the local State where possible, and of cooperation with local units, was reiterated.[31]

Three hundred mechanics, the Delegate of Pakistan noted, did not constitute an armed force.[32] There was some debate over whether members of the Panel should be required to take the United Nations oath, with the result that it was decided that they should.[33] Some delegations expressed doubts about the practicality of the Panel; it would be difficult to keep the list of members up to date, and the nomination in advance of persons who would be qualified for any of the diverse tasks which might arise was a problem.[34] The United States, however, appeared to express the general sentiment, apart from that of the Soviet bloc, that the adoption of the Secretary-General's plan for establishing the Service and Panel would be "distinct progress" towards increasing the efficiency of United Nations Missions. The revised proposal, in the United States view, had "none of the defects which had led to objections on the part of many delegations, including the United States delegation," to Mr. Lie's original plan. There was no question that the Secretary-General had the legal right to reorganize Secretariat services in the fashion proposed, and to provide Observers if requested to do so by United Nations organs; talk of the plans running counter to Article 43 was obviously unfounded.[35]

In short, the Committee displayed considerable consensus in support of the new proposal. An Israeli amendment which would have authorized the Secretary-General to place Field Service personnel at the disposal of United Nations Missions only in response to a General Assembly or Security Council resolution was withdrawn in the face of substantial opposition,[36] including that of the Secretary-General. Lebanese amendments designed to increase local control over the possible arming of the Service and over the nationality

right to recruit and maintain an armed force of its own. The right to have an army remained the exclusive right of States. Even Article 43 of the Charter made no mention of the United Nations right to form an army of its own. That article dealt with the undertaking by Member States ... to make available to the Security Council contingents of their own armed forces. No international army and no international military unit could be founded on the basis of the Charter's provisions."

[31] *Ibid.*, pp. 97, 107, 109–110. Lebanon suggested that the UN organ which appointed the Mission should decide whether local units or Field Service personnel should be employed, rather than leaving this delicate question to the Secretary-General (at p. 112; and see p. 117).

[32] *Ibid.*, p. 97.   [33] *Ibid.*, pp. 97, 112–113, 117.

[34] *Ibid.*, p. 100. The United Kingdom took the lead in espousing these views. For other statements critical of the Panel, see pp. 105, 108–110.

[35] *Ibid.*, pp. 98, 103, 105, 109.   [36] *Ibid.*, pp. 104, 110, 116, 118.

of Panel members were defeated,[37] as was a Polish motion to continue study of the proposal to establish the Field Service and Panel.[38] The resolution on the Field Service proposed by the Special Committee was adopted by a vote of thirty-eight to five, with eight abstentions; that on the Panel, by a vote of twenty-eight to seven, with eighteen abstentions.[39] The General Assembly adopted the resolutions in plenary session on November 22, 1949.[40]

Conclusions

(a) "Acutely conscious of how different things in Palestine could have been had the United Nations had an international force at its disposal,"[41] the Secretary-General initially advanced a plan for the creation of a genuinely international force: a Guard, to be internationally recruited by the Secretary-General, apparently to be under his immediate direction, and to be placed at the disposal of the Security Council – and the General Assembly – if not as a "striking force," then nonetheless as a beginning in "the enforcement of peace." The Guard would, among other things, have truce and plebiscite functions; it would be lightly armed for defensive, and equipped for transport and communications, duties. Mr. Lie's proposal, as delineated in his Harvard speech and his Annual Report, was imaginative, radical, and designed to meet an unquestioned need in a cogent (if not legally unassailable) manner. It was unacceptable.

(b) Even after Mr. Lie retreated somewhat to a more modest proposal, the reception remained cool. As has been pointed out, none of the great Powers supported the substance of the Secretary-General's proposal for the establishment of the Guard; and the sparsity of support in other quarters was notable. The reasons of – and perhaps for – the opposition were varied, and some were not without some merit. It is true that the Charter contains no provision for an internationally recruited force, in contrast with the provision of national contingents; it contains no provision for putting any sort of force at the General Assembly's disposal; yet the truce and plebiscite functions of the Guard – if indeed the Secretary-General's thoughts did not go beyond such – might well have involved the Guard in duties which the Charter contemplated for forces under Article 43. This is not to say that the Secretary-General's plan was lacking in legal basis, but it is to say that legal criticism of it had some foundation. (The same may of course be said of some innovations in United Nations structure which have been carried out.) The financial and practical

---

[37] *Ibid.*, p. 118. [38] *Ibid.* [39] *Ibid.* [40] General Assembly resolution 297 A and B (IV).
[41] Trygve Lie, *In the Cause of Peace* (1954), p. 192.

difficulties were equally real, and possibly more potent. The will to construe the legalities, and to overcome the financial and other practicalities, so as to realize the Secretary-General's plan, was present neither among the great Powers nor among the great voting blocs. Internationalism, or the immediate demands of international events, apparently had just not advanced that far.

(c) The Secretary-General accordingly had no choice but to modify his plan, and this he did materially. The Guard was stripped of its truce and plebiscite functions, its arms, its numbers, probably even of its possibility for growth; placing some of these elements in the Panel was more than dividing the sum in two parts. Indeed, in his concessions to the dispositions of nationalism, the Secretary-General went farther than was required when he proposed that the Field Force be recruited by secondment.

(d) The Secretary-General's revised plan met with broad approval on all sides, particularly as the Field Force was concerned, except the Soviet. The modesty of his revised plan made the immodesty of the Soviet opposition appear the more intemperate.

(e) The Field Force and Panel, while certainly "something useful," hardly constitute that international force which Trygve Lie presciently proposed in 1948, and which Dag Hammarskjöld could have put to such profound use in 1956.

A United Nations "Legion": Introduction

The proposals for a United Nations Field Service and Field Reserve Panel, adopted in 1949, were not designed to, and in fact did not, provide the United Nations with an international police force capable of coercive policing. The Secretary-General's plan for a Guard, especially as it was transformed into the more limited Service and Panel, contemplated not an implement of collective security, but an instrument of peaceful settlement. Its genesis was essentially in the truce experience of Palestine, not the battle experience of Korea. But, in 1951 and 1952, the Secretary-General suggested plans of a different order.

In 1950, under the stimulus of the Korean hostilities, the General Assembly adopted the "Uniting for peace" resolution. That resolution, among other things, constituted a Collective Measures Committee, which, "in consultation with the Secretary-General," was directed to study and report on "methods ... which might be used to maintain and strengthen international peace and security."[42] The Secretary-General, who, throughout the existence of the

---

[42] GAOR, Seventh Session, Supplement No. 17, *Report of the Collective Measures Committee*, 1952, p. 17.

Collective Measures Committee, played a leading, if not the leading, role in the submission of proposals to it, suggested the establishment of a "United Nations legion."

The Plan

As the Secretary-General first proposed his plan for a United Nations Guard in an address at Harvard, so he early spoke of his ideas for a United Nations Legion in a public address before the United Nations Association of Canada:

> Member Governments have been asked to set aside part of their armed forces for United Nations action in case of any future acts of armed aggression. The possibility of creating a separate United Nations Legion composed of volunteers is also being explored.
>
> I have advocated since 1948 the creation of special United Nations forces. As Secretary-General, I feel it is of the utmost importance that the Member Governments agree to provide these forces and that a United Nations Legion also be established, composed of volunteers drawn especially from those countries unable to set aside special United Nations units of their own. These forces should be at the disposal of the Security Council and the General Assembly.[43]

Subsequently, a principal aide of the Secretary-General, Col. Alfred G. Katzin, clarified the proposal further:

> There is no thought on the part of the Secretary-General that a United Nations Legion could be actually organized and operated at the present time as a substitute for national forces acting on behalf of the United Nations ..., or that, indeed, a United Nations Legion could operate independently of such national forces to cope with an aggression, or that it could be of such size and composition as to constitute an international army. Primarily, such a Legion would appear to have practical value and utility as an "organism" within the framework of which additional and supplementary manpower might be organized and through which increased ancillary support and "some combatant support" might be more easily and more rapidly made available by smaller States than would be the case if the extent and nature of their contributions had to await detailed negotiation at the outbreak of an aggression.[44]

The Secretary-General's proposals were submitted to the Collective Measures Committee as "tentative suggestions ... not ... fully developed in their technical aspects."[45] Recognizing that, in resisting aggression, the United Nations could, under existing circumstances, find no substitute for a United Nations force composed of army, navy, and air elements contributed

---

[43] Alfred G. Katzin, "Collective Security: The Work of the Collective Measures Committee," *Annual Review of United Nations Affairs*, 1952 (1953), p. 212.

[44] *Ibid.*, p. 213.   [45] *Report of the Collective Measures Committee* (see note 42), p. 12.

from national forces, the Secretary-General suggested two supplementary techniques of assistance to the UN:[46]

(a) States whose resources would not permit of the contribution of self-contained combat or ancillary units as contemplated in paragraph 8 of the "Uniting for peace" resolution would be invited to consult as to whether, by resort to a United Nations Volunteer Reserve as contemplated by the Secretary-General, or in any other manner, they could alone or jointly with other States similarly placed, organize in advance combatant or auxiliary units (such as labor or transport units) able to be integrated in a United Nations force to resist aggression; and

(b) Potential strength might be added to forces available to any United Nations Executive Military Authority by enlisting, in the military reserve establishments of States willing to participate, the part-time services of individual volunteers. Such a United Nations Volunteer Reserve "in support of United Nations principles to resist aggression"[47] would, in advance, undertake to be trained and held in reserve to that end. Accordingly, the Secretary-General proposed that principles and procedures be developed between the United Nations and States willing to cooperate, whereby use would be made of individual volunteers for United Nations service.

Under the plan, volunteers would be recruited through the existing national military establishments of the participating States. They would be organized into special United Nations Reserve Units or Groups, and maintained in active training or reserve status within national Volunteer Reserve establishments, pending their mobilization for service by the United Nations. Cooperating States would be asked to meet the cost of recruiting, equipping, and training the United Nations Volunteer Reservists as part of their advance contribution to collective security under the United Nations.

Conditions of service by United Nations Volunteer Reservists would be the subject of agreement between the United Nations and the cooperating States, and should, it was proposed, be sufficiently elastic to meet the special needs and requirements of all concerned. Probably, on account of widely differing conditions and circumstances, detailed arrangements would have to be examined and completed on a State-by-State basis. Thus, for example, these arrangements might prescribe that recruits to a United Nations Volunteer Reserve would be available for national service in the same way as any other national reservists. It might similarly be provided that members of

---

[46] *Ibid.*, pp. 12–13.   [47] *Ibid.*, p. 12.

existing national volunteer establishments electing individually to be earmar-ked for United Nations service as United Nations Volunteer Reservists would remain subject to mobilization for national service. It could be provided that volunteers would be mobilized for active United Nations service only if an Executive Military Authority were appointed by the United Nations to resist an act of aggression. It could equally be provided that cooperating States would determine individually whether, for internal security or any other reasons, any volunteers held on their reserve estab-lishments could or could not be released for United Nations service. Again, such States and the United Nations Executive Military Authority would decide between them whether United Nations reservists should be mobilized as part of any force contributed to the Executive Military Authority by the State concerned, or as part of an alternative force, or a combination of both. The proposals should be designed to have the utmost flexibility of application to meet the practical needs of a given situation.

As for command arrangements of United Nations Volunteer Reserve units, the Secretary-General urged that they be worked out with the utmost flexibility to suit the practical needs of cooperating States and the Executive Military Authority. He emphasized the paramount importance of recog-nizing and preserving the international character of the reserve components.

The Secretary-General estimated that "at least 50 or 60,000 volunteers willing to serve the principles of the United Nations might well become available through a United Nations Volunteer Reserve." The Reserve would provide supplementary strength to other forces seconded to a United Nations Executive Military Authority at the time such an Authority was appointed to resist aggression. The Secretary-General submitted that his plan for a Volun-teer Reserve – a force which would be trained in advance on a part-time voluntary basis – if adopted and implemented, would "solve in large part" the financial, as well as the morale, problems inherent in the existence of a standing force inactive for long periods of time (problems of which the critics of his plan for a United Nations Guard had made much and with reason).

The Response

The record of governmental response to the Secretary-General's plan is relatively sparse. Unlike his plan for the Guard, the Legion was not seriously debated in the General Assembly; no Special Committee of the Assembly was constituted to consider it (although the Collective Measures Committee was of course competent to do so and did); and no definitive action was taken, apart from its eventual tabling by the Secretary-General himself.

The Secretary-General did not resourcefully struggle for the acceptance of even a modified version of his plan, as he had in the case of the United Nations Guard. His "tentative suggestions" actually were such; they apparently were advanced by the Secretary-General's representative with considerable caution, and with frank admission of the difficulties that stood in the way of the adoption of them or any other plan which would, in varying measure, provide for an international police force. Colonel Katzin's remarks, while directed towards the problems of an international police force in general rather than those of the Legion in particular, embrace the Legion, and are characteristically enlightening:

> The absence of unanimity among the Great Powers on collective security arrangements, present world tensions, acts of localized aggression, and guerrilla activity in areas of instability make it entirely unrealistic for the United Nations to attempt to pin its hopes on advance pledges of specific forces. Such forces might not bear any relation whatever to the needs of the occasion ... an army of any given size, even though its elements are earmarked in advance for United Nations service, may not be capable of dealing with any aggression which the United Nations is called upon to resist ... while the existence of such armed United Nations forces might, to some extent, allay some public doubts about the effectiveness of the principle of collective security through the United Nations, it would in fact, in all probability, serve very little other purpose ...
>
> There would be undoubted advantage to the United Nations to have information in advance, to the greatest extent possible, of the strength of military forces upon which it could rely in the event that it were faced with the responsibility to conduct an armed action. On the other hand, it must be recognized that in the final analysis, and for so long as universal disarmament is not a major part of any overall United Nations collective-security plan, the United Nations will always have to rely primarily upon the total resources of its Member States to resist an act of aggression. The total resources required may well exceed, in many situations, any small elements of their national armed forces which they might be able safely to earmark specifically in advance for United Nations action ...
>
> The mere existence of an armed force of any given strength is not of itself a guarantee that such a force can be effective, no matter how well equipped. Under conditions of modern warfare, resources of a very far-reaching nature, which extend far beyond the mere "mounting" of a force, are required. Not only must such a force be brought to an area of operations, but it also must be adequately sustained throughout the period of its engagement, whether this extends over weeks, months, or years. Vast ancillary support must be available. Indeed, manufacturing resources of some States in certain circumstances may be required, to a greater or lesser degree, to be directed exclusively or largely to the maintenance of such a force. Commercial shipping and aviation resources may have to be diverted from normal commercial utilization ... It can well be understood,

therefore, without further amplification, that if the United Nations is to face its responsibilities to counter aggression in a practical manner, then, from the outset, it must look to States for more assistance than the mere provision of a given element of armed strength.

But there are also other elements ... which must, under present conditions, govern the capabilities of States to be specific on their advance contributions to the United Nations, no matter how clear their good will or how firm their intention to fulfill their pledges to support the United Nations in resisting aggression.

If we look at the commitments of the Great Powers in the first instance, we shall understand that there are vital strategic considerations which limit their freedom of action. An outbreak of aggression in one area must be considered in relation to other troubled areas and areas of potential aggression. Until there is a fully developed and genuine international security system based on controlled forces and limitation of armaments, the Great Powers individually, rather than the United Nations, will have to assess strategic considerations on a world-wide basis. Especially since the Uniting for Peace Resolution is based on the principle of voluntary cooperation of elements from national armed forces, and bearing in mind that such forces would be mobilized by the United Nations only after the outbreak of aggression, it is clearly a matter of great difficulty for the Great Powers to pledge in advance specific forces for service with the United Nations.

The situation of the smaller States can be somewhat different. But because of their lesser resources and because many of them have regional defense commitments which make it difficult for them to earmark additional specific forces for service with the United Nations, their situation, but for different reasons, has put many of them in much the same position as the Great Powers.[48]

The Secretary-General, in outlining his proposals, stated at the outset that, in his opinion, "the creation of any supra-national self-contained standing force, internationally recruited for a fixed period of full-time service and subject, not to the control of any national government, but to a self-contained United Nations command, was administratively, financially, and militarily impractical at the present time."[49] The Collective Measures Committee's unqualified endorsement of this declaration constitutes one of its few definite reactions to his proposals.[50] The Committee added that, "inasmuch as the Secretary-General's specific proposals do not advocate the organization of a 'legion' in the generally accepted sense of that term, the use of this nomenclature in the context of the present proposals is confusing and misleading and should be abandoned."[51] The Committee observed that it had been unable to give more than "preliminary consideration to the Secretary-General's proposals for a

---

[48] Katzin, "Collective Security," pp. 207–9.

[49] Report of the Collective Measures Committee (see note 42), p. 12.

[50] Ibid. Both the Secretary-General and the Committee took care to limit their statements to the time at which they spoke.

[51] Ibid., p. 12.

United Nations Volunteer Reserve and was not able to take any decision on the merits, in terms either of their political possibilities or of their military feasibility." It concluded that the proposals deserved further consideration by any continuing body the General Assembly might establish and urged each Member State to consider whether, in its own case, certain features of the Secretary-General's proposals would assist it in carrying out the recommendations of the "Uniting for peace" resolution.[52]

The General Assembly's consideration of the report of the Committee was not extended, and references to the Secretary-General's plan were few. Australia, the United States, New Zealand, the Netherlands, and France, in varying degree, supported the plan for a Volunteer Reserve.[53] However, no mention was made of a United Nations Legion or Volunteer Reserve in the resolution adopted by the General Assembly in response to the Collective Measures Committee's report.[54]

The third and, to date, the last report of the Collective Measures Committee, under the caption "Question of a United Nations Volunteer Reserve," declares:

> The second report of the Collective Measures Committee, in dealing with the question of the formation of a United Nations Volunteer Reserve, indicated that the Committee had been able to give only preliminary consideration to the proposals made by the first Secretary-General of the United Nations in this regard. The Committee was subsequently advised that the Secretary-General did not wish, for the time being, to proceed with the proposals. The Committee is of the opinion that no further action or study by it is required on this question.[55]

The Committee in this fashion recorded the Secretary-General's decision, at least "for the time being," to yield to the dual pressures of the depreciation or disinterest of Members, and the doubts of his Secretariat colleagues most closely concerned. For reasons that Governments perhaps did not choose to reveal fully, and for reasons (not necessarily the same) that Colonel Katzin alludes to in the passages quoted from his paper, the verdict, in 1952 and 1953, was that the Secretary-General's plan for a United Nations Legion was not "practical."

---

[52] *Ibid.*
[53] GAOR, Seventh Session, First Committee, 573rd Meeting, March 12, 1953, pp. 400, 442, 448, 453, 461.
[54] General Assembly resolutions 703 (VII), March 17, 1953.   [55] United Nations doc. A/2713.

19

Mini-States and a More Effective United Nations

ℭℌ

Fifty years ago, the First Assembly of the League of Nations demonstrated a higher sense of responsibility than did the General Assembly of the United Nations at its Twenty-Sixth Session, or at its preceding Sessions. The issue then was that of mini-States, an issue which has been very much with the United Nations for the last decade.

Liechtenstein was denied admission to the League by a vote which followed upon a report made to the Assembly. The report noted that:

> Liechtenstein has been recognized de jure by many States. She has concluded a number of Treaties ... The Principality of Liechtenstein possesses a stable Government and fixed frontiers ... There can be no doubt that juridically the Principality of Liechtenstein is a sovereign State, but by reason of her limited area, small population, and her geographical position, she has chosen to depute to others some of the attributes of sovereignty ... Liechtenstein has no army. For the above reasons, we are of the opinion that the Principality of Liechtenstein could not discharge all the international obligations which would be imposed on her by the Covenant.[1]

In 1971, the General Assembly of the United Nations voted to admit Qatar to membership (along with Bahrain and Bhutan). The unanimous recommendation of the Security Council on which this action was based shows no signs of the judiciousness that characterized the League's proceedings of 1920. By 1920, Liechtenstein had been more or less independent for 200 years; by 1971, Qatar had been independent for some weeks. The population of Liechtenstein (not a United Nations Member any more than it was a League Member) is about 21,000; that of Qatar, about 80,000. Qatar's approximately 4,000 square miles – only an approximation, since its frontiers, unlike Liechtenstein's, are not stable and not even fully delimited – are much more

First published in *American Journal of International Law* (1973), 67.
[1] League of Nations, *First Assembly–Plenary Meetings*, Annex C, p. 667.

than Liechtenstein's 62 square miles. They are also far less fertile. Liechtenstein is highly industrialized and richly agricultural; its gross national product compares respectably with Qatar's (which is almost exclusively based on oil); it has no illiteracy and Qatar has much. It has had long if limited experience in international relations; Qatar virtually none.

Why the difference in result? Why are the established European mini-States largely out of the United Nations and the new Asian and African mini-States increasingly in?

It cannot be because the mini-States currently in vogue are any more able to carry out the obligations of the Charter of the United Nations than the older mini-States were able to carry out those of the League Covenant. On the contrary, the obligations imposed upon United Nations Members are much greater than those imposed on Members of the League.

The essential theory of the Covenant was that the League Council would adopt decisions on the basis of unanimity (apart from the disputants) but that the League Members themselves would be left to apply the League Covenant in the light of the findings of League organs. The essential theory of the United Nations is that the Security Council, on which only the five Permanent Members have a veto, can bind all Members, large and small, to take the action the Council decides upon to maintain or restore international peace and security.

The activities of the United Nations are far more diversified, intensive, and expensive than were those of the League. The burdens of meaningful United Nations membership are much more substantial than were those of the League. This is illustrated by the fact that it is United Nations practice for Members to maintain permanent Missions at its headquarters; this was not the custom of the League. Its relatively episodic program did not demand them.

Membership in the United Nations, as Article 4 of the Charter provides, is open to "peace-loving States which accept the obligations contained in the present Charter and, in the judgement of the Organization, are able and willing to carry out these obligations."

What sort of judgment is it that moves the Organization to conclude that Qatar or Bahrain (population, 195,000: area, 231 square miles) is able and willing to carry out the obligations of the Charter – to "fulfil in good faith the obligations assumed by them in accordance with the present Charter," such as the obligation to give the United Nations "every assistance in any action it takes in accordance with the present Charter ..."? Or that the Maldive Islands, admitted to membership in 1965 – population, circa 100,000, capacities to do most anything international, virtually zero – can fulfill

Charter obligations? If the United Nations did not have the improvident rule of paying the cost of transport of five Delegates from each Member to each General Assembly, there is room for doubt whether the Maldives could mount the resources to ferry a Delegation to New York to cast the equal vote it there enjoys with the United States and the Soviet Union. In fact, in 1971, those resources were apparently lacking in any event; no delegation from the Maldives appeared at the Twenty-Sixth Session. Even on so critical and contested an issue as Chinese representation, the Maldives were recorded absent.

When the representative of the United States in the Security Council unwisely supported the admission of the Maldives, he wisely stated:

> Today many of the small emerging entities, however willing, probably do not have the human or economic resources at this stage to meet this second criterion [the ability to carry out Charter obligations]. We would therefore urge that Council Members and other United Nations Members give early and careful consideration to this problem in an effort to arrive at some agreed standards, some lower limits, to be applied in the case of future applicants for United Nations membership.[2]

Secretary-General U Thant expanded upon this theme in 1967. "I would suggest," he submitted in his Annual Report, "that it may be opportune for the competent organs to undertake a thorough and comprehensive study of the criteria for membership in the United Nations, with a view to laying down the necessary limitations on full membership while also defining other forms of association which would benefit both the 'micro-States' and the United Nations."[3]

In December of that year, the United States addressed a letter to the President of the Security Council referring to these remarks of the Secretary-General, suggesting that the time had come to examine the question in terms of general principles and procedures, and further suggesting that the Council's dormant Committee on the Admission of New Members be revived to that end.

But too little has happened since. The United Nations Institute for Training and Research (UNITAR) produced an able study on *Small States and Territories: Status and Problems*.[4] And the Security Council established a Committee of Experts (whose interesting interim report is considered below) to make recommendations on the question. But the Committee has formula-

---

[2] United Nations Security Council, *Official Records*, 1243rd meeting, September 20, 1965.

[3] United Nations doc. A/6701, Add. 1, para. 165, December 13, 1967.

[4] By Jacques Rapoport, Ernest Muteba and Joseph T. Therattil (1971).

ted no recommendations. The suggestions submitted to the Committee reportedly were found by the Legal Counsel of the United Nations not to be consonant with the Charter; the Committee has ceased meeting; and the Security Council has not further considered the problem except in the context of particular applications for membership, which it approves, however doubtful may be the abilities of the applicant to carry out its Charter obligations.

At the meeting of the Committee of Experts of September 26, 1969, the United States submitted a proposal[5] for associate membership in the United Nations, the essentials of which are as follows:

> We note that under Article 4 (1) of the United Nations Charter, peace-loving States that accept the obligations of the Charter and, in the judgement of the Organization, are "able and willing" to carry them out are eligible for membership in the United Nations. We are concerned about the ability of some of these exceptionally small new States to carry out such obligations. We believe membership for them would entail a disproportionately heavy burden. At the same time, we believe that association with the United Nations of States not able to assume all the burdens of full membership is desirable from the standpoint both of their own political, economic and social development, and of the contribution they could make to the attainment of the broad objectives of the United Nations.
>
> Accordingly, the United States proposes that there be established the status of United Nations Associate Member, each recipient of which shall:
>
> (a) enjoy the rights of a Member in the General Assembly except to vote or hold office;
> (b) enjoy appropriate rights in the Security Council upon the taking of requisite action by the Council;
> (c) enjoy appropriate rights in the Economic and Social Council and in its appropriate regional commission and other sub-bodies, upon the taking of requisite action by the Council;
> (d) enjoy access to United Nations assistance in the economic and social fields;
> (e) bear the obligations of a Member except the obligation to pay financial assessments.
>
> The admission to Associate Membership in the United Nations will be effected in accordance with the same procedures provided by the Charter for the admission of Members. States which opt for Associate Membership would submit to the Secretary-General a declaration of willingness to abide by the principles of the United Nations, as set forth in the Charter.

---

[5] United Nations doc. S/9836, Annex 1, June 15, 1970.

On May 25, 1970, the United Kingdom submitted an alternative proposal to the Committee, in the form of a working paper[6] which provided:

The purpose of any arrangement should be to meet the needs of very small States which wish to be Members of the United Nations but which would find difficulty in meeting all the financial and administrative obligations involved.

The aims are first to respect the sovereignty and independence of the States concerned and also to enable them to enjoy the general benefits of membership of the Organization.

Accordingly we suggest for further examination an arrangement whereby a State could voluntarily renounce certain rights (in particular voting and election in certain United Nations bodies) but otherwise enjoy all the rights and privileges of membership. This arrangement (which would not require amendment of the Charter) might be embodied in a declaration to be made by a new State at the time of its application on the following lines:

The State of … hereby applies for membership of the United Nations in accordance with Article 4 of the Charter.

In submitting this application, the State of … expresses its desire to enjoy the privileges and assume the obligations of membership of the United Nations and to be accorded the protection and assistance which the United Nations can provide, in particular with regard to the maintenance of its territorial integrity and political independence; and declares that it does not wish to participate in voting in any organ of the United Nations, nor to be a candidate for election to any of the three Councils established by the Charter or to any subordinate organ of the General Assembly.

On this basis and on the understanding that the assessment of its financial contribution would be at a nominal level, the State of … declares that it accepts the obligations contained in the Charter of the United Nations and solemnly undertakes to fulfil them.

The State of … further understands that it may at any time, after the expiration of one year's notice to the Secretary-General of its intention to that effect and after its acceptance of a revised assessment of its financial contribution, avail itself of those rights of membership the exercise of which it has hereby voluntarily renounced.

We believe this suggestion to be fully compatible with the relevant Articles of the United Nations Charter. If, as a voluntary exercise of its sovereignty, as part of its request for membership, a State renounces the exercise of certain rights of membership in a manner acceptable to the Organization and its other Members, this would not be contrary to the provision of Article 2 (1), which is concerned to safeguard the *sovereign* equality of all the Members. The position would only reflect the free and sovereign choice of that State and the recognition and acceptance by the Organization of the choice made.

[6] *Ibid.*, Annex 2.

The grounds on which the Legal Counsel of the United Nations reportedly found both these proposals incompatible with the Charter have not been made public. It may nevertheless be worthwhile to endeavor to assess their legal and practical merit.

It is clear that the Charter contemplates neither associate membership nor membership coupled with a renunciation of vote.

This is indicated not only by the terms of Article 4, which contains no such special provisions, but also by provisions of three kinds: those which provide for the sovereign equality of the Members; those which provide that Members shall have a vote in specified organs; and those which specify when Members in attendance at an organ shall have no vote.

Thus the Preamble to the Charter speaks of "the equal rights . . . of nations large and small. . ." The Purposes and Principles of the Charter speak of "respect for the principle of equal rights and self-determination of peoples." And Article 2 lists first among the Principles in accordance with which the Organization and its Members shall act: "the sovereign equality of all its Members." Furthermore, Article 78 provides that the relationship among Members of the United Nations "shall be based on respect for the principle of sovereign equality."

If the principle of sovereign equality is applied to mini-States, it may be argued that, if they are accepted as "States" – as they traditionally have been and currently are – which are "peace loving" (they hardly have a choice), and if the Organization's judgment is that they are able and willing to carry out the Charter's obligations, then they must be admitted with equal rights.

The conclusion that a mini-State Member of the United Nations shall enjoy the vote that larger States Members enjoy is reinforced by Article 18, paragraph 1: "Each member of the General Assembly shall have one vote"; Article 27, paragraph 1: "Each member of the Security Council shall have one vote"; and the like provisions of Article 67 in respect of the Economic and Social Council and Article 89 in respect of the Trusteeship Council.

Moreover, it may be argued that, when, under the regime of the Charter, it is intended that a Member have no vote, it is so specified. Thus Article 19 provides that a Member in the requisite arrears in its contributions to the Organization "shall have no vote in the General Assembly." *Per contra*, a Member not in the requisite arrears shall have a vote in the General Assembly. Furthermore, under Articles 31 and 32, a Member State not a Member of the Security Council may be invited to participate in its discussions under certain circumstances, but "without vote." Under Article 69, the Economic and Social Council shall invite any Member to participate "without vote" in its deliberations on any matter of particular concern to that Member.

There are additional, lesser arguments which may be directed against the US proposal. Article 9, paragraph 1 of the Charter provides that: "The General Assembly shall consist of all the Members of the United Nations." May it consist of associate Members as well, without amending the Charter to that effect? Alternatively, if the United States proposal is strained to read as one for "the status" not of associate membership but for an "associate status" for mini-States not involving membership (whether full or associate), then arguably it would have to be modified to conform to the Charter's prescriptions respecting non-Members (most notably, Article 11, paragraph 2; Article 32; and Article 35, paragraph 2).

The United Kingdom proposal clearly is one for membership – membership with a renunciation of rights. It thus may be said to contain the disabilities that the proposal of the United States does, except that, since the mini-States would be "Members," the provisions of Article 9 would be respected, at least formally. It endeavors to deal with provisions such as that of Article 18, paragraph 1 by the means of voluntary renunciation of the right to vote. But may a Member lawfully renounce as fundamental a right as that to vote, not episodically but indefinitely and by a binding legal undertaking?

It may accordingly be maintained that Article 4 of the Charter is exhaustive in its treatment of the subject of membership in the United Nations (apart from the provisions for original membership in Article 3); and that, especially in the light of the foregoing considerations, it is not lawful to afford States other means of becoming parties to the Charter or to enable them to become parties in a status other than that of Member.

If it may be presumed that the Legal Counsel of the United Nations, in criticizing the United States and British proposals, advanced considerations such as these, what may be said in defense of those proposals?

As to the principle of sovereign equality, the Charter itself honors it in the breach. Most notably, under Article 27, only the Permanent Members of the Security Council have a veto. And there are lesser distinctions made in electing Non-Permanent Members of the Security Council – or there would be if the Charter criteria for elections were taken into account, as they are not – not to speak of selecting only certain members for membership in other organs (the Trusteeship Council and, simply in the sense that it is not a committee of the whole, the Economic and Social Council). In short, the Charter applies the principle of sovereign equality where the interests of the Organization are presumed to benefit from it and modifies that principle where the interests of the Organization are presumed so to require. May not that principle be further modified in the case of mini-States?

As to the provisions of the Charter which provide that a Member of the

General Assembly and other organs "shall" have one vote, it may be argued that, as the membership has uniformly interpreted the Charter, a Member is not required to vote. It may abstain, or may be recorded as not partipating or absent. What then is to prevent a Member from uniformly so acting, by renouncing its right to vote indefinitely and in return for a financial undertaking by the Organization? (It should be noted that the British proposal is for indefinite but not irrevocable renunciation of specific rights.)

As to the provisions of the Charter which specify the circumstances in which a Member has no vote, these, on the same reasoning, are no more dispositive. It is established practice – constituting on that account an authoritative interpretation of the Charter – that there is at least one circumstance additional to those set out in the Charter in which Members have no vote: the circumstance in which the absence of a Permanent Member of the Security Council does not constitute a negative vote or veto of a Security Council decision. (It may be added that a circumstance in which a Member "shall have no vote in the General Assembly" – that foreseen in Article 19 – has been deliberately misapplied by the General Assembly, since the Soviet Union, allied States, and France have continued to vote in the Assembly despite the fact their their arrears in payments of contributions exceed the level prescribed by Article 19 to require suspension of vote.)[7]

The British proposal appears to be a most constructive development of the American. It apparently assumes membership by mini-States that are "able and willing" to carry out the obligations of the Charter except for certain financial and administrative obligations. It spells out explicitly what inheres in the proposal of the United States: a voluntary renunciation by the applicant mini-State of voting and electoral rights in return for no or nominal assessments. As the working paper of the United Kingdom stresses, that renunciation would "only reflect the free and sovereign choice" of the mini-State and the recognition and acceptance by the Organization of the choice made. It is not extraordinary for States to renounce rights they otherwise would enjoy under a treaty; this would be such a case. While there are undoubtedly some rights in international law that a State cannot lawfully renounce, does *jus cogens* forbid revocable renunciation of the right to vote?

Legally, then, while the Anglo-American proposals do not conform to the letter of the Charter, and still less are contemplated by it, it may be argued that they are not excluded by it. It may be doubted whether the drafters of the Charter considered the question of mini-States or of associate mem-

---

[7] See (S. M. Schwebel), "Article 19 of the Charter of the United Nations, Memorandum of Law," *American Journal of International Law* (1964) 58, p. 753, and Chapter 20, this volume.

bership at all.[8] Yet the Charter, particularly as it has been interpreted through the subsequent practice of the parties, arguably is open to a construction that would permit the admission of mini-States coupled with a partial renunciation of rights in return for a partial absolution of obligations. It is submitted that the merit of this legal approach is more clearly illustrated by the terms of the British proposal than that of the United States. In a sense, the Security Council would find a mini-State not "able" to fulfill certain financial and electoral obligations; these obligations would be waived, in return for the mini-State's renunciation of certain rights. If the membership of the Council and the Organization at large were willing to treat such an arrangement as within the permissible scope of interpretation of the Charter, there would not seem to be an insuperable legal barrier to their doing so.

Such an interpretation arguably would comport with that cardinal rule of interpretation, that of "effectiveness." For it is clear that the Organization's functioning would be promoted by such an arrangement which, for example, by curbing the influx of voting mini-States, would tend to give more meaning to the provisions of Article 18 for a two-thirds vote in the General Assembly than those provisions otherwise would have.

It should be noted that three of the Regional Economic Commissions of the United Nations, ECAFE, ECLA, and ECA, have members expressly designated as associate members. These associate members lack the right to vote. Among these territories (essentially non-self-governing) are some very small entities which, but for their non-self-governing character, would be mini-States. The fact that subsidiary organs of the United Nations, such as the Regional Economic Commissions, have been able to embrace a category of associate, non-voting membership without Charter provision or amendment to that effect may be viewed as a precedent capable of wider application to membership in the United Nations itself. However, certain Specialized Agencies of the United Nations, notably UNESCO and FAO, found it necessary to amend their constitutions to provide for associate membership, without vote, for territories not responsible for the conduct of their international relations. These examples cut in opposite directions, but their force is in any event limited by the fact that they do not concern independent States.

Of course, both Specialized Agencies of the United Nations and specialized organs of the United Nations, such as UNCTAD and UNIDO, have among their membership States that are not members of the United Nations; and among them are some mini-States. That fact indicates that mini-States

---

[8] Russell and Muther's *A History of the United Nations Charter* (1958) indicates no such consideration.

already can secure some of the benefits of United Nations membership, including the tangible benefits of the United Nations Development Program, without joining the United Nations at all. Nevertheless, the record also demonstrates that that arrangement is not sufficiently attractive to them; nearly all newly independent mini-States have sought and received United Nations membership. It may be cogently maintained that they should indeed be content with less, but the easy grasp of something more has proven too tempting. Suggestions that the United Nations attempt to deal with the problem by codifying the various provisions of this kind, which are extensive, into an "associate status" for mini-States which would entail neither membership nor associate membership make sense, except for the fatal flaw of disinterest by mini-States.

The practical merits of the Anglo-American approach are multiple. Mini-States would enjoy those benefits of membership that should mean the most to them, including the prestige of a kind of membership; they would be absolved of financial burdens which are proportionately heavy; the United Nations would be the more fully representative; but miniscule entities, representing small fractions of mankind, would not vote or serve on bodies in a way that unduly distorts the representative character of those bodies.

In view of the merits of associate membership for mini-States and the demerits of their continued, not to speak of additional, membership in the United Nations, it may be argued that associate membership should be incorporated into the United Nations but by way of Charter amendment rather than liberal interpretation. That naturally would obviate the admitted, substantial difficulties of constituting a category of associate membership without Charter amendment. Since the Permanent Member of the Security Council which at one time was the most vigorous backer of the admission of mini-States to unqualified membership, the United Kingdom, more lately has taken the lead in proposing the measures described above, it presumably would welcome such an amendment; and it is not clear that any other Permanent Member would be disposed to block it by its failure to ratify. It might even be possible to garner a two-thirds vote of the General Assembly to adopt an amendment to be submitted for ratification.

While opening the avenue of associate membership in the United Nations either by amendment or interpretation of the Charter may be seen as belatedly closing the barn door through which too many mini-States have already rushed, it should not be assumed that mini-States themselves necessarily and uniformly would find such arrangements unattractive.

Indeed, in view of the complaints of The Gambia about the burden of assessments,[9] and of the Maldives seeming to have dropped out, even some mini-States already Members might welcome associate membership as a realistic mode of participation in international organization.

[9] Twentieth United Nations General Assembly, *Official Records*, 1332nd meeting, September 21, 1965; Twenty-Second United Nations General Assembly, *Official Records*, 1566th meeting, September 25, 1967.

20

Article 19 of the Charter of the United Nations: Memorandum of Law

Summary

ↄ

This memorandum[1] contains an analysis of the considerations of law involved in the application of Article 19 of the Charter of the United Nations. Its conclusions may be summarized as follows:

A. The first sentence of Article 19, which provides that a Member in arrears to a specified extent "shall have no vote in the General Assembly," entails no decision of the General Assembly to suspend a Member's vote; it is mandatory and automatic in effect. The second sentence, which provides that the General Assembly "may, nevertheless, permit such a Member to vote if it is satisfied that the failure to pay is due to conditions beyond the control of the Member," is permissive in effect.

B. The records of the San Francisco Conference demonstrate the intention of the drafters of the Charter that the application of the first sentence of Article 19 entail no decision of the General Assembly to suspend a Member's vote.

C. The practice of the United Nations confirms the plain meaning of Article 19 and the intention of the Charter's drafters.

D. The fact that a Member is in arrears within the terms of Article 19 is, by established practice, computed and reported by the Secretary-General, or reported by the Committee on Contributions on the basis of the computations of the Secretary-General.

E. Assessments for peacekeeping operations, including those for the United Nations Emergency Force (UNEF) and Organisation des Nations Unies Congo (ONUC), are included in the computation of arrears within the terms of Article 19.

First published in *American Journal of International Law* (1964), 58, p. 753.
[1] Prepared by the Office of the Legal Adviser, Department of State, February, 1964. The memorandum was written by Stephen M. Schwebel in his then capacity of Assistant Legal Adviser for United Nations Affairs.

F. The Committee on Contributions advises the General Assembly on the application of the second sentence of Article 19, a provision which has no bearing on willful failure to pay.

G. Differing interpretations of Article 19 are without merit.

H. The analogous constitutional provisions and practice of the Specialized Agencies similarly show that (*i*) a provision that a Member in arrears "shall have no vote" is mandatory and automatic in effect, and (*ii*) the finding of the fact of arrears is a ministerial, mathematical calculation performed by the Secretariat and accepted by the Assembly without challenge.

The Mandatory and Automatic Application of the Provision That a Member "Shall Have No Vote"

Article 19 of the United Nations Charter provides:

> A Member of the United Nations which is in arrears in the payment of its financial contributions to the Organization shall have no vote in the General Assembly if the amount of its arrears equals or exceeds the amount of the contributions due from it for the preceding two full years. The General Assembly may, nevertheless, permit such a Member to vote if it is satisfied that the failure to pay is due to conditions beyond the control of the Member.

It is plain that the application of the second sentence of Article 19 is permissive: the General Assembly "may ... permit" a Member in the requisite arrears to vote "if it is satisfied that the failure to pay is due to conditions beyond the control of the Member." It has been contended that the application of the first sentence of Article 19 is likewise permissive. It has been suggested that, just as a General Assembly decision is required to implement the second sentence of Article 19, a General Assembly decision is required to implement the first sentence; and that, absent a decision of the General Assembly depriving a Member of its vote, a Member in arrears within the meaning of Article 19 continues to enjoy its voting rights unimpaired. It has been argued that, since suspension of a Member's right to vote in the General Assembly is a matter of great importance, the effecting of suspension requires an exercise of the General Assembly's discretion; it requires a decision and, indeed, a decision on an "important question" (as that term is employed in Article 18), with the result that the taking of that decision requires a vote of a two-thirds majority.

It has otherwise been contended that, even if the mandatory and automatic application of Article 19 is conceded, nevertheless the General Assembly itself must, as a condition of the article's application, first find as a fact that a Member is in arrears within the terms of Article 19; and that the General Assembly's so finding is a determination of an "important question" which, by the terms of Article 18, requires a two-thirds majority of the Members present and voting.

These contentions will be discussed in turn. It will be shown that the terms of the Charter, the proceedings at San Francisco, the provisions of the Organization's Financial Regulations and the practice pursued in accordance with them, the conclusions of the Secretary-General and the President of the Fourth Special Session of the General Assembly, and the analogous constitutional provisions and practice of the Specialized Agencies, all demonstrate that (*a*) the first sentence of Article 19 neither requires nor permits a General Assembly decision to suspend a Member's vote; and (*b*) establishment of the fact of arrears within the terms of Article 19 results from a mathematical computation performed by the Secretary-General in accordance with rules laid down by the General Assembly.

The argument which would assimilate the permissive language of the second sentence of Article 19 to the mandatory language of the first sentence is without merit. The terms of the Charter are clear and decisive. The first sentence of Article 19 provides that a Member of the United Nations in the requisite arrears "*shall* have no vote in the General Assembly." From the fact of the requisite arrears, the consequence of loss of vote follows automatically. The question is not one of the General Assembly's discretion in suspending the voting rights of a Member; the question rather is whether the requisite arrears exist. On the determination of that question more is said below, but, in short, the existence of the requisite arrears is determined by the facts shown by the accounts of the Organization. Given the requisite arrears within the terms of Article 19, a Member has no vote in the General Assembly. "The General Assembly *may*, nevertheless, *permit* such a Member to vote if it is satisfied that the failure to pay is due to conditions beyond the control of the Member."

The mandatory and automatic character of the first sentence of Article 19 emerges with even greater force from a study of the Charter's French text. It provides that a Member of the United Nations in the requisite arrears in the payment of its contributions "ne peut participer au vote à l'Assemblée Générale." The Spanish text provides that such a Member "no tendrá voto." A literal translation from the Russian prescribes that a Member in the requisite arrears "is deprived of the right to vote in the General Assembly." A literal translation from the Chinese provides that such a Member "shall lose its right to vote in the General Assembly."

Where the Charter is meant to be mandatory in effect, it uses mandatory language: the General Assembly "shall." Where the Charter is intended to be permissive in effect, it uses permissive language: the General Assembly "may." Examples could be multiplied. Two further references suffice to supplement that of Article 19: Article 20 provides that the General Assembly "shall" meet in regular annual Sessions. Article 22 provides that the General Assembly "may" establish such subsidiary organs as it deems necessary. The difference is plain, and it is vital.

The pertinence and importance of the Charter's distinction between mandatory provisions and permissive provisions is demonstrated by that Article of the Charter which, in addition to Article 19, relates to suspension of a right: Article 5, which provides for suspension not of the single right of voting in the General Assembly but for suspension "from the exercise of the rights and privileges of membership ..." Article 5 provides:

> A Member of the United Nations against which preventive or enforcement action has been taken by the Security Council may be suspended from the exercise of the rights and privileges of membership by the General Assembly upon the recommendation of the Security Council. The exercise of these rights and privileges may be restored by the Security Council.

It will be noted that Article 5 specifies that a Member against which preventive or enforcement action has been taken "may" – not "shall" but "may" – be suspended. In contrast, Article 19 provides that a Member in the requisite arrears "shall" – not "may" but "shall" – have no vote in the General Assembly.

The second sentence of Article 19 reinforces the conclusion that suspension of vote under that Article requires no decision by the General Assembly. It provides that: "The General Assembly may, nevertheless, permit such a Member to vote if it is satisfied that the failure to pay is due to conditions beyond the control of the Member." Now it is plain that, normally, all Members of the United Nations have the right to vote. Indeed, Article 18, paragraph 1, of the Charter provides that: "Each member of the General Assembly shall have one vote." Thus, there would be no purpose in Article 19 providing that: "The General Assembly may ... permit" a Member in the requisite arrears to vote unless that Member's voting rights in the General Assembly were already suspended. The General Assembly need not grant permission to a Member to do what it is entitled to do. But the General Assembly must "permit" a Member in the requisite arrears to vote if that Member is to be entitled to vote. Without such permission, a Member in the requisite arrears "shall have no vote in the General Assembly."

The records of the San Francisco Conference demonstrate the intention of the drafters of the Charter that the application of the first sentence of Article 19 entail no decision of the General Assembly to suspend a Member's vote. They further demonstrate their intention to accord the General Assembly discretion in the application of the second sentence. Thus, the Revised Report of the Rapporteur (Judge Alfaro of Panama) of Commission II, adopted by the Plenary Session of the San Francisco Conference, declares that:

> The Assembly will be a body on which every member of the United Nations is represented and in which every member has one vote. A member which has fallen two years in arrears on its financial obligations to the Organization, however *will not* be allowed to vote *except by special decision of the Assembly*. On important questions a two-thirds majority will be required, but otherwise decision will be made by a majority vote.
>
> The Assembly *will have the right*, upon a recommendation of the Security Council, to admit new members, *to suspend the rights and privileges of members against which preventive or enforcement action is taken by the Security Council*, and to expel members (*UNCIO*, Vol. 8, pp. 265–266; emphasis supplied).

The first paragraph quoted of the Report of the Rapporteur sets forth the rule that a Member in the requisite arrears "will not be allowed to vote." The exception to the rule is that, "by special decision of the Assembly," a Member whose voting rights are suspended may be allowed to vote. In contrast with this mandatory régime, which is subject only to the special exception of the second sentence of Article 19, "the Assembly will have the right ... to suspend the rights and privileges of members against which preventive or enforcement action is taken by the Security Council." Thus, in treating Article 19, the Rapporteur speaks in mandatory terms. He confines the General Assembly's "decision" to that of allowing a Member in the requisite arrears to vote. But when the Rapporteur turns from Article 19 to Article 5, he purposefully provides that: "The Assembly will have the right" – that is, the discretion – to suspend the rights and privileges of membership.[2]

---

[2] Article 19 has its origins primarily in amendments proposed at San Francisco by the delegations of India, the Netherlands, and Australia (*UNCIO, Documents* (1945), Vol. 8, pp. 508–509). These amendments all import that a Member in the requisite arrears has no vote, with no decision of the General Assembly being taken to deprive it of its vote. Committee II/1 of the San Francisco Conference, in response to these amendments, recommended "that States failing to fulfill their financial obligations should be deprived of all voting rights in the Assembly as long as they are in arrears. In its discussions of this matter, the experience of the League of Nations was cited as indicating the need for such a penalty ... It also recommends that the General Assembly should be empowered to waive this penalty if the default of a member is due to causes beyond its control" (*ibid.*, p. 453). The Committee accordingly proposed the following provision:

> Each member of the Organization shall have one vote in the General Assembly. A member which is in arrears in the payment of its financial contributions to the Organization shall have no vote so long as its arrears amount to its contributions for two full years. The General Assembly may waive the

The practice of the United Nations in respect of the mandatory and automatic character of Article 19, while slender, is nevertheless illuminating. It shows that no affirmative action is expected of the General Assembly in application of the first sentence of Article 19. At the opening of the Fourth Special Session of the General Assembly on May 14, 1963, Haiti was in arrears within the terms of that Article. The Secretary-General of the United Nations accordingly wrote a letter to the President of the General Assembly, dated May 14, 1963, as follows:

> Dear Mr. President,
>
> At the present time one Member State, Haiti, is in arrears in the payment of its financial contribution to the United Nations within the terms of Article 19 of the Charter which provides as follows:
>
>> A Member of the United Nations which is in arrears in the payment of its financial contributions to the Organization shall have no vote in the General Assembly if the amount of its arrears equals or exceeds the amount of the contributions due from it for the preceding two full years. The General Assembly may, nevertheless, permit such a Member to vote if it is satisfied that the failure to pay is due to conditions beyond the control of the Member.
>
> The arrear contributions due from the Government of Haiti exceed by $22,400 the amount of the contributions due from it for the preceding two full

penalty if it is satisfied that the reasons for delay in payment are beyond the control of the State in question.   (*Ibid.*, p. 457.)

The Secretariat of the Conference suggested, in transmitting this text to the Coordination Committee, that it be revised to substitute for the words "waive the penalty" the words "restore the privilege of voting" (*UNCIO, Documents* [1954], Vol. 18, p. 174). The Coordination Committee, which could make no substantive change in the draft provisions, being confined to questions of organization, language clarification, and consistency of committee decisions (see Russell and Muther, *A History of the United Nations Charter* [1958], p. 641), recast the second sentence of what became Article 19 substantially as it appears in the Charter. In the course of so doing, a discussion took place among three of its fourteen members with regard to the wording of the second sentence, in which the discretionary nature of the General Assembly's authority under that sentence was restated (*UNCIO, Documents* [1954], Vol. 17, p. 54). Subsequently, the Soviet member of the Coordination Committee, Professor Golunsky, in referring to the intention to restrict loss of vote to the General Assembly, stated that the Article "clearly meant that the Members in arrears could not vote in the General Assembly" (*ibid.*, p. 350). The final, governing interpretation of Article 19 at San Francisco, which was unanimously adopted by the Conference's Ninth Plenary Session (*UNCIO, Documents* [1945], Vol. 1, p. 623), is the Revised Report of the Rapporteur of Commission II which is quoted in the body of this memorandum.

Of further interest is the Department of State's *Report to the President on the Results of the San Francisco Conference* of June 26, 1945: "The Conference made only one change of substance in the portions of the Dumbarton Oaks texts relating to the structure and proceedings of the General Assembly itself. This was to add a provision depriving a Member of the right to vote if it is two years or more in arrears in the payment of its financial contributions. This amendment, which was submitted in various forms by five different Delegations, was adopted with the overwhelming support of the representatives of nations large and small. In order to prevent undue hardship, it has been provided that the General Assembly should have the power to waive the penalty if the non-payment of contributions is due to causes beyond the control of the Member in question (Article 19)" (p. 60).

years, and a payment exceeding that amount would be necessary in order to reduce the arrears below the limit specified in Article 19.

Yours sincerely,
U Thant
Secretary-General

The President of the General Assembly replied to the Secretary-General by letter dated May 15, 1963, as follows:

Dear Mr. Secretary-General,

I have received your letter of 14 May 1963, informing me that, at the opening of the Fourth Special Session of the General Assembly, Haiti was in arrears in the payment of its financial contribution to the United Nations within terms of Article 19 of the Charter. I would have made an announcement drawing the attention of the General Assembly to the loss of voting rights in the Assembly of the Member State just mentioned, under the first sentence of Article 19, had a formal count of vote taken place in the presence of a representative of that State at the opening plenary meeting. As no such vote took place, and as the representative of Haiti was not present, this announcement became unnecessary.

I am transmitting a copy of your letter and of my present reply to the Chairman of the Fifth Committee at the present Special Session so that he may be informed of the situation which will give rise to the loss of voting rights in the Fifth Committee of the Member concerned if the situation is not previously rectified. I am informed, in this respect, that the representative of Haiti will very shortly make the payment necessary to render the first sentence of Article 19 inapplicable.

Yours sincerely,
Muhammad Zafrulla Khan
President
Fourth Special Session of
the General Assembly

The foregoing exchange of letters was transmitted to the Permanent Missions of States Members of the United Nations for their information, by note dated May 20, 1963.

The President of the General Assembly, in the course of a television interview on May 19, 1963, had occasion to amplify the view contained in the letters of May 14 and 15. Questions put to the President, and his answers, follow:

Question: Sir, as you know, the Charter of the United Nations provides sanctions or punitive measures against any country which falls in arrears to the extent of two years' default in its dues. Do you believe that sanction should be applied now to countries which are or will be in default, such as Haiti was until the other day, or that it should be applied against say the Soviet Union which is likely to be in serious default in the near future?"

Mr. Zafrulla Khan: The matter has nothing to do with my opinion or belief. The Article is perfectly clear. Article 19 of the Charter says that when that situation arises which you have mentioned, that a Member is in default up to a certain point, it has no vote in the Assembly. It is not for me to decide whether it has or it hasn't. The English version says it shall have no vote and the French version says it cannot vote. It applies automatically.

The second portion of the Article provides, however, that the Assembly might, as it were, suspend the operation of the first part if it finds that the default was due to conditions over which the defaulting member has no control. But so far as the first part is concerned, it comes into force automatically when that situation arises.

Question: In other words, if Haiti had shown up on the first day of the Session and been in arrears as it was, you would not have allowed Haiti to vote?

Mr. Zafrulla Khan: If a vote had been taken and Haiti had been present, I would have had to announce that Haiti would not be able to participate in the vote.

Question: And if the Soviet Union in a year or two – next year, for instance – is sufficiently in arrears to lose its vote – would you deprive it from exercising its vote?

Mr. Zafrulla Khan: It has nothing to do with any particular Member. All Members stand on the same footing.

Question: Is there a general feeling in the General Assembly that any country that falls in [the requisite] arrears must automatically be deprived of its vote?

Mr. Zafrulla Khan: I do not know whether that is the feeling in the Assembly or not, but that is what the Charter says.

The Government of Haiti, in the course of the Fourth Special Session of the General Assembly, paid a portion of its arrears sufficient to absolve it from the application of Article 19. It did so before its delegation appeared at any meeting of the Assembly's Plenary Session or any meeting of the single Main Committee then sitting, the Fifth Committee.

The application of Article 19 also arose in 1958. The Report of the Committee on Contributions to the Thirteenth Session noted the fact that, at the time of its Report, which was dated August, 1958, Bolivia had not paid part of its contribution for 1955, as well as its total contributions for 1956, 1957, and 1958. The Report continued: "The attention of the General Assembly is therefore invited to the terms of Article 19 of the Charter, which provides: ..." (A/3890, p. 5). As the Secretary-General later stated: "Before the opening of the General Assembly session, arrangements had, however, been made by the Member State concerned for payment of the outstanding arrears" (*ICJ Pleadings, Certain Expenses of the United Nations (Article 17, paragraph 2 of the Charter*, p. 54).

The practice of the United Nations in implementing Article 19 is in most respects scant because the very great majority of Members have paid their assessments or, being in arrears, have nevertheless paid enough to avoid that

Article's application. Thus, while there were, shortly before the Fourth Special Session of the General Assembly convened in 1963, ten Members in arrears within the terms of Article 19, nine of them made payment sufficient to avoid the Article by the time the Session opened. (The tenth Member was Haiti.) Among them were Hungary and Cuba – Members whose liability under Article 19 was subject to the inclusion in the computation of their arrears of assessments for ONUC and UNEF.

What does the practice of the Organization indicate? It shows that Members in arrears within the terms of Article 19 have recognized the mandatory and automatic force of that Article by not even appearing in Plenary Session and in Main Committee. The Charter requires that a Member in the requisite arrears shall have no vote in the General Assembly. It does not oblige such a Member to refrain otherwise from participating in the Assembly's proceedings. But such has been the deference to Article 19 that Members falling within its terms have managed to make sufficient payment in time to avoid its application or, failing that, were absent from the proceedings of the Assembly, both in Plenary Session and in Main Committee, until making payment.[3]

The computation of arrears under Article 19

The terms of the Charter, the provisions of the General Assembly's Rules of Procedure and of the Financial Regulations, the extensive, established practice followed in pursuance of those Rules and Regulations, and the large body of analogous practice of the Specialized Agencies combine to demonstrate that establishment of the fact of arrears within the terms of Article 19 is not a matter of General Assembly decision. What is required for loss of vote is not a determination of the fact of arrearage, but the mere existence of the requisite arrears. The calculation and report of their existence by the Secretary-General is the result of his routine and required implementation of the Financial Regulations. It is a question not of General Assembly decision, but of accounting computation.

By the terms of Article 19, a Member in arrears in the payment of its financial contributions to the Organization shall have no vote in the General

---

[3] The practice of the Organization, as exemplified in the Haitian case, also confirms that suspension of vote under Article 19 applies to the Main Committees of the General Assembly. In transmitting the exchange of letters between the Secretary-General and the President to the Chairman of the Fifth Committee, "so that he may be informed of the situation which will give rise to the loss of voting rights in the Fifth Committee of the Member concerned if the situation is not previously rectified," the President both reaffirmed the automatic and mandatory effect of Article 19 and took note of that Article's embracing the Main Committees, as well as Plenary Session, of the General Assembly.

Assembly only "if the amount of its arrears equals or exceeds the amount of contributions due from it for the preceding two full years." Thus the finding of whether a Member is in arrears within the terms of the Article requires a totaling of the amount of its arrears on contributions due from it, a totaling of the amount of contributions due from it for the preceding two full years, and the mathematical conclusion as to whether the first sum equals or exceeds the second. This is an arithmetical, not a political, decision. It is no more required to be made by the General Assembly than is any other computation in which the Secretary-General, by reason of his position as "the chief administrative officer of the Organization," must engage.

This is not to say that the ascertainment of arrearage within the terms of Article 19 is beyond the General Assembly's control. On the contrary, the General Assembly has adopted rules, general and impartial in nature, which the Secretary-General is obliged to apply. The General Assembly's Rules of Procedure provide, in Rule 153, that: "The General Assembly shall establish regulations for the financial administration of the United Nations." Rule 161 assigns to the Committee on Contributions the task of advising the General Assembly on the scale of assessments "and on the action to be taken with regard to the application of Article 19 of the Charter." The Financial Regulations which the General Assembly has unanimously adopted provide that they "shall govern the financial administration of the United Nations" (Regulation 1.1). Rule 101.1, promulgated in pursuance of the Financial Regulations, notes that: "The Controller shall be responsible for the administration of these Rules, on behalf of the Secretary-General." Regulation 11.1 provides that: "The Secretary-General shall maintain such accounting records as are necessary and shall submit annual accounts." Pursuant to that regulation, Rule 111.4 provides that the financial statements which shall be prepared "at intervals as prescribed by the Controller" shall include supporting schedules on: "Status of Members' contributions and advances." Such statements are in fact prepared monthly and circulated as official documents.[4] They show, for each Member, the status of advances to the Working Capital Fund and of "contributions due" to the United Nations Regular Budget, the UNEF Special Account, and the Congo *ad hoc* Account. The total amounts due from each Member under each account are given. The authority, and accuracy, of the Secretary-General in making such computations are not known to have been challenged by any Member. Furthermore, Regulation 5.7 provides:

---

[4] See, for example, "Statement on the Collection of Contributions as at December 31, 1963," ST/ADM/SER.B/183.

The Secretary-General shall submit to the regular session of the General Assembly a report on the collection of contributions and advances to the Working Capital Fund.

The Secretary-General accordingly is required by the Financial Regulations to report to the General Assembly on the status of Members' arrears, a report which may refer to the status of their arrears within the terms of Article 19. Thus the Report of the Secretary-General on the Collection of Contributions as at September 14, 1959 declares:

> As at 14 September 1959, the contributions payable by Member States for the years prior to 1957 have been paid in full, and for 1957 the amounts outstanding represent in all cases less than the total contributions due for that year. At the present time therefore, no Member State is in arrears in the payment of its financial obligations to the Organization to the extent that Article 19 of the Charter would apply. (A/C.5/778, p. 1.)

Regulation 5.7 governs the submission of a report on the collection of contributions "to the regular session of the General Assembly." When the General Assembly otherwise meets, the Secretary-General has, as occasion required, informed it of the occurrence of the fact of arrears within the terms of Article 19. Thus in the Haitian case in 1963, at the General Assembly's Fourth Special Session, the Secretary-General brought the fact of that Member's arrears to the attention of the General Assembly by letter addressed to its President. The President's letter in response to that of the Secretary-General accepted the Secretary-General's computation of arrears within the terms of Article 19.

The Committee on Contributions, on the basis of the Secretary-General's reports, likewise may report the occurrence of the fact of arrears within the terms of Article 19. As noted above, the Committee, in 1958, recorded that, as of the August date of its Report, Bolivia was in the requisite arrears. The Committee has regularly reported the contrary. For example, its Report to the Eighteenth Session of the General Assembly states: "As at present no Member State is in arrears in the payment of its contributions to the extent that Article 19 would apply, no action of the Committee was required in this respect" (A/55100, p. 4). The role of the Committee on Contributions is not confined to noting the fact of arrears as computed by the Secretary-General, however. Its advice, pursuant to Rule 161 of the Rules of Procedure, clearly concerns the question of whether a Member's failure to pay is due to conditions beyond that Member's control. Since the prime function of the Committee is to advise the General Assembly on the scale of the apportionment of expenses, the Committee is well fitted to advise on a claim that a

Member is not able to pay its assessments "due to conditions beyond the control of the Member." Because the Committee on Contributions is not characteristically in session on the day of the opening of the General Assembly, it falls to the Secretary-General to report the latest facts of arrearage to the presiding officer of the General Assembly when it first meets.

The respective functions of the Secretary-General and the Committee on Contributions in respect of Article 19 are admirably set forth in the Dossier Transmitted by the Secretary-General to the International Court of Justice in the course of its advisory proceedings on *Certain Expenses of the United Nations.* Under the heading "Application of Article 19 of the Charter (Arrears on contributions)," the Note by the Controller declared:

58. The General Assembly, in establishing the Committee on Contributions, an expert committee, prescribed that the Committee's functions should include advising it "on the action to be taken with regard to the application of Article 19 of the Charter" . . .

59. In compliance with this directive, the Committee on Contributions has considered at each of its sessions a report by the Secretary-General on the collection of contributions which included a detailed statement of the amounts due from each Member State in respect of its financial contributions to the Organization . . .

64. On the basis of the status of the contributions at the time of its meetings, usually August of each year, the Committee on Contributions has reported annually to the General Assembly that no action was required by the General Assembly in respect of the application of Article 19, except in 1958, when the Committee on Contributions, referring to the arrears of one Member State, invited attention to the terms of Article 19 of the Charter. Before the opening of the General Assembly session, arrangements had, however, been made by the Member State concerned for payment of the outstanding arrears. In 1960, when the session of the Committee on Contributions opened on 17 October, the Secretary-General's report (A/C.5/825) on the Collection of Contributions as at 20 September 1960, submitted in compliance with Financial Regulation 5.7 to the fifteenth session of the General Assembly contained the following paragraph:

As of this date, one Member State is in arrears in the payment of its contributions to the extent that Article 19 of the Charter might be deemed to apply, no payments having been received in respect of the years 1958, 1959, or 1960. Assurances have been given, however, on behalf of the Government of the Member State in question that a payment is in transit which will reduce its outstanding arrears below the stipulated limit.

As the payment referred to in this paragraph was received, no further action was called for.   (*Pleadings*, pp. 53–55).

Those who contend that the General Assembly must itself find the fact of arrearage within the terms of Article 19 cannot contest the established character of the contrary practice described. They cannot deny that the General Assembly, in its adoption of the pertinent Rules of Procedure and Financial Regulations, has authoritatively interpreted the procedure for the application of Article 19 which implementation of that Article entails. Moreover, the extensive analogous practice of the Specialized Agencies in applying constitutional provisions virtually identical to Article 19 is uniform in demonstrating that establishment of the fact of arrears always is a ministerial act of mathematical calculation, performed by the Director General of the Agency concerned; it never is a matter of determination by the Assembly of the Agency (see the Appendix to this memorandum).

Persuasive as established, unchallenged practice is, it could nevertheless be urged that there could be a difference of view between a Member and the Secretary-General on the amounts which the Member has in fact paid the Organization; a question which, arguably, would be for the General Assembly to settle. There could be other differences on which the General Assembly might arguably be required to pass, such as whether the Member is due a credit for claims or services which should be set off against unpaid contributions; or whether the allocation of credits and debts between Members formerly part of a single Member State is correct. Since such conceivable differences of view between the Secretary-General and a Member are of no practical moment to the application of Article 19 in 1964, they may be put aside. However, it actually is argued that there are differences of view between certain Members and the Organization as to whether certain financial contributions as to which the Secretary-General lists such Members as being in arrears are indeed so; that is to say, whether such Members are bound, as a matter of legal obligation, to pay certain financial contributions to the Organization. This is a question which, by reason of Article 17 of the Charter, is determined by the General Assembly. Insofar as it is pertinent to the implementation of Article 19 in 1964, it is a question which has already and amply been determined by resolutions of the General Assembly.

It has, in particular, been contended that Article 19 does not apply to arrears on assessments for peacekeeping operations, notably those for UNEF and ONUC. That contention plainly is in error. Nothing in the Charter, or its drafting history, indicates that Article 19 does not embrace peacekeeping expenses.[5] Article 19 refers to Members' "financial contributions to the

---

[5] Mexico urged the contrary, in a construction of the records of the San Francisco Conference which the Secretary-General described as "a misinterpretation of the discussions at San Francisco" (General Assembly, Fifteenth Session, *Official Records*, 839th Meeting of the Fifth Committee, p. 59. See, for the

Organization," which certainly appear to include contributions for peace-keeping expenditures. As Secretary-General Dag Hammarskjöld stated to the Fifth Committee: "All expenses of the Organization within the meaning of Article 17, paragraph 2, were subject without exception to the sanctions provided for in Article 19."[6]

As the Secretary-General thus indicated, the "financial contributions" specified in Article 19 equate with the "expenses" referred to in Article 17, paragraph 2. That paragraph provides that: "The expenses of the Organization shall be borne by the Members as apportioned by the General Assembly." In its advisory opinion of July 20, 1962, the International Court of Justice reached the conclusion that the expenditures authorized by the General Assembly for peacekeeping operations in the Congo and the Middle East "constitute 'expenses of the Organization' within the meaning of Article 17, paragraph 2, of the Charter of the United Nations."[7]

On December 19, 1962, the General Assembly, by a vote of 76–17–8, adopted resolution 1854 (XVII) by which it "accepts the opinion of the Court on the question submitted to it." It was understood that the Assembly, by accepting the Court's opinion, thereby confirmed that peacekeeping assessments for ONUC and UNEF are "expenses of the Organization" and, hence, included in the "financial contributions to the Organization" to which Article 19 refers. This is emphasized by the Assembly's rejection of an amendment to resolution 1854, submitted by Jordan, to substitute "takes note of" for "accepts." The Delegate of Jordan, in so moving, explained that the Jordanian amendment was designed to avoid inclusion of ONUC and UNEF assessments in the computation of liability under Article 19.[8] Sixty-eight Members voted against the Jordanian amendment, twenty-eight for, and fourteen abstained. Thus, any question about whether peacekeeping assessments, including those for ONUC and UNEF, are within the scope of

---

verbatim text of the statement of the representative of Mexico, A/C.5/862, pp. 30–34). The Mexican argument was submitted in its verbatim text to the International Court of Justice in the Dossier Transmitted by the Secretary-General in the advisory proceedings on *Certain Expenses of the United Nations (Pleadings, Oral Arguments, Documents, Certain Expenses of the United Nations* [Article 17, paragraph 2 of the Charter], 1962, p. 90). It was restated and endorsed in the Written Statements submitted to the Court by the Republic of South Africa (*Pleadings*, p. 260) and the Union of Soviet Socialist Republics (*Pleadings*, p. 273). The Mexican argument was rebutted by the Written Statements of Australia (*Pleadings*, pp. 233–238) and the United States of America (*Pleadings*, pp. 207–209) and the Oral Statement of Sir Kenneth Bailey (Australia) (*Pleadings*, pp. 372–377). It was not accepted in any degree by the Court (*Certain Expenses of the United Nations, Article 17, paragraph 2, of the Charter*), Advisory Opinion of July 20, 1962, (*ICJ Reports 1962*, p. 151).

[6] 839th Meeting of the Fifth Committee (see note 5).   [7] *ICJ Reports 1962*, pp. 151, 179–180.

[8] General Assembly, Seventeenth Session, *Official Records*, 964th meeting of the Fifth Committee, para. 4; see also, verbatim text, Press Release PM/4197 of December 6, 1962, at p. 3.

Article 19 was answered affirmatively, overwhelmingly and definitively by the Seventeenth Session of the General Assembly.

It has been shown that the fact of arrears within the terms of Article 19 is computed and reported by the Secretary-General (or reported by the Committee on Contributions acting on the basis of accounts kept by the Secretary-General). It has been shown that, in making this computation, the Secretary-General acts in response to the impartial, standing requirements of the Rules of Procedure and the Financial Regulations, which have been adopted without regard to the particular case and in advance of its occurrence. It has been shown that, in the computation of such arrears, the assessments that are the prime focus of controversy, those for UNEF and ONUC, necessarily are included. It has been shown that the Secretary-General is obliged, by the terms of the Regulations, to communicate his findings to the General Assembly. It has been shown that – putting aside the possibility of exculpation pursuant to the second sentence of Article 19 – once the fact of a Member's being in the requisite arrears obtains, the Member "shall have no vote in the General Assembly." In the light of these showings, it may be asked: once the General Assembly is informed of the fact of the requisite arrearage, what fact, if any, is it required to establish? What decision is it required, or permitted, to take? Apart from a decision to exculpate the Member pursuant to the conditions of the second sentence of Article 19, it is plain that the Assembly is neither obliged nor permitted to take a decision establishing the fact of the requisite arrearage, any more than it is obliged or permitted to take a decision suspending such a Member's vote. Thus the question of whether such a decision is to be taken by a simple majority or a majority of two-thirds does not arise. Consideration of whether such a decision is a "budgetary question," or a "suspension of the rights and privileges of membership," or is otherwise an "important question" is immaterial; there is no such decision at all.

To be sure, the General Assembly is required to be informed of the fact of arrearage which gives rise to the suspension of a Member's vote, not only by the terms of the Financial Regulations but by the clear import of the second sentence of Article 19. Thus the President of the Fourth Special Session rightly stated that, had the Member in the requisite arrears been present and had there been a vote, he would have made an announcement drawing the attention of the General Assembly to the loss of voting rights. Is such an announcement subject to a point of order?

Rule 73 of the Rules of Procedure provides that, during "the discussion of any matter," a representative may rise to a point of order, which shall be immediately decided by the President. A representative may appeal against the President's ruling. Rule 73 further provides: "The appeal shall be immediately put to the vote and the President's ruling shall stand unless overruled by a majority of the Members present and voting. A representative rising to a point of order may not speak on the substance of the matter under discussion."

Thus should one or more Members be in the requisite arrears when the General Assembly meets in 1964, and the presiding officer accordingly states to the General Assembly that certain named Members, being so, "have no vote in the General Assembly" unless it should permit such Members to vote because it is satisfied that failure to pay is due to conditions beyond their control, that announcement could give rise to a point of order. That point of order "shall be immediately decided by the President in accordance with the rules of procedure" – Rules which, in turn, give effect to the provisions of the Charter. Should a representative appeal against the President's ruling, the appeal shall be immediately put to the vote and the President's ruling shall stand unless overruled by a simple majority of the Members present and voting. Actually, such a challenge would be irregular. The Charter does not contemplate that its provisions shall be subject to points of order. But, nevertheless, should a point of order be raised and pressed, it must be disposed of in accordance with the Charter's terms and the Rules of Procedure. A procedural mechanism exists through which the President's announcement that a Member in the requisite arrears has no vote may be challenged; but the only vote which would be substantively in accord with the law of the Charter would be that in support of the President's ruling. It may be noted, in this regard, that, in the many cases in which announcement or other communication has been made in the Specialized Agencies that certain Members have no vote because of financial default, such announcement has never been challenged.

Where, pursuant to the second sentence of Article 19, there is a motion to permit a Member to vote, the advice of the Committee on Contributions should be sought, in accordance with Rule 161. Thus, in the event of such a motion, the Committee should be urgently convened. Pending its report, the vote of any Member in arrears under Article 19 shall, consonant with Article 19's mandatory terms and the analogous procedures of the Specialized Agencies, remain suspended. However, should the Committee on Contributions, in its Report to the General Assembly, already have advised it on the Member's claim for exculpation, the General Assembly will be in a position to act immediately on a motion to permit that Member to vote.

It should be noted that the criterion for exculpation under the second sentence of Article 19 is objective. The General Assembly, to permit a Member to vote under Article 19, must be satisfied that failure to pay is "due to conditions beyond the control of the Member." Moreover, the exculpation provision of Article 19 can have no application where the Member in arrears asserts not that failure to pay is due to conditions beyond its control, but that it deliberately has not paid certain assessments upon it. Whatever the reason for willful failure to pay its financial contributions, the second sentence of Article 19 has no application to it.

Certain contentions have been advanced by Members of the United Nations which are not consistent with the views set forth in this paper. The Union of Soviet Socialist Republics addressed a letter to the Secretary-General dated June 10, 1963 (document A/5431), primarily concerning the Haitian precedent. The Czechoslovak Socialist Republic addressed a note verbale of similar substance to the Secretary-General on June 17, 1963 (document A/5433). Their views may be summarized as follows:

(*a*) The application of the first sentence of Article 19 is not mandatory and automatic but requires a decision by the General Assembly.

(*b*) That decision is to be taken by a two-thirds majority of the Members present and voting, since Article 18, paragraph 2 specifies such a majority for "the suspension of the rights and privileges of membership."

(*c*) Arrears on the payment of assessments for ONUC and UNEF, if not indeed peacekeeping expenses generally, may not be included in the computation of liability under Article 19.

Points (*a*) and (*c*) have already been discussed fully above. As to point (*b*), it is true that, pursuant to Article 18, paragraph 2, a decision on "the suspension of the rights and privileges of membership" requires a two-thirds vote. However, since the application of the first sentence of Article 19 is mandatory and automatic, it requires no "decision." Thus the question of whether such a decision is to be taken by a simple majority or a majority of two-thirds does not arise. Equally, as noted, there is no decision of the General Assembly on the fact of arrears. Moreover, the reference of Article 18, paragraph 2 to "the suspension of the rights and privileges of membership" is not to Article 19, which speaks neither of suspension nor of the rights and privileges of membership, but to Article 5, which provides that a Member "may be suspended from the exercise of the rights and privileges of membership" by the General Assembly upon the recommendation of the Security Council. This is confirmed by the following phrase of Article 18, paragraph 2, which provides for a two-thirds vote on "the expulsion of Members," a provision which, in turn, is linked to the provision of Article 6 for expulsion of

Members by the General Assembly upon the recommendation of the Security Council.[9]

The analysis contained in this memorandum is confirmed by the leading monograph in the field, that of the distinguished Indian scholar and public servant, Dr. Nagendra Singh, President of the Third Assembly of IMCO and a member of the Institut de Droit International. In his work on *Termination of Membership of International Organizations* (1958), Dr. Singh concludes:

> It is essential to examine the constituent instrument to see if suspension is mandatory or permissive. Thus on a correct interpretation of Article 13(4) of ILO, the suspension of the voting rights of a defaulting member State is mandatory as the stipulation is "a member *shall* have no right to vote". The United Nations Charter also visualizes mandatory suspension of voting rights in the event of financial default of a certain magnitude, specified in Article 19. However, Article 5 provides a permissive type of suspension when preventive or enforcement action has been taken against a member by the Security Council, because the words used are "may be suspended", as against Article 19 which runs "shall have no vote in the General Assembly". However, both in ILO, Article 13(4), and United Nations Charter, Article 19, though mandatory suspension is prescribed in the event of financial default of a certain magnitude, power is given to the Conference and the General Assembly respectively by a two-thirds majority to permit a defaulting member to exercise its rights of vote, provided the Conference of ILO or the General Assembly of the United Nations are satisfied that the failure to pay is due to conditions beyond the control of the member. This has the effect of introducing an element of discretion into an otherwise mandatory provision regarding suspension.
>
> However, a number of constituent instruments provide a permissive type of suspension. For example, WHO Article 7 provides "the Health Assembly *may* suspend ... the voting privileges". In these constituent instruments, a mere permissive type of suspension exists at the discretion of the appropriate organ authorized to exercise this right.[10]

[9] Professor Kelsen states that the provision in Article 18, paragraph 2 on "the suspension of the rights and privileges of membership" does not refer to Article 19: "the formula probably refers only to the suspension of the rights and privileges of membership provided for in Article 5" (*The Law of the United Nations* [1950], p. 719).

[10] At page 45. Professor Kelsen's earlier treatise on *The Law of the United Nations* interprets Article 19 in a manner differing from the foregoing analysis. His position is that the General Assembly, "by a decision not expressly provided for in Article 19, establishes the fact that a Member is in arrears in the payment of its financial contributions to the Organization and declares the exercise of the right of this Member to vote in the General Assembly suspended" (p. 719). This meaning of Article 19, Professor Kelsen states, is "formulated in a technically insufficient way" (by the Charter) (*ibid.*).

It is submitted that, on the contrary, Article 19 means just what it says. Its first sentence provides for no decision by the General Assembly, and none is to be read into it. The mandatory and automatic character of the first sentence of Article 19 has been amply demonstrated above. It has equally been shown that, in accordance with the Financial Regulations and the General Assembly's Rules of Procedure, as well as the analogous practice of the Specialized Agencies, it is the Secretary-General, or the Committee on Contributions acting on data supplied by the Secretary-General, who, on the basis of the Organization's accounts, finds as a fact that a Member is in the requisite arrears.

APPENDIX ON THE PRECEDENT OF THE SPECIALIZED AGENCIES

The extensive history of application by the Specialized Agencies of provisions substantially identical to Article 19 is especially illuminating. It demonstrates, first, that implementation of a provision of the order of Article 19 entails no decision by the Assembly of the Agency, its effect being mandatory and automatic; and, second, that the finding of the fact of existence of the requisite arrears is made, as a matter of ministerial, mathematical calculation, by the Secretariat of the Agency.

The Constitutions of four of the Specialized Agencies – the International Labor Organization (ILO), Food and Agriculture Organization (FAO), United Nations Educational, Scientific, and Cultural Organization (UNESCO), and International Maritime Consultative Organization (IMCO) – as well as the International Atomic Energy Organization (IAEA) contain provisions parallel to Article 19. Article 13, paragraph 4 of the Constitution of the ILO provides:

> A Member of the Organisation which is in arrears in the payment of its financial contribution to the Organisation shall have no vote in the Conference, in the Governing Body, in any committee, or in the elections of members of the Governing Body, if the amount of its arrears equals or exceeds the amount of the contributions due from it for the preceding two full years: provided that the Conference may by a two-thirds majority of the votes cast by the delegates present permit such a Member to vote if it is satisfied that the failure to pay is due to conditions beyond the control of the Member.

Article IV, paragraph C.8 (*b*) and (*c*) of the Constitution of the UNESCO provides:

> (*b*) A Member State shall have no vote in the General Conference if the total amount of contributions due from it exceeds the total amount of contributions payable by it for the current year and the immediately preceding calendar year.
>
> (*c*) The General Conference may, nevertheless, permit such a Member State to vote, if it is satisfied that the failure to pay is due to conditions beyond the control of the Member Nation.

Article III, paragraph 4, of the Constitution of the FAO provides:

> Each Member Nation shall have only one vote. A Member Nation which is in arrears in the payment of its financial contributions to the Organization shall have no vote in the Conference if the amount of its arrears equals or exceeds the amount of the contributions due from it for the two preceding financial years. The Conference may, nevertheless, permit such a Member Nation to vote if it is

satisfied that the failure to pay is due to conditions beyond the control of the Member Nation.

Article XIX, paragraph A, of the Statute of the IAEA provides:

A member of the Agency which is in arrears in the payment of its financial contributions to the Agency shall have no vote in the Agency if the amount of its arrears equals or exceeds the amount of the contributions due from it for the preceding two years. The General Conference may, nevertheless, permit such a member to vote if it is satisfied that the failure to pay is due to conditions beyond the control of the member.

Article 42 of the Convention of the IMCO provides:

Any Member which fails to discharge its financial obligation to the Organization within one year from the date on which it is due, shall have no vote in the Assembly, the Council, or the Maritime Safety Committee unless the Assembly, at its discretion, waives this provision.

Where the decision to suspend the vote of a Member excessively in arrears is, contrary to the provisions which obtain in these four Specialized Agencies and the IAEA, left to the Assembly of a Specialized Agency, the constitutions of such Agencies (World Health Organization [WHO], World Meteorological Organization [WMO], and the International Civil Aviation Organization [ICAO]) expressly so provide. Thus Article 7 of the Constitution of the WHO gives the Health Assembly discretion to suspend the vote of a Member in arrears; it does not provide that a defaulting Member "shall have no vote" but that the Health Assembly "may, on such conditions as it thinks proper, suspend the voting privileges." Article 31 of the Convention of the WMO provides not that a Member which fails to meet its financial obligations "shall have no vote" but that "the Congress may by resolution suspend it from exercising its rights and enjoying its privileges."[11] Article 62 of the Convention on International Civil Aviation provides not that a Member in the requisite arrears "shall have no vote" but that: "The Assembly may suspend the voting power in the Assembly and in the Council of any contracting State that fails to discharge within a reasonable period its financial obligations to the Organization."[12] The language of these constitutional provisions, providing for the discretion of the plenary organs of the Agencies concerned to take or not to take a decision suspending voting privileges, lends emphasis to the contrasting language of Article 19 of the Charter. It demonstrates that, had it

---

[11] Nevertheless, by resolution 6 (Cg-III), the Congress adopted an automatic standard, which has been automatically applied.

[12] The Assembly had adopted resolutions for limited terms containing an automatic standard: *cf.* resolutions A 1–56 and A 6–2.

been the intention of the Charter's authors to accord the General Assembly such discretionary power, Article 19 would have been drafted otherwise. As it is, the mandatory and automatic intent of Article 19 emerges the more clearly.

The application by the ILO of Article 13, paragraph 4 has been in accordance with detailed, dispositive Standing Orders of the International Labor Conference. The text of those Orders is of extreme interest, and is quoted in full below.[13]

Pursuant to them, it is the Director General who finds as a fact that a Member is in arrears within the terms of Article 13, paragraph 4. He brings this fact to the attention of the Financial and Administrative Committee of the Governing Body by a written report. For example, G.B. 157/F.A./D.1/5, of November, 1963, states that the "arrears due" from two Members "exceed the amount of the contributions due from them for the past two full years (1961 and 1962). Both of the above-mentioned States are, therefore, subject to the provisions of paragraph 4 of Article 13 of the Constitution" (at pp. 1–2). G.B. 155/F.A./D.2/5 of May–June 1963 has an identical statement by the Director General in respect of eight Members in the requisite arrears. A

---

[13]   Section D

Disqualification from Voting of Members Which Are in Arrears in the Payment of Their Contributions to the Organization.

Article 29

Notification to Member in Arrears

1. If the Director-General finds that the amount of the arrears due from a Member of the Organization which is in arrears in the payment of its contribution to the Organization will, in the event of no payment being received from the Member during the succeeding three months, increase so as to equal or exceed the amount of the contribution due from that Member for the two full years preceding the expiration of the said period of three months, he shall send to the Member in question a communication calling its attention to the terms of article 13, paragraph 4, of the Constitution.

2. When the amount of the arrears due to the International Labor Organization from a Member which is in arrears in the payment of its contribution to the Organization equals or exceeds the contribution due from that Member for the preceding two full years, the Director-General shall notify the Member in question of this fact and call its attention to the terms of article 13, paragraph 4, of the Constitution.

3. Contributions are due on 1 January of the year to which they relate, but the year in respect of which they are due shall be regarded as a period of grace and a contribution shall be regarded as being in arrears for the purpose of this article only if it has not been paid by December 31, of the year in respect of which it is due.

Article 30

Notification to Conference and Governing Body
that Member is in Arrears

The notification provided for in paragraph 2 of article 29 shall be brought by the Director-General to the attention of the next sessions of the International Labor Conference, the Governing Body, and any other committee of the International Labor Organization in which the question of the right to vote of the Member concerned may arise, and to the attention of the electoral colleges provided for in articles 49 and 50 of the Standing Orders of the Conference.

similar statement of arrears in contributions is inserted in the Provisional Record of the Conference (for example, Provisional Record No. 4 of the 47th Session of the Conference, at p. XX).

The Director General's finding of the fact of the requisite arrearage, and the consequent automatic suspension of the vote of the Member in question, has repeatedly taken place. No verbal announcement is made to the ILO body in question of the loss of vote of the Member. But such a Member does not participate in the vote; its name is not called on a record vote; its Delegates are left out of the calculation of the quorum. In only one of many cases of automatic loss of vote does a question seem to have been raised. In a

Article 31
Procedure Where Proposal is Made to Permit Member in Arrears to Vote

1. Any request or proposal that the Conference should nevertheless permit a Member which is in arrears in the payment of its contributions to vote in accordance with article 13, paragraph 4, of the Constitution shall be referred in the first instance to the Finance Committee of the Conference, which shall report thereon as a matter of urgency.
2. Pending a decision on the request or proposal by the Conference, the Member shall not be entitled to vote.
3. The Financial Committee shall submit to the Conference a report giving its opinion on the request or proposal.
4. If the Finance Committee, having found that the failure to pay is due to conditions beyond the control of the Member, thinks fit to propose to the Conference that the Member should nevertheless be permitted to vote in accordance with article 13, paragraph 4, of the Constitution, it shall in its report:
    (a) explain the nature of the conditions beyond the Member's control;
    (b) give an analysis of the financial relations between the Member and the Organization during the preceding ten years; and
    (c) indicate the measures which should be taken in order to settle the arrears.
5. Any decision which may be taken by the Conference to permit a Member which is in arrears in the payment of its contribution to vote notwithstanding such arrears may be made upon the Member complying with any recommendations for settling the arrears which may be made by the Conference.

Article 32
Period of Validity of a Decision to Permit Member in Arrears to Vote

Any decision by the Conference permitting a Member which is in arrears in the payment of its contributions to vote shall be valid for the session of the Conference at which the decision is taken. Any such decision shall be operative in regard to the Governing Body and committees until the opening of the general session of the Conference next following that at which it was taken.

Article 33
Cessation of Disqualification from Voting

When, as a result of the receipt by the Director-General of the International Labor Office of payments made by a Member, article 13, paragraph 4, of the Constitution ceases to be applicable to that Member:
(a) the Director-General shall notify the Member that its right to vote is no longer suspended;
(b) if the International Labor Conference, the Governing Body, the electoral colleges provided for in articles 49 and 50 of the Standing Orders of the Conference, or any committee concerned, has received the notification provided for in article 30 of the present section, the Director-General shall inform it that the right to vote of the Member is no longer suspended.

record vote on the readmission of Japan to the ILO, the following exchange took place in the Conference:

> *Interpretation*: Mr. MATEEV (*Government delegate, Bulgaria*). The Bulgarian delegation has not been asked to vote.
>
> *Interpretation*: The PRESIDENT. Under Article 13, paragraph 4, of the Constitution, "a Member of the Organisation which is in arrears in the payment of its financial contribution to the Organisation shall have no vote in the Conference, in the Governing Body, in any committee, or in the elections of members of the Governing Body, if the amount of its arrears equals or exceeds the amount of the contributions due from it for the preceding two full years".
>
> It is at the Bulgarian delegate's request that I have recalled this provision. I hope that my successor will not have the painful duty of repeating this reminder, and I hope that by then Bulgaria will have paid the contributions, which should be easy, since we have learnt that Bulgaria is at present enjoying very great prosperity.

That settled the matter.[14]

The application of the loss-of-vote provision of Article IV.C.8 of the UNESCO Constitution is of special interest, since that provision was drafted in pursuance of an instruction of the General Conference to the Director-General to recommend "any measures necessary to ensure payment of contributions from Member States, bearing in mind the provisions of Article 19 of the Charter of the United Nations."[15] The General Conference further resolved that:

> On 1 January of each year the Director-General shall notify any Member State which by virtue of non-payment of contributions would not be entitled to vote in the next Session of the General Conference that the State in question has failed in its financial responsibilities to Unesco; that this fact will be reported to the next session of the General Conference where the State in question will not be entitled to vote unless payment has been made prior to the date of such Conference, or the Conference decides otherwise under Article IV/C/8 (*c*) of the Constitution.
>
> (Fifth Session, resolution 18.31.)

The Director General computes the existence of arrears within the terms of Article IV.C.8, and expressly communicates that fact to the General Conference in his Report on the Collection of Contributions. For example, at the Eleventh Session, the Director General's report listed five Members in arrears for 1958 and earlier, and stated:

> The attention of the above-mentioned Member States has been drawn to the provisions of Article IV.C.8 of the Constitution which governs the right to vote of Member States. The application of this Article at the eleventh session of the

---

[14] International Labor Conference, *Record of Proceedings of the 34th Session*, 1951, p. 220.
[15] Records of the General Conference, Second Session, p. 40.

General Conference will affect any Member State which is in arrears for the year 1958 or earlier. (11 C/ADM/5, p. 2.)

The Director General's report to the Twelfth Session made the same finding in the same terms in respect of four Member States (12 C/ADM/9, pp. 1–2).

In response to the Director General's report, the President of the General Conference declares at the First Plenary Meeting that the Members in question "have not the right to vote at this session of the General Conference." An example of the President's statement merits quotation in full:

> The *PRESIDENT* [Translation from the French]: It is now my duty to make a statement about arrears in payment of contributions and their effect on the right to vote of Member States at this session of the General Conference.
>
> Under Article IV, paragraph 8 (*b*) of the Constitution, the right of Member States to vote is contingent upon payment of their contributions. Paragraph 8 (*b*) reads as follows:
>
> "A Member State shall have no vote in the General Conference if the total amount of contributions due from it exceeds the total amount of contributions payable by it for the current year and the immediately preceding calendar year."
>
> At present, four Member States have not the right to vote at this session of the General Conference, since the total amount of contributions due from them exceeds the total amount of contributions payable by them for the current year and the immediately preceding calendar year. These four States are Bolivia, China, Honduras and Paraguay. Paragraph 8 (*c*) of Article IV, however, states that the General Conference may nevertheless permit such a Member State to vote, if it is satisfied that the failure to pay is due to conditions beyond the control of the Member Nation.
>
> The delegations of the States concerned will therefore have to decide whether they should request the General Conference to apply this paragraph. Such requests, if not already submitted to the Director-General, should be addressed without delay to the President of the General Conference, who will transmit them to the Administrative Commission, to which such requests are normally referred.
>
> (*Records of the General Conference*, Eleventh Session, p. 52.)

The President's announcement that Members "have not the right to vote" has not been challenged. Rather, the mandatory and automatic application of Article IV.C.8 has been treated by the Secretariat, the President of the General Conference, and all Member States as plain and incontestable. The computation of the requisite arrearage by the Director General has similarly not been questioned. While there have been a number of instances where Member States, being automatically deprived of their votes, subsequently have been permitted by the General Conference to vote in response to a motion to exculpate them pursuant to the second sentence of Article IV.C.8, such Members, being without the right to vote, naturally have not voted on the motion to exculpate them.

In the International Atomic Energy Agency, the Director General determines the fact that a Member State is in arrears in its contributions within the meaning of Article XIX.A of the Statute. His computation is communicated to the General Conference by a "Note by the Director-General," which is issued in pursuance to Financial Regulation 6.07:

> The Director-General shall submit to each regular session of the General Conference through the Board of Governors a report on the collection of contributions and of advances to the Working Capital Fund.
>
> (INFCIRC/8/Add.1.)

The similarity of this regulation to that of Financial Regulation 5.7 of the United Nations will be noted. The Director General's note is issued on the day of the opening of the regular Session of the General Conference and shows the status of financial contributions as of the day before. One example of the relevant passage of his note follows:

> From the above tables, and that in Annex B, it will be noted that three Members, namely Cuba, Honduras and Paraguay have not paid their advances to the Working Capital Fund, nor any part of their contributions for 1958 and 1959. Article XIX.A of the Agency's Statute provides that:
> "A member of the Agency which is in arrears in the payment of its financial contributions to the Agency shall have no vote in the Agency if the amount of its arrears equals or exceeds the amount of the contributions due from it for the preceding two years. The General Conference may, nevertheless, permit such a member to vote if it is satisfied that the failure to pay is due to conditions beyond the control of the member."
> On 5 July 1960 the Director-General telegraphed the three Governments concerned about their arrears inviting their attention to the provisions of Article XIX.A of the Statute, but no payments have so far been received, although the Government of Honduras has telegraphed the Director-General indicating that it will make the necessary payments in time to preserve its voting rights in the General Conference during the fourth regular session.
>
> (GC [IV] 126, Annex A, pp. 1–2)

Another example lists: "States to which Article XIX.A of the Statute applied on 23 September 1963 (noon)" (GC [VII]/243, Annex B, p. 3).

No further communication is made to the General Conference, either by the Director General or by the President. The delegation concerned is informed by the Secretariat orally that it has no vote. The voting officers of the Secretariat are instructed not to call the Member's name in any roll-call vote, and, to prevent error, the roll-call lists are overprinted to block out the names of the Member States affected. Voting officers are further instructed not to distribute ballot papers to such Members nor to count their votes should they attempt to vote on a show of hands. There has never been a challenge to this procedure of automatic and mandatory application of Article XIX.A, though it has been applied at four General Conferences from 1960 through 1963, to nine Member States, only one of which subsequently has been exculpated pursuant to the second sentence of Article XIX.A. The Member State exculpated was not permitted to vote on the motion to exculpate.

The FAO has a similar history of the mandatory and automatic application of its loss-of-vote provision, upon the computation by the Director General of the existence of the requisite arrears. The Director General reports to the Finance Committee on the status of arrears; the Committee reports to the Council, which in turn reports to the Conference. At a meeting of the General Committee of the Conference, the Secretary-General of the Conference announces which Members have no vote. In the absence of any recommendation by the General Committee for the application of the exculpatory clause of Article III, paragraph 4, such Members are treated as not having the right to vote. No formal announcement is made to the Conference, but the delegations of the Members in question are privately informed. No account is taken of their vote in a show of hands; the names of Members whose voting rights are suspended are not called in a roll-call vote. When there is a secret ballot, the names of Members whose voting rights are suspended are not called and they are not given a ballot paper.

In 1959, the delegation of Bolivia protested its not having been called upon to vote. It set forth the conditions beyond its control which, in its view, led to its failure to pay its assessments (C.59/PV/9). The Chairman then made reference to the provisions of Article III, paragraph 4, and the matter was referred to the General Committee. The Chairman subsequently announced that the General Committee had considered the circumstances of Bolivian default and had arrived at the conclusion "that the circumstances so set out justify the position in which the Bolivian Government finds itself . . . it has, therefore, decided to recommend to the Conference that the rights of Bolivia to participate fully in this conference, with the concomitant right to vote, should be restored" (C.59/PV/11). This recommendation was accepted in 1959, and again in 1961 (C.61/PV/9). The Eleventh Session of the Conference in 1961 also treated the voting rights of Paraguay as automatically suspended, but took no action to restore them. Again, at its Twelfth Conference in 1963, Bolivia and Paraguay were in the requisite arrears. Paraguay's vote was treated as automatically suspended, there being no vote of the Conference withdrawing it, and, while Paraguay was represented at the Conference, it on no occasion sought to vote. Waiver of Bolivia's suspension was sought on Bolivia's behalf by application of the exculpatory clause of Article III, paragraph 4. Exculpation was not granted and, since Bolivia's vote was treated as automatically suspended, it did not vote at the Conference.

Pursuant to Financial Regulation 5.10 of the Inter-Governmental Maritime Consultative Organization, the Secretary-General is required to report to each Session of the Assembly, the Council, and Maritime Safety Committee on the application of Article 42 of the Convention. For example, the Secretary-General stated, in his "Report on the Application of Article 42 of the Convention" to the Third Session of the IMCO Assembly, "that at the time of preparing this document Article 42 of the Convention is applicable to the following Members" (listing seven) (A/III/4). The disposition of the Secretary-General's report at that session is described in the summary record as follows:

> After informing the Assembly that Argentina had now paid up in full, the PRESIDENT inquired whether there were any objections to the application of Article 42 of the Convention in respect of the six countries which had not discharged their financial obligations for the previous year. There being no objections, it was *decided* that Article 42 should be applied to the following Members: Dominican Republic, Ecuador, Haiti, Honduras, Indonesia and Panama. (A.III/SR.1, pp. 8–9.)

It will be recalled that the waiver provision of Article 42 of the IMCO Convention is more liberal than the exculpatory clause of Article 19 of the Charter (above, paragraph 37). The announcement by the President that a Member shall have no vote unless the Assembly decides "at its discretion" to waive the provision has never been challenged by any Member. Nor has question ever been raised about the Secretary-General's making the computation of the requisite arrearage which leads to the automatic loss of vote under Article 42.

21

The United States Assaults the ILO

လာ

David A. Morse, after twenty-two years of distinguished service as Director General of the International Labor Office, was succeeded in May, 1970, by C. Wilfred Jenks. The election of Dr. Jenks, then Principal Deputy Director General and an official of the ILO for almost forty years, although closely contested, was widely welcomed, not least by international lawyers, among whom Dr. Jenks had long been so eminent. The United States supported Dr. Jenks's election.

On July 31, 1970, Congressman John R. Rooney of New York, submitting that "this bird Jenks thinks he has inherited the ILO lock, stock and barrel,"[1] concluded that "Mr. Jenks needs to be rocked. I know of only one way to rock him, cut off his water."[2] Congressman Rooney suggested that the Assistant Secretary of State for International Organization Affairs telephone the Chief of the United States Mission in Geneva, "Ambassador Rimestad and tell him to hotfoot it over to Mr. Jenks and tell him before nightfall that there will be no money for the ILO."[3] Congressman Rooney did not wish the purposes of this threat to be concealed. On the contrary, he declared that "Mr. Jenks should have a copy of this record air mailed to him as soon as it is printed ... Maybe it will help him[4] ... He might change his mind. I will lay odds that he eventually will."[5]

The subject of the change so to be induced in the mind of the ILO's Director General was the appointment of an Assistant Director General of Soviet nationality (who ranks eighth in the ILO hierarchy, and who heads a department concerned with social security and maritime and certain other affairs). In June, in the course of a conversation with the Deputy Under Secretary for International Affairs of the US Department of Labor, George

---

First published in *American Journal of International Law* (January, 1971), 65, 1.

[1] *Hearings before a Sub-committee of the Committee on Appropriations, House of Representatives, 91st Congress, 2nd Session, "Additional Testimony on the International Labor Organization,"* p. 79.

[2] *Ibid.*, p. 69.   [3] *Ibid.*, p. 76.   [4] *Ibid.*, p. 70.   [5] *Ibid.*, p. 77.

H. Hildebrand, about the appointment of a US national to the senior directorate of the ILO (there being none with the departure of Mr. Morse), Dr. Jenks informed him of his intention also to appoint a Soviet Assistant Director General.[6] That in turn led to consultations among the US labor, employer, and governmental representatives in the ILO and to the calling of extraordinary Hearings before a Sub-Committee of the Committee on Appropriations of the House of Representatives on July 31, at which Congressman Rooney made the remarks quoted above.

His remarks, in turn, appear to have been stimulated by the testimony of George Meany, President of the American Federation of Labor, Congress of Industrial Organizations (AFL–CIO), Edwin P. Neilan, US Employer Delegate to the ILO, and Mr. Hildebrand, who substantially supported suggestions by Congressman Rooney[7] that payment of ILO assessments by the United States be cut off.[8] The purpose of withholding funds was candidly stated to be the exertion of pressure upon the Director General so as to lead him not to appoint, or to vacate the appointment, of a Soviet Assistant Director General. Mr. Neilan suggested that "the delinquency [of the United States in withholding its payment] is not going to accomplish the purpose unless it is accompanied by a clear statement of the reason for it";[9] whereupon Congressman Rooney remarked that the record of the Sub-Committee's Hearings would be airmailed to the Director General. That record manifests not only opposition to the appointment of a Soviet Assistant Director General but disapproval of what was alleged to be disproportionate Soviet influence in the International Labor Organization and in the International Labor Office. It was claimed that the Soviet Union gets what it wants in the ILO by threatening to withhold its 10 percent contribution to the budget; and the Sub-Committee appeared to take up the suggestion that the United States would exert even more influence if those directing the ILO could be brought to appreciate that the United States could withhold its 25 percent contribution.[10] The appointment of a Soviet representative was, in Mr. Meany's view, "the last straw."[11] Not only was the Organization inordinately influenced by the Soviet Union; in Mr. Meany's view, "it is quite obvious that the [International Labor] office is, and has been for some time, in the Russians' corner."[12]

By the time of the Sub-Committee's Hearings, the House of Representa-

---

[6] *Ibid.*, p. 71.

[7] *Ibid.*, pp. 59, 68–69. Mr. Hildebrand preferred the threat of withholding payment of US assessments to actual withholding (*ibid.*, p. 76). The representative of the Department of State, Samuel De Palma, Assistant Secretary of State for International Organization Affairs, opposed deletion of appropriations for the ILO (at pp. 74–75, 78).

[8] *Ibid.*, pp. 5, 59.   [9] *Ibid.*, p. 70.   [10] *Ibid.*, pp. 59, 66.   [11] *Ibid.*   [12] *Ibid.*, p. 75.

tives had already adopted a Bill containing, among other appropriations, the remaining half of the ILO assessment for 1970. Nevertheless the Sub-Committee decided to invite the Senate Appropriations Committee, which had not yet acted, to strike that sum of $3,758,875 from the Bill. This the Committee, led by Senator John L. McClellan, agreed to do, coupling this action with the recommendation that "the proper legislative committee review the continued participation of the United States in this organization."[13]

When these recommendations came before the Senate, Senator Javits moved vigorously to restore the ILO appropriation. He noted that the United States "is bound as a matter of law to pay the assessments for the ILO duly made upon it."[14] He cited a number of reasons (among them, the thrust of the advisory opinion of the International Court of Justice in the case of *Certain Expenses of the United Nations*) why failure to pay would detract from the interests of the United States and the United Nations community.

In reply, it was maintained that the ILO was deluged with Communist propaganda;[15] that some other Members were in arrears, and that the United States would lose its vote in ILO organs only after the amount of its arrears were to equal or exceed the amount of contributions due from it for the preceding two full years, and that, accordingly, failure to pay would not be a treaty violation;[16] that Soviet nationals are appointed to international Secretariats upon the nomination of a single candidate for the post in question, while the United States is "discriminated against" since it has to submit a number of candidates;[17] and that representation of Soviet workers' and employers' representatives in the ILO, as well as the manner of choice of Soviet members of the Secretariat, represents a "double standard."[18]

At the conclusion of the debate, and before the vote, Senator McClellan asked unanimous consent to have printed in the Record a letter from William B. Macomber, Jr., Deputy Under Secretary of State of Administration, which, however, Senator McClellan refrained from reading out. Nor apparently did the Senator give his colleagues indication of the letter's contents. Mr. Macomber wrote that, if the cut in the ILO appropriation were adopted,

> serious legal consequences will follow ... the United States has undertaken an international legal duty to pay the share of the budget that has been voted by the ILO General Conference and ... we would be in violation of that obligation if we did not pay our full assessment.[19]

---

[13] *Congressional Record*, Senate, August 24, 1970, at S14103.   [14] *Ibid.* at S14094.
[15] *Ibid.* at S14097.
[16] *Ibid.* at S14098.   [17] *Ibid.* at S14103.   [18] *Ibid.* at S14105.   [19] *Ibid.* at S14106.

After referring to the *United Nations Expenses Case*, Mr. Macomber noted that "non-payment of our dues to the ILO could, of course, lead to the question being raised again in the International Court of Justice." And, he concluded, non-payment "would seriously weaken the ability of the United States to exert influence within the organization."[20] The vote to sustain the deletion of funds for the ILO was forty-nine to twenty-two, twenty-nine Senators not voting.[21] The Senate-House Conference Committee and the House of Representatives subsequently upheld the deletion (some three weeks after the Soviet Assistant Director General took office in September, 1970).[22]

In the light of these actions, it is clear that the United States has violated international law on two counts.

First, it has violated its explicit obligation to respect the international character of the responsibilities of the Director General of the ILO. As do the comparable provisions of the United Nations Charter, the ILO Constitution provides that: "The responsibilities of the Director-General and the staff shall be exclusively international in character" and that:

> In the performance of their duties, the Director-General and the staff shall not seek or receive instructions from any government or from any other authority external to the Organization ...
>
> Each Member of the Organization undertakes to respect the exclusively international character of the responsibilities of the Director-General and the staff and not to seek to influence them in the discharge of their responsibilities.[23]

Among those responsibilities is the appointment of staff by the Director General under regulations approved by the Governing Body (regulations followed to the letter in this case). Thus, insofar as it seeks by the threat or use of non-payment to induce the Director General to vacate his appointment of a Soviet Assistant Director General or otherwise to adjust his policies to the will of the United States, the latter thereby endeavors to influence, and indeed instruct, the Director General contrary to this important international legal obligation. As the record of the House Hearings and Senate and House debate

---

[20] *Ibid.*   [21] *Ibid.*

[22] *Congressional Record*, House, October 6, 1970, at H9622–9633. Congressman Rooney then stated "that we belonged to an organization that has become dominated by Communists. It is now nothing but a stage for Communist propaganda, and there is no reason why our taxpayers should be paying 25 percent of every dollar of cost of keeping that organization alive" (at H9623). In response to Congressman Frelinghuysen's statement that the reduction in the appropriation would cause "a default by the United States on an assessment which has already been levied against it," Congressman Rooney replied: "There is not any question about that. That is exactly what we want to do, is it not?" (at H9631).

[23] Article 9, paras. 4 and 5.

makes clear, this is precisely what the Congress had in mind. While the Department of State did not favor the course of action initially threatened and then implemented by the Congress, it has officially communicated that action to the Director General; and failure to pay an assessment in any event must be a matter of public and official record.

Representations by States to the Secretary-General of the United Nations and the Directors General of the Specialized Agencies about Secretariat appointments are a commonplace. That, however, is not sufficient to legalize the pressures exerted by the United States in this instance. It is one thing for a State to express preferences to an international official about aspects of his official functions, including staff appointments (almost invariably about appointments of its own nationals); it is quite another for a State to inform an international official that, unless he takes or refrains from taking a specific action, that State will commit against the Organization a specific, grave, and, in this case, patently illegal injury. A clearer case of a State endeavoring to influence and instruct an international civil servant contrary to its international obligations would be hard to conceive.

Second, the United States has failed to meet its obligation under the Constitution of the ILO to pay assessments upon it. Article 13 of the Constitution provides that the expenses of the ILO "shall be borne by the Members." That this provision imports what the ILO Constitution elsewhere describes as "financial obligations"[24] is the plainer view of the interpretation of precisely that provision of the United Nations Charter by the International Court of Justice in its advisory opinion on *Certain Expenses of the United Nations*.[25]

This willful failure of the United States to pay an ILO assessment, whose validity and legally binding character is not open to serious challenge, in a sense surpasses the violation of international law committed by the USSR and allied states and France in failing to pay certain peacekeeping expenses of the United Nations. Those countries alleged (however unjustifiably) that the assessments in question were unlawful, a contention which the International Court of Justice did not sustain. But the United States can allege no illegal act to give a color of legality to its own. It does not challenge the validity of any ILO assessments. The policy which the Congress has so far embraced is simply to withhold all unpaid contributions until ILO policies are reshaped to suit it.

At the time when the United States ceased to press for the application of Article 19 of the United Nations Charter to the United Nations delinquents,

---

[24] Article 2, para. 5.
[25] *ICJ Reports 1962*, pp. 158, 164; *American Journal of International Law* (1962), 56, p. 1053.

it declared that it reserved the right not to pay future United Nations assessments if strong and compelling reasons existed for non-payment.[26] Whatever the legal force of that declaration – a question of considerable complexity and interest – the continuing delinquency of certain States in their United Nations payments cannot justify a default of the United States in the ILO. Moreover, in the ILO there are no exceptions to collective financial responsibility to which US non-payment may reasonably be claimed to be responsive. Indeed, the very rationale of the United States declaration in the United Nations is lacking in the ILO, for, unlike the United Nations, the International Labor Organization has consistently and automatically deprived Members in the requisite arrears of their votes in ILO bodies.[27] It has not maintained a double financial standard. The deplorable double standard which the United Nations itself has maintained in respect of the payment of financial obligations due it and in the application of Article 19 has contributed to the broader undermining of the principle of collective financial responsibility in the world of international organization. But that hardly justifies the United States in making this singular contribution of its own in an ILO context.

It remains to comment upon the arguments advanced in the Congress in support of cutting off payments to the ILO. The contention that the ILO suffers a surfeit of Communist propaganda has no legal force; politically, the sensible course is to answer such propaganda rather than facilitate it by a process of United States retreat. The suggestion that because some Members are in arrears, the United States may lawfully be, rebuts itself, the more so in any organization where delinquents in the requisite arrears suffer the prescribed suspension of vote. Nor is there substance to the contention that, since two years' worth of delinquency must accrue before an ILO Member loses its vote, non-payment of lesser sums is lawful; this confuses violation of the law with imposition of a sanction responsive to the violation.

The other arguments are more consequential. The United States has reason to complain that the Soviet Union is permitted to submit the name of but one candidate for a position in an international secretariat; this process in fact

---

[26] "[We] must make it crystal clear that if any member can insist on making an exception to the principle of collective financial responsibility with respect to certain activities of the Organization, the United States reserves the same option to make exceptions if, in our view, strong and compelling reasons exist for doing so. There can be no double standard among the members of the Organization." Ambassador Arthur J. Goldberg, in an address to the United Nations Special Committee on Peacekeeping Operations, August 16, 1965, United Nations doc. A/AC.121/PV.15, pp. 3–15; reprinted in 53 *Department of State Bulletin* (Sept. 13, 1965), 454, 456; excerpted in *American Journal of International Law* (1966), 60, p. 104 at p. 106.

[27] See "Article 19 of the Charter of the United Nations: Memorandum of Law," by the Office of the Legal Adviser, Department of State, in *American Journal of International Law* (1964), 58, pp. 752, 772–776.

tends to enable the USSR to select those of its nationals who are to be employed by international organizations, contrary to Article 101 of the United Nations Charter and comparable clauses of the constituent instruments of the Specialized Agencies. However, the situation would not be materially different if the USSR were to submit several names for a post; the fact is that, in any totalitarian society, an international organization will have grave difficulty in freely recruiting and holding Secretariat members.

It is of course also true that Soviet workers' and employers' organizations are not free and representative in the sense in which they are in democratic countries; they hardly comport with the tripartite plan of the ILO.[28] But again the fact is that, in too much of the world, realities are not consonant with the structure of the ILO or the ideals of the United Nations. If the Soviet Union and other non-democratic (including non-Communist) States are to be Members of the ILO and the United Nations, if universality is to be put above purity, then it is plain that, up to a point, a "double standard" will have to be accepted; a standard in which many non-democratic States are prone to violate their international obligations more pervasively and importantly than democratic States characteristically do. The cure for this is not for democratic States to join in subverting international law and organization. Rather, it is for democratic States to fight the double standard by every lawful means; it is for democratic States to adhere to their international obligations and to strengthen the international organizations which are so important to the implementation of those obligations.

Universality is not of course the paramount goal. An international organization is meant to promote its purposes, not diffuse them. There is and will be a tension between universality and effectiveness which generalizations cannot resolve. There may come a point in a given international organization where violation by some Members of their obligations will require others reciprocally to withhold performance of theirs.

What is clear in this case of assault by the United States Congress on the ILO is that a sense of proportion, of intelligent and practical purpose, of

---

[28] Nevertheless, the International Labor Organization in 1946 extended a warm invitation to the USSR to rejoin the ILO. The employers' representatives noted that the existing ILO Constitution had permitted the appointment of a representative "of socialized management when the USSR was a Member of the Organization ... If the USSR resumed membership of the Organization, and the Employers' representatives shared the general desire that it should do so, it would naturally appoint as Employers' delegate a representative of the socialized management of the USSR." The Conference Delegation on Constitutional Questions unanimously concluded that "appropriate provision for the representation of socialized management and of different sections of the labor movements of Member States can be made within the framework of the present system of representation." Report II (1), pp. 91–94, quoted in International Labor Organization, Record of Proceedings of the 29th International Labor Conference, 1946, pp. 358–359.

legality, has been lamentably lacking. It is to be hoped that this gross display of international insensitivity and illegality will have been reversed by the time these comments appear in print; the longer it is prolonged, the greater will be the damage to the ILO, to international law and organization, and to the interests of the United States.

22

Goldberg Variations

❦

In his maiden address to an organ of the United Nations on August 16, 1965, then Ambassador Arthur J. Goldberg, the newly appointed Permanent Representative of the United States of America to the United Nations, made a statement which marked a watershed in United Nations history. Until that statement, the United States, together with the United Kingdom, had led a majority of the membership of the Organization in a determined effort to uphold the financial authority of the United Nations. That effort particularly was manifested in the policy of seeking to induce Member States which were delinquent in the payment of their assessed financial contributions to the Organization to pay those assessments; and, in the event of their continued refusal to pay, to apply to them the sanction prescribed by the terms of Article 19 of the United Nations Charter, which provides that: "A Member of the United Nations which is in arrears in the payment of its financial contributions to the Organization shall have no vote in the General Assembly if the amount of its arrears equals or exceeds the amount of contributions due from it for the preceding two full years."

The Soviet Union, some Eastern European Members, and France maintained that they were not legally bound to pay assessments upon them for peacekeeping operations, i.e., the United Nations Emergency Force in Sinai (UNEF) and the United Nations Operations in the Congo (ONUC). The question of whether the resolutions of the General Assembly authorizing expenditures for those operations gave rise to an obligation of the States so assessed to pay was the essence of an advisory opinion requested of the International Court of Justice. The Court, in an opinion which was important in more than one respect, held:

> By Article 17, paragraph 1 [of the United Nations Charter], the General
> Assembly is given the power not only to "consider" the budget of the Organi-

First published in M. Rama-Montaldo (ed.), *Liber Amicorum: Estudios en homeaje a los 75 años del Profesor Eduardo Jiménez de Aréchaga* (1994).

zation, but also to "approve" it. The decision to "approve" the budget has a close connection with paragraph 2 of Article 17, since thereunder the General Assembly is also given the power to apportion the expenses among the Members and the exercise of the power of apportionment creates the obligation, specifically stated in Article 17, paragraph 2, of each Member to bear that part of the expenses which is apportioned to it by the General Assembly. When those expenses include expenditures for the maintenance of peace and security, which are not otherwise provided for, it is the General Assembly which has the authority to apportion the latter amounts among the Members.[1]

The Court consequently concluded that Member States were legally bound to pay the peacekeeping assessments at issue.

The General Assembly accepted the Court's opinion. However, the Soviet Union and France were among the Members that voted against the resolution so stating and they maintained their position that the General Assembly had no authority under the Charter to obligate Member States to contribute to the payment of peacekeeping expenses.

During the calendar year 1964, the arrears of several Members of the United Nations, including the Soviet Union, exceeded their assessed contributions for 1962 and 1963. The United States, the United Kingdom, and like-minded States mounted a diplomatic campaign of exceptional vigor designed to ensure that, when the General Assembly met in 1964, the mandatory and automatic provisions of Article 19 would be applied to those Members which by then continued to be in the requisite arrears. That campaign was no less energetically opposed by the Soviet Union and France. The result was that, in 1964, the General Assembly met and conducted only the most essential Organizational business, without voting. Avoidance of voting essentially avoided taking a decision on the application of Article 19.

By the summer of 1965, it was clear that this equivocal expedient had failed to achieve either payment of unpaid assessments or sufficient willingness among the majority of the membership to apply the Charter's sanction for non-payment. Accordingly, Ambassador Goldberg was instructed to say:

> The United States had regretfully concluded that, at the present stage in the development of the United Nations, the General Assembly was not prepared to carry out the relevant provisions of the Charter, that is, to apply the loss-of-vote sanction provided in Article 19. The intransigence of a few Member States and their unwillingness to abide by the rule of law had created that state of affairs, and while the United States continued to maintain that Article 19 was applicable in present circumstances, it recognized that the consensus of opinion in the Assembly was against application of the Article and in favour of having the Assembly

---

[1] *Certain Expenses of the United Nations (Article 17, paragraph 2, of the Charter)*, *ICJ Reports 1962*, p. 164.

proceed normally. The United States would not seek to frustrate that consensus, since it was not in the interest of the world to have the Assembly's work immobilized ... At the same time, if any Member State could make an exception to the principle of collective financial responsibility with respect to certain United Nations activities, the United States reserved the same option to make exceptions if, in its view, there were strong and compelling reasons to do so. There could be no double standard among the Members of the Organization.

The effect of failing to apply Article 19 was to impair the exercise by the Assembly of certain prerogatives granted to it under the Charter. Since the United States sought to strengthen the United Nations by adhering to the sound principles laid down in the Charter and the Assembly's attitude had developed contrary to the views which the United States still held to be valid, the United States disclaimed responsibility for the Assembly's attitude.[2]

This statement was a watershed because, up to the time of its making, the United States had put its full weight behind the faithful payment of United Nations assessments, upon it and upon other Members; thereafter, the flow has been dominantly downhill. The United States was eventually to become the most conspicuous among the many Members of the Organization which are in arrears in the payment of their assessed contributions to the budget of the United Nations.

The political and financial significance of this change in United States policy accordingly has been profound. The repeated and far-reaching failures of the United States to pay assessments, which were most acute in the 1980s, did not invoke the "Goldberg Reservation" by way of legal justification. Nor have the largest of those failures fallen within the terms of that Reservation in any event; they did not constitute "an exception to the principle of collective financial responsibility with respect to certain United Nations activities" – although such exceptions for certain United Nations activities repeatedly have been asserted by the United States – but across-the-board withholdings. Nevertheless, the perceptions in the Congress of the United States about the legal obligations of the United States to pay assessments upon it appear to have been vitally affected by the refusal of the General Assembly to apply the terms of the Charter to the 1964 delinquents. The idea seems to have become prevalent in Congressional circles that what is sauce for the goose is sauce for the gander. How those perceptions may have been affected, if at all, by the payment, some twenty years later, of these very same, outstanding peacekeeping assessments by the Soviet Union and France, is unclear. What is clear is that, to this day, and unlike the situation which prevailed before 1964, the Congress of the United States does not appear to

---

[2] United Nations doc. A/5916/Add. 1, p. 86 (1965), reprinted in Whiteman, *Digest of International Law* (1968), 13, p. 495.

take seriously the international legal obligations of the United States to pay assessments upon it, whether those of the United Nations, the International Labor Organization, or other international governmental organizations of which the United States is a member. A major reason for this state of affairs appears to be the failure of the General Assembly to sustain the Organization's budgetary authority in the Article 19 confrontation of 1964, a confrontation which attracted great public and press attention at the time.

However significant the political and financial impact of the outcome of that confrontation, and of the Goldberg Reservation which marked its end, the legal problems posed by the reservation remain. Quite apart from the politics of the matter, is the Government of the United States, on the basis of the Goldberg Reservation, legally entitled to withhold payment of contributions assessed by the United Nations upon it? That is the question to which the remainder of this paper is addressed.

The principle of reciprocity is a dominant one in international law as it is in international relations. At first sight, the proposition that, if the Soviet Union and some other Members were in effect permitted by the General Assembly to withhold payment of assessments upon them, the United States should be permitted to withhold payment of assessments upon it, is plausible. And there is ground for concluding that the delinquents of 1964 were permitted by the General Assembly to withhold payment of assessments, in that the mandatory sanction prescribed by the Charter to deal with such delinquency was not applied by the effective decision (or indecision) of the General Assembly. Moreover, the practice of arrearage in the payment of United Nations assessments has become widespread. Nevertheless, as a matter of law, the proposition is open to serious question.

The observance and non-observance of Charter obligations is a question of the law of treaties, the Charter being the paramount treaty of the era. That law is codified by the provisions of the Vienna Convention on the Law of Treaties. While the United States is not a party to that Convention (which is in force), for reasons, it is understood, of an internal political nature, it recognizes the provisions of the Vienna Convention to be generally reflective of customary international law. Article 42 of the Vienna Convention provides that the suspension of the operation of a treaty may take place only as a result of the application of the provisions of the treaty or of the Vienna Convention. The United Nations Charter itself contains no provision for suspension of obligations on which the Goldberg Reservation may be said to be based. And it is difficult to fit that Reservation within the confines of the Vienna Convention.

Article 60 of the Vienna Convention, entitled "Termination or suspension of the operation of a treaty as a consequence of its breach," provides in pertinent part:

> 2. A material breach of a multilateral treaty by one of the parties entitles:
>   (a) the other parties by unanimous agreement to suspend the operation of the treaty in whole or in part or to terminate it either:
>   (i) in the relations between themselves and the defaulting State, or
>   (ii) as between all the parties;
>   (b) a party specially affected by the breach to invoke it as a ground for suspending the operation of the treaty in whole or in part in the relations between itself and the defaulting State;
>   (c) any party other than the defaulting State to invoke breach as a ground for suspending the operation of the treaty in whole or in part with respect to itself if the treaty is of such a character that a material breach of its provisions by one party radically changes the position of every party with respect to the further performance of its obligations under the treaty.
> 3. A material breach of a treaty, for the purposes of this article, consists in:
>   (a) a repudiation of the treaty not sanctioned by the present Convention; or
>   (b) the violation of a provision essential to the accomplishment of the object or purpose of the treaty.
> 4. The foregoing paragraphs are without prejudice to any provision in the treaty applicable in the event of a breach.

(The Vienna Convention on the Law of Treaties between States and International Organizations or between International Organizations duplicates these provisions with the addition, after "defaulting State," of the words: "or international organization.")

Applying these provisions to the facts of the case under discussion, is the United States entitled to withhold payment of United Nations assessments upon it in reliance upon the Goldberg Reservation?

It may be initially incidentally observed that the provisions of Article 60 are specified in paragraph 4 to be without prejudice to any provision of the treaty applicable in the event of breach. In the instant case, it follows that Article 19 of the Charter is not prejudiced by the force of Article 60 of the Vienna Convention, as indeed it has not been. In so far as Article 19 was not observed with respect to the failure of the Soviet Union and other States to pay peacekeeping assessments – and Article 19 was not observed – that inobservance of course was unrelated to the provisions of the Vienna Convention, which moreover was not in force at the time the General Assembly may be said to have initially acquiesced in the breach of Article 19 (and Article 17) of the Charter. It should be added that Article 19 is by no means a dead letter. The Secretary-General of the United Nations has affirmed its mandatory and automatic applicability in other cases and it has been effectively applied by the General Assembly on a number of occasions.[3]

Was the breach by the Soviet Union, France, and other Members of their obligations to pay assessments upon them which had been found by the International Court of Justice to be within the scope of Article 17 of the Charter a "material breach" of treaty within the terms of paragraph 3 of Article 60 of the Vienna Convention? It is believed that the answer to that question is positive. Their repudiation of their obligation under Article 17 was not sanctioned by the Vienna Convention (as by a "fundamental change of circumstances" under Article 62). And their violation of a Charter obligation appears to constitute the violation of a provision of a treaty essential to the accomplishment of its object or purpose. Clearly the United Nations cannot attain its objects or purposes if it lacks the financial resources to do so as a result of Members' refusal to pay the assessments upon them.

It could be argued to the contrary that, despite the refusal of some Members to pay their peacekeeping assessments (and certain assessments of the regular budget), the United Nations has been able to accomplish its objects and purposes in some measure, and that therefore their refusal was not "essential." But if their refusal to meet their assessments, in its financial dimensions of itself serious, is regarded, as it should be regarded, as part of and stimulus for the larger and graver financial problems which have burdened the Organization for years, and which today do inhibit the accomplishment of its objects and purposes, then the breach of Charter obligations flowing from failure to pay peacekeeping expenses – and from the failure of the General Assembly to apply the mandatory sanction therefor – may reasonably be treated as material. Most fundamentally, the practice of some Members in effectively reserving to themselves the judgment as to whether assessments upon them are obligatory – at any rate, whether and when they are paid – is destructive of treaty obligations which are essential to the accomplishment of the objects and purposes of the Charter. When, as in the confrontation over the application of Article 19, the General Assembly itself may be said to have acquiesced in the breach by failing to apply the prescribed mandatory sanction to deal with that breach, and does so because of positions maintained by the Members in breach, the breach is all the more material.

Having dealt with paragraphs 3 and 4 of Article 60, there remains paragraph 2, the salient provision. Subparagraph (a) is obviously inapplicable: the parties to the Charter have not in fact unanimously agreed to suspend or

---

[3] See the Note Verbale dated July 26, 1968 from the Secretary-General addressed to the Permanent Representative of the Union of Soviet Socialist Republics, to which is attached a legal opinion of the United Nations Legal Counsel, United Nations doc. A/7146, reproduced in *International Legal Materials* (1968), 7, pp. 1187–1192.

terminate the operation of the Charter. Is subparagraph (b) apposite, i.e., could the United States maintain that it is "a party specially affected by the breach" of the Soviet Union, France, and certain other Members, acquiesced in by the General Assembly, so that the United States is entitled to suspend in part the operation of the Charter, namely, in respect of its obligations under Article 17, paragraph 2 of the Charter to bear its apportionment of the expenses of the Organization?

It is difficult to see how the United States – even in its special position as a Permanent Member of the Security Council – could make out the argument that the failure of the Soviet Union, France, and some other States to pay peacekeeping assessments, and the associated failure of the General Assembly to apply the sanction for the accrual of the resultant arrears, "specially affected" the United States. It affected it, as it affected all Members who have a stake in the faithful performance of Charter obligations and the financial integrity of the Organization. But those were not special effects. Thus Article 60, paragraph 2(b) of the Vienna Convention does not appear to furnish ground for the United States to suspend operation of Article 17 of the Charter: certainly not "in the relations between itself and the defaulting State" – an irrelevant relationship – and not even in the relations between itself and the United Nations.

What of Article 60, paragraph 2(c)? May the United States pursuant to that provision invoke the breach by the Soviet Union and other Members as a ground for suspending the operation of part of the treaty – namely, Article 17, paragraph 2 of the Charter – with respect to itself because the treaty is of such a character that "a material breach of its provisions by one party radically changes the position of every party with respect to the further performance of its obligations" under the Charter?

It cannot be established that the material breach by some States of their obligations under Article 17, and the associated breach by the General Assembly of its obligations under Article 19, radically changed the position of every party to the Charter in respect of the further performance of its Charter obligations. However serious and prolonged the failure to pay peacekeeping assessments, the result was not an increase in the assessments of the membership as a whole, or in the assessments of every party to the Charter, still less a radical increase, but rather the amassing of debt by the United Nations. Much of that debt was owed to certain Members of the United Nations who sustained peacekeeping expenses, as by the provision of troops, for which they were not repaid; arguably their position was radically changed. But the position of every party to the Charter was not radically changed.

However, it could be argued that the accrued debt of the United Nations hobbles the maintenance and launching of peacekeeping and other United Nations operations and in that way the position of every Member of the Organization has been radically changed. That is not an argument which, on the facts, is easily established. For many years after the 1964 confrontation over the application of Article 19 to certain Members in arrears within the terms of that article, peacekeeping operations were in fact launched and sustained by the United Nations, and still are, in increasing measure. Expenses have been assessed by the General Assembly after prior authorization by the Security Council, or have been met by voluntary contributions. By this and other expedients, the United Nations has managed or muddled through, although arrearages are large. Thus while the Organization has suffered from financial shortfalls, in peacekeeping and in other spheres, it cannot be concluded that the position of every party to the Charter has been radically changed by the defaults in question. Moreover, "the position of every party with respect to its obligations" under the Charter has not in any event been radically changed by the material breach in question. Insofar as Members are assessed, they remain legally bound to pay their assessments, i.e., their obligations are intact. While that conclusion is not unarguable, it is, for the reasons set out in this analysis, believed to be the better view of the matter.

There are other provisions of the Vienna Convention which might be seen as pertinent to the present analysis, notably Article 62, on fundamental change of circumstances. Article 62, paragraph 1, of the Convention provides:

1. A fundamental change of circumstances which has occurred with regard to those existing at the time of the conclusion of a treaty, and which was not foreseen by the parties, may not be invoked as a ground for terminating or withdrawing from the treaty unless:
   (a) the existence of those circumstances constituted an essential basis of the consent of the parties to be bound by the treaty; and
   (b) the effect of the change is radically to transform the extent of obligations still to be performed under the treaty.

Article 62, paragraph 3 provides that, where a party may invoke a fundamental change of circumstances as a ground for terminating or withdrawing from a treaty it may also invoke the change as a ground for suspending the operation of the treaty.

If it is accepted (as it should be) that the content of Articles 17 and 19 of the Charter constituted an essential basis for the consent of the parties to be bound by the Charter, and that the violation of these provisions with impunity was not foreseen, for essentially the reasons set out in respect of Article 60 of the Vienna Convention, it is difficult to see how the outcome of the confrontation of 1964 on peacekeeping assessments and the application of Article 19 "radically transformed the obligations still to be performed" under the United Nations Charter, for the reasons stated above. Moreover, under Article 62 of the Vienna Convention, the United States could not suspend performance of its obligations under Article 17, paragraph 2 of the Charter alone but only suspend its obligations under the Charter as a whole, unless the ground relates solely to particular clauses of the treaty where those clauses "are separable from the remainder of the treaty" and it appears that acceptance of those clauses was not an essential basis of the consent of the parties to be bound by the treaty as a whole. But the provisions of Article 17 are hardly separable; and they were essential to the acceptance of the Charter. Thus "fundamental change of circumstances" no more neatly fits invocation of the Goldberg Reservation than do the provisions of Article 60 of the Vienna Convention.

In sum it is very doubtful that the law of treaties, as codified in the Vienna Convention on the Law of Treaties of 1969, and supplemented by the companion Vienna Convention on the Law of Treaties between States and International Organizations or between International Organizations of 1986, provides ground for the conclusion that, by reason of invocation of the Goldberg Reservation, the United States is legally entitled to withhold payment of assessments by the United Nations.

As distinguished a scholar of international law and the United Nations as Professor Thomas M. Franck appears to have another view, though not expressly related to the law of treaties. Observing that the assessment system of the United Nations is not "particularly moral or principled," Professor Franck concludes that

> there is nothing immoral or unprincipled about a State refusing to pay for cogent reasons of national self-interest.
>
> Nor is such refusal illegal. Although the International Court in 1962 opined that there was a legal obligation to pay, an opinion duly adopted as the view of the Assembly, the norm fell into desuetude once the Assembly refused to discipline the defaulting Soviets . . .
>
> It may fairly be concluded that the theoretical "obligation to pay" died on the floor of the Assembly in 1965. Since each UN organ is free to interpret the Charter, the Assembly was within its rights in refusing to apply the Court's advisory opinion. No formal resolution adopting the opinion can outweigh the actual practice. In effect, the Assembly has yielded to the Soviet Union's (and 29 other nations') stated refusal to pay for activities it opposed or regarded as violative of the Charter. Therefore, it is now open to any State to refuse payment on the ground that a UN activity is beyond the powers of the organ that authorized it, and against that State's interest.[4]

[4] Thomas M. Franck, *Nation Against Nation* (1985), p. 259.

Professor Franck's conclusion cannot be dismissed, despite the analysis set out above. While it is not supported by the law of treaties as codified in the Vienna Convention, it is undeniable that "the actual practice" of widespread arrearage in the payment of assessed contributions has been maintained. On that basis, there is ground for the argument that the obligation to which Article 17 of the Charter gives rise has fallen into desuetude. But what is, it is believed, more persuasive is that the membership at large, including the United States, has continued to recognize that assessments are binding. Thus, when Members fall in arrears within the terms of Article 19, it is a recurrent practice for them to seek exculpation under that article; they do not maintain that assessments are not binding but that "the General Assembly may, nevertheless, permit such a Member to vote if it is satisfied that the failure to pay is due to conditions beyond the control of the Member." The official position of the membership of the United Nations as a whole is one of recognition of the binding character of assessments, not one of denial of that character.

Assessments are made on Members globally and not for specific budgetary items, so that withholding in response to items of the budget of itself is not specific in effect (however specific may be the objection voiced by the withholding Member). More than this, the larger defaults of the United States over the years have not been attributed to objectional particulars of assessments upon it or to the objectionable character of the expenditures in question but to more general objections by the United States Government or Congress to aspects of United Nations operations, e.g., a budgetary process which gives inadequate weight to the position of the major contributors and excessive weight to the position of a majority of the membership whose financial contributions are minor.

Some progress has been made in recent years to meeting those objections, and towards meeting more generalized reservations about the United Nations which became current in the United States and elsewhere. For its part, the United States has made a substantial start in the payment of its arrears, which it has undertaken to discharge in full, and which it has been paying off in installments; and it is largely meeting current assessments (but not altogether currently, since for some years the United States has paid assessments due on January 1 after October 1 of the year in question). As noted, the Soviet Union and France paid the contentious peacekeeping assessments many years after they were levied, but in the case of Russia and of the successor republics of the USSR, fresh arrearages have arisen, apparently not for reasons of principle or policy but because of economic difficulties.

The results of the accrual of withholdings by the United States, and the arrearages of a very large number of other Members in varying but in some cases consequential amounts, have subjected the Organization to a state of continuing financial crisis. Overcoming that crisis, and placing the United Nations on a sound financial footing, is one of the more pressing of contemporary international problems. The Goldberg Reservation, however understandable when made, and however politically appealing it may have been when made, does not furnish persuasive legal justification either for avoiding or for exacerbating that problem, particularly as in practice it has magnified over the years.[5]

---

[5] For an analysis generally consistent with that set out in this paper, see the report prepared by Professor Frederick L. Kirgis, Jr., for the Special Working Committee on United Nations Relations of the American Society of International Law, published in the Society's *Newsletter* of July–September 1989, pp. 4–5.

PART IV
International Contracts and Expropriation

☙

23

Report of the Committee on Nationalization of Property of the American Branch of the International Law Association

A Response by the Committee on the Nationalization of Property of the American Branch to the Questionnaire of the International Committee on Nationalization

ॐ

Introduction

The Committee on the Nationalization of Property was created by the American Branch of the International Law Association. The American Branch requested the Committee to study the problem of nationalization of the property of aliens, as it concerns international law. The Committee is composed of lawyers whose experience, taken collectively, represents service as Government officials, teachers, and practitioners.

The members of the Committee live and work in a community whose foundations were built with capital funds from abroad. As the United States developed and industrialized, its citizens created financial resources and managerial and scientific techniques. A proportion of these funds and techniques are assets which may be used with assets of other countries to develop world trade and provide an increasing level of industrial development in other parts of the world. The assets other peoples possess include raw materials and natural resources, in many instances far beyond the foreseeable requirements of the States in which they are found. In some cases they include capital, and, in more cases, skills. The market potential of all countries of itself is an asset awaiting further development for mutual benefit.

In the ever-shrinking world community, whose population is estimated to be increasing by 70,000 per week, it is in the mutual interest of the United States and other States to maintain free association to develop the general

The Report was first published in *Proceedings and Committee Reports of the American Branch of the International Law Association 1957–1958*, p. 61. The Appendix to the Report, containing the Committee's answers to the Questionnaire of the International Committee, is omitted. James N. Hyde was Chairman of the Committee.

level of productivity. All countries will gain by the mutual development of their natural, agricultural, and industrial resources; no country can best attain these ends alone. Economic interdependence is universal and acute.

Political differences in the world are deep and complex. This fact in itself is a reason for an approach that continues to offer foreign capital and skills for creative and cooperative use in worldwide economic development. Of course no State need agree to such a joint use of respective capacities. Yet, when it does, certain obligations come into being. It is appropriate to consider what they are and how they can be determined.

In the United States, a vital proportion of the capital available for potential investment abroad is in private hands. The management of private corporations, as trustees for that broad segment of the general public who are stockholders, largely determines the disposition of such capital. Corporate management must evaluate what contribution capital sent abroad will make to the success of the enterprise, as well as the risk that the venture may be frustrated.

The Committee accordingly is concerned with the bases for a fair and continuing relationship between existing, as well as future, foreign private investment and the State which explicitly or implicitly invites its use, in combination with its own assets. It is appropriate and necessary to look to international law for the concepts and methods that will provide a framework for such a fair and continuing relationship.

The wrongful taking of alien property interests represents the frustration and failure of joint plans reaching across borders. It is the task of law to discourage the wrong, and, where it occurs, to right it.

The Law

Definitions

The problem of central concern is the taking by a State of alien interests, legal or equitable, in property and contract.

We are concerned with private interests. Foreign investment by Governments and their agencies is important. But peacetime maltreatment of public investment, in an era of invasion of private foreign property interests, has not been conspicuous.[1]

We use the word "taking" advisedly and consistently. We employ it as a substitute for the words "nationalization" and "expropriation."

To "nationalize" may carry connotations of broad social and economic

---

[1] For example, no loans of the International Bank for Reconstruction and Development, or of the Export–Import Bank, are known to have been repudiated.

measures designed to refashion the fundamental structure of a community. It imports a presumption of what may be a question: whether the taking is for a public purpose. The term "expropriation" is perhaps prejudicial as well, carrying as it may implications of class conflict. The word "taking" is impartial, broad, and descriptive.

Our use of the word "taking" is subject to a single reservation. A taking need not be total; title need not pass. To fall within the ambit of our analysis, a taking may well involve lesser measures which have the effect, in whole or in part, of an appropriation or destruction by the State of alien interests in property and contract. Among such measures may be sequestration, custodianship, breach by a State of a contract with an alien, arbitrary measures of taxation and exchange control, oppressive administrative proceedings, State-sponsored boycott, forced dissolution of a corporation, invasion of a company's managerial prerogatives, or compulsory sale of its stock. These examples are but illustrative of the fact that the opportunities of the State either to regulate or to abuse the rights of foreigners are manifold. We use the word "taking" with the potential of such abuse in mind.

It is with international law that we are concerned. International law, in its present state of evolution, is not substantially applicable to the treatment by a State of its own nationals. The human rights provisions of the United Nations Charter may be argued to invest the individual under international law with rights against his State, but even if this is true in the sphere of property rights we shall nevertheless consider interests of aliens alone. However, we speak of alien rights in the sense of indirect as well as direct legal rights. Thus, the interests of foreigners in a corporation cannot be disregarded by a State because that corporation is its national.

We do not deal with the law of war and its effects upon alien property and contractual interests. This is by no means to say that we regard a national proclamation of a state of emergency, or the recommendation of United Nations measures of pacific settlement, or the taking of police action within or without the United Nations, or war itself, as necessarily validating treatment of alien interests which would be otherwise unlawful.

Principles

In the Committee's view, three basic principles of international law govern the treatment of alien interests in property and contract:

(*a*) International law is supreme over municipal law.

(*b*) The taking of alien interests must be accompanied by full compensation.

(*c*) States are bound to perform their treaties with States and contracts with aliens in good faith.

Our fundamental assumption is the supremacy of international law. Thus, our approach is characterized by a recognition of the distinction between the power of States and the rights and duties of States. In the present stage of international law and life, not all that States have and exercise the *power* to do is necessarily right or creative of rights. The practice of States, a source of international law, must be approached with discrimination. The suffering of wrongs must not be confused with acquiescence in the assertion of rights. Above all, incantations of "sovereignty" must be regarded as the derision of law they so often are meant to be.

The supremacy of international law over municipal law may be summarily illustrated. Thus, the Permanent Court of International Justice held in the case of *Free Zones of Upper Savoy* that "it is certain that France cannot rely on her own legislation to limit the scope of her international obligations ..."[2] The Court held similarly in its opinion on *Treatment of Polish Nationals in Danzig* that "a State cannot adduce as against another State its own Constitution with a view to evading obligations incumbent upon it under international law ..."[3]

The application to alien property interests of this axiom of the supremacy of international law was emphasized by the Government of the United States in its diplomatic exchange with the Government of Guatemala over the taking of United Fruit Company property:

> The Government of the United States does not controvert in the slightest the proposition that the Act of Congress of the Republic of Guatemala ... constitutes an act of sovereignty inherent in Guatemala. Every act of the Guatemalan Government constitutes a sovereign act, as do the acts of every other sovereign Government, including the acts of the Government of the United States. But to state that no sovereign act of a Government affecting foreign States or their nationals is open to discussion, or question, as to its validity under international law, because it is a sovereign act, is to say that States are not subject to international law. One has only to look at the diplomatic records of any Government over any period of time to see that such sovereign acts are constantly discussed and held up to scrutiny by other members of the family of nations with whom they treat for determination as to whether they measure up to or fall below the standards required under international law.
>
> The obligation of a State imposed by international law to pay just or fair compensation at the time of taking of property of foreigners cannot be abrogated from the international standpoint by local legislation. If the contrary were true, States seeking to avoid the necessity of making payment for property expropriated from foreign nationals could avoid all pecuniary responsibility simply by changing their local law. Every international obligation could thus be wiped off

[2] PCIJ, *Series A/B, No. 46*, p. 167 (1932).   [3] PCIJ, *Series A/B, No. 44*, p. 24 (1932).

the books. But international law cannot thus be flouted. Membership in the family of nations imposes international obligations.[4]

Whatever the position under municipal law, it is to the standards of international law which States, in their treatment of alien property interests, must adhere.

Yet the logical application of this root concept is far from axiomatic. In the field of private international law, its implementation is sustained by the courts and authorities of some States, denied by those of others, and ignored by still others. Some courts refuse to exercise jurisdiction to restore property and contractual rights taken in violation of international law; others do not.

In the view of the Committee, the problems of private international law posed in the Questionnaire may be met with relative simplicity, and with a complete regard for the advancement of international law and welfare, by rigorous application of the principle of the supremacy of public international law. It is, in our submission, unsound to maintain that the State is responsible under international law for the violation of alien property and contractual interests but that, under its rules of private international law which are alleged to be municipal rules alone, its courts may subvert that international law by which the State as a whole is bound. Whatever doctrinal validity the dichotomy between private international law and public international law may have, it is insufficient to overcome the needs of the international community. Public international law is not only to be described but applied. A principal forum of its application, especially in the field of alien property and contractual interests, is and should increasingly be the municipal courts of States.

Authority for this view is found not only in contemporary practice – which admittedly is in conflict – but in the principle of law which underlies it: that no legal right can spring from a wrong. Thus, where a State violates international law in its taking of alien interests, it and its successors who take with knowledge do not come into court with clean hands. They have no claim, basing it as they do upon a misuse of sovereign power, to the application on their behalf of the sovereign rights of the State which has jurisdiction over the *res*. This is so whether or not the *res* was within the territory of the taking State at the time of taking.

A second fundamental principle is that the taking of alien interests must be accompanied by full compensation. To the extent that alien interests are taken without the payment of prompt, adequate, and effective compensation, there is confiscation – public seizure of private rights which, in essence, does not

---

[4] *Department of State Bulletin* (September 14, 1953), 29, pp. 358, 360.

differ from that private seizure of private rights that the legal systems of all civilized societies prohibit. "No one," the United Nations Universal Declaration of Human Rights proclaims, "shall be arbitrarily deprived of his property."[5] This basic requirement – full compensation, promptly and effectively paid – has received repeated expression in legal principle and in positive law. It is linked with the principles of unjust enrichment and acquired rights. The concept of unjust enrichment is fundamental to Roman law, civil law, and is today acknowledged in Anglo-American law. It is embedded in international law, in substance and in terms.[6] In substance, it equates with "the principle of respect for vested rights" to which the Permanent Court of International Justice repeatedly lent its authority.[7]

The Committee recognizes that the taking of alien interests has not consistently been characterized by compensation which is either prompt, or adequate, or effective. But it does not see in these violations of the principle of unjust enrichment the establishment of a new principle of not-so-unjust enrichment. The arbitrary divesting of rights does not vitiate the principle of respect for vested rights. International political settlements for less than full compensation are not legal precedents that prejudice the international law rule requiring payment of full compensation.

Some argue that the "capacity" of the taking State to pay should govern not its possibility of taking but the amount of compensation due. But it is not apparent why, if the taking is proportionately large, the obligation to compensate should be disproportionately small. Such achievements as nationalization may have are too controversial to admit the assumption that a large-scale taking is necessarily a national good meriting special dispensation. Still less can the Committee see why, even if the contentious economic justification of large-scale taking were to be established, the foreign investor should bear the burden of a State's experimentation. By hypothesis, the foreigner whose presence is expressed in his property and contractual interests will be absent once his interests are taken; he will not share in the national social advantage of a large-scale taking, even assuming such advantage to exist. As against the international investor, a national taking accompanied by less than full compensation represents injustice compounded.

If a State receives a gift from the Government or the people of another State, it is entitled to treat it as such. Is it equally entitled to treat foreign

---

[5] Article XVII.

[6] See, for example, *Lena Goldfields, Ltd. Arbitration*, 36 Cornell L.Q., pp. 42, 51 (1950–1951).

[7] See, for example, *Case Concerning Certain German Interests in Polish Upper Silesia (Merits)*, PCIJ, Series A, No. 7, pp. 21–22 (1926).

investments as gifts? The obvious answer leads to the ineluctable conclusion: if a State takes property of foreigners, it must provide fair compensation.

A standard of fairness is not beyond the reach of international legal technique. It is simpler to establish than a standard which falls short of the fair. For example, Article 6 of the Treaty of Friendship, Commerce, and Navigation between Japan and the United States provides:

> Property of nationals and companies of either Party shall not be taken within the territories of the other Party except for a public purpose, nor shall it be taken without the prompt payment of just compensation. Such compensation shall be in an effectively realizable form and shall represent the full equivalent of the property taken; and adequate provision shall have been made at or prior to the time of taking for the determination and payment thereof."[8]

It is equally axiomatic that a public taking of alien interests must be not only fully compensated but also (a) for a public purpose and (b) not based upon an arbitrary and unreasonable classification violative of fundamental human rights. Subject to the principle of respect for acquired rights, a State lawfully may reserve certain areas of a nation's economic endeavor to its nationals. But, under international law, a State may not take foreign interests as a measure of political reprisal. Nor may a State use its public power to take alien interests for private profit, or for other ends than those directly related to public purposes.

A third and fundamental principle is that States must perform their treaties with States and contracts with aliens in good faith. The principle of *pacta sunt servanda* is of the essence of the supremacy of international law. "No case is known in which any tribunal ever repudiated the rule or questioned its validity."[9] There is, in fact, no dispute over a State's being bound to carry out in good faith the obligations it assumes by treaty. These obligations embrace the field of treatment of alien property and contractual interests as well as other areas of international law. A taking in violation of a treaty, as the Permanent Court of International Justice held in the *Chorzow Factory* case, is "unlawful" and "illegal."[10]

While the legal force of a treaty restriction upon a taking by a State of alien interests is uncontested, the international legal impact of restrictions contained in contracts between States and aliens is a matter of dispute. In the view

---

[8] [1953] 4 *US Treaties, etc.* (II), pp. 2068–2069.

[9] "Law of Treaties," *Harvard Research in International Law, American Journal of International Law Supplements* (1935), 29, p. 977. The authorities collected by the Harvard Research in support of the rule of *pacta sunt servanda* are extensive and conclusive.

[10] *Case Concerning the Factory at Chorzow (Claim for Indemnity, Merits), PCIJ*, Series A, No. 17, p. 47 (1928). See also *Case Concerning Certain German Interests in Polish Upper Silesia (Merits)* (above, note 7), at p. 21.

of the Committee, an approach which is both principled and progressive would admit no such dispute; the contractual obligations freely assumed by a State are no less binding than its treaty obligations. This would be true even if the following were not:

> International law today recognizes that individuals and other subjects are directly entitled to international rights ... the alien is internationally recognized as a legal person independent of his State; he is a true subject of international rights.[11]

In the case of *Losinger & Co.*, Switzerland declared: "The principle *pacta sunt servanda* ... applies not only to agreements directly concluded between States, but also to those between a State and foreigners ..."[12] Yugoslavia, its opponent, while denying any violation of that principle, maintained that the breach by a State of a contract with an alien of itself did not engage that State's international responsibility.[13] A settlement made it unnecessary for the Permanent Court to rule and, in fact, no conclusive international judgment on the question exists. Nor is a consistent pattern formed by the practice of States in other instances of dispute over the violation of contracts between States and aliens, such as the Anglo-Iranian Oil Company and Suez cases.

It is noteworthy, however, that more than one effort at codification of the law governing the treatment of alien interests has substantially viewed the breach of such contracts as a breach of international law. Thus, the Harvard Research declares:

> A State is responsible if an injury to an alien results from its non-performance of a contractual obligation which it owes to the alien, if local remedies have been exhausted without adequate redress.[14]

The Bases of Discussion drawn up in 1929 by the Preparatory Committee of The Hague Conference for the Codification of International Law submitted:

> A State is responsible for damage suffered by a foreigner as the result of the enactment of legislation which directly infringes rights derived by the foreigner from a concession granted or a contract made by the State.

---

[11] United Nations doc. No. A/CN.4/96, 51, 58; International Law Commission, "International Responsibility," Report by F. V. Garcia-Amador, Special Rapporteur.

[12] *PCIJ, Series C, No. 78*, p. 32 (1936); translation supplied.

It is submitted that the Swiss view is unassailable; that, as a matter of principle, there is no difference whatsoever in this respect between treaties and contracts. As a matter of practice, support for the Swiss view, while mixed, is nevertheless substantial. In the arbitration between Losinger & Co. and the Kingdom of Yugoslavia, which antedated the proceedings before the Permanent Court, the umpire forcefully upheld "the principle of fidelity to contract ... *Pacta sunt servanda*" (*ibid.*, p. 83).

[13] *Ibid.*, pp. 242, 333, 334.

[14] 23 *American Journal of International Law Supplement* (1929), 23, p. 167. See Dunn, *The Protection of Nationals* (1932), p. 166.

It depends upon the circumstances whether a State incurs responsibility where it has enacted legislation general in character which is incompatible with the operation of a concession which it has granted or the performance of a contract made by it.[15]

More recently, Professor de La Pradelle, as Rapporteur of the Institute of International Law, advanced a draft that provided:

Nationalization ... shall respect obligations validly entered into, whether by treaty, or by contract ..."[16]

While the Hague Conference did not come to consider the former drafts, and the Institute was unable to achieve agreement upon the latter, they lend weight to the view which this Committee espouses: that the taking of alien contractual rights by a State of itself is a breach of international law.[17] Parties normally contract in the expectation of performance. When a State, through its interjection of sovereign power, steps out of the role of contractor and upsets that expectation, it violates international law.

No Government would suggest that it has a legal right to breach a loan agreement it concludes with the International Bank for Reconstruction and Development. Can it seriously be contended that a Government has the legal "right" to breach a loan agreement with the Chase Manhattan Bank? Acceptance of the argument that the former contract is intergovernmental, and consequently governed by international law, while the latter has but one Government as a party, and consequently is governed by municipal law, even if formalistically satisfying – as it is not – adds nothing to the rule of international law. It may detract from the flow of international investment.

---

[15] League of Nations doc. C.75.M69.1929.V., p. 33. The Bases of Discussion contain a similar clause concerning executive acts (*ibid.*, 59). What the Preparatory Committee described as "the prevalent opinion" expressed in its draft was based upon the responses of twenty-three governments to its questionnaire.

[16] *Annuaire de l'Institut de droit international 1952*, 44, Part 2, pp. 305–318; translation supplied.

[17] See *Serbian and Brazilian Loan Cases*, PCIJ, Series A, Nos. 20 and 21 (1929), and comment upon by Lipstein, *The Place of the Calvo Clause in International Law*, British Year Book of International Law (1945), 22, pp. 130, 134, and *International Fisheries Co. (USA) v. United Mexican States*, 4 Reports of International Arbitral Awards (1931), pp. 691, 699, as well as the *El Triunfo Case (US v. El Salvador* [1901], *Foreign Relations US* (1902), pp. 838, 871; *Turnbull et al. (US v. Venezuela)*, Ralston and Doyle, *Venezuelan Arbitrations of 1903*, pp. 239, 242, 244; the *Landreau Claim (US v. Peru*, 1922), 1 *Reports of International Arbitral Awards*, pp. 349, 356, 364; the *Shufeldt Claim (US v. Guatemala*, 1930), 2 *Reports of International Arbitral Awards*, pp. 1081, 1097–1098; *The Administration of Posts and Telegraphs of the Republic of Czechoslovakia v. Radio Corporation of America* (1932), *American Journal of International Law* (1936), 30, pp. 523, 530–532, 534; *Radio Corporation of America v. The National Government of the Republic of China* (1935), 3 *Reports of International Arbitral Awards*, pp. 1623, 1627; *North American Dredging Company of Texas (USA) v. United Mexican States* (1926), 4 *Reports of International Arbitral Awards* 26, 35; *Harry H. Hughes (USA) v. United Mexican States* (1930), *ibid.*, pp. 617, 621; and Dunn, *The Protection of Nationals*, pp. 165–167.

The unsoundness of treating the legal rights arising from contracts between States and aliens as being of a lower order than those arising from agreements between Governments or their agencies merits further illustration. Afghanistan recently granted the Soviet Techno Export Organization rights to explore for oil in Afghanistan. A breach by Afghanistan of the pertinent agreement would be a breach of international law.[18] But a contract by Afghanistan with a privately owned oil company, for the same object, of the same substance, upon the same terms, breached in the same way, by the same State, would not be a breach of international law in the eyes of some formalists. In fact, some would go so far as to say that if the contract were governed by Afghanistan law and that law were altered to authorize the contract's breach, no law, international, municipal, or other, would be violated by breach.

Questionable conclusions such as these may be reached, at the price of practical deterrence of private capital investment. In the Committee's view – which has significant support in municipal law – States no less than individuals are bound by their contracts.[19] This is so even if, in a given case, a contract between a State and an alien happens to be governed by the contracting State's municipal law. But whatever differences there may be about the law relating to a State's performance of contracts with aliens, there can be no dispute about the fact that performance is in the universal interest. The interest in a maximum flow of international capital and trade is, as a matter of economic fact, and as between borrower and investor, buyer and seller, wholly mutual. International contracts are a primary means of imple-

---

[18] This certainly would be the case were the agreement between the Government of Afghanistan and the USSR. It probably would be the case were the agreement between the Afghanistan Government and an "independent" Soviet state agency.

[19] In *Perry v. United States*, the Supreme Court held:
>The United States are as much bound by their contracts as are individuals ... When the United States, with constitutional authority, makes contracts, has rights and incurs responsibilities similar to those of individuals who are parties to such instruments ... The [contrary] argument ... is in substance that the Government cannot by contract restrict the exercise a sovereign power. But the right to make binding obligations is a competence attaching to sovereignty"
>
>   (294 US 330, 351, 352, 353 [1934]).

In *Robertson v. Minister of Pensions*, it was similarly held:
>The next question is whether the assurance is binding upon the Crown. The Crown cannot escape by saying that estoppels do not bind the Crown, for that doctrine has long been exploded. Nor can the Crown escape by praying in aid the doctrine of executive necessity, i.e., the doctrine that the Crown cannot bind itself so as to fetter its future executive action ... the Crown is bound by its express promises as much as any subject ... The defence of executive necessity is of limited scope. It only avails the Crown where there is an implied term to that effect, or that is the true meaning of the contract.   ([1948] 2 All E.R. 767, 770.)

See also the multinational authorities cited by Mann, "The Law Governing State Contracts," *British Year Book of International Law* (1944), 21, pp. 11, 13–14, n. 10.

menting that interest. Unilateral repudiation or alteration by States of their contracts with aliens hardly promote that interest or the conclusion of contracts which is its expression.

Is "nationalization" a valid legal excuse for the breach by a State of its contracts with foreigners? The Permanent Court of International Justice, in the *Chorzow Factory* case, responded negatively, where a treaty restricted a taking. The International Court of Justice has been denied opportunity to respond where a contract restricted a taking – a fact which suggests that States that have breached contracts with foreigners lack confidence in the legality of their actions. In the view of the Committee, restrictions upon the taking of alien interests may be found in a treaty; they may be expressed or implied by contract; in either case, international law requires they be respected. The breach by a State of a contract with an alien is no less illegal because it is complete. The taking of contract interests cannot be legal where the breach of contract interests is illegal.

It follows that, while the measure of compensation which conditions a State's taking of alien interests not protected by treaty or contract[20] is prompt, adequate (full), and effective compensation, the consequences flowing from a State's breach of a treaty or contract are otherwise. As the Permanent Court pointed out in the *Chorzow Factory* case, an equation between the indemnity due in a lawful taking and that due in an unlawful one would be "unjust." Rather, the Court held, the consequences of "unlawful dispossession" are to be assessed as follows:

> The essential principle contained in the actual notion of an illegal act – a principle which seems to be established by international practice and in particular by the decisions of arbitral tribunals – is that reparation must, as far as possible, wipe out all the consequences of the illegal act and reestablish the situation which would, in all probability, have existed if that act had not been committed. Restitution in kind, or, if this is not possible, payment of a sum corresponding to the value which a restitution in kind would bear; the award, if need be, of damages for loss sustained which would not be covered by restitution in kind or payment in place of it – such are the principles which should serve to determine the amount of compensation due for an act contrary to international law.[21]

---

20 A contract may be implied as well as express. Thus, if a State invites foreign investment pursuant to the terms of a given law, its right unilateral to alter that law, in derogation of investment made in reliance upon it, is open to question. Not only may the principles set forth above govern such a situation, but the further principle of estoppel or *préclusion* may be applicable.

21 *Chorzow Factory (Merits)* (above, note 10), p. 47. The draft submitted to the Institute of International Law provided: "Nationalization ... shall respect obligations validly entered into, whether by treaty, or by contract. Failing such respect, there will be a denial of justice giving the right not merely to payment of full compensation, but to damages of a punitive character" (*Annuaire* [see note 16]).

Thus, the remedy for breach by a State of a contract with an alien, whether designated as a breach or a taking or as expropriation or nationalization, is in the nature of specific performance. Where performance actually is no longer possible, then the foreign contractor must be placed as nearly as possible in the position he would have enjoyed absent the breach, that is to say, he is entitled to the profits he would have earned had not his contract rights been taken.

Procedures

Procedures for the application of the foregoing principles are secondary only to the principles themselves. International law is characterized by an assertion of rights coupled with an absence of remedies. The consequent fragility of international law needs no elaboration. Any effort to strengthen the rule of law must consider procedure with substance, enforcement with prescription.

The rights of aliens in property and contract traditionally have been considered – to the extent that they have been judicially considered at all – in the first instance in municipal courts, and in the second in international courts or arbitral tribunals.

Traditionally, international law, with an understandable emphasis upon the rule of exhaustion of local remedies, and an awareness of the lack of alternative judicial fora, placed principal reliance upon municipal tribunals. It was assumed that an alien investing in a country subjected himself to the protection and obligations of the law of the State in which he invested. It was assumed that not only would the alien be required to seek redress for injuries in the local courts but that justice would be done. Only where there was a "denial of justice" might international law come into play, by means of the diplomatic intervention of the State whose national the alien was.

In the traditional view, if a State were to take an alien's interests by legislative or executive action not subject to genuine judicial challenge, this of itself would constitute, as a denial of justice, a violation of international law. Since, in fact, all too often violations of alien interests by a State have been characterized by a lack of effective judicial redress, those who have denied that international law automatically is breached by the arbitrary breach by a State of its contract with an alien have nevertheless tended to affirm that such breaches in practice do violate international law.

These traditional patterns are not without merit. The local remedies rule, which never applied where local remedies did not exist, is a reasonable one. Standards of international behavior have not so far deteriorated that it may be assumed that an alien may never have his day in the court of any foreign State on terms of equality not only with that State's nationals but with the State itself.

Yet, the expanding pace of world development, the rising level of international trade, the increasing demand for foreign capital, the immensity of certain capital commitments, the growth of large international corporations, and the multiplication of sovereignties, in uneasy combination with a contradictory and costly contempt in some cases for alien property and contractual interests, have led to a search for new procedures for the lawful disposition of disputes. At the same time, the weakness of the traditional appellate recourse – that of the home State's diplomatic intervention – has become the plainer. While the United Nations Charter has imposed restrictions upon the resolution of international disputes by force, States generally have not accepted complementary procedures for the resolution of disputes through law.

Dissatisfaction with the procedures for the settlement of alien property and contractual disputes has embraced another sphere as well, that of the municipal courts of States other than the State alleged to have breached alien interests. The actions of municipal courts in dealing with such breaches are inconsistent and confused. Concepts of territoriality, act of State, sovereign immunity, and public policy have dissonantly clashed.

The Committee accordingly sees the procedural problem as threefold:

(1) A new international court of arbitration should be established, to which alien holders of property and contractual rights would have equal access with States.[22] Such a court, designed to resolve disputes between States and aliens,[23] should be a fully constituted tribunal, akin to the International Court of Justice rather than to the Permanent Court of Arbitration. It should be animated by those general principles of law recognized by civilized nations upon which the International Court of Justice itself is authorized to draw. It might embody specialized panels competent to deal with technical disputes, such as those turning upon matters of taxation or accounting or the particular techniques of an industry.

Such a court would supply the advantages of arbitration to the many alien investors whose interests are not contractual or whose contracts do not provide for *ad hoc* arbitration. The Committee recognizes the danger of undue proliferation of international machinery. But it believes that the creation of a tribunal of this kind, open to all alien investors and all States, would fulfill a need that is not otherwise met. This would be preferable, in its view, to amendment of the Statute of the International Court of Justice that would accord access to aliens.

---

[22] While the Committee is concerned with rights in property and contract, it does not mean to suggest that aliens other than investors should not enjoy increased international procedural status for the protection of other human rights.

[23] The field of international commercial arbitration between private parties is of course well developed.

Thus the Committee would modernize the rule of exhaustion of local remedies – a rule which, in any case, it views as procedural. The alien investor should, and in varying degrees does, have municipal judicial recourse against the violation of his rights. Where local remedies are or reasonably promise to be effective, the alien should have the option of employing them. He will tend to exercise that option to the extent that local remedies are in fact prompt and adequate. Municipal litigation generally is less expensive than international litigation. But where the State, if not through maladminist-ration of the judicial process, then through the enactment of legislation or decree alters the municipal law which, it argues, governs the rights of the alien investor, then municipal courts provide no remedy.[24] It is in cases such as these – and there will be others – in which the alien will wish to exercise the option, with which he should be endowed, of recourse to an alternative forum of the first instance, the new international court of arbitration. The local remedies rule thus would acquire a new dimension, for the alien would be required either to exhaust municipal remedies or the remedies of the international court of arbitration before the diplomatic intervention of his State would be permissible.[25]

A new international court of arbitration finds promising precedent in the experience of *ad hoc* arbitration between States and aliens. The major inter-national investments of the twentieth century often have carried with them provision for the constitution of arbitral tribunals. These tribunals, to which the contracting State and the contracting alien have access on a basis of equality, directly adjudicate disputes between States and aliens, by applying municipal law,[26] international law, or those general principles of law recog-nized by civilized nations which are a source of international law.

It is in any case clear that the law such tribunals find to be controlling cannot be municipal law as the contracting State may amend it in derogation of the rights it has accorded the investor. This is implied in the very constitution of a tribunal distinct from the State's judicial structure, and is made explicit in a number of concession agreements. It is plain that, when an alien investor enters into a contractual arrangement with a State which is interwoven with the law of that State, the parties contract under the

---

[24] The instances where courts are empowered to strike down the promulgations of legislature or executive are exceptional.

[25] Where the alien already enjoys the advantages of arbitration by the terms of his contract with the State, he is not bound to do more than exhaust the remedy arbitration provides. Should the State refuse to arbitrate, local remedies would thereby be exhausted, and the diplomatic intervention of the alien's State would be in order.

[26] Of the contracting State or of the contracting alien's State, or both (as in *Radio Corporation of America v. The National Government of the Republic of China* [see note 17]).

assumption that it is the law as it exists at the time of contract, and not as it may later be amended, which applies to their relations and to any judicial resolution of them.[27]

Such *ad hoc* tribunals provide not only an effective means of settlement of disputes between States and aliens but a clear-cut test of the honoring by a State of its obligations under international law. If, as in the case of Iran, the State which purports lawfully to take the property of an alien refuses to submit its action to the adjudication of the arbitral tribunal whose competence it earlier accepted, its action constitutes an undeniable denial of justice. A new international court of arbitration would embody the advantage of this test as well.

(2) The need on the inter-State level is not the creation of new machinery but the use of that which exists. The International Court of Justice and its predecessor have played an effective role in the protection of the rights of States and alien investors alike, insofar as the Court has been permitted to do so.[28] The jurisdiction actually accorded the Court has been regrettably constricted. In fact, the principal post-World War II disputes over the treatment of alien property and contractual interests have been withheld from the Court's judgment. The taking of alien interests repeatedly has been left to the arena of unsatisfactory settlement, international disturbance, or unheeded injustice. The Committee particularly regrets that the Government of the United States so far has chosen to contest the jurisdiction of the Court in the *Interhandel* Case.

The problem – fundamental to international law – of the Court's compulsory jurisdiction is substantially one in which virtually all States are guilty, and some guiltier than others. The Committee submits that the international legal character of the views, the arguments, and the proposals to be advanced at this Conference of the International Law Association should be tested against the willingness of those who advance them to have their respective States bound by the Court's effective and compulsory jurisdiction.

It has been noted that no authoritative judicial ruling exists on certain of the principal issues under discussion. The International Court of Justice has been denied more than one opportunity to render such a ruling. It is in the incontestable interest of the rule of international law that future opportunities should not be lost.

---

[27] This is not to say that the law-making body of a State may generally deny to subsequent legislatures the right to legislate. But it is to say that a State may bind itself not to adopt, or so apply, legislation as to violate its obligations, whether they spring from treaty or contract.

[28] Inter-State arbitration presents a promising alternative. A number of economic treaties concluded by the United States in recent years contain provision for arbitration of disputes.

(3) A third and vital forum is the municipal courts of States other than the State whose treatment of the alien's interests is challenged. In this sphere, as has been indicated above, it is the Committee's belief that it is incumbent upon municipal courts to apply public international law. Municipal courts should recognize no title as arising, and none of the effects of ownership flowing, from a taking of alien interests in violation of international law.

15. As a Committee of lawyers, dedicated to the judicial process, we place our emphasis upon judicial settlement. But we recognize that the sanctions which the effective enforcement of international law may require may be not only judicial. In fact, judicial sanctions themselves may require executory sanctions. It is accordingly submitted that measures, short of the use or threat of use of armed force, to sustain international law not only are lawful but, in certain cases, may be imperative. In the sphere of treatment of alien property and contractual rights, as throughout international life, the problem of strengthening the role and the rule of law is a principal problem of our age.

24

The Story of the United Nations Declaration on Permanent Sovereignty over Natural Resources

୧୨

The United Nations General Assembly adopted at its Seventeenth Session a resolution which, the Delegate of Bulgaria complained, comprised "a charter of foreign investment."[1] The resolution,[2] entitled "Permanent Sovereignty over Natural Resources," is the capstone of more than ten years of consideration of the subject by the General Assembly, the Human Rights Commission, the Economic and Social Council and a special Commission on Permanent Sovereignty over Natural Resources.[3] It was adopted by a vote of eighty-seven in favor, two opposed and twelve abstentions. The United States voted with the majority; France and South Africa were the two dissenters; and the Communist bloc (including Cuba) and, for varying reasons, Ghana and Burma, abstained.

The resolution reads:

The General Assembly,

Recalling its resolution 523 (VI) of 12 January 1952 and 626 (VII) of 21 December 1952,

Bearing in mind its resolution 1314 (XIII) of 12 December 1958, by which it established the Commission on Permanent Sovereignty over Natural Resources and instructed it to conduct a full survey of the status of permanent sovereignty over natural wealth and resources as a basic constituent of the right to self-determination, with recommendations, where necessary, for its strengthening, and decided further that, in the conduct of the full survey of the status of the permanent sovereignty of peoples and nations over their natural wealth and resources, due regard should be paid to the rights and duties of States under

---

First published in *American Bar Association Journal* (May 1963), p. 463. Copyright 1963 American Bar Association, reprinted by permission of the *ABA Journal.*

[1] United Nations General Assembly, Seventeenth Session, Second Committee, Provisional Summary Record of the 859th Meeting, UN doc. A/C.2/SR.859, 5.

[2] General Assembly resolution 1803 (XVII) of December 14, 1962.

[3] See Hyde, "Permanent Sovereignty over Natural Wealth and Resources," *American Journal of International Law* (1956), 50, p. 854.

international law and to the importance of encouraging international cooperation in the economic development of developing countries,

Bearing in mind its resolution 1515 (XV) of 15 December 1960, in which it recommended that the sovereign right of every State to dispose of its wealth and its natural resources should be respected,

Considering that any measure in this respect must be based on the recognition of the inalienable right of all States freely to dispose of their natural wealth and resources in accordance with their national interests, and on respect for the economic independence of States,

Considering that nothing in paragraph 4 below in any way prejudices the position of any Member State on any aspect of the question of the rights and obligations of successor States and Governments in respect of property acquired before the accession to complete sovereignty of countries formerly under colonial rule,

Noting that the subject of succession of States and Governments is being examined as a matter of priority by the International Law Commission,

Considering that it is desirable to promote international cooperation for the economic development of developing countries, and that economic and financial agreements between the developed and the developing countries must be based on the principles of equality and of the right of peoples and nations to self-determination,

Considering that the provision of economic and technical assistance, loans and increased foreign investment must not be subject to conditions which conflict with the interests of the recipient State,

Considering the benefits to be derived from exchanges of technical and scientific information likely to promote the development and use of such resources and wealth, and the important part which the United Nations and other international organizations are called upon to play in that connexion,

Attaching particular importance to the question of promoting the economic development of developing countries and securing their economic independence,

Noting that the creation and strengthening of the inalienable sovereignty of States over their natural wealth and resources reinforces their economic independence,

Desiring that there should be further consideration by the United Nations of the subject of permanent sovereignty over natural resources in the spirit of international cooperation in the field of economic development, particularly that of the developing countries,

Declares that:

1. The right of peoples and nations to permanent sovereignty over their natural wealth and resources must be exercised in the interest of their national development and of the well-being of the people of the State concerned.
2. The exploration, development and disposition of such resources, as well as the import of the foreign capital required for these purposes, should be in conformity with the rules and conditions which the peoples and nations freely

consider to be necessary or desirable with regard to the authorization, restriction or prohibition of such activities.

3. In cases where authorization is granted, the capital imported and the earnings on that capital shall be governed by the terms thereof, by the national legislation in force, and by international law. The profits derived must be shared in the proportions freely agreed upon in each case, between the investors and the recipient State, due care being taken to ensure that there is no impairment, for any reason, of that State's sovereignty over its natural wealth and resources.

4. Nationalization, expropriation or requisitioning shall be based on grounds or reasons of public utility, security or the national interest which are recognized as overriding purely individual or private interests, both domestic and foreign. In such cases the owner shall be paid appropriate compensation, in accordance with the rules in force in the State taking such measures in the exercise of its sovereignty and in accordance with international law. In any case where the question of compensation gives rise to a controversy, the national jurisdiction of the State taking such measures shall be exhausted. However, upon agreement by sovereign States and other parties concerned, settlement of the dispute should be made through arbitration or international adjudication.

5. The free and beneficial exercise of the sovereignty of peoples and nations over their natural resources must be furthered by the mutual respect of States based on their sovereign equality.

6. International cooperation for the economic development of developing countries, whether in the form of public or private capital investments, exchange of goods and services, technical assistance, or exchange of scientific information, shall be such as to further their independent national development and shall be based upon respect for their sovereignty over their natural wealth and resources.

7. Violation of the rights of peoples and nations to sovereignty over their natural wealth and resources is contrary to the spirit and principles of the Charter of the United Nations and hinders the development of international cooperation and the maintenance of peace.

8. Foreign investment agreements freely entered into by, or between, sovereign States shall be observed in good faith; States and international organizations shall strictly and conscientiously respect the sovereignty of peoples and nations over their natural wealth and resources in accordance with the Charter and the principles set forth in the present resolution.

II

Welcomes the decision of the International Law Commission to speed up its work on the codification of the topic of responsibility of States for the consideration of the General Assembly;

Requests the Secretary-General to continue the study of the various aspects of permanent sovereignty over natural resources, taking into account the desire of Member States to ensure the protection of their sovereign rights while encouraging international cooperation in the field of economic development, and to report to the Economic and Social Council and to the General Assembly, if possible at its Eighteenth Session.

Sovereignty over Resources Is Theme of Resolution

It will be seen that much of the resolution consists of affirmation and reaffirmation of the permanent sovereignty of States over their natural wealth and resources. "The principle of the sovereign rights of nations over their own resources," the Delegate of Burma remarked, "would seem so obvious as not to require elucidation."[4] The United States, for its part, did not favor the United Nations setting about to expound the obvious. Thus it opposed the creation of the Commission on Permanent Sovereignty over Natural Resources, which was the author of the draft resolution on which the Seventeenth Session centered its debate. However, once the Commission was established, the United States participated actively as a member and played a leading role in the General Assembly's consideration of the subject. With respect to the resolution's primary theme, the United States Delegation more than once assured the Assembly that it "wholly supports every country, including our own, enjoying the full benefit of its natural resources."[5]

It was widely recognized that the importance of the resolution would lie not so much in its abstract assertions of sovereignty as in the concrete conditions laid down for the exercise of that sovereignty. Had the resolution simply consisted of recitals of sovereign rights, without due regard to sovereign obligations, the United States presumably would have opposed it as it did an earlier resolution on the subject.[6] As it was, the draft resolution proposed by the Commission did contain recognition of the obligations of States under international law in their treatment of foreign property.[7] However, there were gaps in the Commission's draft which the United States, together with the United Kingdom, sought to fill. These gaps were discussed in a report of the American Bar Association's Standing Committee on Peace and Law Through United Nations, and were the subject of a resolution adopted by the Board of Governors of that Association urging the United States Government to oppose any international declaration "dealing with the nationalization or other taking of private property ... unless it

---

[4] United Nations doc. A/C.2/SR.850, p. 10.

[5] United Nations General Assembly, Seventeenth Session, Provisional Verbatim Record of the 1193rd Meeting, A/PV.1193, p. 31.

[6] General Assembly resolution 626 (VII) of December 21, 1952.

[7] *Cf.* the second preambular paragraph and operative paragraph 3 of the resolution adopted, which in its references to international law is identical to the Commission's draft.

provides for non-discriminatory treatment . . . and contains provision for prompt, adequate and effective compensation." They had aroused considerable concern in the international legal and business community. They were of concern to the United States Government as well.

The draft resolution was seen to be deficient in three prime respects. First, its standard of compensation for the taking of foreign property was "appropriate compensation, in accordance with the rules in force in the State taking such measures in the exercise of its sovereignty and in accordance with international law."[8] In the view of the United States, appropriate compensation in accordance with international law is "prompt, adequate and effective" compensation. The United States, so interpreting the word "appropriate," proposed an amendment which, if adopted, would have made explicit the meaning which it held the resolution to contain.

Second, while the draft resolution provided that where a State authorizes the import of foreign capital "the capital imported and the earnings on that capital shall be governed by the terms thereof, by national legislation in force, and by international law,"[9] it did not expressly affirm that foreign investment agreements shall be faithfully observed. The United States proposed an amendment to that effect.

Third, the Commission's draft provided that in any case where the question of compensation for a taking of foreign property gave rise to a controversy, "national jurisdiction should be resorted to. Upon agreement by the parties concerned settlement of the dispute may be made through arbitration or international adjudication."[10] Since the United States believed that this language was open to interpretation that national jurisdiction supplies exclusive recourse for the foreign investor, which could be varied only by agreement reached after a dispute had arisen to arbitrate or internationally adjudicate that dispute, the United States further moved to preclude that interpretation.

These three deficiencies were mitigated or overcome at the General Assembly's Seventeenth Session. At the same time, two far-reaching Soviet amendments, which would have destroyed the resolution's balance by exaggerating sovereign prerogatives and asserting an "inalienable right" to "unobstructed . . . expropriation"[11] were defeated. Also defeated or withdrawn were amendments running counter to those whose purpose was to remedy the draft resolution's three deficiencies and motions to refer the draft resolution to a reconstituted Commission on Permanent Sovereignty over

---

[8] United Nations doc. A/C.2/L. (earlier reproduced as E/3511, Annex), operative paragraph 4.
[9] *Ibid.*, operative paragraph 3.
[10] *Ibid.*, operative paragraph 4.   [11] United Nations doc. A/5344/Add. 1, p. 6.

Natural Resources. The United Kingdom, which had introduced a number of constructive amendments, withdrew them in the interest of achieving the widest measure of agreement and instead joined with the United States in proposing the two amendments discussed below. The history of a third amendment which the United States had introduced earlier to the passage on appropriate compensation is as follows.

"Prompt, Adequate and Effective Compensation"

The United States proposed that that phrase read: "the owner shall be paid appropriate – prompt, adequate and effective – compensation."[12] At the same time, Afghanistan proposed that: "the owner shall be paid adequate compensation, when and where appropriate."[13] The Soviet amendment would have inserted at the beginning of operative paragraph 4 the statement that the General Assembly:

> confirms the inalienable right of peoples and nations to the unobstructed execution of nationalization, expropriation and other essential measures aimed at protecting and strengthening their sovereignty over natural wealth and resources."[14]

In introducing the United States amendment, Ambassador Philip M. Klutznick stated that it was "designed to make explicit what is already implicit in ... operative paragraph 4. In the view of the United States, the words 'appropriate compensation' can only mean prompt, adequate and effective compensation."[15] With this, the delegate of Hungary disagreed:

> It was not correct to say that nationalization with the payment of compensation was a generally acceptable principle; the fundamental principle was that of State sovereignty. Any decision relating to whether and how much compensation should be paid was essentially an international affair of the State concerned, which therefore was the sole judge in the matter and could brook no outside interference whatsoever in the exercise of its sovereignty. The basis of any right to compensation was not some rule of international law but the relevant legislation of the State concerned ... The concept of prompt, adequate and effective compensation, which the United States wishes to impose and codify as a sort of international law, would be flagrantly unjust to emerging nations.[16]

Similar views were advanced by other Communist States. But they received no articulated support in the non-Communist world. Various countries viewed this and other United States amendments as unnecessary,

---

[12] *Ibid.*, p. 4.   [13] *Ibid.*   [14] *Ibid.*, p. 6.
[15] US Mission to the United Nations, press release No. 4091, p. 6.
[16] A/C.2/SR.846, p. 4.

while others supported what they saw as desirable clarifications of the draft resolution's existing intent. The Delegate of Madagascar, while supporting the other United States amendments, characterized the specification of "prompt, adequate and effective" as "unnecessary." He stated that "compensation could not but be adequate; as to the promptness of compensation, the very idea of international cooperation demanded that the financial situation of the State concerned should be borne in mind and that it should be given time, if necessary, to make the payment."[17] This was as far as direct criticism of the United States amendment – apart from Communist criticism – went.

All Except Soviets Withdraw Amendments

Nevertheless, there was considerable sentiment in the Committee for the withdrawal of all amendments and the adoption of the draft resolution as it stood. The United States and the United Kingdom endeavored to meet that sentiment halfway. As noted, the United Kingdom withdrew its amendments and joined the United States in a reformulation of the two amendments concerning the binding character of foreign investment agreements and recourse to arbitration; and, in the light of the discussion that had taken place, the United States withdrew its amendment specifying prompt, adequate, and effective compensation. In doing so, Ambassador Klutznick stated that the United States delegation "was confident that the expression 'appropriate compensation' in operative paragraph 4 of the draft resolution would be interpreted as meaning, under international law, prompt, adequate and effective compensation. Thus it now merely proposed, for purposes of clarification," its remaining two amendments.[18] At the same time, the Delegate of Afghanistan, "in the same spirit of compromise that had been demonstrated by the United Kingdom and United States delegations,"[19] withdrew his Delegation's amendment.

The Delegate of the Soviet Union did not evidence a like spirit. The Soviet amendment, providing for "unobstructed ... expropriation," was put to a vote, first in Committee and, having been defeated there, then in Plenary Session. In that latter, determinative test, it was rejected by forty-eight votes against, thirty-four in favor and twenty-one abstentions. Among the Delegations favoring the Soviet amendment, twenty-three were not Communist.[20] It should be noted that, after the vote in Committee on the resolution, the United States representative, Seymour M. Finger, stated that his delegation "is pleased that this Committee has reaffirmed the traditional inter-

---

[17] *Ibid.*, pp. 5–6.   [18] A.C.2/SR.850, p. 7 (as corrected).   [19] *Ibid.*   [20] A.PV.1193, p. 76.

national law providing for appropriate – that is to say, prompt, adequate and effective – compensation in case of expropriation and the like."[21] No member took exception to this statement.

On the basis of this mixed but predominantly favorable record, it is submitted that the force of the United States view that appropriate compensation in accordance with international law means prompt, adequate, and effective compensation was enhanced by the General Assembly's treatment of the resolution. Moreover, the terms of that resolution – "the owner *shall* be paid appropriate compensation" – when coupled with withdrawal of the Afghan and defeat of the Soviet amendments, make it plain that payment of appropriate compensation is a matter not of discretion but of obligation.

Binding Character of Investment Agreements

The first of the two principal amendments which the United States and the United Kingdom jointly proposed was to insert after the first sentence in operative paragraph 3 a sentence providing: "Agreements freely entered into shall be faithfully observed."[22] This "generally accepted principle," Ambassador Klutznick said, which was already "implicit in operative paragraph 3,"[23] applies "alike to agreements between States, States and international organizations and States and private foreign investors."[24] It "merely reaffirmed a principle endorsed by all nations which accepted the United Nations Charter," Ambassador Schweitzer of Chile added (apparently in a reference to Article 2, paragraph 2).[25] The Delegate of Panama also approved the proposal, but suggested that it be placed at the beginning of operative paragraph 8, and worded as follows: "Agreements freely entered into by States and international organizations or States and foreign investors shall be faithfully observed."[26] The co-sponsors accepted Panama's suggestion,[27] which, Panama said, was advanced in the hope of promoting general agreement.[28] Panama withdrew its proposal, however, when it emerged that its suggestion would not achieve that result. That it would not was made clear by Iraq, which "considered that agreements between States and companies were straightforward contracts which were adequately protected by the national legislation of sovereign States and that it was therefore unnecessary

---

[21] US Mission to the United Nations, press release No. 4113, p. 1.   [22] A/5344/Add. 1, p. 7.

[23] A/C.2/SR.851, p. 16.

[24] A/C.2/CR.850, p. 7 (as corrected).

[25] *Ibid.*, Article 2, paragraph 2, provides: "All Members ... shall fulfill in good faith the obligations assumed by them in accordance with the present Charter."

[26] A/C.2/SR.850, pp. 8–9.   [27] *Ibid.*, p. 12.   [28] A./C.2/SR.852, pp. 6–7.

to stress the need for their observance in an international instrument,"[29] and, for its own reasons, by the Soviet Union.[30] For its part, Algeria submitted an amendment (more fully discussed below) which would have inserted as a preamble:

> *Considering* that the obligations of international law cannot apply to alleged rights acquired before accession to full national sovereignty of formerly colonized countries and that, consequently, such alleged acquired rights must be subject to review as between equally sovereign States."[31]

Intensive negotiations then began between the representative of Algeria and representatives of the United States and the United Kingdom which resulted in an agreement to amend the resolution so as to make clear that it is without prejudice to questions of succession of States and Governments. As an element of that agreement, the two-Power amendment was revised to read: "Foreign investment and technical assistance agreements freely entered in to by sovereign States shall be observed in good faith."[32]

Some Members Object to US–UK Amendment

This revision did not satisfy certain Members, however, who maintained their objection to any affirmation of the binding character of agreements between States and private foreign investors. The Delegate of Lebanon, for example, declared that he "did not consider that agreements between sovereign States could be equated with agreements concluded between a Government and a domestic or foreign company. Agreements of the latter sort did exist, but they were subject to national jurisdiction and could sometimes be modified by national legislation, even in cases not involving nationalization."[33] Lebanon, joined by Syria, accordingly moved to replace the words of the US–UK amendment, "by sovereign States," with "between sovereign States."[34] "The real point at issue," the Delegate of Lebanon contended, "was that contracts entered into by sovereign States with private firms should not be subject to international jurisdiction."[35]

Taking issue with this viewpoint, the United States and the United Kingdom revised their amendment for the last time to provide: "Foreign investment agreements freely entered into by, or between, sovereign States shall be observed in good faith."[36] Lebanon and Syria moved to delete the words "by, or." Their motion was defeated by a vote of forty-seven to

---

[29] A/C.2/SR.851, p. 15.   [30] *Ibid.*, pp. 17–18.   [31] A/5344/Add. 1, p. 8.   [32] *Ibid.*, p. 9.
[33] A/C.2/SR.856, p. 3.   [34] A/5344/Add. 1, p. 11.   [35] A.C.2/SR.858, p. 5.
[36] A/5344/Add. 1, p. 12.

thirty-three, with eleven abstentions.[37] The US–UK amendment was then adopted by fifty-three votes in favor, twenty-two opposed and fifteen abstentions.

Statements following the vote were as interesting as those that preceded it. On the one hand, after the resolution's adoption in Plenary Session, Iraq reiterated that it regarded "agreements signed between companies and sovereign States as simple contracts, governed and protected by domestic national laws of sovereign States." Iraq saw no reason for reference to their observance in an "international instrument."[38] On the other hand, the Delegate of Australia expressed the view in Committee that "the obligations deriving from agreements between two States were not fundamentally different from those deriving from contracts between a State and a private individual or company."[39] And the representative of the United States declared:

> My delegation is especially gratified that this Committee has affirmed the binding character of foreign investment agreements, whether these agreements are for arbitration of disputes or are of a more comprehensive character, and whether these agreements are concluded between States, or between States and international organizations, or States and private foreign investors.[40]

National and International Remedies Are Discussed

The draft resolution submitted by the Commission on Permanent Sovereignty over Natural Resources did not provide generally for the settlement of investment disputes. However, in its paragraph concerned with "nationalization, expropriation or requisitioning" it provided that: "In any case where the question of compensation gives rise to a controversy, national jurisdiction should be resorted to. Upon agreement by the parties concerned settlement of the dispute may be made through arbitration or international adjudication."[41]

This wording was seen by the United States as open to three difficulties. First, the use of the words "resorted to" might be said to import that national jurisdiction provides the only recourse of the foreign investor both in the first and last instance. It accordingly could be interpreted as precluding the exercise of diplomatic protection by the State of which the foreign investor is a national. Second, the wording of the sentence beginning "Upon agreement" could be construed as meaning that only an agreement arrived at after, and not before, a dispute had arisen for arbitration or international adjudi-

---

[37] *Ibid.*, p. 17.　　[38] A/PV.1194, p. 17.　　[39] A/C.2/SR.859, p. 10.
[40] Press release No. 4113, p. 12.
[41] See note 8 above.

cation of that dispute was to be implemented. Even then, the Commission's draft provided that, upon agreement, settlement of the dispute "may" be made through arbitration or international adjudication. Third, the Commission's wording did not appear to take account of a situation in which the parties had agreed to pursue arbitration or international adjudication in lieu of local remedies.

Accordingly, the United States proposed to reword the pertinent sentences to read:

> Where a question of compensation for nationalization, expropriation or requisitioning gives rise to a controversy, local remedies should first be exhausted in accordance with international law, unless the parties have agreed to international adjudication or other method of settlement.[42]

That proposal was, in the consolidated US–UK amendment, revised to provide:

> In any case where the question of compensation gives rise to a controversy, national jurisdiction should be exhausted. Where, however, there is agreement to that effect by the parties concerned, settlement of the dispute shall be made through arbitration or international adjudication.[43]

Three important amendments to the revised US–UK text were moved.

Mauritania proposed to substitute the words "should be resorted to" for "shall be exhausted."[44] That amendment narrowly failed of adoption.[45] Inclusion of provision for the exhaustion of national jurisdiction clearly indicates that the right of diplomatic recourse is preserved.

Lebanon and Syria proposed to insert after the words "there is agreement" the words "between sovereign States," and to delete "by the parties concerned."[46] Thus arbitration agreements between States and parties other than States – such as those characteristically contained in concession contracts – would have been excluded. This amendment was defeated by a vote of thirty-eight to thirty, with twenty-four abstentions. The wording finally adopted – "agreement by sovereign States and other parties concerned" – clearly embraces agreements between States, between States and international organizations, and States and private parties.

Jordan, Morocco, and Thailand proposed to amend the passage to provide: "National jurisdiction should be exhausted. However, if no settlement is

---

[42] A/5344/Add. 1, p. 4. The United Kingdom proposed an amendment meant to achieve similar results (*Ibid.*, p. 6).

[43] *Ibid.*, p. 7.

[44] A/PV.1193, p. 76. When this amendment was proposed in Plenary Session, the text provided "shall be exhausted."

[45] *Ibid.*   [46] A/5344/Add. 1, p. 11.

reached thereunder, and there is agreement to that effect by the parties concerned."[47]

The United States and the United Kingdom were unwilling to accept this proposal, since it would have implied that an agreement to arbitrate or internationally adjudicate never could stand in lieu of local remedies, even if such substitution were the intention of the parties. At the same time, it was not the intent of the US–UK amendment necessarily to substitute arbitration or international adjudication for the pursuit of local remedies. The representative of the United States noted that, as regards international adjudication, the US–UK text envisages "the possibility of recourse to international adjudication after national jurisdiction had been exhausted."[48] Thus, in response to the views of the sponsors of the sub-amendment,[49] and of the Delegates of Malaya[50] and Ethiopia,[51] the United States and the United Kingdom revised the joint amendment so as not to prejudice the question of whether arbitration or international adjudication stand in place of local remedies. This would be determined on the facts of each case. Jordan, Morocco, and Thailand accordingly withdrew their amendment.[52] The US–UK text finally read:

> In any case where the question of compensation gives rise to a controversy, national jurisdiction shall be exhausted. However, upon agreement by sovereign States and other parties concerned, settlement of the dispute should be made through arbitration or international adjudication.[53]

It is important to note that the United States and the United Kingdom proposed this language on the understanding that the words "However, upon agreement" embrace agreements to arbitrate or adjudicate which antedate, as well as those which follow upon, the existence of a dispute.[54] This understanding was acknowledged by the delegate of the United Arab Republic in explaining his vote after the adoption of the resolution in committee, when he expressly stated that this passage of the resolution covered agreements which "existed."[55]

It should be added that, as suggested by the United States representative, the prescription of operative paragraph 8 that "foreign investment agreements freely entered into by, or between, sovereign States shall be observed

---

[47] *Ibid.*, p. 11. [48] A/C.2/SR.858, p. 5.

[49] As expressed by the Delegate of Morocco, A/C.2/SR.855, p. 21 and A/C.2/SR. 856, p. 5.

[50] A/C.2/SR.856, p. 5. [51] *Ibid.*, pp. 6–7. [52] A/5344/Add. 1, pp. 10–11.

[53] A/5344/Add. 1, pp. 11–12.

[54] The original United Kingdom amendment, which was designed to ensure that existing agreements to arbitrate or adjudicate were covered by the resolution, used the very words: "However, upon agreement ..." A/5344/Add. 1, p. 6.

[55] A/C.2/SR.859, p. 13.

in good faith" applies as much to arbitration and adjudication agreements as to other provisions of foreign investment agreements.[56]

State Succession Problems Provoke a Compromise

The preambular paragraph proposed by Algeria, declaring that the obligations of international law "cannot apply to alleged rights acquired before accession to full sovereignty of formerly colonized countries,"[57] was not acceptable to the United States and the United Kingdom. However, those Delegations had no objection to stating that the resolution does not pass upon problems of State and governmental succession as they relate to acquired rights. Accordingly, they worked out a compromise with the Delegate of Algeria providing for the withdrawal of his amendment in return for the inclusion of what were to become preambular paragraphs 5 and 6, and the amendment of the clause on the observance of foreign investment agreements to specify agreements concluded by "sovereign States." It was clearly understood that agreements concluded by States other than sovereign States and property rights acquired under colonial rule were in no way prejudiced by passage of the resolution. As the delegate of the United States put it in proposing the revised US–UK amendments: "The text now clearly was without prejudice to any aspect of State succession and to rights acquired in former colonial territories."[58]

Soviet View of Sovereignty Is Defeated

One of the several Soviet amendments to the Commission's draft would have had the General Assembly declare that it:

> Unreservedly supports measures taken by peoples and States to reestablish or strengthen their sovereignty over natural wealth and resources, and considers inadmissible acts aimed at obstructing the creation, defense and strengthening of that sovereignty.[59]

The proposed amendment gave rise to little comment in committee. Apparently a number of members regarded it as just one more incantation of sovereignty, as one more invocation of the resolution's theme which did no harm. Others saw its terms as so extreme that they did not take the proposal seriously. To the surprise of much of the Committee, the amendment, in one

---

[56] See the US statement quoted above at p. 403, and note 40.　　[57] A/5344/Add. 1, p. 8.

[58] A/C.2/SR.854, p. 11.

[59] A/5433/Add. 1, p. 7.

of twenty-six votes in the course of an extended night session, was adopted by forty-three to thirty-two, and sixteen abstentions. Its approval led the United States and the United Kingdom to vote against the resolution as a whole in committee.

When the resolution came before the Plenary Session for definitive action, a separate vote was taken on the retention of the Soviet passage, then operative paragraph 5 of the resolution. Speaking in favor of its deletion, Ambassador Klutznick declared:

> Now putting aside operative paragraph 5, the draft resolution strikes a healthy balance between the rights and obligations of sovereignty. The exercise of sovereignty, with respect to natural resources as otherwise, requires respect for the rights of others as well as one's own rights. This the resolution recognizes, except in operative paragraph 5. That paragraph, in its own terms, its "unreserved". It does not make sense painstakingly to compose a draft resolution which sets forth the rights and obligations of States, which affirms their sovereignty and the modalities of the exercise of that sovereignty and, at the same time, declares unreserved support for measures to "re-establish or strengthen their sovereignty over natural wealth and resources".
>
> To support unreservedly "measures" may be taken to imply any measures, including measures in violation of international law, in violation of treaties, in violation of contracts, in violation of the demands of economics, in violation of the international interest, in violation of the true national interest. To support unreservedly measures to re-establish or strengthen sovereignty over natural wealth and resources is to suggest that any measures in exercise of sovereignty are legitimate in form, however illegitimate they may be in substance.[60]

The Soviet-sponsored paragraph was struck out by a vote of forty-one opposed to retention, thirty-eight in favor, and fifteen abstentions. Failing to muster a simple majority, it fell far short of the necessary two-thirds majority. It should be noted that before the resolution was voted on in Plenary Session the Assembly decided that the resolution concerned an "important question," accordingly requiring for adoption a two-thirds majority of the members present and voting.

Declaration Is Judged as Generally Favorable

There is much more in the resolution that merits comment, not all of it favorable. It should be recognized that the resolution incorporates certain passages of an autarchic and statist tenor, such as the penultimate preambular paragraph (a Soviet proposal): "*Noting* that the creation and strengthening of

[60] A/PV.1193, p. 32.

the inalienable sovereignty of States over their natural wealth and resources reinforces their economic independence."

The fourth preambular paragraph is in the same vein and from the same source. The United States voted against the inclusion of these passages.[61] While deploring their adoption, the United States Delegation viewed these and other undesirable passages of the resolution as outweighed by the resolution's positive elements.

Among those positive elements which have not been discussed above is the provision that foreign capital shall be governed by the terms of its import, by national legislation, and "by international law." As Ambassador Adlai E. Stevenson points out in a letter to the Secretary of the American Bar Association, the resolution thus "incorporates by reference the requirement of international law that the foreign capital shall not be subjected to discriminatory treatment."[62]

Also noteworthy are the profit-sharing provisions (operative paragraph 3) and the provision that a taking of private property must be for a public purpose (operative paragraph 4). The provision of the profit-sharing clause that "profits derived must be shared in the proportions freely agreed upon, in each case" is a specific application of the binding character of foreign investment agreements which the resolution more generally affirms.

Speculation on the effects of the resolution would be premature. It should be noted, however, that, while the resolution is not binding on Member States, it expresses the views of the great majority of the nations of the world. Cast in the form of a declaration, which in United Nations usage is meant to give a resolution particular weight, it represents a consensus of the economically developed and less developed countries. The fact that that consensus includes positive recognition of the obligation to pay compensation where property is taken, to observe investment agreements and agreements to arbitrate, and to abide by other requirements of international law should contribute to the enhancement of the international investment climate.

[61] A/5344/Add. 1, pp. 13–14.   [62] Letter of December 21, 1962, to Joseph D. Calhoun.

25

Speculations on Specific Performance of a Contract between a State and a Foreign National

☙

Under what circumstances is, or should be, specific performance available to parties to a contract between a State and a foreign national?

The answer to that question is speculative, since the law directly in point is sparse. Nevertheless, resort to municipal law sources and analogies, and consideration of such relevant international law as there is, suggests that circumstances exist, or should exist, in which the remedy for breach of a contract between a State and a foreign national is specific performance. Moreover, where the contract in dispute provides for arbitration of a quasi-international character, the case for specific performance may be strengthened. Specific performance, it will be suggested, is a remedy to be applied selectively in the application of international contracts as in other contracts. But it has, or should have, its place – a place of importance.

The Governing Law

The question of the remedies which the law affords for violation of a contract depends on what law governs the contract and upon the terms of the contract itself. Putting aside a contractual indication of remedies, we are brought to the question of what law governs contracts between States and foreign nationals. To that question there is no ready answer. The answer plainly depends upon the contract in question. Such a contract may be, and generally is, governed by the municipal law of the contracting State. It may, however, be governed by the municipal law of another State, notably that of the nationality of the foreign contractor. It may, otherwise, be governed by the shared principles of law of more than one State. Or the contract may be governed by the general principles of law – certain of those famous, not easily fixed "general principles of law recognized by civilized nations." Or the contract may be governed by international law.

This discussion does not propose to examine the question of the proper law of a contract between a State and a foreign national. For our purposes two conclusions will suffice:

1. The proper law of such an international contract may be any of the possibilities suggested above.
2. Whatever the governing law, certain kinds of violations of such contracts give rise to State responsibility under international law.

International Wrongs and Remedies

Let us pursue the latter conclusion. There is a considerable measure of agreement that, where a State violates a contract with a foreign national in an "arbitrary" or "tortious" manner or where there has been a "denial of justice" in the courts of the respondent State in respect of an alleged breach of an international contract, the contracting State violates international law. Agreement is less widespread on what constitutes an arbitrary or tortious breach. Professors Sohn and Baxter, in their notable *Convention on the International Responsibility of States for Injuries to Aliens*, have set forth perceptive criteria for that determination.[1]

Some thirty years ago, Professor Dunn set forth a broader criterion.[2] He submitted that the meaning of the cases is that, where a State steps out of its role of commercial contractor and applies its sovereign power to upset the expectations of contractual performance which must be assumed to have motivated the parties, it incurs international responsibility. Professor Dunn's thesis has been reaffirmed and elaborated by Lowell Wadmond, in an address in London to the American Bar Association.[3] Several scholars have put forth still other, more limited interpretations of the law as to the circumstances giving rise to international responsibility.[4]

There is considerable and consequential difference of view as to what is arbitrary or tortious breach by a State of a contract with a foreign national. It is enough for the purposes of this discussion to note the wide agreement that

---

[1] "Convention on the International Responsibility of States for Injuries to Aliens" (Final Draft with Explanatory Notes), published in F. V. Garcia Amador, Louis B. Sohn, and R. R. Baxter, *Recent Codifications of the Law of State Responsibility for Injuries to Aliens* (1974), pp. 222–224.

[2] F. S. Dunn, *The Protection of Nationals* (1932), pp. 163–169.

[3] Republished as "The Sanctity of Contract Between a Sovereign and a Foreign National," Southwestern Legal Foundation, *Selected Readings on Protection by Law of Private Foreign Investments* (1964).

[4] See, for example, A. A. Fatouros, *Government Guarantees to Foreign Investors* (1962), p. 232 ff.

there are circumstances, in addition to that of a denial of justice, where violation of an international contract by a State will be deemed arbitrary and, accordingly, in violation of international law. That being true, the question of what remedies lie for violation of an international obligation is relevant to the subject before us, even though the proper law of the particular contract is not international law.

Specific Performance in Municipal Law

Before pursuing the question of specific performance as a remedy for the violation of an international obligation, let us glance at specific performance in municipal law. We can do no more than glance, for the subject is vast and variable. The conditions under which specific performance is afforded differ, not only with the system of law but with the type of contract involved. The principles applicable to governmental contracts may not be the same as those applied to contracts in which none of the parties has governmental character.

In Anglo-American law the limitations on according specific performance are, of course, great. The norm is damages; the exception is specific performance. Only where damages are an inadequate remedy may specific performance be granted. Thus, where there is a contract for the sale of land, either buyer or seller may secure a decree ordering specific performance. Land is assumed not to have a clearly defined market price, and each piece of land is regarded as unique. Where a contract is for the sale of goods, specific performance generally is granted only where the chattel is unique or irreplaceable. However, the Uniform Sales Act broadens the traditional rule in most states of the United States, permitting courts to direct that a contract for the sale of specific and ascertained goods shall be performed specifically, without giving the seller the option of retaining the goods on his payment of damages. It also adds to the right of the seller to win a kind of specific performance. And contracts not to compete may be enforced specifically.

Since adequacy of damages is the governing criterion, it might be supposed that, where the debtor lacks the resources to pay damages, the creditor should be awarded specific performance. In some cases courts have so held. However, the question is complex and may relate to the law concerning preferences among creditors. Where the debtor cannot pay damages, specific performance is not necessarily accorded.

The restricted role of specific performance in Anglo-American law is, of course, rooted in the historical distinctions between law and equity. While that role has logic as well as history to commend it, specific performance need not be so restricted. And in some other systems of law, it is not.

In German law, the Civil Code neither sets the money judgment for damages as the norm nor places upon the injured party the burden of establishing inadequacy of money damages, if he elects to seek specific relief. Rather, that code "asserts a precisely opposite principle – that specific performance of all obligations ... is normal and damages are to be awarded only in types of cases where specific performance is not possible or where the injured party gives notice ... of his election to take money compensation."[5]

In France, still another path has been taken. There specific performance is normal and available to enforce promises to transfer specific assets – goods as well as land – wherever execution is physically possible. The test is not the adequacy of money damages. But, where the contract is one not for the transfer of specific assets but for the doing of a specific act, the only sanction in France is a money judgment.[6]

What about contracts between Governments and their nationals? Is the remedy of specific performance accorded?

This, again, presents a large question, susceptible of much comparative research and reflection. No informed answer is proffered. It seems safe to hazard, however, that specific performance is awarded infrequently to an injured party whose grievance is against a Government or a governmental authority.[7] Governments, because they are Governments, tend, in their municipal law, to be accorded a freedom of action which that law does not grant other parties whose responsibilities are not governmental. That freedom of action could be constrained unduly by compelling Governments specifically to perform their contracts. Where the Government claims that its breach of contract with a private party is impelled by considerations of the public interest, the public interest may not, in fact, permit specific performance by the Government. This is not to say that the public interest will not require the payment of monetary compensation to the private party – for an element of the public interest is the public interest in protecting contracts. The credit of the Government is a public asset; its dissipation is a public loss. Nor does regard for the public interest equate with disregard for the private interest. A balance must be struck between the necessities of governmental freedom of action and of the maintenance of the public credit; between advancement of the public interest and respect for the private interest which has contracted with the public interest for their mutual benefit.

---

[5] Dawson and Harvey, *Contracts and Contract Remedies* (1959), p. 103. [6] *Ibid.*, p. 104.

[7] See J. D. B. Mitchell, *The Contracts of Public Authorities, A Comparative Study* (1954), pp. 20–21, 156, 232–233.

Both in Anglo-American and civil law, that balance appears to incline against according specific performance by the State.[8]

Specific Performance in International Law

Let us turn now to the question of the availability of specific performance as a remedy for violation of a contract between a State and a foreign national.

The Permanent Court of International Justice, in its famous holding in the case concerning the *Factory at Chorzow*, declared:

> The essential principle contained in the actual notion of an illegal act – a principle which seems to be established by international practice and in particular by the decisions of arbitral tribunals – is that reparation must, as far as possible, wipe out all the consequences of the illegal act and reestablish the situation which would, in all probability, have existed if that act had not been committed. Restitution in kind, or, if this is not possible, payment of a sum corresponding to the value which a restitution in kind would bear; the award, if need be, of damages for loss sustained which would not be covered by restitution in kind or payment in place of it – such are the principles which should serve to determine the amount of compensation due for an act contrary to international law.[9]

Interpreting this holding, the Committee on Nationalization of Property of the American Branch of the International Law Association states:

> Thus, the remedy for breach by a State of a contract with an alien, whether designated as a breach or a taking or as expropriation or nationalization, is in the nature of specific performance.[10]

As noted above, every violation of a contract between a State and a foreign national is not an act contrary to international law. Only those acts which are arbitrary or tortious (or involve a denial of justice) contravene international law. When such violation takes place, it may be contended that the remedy to be accorded is specific performance. And, "Where performance actually is no longer possible, then the foreign contractor must be placed as nearly as possible in the position he would have enjoyed absent the breach, that is to say, he is entitled to the profits he would have earned had not his contract rights been taken."[11] However, if the breach of contract is not arbitrary and if the proper law of the contract is not international law, the parties are remitted to such remedies as the contract's proper law may afford.

---

[8] *Ibid.*

[9] *Case Concerning Factory at Chorzow, Merits, Judgment No. 13, 1928, PCIJ, Series A, No. 17*, p. 47.

[10] American Branch of the International Law Association, *Proceedings and Committee Reports, 1957–1958* (1958), p. 72.

[11] *Ibid.*, pp. 72–73.

Even if the *Chorzow Factory* case read, as the American Branch of the ILA reads it, as calling in the first place for specific performance of a contract between a State and a foreign national, is this proposition sound? The proposition, as interpreted in these remarks, is limited to cases of arbitrary exercise of governmental power – of intervention by the contracting State to upset the parties' expectations of performance. Now it has been noted that, in municipal law, the exercise of governmental power, at least in some cases, tends to be protected against a decree of specific performance. If this is the case, should the result differ when the State's contract is with a foreign national rather than its citizen?

The *Chorzow Factory* case, in a sense, contains an answer. But that answer is formalistic and not fully satisfying. The Court there points out that, where there is a wrong under international law involving a foreign national, "the rules of law governing the reparation are the rules of international law in force between the two States concerned, and not the law governing relations between the State which has committed a wrongful act and the individual who has suffered damage."[12]

A related consideration is that a State may not invoke its municipal law as a defense to violation of international law. As the arbitral tribunal held in the *Norwegian Shipowners Claims*:

> "Restraint of princes" ... cannot be invoked by the United States against the Kingdom of Norway in defence of the claim of Norway ... No State can exercise towards the citizens of another civilized State the "power of eminent domain" without respecting the property of such foreign citizen or without paying just compensation as determined by an impartial tribunal, if necessary.
>
> This remark applies to the contract [found to be "taken" by the United States].[13]

It is, of course, elementary that domestic exigencies do not free a State from its international obligations. More concrete distinctions between a State's contracts with its citizens and those with foreign nationals are these. Where, in contracting with its national, a State is accorded by municipal law a particular power to intervene and a peculiar immunity from imposition of a decree of specific performance, such privileges and immunities may be defended on the ground that the private contracting party, as a subject of the law of the State, will share in the public good assumed to flow from the State's action. His particular rights are prejudiced, but the public of which he

---

[12] See above, note 9, p. 28.
[13] Norwegian Shipowners' Claims (Norway v. United States, 1922), *United Nations Reports of International Arbitral Awards*, Vol. I, p. 338.

is a part gains, and, in the larger sense, he benefits in some measure. By hypothesis, however, the foreigner whose presence is expressed in his property or contractual interests will be absent to the extent that his interests are taken. He will not share in the national social advantage of the State's taking, assuming it to exist.[14]

The contracting foreigner admittedly may place himself within the reach of the municipal law of the contracting State by entering into a contract with it. Nevertheless, international law protects him against the arbitrary action of the foreign State. And the fact that the foreign national normally is not within the jurisdiction of the contracting State until he contracts with it suggests a further consideration: the flow of international capital will be maximized by respect for international contracts. As the General Assembly of the United Nations declared:

> Foreign investment agreements freely entered into by, or between, sovereign states shall be observed in good faith.[15]

Good faith observance of international contracts imports performance of the terms of the contract by both parties. Where there is a breach of contract, the remedy to repair it may be specific performance – especially where it is the only remedy which can repair it effectively. If a State, as is sometimes the case, lacks the capacity to pay the damages it would be obliged to pay were monetary compensation required, it may be said that good faith requires the contract to be performed specifically. The considerations of creditors' preferences which support a contrary municipal rule will not tend to have comparable force in the international sphere, nor, for that matter, whenever a Government's specific performance is sought.

The foregoing considerations of equity and economic advantage suggest that the case for according specific performance may be more compelling as respects a contract between a State and a foreign national than as respects one between a State and its citizen. Admittedly, the distinctions between the cases are not conclusive. And, whatever their force, the fact that specific performance normally is not afforded against a State in the national sphere suggests that it normally will not be accorded in the international sphere. An international lawyer would not counsel his international client prudently were he to advise that specific performance is a remedy to be expected.

There is, however, a further, quite distinct consideration which strengthens the case for specific performance.

---

[14] See above, note 10, p. 67.
[15] United Nations General Assembly, *Official Records*: Seventeenth Session, resolution 1803 (XVII).

The Impact of Arbitration

Many contracts between States and aliens contain arbitration clauses, often providing for a kind of quasi-international arbitration. A typical clause provides that:

> If any doubt, difference or dispute shall arise between the Government and the Company concerning the interpretation or execution of this contract ... or the rights and liabilities of the parties hereunder, it shall, failing any agreement to settle it in another way, be referred ... to arbitration.[16]

Each party appoints an arbitrator. They, in turn, appoint an umpire; and, failing their agreement upon an umpire, he is appointed by the President of the International Court of Justice or other impartial authority.

Such an arbitral tribunal has no power to enforce its judgments – though its awards may be enforceable by separate municipal proceedings. It can, as easily, require or not require the parties – the Government and the foreign national – to perform specifically or to pay damages. What, in fact, do such tribunals do?

A review of arbitral awards rendered in cases between Governments and foreign nationals indicates that such arbitral tribunals tend to render awards in the nature of declaratory judgments.[17] These awards are binding and final. They say that the rights of the parties are such-and-such; that the Government has the right to this part of the seabed and the concessionaire the right to that; that the Government cannot award certain rights to a third party, since it has earlier awarded the same rights to the foreign contractor; and the like. The tribunals resolve disputes over "the interpretation or execution" of international contracts by ruling how they shall be interpreted and, in effect, how they shall be executed. The parties to such arbitrations subsequently have performed their contracts accordingly. How far removed is this process – this effective remedy – from that of specific performance? Actually, it is very close.

There are, of course, cases in which arbitral tribunals award damages. In some cases they are asked to do so. This is true particularly where the arbitration is not between the Government and the company but between the contracting Government and the Government of the State of which the

---

[16] Aramco Concession Agreement (1933), Article 31. Note that the Aramco Concession Agreement contains a certain contractual indication of remedies; i.e., damages payable by Aramco for breach of its obligations.

[17] See, for example, *Saudi Arabia v. Arabian American Oil Co.* (1958), *International Law Reports*, Vol. 27, p. 117; *Petroleum Development Ltd. v. Sheikh of Abu Dhabi* (1951), 1951 *International Law Reports*, p. 144; *Petroleum Development (Qatar) Ltd. v. Ruler of Qatar* (1950), *ibid.*, p. 161.

company is a national. Why is this? Because an intergovernmental arbitration over claims arising out of a contract between a Government and a foreign national typically takes place when the contract has been ruptured gravely; when the foreign national has given up attempting to implement the contract, alleging governmental interference; when the contracting Government has declared the contract at an end, alleging default by the foreign national; and the like. By this time, the hour for specific performance usually has passed; management may have changed hands; the claims and counter-claims tend to be for damages.

This is not, however, to say that specific performance can never be the remedy in such cases. Still less is it to say that specific performance should not be the remedy in the many cases where, despite dispute, the contractual relationship is in process of daily implementation. On the contrary, specific performance may well be the remedy which is more than a cure – the remedy which can give new life to the living law of a contractual relationship.

26

On Whether the Breach by a State of a Contract with an Alien is a Breach of International Law

ود

The question of whether the breach by a State of a contract between that State or its agency and an alien is a breach of international law has long divided States and scholars. For example, in the *Ambatielos* case, the Greek Government maintained that the contract between His Majesty's Government in the United Kingdom and Mr. M.N.E. Ambatielos

> was one between a State and a foreign national, with the result that, according to the admitted principles of international law, the Government of the State incurs a direct responsibility on breach of the contract, for which the Government of the foreign national thereby injured is entitled to seek redress.[1]

Greece invoked Professor Borchard's conclusion that:

> It is a rule, which it is believed has been accepted generally, that the contracts entered into by a State with foreigners, create obligations which the State must fulfil. With reservations as to the exhaustion of local remedies it will be responsible for the non-execution towards the foreign State.[2]

These contentions were resisted by the British Government. In the *Ambatielos* proceedings, it maintained that:

> It is plain that, according to the well-settled principles of international law, the fact that one party to the contract was a Greek national and the other a department of His Majesty's Government in the United Kingdom, does not entitle the Greek Government, as is suggested in your note, to seek redress on behalf of its national on the ground of breach of contract. This question whether there was a breach of contract has been finally decided by the tribunal to which the parties agreed to refer it, and the only ground on which the Greek Government might be entitled to make diplomatic representations to His Majesty's Government would (subject always to the consideration that Monsieur Ambatielos did not make use of his

First published in P. L. Zanardi, A. Migliazza, F. Pocar, and P. Ziccardi (eds.), *International Law at the Time of its Codification: Essays in Honour of Roberto Ago* (1987).

[1] *ICJ Pleadings, Ambatielos Case* (Greece v. United Kingdom), p. 71.   [2] *Ibid.*, p. 84.

right of appeal and had therefore not exhausted his legal remedies) be that the decision in question constituted a denial of justice in the sense which international law recognizes as involving the responsibility of the State concerned.[3]

The position of the British Government was more fully recalled by the late Sir Gerald Fitzmaurice (who was one of the British counsel in the arbitral proceedings to which the judgment of the International Court of Justice led) in the following terms. Sir Gerald was commenting upon passages in the opinion of Judge Sir Hersch Lauterpacht in the *Norwegian Loans* case, to one of which reference is made below. In the course of Sir Gerald's comment, he quotes from the unpublished pleadings in the arbitral (third) phase of the *Ambatielos* case, in a fashion which illuminates this paper.

(2) BREACHES OF STATE CONTRACTS ENTERED INTO WITH FOREIGNERS

It will be noticed that it is implicit in the passages cited under the preceding head that an alleged breach by a Government of a contract with a foreigner is *prima facie* a matter that raises issues under international law, and is therefore in principle a matter of international jurisdiction. However, in view of his finding on the jurisdictional aspects of the *Norwegian Loans* case, Lauterpacht was not called upon to go into the substantive question of whether the alleged breach of contract would in fact have involved a violation of international law. Therefore it would be wrong to attribute to him the view that if there is in fact a breach by a State of a contract between itself and a foreign national or corporate entity, a breach of international law is thereby *ipso facto* constituted, even in the absence of any denial of justice such as would result if, for instance, a right of action were not afforded to the foreigner in the local courts, or if, such a right being afforded, the decision were given against him on manifestly dishonest grounds.

It is clear that, *failing any denial of justice in the courts*, no breach of international law can arise from the mere breach of a contract between an individual *national* (or national entity) of the country concerned and a foreigner – or from a decision given in such a case against the foreigner (unless of course it is clearly motivated by xenophobic considerations – in which event it constitutes a denial of justice). It may be slightly less obvious that there is no breach of international law arising from the breach of contract *per se*, where the contract is between the local *Government* and a foreigner, and where a breach on the part of the Government is alleged; but, to cite from the United Kingdom counter-case in the third phase of the Ambatielos case, paragraph 269, "It is generally accepted that, so long as it affords remedies in its Courts, a State is only directly responsible, on the international plane, for acts involving breaches of contract, where the breach is not a simple breach ... but involves an obviously arbitrary or tortious element, e.g. a confiscatory breach of contract – where the true basis of the international claim is the confiscation, rather than the breach *per se*." Thus Hyde (*International Law*, 1st

---

[3] *Ibid.*, pp. 106–107.

ed. vol. I, p. 549), referring to the practice of the United States, says that "a breach of contract must constitute also a tort in order to be regarded as internationally illegal conduct"; and Eagleton (*The Responsibility of States in International Law*, p. 164) citing Hyde, adds: "In these cases the basis for the claim is to be found in the fact that the circumstances accompanying the breach of contract constitute in themselves internationally illegal conduct."

It may well be that had the Court found itself competent in the *Norwegian Loans* case, and had it gone on to determine the merits, Lauterpacht would have considered that a failure by a government to honor a gold clause in a contract with a foreigner involved a sufficiently tortious element to bring the case within the above-mentioned principle. But this cannot be assumed, and the matter seems sufficiently important and controversial to warrant this *caveat* against reading too much into his remarks on what was, as it then stood before him, a purely jurisdictional issue.[4]

While still other States and scholars have not accepted the position which Sir Gerald sets forth, and while State practice is unquestionably uneven, it is believed that the weight of such international judgments as have been brought to bear on the question supports his view.

One may characterize Sir Gerald's – and the British – position as the median position. At one extreme is the position espoused by Greece in the *Ambatielos* case, namely, that the breach by a State of its contract with an alien is of itself a breach of international law. That that position is not an isolated one is illustrated by the contentions which Switzerland earlier advanced before the Permanent Court of International Justice in the *Losinger & Co.* case, where it maintained that:

> The principle *pacta sunt servanda* ... must be applied not only to agreements concluded directly between States, but also to agreements between a State and an alien; precisely by reason of their international character, such agreements may become the subject of a dispute in which the State takes the place of its nationals for the purpose of securing the observance of contractual obligations existing in their favor. The principle *pacta sunt servanda* thus enables a State to resist the non-performance of conventional obligations assumed by another State in favor of its nationals.[5]

In further support of Greece's contentions, there may be cited the bases of discussion prepared by the Preparatory Committee of The Hague Codification Conference:

---

[4] Sir Gerald Fitzmaurice, "Hersch Lauterpacht – The Scholar as Judge," Part I, *British Year Book of International Law* (1961), 37, pp. 1, 64–65.

[5] *Losinger & Co.* case, PCIJ, Series C, No. 78, p. 32.

Basis of discussion No. 3

A State is responsible for damage suffered by a foreigner as the result of the enactment of legislation which directly infringes rights derived by the foreigner from a concession granted or a contract made by the State.

It depends upon the circumstances whether a State incurs responsibility where it has enacted legislation general in character which is incompatible with the operation of a concession which it has granted or the performance of a contract made by it.

Basis of discussion No. 8

A State is responsible for damage suffered by a foreigner as the result of an act or omission on the part of the executive power which infringes rights derived by the foreigner from a concession granted or a contract made by the State.

It depends upon the circumstances whether a State incurs responsibility when the executive power has taken measures of a general character which are incompatible with the operation of a concession granted by the State or with the performance of a contract made by it.[6]

At the other extreme is the position that the breach of a contract between a State and an alien does not give rise to a violation of international law, at any rate if the contract is governed by the law of the contracting State.[7] This position perhaps is found more in what States do not say – but sometimes do – than in what they do say. The *travaux préparatoires* and terms of the United Nations General Assembly's "Charter of Economic Rights and Duties of States" provide an illustration of the current unwillingness of an apparent majority of States to recognize, at any rate in such a document adopted in such a forum, any obligations under international law arising out of contracts between States and aliens. (Yet it should be recalled that, a decade earlier, the General Assembly adopted resolution 1803 [XVII], which provides that: "Foreign investment agreements freely entered into by, or between, sovereign States shall be observed in good faith" – a provision that embraces contracts concluded by States with aliens.)

The median position to which the quotation of Sir Gerald Fitzmaurice gives expression has recently received considered endorsement by the American Law Institute, which, in 1986, adopted its revised *Foreign Relations Law of the United States.* Section 712 provides:

Economic Injury to Nationals of Other States

A State is responsible under international law for injury resulting from:

(1) a taking by the State of the property of a national of another State that is (a)

---

[6] League of Nations publication *V. Legal, 1929 V.3* (document C.75.M.69.1929.), pp. 33 ff. It should be noted that there was no provision on this subject in the draft approved in first reading by the Third Committee of the Conference, and that no convention on State responsibility was adopted.

[7] For an able exposition of this position, see A. A. Fatouros, *Government Guarantees to Foreign Investors* (1962).

not for a public purpose, or (*b*) discriminatory, or (*c*) not accompanied by provision for just compensation . . .

(2) a repudiation or breach by the State of a contract with a national of another State

(*a*) where the repudiation or breach is (i) discriminatory; or (ii) motivated by other non-commercial considerations and compensatory damages are not paid; or

(*b*) where the foreign national is not given an adequate forum to determine his claim of breach or is not compensated for any breach determined to have occurred;

(3) other arbitrary or discriminatory acts or omissions by the State that impair property or other economic interests of a national of another State.

The commentary on this section provides:

> h. *Repudiation or breach of contract by State.* A State party to a contract with a foreign national is liable for a breach of that contract under applicable national law, but not every repudiation or breach by a State of a contract with a foreign national constitutes a violation of international law. Under Subsection (2) a State is responsible under international law for such a repudiation or breach only if it is discriminatory ... or if it is akin to an expropriation in that the contract is repudiated or breached for governmental rather than commercial reasons and the State is not prepared to pay damages. A repudiation or failure to perform is not a violation of international law under this section if it is based on a *bona fide* dispute about the obligation or its performance, if it is due to the State's inability to perform, or if the State's non-performance is motivated by commercial considerations and the State is prepared to pay damages.

It will be observed that the revised *Foreign Relations Law of the United States* does not accept the contention that the breach by a State of its contract with an alien necessarily constitutes a breach of international law – and rightly so; rightly, because such a contract is not an instrument of international law whose breach thereby gives rise to a violation of international law. But neither does it accept the position that, since a contract between a State and an alien is typically (though by no means invariably) governed by the law of that State, the State is free under international law to absolve itself of its obligations towards the alien by altering the content of the governing law or by otherwise evading the terms of its commitments. Rather, it adheres to the position, which has considerable support in doctrine and practice, that if a State repudiates or violates its obligations under a contract with a foreign national, it is responsible for such a violation "only if it" – the breach – "is discriminatory ... or if it is akin to an expropriation in that the contract is repudiated or breached for governmental rather than commercial reasons ..." An indication of doctrinal support for this position is found in the references provided above by Sir Gerald Fitzmaurice; perhaps that support was most extensively and ably developed by the late Professor F.S. Dunn in his seminal study on *The Protection of Nationals: A Study in the Application of International Law* (1932).[8]

As observed above, a contract between a State and an alien is not an instrument of international law; it does not give rise to obligations under the law of treaties. In the words of F.K. Nielsen in *The United States of America on behalf of Singer Sewing Machine Company v. The Republic of Turkey*:

> It cannot be said that the law of nations embraces any "Law of Contracts" such as is found in the domestic jurisprudence of nations. International Law does not prescribe rules relative to the forms and legal effect of contracts ... But ... that law may be considered to be concerned with the action authorities of a Government may take with respect to contractual rights. It is believed that in the ultimate determination of responsibility under international law, application can properly be given to principles of law with respect to confiscation, and that the confiscation of the property of an alien is violative of international law. If a Government agrees to pay money for commodities and fails to make payment, the view may be taken that the purchase price of the commodities has been confiscated, or that the commodities have been confiscated.[9]

It should be recalled that there is no more firmly established principle of international law than that a State cannot plead its national law in derogation of its international obligations. Action or inaction by a State *vis-à-vis* an alien may be perfectly lawful in terms of its municipal law, but still engage its international responsibility. There is no need to document this fundamental conclusion, which is contained and elaborated in a multiplicity of authorities. But to take one outstanding example in the codification processes of the International Law Commission of the United Nations in which Roberto Ago has played so extended and pre-eminent a part, the title, "Irrelevance of municipal law to the characterization of an act as internationally wrongful," introduced Judge Ago's draft convention on State responsibility on this point. The draft article he proposed, with the ample authority of the Permanent Court of International Justice and the International Court of

---

[8] See also, among other studies, R. Y. Jennings, "State Contracts in International Law," *British Year Book of International Law* (1961), 37, p. 156; K. S. Carlston, "Concession Agreements and Nationalization," *American Journal of International Law* (1958), 52, p. 260; and C. F. Amerasinghe, "State Breaches of Contract with Aliens and International Law," *ibid.*, (1964), 58, p. 881. See also Lowell Wadmond, "The Sanctity of Contract Between a Sovereign and a Foreign National," printed in The Southwestern Legal Foundation, *Selected Readings on Protection by Law of Private Foreign Investments* (1964), p. 139, especially the cases cited at p. 160, note 35.

[9] *American–Turkish Claims Settlement under the Agreement of December 24, 1923, Opinions and Report*, prepared by Fred K. Nielsen, 1937, p. 491.

Justice marshaled in its support, read: "The municipal law of a State cannot be invoked to prevent an act of that State from being characterized as wrongful in international law."[10] The draft convention adopted by the International Law Commission provides, in Article 4:

> An act of a State may only be characterized as internationally wrongful by international law. Such characterization cannot be affected by the characterization of the same act as lawful by internal law.[11]

Judge Lauterpacht's holding in his Separate Opinion in the *Norwegian Loans* case, referred to above by Fitzmaurice, bears recalling:

> The question of conformity of national legislation with international law is a matter of international law. The notion that if a matter is governed by national law it is for that reason at the same time outside the sphere of international law is both novel and, if accepted, subversive of international law. It is not enough for a State to bring a matter under the protective umbrella of its legislation, possibly of a predatory character, in order to shelter it effectively from any control by international law. There may be little difference between a Government breaking unlawfully a contract with an alien and a Government causing legislation to be enacted which makes it impossible for it to comply with the contract.

In the same case, Judge Lauterpacht observed that:

> The question of the treatment by a State of the property rights of aliens – including property rights arising out of international loans – is a question of international law ... The Hague Convention of 1907 for the Pacific Settlement of International Disputes ... refers expressly, as suitable for arbitration before the Permanent Court of Arbitration, to disputes "arising from contract debts claimed from one Power by another Power as due to its nationals."[12]

Judge Lauterpacht's reference to property rights arising out of international loans applies no less to property rights arising out of international contracts at large.

Accordingly, there is more than doctrinal authority in support of the conclusion that, while mere breach by a State of a contract with an alien (whose proper law is not international law) is not a violation of international law, a "non-commercial" act of a State contrary to such a contract may be. That is to say, the breach of such a contract by a State in ordinary commercial intercourse is not, in the predominant view, a violation of international law, but the use of the sovereign authority of a State, contrary to the expectations

---

[10] *Yearbook of the International Law Commission 1971*, Volume II, Part One, pp. 226, 233.
[11] *Yearbook of the International Law Commission 1973*, Volume II, p. 184.
[12] *ICJ Reports 1957*, pp. 37, 38.

of the parties, to abrogate or violate a contract with an alien, is a violation of international law.

Thus, in the *Shufeldt Claim (United States of America on behalf of P.W. Shufeldt v. The Republic of Guatemala* [1930]), the case turned on the legality under international law of Guatemala's abrogation, by legislative and executive action, of a chicle concession contract. The United States maintained that: "The arbitrary cancellation of the concession by the Government of Guatemala through legislative and executive action" fell short of "the standards required by international law."[13] It claimed that: "The property rights of the claimant were arbitrarily confiscated and destroyed by the Guatemalan Government, and that Government is bound to make compensation therefor. The obligation to make such compensation is not affected, excused or discharged by any considerations of alleged national interests motivating that Government to effect such confiscation and destruction."[14] Guatemala challenged the *locus standi* of Shufeldt, and maintained that the contract was "illegal void and a nullity *ab initio*" on various grounds of its having been contrary to the law of Guatemala; that the contract was "abrogated, cancelled and avoided under the terms thereof" by reason of the grantees failing to comply with it; and that the decree of the Guatemalan National Assembly abrogating the contract "was the constitutional act of a sovereign State ... not subject to review by any judicial authority."[15] The Arbitrator, Sir Herbert Sisnett, held that the contract had been approved by the National Assembly; that, since the Guatemalan Government had acted for six years in recognition of the validity of the contract, it was in any event precluded from denying its validity, a position which he found to be "in keeping with the principles of international law,"[16] and that

> it is perfectly competent for the Government of Guatemala to enact any decree they like and for any reasons they see fit, and such reasons are no concern of this Tribunal. But this Tribunal is only concerned where such a decree, passed even on the best of grounds, works injustice to an alien subject, in which case the Government ought to make compensation for the injury inflicted and can not invoke any municipal law to justify their refusal to do so.[17]

The Arbitrator further held that, if the grantees had contravened the contract, the Government took no steps then to cancel it or to refer the dispute to arbitration as the contract provided, but continued to recognize the validity of the contract and to receive benefits under it; and that in any event

[13] Department of State, *Shufeldt Claim*, Arbitration Series No. 3, 1932, 73.   [14] *Ibid.*, p. 76.
[15] *Ibid.*, p. 365.
[16] *United Nations Reports of International Arbitral Awards* (UNRIAA), Volume II, pp. 1081, 1094.
[17] *Ibid.*, p. 1095.

the Government could not "set up this alleged breach as the cause of the cancellation in face of the provisions of the decree."[18] The Arbitrator further held that: "There can not be any doubt that property rights are created under and by virtue of a contract" and that Shufeldt possessed "the rights of property given to him under the contract."[19] He continued:

> The Guatemala Government contend further that the decree ... was the consti-
> tutional act of a sovereign State ... and is not subject to review by any judicial
> authority. This may be quite true from a national point of view but not from an
> international point of view, for "it is a settled principle of international law that a
> sovereign can not be permitted to set up one of his own municipal laws as a bar to
> a claim by a sovereign for a wrong done to the latter's subject."[20]

In the light of these holdings, the Arbitrator concluded that, in these circumstances, Shufeldt had a right to pecuniary indemnification for the taking of his contractual rights.

There are a number of arbitral awards which are in accord with the conclusion for which the *Shufeldt* case is authority, namely, that the non-commercial use of sovereign authority to abrogate or violate a contract with an alien gives rise to responsibility under international law. Among such cases are *Company General of the Orinoco (France) v. Venezuela* (1905)[21]; the *George W. Hopkins* case (1926)[22]; *International Fisheries Company (USA) v. United Mexican States* (1931)[23]; *George W. Cook (USA) v. United Mexican States* (1927)[24]; *Saudi Arabia v. Arabian American Oil Company* (1958)[25]; *BP Exploration Company (Libya) Limited v. Government of the Libyan Arab Republic* (1972)[26]; *Texaco Overseas Petroleum Company v. Government of the Libyan Arab Republic* (1977)[27]; *In the Matter of Revere Copper and Brass, Inc. and the Overseas Private Investment Corporation* (1978)[28]; *Agip Company v. Popular Republic of the Congo* (1979)[29]; *Framatome et al. v. Atomic Energy Organization of Iran* (1982)[30]; *Elf Aquitaine Iran v. National Iranian Oil Company* (1982)[31]; and

---

[18] *Ibid.*, p. 1096.   [19] *Ibid.*, p. 1097.   [20] *Ibid.*, p. 1098.

[21] J. H. Ralston, *Report of the French–Venezuelan Mixed Claims Commission 1902*, pp. 244, 359–365.

[22] *UNRIAA*, Volume IV, pp. 41, 46.   [23] *Ibid.*, pp. 691, 699.   [24] *Ibid.*, pp. 213, 215–216.

[25] *International Law Reports*, Vol. 27, pp. 117, 168, 172, 192, 227.

[26] *International Law Reports*, Vol. 53, pp. 297, 329.

[27] *Ibid.*, pp. 389, 470–471, 473–477, 479, 480–482.

[28] *International Law Reports*, Vol. 56, pp. 258, 271–275, 282–283, 290.

[29] *International Legal Materials* (1982), Vol. 21, pp. 726, 734–737.

[30] The award was initially published under the title *Company Z and Others (Republic of Xanadu v. State Organization ABC (Republic of Utopia)*, *Yearbook Commercial Arbitration* (1983), 7, p. 94. The award was published under its true name and in its original French in *Clunet, Journal du Droit International* (1984), p. 58.

[31] *Yearbook Commercial Arbitration* (1986), 11, p. 98.

Judge Charles N. Brower's Separate Opinion in the interlocutory award in *Sedco, Inc., and National Iranian Oil Company and Iran* (1986).[32]

While it is not practicable in this paper to comment upon all of these cases in the fashion in which pertinent passages of the arbitral award in the *Shufeldt* case have been summarized, it may be observed that, in the leading case of Saudi Arabia v. Arabian American Oil Company, the arbitral tribunal held that the concession agreement of 1933 between Saudi Arabia and Aramco was not governed by public international law. It held that it derived its judicial force from the legal system of Saudi Arabia. In the governing circumstances, it found the concession agreement to be the fundamental law of the parties, "which has the effect of conferring acquired rights."[33] It continued:

> By reason of its very sovereignty within its territorial domain, the State possesses the legal power to grant rights which it forbids itself to withdraw before the end of the Concession, with the reservation of the Clauses of the Concession Agreement relating to its revocation. Nothing can prevent a State, in the exercise of its sovereignty, from binding itself irrevocably by the provisions of a concession and from granting to the concessionaire irretractable rights. Such rights have the character of acquired rights. Should a new concession contract incompatible with the first, or a subsequent statute, abolish totally or partially that which has been granted by a "previous law or concession, this could constitute a clear infringement, by the second contract, of acquired rights or a violation, by the subsequent statute, of the principle of non-retroactivity of laws, with the only exception of rules of public policy. This is because a legal situation acquired by virtue of a previous special statute cannot be abrogated by a subsequent statute – *generalia specialibus non derogent* – unless the legislator has expressly given retroactive effect to such statute, which the State cannot do in respect of concessions, without engaging its responsibility.[34]

The particular contribution of the quoted passages of the Restatement of the *Foreign Relations Law of the United States* is that it gives specific content to the widely accepted doctrine that a State is responsible under international law if it commits not any breach, but an arbitrary breach, of a contract between that State and an alien. What is "arbitrary"? It is a breach "for governmental rather than commercial reasons." If a State, acting in a commercial capacity as any other contractor, breaches a contract with an alien, it

---

[32] *International Legal Materials* (1986), Vol. 25, pp. 629, 647–648. See also, for an award which affirms the principle *pacta sunt servanda* applicable to a contract which the tribunal found to run between a foreign contractor and a State, *SPP (Middle East) Limited, Southern Pacific Properties Limited and the Arab Republic of Egypt, The Egyptian General Company for Tourism and Hotels* (1983), *International Legal Materials* (1983), Vol. 22, pp. 752, 770–771, 774, 776 (annulled by the Paris Court of Appeal on another ground).
[33] *International Law Reports*, Vol. 27, p. 168.   [34] *Ibid.*

does not violate international law. As it was well put in the *International Fisheries Company* case cited above:

> If every non-fulfilment of a contract on the part of a Government were to create at once the presumption of an arbitrary act, which should therefore be avoided, Governments would be in a worse situation than that of any private person, a party to any contract.[35]

At the same time, the Mexican–USA General Claims Commission in this award recognized that, where a State's cancellation of a contract was "an arbitrary act, a violation of a duty abhorrent to the contract," that "in itself might be considered a violation of some rule or principle of international law."[36]

Examples of repudiation or breach by a State of a contract with an alien for governmental rather than commercial reasons are not unusual. The salient illustration is the repudiation by a State of a contract with an alien in the course of nationalization of an industry or the taking of the particular interests of the alien. Where the State does not pay damages that compensate for the breach of the alien's contractual rights, such a breach of contract certainly gives rise to responsibility under international law. Indeed, when the State employs its legislative or administrative or executive authority as only a State can employ governmental authority to undo the fundamental expectation on the basis of which parties characteristically contract – performance, not non-performance – then it engages its international responsibility.

It is recognized that this conclusion is the opposite of an approach which is currently accepted in some quarters, namely, that if a State employs its governmental authority in order to promote the national public welfare in a manner which overrides the contractual rights of an alien, the international responsibility of the State is not incurred.[37] It is believed that that approach is in error, not only for the legal reasons set out above, but because the alien, by definition, is not part of the national public whose welfare the State promotes. He is a sojourner in the community ruled by the State and, if it casts him or his rights out, then the State is obligated in equity as well as under international law to repair the resultant situation, whether by payment of compensation, restitution, or specific performance of its contract.

---

[35] *UNRIAA*, Volume IV, pp. 691, 700. [36] *Ibid.*, p. 699.

[37] For an excellent exposition of this viewpoint, see Oscar Schachter, *International Law in Theory and Practice, Recueil des Cours*, Volume 178 (1982–V), pp. 311–312.

27

Some Little-Known Cases on Concessions

✧

As Professor Jennings observed, "The particular topic of State contracts impinges upon some of the hardest questions of international law."[1] He concluded that:

> This part of international law, like so many other branches of the law, is in great need of elaboration. This can best be accomplished by its application to concrete cases t y arbitral tribunals. There is a wealth of material from which the law could by this means be developed.[2]

The purpose of this article is to mine some of the material to which Professor Jennings refers. It will set forth the awards in eleven cases involving international concession contracts. Ten of these are awards of arbitral tribunals adjudicating controversies between the granting State and the concessionaire; the eleventh, though consisting of Thai municipal decisions, is included because of interesting aspects of the decisions in a case involving a foreign concessionaire. Wherever possible, the arguments of the parties are described. None of these cases has, to the authors' knowledge, been published previously, except, in some instances, in privately printed form.

The principal topics dealt with in the awards may be summarized as follows: the juridical character of a concession contract (Sections I, II, III, IV); the principles governing the interpretation of State contracts (Sections I, II, III, IV); the general principles of law recognized by civilized nations (Sections I, IV, V); State succession to concessionary obligations (Sections I, V); the assignment of concessionary rights (Sections I, V); the right of independent

Written with Dr. J. Gillis Wetter. First published in *The British Year Book of International Law 1964* (1966), 40.

The authors wish to express their appreciation for research grants of the Svenska Handelsbanken's Social Science Research Fund and of the International Law Fund, and for the aid of Dr. Nicolas Tazedakis of the Athens Bar in securing the texts of some of the awards reported.

[1] "State Contracts in International Law," *British Year Book of International Law* (1961), 37, p. 156.

[2] *Ibid.*, p. 182.

management of the concessionary enterprise (Section II); expropriation of contractual rights and the State's power to renounce its contractual obligations (Sections I, II, III, IV); the application of *rebus sic stantibus* to concession contracts (Section II); and the nature of the compensation due upon breach or revocation of a concession contract (Sections II, IV, V).

I

The *Watercourses in Katanga* Case (*Compagnie du Katanga v. The Colony of the Belgian Congo, 1931*)[3]

In 1891 the Independent State of the Congo (the Congo Free State) took possession of Katanga. On March 12, 1891 it entered into a convention with certain Belgian interests providing for the establishment of a corporation under Belgian company law. The Company, which was incorporated under the style of the *Compagnie du Katanga*, was to have as its object the exploration of a defined territory, the establishment of lines of communication, and the exploitation of the territory's natural resources. In return for the obligations which the Company assumed of carrying forward these activities, it was granted the full ownership of one-third of the tracts of State land (*terrains*) situated in the territory covered by the convention, and a concession, for a period of ninety-nine years, to exploit the sub-soil of the land thus granted.[4]

On June 19, 1900 the Independent State of the Congo and the *Compagnie du Katanga* entered into a convention providing for the establishment of the so-called *Comité Spécial du Katanga* to which was entrusted the management, for the parties' joint account, of the tracts of land belonging to them at that time. The profits and other benefits that might be derived from the development of the land were to be divided between the parties in the proportion of two-thirds for the Independent State and one-third for the Company.

By a law of October 18, 1908 Belgium, after having annexed the Independent State and transformed it into a Colony, assumed responsibility for all its obligations. These obligations were set out in an annex to the law, in which the convention with the *Compagnie du Katanga* was specifically mentioned. In

---

[3] While, at the time of arbitration, the concessionaire, though partly foreign owned, was of the nationality of the disputant State, it should be noted that the concession was originally granted to the Company by a foreign State, the Independent State of the Congo. The briefs and the award have been released for publication by courtesy of the *Compagnie du Katanga*.

[4] Article 9 of the convention stipulated that: "L'Etat concède à la Compagnie du Katanga, en pleine propriété, le tiers des terrains appartenant au domaine de l'Etat situés dans les territoires visés dans la présente convention."

the same law, Belgium undertook to "respect acquired and legally recognized rights of third parties, whether indigenous or non-indigenous."

The Colony of Belgian Congo issued a decree of June 13, 1913, which stipulated, *inter alia*, that the river-beds of all lakes and watercourses, whether navigable and floatable[5] or not, belonged to the Colony. The decree furthermore subjected these watercourses to regulatory controls and established a licensing procedure for their use. It was this decree that gave rise to the dispute between the parties.

The Company maintained that the decree of 1913 violated the terms of the convention of 1891 insofar as the Colony claimed the ownership of the watercourses situated within the territory envisaged in the convention, including that one-third of the whole territory of Katanga which had been granted to the Company in full ownership. The Colony denied the Company's claim and contended that the decree of June 13, 1913 had general and mandatory application, since the watercourses had never been included in the Company's concession but had always been reserved for the exclusive ownership of the State.

This dispute was referred to arbitration pursuant to a *compromis* of October 8, 1930.[6] In their pleadings, the parties adduced the following arguments.

The Company's Case

The Company first distinguished navigable and non-navigable streams. It maintained that, until the decree of June 13, 1913 had been enacted, the unnavigable and unfloatable watercourses were susceptible to private appropriation and could also under general principles of law be the subject of legal transfer; they were not open to everybody's use, and did not belong to the public domain; only navigable and floatable watercourses were within the public domain.

The Company further argued that it had been granted one-third of the tracts of land in full ownership and for valuable consideration. In the 1891 convention the expression "tracts of land" (*terrains*) should be understood in its usual sense as meaning land together with all that the land contained and all the elements of which it was composed, including such watercourses as were susceptible of private appropriation and trees, bushes, dams, hills, and rocks.

The Company further stated that Article 1 of the convention of June 19, 1900 had vested the *Comité Spécial du Katanga* with special powers of administration, management, and assignment of property rights without any

---

[5] The French phrase is *navigables et flottables*.

[6] The Tribunal was composed of M. Louis Braffort, M. Léon du Bus de Warnaffe, and M. René Marcq. The Award was rendered on December 11, 1931, in Brussels. The translation is the authors'.

exception; and that Article 5 of that convention provided that all profits derived from the territory's development, as well as all expenses of any kind, should be divided between the parties in the proportion of two-thirds for the Independent State and one-third for the Company. Moreover, Article 6 provided that at the expiration of the convention, the interests then remaining should be divided between the parties in the same proportions.

Accordingly, the exclusive right to transfer or to permit the use of those unnavigable and unfloatable watercourses in Katanga which traversed the territories belonging to the State and the Company had been reserved for the *Comité Spécial* which could exercise these rights only for the benefit of the two parties to the agreement.

The Company noted that, in accordance with its powers, the *Comité Spécial* had entered into an agreement of October 30, 1906 with *Union Minière du Haut-Katanga*. That agreement gave *Union Minière* the right to exploit the falls and cataracts in rivers situated in the south of Katanga for the production of power. In return, *Union Minière* had undertaken to furnish to the *Comité Spécial* at cost price such power as the *Comité* might deem necessary; and in addition *Union Minière* transferred shares of its stock to the *Comité*.

The Company then drew attention to the fact that Belgium, pursuant to its undertakings in the law of October 18, 1908, accepted responsibility for the obligations assumed by the Independent State, among which the convention concluded with the *Compagnie du Katanga* was specifically included; Belgium's annexation of the Independent State could therefore not have the effect of modifying such legally recognized rights as the *Compagnie du Katanga* and the *Comité Spécial* possessed in regard to the unnavigable and unfloatable watercourses.

This being the case, the Company maintained that the effect of the provisions of the decree of 1913 was to purport to appropriate for public use watercourses which had already been transferred to the *Compagnie du Katanga*.

The Company argued further that the Colony invoked in vain its police power over the watercourses. While, in the course of exercising its governmental authority, the Colony might issue regulations governing watercourses, it could not in exercising its police powers appropriate property belonging to others, nor could it unilaterally revoke its contractual undertakings. A State's police power, the Company argued, must be distinguished from the right to exploit, administer, manage, and assign, and is altogether separate from the authority to transfer rights from one private party to another.

Accordingly, since the subject matter of the dispute was economic rights capable of being freely transferred, the State's granting of a concession (*le droit de concession*) included the concessionaire's right to transfer the property or the yield thereof to a third party. The grant of a concession is an exercise of property rights and confers on the owner the right to derive profits and to collect fees.

The Company submitted, in conclusion, that, while it was understandable that the Colony desired to apply a uniform system for the regulation of the unnavigable and unfloatable watercourses in the whole of the Congo, the Colony could not proceed to attain this end by action which in reality constituted expropriation without compensation and amounted to a unilateral revocation of its undertakings.

The Colony's Case

The Colony denied that the Company had any claim. The Company's submission that the watercourses had been transferred to its ownership by the convention of 1891 seemed to be based on three contentions: first, that under the common law applicable in 1891 in the Colony, the unnavigable and unfloatable watercourses constituted property of riparians; secondly, that the parties to the convention of 1891 relied on this rule of the common law as a law supplementing their expressed intention; and thirdly that the decree of 1913 had not modified this régime. None of these contentions, argued the Colony, was well founded.

In regard to the first contention, the Colony stated that an Ordinance of May 14, 1886 stipulated that "where a subject-matter is not regulated by a decree, a resolution or an ordinance already promulgated, disputes over which the courts of the Congo have jurisdiction shall be resolved with reference to local customs and general principles of law and equity." Accordingly, if a litigation had been instituted at the time between the *Compagnie du Katanga* and the Independent State, it ought to have been resolved according to "local customs and general principles of law and equity." However, this amounted only to a *petitio principii*, since in 1886 the Congo was an independent State which, in international law, was not linked in any way with Belgium but was open to pioneers and merchants of all nations; and which applied to all comers the same rules of law. Indeed, the terms employed in the decree of May 14, 1886 excluded any preference for Belgian legislation.

The Colony argued, moreover, that, even were it supposed that Belgian legislation contained legal principles applicable in the Congo, the matter at issue would still be resolved against the Company. Under Roman law, only watercourses without importance, or temporary ones, could be the object of private ownership. Under customary law, at least according to the principles of the Napoleonic Code, the ownership of all watercourses would be reserved for the State, and the French *Cour de Cassation* had on repeated occasions interpreted the provisions of the *Code Civil* to mean that watercourses could not be privately appropriated. While it was a fact that French legislation in 1898 had inaugurated a new system by transforming the ownership of river-beds of unnavigable and unfloatable watercourses to the riparians, the Belgian *Cour de Cassation* had continued to adhere to the doctrine previously enunciated by the French *Cour de Cassation*. Hence, even on the hypothesis that Belgian law was applicable, the Company could not claim any ownership over the watercourses in Katanga.

As to the second contention, the Colony retorted that there was no reason for supposing that the parties to the convention of 1891 had intended that the law applicable at the time should continue to govern all the future effects of the convention on all points which had not been expressly provided for by the parties. It was certain in any event that, in regard to this matter, the parties had not expressly provided that the common law should govern unforeseen effects of the concession. In any case it was necessary to consider more closely the state of the Congolese law at the time of the convention. In this connection, the Colony stressed that it must be realized that the purpose of the Ordinance of May 14, 1886 was not to define the law of the Congo by reference to local customs, general principles of law and equity. The Ordinance confined itself to providing that as long as a subject matter was not regulated by promulgated legislative acts – as long as the law of the Congo had not been created – in the expectation of such creation, and in the course of its gestation, but only then, the judge should apply such customs and principles.

Thus, in the last century, the law of the Congo was but an emerging law in process of formation, and its rules could be created only gradually through progressive legislation. Accordingly, if the parties in 1891 envisaged the common law as being incorporated in this convention, it was the common law, such as it existed at that time, which was of a singularly provisional and indeterminate character.

In addition, it was inconceivable that the Independent State of the Congo could at that moment (and still less could Belgium in 1908 when it assumed the Independent State's contractual undertakings) surrender its sovereignty and compromise its future by establishing in perpetuity, and without the possibility of change, the legal régime of those lands in the territories which had been subject to transfer in accordance with the vague and controversial rules of law prescribed in the Ordinance of 1886.

In opposing the third of the Company's contentions, the Colony submitted that the issue was not, as the Company had maintained, whether the decree of 1913 violated the principle of non-retroactive application of law. On the contrary, this decree clearly constituted an act through which the legislature of the Congo realized the plans envisaged in the Ordinance of 1886 and gave the colonial law, which was until then in process of development, a settled form (*sa forme organisée*). This being the case, it would, in the submission of the Colony, be impossible to view the decree of 1913 as embodying legal provisions applicable only to lands which had not yet been subject to any concessionary grant. The legislature's intention had certainly been to apply these rules to the whole colonial territory; moreover, it was difficult to see how it would be possible to subject to different régimes, on the one hand those territories which had not yet been the subject of transfer, and, on the other hand, the millions of hectares of land which had been transferred, and moreover the property of the indigenous population as well. Thus, any land law must have for its aim and purpose either to establish or to change the régime as a whole, and must for this very reason apply even to previously acquired property rights. It was difficult to understand why property rights acquired from the State should enjoy the privilege of being exempted from such a law in contradistinction to property rights acquired in another manner. Hence, the Colony submitted, it must be recognized that the decree of 1913 did apply to the lands transferred to the *Compagnie du Katanga*.

Lastly, the Colony disputed the Company's submission that the decree of 1913 amounted to expropriation and could consequently not be enforced except against payment of just and prior compensation. The Colony maintained that an expropriation is a special act through which the public authority appropriates specific property; but that a general act through which the legislature determines the scope and extent of property rights has not such a character.

The Colony concluded by submitting that, if the Tribunal should find that the watercourses could be the subject of private ownership, it ought nevertheless to hold that this decision left intact the Colony's sovereign rights and, in particular, the right to require advance governmental permission for the establishment, discontinuance, or modification of any works affecting watercourses, whether permanent or temporary, of such a character as to influence in any manner the flow of the watercourses.

The Award of the Arbitration Tribunal

The Tribunal stated that it was necessary initially to determine exactly what rights the Company had acquired by virtue of the 1891 convention. For this

442

purpose it must first establish whether the unnavigable and unfloatable watercourses in the Colony did or did not belong to the public domain in March 1891, and whether they were capable of private appropriation. To answer this question it was necessary to investigate what solution a judge faced with the issue in 1891 would have given to the dispute. Article 2 of the Ordinance of the General Administrator of July 1, 1885 stipulated that vacant land should be considered as belonging to the State, but there did not exist on that date any other text giving certain parts of the territory the character of public domain; moreover, the Act of Berlin of February 26, 1885, which established the right of free navigation on the rivers of the Congo, was restricted to navigable watercourses. Hence, at that time, there was no legal text applicable to the Colony which prescribed that unnavigable and unfloatable watercourses fell within the public domain.

The Tribunal next examined the question of the applicable law. Referring to Article 1 of the Ordinance of May 14, 1886, it held that there could be no question of invoking local customs – and the parties had not indeed done so – since these customs applied only to land owned by indigenous communities and not to State territory, and since the conventions with the Company comprised only land which belonged to the State and to which the indigenous population had no rights. Discussing the concept of general principles of law the Tribunal declared:

> Where a subject-matter is not regulated by a decree, a resolution or an ordinance already promulgated, disputes over which the courts of the Congo have jurisdiction shall be resolved with reference to local customs and general principles of law and equity.
>
> While general principles of law are understood to mean dominating legal concepts of the most developed municipal legal systems, it must be recognized that the author of the Ordinance thought that Belgian law must, in case of divergency, prevail over the law of other nations having the same degree of civilization.
>
> Under the general principles of law accepted in Belgium, "the fact that an object is destined for public use does not suffice to make it part of the public domain; it must have been incorporated into the public domain by law, or it must serve without distinction for the use of all". (Cass. c. 21 janvier 1926, Pas. 1926 I. 188.)
>
> Again, if, as the Colony submits, general principles must be understood to mean not Belgian law but the law common to all countries which have arrived at the same degree of civilization as Belgium, it must be recognized that this 'common law' does not reserve for the public domain unnavigable and unfloatable watercourses. (*Cf. Pasimonie* 1877, p. 88.)
>
> A comparative study of these laws shows that one segment of the legislation and legal doctrine persists in denying that unnavigable and unfloatable watercourses

constitute riparian property, but that there exists near unanimity in favor of the legal possibility of admitting private appropriation of these watercourses.

Thus, under general principles of law, the watercourses at issue, being neither navigable nor floatable, could in 1891 be granted to private subjects as private property.

This conclusion derives particular support in the present case from the fact that the grantor in the Convention of 1891 was the Sovereign King, absolute monarch, uniting in his own person the legislative and executive powers and that he had the power to fix liberally, explicitly or implicitly, the substance of the territory susceptible of private appropriation within the sole boundaries of the provisions of the Act of Berlin and the very nature of things.

Having thus established that the watercourses could have been appropriated for private use, the Tribunal considered whether the watercourses were in fact comprised in the convention of 1891. The word used in the convention, it will be recalled, was "tracts of land" (*terrains*). The Colony had argued that this word should be given a restrictive meaning and should be understood to designate only the soil, excluding watercourses. The Tribunal first stated certain general principles which should in its opinion govern interpretation of the convention. It declared:

> The general principles of law and equity make it incumbent upon the judge for the purpose of determining the object, the scope or the range of an agreement, to investigate the common intention of the parties, bearing in mind the state of affairs at the time of the conclusion of the agreement, and considering the circumstances, the personalities of the parties and the aim pursued by each of them in contracting.

> Given the extremely general aim and scope of this Convention – the extent of the concessions made to the *Compagnie du Katanga* in consideration of manifold and burdensome obligations – the nature of these obligations, which imposed upon the Company particularly the exploitation in full of the property granted to it – it is not possible to understand the term "terrains" in a restricted sense, which moreover the concept does not bear; and to maintain that it should not apply directly to everything which was comprised in the private domain of the Independent State.

> On the other hand the Sovereign King, who was the grantor and who was concerned with the urgent necessity of occupying and developing the territory of Katanga, and who was mindful of the considerable and burdensome efforts which this occupation and administration would entail, wished to secure for the organization, the heads of which had given him distinguished support in his glorious enterprise and who continued to extend to him the collaboration which he considered indispensable, satisfactory means and rewards in establishing between this organization and the State a true division of all the elements of this territory susceptible by their nature of private appropriation.

> The Belgian nationals who extended their collaboration also wished to obtain a just compensation for the extensive services which they undertook to perform.

444

This joint intention of the parties manifests itself clearly in Article 10 of the Convention of 1891, which stipulated that "the territory of the State ... shall be divided into tracts of land comprising in longitude and in latitude six geographical minutes."

The Tribunal next considered the argument adduced by the *Compagnie du Katanga* which related to the granting in 1906 by the *Comité Spécial du Katanga* of a concession to the *Union Minière du Haut-Katanga*. This concession, as stated by the *Compagnie du Katanga* in its pleadings, granted the *Union Minière* the right to exploit falls and cataracts of rivers situated in that part of Katanga which was the subject of its concession. The concession was ratified by decree of the sovereign King. The concession to the *Union Minière* was expressly granted "in conformity with the Convention of 19 June 1900," i.e., the convention between the Independent State of the Congo and the *Compagnie du Katanga* providing for the setting up of the *Comité Spécial du Katanga*.

The Tribunal concluded that these facts alone sufficed to negate the argument adduced by the Colony to the effect that the convention with the *Union Minière* had been entered into by the *Comité Spécial* not in its capacity of agent for the Independent State and the *Compagnie du Katanga* and in conformity with the convention between them of June 19, 1900, but by virtue of an Act of December 6, 1900 by which the Independent State delegated to the *Comité* the exercise of public authority. Furthermore, it was only on January 6, 1920 that the Minister of the Colonies, while recognizing that the unnavigable and unfloatable watercourses had been subject to private appropriation up to 1913, claimed that the *Compagnie du Katanga* and the *Comité Spécial du Katanga* had received land only and that, if the *Comité Spécial* had given *Union Minière* the right to utilize the falls in *Haut-Katanga*, the *Comité* had acted on the strength of the delegation to it of the right to exercise a public authority.

The position of the parties at the time of the conclusion of the convention having been determined, the Tribunal next examined whether any acts had taken place after 1891 which were capable of modifying the rights of the parties and which a court must now apply to the dispute. The Tribunal then referred to the fact that the decree of June 30, 1913 stipulated that "the bed of every lake and of every other watercourse, whether navigable or floatable or not, belongs to the Colony."

The Tribunal, in discussing the effect of this decree, emphasized that Belgium, by a law of October 18, 1908, had assumed responsibility for all the obligations previously undertaken by the Independent State of the Congo, and particularly those specified in Annex A to that law, among which was the convention of 1891; and that Belgium had by the same law undertaken to respect the legally acquired rights of third parties, whether indigenous or not. Therefore, the obligations flowing from the convention of 1891 had been assumed by Belgium and had the force of law. The Tribunal concluded:

> Without going into the question whether the State of Belgium was empowered to reject purely and simply by a decree obligations solemnly accepted by it, in connection with the rights accruing to the State from the cession of the Congo by the Sovereign King, it suffices to mention that Article 7 of the Colonial Charter of 18 October 1908 provided that "the King shall exercise the legislative power through decrees except with regard to matters which are regulated by law" and that "the courts and tribunals shall apply decrees only to the extent that they do not contravene laws".
>
> In these circumstances, the decree of 1913 is inapplicable to the Convention of 1891, which was incorporated in the Colony's legislation.

The Tribunal accordingly decided that the unnavigable and unfloatable watercourses were comprised in the tracts of land granted to the *Compagnie du Katanga*; that they were embraced by the convention of 1900 creating the *Comité Spécial*; that the *Comité Spécial* was invested with the power of protecting and directing the joint exploitation of these watercourses and had the most extensive rights to assign them; that the decree of June 20, 1913 did not impair the acquired rights of the *Compagnie du Katanga* as they were established through concessions and the convention of June 19, 1900; and that the *Comité Spécial* had the exclusive right to levy charges on users. The Tribunal further held that, as the parties had not raised the matter, it could not order the Colony to reimburse charges collected by it from users of the watercourses.

Lastly, the Tribunal decided that the rights thus recognized as belonging to the *Compagnie du Katanga* left intact public regulatory power over the watercourses in question.

Conclusions

The *Watercourses in Katanga* case, a landmark in the concession system applied by Belgium in the Congo, is of considerable interest despite its now archaic colonial flavor; for the award, which was unanimous, contains a number of noteworthy points.

First, the Tribunal drew upon general principles of law recognized by civilized nations in deciding a key issue: whether watercourses of the kind in dispute were subject to private appropriation. This was in 1931 when the relevance of general principles of law in the interpretation of international concession contracts had not been widely espoused.

Second, the Tribunal, in interpreting the terms of the concession, had recourse to principles that would seem to be universally accepted in the construction of agreements to which both parties are equal in a legal sense. Thus it relied heavily on the common intention of the parties, having regard to the position at the time of the conclusion of the convention and the aims pursued by each of them in contracting. Applying these methods of interpretation to the concession, the Tribunal declined to give the word *terrains* a restrictive meaning. It did not hold that concessions are to be interpreted restrictively in favor of the granting State. On the contrary, it emphasized that the concession was extremely general in scope and granted extensive rights to the concessionaire Company in return for the Company's assumption of far-reaching obligations. (However, it should be noted that the Company's rights were so extensive as to partake of quasi-governmental powers akin to those accorded the great trading companies of an earlier concessions era. This fact could be said to detract from the significance of the Tribunal's tending to place the parties on an equal plane, for in a measure, they actually were so. Nevertheless, at the time of the award – as perhaps contrasted with the situation as it may have existed in the days of the Independent State of the Congo – the Company was clearly a company and the State clearly a State.)

Third, the Tribunal ruled that a decree which purported to establish the State's ownership of and regulatory authority over properties whose ownership was claimed by the concessionaire did not impair the acquired rights of the Company in respect of those properties. The Company retained ownership and the right of assignment. Moreover, while the Colony urged that, in any event, the decree could be justified as an exercise of its police power, the Tribunal did not accept that contention. The Tribunal held that, in the light of the obligations assumed by Belgium upon its annexation of the Congo, the Colony's decree could not derogate from rights granted by the Independent State of the Congo, and that the Colony's undoubted regulatory powers must be so construed. Thus the Tribunal at the same time recognized and restricted the sweep of the Colony's regulatory authority.

For the above reasons, the award in the *Watercourses in Katanga* case is an addition of some importance to the limited body of case law in which the bases of the relationship between a State and a concessionaire have been the explicit focus of judicial examination. This is true despite features peculiar to the Congo concessions régime – features which gave the concessionaire broad exploitative powers which are not characteristic of modern concession contracts.

II

Some Arbitral Awards Concerning a Greek Utility Concession of 1925[7]

In October 1925 an agreement was entered into by the Government of Greece with the *Syndicat d'Etudes et Entreprises* and the Power and Traction Finance Company Ltd. By the terms of the convention, the concessionaires were granted certain rights and undertook certain obligations in respect of the supply of electricity and transport services in Greece. Pursuant to the convention, the concessionaires, who took over operations of previous concessionaires, formed companies to carry out their undertakings, namely, the Hellenic Electric Railways, the Electric Transport Company, and the Athens Piraeus Electricity Company.

A number of disputes relating to the interpretation of the agreement arose, and were submitted to arbitration in accordance with Article 49 of the agreement which provided:

> Any and every dispute, difference or question which may arise at any time between the State and the Company or the Concessionaires touching the construction meaning or effect of this concession or of any clause or thing herein contained or the rights and liabilities of the parties hereunder or otherwise howsoever relating to the premises shall be referred to the arbitration of three arbitrators of whom one shall be nominated by the State and one by the Company or the Concessionaires and the third who shall act as Chairman shall be chosen by the other two.
>
> Each of the parties shall nominate an arbitrator within one month of the receipt of a notification in writing from the other party that a difference has arisen.
>
> If the two arbitrators first appointed fail to agree on a chairman then the Chairman shall be the Director of the International Labor Office of the League of Nations or a person nominated by him.
>
> The parties hereby undertake to abide by the decision of the arbitrators so appointed. The expenses of any arbitration shall be borne and paid as the arbitrators may direct. No action shall be brought by the Company or the Concessionaires against the State or by the State against the Company or the Concessionaires until an award of the arbitrators has been made and then only for the amount of such award or for the purpose of giving effect thereto as the case may be.

---

[7] The cases reported in this section are drawn (with two exceptions) from a privately printed booklet, edited by the Athens Piraeus Electricity Company Ltd., entitled *Arbitral Awards Issued in Application of Article 49 of the Agreement in Regard to the Supply of Electricity and Transport Services Dated 17 October 1925* (1941). The booklet contains thirteen awards, of which four of primary interest are reported here. Notes on one remaining award, and on two further awards rendered in 1956 and 1961, are also included.

Ad hoc tribunals were constituted to resolve each of these disputes.

The *Staff Regulations* Case (*Government of Greece v. Hellenic Electric Railways Ltd., 1928*)[8]

The issues in this case, as the Tribunal had occasion to stress, were far from clear. In fact, the arbitrators' initial task was to define the dispute in the light of the voluminous documentation submitted to it in evidence. At their first sitting, they proposed, and the parties accepted, the following statement which served the function of a *compromis*:

> Quelles sont la portée et la valeur des mots "droits acquis" pour le personnel et quelles sont l'étendue ou les limites des "obligations assumées" par la Société, tant en vertu de l'article 6 du décret-loi du 16 octobre 1925 et de la lettre complémentaire du 14 octobre 1925 que de l'article 12 de la convention qui garantit l'indépendance administrative et financière (financial) de la Société?

Article 6 of the Decree-Law of October 16, 1925 referred to in this statement read as follows:

> Les concessionnaires et les sociétés successeurs prennent l'engagement d'observer toutes les obligations des sociétés existantes envers leur personnel grec, en tant que ces obligations existaient à la signature de la convention ratifiée par le présent décret, et sont basées sur des prescriptions des lois helléniques ou sur des accords particuliers entre ces sociétés et leur personnel.

The letter of October 14, 1925 from the Company to the Ministry of Communications, also referred to in the statement, read as follows:

> Afin d'éclaircir et compléter les engagements assumés par nous suivant art. 6 du décret législatif concernant la ratification de la convention entre l'Etat et nous-mêmes "relative à la fourniture d'électricité et aux transports", nous avons l'honneur de vous faire savoir que les nouvelles sociétés à constituer par nous prendront l'engagement suivant : en cas de renvoi, à la suite de suppression de poste, de n'importe quel employé du personnel actuel, hellénique et titularisé des sociétés d'électricité et des transports existantes dont fait mention notre convention, la Société s'engage à offrir à l'employé renvoyé un poste dans une autre de ses entreprises, avec des émoluments non pas inférieurs à ceux perçus par lui lors du renvoi, ou si elle ne fait pas cela, à verser à l'employé ainsi renvoyé une indemnité fixée aux appointements d'un mois pour chaque année de son service dans l'entreprise d'où il est renvoyé, en tout cas cette indemnité ne pouvant pas être inférieure aux appointements de trois mois. Cette indemnité sera versée à la place de celle fixée par la loi 2112, mais elle sera indépendante des versements éventuellement dus à l'employé par des caisses de retraite ou de prévoyance existantes.

---

[8] The Tribunal was composed of M. Albert Thomas, Director of the ILO, as President, and Messrs. Demetrios Schinas and Percy Horsfall. The award was rendered in Geneva on March 6, 1928.

L'engagement assumé en vertu du présent a la même vigueur comme s'il était compris dans la convention.

As to Article 12 of the convention, it provided:

Except as otherwise specifically provided in this concession nothing in this concession shall be deemed to restrict the financial and administrative independence of the Company or to restrict the right of the Company to carry on its undertaking until 31 December 1985 in the ordinary course of business.

The Company submitted that certain actions taken by the Greek authorities contravened Article 12 of the convention and the rights granted to the Company by virtue of the explanatory letter of October 14. In the first place, the Minister of Communications, invoking certain provisions in a Greek regulation of 1917 (*Règlement général du personnel des services extérieurs*), had nominated three persons as representatives on the *conseil d'avancement* of the Company's staff. The Company objected that the provisions of the regulations violated the administrative independence of the Company and could not be applied to it. The Minister contended, however, that the administrative independence which the Company was to enjoy under Article 12 of the convention had been rendered inoperative by Article 6 of the Decree-Law by which the convention was ratified. Furthermore, were the Company to put regulations concerning its own personnel into effect, as it had proposed to do, such regulations would be illegal under a Greek law. The Company contended, however, that the Greek law in question could apply only to the former companies which had operated the services before the convention of 1925 was concluded.

In the second place, the Minister of Communications had made a request that an employee who had completed his military service be reinstated in his position with the Company pursuant to a provision of the *Règlement général*. The Company refused to comply with this request, again contending that it impinged upon its administrative independence pursuant to Article 12 of the convention. The Minister responded by stating that the relationship between the Company and its employees was governed by Article 6 of the Decree-Law ratifying the convention which must be viewed as having superseded Article 12 of the convention in the event that the two provisions conflicted. Accordingly, all Greek regulations having the force of law which applied to Greek railways and tramways would, in the Minister's submission, be equally applicable to the Company. The Company eventually drew up its own staff regulations and submitted that the sole question which could be arbitrated in the case was whether these regulations respected the vested rights of the employees who had been transferred from the previous concessionary undertakings. The Government, in expressing disagreement with this view, demanded the institution of arbitration and insisted in addition that any staff regulations adopted by the Company must be approved in advance by the Minister of Communications.

In discussing the facts and issues of the case, the Tribunal stated that the first question to be decided was: what were the employees' vested rights which were envisaged in Article 6 of the Decree-Law ratifying the convention? In the submission of the Company, these rights were limited to those referred to in the explanatory letter of October 14, 1925, i.e., an obligation to re-employ on equal or better terms certain categories of employees dismissed as a result of abolition of posts, or, failing this, to give such employees a minimum of three months' salary. In the Government's view, however, the vested rights of the employees of the companies that were to be reorganized pursuant to the convention had a much greater scope, and encompassed all working conditions, including advancement, and stability of employment, i.e., in short the entire situation of existing employees at the time of the execution of the convention, which, it was argued, the Company had an obligation to preserve. In particular, the Government submitted that Article 6 of the Decree-Law obliged the Company to apply the provisions of the *Règlement général* of 1917.

The Tribunal held that, in the circumstances, the broader interpretation of vested rights seemed to be correct and the restrictive interpretation advanced by the Company unacceptable. This did not mean, however, that all the provisions of the Greek regulations had the effect of creating vested rights for the employees. In particular, the right conferred on the Government to appoint representatives on the staff councils did not, in the Tribunal's view, amount to vested rights of the employees.

The Tribunal went on to state that it might have been possible to decide what specific articles in the regulations of 1917 could be deemed to create vested rights. However, the issue had been broadened, and the next matter to be decided was whether the Company was in principle obliged to observe the conditions of general regulations issued in virtue of enabling regulations of 1912 (as amended in 1914) and in particular whether the Company was obliged to submit its own staff regulations to the Government for approval. In other words, did the administrative and financial independence guaranteed to the Company give it entire freedom to regulate the working conditions of its employees and its relations with them without any intervention of the Government? The issue thus turned on a construction of the principle of administrative and financial independence.

Greece had contended that Article 6 of the Decree-Law diminished or even suppressed the independence recognized in Article 12 of the convention. In Greece, the Government argued, the legislative authorities, when ratifying a convention entered into by a Minister, had the right to add to or derogate from the provisions of the agreement, by inserting new provisions if necessary. If the contracting company did not formally object to such changes, it was deemed to have accepted them. Accordingly, Article 6 of the Decree-Law had in fact replaced Article 12 and had subjected the Company to a duty strictly to observe all Greek laws and regulations pertaining to the matters at issue.

The Tribunal ruled that it was impossible to accept this argument since it could not admit that two articles having equal force of law and issued on the same day were in direct contradiction; if they were so, the legislative authorities had to make this clear beyond doubt. More especially must this be the case since the Company had attached particular importance to the formula adopted in Article 12. The principle enshrined in that formula must therefore have a real and positive meaning. The Tribunal stated:

> Il nous paraît impossible d'adhérer à une argumentation de cette nature. Sans doute ne saurait-on parler ici de modifications apportées unilatéralement par l'Etat, puissance publique, aux engagements souscrits par l'Etat contractant, étant donné que la convention n'était pas conclue définitivement avant d'être promulguée, et que des réserves pouvaient donc être formulées en temps utile par le décret-loi du 16 octobre 1925. Mais en la circonstance, l'argumentation de l'Etat paraît inacceptable, puisque le décret-loi indique que les articles de la convention ont, par l'acte de ratification, acquis force de loi, et qu'on ne saurait admettre que deux articles ayant également force de loi et édictés le même jour par la même autorité, soient ainsi en contradiction directe, l'un annulant l'autre. Peut-être précisera-t-on qu'en vertu de la reconnaissance des droits acquis qu'impose l'article 6, cet article limite, au moins en fait et pour une part, l'indépendance de la Société. Nul ne songe à le nier, mais on ne saurait en déduire qu'en dehors de cette reconnaissance des droits acquis, il constitue une sorte de limitation générale pour les applications à venir. Il aurait fallu, dans ce cas, que l'autorité législative indiquât avec précision ces limites; et elle ne l'a pas fait.
>
> L'Etat a également fait valoir qu'il respectait l'indépendance administrative et financière de toutes les sociétés concessionnaires en général, et que la formule d'indépendance inscrite à l'article 12 était sans portée particulière. C'est une interprétation qui ne saurait davantage être admise. La Société a attaché, en toutes circonstances, soit au moment de la négociation primitive, soit en mars 1927, lors des négociations nouvelles, une importance particulière à obtenir cette formule qui doit évidemment posséder un sens réel et positif.

However, it was equally impossible to admit, the Tribunal continued, that Article 12 granted the Company, as the latter contended, unrestricted freedom in relation to its personnel. It was inconceivable that a State granting a public utility concession for a term of sixty years could have absolutely renounced for the whole of this period the right to control the conditions of work by a text as vague as that of Article 12. In the circumstances, the Company must be deemed to have accepted Greek traditions in the labor field which contemplated a measure of public intervention. Had it wished to be exempted from Greek laws and regulations in their totality, this would have had to be stated in precise terms:

> Mais la Société a, de son côté, prétendu qu'en vertu de l'article 12, elle devait posséder une liberté sans réserve pour l'établissement du statut de son personnel. Il nous paraît également impossible d'admettre que, par le simple vote de l'article 12, cette indépendance totale ait été accordée à la Société. Il paraît impossible d'imaginer qu'un Etat concédant des services publics renonce pour soixante années, d'une manière absolue, à tout contrôle des conditions du travail. Il paraît impossible qu'il déclare, par un texte aussi vague, que la Société peut jouir d'une liberté totale à l'égard des lois et règlements qui régissent toutes les autres sociétés de même nature.
>
> Peut-être, la tradition britannique de la pleine liberté d'accord entre employeurs et employés, même dans les services concédés, a-t-elle guidé les négociateurs de la Société, et leur a-t-elle fait négliger de demander des précisions quant à l'indépendance vis-à-vis des lois et règlements concernant les sociétés de transport. Ils ne pouvaient cependant ignorer la tradition hellénique, semblable à celle de beaucoup d'autres pays, tradition datant déjà de plusieurs années avant la guerre et qui consacre, au contraire, l'intervention des pouvoirs publics, au nom de la sécurité ou de l'ordre public, dans la réglementation des conditions du travail du personnel des entreprises concédées. Si leur désir était d'être dispensés de l'observation de l'ensemble de ces lois et règlements, il est surprenant qu'ils n'aient pas demandé, sur ce point, des exceptions précises, alors que pour les lois fixant des conditions techniques d'exploitation, la convention prévoit expressément des exceptions.

The Company attempted to distinguish between laws applicable to all industries, such as laws respecting working hours, prevention of accidents, hygiene, social insurance, etc. – to which it would submit – and laws which applied to particular industries, such as railways, from which it claimed to be exempt. This distinction could not, in the opinion of the Tribunal, be accepted.

For these reasons, the Tribunal concluded that the underlying issue, i.e, whether the Company had to submit its staff regulations to the Government for approval, must be answered in the affirmative since the Greek enabling legislation was of a general character.

This conclusion did not, however, fully resolve the differences which had given rise to the arbitration; for it remained to consider in what respects the Government was to have a right to refuse its approval of provisions contained in the staff regulations. Thus, the Government could not, in the view of the Tribunal, insist that these provisions be in complete conformity with the general regulations in force in Greece:

> Il ne fait pas de doute pour nous (et il semble maintenant admis par l'Etat) qu'on ne saurait exiger en vertu de l'indépendance administrative reconnue à la Compagnie, que ce règlement soit conforme en tous points au règlement général.

The general principles to be adhered to by the Government in passing upon the staff regulations were stated by the Tribunal as follows:

> L'Etat, sans doute encore, devra insister auprès de la Société pour qu'elle admette certaines dispositions qui lui semblent conformes aux conditions normales de l'industrie ou aux dispositions générales imposées à d'autres sociétés concessionnaires. Mais il ne pourrait, sans violer l'indépendance qu'il a reconnue par contrat, c'est-à-dire sans violer ses engagements contractuels par un abus de la puissance publique, imposer des conditions autres que celles qui, en vertu de la loi ou en raison de pratiques normales, sont imposées à toutes les industries ou à une catégorie d'industrie. L'examen du règlement par le Ministère a donc essentiellement pour objet de constater que le règlement respecte toutes les lois générales d'ordre public ou établies dans l'intérêt supérieur de la collectivité.

In outlining practical solutions for certain of the Government actions which had given rise to the disputes at issue, the Tribunal underlined that these solutions would respect Greek laws and the Company's proper interests.

The *Truncated Arbitral Tribunal* Case *(Government of Greece v. Hellenic Electric Railways Ltd., 1930)*[9]

In this case the issue was set out in a *compromis* drawn up by the parties:

> 1° – la manière dont doit être résolu un différend si l'une des parties ne désigne pas d'arbitre ou ne désigne cet arbitre qu'après l'expiration des délais fixés à l'article 49 de la convention du 17 octobre 1925;
> 2° – le point de départ du délai de 30 jours fixé à l'article 49 sus-indiqué.

The arbitration clause of the Convention did not provide for the contingency that one of the parties might not designate its arbitrator within the prescribed time-limit and various solutions for this problem were ventilated before the Tribunal. The latter proposed that the parties should agree to invest the Director of the International Labor Office with the competence to designate an Arbitrator on behalf of the defaulting party. Recognizing that this procedure went beyond Article 49 of the convention, the parties reques-

---

[9] The Tribunal was composed of M. Albert Thomas, as President, and Messrs. André Zakkas and René Bresnard. The award was rendered in Geneva on February 10, 1930.

ted the Tribunal to embody the arrangement in an award so as to give it a binding character; and it was so decided.

The second point raised in the *compromis* was resolved in a similar manner, by means of an agreed arrangement to the following effect:

> Sur la seconde question, celle du point de départ du délai prévu à l'alinéa 2 de l'article 49 de la convention, le collège arbitral décide que l'avis écrit destiné à constater le désaccord devra être signifié à la partie adverse sous la forme d'un exploit d'huissier; du lendemain de la signification de cet exploit partira le délai de 30 jours au cours duquel chacune des parties devra désigner son arbitre.

The *Ten Lepta Charge* Case (*Hellenic Electric Railways Ltd. v. Government of Greece, 1930*)[10]

The issue in this case was whether the tax exemption clauses contained in the convention of 1925 exempted the Company from the payment of a special charge on railway tickets imposed by a Greek law of 1929. Articles 24 and 25 of the convention established various tax exemptions for the concessionaires. Article 25 provided, *inter alia*, that taxes levied on fares might in no case exceed a total of 5 percent:

> The State shall be entitled to impose taxation ... on travellers as such on the Company's railway, tramway or omnibus routes provided that the total of any taxes so imposed including the expenses of control shall at no time exceed 5 per centum ... on fares (calculated before the addition of such tax).

The Athens–Piraeus Railway Company, whose operations were taken over by the Hellenic Electric Railways Ltd., by virtue of the convention, was, according to an agreement with Greece, to pay taxes levied on railway tickets up to a maximum of 5½ percent. On December 23, 1925 a Decree-Law was promulgated providing for the setting-up of a special fund for retired railway employees. Contributions to the fund were levied in the form of charges on railway tickets of different amounts on different railways; a charge of 10 lepta per ticket was fixed for the line between Athens and Piraeus, which was run by the Company.

In April 1926 the Company had decided, with effect from April 1, the date on which it took over the operations of the railway, not to levy the extra charge of 10 lepta on each ticket since it was in excess of the 5 percent taxation which was stipulated as a maximum in Article 25; from that date the Company would add only a 5 percent tax charge on each ticket, and not 5½ percent as the previous operator of the railway had done, since the conven-

---

[10] The Tribunal had the same composition as in the *Truncated Arbitral Tribunal* case. The award was rendered in Geneva on March 18, 1930.

tion of 1925 must be deemed to have superseded previous laws. While the Government contended that the 10-lepta charge was not a tax but a social contribution, the Company maintained that imposition of the charge was at variance with the convention since its provisions could not be circumvented merely by giving a different name to charges imposed by legislation. The Minister of Communications, asked to give his opinion on the matter to the Minister of Finance, upheld the position taken by the Company.

A new Decree-Law issued on November 5, 1927, which confirmed and incorporated the Decree-Law of December 23, 1925, provided specifically that the charges on railway tickets were not levied by the Government but constituted social contributions. A law was promulgated in 1929 which reproduced the provisions of the Decree-Law of 1927 and provided that the charges in question were payable to a special pension fund. When the Company persisted in its claim that it was exempt from paying the charge, the Government took up the position that the general question of the applicability of the Greek legislation to the Company had already been decided by the Arbitral Tribunal in the *Staff Regulations* case reported above.

The Tribunal initially considered the distinction advanced by the Government between taxes and social charges contributed to a special fund for retired employees, holding that it was impossible to delimit with exactitude the meaning of the concept "tax." It attached particular importance to the fact that the charge was levied for a public purpose; even if the charge was not a tax in the most rigorous sense of the word, it was at least to be viewed as a tax in the general sense of terminology employed in Article 25. Since the limit of 5 percent established in Article 25 for charges levied on railway tickets had already been reached, it found that the charge exceeded the contractual limits and violated the convention. It said:

> Il est incontestable que la distinction opérée par l'Etat repose sur une analyse très sérieuse des faits. Cependant, la conclusion qu'il tire de cette analyse peut être mise en doute. Les définitions de l'impôt varient sensiblement suivant les auteurs et le collège arbitral ne prétend pas exprimer sur ce point une doctrine de portée générale. Il doit constater cependant que la taxe de 10 lepta établie par la loi 3828 présente les caractères habituels d'un impôt en ce sens qu'elle constitue une prestation pécuniaire sans contre-prestation correspondante (à la différence des taxes proprement dites), que cette prestation est perçue par des moyens de contrainte juridique, suivant des règles légales déterminées et que sa destination est d'utilité publique. C'est sans doute ce dernier élément qui est contesté par l'Etat lorsqu'il allègue l'affectation spéciale du produit de la taxe. Cependant, cette affectation spéciale ne fait pas disparaître, semble-t-il, le caractère d'utilité publique de la taxe. Celle-ci est représentée par l'Etat lui-même comme une 'charge sociale'; n'est-il pas évident qu'une charge sociale a un caractère d'utilité publique?

Et l'Etat, en établissant la taxe de 10 lepta, n'a-t-il pas agi au nom de la solidarité sociale qui constitue une des raisons d'être de l'activité de l'autorité publique? ...

Pour ces raisons, il semble au collège arbitral que la taxe instituée par la loi 3828 est un impôt, si non dans le sens le plus rigoureux du terme (et sur ce point la discussion pourrait être sans fin), tout au moins dans le sens général qui résulte de la terminologie employée par l'article 25, paragraphe 2 de la convention (texte anglais). Le collège arbitral estime qu'en fait et en droit la taxe de 10 lepta est un impôt d'une nature particulière, et il constate que son mode de perception est exactement celui que prévoit et réglemente l'article, alinéa 2, de la convention. La limite de 5% prévue par cette disposition s'applique donc à cette taxe et, comme ladite limite se trouvait atteinte avant l'établissement de la taxe de 10 lepta, il y a lieu de conclure que la taxe instituée par la loi 3828 excède la limite contractuelle acceptée par l'Etat et se trouve en contradiction avec la convention du 17 octobre 1925.

The Government did not confine its argument to a discussion of whether or not imposition of the 10-lepta charge was compatible with the terms of Article 25 of the convention. It also submitted that the convention was not an ordinary contract in the sense of the civil law but a public utility concession (*concession de service public*). Such a concession, it argued, did not abolish legislative sovereignty, and the conditions attached to the convention could be unilaterally modified by a law having the general and impartial nature which characterizes a law.

This argument was expressly rejected by the Tribunal, which stated that legislative modifications of the conditions of a public utility concession must not have effects harmful to the concessionaire, and, if they did, the concessionaire would have a right to obtain compensation for the damage resulting from such action. Whether or not the convention was a public utility concession or a civil law contract, it was indisputable that it contained *bona fide* undertakings which should be respected:

Sans doute, l'exercice de la souveraineté législative, modifiant les conditions de la concession d'un service public ne doit pas avoir pour effet de léser le concessionnaire, et s'il était ainsi, ce dernier serait en droit d'obtenir la réparation du préjudice résultant de la modification de la concession.

Le collège arbitral ne croit pas nécessaire de formuler des considérations théoriques sur la valeur du principe de la souveraineté législative allégué par l'Etat Hellénique. La convention du 17 octobre 1925 est-elle plus une concession de service public qu'un contrat civil? De l'avis du collège arbitral, cette distinction importe peu. Que la convention soit une concession de service public ou un contrat de droit civil, il est incontestable que, dans l'un et l'autre cas, elle comporte des engagements *bona fide* qui doivent être respectés. A cet égard, le collège arbitral constate que l'alinéa 2 de l'article 25 de cette convention constitue une disposition précise, et il estime que le mécanisme comportant la taxe de 10 lepta instituée, tant par la loi 3828 que par les décrets antérieurs, n'est pas compatible avec cette disposition.

The Tribunal, having thus in clear terms resolved the issues presented in the arbitration, went further, feeling compelled to assist in establishing the broad lines of an agreement for the future which would be respected by both parties and serve to prevent further disputes. In doing so it was mindful particularly of the general conclusions reached in the *Staff Regulations* case; for in its opinion the two awards, seen together, posed the problem of whether the convention would prevent the enactment by Greece of general social insurance schemes. The Tribunal was of the view that the Company ought in principle to participate in the social insurance envisaged in the law which imposed the 10-lepta charge.

As a result of discussions before the Tribunal, the Company submitted a declaration in which it acknowledged that Article 25 of the convention did not exempt the Company from paying such contributions as a general social insurance law might impose upon employers. The Company proposed a formula for increasing the price of its tickets which would yield a total of 2,000,000 drachmas per year, half of which would be paid to the special fund, and the rest to a retirement fund for the Company's employees. The Tribunal held that this proposal appeared to constitute a practical solution to the difficulties which had given rise to the arbitration.

The *Safety and Control Regulations* Case (*Government of Greece v. Hellenic Electric Railways Ltd. and Electric Transport Company Ltd., 1930*)[11]

Article 46 of the convention stipulated that the concessionaires should adopt certain safety regulations to be approved by the Minister of Communications. The Article read, in part:

> Les concessionnaires ou la Société d'accord avec le Ministre des Communications établiront des règlements pour la protection du public et de la Société. Ces règlements seront en vigueur à partir de la date de leur publication comme s'ils étaient insérés dans la présente convention, et aucune modification ou addition auxdits règlements ne sera valable sans leur acceptation préalable par la Société.

Draft regulations prepared by the Companies did not meet with the Government's approval, and the matter was submitted to arbitration.

Eighty clauses of the draft regulations were in dispute, and the Tribunal, which rendered a unanimous award, considered its task to be to render a final

---

[11] The Tribunal was composed of M. Maison, as President, and Messrs. Politis and Besnard. The award was rendered in Paris on June 5, 1930.

decision on the wording of each of these clauses. In view of the magnitude of this task, the Tribunal stressed that it could only state the general principles adhered to by it in fixing the wording of each clause. It did not feel bound to adopt either of the contradictory proposals advocated by the parties but considered itself at liberty to adopt, if necessary, a text of its own.

The Tribunal took the position that, if the basis of its decision must be respect for the convention, equally the Government could only be precluded from imposing necessary security measures in virtue of a specific provision of the convention:

> Le collège arbitral a estimé que la base de sa sentence devait être le respect de la convention du 17 octobre 1925. Il a considéré également que le droit d'intervention de l'Etat Hellénique n'était limité que dans les cas prévus par des dispositions explicites de la convention, et que son indépendance restait entière pour imposer les mesures nécessaires à la sécurité, à la police ou à l'ordre public, dans tous les cas où ces mesures ne seraient pas contraires à une prescription de la convention.

The Companies argued that extensive control by the Government over the safety regulations would infringe upon their right freely to administer their enterprise, as laid down in clause 12 of the convention, which, it will be recalled, was at the heart of the arbitration in the *Staff Regulations* case. The Tribunal held, however, that the rights granted to the Companies should be given a restrictive interpretation, and that controlling action by the Government was barred only where such limitations upon its regulatory powers were expressly stipulated. Where the provisions of the convention were not precise, an attempt should be made to reconcile the public interest and the interests of the Companies.

> Les arbitres ont estimé que le régime fait par la convention à la Société est un régime d'exception qui doit être interprété de droit étroit, et que, par conséquent, le droit d'intervention de l'Etat Hellénique n'est limité que dans les cas où des dispositions de la convention le précisent explicitement ...
>
> Le collège arbitral a estimé que dans les cas où les prescriptions de la convention n'avaient pas un sens net et précis et où il pouvait subsister un doute sur la portée exacte du texte, il devait l'interpréter dans le sens le plus pratique, et de manière à concilier, dans toute la mesure possible, l'intérêt public et celui des deux parties.

Case Concerning Collection of a Pension Fund Charge (Government of Greece v. Athens–Piraeus Electricity Company Ltd., and the Electric Transport Company Ltd., 1933)[12]

This arbitration related to issues already considered in the *Staff Regulations*

---

[12] The Tribunal was composed of M. Louis de Brouckère, President, M. André Mater and Mr. Zakkas. The award was rendered in Geneva on March 1, 1933.

and the *Ten Lepta Charge* cases. Pursuant to the award in the latter case, Greece had promulgated a law implementing the arrangement sanctioned in the award under which pension-fund charges were to be added to the cost of tickets. The issue in the present arbitration was whether it was implied in the *Ten Lepta Charge* award that the Company's approval was necessary in regard to the manner in which the pension-fund charges were to be collected. The Tribunal was unanimous in holding that, while the Company's approval was not strictly necessary, it was highly desirable that the Government and the Company reach agreement on the matter. The parties to the arbitration were accordingly directed to initiate negotiations with a view to reaching such an agreement. Meanwhile, the manner of collecting the charges prescribed in Greek legislation should apply:

> Considérant que s'il n'est pas établi, en droit, qu'un accord préalable entre les Sociétés demanderesses et l'Etat soit indispensable quant aux modalités de perception des contributions au compte spécial ainsi qu'aux facilités tarifaires corrélatives à accorder éventuellement aux Sociétés, il n'en reste pas moins qu'un tel accord est, en équité, hautement désirable et de nature à contribuer à la bonne entente nécessaire à la marche normale du service; ...
>
> Renvoient les parties à s'entendre sur les modalités de perception des contributions aux fins de participation au compte spécial des retraités des chemins de fer institué par la loi numéro 3828 du 29 janvier 1929, ainsi que sur les facilités tarifaires corrélatives à accorder éventuellement aux Sociétés;
>
> Décident, en outre, vu l'urgence, que, jusqu'à réalisation dudit accord entre les parties, le paiement des contributions visées aux décrets des 8 septembre et 18 novembre 1932 sera effectué par provision suivant le mode de perception prévu par lesdits décrets.

The *Tunnel Indemnity* Case (*Hellenic Electric Railways Ltd. v. Government of Greece, 1933*)[13]

The award is lengthy and complex but only one of its aspects requires to be noted here. The concessionaires undertook to construct an underground railway tunnel and were granted a right of expropriation for that purpose. Indemnities were to be fixed by a process in which the ultimate decision lay with the Greek courts, and were payable for damage caused to pipes, buildings, etc. The convention provided:

> The passage of a tunnel under any houses or other buildings shall not be held to create an obligation of indemnity by the Company except in the event of actual damage being caused to such houses or buildings.

---

[13] The Tribunal was composed of M. Emile Kirchhofer, President, and Messrs. Jen Youpis and Alexandre Wamwetzos. The award was rendered in Lausanne on July 19, 1933.

460

The Company moved for a declaration to the effect that, if the Company were ordered by the Greek courts to pay to holders of expropriated property damages for lost profits, the Greek Government should be liable to reimburse the Company to that amount.

The Tribunal ruled against the Company, holding, *inter alia*, that the case could not be considered one in which the Government was taking action harmful to the concessionary rights granted in the concession. Had this been the case, the concessionaire would have been entitled to compensation. Moreover, the doctrine of *rebus sic stantibus*, invoked by the Company, could not provide support for its claim. The Tribunal indicated, however, that, in certain circumstances, the doctrine of *rebus sic stantibus* could be properly invoked in aid of a concessionaire:

> Il n'est pas davantage possible d'assimiler une interprétation erronée de la convention par le juge à l'acte, administratif ou même législatif, par lequel l'Etat, le sachant et le voulant, aggrave sensiblement les charges du concessionnaire, telles qu'elles résultent de la concession, – cas dans lequel la doctrine et la jurisprudence reconnaissent au concessionnaire le droit à une indemnité. L'Etat n'a pas à répondre des prononcés rendus par les autorités judiciaires en toute indépendance dans l'exercice de leurs fonctions et en vertu de leurs attributions. Et l'on ne peut reprocher, dans la présente cause, au Gouvernement, d'avoir omis un acte que les circonstances lui eussent fait un devoir d'accomplir. Du reste, la seule voie d'intervention ouverte à l'Etat, à savoir au pouvoir exécutif et au pouvoir législatif, ce serait la voie de l'interprétation légale. Mais on ne conçoit pas que l'Etat ait l'obligation d'édicter une loi interprétative (avec effet rétroactif), lorsqu'il s'agit, non pas de remédier à une jurisprudence constante qui, de l'avis du législateur, nuit gravement à l'intérêt public, mais seulement de parer à l'éventualité que le juge pourrait mal appliquer la convention ... ou l'interpréter dans un sens plutôt que dans l'autre ...
>
> La théorie de l'imprévision ou de la *clausula rebus sic stantibus*, appliquée parfois en matière de concessions, ne vient pas à l'appui des conclusions de la Société, qui tendent au remboursement total des indemnités qu'elle devrait verser pour des dommages négatifs.
>
> Cette théorie pose, entre autres conditions, que des faits imprévisibles aient bouleversé l'activité économique de la Société concessionnaire, au point de la mettre dans l'impossibilité d'accomplir sa tâche d'utilité publique, en sorte que l'Etat (ou la Commune) doit lui venir en aide, d'une manière ou d'une autre.
>
> Cette hypothèse n'est point réalisée en l'espèce, et il ne peut en être question actuellement; l'avenir restant naturellement réservé pour le cas, d'ailleurs fort peu probable, où des condamnations de la Société à la réparation de dommages négatifs licites la mettraient dans une situation justifiant l'application de la théorie de l'imprévision. Il convient en outre de noter qu'aux termes de son contrat passé avec les entrepreneurs le 25 août 1927, la Société a le droit de se décharger sur eux de tous dommages-intérêts, y compris les indemnités pour dommages négatifs licites.

The *Obsolete Tramways* Case *(Electric Transport Company Ltd. v. Government of Greece, 1956)*[14]

By the 1925 convention the Company had been granted the exclusive right to construct and operate tramway services in districts of Athens. Those services deteriorated during the war and in postwar civil disturbances. The Company planned to replace the obsolete tramway lines with bus services, but failed to reach agreement with the Government on the terms for doing so. The Government intervened and tore up the tracks of two lines of tramways. The Tribunal held, *inter alia*, that, even although the State necessarily possessed the power to decide in the last resort upon questions bearing upon the satisfaction of public requirements, the tearing up of the tracks was a breach of the administrative independence with which the Company was invested by the terms of the convention.

> Considérant que l'Etat détient nécessairement le pouvoir de décider en dernier ressort dans des matières qui touchent à la satisfaction de besoins publics, tel que le transport d'une population concentrée et que, par conséquent, rien ne peut empêcher l'Etat, s'il le juge à propos, dans un but d'utilité publique, d'imposer une mesure contraire aux vues d'un cocontractant, notamment d'un concessionnaire;
>
> Considérant, par conséquent, que la Société devait accepter en tant que mesure provisoire, l'interruption de la circulation des tramways en raison de la réfection des rues, mais qu'elle n'avait pas à accepter la suppression définitive des tramways avant qu'ils soient remplacés par les trolleybus;
>
> Considérant que l'Etat Hellénique, au cours de la nuit du 15 ou 16 novembre 1953, a fait enlever de force, et sous la protection de la police, des voies ferrées que la Société requérante tenait à conserver à tout prix, afin de ne pas interrompre la circulation;
>
> Considérant que cet enlèvement définitif par la force constitue une voie de fait par opposition à la voie de droit, qu'une telle voie de fait est contraire à l'indépendance que l'article 12 de la Convention garantit à la Société, étant donné que cette indépendance, dite administrative, comprend de toute évidence l'indépendance d'ordre technique ...

The Tribunal noted that the interruption of normal traffic on the two lines resulted in a diminution of the Company's revenues and held that the Government was required to pay the Company an indemnity sufficient to place it in the situation in which it would have been had the Government's "error" not been committed.

---

[14] The Tribunal was composed of Judge Paal Berg, President, and Judge Andonios Floros and M. André Mater. The award was rendered in Geneva on May 17, 1956.

The *Real Property Tax Exemption* Case *(Hellenic Electric Railways Ltd. v. Government of Greece, 1961)*[15]

Article 25 of the 1925 convention afforded the Company a tax exemption which provided that the Company was "exempte pendant la durée de la concession de toute imposition déjà en vigueur ou à lever à l'avenir sur le capital ou sur le revenu et spécialement de l'impôt sur les immeubles, de l'impôt sur la plus-value automatique des biens meubles et immeubles ..." By a law of April 10, 1953 it was provided that tax exemption on the income from buildings enjoyed by concessionary enterprises and public services was to be limited only to income produced by the direct utilization of such buildings for the purposes of the enterprise. On July 23, 1954 a new convention was signed by the parties which reaffirmed that Article 325 of the 1925 convention remained in force and which provided that the Company had the right to develop real property for any purpose, on the condition that such development did not impair the functioning of the railway.

Thereafter, the Company claimed reimbursement of the amounts it had paid the Greek Government in taxes on income from real property since the enactment of the 1953 law. The Government declined to pay, maintaining that the exemption provided for in Article 25 was limited to income deriving from the concessionary enterprise. The Company instituted arbitration, claiming that the exemption embraced all its income, regardless of origin, including that flowing from the renting of real property to third parties.

The Tribunal noted that resolution of the question depended upon the meaning of Article 25, read in the context of the convention as a whole. It further noted that the Government did not claim to have altered the régime of the 1925 convention. The fact that the Government had not sought to collect the taxes in dispute until 1953 meant little, for the Government might not have been aware of the facts concerning the use of properties owned by the Company.

The Tribunal held that, taken by itself, Article 25 appeared to provide a tax exemption of very extensive scope. However, the convention as a whole was designed to provide the public with a specified service. All the activities of the Company for which the convention provided related to that service. The 1954 convention, in providing that the Company might develop real property for any purpose, did not deal with the question of taxation of income from real property. Thus Article 25 should be read as relating to income deriving from the public service performed by the Company.

[15] The Tribunal was composed of Judge Carlo Pometta, President, and Messrs. Andréas Chatziadaris and Michel Pesmazoglu. The award was rendered in Lausanne on June 22, 1961.

The Tribunal added that a tax exemption was legitimate insofar as the State was freed from the performance of a task which the concessionaire discharged in return for its exemption. But an exemption of very extensive scope, applying to no matter what source of income, would be hard to reconcile with the general principle that, absent any indication to the contrary, fiscal privileges are not to be extensively interpreted.

In the light of these conclusions, the Tribunal held that the tax exemption covered income from buildings which directly related to the enterprise, or had in the past done so, as well as buildings which indirectly related to it (such as housing for certain employees of the railway). The exemption was held not to embrace income from properties rented to third parties, whose use was not related to the railway's service. The parties were remitted to working out the sum due to the Company by way of reimbursement in application of the Tribunal's holding.

Conclusions

The foregoing cases are of great interest in their demonstration of the central role arbitration can play not only in the settlement of disputes under an international concession contract, but also in the nourishment of the contractual relationship *ex aequo et bono*. The Tribunals' decisions are significant: e.g., their definition of the meaning of a concessionaire's administrative independence and its relationship to legislative authority; their interpretation of the scope of a tax immunity; the need to interpret public-service concessions, like other contracts, in good faith; the limited right of legislative modification of concession rights with the consequent duty to pay compensation; the doctrine that contractual limitations upon the State's regulatory powers must be express. Coupled with these holdings of law is a form of judicial legislation, either expressly invited by the parties or accepted by them. In this way the parties overcame a lacuna in their arbitral procedure by a ruling of the Tribunal. Again, while the Company was exempted from the imposition of a particular social-service charge, the Tribunal found itself compelled to assist in establishing the ambit of future arrangements which would permit an agreed mode of participation by the Company in a social insurance plan. Finally, the Tribunal went so far as to contemplate the application of the doctrine of *rebus sic stantibus*, not to assist the State in escaping from its obligations but to assist the Company in receiving a fair return on its investment in circumstances where unforeseeable occurrences overturn the economic basis of the enterprise.

III

The *Teak Forest Concession* Case *(Borneo Company Ltd. v. The Ministry of Agriculture and the Forestry Department of Thailand, 1961)*[16]

The Borneo Company Ltd. was the holder of two concessions, granted by the Government of Thailand on November 16, 1939, which gave the Company sole rights for a period of fifteen years as from June 1, 1940 to exploit defined teak-forest areas.

The terms of these "Agreements of Teak Forest Concession" were substantially the same and *inter alia* they provided:

Article 1. This Concession is issued subject to the laws and regulations which are now in force or which shall be brought into force in the future and the Grantee shall not be entitled to claim exemption therefrom by reason of any of the terms of this Concession.

Article 2. For every log which the Grantee shall extract from the said forest in accordance with the terms of this agreement the Grantee shall pay to the Grantor a fee according to the size of the logs as provided in Article 3 hereof at such time and at such place and in such manner as the Grantor or his duly appointed representative shall notify in writing from time to time and will also pay any other fees or charges which may become payable.

When the Grantee shall have paid all such monies to the Grantor as above provided and the Forest Officials shall have marked the logs as evidence that the Grantee has made payment then the property in the said logs shall be considered to have passed to the Grantee.

Article 3. Unless otherwise hereinafter provided the following shall be the rates of payment to the Grantor for each log in accordance with the following sizes and rates:

Class A. For logs measuring 5.49 metres upwards and having a cubic content from 1.13 cubic metres and upwards at the rate of Tcs 8.28 per cubic metre.

Class B. For logs measuring 5.49 metres upwards and having a cubic content of less than 1.13 cubic metres at the rate of Tcs 5.65 per cubic metre.

Class C. For logs measuring less than 5.49 metres at the rate of Tcs 3.53 per cubic metre.

---

[16] Judgment of the Court of Appeal of Thailand in Civil Case No. 1178/2502 (1959), Red Case 178/2503 (1960), February 17, 1960. Judgment of the Grand Council of the Supreme Court of Thailand (The Dika Court) in Case No. 1363/2504 (1961), November 28, 1961. The case has been made available by courtesy of the Borneo Company Ltd., and an English translation has been made with the cooperation of the Company.

PROVIDED ALWAYS that if during the term of this Concession it shall appear that teak or teak rafts of medium quality have an average market price in Bangkok higher than Tcs 45 per cubic metre and such price shall continue for a reasonable time the Grantor may increase the rate as provided in Class A above to an extent not exceeding 20 per cent of the rate therein mentioned and written notification calling for such increased rate shall be given from time to time by the Grantor to the Grantee in respect of the timber extracted under this agreement for each group or raft and from when the same shall be payable independently of where the logs in respect of which such payments are to be made may be at the time but the logs must be those in respect of which royalty has not yet been paid.

And if at any time the average price of teak or teak rafts of medium quality shall fall in the Bangkok market below Tcs 45 per cubic metre the Grantee is entitled to apply to the Grantor for the price to be reduced from the increased price to the original price hereinbefore provided in respect of logs for which the royalty has not yet been paid.

As regards the rates of payment which the Grantee must pay under the term above-mentioned, after five years from the date of the grant of this Concession the classification as regards size and rates of payment shall be changed as follows:

Class A. For logs having a cubic content from 1 cubic metre upwards.

Class B. For logs having a cubic content less than 1 cubic metre to half a cubic metre.

Class C. For logs having a cubic content less than half a cubic metre.

As regards the rate which the Grantee shall pay under the new classification the Grantor shall fix the same on a basis of the former rate having consideration for the quantity of timber and the amount of money which the Grantee has already paid or shall be under the obligation of paying during the first five years of this Concession. The change in the rate thus provided for may exceed or be lower than the original rate but in no case shall such increase or decrease exceed 5 per cent of the original rates fixed in this clause.

The measurement and calculation of the cubic contents of logs for the purposes of this article shall be in accordance with the scales and rates of the Forestry Department. In determining the length of a log measurements shall be taken from one extreme end of the log to the other extreme end and metric measurements shall be used in all cases and when the cubic contents of the log have been been calculated they shall be accepted in full without any reduction.

Article 4. In addition to all sums payable under Article 3 hereof the Grantee undertakes to pay all taxes and fees leviable under any laws or customs now in force or which hereafter shall come into force in relation to the teak trade. In addition the Grantee agrees to make all special payments in respect of rights granted to him under this agreement and also for expenses in regard to the replanting of the said forest as paid by the Grantor. Payments under the last two headings shall be arranged separately and in advance.

As from 1947, revised royalty rates (Baht. 9.74, 5.65, and 3.53) were applied in conformity with Article 3 of the concession. On August 21, 1951 the Ministry of Agriculture, by virtue of powers conferred in the Forestry Act of 1941, as amended in 1951, issued a notification fixing new royalty rates for teak in the whole of Thailand substantially higher than those applied to the Company since 1947 (Baht. 50, 40, and 20 for classes A, B, and C, respectively) and demanded the payment of the increased rates from the concessionaire. While protesting against the increased rates, the Company agreed to pay, and did pay, the royalty claimed "by way of amicable settlement but without prejudice to the terms and conditions of the concessions." On November 30, 1953, the Ministry of Agriculture required the concessionaire to pay, in addition, forest maintenance charges at a rate equal to the royalty for timber worked under the concessions. The Company objected that this order was in violation of Article 3 of the concession but, pending decision by the competent courts, paid the forest maintenance charges under protest.

The Company – while not disputing the Government's right to levy charges of this nature – brought a claim against the Government for refund of part of the forest improvement charges paid under protest, contending that the rates to be regarded as bases when calculating the maintenance charges should be those rates at which the Company was liable to pay under Article 3 of the concessions.[17] The Company's claim was based primarily on two grounds. First, the Company contended that it was against the spirit of the Forestry Act of 1941 and *ultra vires* for the Ministry of Agriculture to fix the royalty for teak as done by the order of August 21, 1951. Second, the Company argued that, even were the order valid, the rates so fixed could not apply to the Company working under a concession which was to be considered as granted under the Forestry Act of 1941 and that, therefore, it had to pay only such royalty as was fixed in the concession. The Company submitted that it could not be inferred from the Forestry Act, which empowered the Ministry of Agriculture to fix royalties, that the Minister had power to cancel or modify rates fixed by the Government.

The Government contended that, under the terms of the concession, the working of the forests must be done in accordance with the Forestry Act and any ministerial regulations, stipulations, and notifications issued by virtue of the Act. The Government stressed that the concessionaire, in Article 2 of the concession, expressly undertook to "pay any other fees or charges which may become payable." It maintained also that imposition of the forest mainte-

---

[17] While the concessions had a term of fifteen years and were therefore due to expire in 1955, they have since continued in force by virtue of an understanding reached between the Company and the Government.

nance charges was not in any way morally reprehensible since the prices of teak between the time when the concession was granted and the time when the charges were imposed had risen many tens of times and that the Company had, in any case, enjoyed considerably greater privileges than small Thai permit holders.

The Company's claim was dismissed by the court of first instance, on the ground that the concessions clearly prescribed that the laws and regulations promulgated after the granting of the concessions would be applicable to them. The decision was challenged by the Company in the Court of Appeal of Thailand, which rendered a judgment favorable to the Company.

The judgment of the Court of Appeal was based on its conclusion that the text of the concession must be taken as the basis for deciding the case. The Court held in this regard:

> The next issue in dispute concerns whether a concession is a contract or not. On this point, this Court is of the opinion that a concession is a juristic act. Although it concerns rights accorded by the Government, nevertheless there is an agreement which determined various duties and conditions binding the parties to abide by same. Upon the agreement being entered into, neither party could cancel or alter the terms unilaterally, without the consent of the other party, or due to the latter's fault ... Therefore, whether a concession would be regarded as a contract or not does not matter. The main point lies in the fact that the text of the concession must be taken as the basis for deciding the case.

The Court next examined the issue whether the forest maintenance charges should be deemed to constitute a royalty (as the Company argued), or a tax (as the Government contended). The Court, in interpreting the concession, particularly Articles 1–4, "in the spirit of the parties relating to the granting and the acceptance of the concessions," concluded that the forest maintenance charges were in the nature of a royalty, and that Article 4 of the concession envisaged other taxes or fees and should not be interpreted to mean that the Government might arbitrarily collect increased charges by classifying them as taxes. The operative part of the judgment of the Court of Appeal read as follows:

> Upon considering the text of the aforesaid articles of the concessions, it can be seen that article 1 is an introduction of generality prescribing that the concession must be under the laws and regulations prevailing at that time and which may prevail in the future. This is natural because, even without such a term, the parties are necessarily liable to be subject to laws notwithstanding when they are enacted. But, particularly concerning taxes, the rates fixed in article 3 are precise both for the present and the future, and such rates are not in conformity with the Internal Tariff Act, 1893. Therefore, it can be seen that the parties have the intention of

leaving the taxes as prescribed in article 3 of the concessions ... The provisions in article 1 are, then, not meant to change the terms laid down in article 3, but only mean that the concessions should be subject to any laws which will be enacted in the future; for instance to pay income tax or any taxes which have been modified or amended.

Upon being granted concessions for exploitation of natural resources or licences for industrial operations, the concessionaire should take into consideration the capital to be invested and the machinery, implements, including expenditures and taxes and duties to be paid during the period of the concession granted: this should have been estimated beforehand. Therefore, it is necessary to fix exactly the terms and conditions. If the concessionaire did not receive assurance in such matters, it would be difficult to find someone who dared to ask for any concession or to carry out industrial operations. Thus the policy of inducement of foreign capital to be invested would be affected, and would result in considerable prejudice to the Government. Moreover the Forestry Act, which empowers the Minister of Agriculture to fix the rates of royalty, has prescribed this in general, not just for concessions, and did not fix rigid rates; only that they should not be levied at more than 50 Baht per cubic metre. Therefore, the said notification does not cover the plaintiff's concessions, because the Ministry of Agriculture has agreed with the plaintiff in a precise manner about taxes in the present and the future. To issue any notification of amendment contrary to such agreement will be in conflict with it and with the spirit of concessions; the fact that the plaintiff has agreed to pay the royalty in conformity with the new rates cannot be interpreted to mean that he is bound to pay forest promotion fees at such rates, because the plaintiff has throughout protested against such payment, which is meant to cover expenditures necessary for the planting of teak seedlings. According to article 4 of the concessions, it is prescribed that, besides the amount which the concessionaire would have to pay according to article 3 in case he should have to pay taxes or fees prevailing in the teak trade, necessary for obtaining concession rights, or the cost of the planting of teak seedlings, the concessionaire would have to pay in either case only in accordance with an agreement to be reached separately with the grantor. Therefore, the provisions in article 4 become clear, in that what has been said about abiding by the law and regulations which may be enacted in the future, as in article 1, is meant for other taxes or fees, apart from what is prescribed in article 3; and that the collection to be effected must be agreed upon beforehand as in article 4; it does not mean that authorization is given to the grantor to make collection arbitrarily.

With regard to the defendants' argument that the price of teak logs has increased approximately thirtyfold, and that they have collected forest promotion fees according to the rates of the royalty newly enforced and deemed appropriate, this Court is of the opinion that such argument cannot be applied to the plaintiff for making the said payment, because the initial agreement may not anticipate that the price of teak logs would be considerably increased in such manner. The prescription of the rates in the concessions is an estimate on the future; if such estimate were erroneously made, it could not be altered unilaterally. In the event of the price of teak logs being reduced, the concessionaire could not ask for a reduction in taxes lower than the rates fixed in the concessions.

A further appeal was made to the Supreme Court of Thailand. The Grand Council of this Court reversed the judgment of the Court of Appeal and dismissed the Company's claim.

The Court, in so deciding, held that the Company was liable to pay such charges as might be imposed by legislation. The Court – apart from rejecting the *ultra vires* argument – stressed that this conclusion was in conformity with the wording of Article 1 of the concessions. It said:

> The general meeting of the Supreme Court is of the opinion that, although in the past, the imposition of royalty was effected by the procedure of requiring concessionaires to enter into the contract of concessions, with the enforcement of the Forestry Act the system of royalty collection has changed into the form of direct imposition by legal powers similarly to other taxes and duties of the State. Hence, whatever rate is specified by the Act, it has to be complied with. The fact that the Minister having executive powers over the Forestry Department previously agreed to accept the terms of the contract of the concessionaire in regard to the rate of royalty to be paid by no means serves as a cause for limiting the legislative power of the State to promulgate laws to other effects ...
>
> Having found that the royalty rate as specified by the Minister of 50 Baht per cubic metre is as effective as if it were an enactment, the general meeting of the Supreme Court therefore is further of opinion that the royalty rates according to the concessions of the concessionaire can no longer be held valid, since there has been an enactment to the contrary.
>
> In addition, it will be seen that this case comes under the condition of article 1 of the concessions by which the concessionaire has agreed that: "This concession is issued subject to the laws and regulations which are now in force or which shall be brought into force in the future and the Grantee shall not be entitled to claim exemption therefrom by reason of any of the terms of this concession".
>
> Hence the general meeting of the Supreme Court is of the opinion that the royalty rate demanded for collection from the plaintiff by the defendant at 50 Baht per cubic metre is legitimate. The plaintiff may not use the concessions as a pretext for exemption from having to comply with it. The defendant's petition is justified. The ruling of the Appeal Court is contrary to the opinion of the Supreme Court.

The *Teak Forest Concession* case, if it concerns the classic problem of the confrontation of concessionary rights and governmental power, is singular in other respects. It is unusual for a concessionaire to submit, expressly and in such sweeping terms, to the future exercise of legislative power (Article 1). It is unusual for the concessionaire, in agreeing upon the fee (i.e., royalty) due, to undertake that it will also pay "any other fees or charges which may become payable" (Article 2). It is unusual for the concessionaire to undertake not only that it will pay a specified royalty but also that it will pay "all taxes and fees leviable under any laws or customs now in force or which hereafter shall come into force in relation to the teak trade" (Article 4). In the light of these undertakings the holding of the Court of Appeal that the text of the contract was central, and that that text, which precisely specified royalties, could not be interpreted to mean that charges amounting to royalties could be imposed at the Government's will, constitutes a striking affirmation of the force of the concessionary relationship. The contrary decisions of the court of first instance and of the Supreme Court not surprisingly rely on Article 1. The judgment of the Supreme Court is of further interest in that it based its decision first of all not on the ample escape clauses which the concession contracts afforded the Government, but on what it apparently regarded as the overriding force of legislative enactment, despite provisions in the concession to the contrary.

However, the basis of this holding does not clearly appear. The Supreme Court might have reached this conclusion on the theory that the State's legislative power cannot be legally restricted by a governmental contract with a private party (even though an alien).[18] Equally, it might have so decided on the ground that an executive grant of a concession was governed by subsequent legislation: "The fact that the Minister having executive powers over the Forestry Department previously agreed to accept the terms of the contract ... by no means serves as a cause for limiting the legislative power of the State to promulgate laws to other effects." Nevertheless, had the executive acted within the scope of its authority (and the contrary does not appear), the executive character of the grant of the concession should not have affected the Court's judgment.

IV

The *Greek Telephone Company* Case (*Greek Telephone Company v. Government of Greece, 1935*)[19]

On February 8, 1930 two contracts were concluded between the Greek Government and Siemens & Halske AG, subsequently confirmed by a special

---

[18] It will be recalled that the Company's alienage was referred to by the Government in its argument.

[19] The Tribunal was composed of Professor George S. Streit, President, and Messrs. Kyriakos Anagnostopoulos and Anastasios P. Papaligouras. The award was rendered at Kifissia on January 3, 1935. This section is based on the German texts of the concessions and on a German translation of the Greek original of the arbitral award. Translations from German are Dr. Wetter's.

law.[20] The Main Agreement was entitled "Agreement for the Construction, Maintenance and Operation of the Urban and Suburban Telephone Communications in Greece." It provided for the construction by Siemens & Halske AG of a modern telephone system in Greek towns and suburban areas specified in the Agreement and for the maintenance and operation of this network by a Greek subsidiary of Siemens & Halske to which its rights with respect to the maintenance and operation of the system were to be assigned. The Greek subsidiary company was to have the exclusive right to operate the system over a period of thirty-eight years, but the Government had the right at its option to take over the system after thirteen years against payment of a price to be fixed in accordance with principles laid down in the Agreement.

The Supplemental Agreement was entitled "Agreement for the Construction, Maintenance and Operation of a Long-Distance Telephone Network in Greece." This contract was subsidiary to the Main Agreement and incorporated by reference a number of its provisions. The object of the Supplemental Agreement was, as defined in Article 1:

> The purpose and object of the Supplemental Agreement is:
>
> (A) The creation by the concessionaire on behalf and for the account of the State of a modern long-distance telephone network in Greece, including appertaining telephone stations, such as specified in article 2, which shall remain in the ownership of the State.
>
> (B) The maintenance and operation of this long-distance telephone network by the successor to the rights and obligations of the concessionaire.

Article 2, paragraph 1 provided that the concessionaire should rebuild and put in working order such of the long-distance lines as were to be listed in a document to be drawn up by agreement between the parties within two months after the execution of the Agreement. Under paragraph 2 specifications of the long-distance telephone lines to be newly constructed by the concessionaire were to be agreed upon within the same period of time. Then under paragraph 3 the concessionaire was to connect the new town systems with the long-distance network with a view, particularly, to ensuring technical uniformity in the two systems.[21] Article 11 provided, *inter alia*:

---

[20] *Vertrag über die Errichtung, die Instandhaltung und den Betrieb von Fernsprechanlagen für den Orts- und Vorortsverkehr Griechenlands; Zusatzvertrag über die Errichtung, die Instandhaltung und den Betrieb des Fernleitungsnetzes in Griechenland.* The two contracts were ratified by the Greek law No. 4547, published in the Government Gazette, Issue A, No. 134 of April 30, 1930.

[21] Article 2 read in part:

　1. The concessionaire undertakes to reconstruct and put in working order such of the already existing long-distance telephone lines as will be specified by agreement between the Ministry of Communications and the concessionaire within two months of the execution of this Agreement, it being understood that all modern technical devices shall be built into the system . . . to the extent that such

The Company [i.e., the Greek subsidiary company] shall maintain in operating condition and operate for the account of the State the long-distance telephone network to be put in working condition and to be newly built by the concessionaire [i.e., Siemens & Halske] pursuant to article 2, paragraphs 1 and 3, including telephone stations and public telephone booths, as from the completion of all reconstruction work and new construction and until the end of the thirteenth year after ratification of the Agreement.

Lastly, Article 13 incorporated by reference many of the provisions of the Main Agreement.

The concessionaire duly executed the works foreseen in the Main Agreement and took over the operations of the urban and suburban telephone network of Greece. With regard to the long-distance telephone network, it appears that, at the Government's request, the Government in fact performed some of the construction work itself. After the old lines had been repaired and put in proper order and the new lines had also been completed, the Company requested that, in accordance with the terms of the Supplemental Agreement, the maintenance and operation of the whole long-distance network in Greece be transferred to it. The Government, however, declined to allow a transfer, contending that the Company had no right to take over the operation of the whole long-distance telephone network. Negotiations for a settlement of the dispute failed and the Company then instituted arbitration proceedings in accordance with the applicable arbitration clause.

The Company's claim was grouped into three parts. First, it claimed that the Company, by virtue of Articles 11 to 13 of the Supplemental Agreement, had a duty to put in working order and to operate for the Government's account the whole of the State's long-distance telephone network, including telephone stations and installations for public use. Second, it claimed that the Government was under a duty to transfer the whole network to the Company as from the date on which the reconstruction and construction works had been completed. Third, it claimed that the Government was liable *vis-à-vis* the Company for all damage caused to the Company by the Government's refusal to allow a transfer of the system.

The Government denied that it was under a duty to transfer the long-distance network to the Company and rested its case on three grounds. First,

---

devices appear feasible and economical . . .

2. The concessionaire undertakes to construct in the same manner such new long-distance telephone lines and stations as will be specified by agreement between the Ministry of Communications and the concessionaire within two months of the execution of this Agreement.

3. The concessionaire undertakes to construct all long-distance lines which will be required for linking new local networks to the long-distance network, and in so doing shall ensure the same technical uniformity as referred to in paragraph I.

it maintained that the Supplemental Agreement was unclear and incomplete. Second, it contended that it was in consequence impossible to bring that Agreement into operation as its implementation would mean the transfer to the Company of only a part of the long-distance network so that the result would be the operation of dual long-distance telephone communications systems, which would be impracticable. Third, it contended that the Supplemental Agreement was not a two-sided contract establishing a mutuality of rights and obligations but, in the Government's words, *ein hinkender Vertrag (negotium claudicans)*, thus operating in favor of the Government insofar as the maintenance and operation of the long-distance network was concerned. Thus, the Government denied that the Company had a right to maintain and operate for the account of the State the whole long-distance telephone network of Greece and also disclaimed any liability toward the Company for any damage caused to it by its not being accorded the direction of the network.

The Tribunal stated that doubts might be entertained about the proper meaning of Articles 1 and 2 and 11 to 13, having regard particularly to the history of the contract. It then went on:

> It is a general rule of law that preference shall be given to that interpretation which accords with the wording of contractual provisions (see in this regard Windscheid I, paragraph 21, n. 3. Also Arndt-Kyriakos paragraphs 1 and 7, and in addition Aubryet Bau I, paragraph 40, Oekonomides I, paragraph 9, n. 4, Krassas I ff. c, paragraph 25, pp. 88).

Next, it summarized Articles 1 and 2 of the Supplemental Agreement and stressed particularly that the network which was to be transferred to the Company under Article 1 was that which was to be delimited by an arrangement made pursuant to Article 2. On the basis of an exposition of these articles, it held that there was no support for the Government's contention that the legal relationship between the parties was an unequal one (*negotium claudicans*) and that the Government was not, on that ground, bound to transfer the network to be reconstructed or newly built; for this contention found no support in any contractual provision.

On the other hand, the Tribunal considered it to be clear from Articles 1 and 2, seen in conjunction, that it was only a part of the long-distance network which the Company had a right to take over and to maintain and operate, i.e., that to be specified in a special document to be agreed upon in accordance with Article 2. Thus, the very wording of these articles, in the Tribunal's opinion, contradicted the Company's claim that the entire long-distance network should be transferred to it. At the same time, it was evident that the Company had an indisputable right to operate part of the system.

The Tribunal next considered whether the Government was in fact unable to transfer that part of the network to the Company. It recognized that experience in other countries showed that it was not impossible *per se* to entrust the operation of a telephone system to several different companies. However, it felt bound to accept the Government's argument that difficulties might be caused by the transfer of only those parts of the network to the Company which it had a contractual right to take over, reserving the rest for operation by the Government, since those parts of the network which had been constructed in pursuance of arrangement made under Article 2 did not form independent units; moreover, several of the lines so situated had in fact been constructed by the Government. With respect to the latter, the Company had argued that, while it was true that the Government had in fact executed some of the works originally allocated to the Company, this had been done under a special understanding in which the Company had reserved its rights to take over the operation of the whole system after completion. The Tribunal found, however, that an intention on the Government's part to permit the Company to manage the whole system had not been established. It was thus, in the Tribunal's opinion, doubtful whether the Government had a contractual duty to transfer those parts of the network which had been constructed by the State.

The conclusion of the Tribunal was that it did not seem practicable, in the light of these difficulties, to order that the whole long-distance telephone network be transferred to the Company for maintenance and operation, but rather only those parts which formed the main communication lines of the country and which could be operated independently of other parts of the network. It decided that one such independent line was the line between Corinth, Athens, and Thessaloniki with its appurtenant stations, which was said to be the most important line in Greece and the one generating the greatest revenue. It stated that the Company ought to be materially and morally satisfied with this solution and that, in fact, the transfer to the Company of a number of other long-distance lines would constitute an actual burden for it, since such isolated lines could not be profitably operated.

The Tribunal further held that the Company had a right to have transferred to it all lines which had been rebuilt or newly constructed by it, but since, as already held, a transfer of these lines would be difficult, it was entitled to obtain full compensation for the failure of the Government to transfer those lines. Although it was not clear whether the Company had a right to have transferred to it those parts of the network which, contrary to original arrangements, had in fact been built by the Government, the Tribunal decided that the Company was entitled to reasonable compensation for not obtaining operational use of those lines in view of the reservations made by the Company when permitting the Government to reconstruct them.

The Tribunal adduced the following reasons in support of its decision that the Government had a right to decline to transfer to the Company all the parts of the network which the latter under the Supplemental Agreement had a right to operate:

> The arbitrators are of the unanimous opinion that the State has the right to refuse a transfer of the maintenance and operation to the Company by virtue of the general principle of public law that under contracts concluded between a State and third parties, the State, in spite of being contractually bound, retains its superiority vis-à-vis the other party and is always entitled, when important State interests so demand, to renounce the contract, on the condition that it pay due compensation to the contracting party. (See in this respect, Jeze, *Les principes généraux du droit administratif, – Le fonctionnement des services publics*, 1926, p. 299. Also: Hauriou, *Précis de Droit Administratif et de Droit Public*, 1927, p. 797.)
>
> In case of such a refusal by the State, it is liable in damages to the Company and must compensate it for what it would have obtained, had the operation been transferred to it.
>
> The whole spirit and structure of the Agreement indicate that the damages shall be assessed on the basis of the provisions of article 11 of the Supplemental Agreement, i.e., by calculating the share to which the Company would be entitled, after deduction of the expenses for the maintenance and operation; this formula will thus govern not only the calculation of the precise revenue to which the Company would be entitled but also the assessment of an equitable amount of damages due.

In the oral hearings the Company had renounced its claim that the compensation payable to it should be fixed by the Tribunal, stating that it would be satisfied with a declaration in principle of its right to obtain damages. The Tribunal accordingly ordered the transfer to the Company of the Corinth–Athens–Thessaloniki line with its stations. It declared, at the same time, that the Government had a right to refuse, when important State interests so demanded, to transfer the maintenance and operation of the whole of the long-distance network to the Company, provided that, in that case, the Company would be entitled to obtain full compensation, to be duly agreed between the parties and to be calculated as from June 27, 1934 until the end of the thirteenth year after the ratification of the Agreement. Finally, it declared that the Company was entitled to reasonable compensation for the lines constructed by the Government in accordance with the special arrangement and not transferred to the Company.

The *Greek Telephone Company* case, while not the most lucid of awards,[22] is

[22] The pleadings of the parties, which might shed light on passages of the award, regrettably are not available. The description of the parties' arguments has been drawn from the award itself.

of interest in more than one respect. The award does not specify the proper law of the contract. At one point it relies on Greek authorities; at another, it refers to French authorities. It speaks of "a general rule of law" and of "a general principle of public law" as governing principles of interpretation; in so doing, the Tribunal (at any rate in its public-law reference) comes near to relying on "the general principles of law recognized by civilized nations." Nowhere, however, does the Tribunal appear to give any weight to the foreign character of the private party with which the State has contracted (and as other cases examined in this article indicate, the Tribunal is not alone in giving no weight to this element).

The Tribunal rejects the argument that the contractual relationship between a State and a private party is of a leonine character, the advantage being with the State. Nevertheless, it holds that "the State, in spite of being contractually bound, retains its superiority *vis-à-vis* the other party and is always entitled, when important State interests so demand, to renounce the contract, on the condition that it pays due compensation to the contracting party." If the State is so entitled "on the condition" that it pays due compensation, then presumably, in the Tribunal's view, it is not so entitled where it fails to discharge that condition. When and how that condition must be met the Tribunal had no occasion to consider.

What compensation would be due compensation is indicated by the Tribunal: the Company must be compensated "for what it would have obtained" had the contract been implemented by the State. That is to say, the Company is entitled to full compensation equal to the profits it would have received had the contract been performed for the whole of its life.

V
The *Palestine Railway* Case *(Société du Chemin de Fer Ottoman de Jaffa à Jérusalem et Prolongements v. Government of the United Kingdom, 1922)*[23]

The *Palestine Railway* arbitration took place pursuant to a *compromis* between the British and French Governments entered into in accordance with the Treaty of Sèvres of August 10, 1920. While a party to the *compromis*, the French Government did not take part in the proceedings, in which the parties

[23] The Tribunal was composed of Judge F. V. N. Beichmann, President, and Messrs. H. Osborne Mance and Ferdinand Mayer. The agent for the British Government was Mr. Orme B. Clarke, CBE; the agent for the Company was Colonel A. J. Barry, CBE. Two awards were rendered in Paris, a preliminary decision of May 29, 1922 and an award of October 4, 1922. The awards and the parties' Memorials are unpublished but privately printed. Stuyt's *Survey of International Arbitrations* (1939), p. 348, lists printed texts in the Peace Palace Library. Texts are also to be found in the Harvard Law Library.

were the *Société du Chemin de Fer Ottoman de Jaffa à Jerusalem et Prolongements* (a French enterprise), as claimant, and the United Kingdom Government, as respondent.

Article 311 of the Treaty provided:[24]

> In territories detached from Turkey to be placed under the authority or tutelage of one of the principal Allied Powers, Allied nationals and companies controlled by Allied groups or nationals holding concessions granted before 29th October, 1914, by the Turkish Government or by any Turkish local authority shall continue in complete enjoyment of their duly acquired rights, and the Power concerned shall maintain the guarantees granted or shall assign equivalent ones.
>
> Nevertheless, any such Power, if it considers that the maintenance of any such concessions would be contrary to the public interest, shall be entitled, within a period of six months from the date on which the territory is placed under its authority or tutelage, to buy out such concession or to propose modifications therein: in that event it shall be bound to pay to the concessionaire equitable compensation in accordance with the following provisions.
>
> If the parties cannot agree on the amount of such compensation, it will be determined by Arbitral Tribunals composed of three members, one designated by the State of which the concessionaire or the holders of the majority of the capital in the case of a company is or are nationals, one by the Government exercising authority in the territory in question, and the third designated, failing agreement between the parties, by the Council of the League of Nations.
>
> The Tribunal shall take into account, from both the legal and equitable standpoints all relevant matters, on the basis of the maintenance of the contract adapted as indicated in the following paragraph.
>
> The holder of a concession which is maintained in force shall have the right, within a period of six months after the expiration of the period specified in the second paragraph of this Article, to demand the adaptation of his contract to the new economic conditions, and in the absence of agreement direct with the Government concerned the decision shall be referred to the Arbitral Commission provided for above.

The Company had obtained a concession from the Imperial Turkish Government in 1888,[25] granting the right to construct and operate a railway, about 80 kilometres long, from Jaffa to Jerusalem. The duration of the concession was seventy-one years, and it was therefore due to expire in 1959. Article 18 of the convention, and Article 20 of the *Cahier des Charges*,

---

[24] The Treaty had not been ratified at the time when the *compromis* was signed. The British and French Governments nevertheless agreed that the arbitration should proceed on the assumptions that the Treaty had been ratified and that Palestine had been placed under British mandate.

[25] "Convention entre le Ministre du Commerce et des Travaux Publics agissant au nom du Gouvernement Impérial, et Youssouf Navon Effendi," dated October 29, 1888, later assigned to the Company, to which was attached a *Cahier des Charges* of the same date; Supplemental Agreement of August 4, 1914.

stipulated that, on the termination of the concession, the railway was to be handed over by the concessionaire to the Government in good condition without payment for the track and fixed properties. The rolling stock, fuel, stores, and all movable property were to be acquired by the Government at a price to be fixed by experts. While the original agreement stipulated a right for the Government to purchase the railway before the expiration of the concession on certain terms, this provision was deleted in a supplemental agreement of 1914. In 1920 the British Government informed France of its intention to purchase the railway under the provisions of Article 311 of the Treaty of Sèvres and negotiations took place between representatives of the Company and British authorities regarding the price to be paid. These negotiations having proved abortive, the question of compensation was referred to arbitration in accordance with the governing *compromis*.

The Company, in its general statement of claim, declared that it would prefer to have its railway returned to it and to resume its operations and the enjoyment of its concession:

> As, however, the British Government had decided to exercise the rights conferred upon it under the Treaty of Sèvres to purchase the concession, such purchase must undoubtedly include all rights conferred on the concessionaires under their contracts and the provisions of the Treaty of Sèvres.[26]

The Company claimed that compensation should be paid to it under the following headings:

(*A*) The commercial value of the railway as a going concern, comprising:
  (1) The value of the physical railway line and plant;
  (2) The additional value of the rights and powers under the concession, including the right and power to earn profits;
(*B*) Compensation for loss of revenue during the period for which the Company has been deprived of its railway;
(*C*) Compensation to staff and sundry expenses.[27]

The British Government made an application to the Tribunal contending that

> for the purpose of assessing the compensation payable to the Claimants by the Respondents for the buying out of their concession, the Tribunal should not take into account the value of the physical railway line and fixed properties as set out ... in [the Company's] General Statement of Claim.[28]

---

[26] (Amended) General Statement of Claim, p. 9.   [27] *Ibid.*, pp. 9–10.
[28] Memorial of May 6, 1922, p. 1.

479

It requested the Tribunal to decide this issue by a preliminary decision "in order to save time and, if possible, to obviate the expenditure of a considerable sum of money upon a line of inquiry which, in their submission, is irrelevant."[29]

The Tribunal indicated its willingness to hear this application and ordered the respondents to file a Memorial in support of their contentions, which they did. The Company filed an answer, and a hearing took place, after which the Tribunal gave a Preliminary Decision on May 29, 1922.

The British Government submitted that it would clearly be wrong to base an assessment of the compensation on the replacement value of the railway line itself and fixed properties:

> The Respondents desire to emphasize the fact that the Tribunal's duty is to assess compensation for the revocation of a concession, not to measure the value of any property in the strict sense of the word. Under the concession the Claimants have certain limited rights: they have no property of which they are free to dispose. They have built the line knowing full well that, at the termination of the concession, it would pass to the Turkish Government, and they did so trusting that the profits of working the line, and those profits only, would be sufficient to pay interest upon and to amortize the capital embarked in the undertaking. As soon as the line was built in compliance with the stipulations of the concession, the Claimants could only make use of it as a machine for making profits. At no time during the continuance of the concession could the line or fixed properties have been sold. If the Claimants had removed a single rail and sold it, they would have had simultaneously to replace it. The Claimants could never have obtained from anybody the reproduction value of any part of the line or fixed properties. Even if the Claimants had been under no obligation to hand over the line and fixed properties on the expiration of the concession, this would be true: *a fortiori* it is true when that obligation exists.
>
> The reproduction value of a railway exists at all times while the concession is still in force. If the Claimants' contention is correct, this value must be allowed as compensation whatever the remaining life of the concession may be at the moment of revocation. The fallacy of such a method of assessment becomes obvious if it be supposed that compensation is being assessed for the buying out of two otherwise similar concessions, one of which has a remaining life of 50 years and the other a remaining life of five years. It would be absurd to give the same compensation in both cases: and this serves to show that compensation should be assessed in respect of the revocation of a right, not of the loss of property ...
>
> Thus, if the Claimants had been permitted to resume exploitation of the railway, they would, having regard to their rights and obligations, have stepped into either a *damnosa hereditas* or into a more or less profitable business. If the Tribunal come to the conclusion that the Claimants could not have made any

---

[29] *Ibid.*, p. 5.

profits during the remaining years of their concession, it seems clear that they have been deprived of something which has no value and that, accordingly, no compensation whatsoever should be payable. If, on the other hand, the Tribunal form the opinion that the Claimants could have made profits, equally clearly they have been deprived of a valuable right. If the Claimants' contention is correct, viz., that the compensation payable depends upon the value of the physical line and fixed properties, it would follow that they would be entitled to receive even if they could have made no profit, compensation for being deprived of a right the exercise of which could only have resulted in a loss. There could obviously be no equity in such a situation.

The Respondents lay stress on the principle which is implied by the use of the word "compensation" in the relevant article of the Treaty of Sèvres. Compensation is a make-weight: it is the equivalent of what the compensated party has lost and is not connected with what the compensating party may have gained.

The Tribunal should not confuse the benefits that the Claimants are relinquishing and the benefits that the Respondents, who are buying out their rights, are obtaining. The Tribunal will be given an entirely false meaning to the word "compensation" if the transaction is looked at otherwise than from the point of view of the loss (if any) which the Claimants have sustained.[30]

In the oral hearings, the British agent elaborated upon this argument and presented a series of Opinions of leading jurists of England, France, the United States, Germany, and Belgium as evidence of the legal principles which would be applicable to the assessment of compensation if the arbitration proceedings were conducted under the respective systems of law pertaining to those countries.[31] The British agent did not "suggest that the law of any particular country is binding on the Tribunal, but it [was] submitted that a legal principle common to a number of countries constitutes an authority which the Tribunal should not lightly disregard."[32]

The Company submitted in its answer that the British agent appeared to contend that the claimants had nothing of which they were at any time competent to dispose and that, accordingly, the physical value of something which they could under the terms of their grant possess and enjoy only for a limited period was non-existent:

The fallacy of this reasoning is, so the Claimants submit, apparent. The fact that at the expiration of the life of the concession the fixed property must be handed over to the Turkish Government might conceivably have this result that as the life of the concession draws on the original cost of the fixed properties should be written off so as to ensure that when the concession expires their value should be shown to

[30] *Ibid.*, pp. 3–5.
[31] The Opinions were rendered by Sir John Simon, M. Ed. Clunet, Mr. Newton Crane, Dr. Siegfried Spier, and M. G. de Leval. They have not been available to the authors.
[32] Memorial of May 6, 1922, p. 5.

be nil, but it can surely not justify the conclusion that no regard can be had to its physical value.

Further the Respondents are in error when they state that it was not open to the Claimants at any time during the life of the concession to sell or dispose of the fixed properties. It is submitted that there was nothing to prevent them from doing so although no doubt in that event the purchasers would be obliged to fulfil the terms of the grant.

The fact that at the end of the concession the railway would become the property of someone else, does not mean that the railway could under no circumstances be sold. Again, if the contentions of the Respondents be correct it would follow as indeed is stated in Clause 7 of the Memorial that if the probability was that no profits in respect of the railway would be earned during the future, the Respondents could take over the line, without paying for it; as a *reductio ad absurdum* that if losses were to ensue the Respondents would be entitled to receive from the Claimants compensation for relieving the Claimants against such loss.

The question as to the principles upon which compensation for compulsory purchase ought to be assessed has frequently arisen before the English Courts, and it has been for many years firmly established that the value to be ascertained is the value of the property expropriated at the time of expropriation with all its existing advantages and with all its possibilities including its special adaptability.

One of the first elements of the value so to be ascertained is, so the Claimants submit, the reproduction value of the property expropriated. It is unnecessary for the present purpose for the Claimants to show what other elements must be reckoned with, and they are content therefore, to emphasize their assertion that whether or not the Tribunal is bound by this or that particular law, the general basic principle of fairness and equity is that lawful owners of property should only be forcibly expropriated of what they possess on the terms that in addition to other compensation the cost to the British Government to reproduce in 1921 a line of equal quality and in similar condition to that which existed at the beginning of the war must certainly be included as an item in such compensation.[33]

In oral argument, counsel for the Company relied on correspondence exchanged between the British and French Governments before the *compromis* was signed, and urged that this correspondence be taken into account in interpreting the terms of Article 311 of the Treaty of Sèvres. He further submitted that: "The Tribunal is not bound by British or by any other law but that it is perfectly free to take into account any elements which, in its opinion, are material to the determination of fair and equitable compensation."[34] Among these elements there entered, he submitted, the reproduction cost of the line.

The Tribunal, in a unanimous award, accepted the contentions of the

---

[33] Answer of May 18, 1922, pp. 3–4. [34] Preliminary Decision of May 29, 1922, p. 18.

British Government and rejected the Company's claim that the compensation be assessed on the basis of the value of the physical properties. It held:

> The Tribunal considers that the text of article 311 of the Treaty of Sèvres leaves it open to the Tribunal to decide freely what are the material elements which should be taken into consideration "on the basis of the maintenance of the contract adapted". The Tribunal is not therefore bound by the opinions which may have been expressed in the negotiations prior to the agreement. Even if the method of procedure envisaged by the British Government in its letter of 22nd September 1920 had been accepted by the French Government – which does not appear to be the case judging by the note dated 20th July 1921 – the Tribunal can only adhere to the conditions of article 311 of the Treaty of Sèvres which, as a result of the agreement arrived at, is to form the basis of its decision.
>
> In accordance with these conditions, account must be taken of the situation in which the Company would have found itself if the British Government had not decided to exercise the option provided for in article 311. On this point there appears to be no doubt that, being obliged by the above quoted articles of the Convention and of the "Cahier des Charges" to hand over to the Turkish Government, without payment, at the termination of the concession, the railway line with its fixed properties as defined in article 20 of the "Cahier des Charges", the Company would only have been entitled to the profits which could be earned by the operation of the line for the duration of the concession. If its profits had not been sufficiently high to cover the present value (reproduction cost) of the line with its fixed properties, the Company would not have had any right to be refunded the difference.
>
> The Tribunal further considers that the amount of the said profits does not depend on the above value. Consequently, this value cannot, in the opinion of the Tribunal, enter into account in the determination of the compensation to be awarded to the Claimants.[35]

The Company was granted a certain period for amending its claim, and the British Government the same period for preparing a reply to it.

The Company accordingly filed an amended general statement of claim, in which it claimed compensation under the following headings:

1. Compensation in respect of the period of Turkish occupation of the railway and of the loss and damage occasioned to it during such occupation;
2. Compensation in respect of the period of British occupation of the railway and of the loss and damage occasioned to it during such occupation;
3. Compensation for profits which could be earned by the operation of the line during the remainder of the concession;
4. Compensation for rolling stock, payments to staff and miscellaneous.

[35] *Ibid.*

The greater part of the compensation claimed, £E.1,105,709 (equivalent to £1,134,060.10s.3d.)[36] out of a total of £E.1,696,452 (equivalent to £1,739,950.15s.5d.), related to loss of profits. That point was divided into two subheadings, i.e., (1) loss of profits which would have been derived from the carriage of traffic as calculated by applying the normal prewar rate of increase, and (2) loss of profits which would have been derived from the additional increase in traffic over and above the normal prewar rate, owing to the more favorable conditions under which the railway would have been operated because of the stability and better conditions which would be the result of the British mandate over Palestine.

The British Government contested not only the figures arrived at by the Company but also the principles used by it in assessing the amount of compensation. It declined to accept the Company's submission that the British Government should, by reason of the purchase of the railway, be subrogated in the Company's rights against the Turkish Government in respect of claims for use and damage done to the railway during the Turkish occupation. The British Government submitted:

> The Claimants contend that, by reason of the buying out of their concession by the Respondents, the Respondents will be substituted for the Claimants and will acquire the rights of the Company against the Turkish Government, for the loss of which the Company should be compensated by the Respondents. This reasoning is fallacious and depends upon a misconception of the transaction which is being carried out. In buying out the Claimants' concession, the Respondents do not become the assignees or inheritors of all the rights and liabilities of the Company; they merely antedate the situation which would arise when the concession expires by effluxion of time, whereupon the right of the Company to operate the railway ceases and the railway line and fixed properties pass to the Government.
>
> After the buying out of the Company's undertaking, the Company will not cease to exist, and will retain their previously acquired rights and liabilities other than the rights expropriated as aforesaid. By their action, the Respondents will have done nothing to prejudice the Company in meeting liabilities or in claiming debts which have accrued due to them; the obligations and rights of the Company in respect of such matters will remain unimpaired.
>
> It follows that the Claimants will, after the completion of the buying out of their undertaking, remain as before the only party entitled to prosecute their claim for damages against the Turkish Government and that the Respondents can have no *locus standi* to make any claim against the Turkish Government in respect thereof.[37]

---

[36] The rate of exchange used by the authors for computing Egyptian pounds into English pounds is £E.1/£0,975 (applicable in October 1922).

[37] Reply of July 21, 1922, pp. 3–4.

The British Government also emphasized that the railway was practically destroyed at the time that it came into its hands and that the value of the concession was diminished by the amount which it would have cost the Company to put the railway into working order.

One of the bases used by the Company for calculating the compensation was that the maximum rates provided for in the *Cahier des Charges* would be increased. The British Government, while not contesting that the rates might be adjusted, stated:

> There [was] no obligation upon [the Government] so to adapt the concession as to ensure that the net profits to the Concessionaire should be the same as those which, at parity of exchange, he earned before the war. Particularly is this true of a public utility company whose charges to the public must be measured by considerations of which the net profit to the shareholders is by no means the first.
>
> The right and duty of the State to regulate the profits earned by a private enterprise which carried on an undertaking of public utility is recognized throughout the world.[38]

The Company had also claimed "the usual allowance" of 10 percent for compulsory purchase. The British Government disputed this claim, saying:

> An allowance of 10 per cent for compulsory purchase cannot be claimed. The terms upon which compensation is to be assessed are laid down in Article 311 of the Treaty, beyond which the Tribunal are not entitled to go, and those terms do not admit of any such allowance being made.[39]

With regard to the Company's contention that its revenue would substantially increase because of the greater prosperity which might be expected in Palestine under British mandate, the British Government replied:

> This prosperity, if it comes to pass, is one of the "new economic conditions" which must be taken into account in adapting the Claimants' contract. If the development of Palestine is to result in certain economic conditions which in themselves conduce to the making of large profits by the Claimants in the operation of their undertaking, this factor must be set off against the other and unfavorable economic factors upon which a claim for a modification of the fares and rates laid down in the Cahier des Charges may be supported. The Claimants cannot be entitled to take into account in the adaptation of the contract all the factors which tend to show that their maximum charges should be increased, while ignoring all those which tend in the opposite direction.[40]

The British Government finally offered to pay in settlement, as a matter of equitable compromise, a sum of Frs. 12,950,000 (equivalent to £223,275.17s.3d.),[41]

---

[38] *Ibid.*, p. 8.   [39] *Ibid.*, p. 14.   [40] *Ibid.*, p. 12.

[41] The rate of exchange used by the authors for computing French francs into English pounds is £1/58 frs. (applicable in October 1922).

as representing the approximate value to the Claimants of their concession. Accepting this figure is approximately equivalent to assuming that the Company could have earned its debenture interest, 5 per cent on the ordinary shares and the sum necessary to repay debentures and ordinary capital at par at the end of the concession.[42]

From this amount should, however, be deducted the cost of repairing the railway, which could be recovered by the Company from the Turkish Government.

The Company disputed, *inter alia*, the position taken by the British Government on the question of subrogation in the Company's claims against the Turkish Government:

> The Respondents contend that after the buying out of the Company's undertaking the Company will not cease to exist but will remain as before the only party entitled to prosecute their claim against the Turkish Government. The Company on the other hand maintain that their right to claim compensation from the Turkish Government will pass to the British Government on the completion of the purchase of the Company's undertaking. The Company submit it would be inequitable to force them to continue in existence with all the attendant costs of administration solely for the purpose of prosecuting the Turkish claim. They point out that by that time the action of the British Government will have deprived them of the revenue out of which the costs of administration have hitherto been met.[43]

After the oral hearings, the representatives of the parties announced that they had agreed on a settlement of all the matters in dispute between them and submitted to the Tribunal the text of the award which by consent they requested the Tribunal to make. This text, which thus constituted the award, read as follows:

> By consent, we award, that the amount to be paid to the Claimants as compensation for the buying out of the Concession and in satisfaction of all claims by the Claimants against the British Government or by the British Government against the Claimants, shall be the sum of £565,000 sterling.
>
> The sum of £103,368 sterling, having been already paid on account, the British Government shall pay to the Claimants the sum of £200,000 sterling on or before the 22nd October 1922; £87,210 sterling on the 1st October 1923, £87,210 sterling on the 1st October 1924, and £87,210 sterling on the 1st October 1925, together with interest on the last three sums at 5 per centum per annum from the 1st October 1922 until payment.
>
> The right to any claim for compensation against the Turkish Government is to pass to the British Government.
>
> The Claimants shall execute any documents which may be necessary to effect

[42] *Ibid.*, p. 15.   [43] Rejoinder of August 10, 1922, p. 2.

such transfer and shall give all assistance that may be reasonably required by the British Government for the prosecution of the said Claim, provided that the British Government shall indemnify the Claimants against all expenses necessarily incurred by them in respect thereof.[44]

It appears from the terms of the settlement that the Company accepted a sum equivalent to about twice that originally offered by the British Government, but amounting to less than a third of its initial claim.

The case is of high interest because of the holding that the basis of compensation due to a concessionaire for premature termination of its contractual rights is lost profits; and that, where the concession contains a provision that fixed properties shall be transferred free of charge to the Government at the expiry of the concession term, compensation payable to the concessionaire shall not take account of the physical value of the fixed assets. Concession contracts often contain provisions for the transfer of fixed assets without charge to the Government upon the concession's expiration. Such clauses are characteristically found not only in public-utility concessions, but in extractive concessions. In the *Palestine Railway* case the parties and the Tribunal agreed on the relevance of lost profits (though the concessionaire would have added the replacement value of fixed assets). The settlement reached apparently took estimated lost profits as its basis. The sole caveat seems to have been the British Government's caution that the profits of a public utility are subject to governmental regulation.

The *Greek Telephone Company* case similarly took lost profits as the measure of damages.

Application of this plausible principle to other disputes between Governments and concessionaires would be of profound importance – and, in some cases, would involve great difficulty. Where, for example, a State expropriates a profitable oil concession which has forty years to run, and which contains, as oil concessions generally do, a provision by which the concessionaire is obliged to transfer fixed assets to the Government free of charge upon the concession's expiration, it will be to the evident advantage of the concessionaire to contend that the measure of compensation is lost profits. The difficulties are principally two. First, calculation of profits over such a long period, in the light of the uncertainties of economics, politics, and technology, is highly problematical. Second, the capacity of the State to pay compensation measured by lost profits may be questionable – certainly in the short run, perhaps even in the long run. If the State is to pay the concessionaire a full measure of the profits lost by it, it might be under an obligation to

---

[44] Award of October 4, 1922.

pay all of the profits earned by the State on the enterprise (and possibly more, were the company able to show that its profits would surpass those earned by the Government). This being the case, it might be asked why the Government should trouble to expropriate? The answer, of course, is, first, that Governments expropriate for political as well as economic reasons, and second, that they do not in fact – whatever their obligation in law – always pay full compensation, whether calculated in terms of lost profits or otherwise.

The difficulties of applying lost profits as a measure of damages do not necessarily suggest that that measure is inappropriate. It may rather suggest that expropriation in the particular case is inappropriate. Other conclusions may, of course, also be reached, for example, that less than full compensation is payable. At any rate, the *Greek Telephone* and *Palestine Railway* cases have their place in any attempt to formulate the applicable legal principles.

While the Tribunal did not pass upon the question of the law to be applied, except in its reference to Article 311 of the Treaty, it is of interest, finally, to note that the parties relied on "legal principles common to a number of countries." This was the express submission of the British Government,[45] while the Company invoked not "this or that particular law" but "the general basic principle of fairness and equity,"[46] concluding that: "The Tribunal is not bound by British or any other law but that it is perfectly free to take into account any elements which, in its opinion, are material to the determination of fair and equitable compensation."[47] In this the parties, if not the Tribunal, once more came close to relying on the general principles of law recognized by civilized nations.

---

[45] Memorial of May 6, 1922, p. 5.   [46] Answer of May 18, 1922, pp. 3–4.
[47] Preliminary Decision of May 29, 1922, p. 18.

28

Commentary on "Social Discipline and the Multilateral Enterprise" and "Security of Investment Abroad"

❧

I wish to congratulate Steven Pfeiffer and his colleagues for arranging this session under the chairmanship of Professor Rosalyn Higgins, in which issues of international law figure. It is important that members of the practicing bar consider problems of international law, for at least two reasons.

One reason is that such problems arise in the course of practice, for most lawyers occasionally if at all, for an increasing number of lawyers, more frequently. Issues of security of foreign investment and international environmental protection by no means are the exclusive province of governmental ministries and of international institutions such as the International Court of Justice. They are encountered in private practice more and more.

The second reason is that education in and exposure to international law is no less important to the practicing lawyer than is his education in and exposure to constitutional law. The number of lawyers who may have a constitutional case in the course of their practice may be small but study of constitutional law is taken for granted. It is part of the general education of any lawyer. Not dissimilarly, international law also plays a role in the framework and fabric of international life. The literate lawyer who is a citizen of the world and a participant in its international economic processes should no more ignore and be ignorant of international law than should the lawyer who is engrossed in municipal practice ignore and be ignorant of constitutional law.

I wish also to congratulate Ambassador Christopher Pinto and Mr. Elihu Lauterpacht on their substantial and acute papers. I have been asked to comment upon them. They are too substantial to permit comprehensive comment; permit me to remark upon a few elements of Ambassador Pinto's paper which I found particularly stimulating, and to say a word or two about Mr. Lauterpacht's paper, a text of which I saw just yesterday.

First published in International Bar Association, Section on Energy & Natural Resources Law, *Energy Law '90* (1991), London, Graham & Trotman.

In the introduction to his paper, Ambassador Pinto writes that:

Few would deny that the behavior of foreign companies themselves has contributed substantially towards obscuring their positive contribution to the quality of life within a host State, and generating attitudes of wariness or suspicion, cynicism or hostility. All the items on a formidable list of misconduct by foreign companies can surely be documented, perhaps even as having occurred within a single State perhaps even within a single company.

Ambassador Pinto concludes his introductory observations by stating that the protean nature of the multinational enterprise, its alien and little-understood nature, and the attitudes and conduct of the multinational enterprise have brought together governments of a wide range of political persuasions "in attempts to devise ways and means of introducing elements of social discipline into the conduct of the multinational enterprise or transnational corporation."

I am not a student of the behavior of transnational corporations, though I have seen a fair amount of that behavior over the years, as a practicing lawyer, Government official, arbitrator and judge. My impression – and I am now about to speak impressionistically – is that problems respecting the perception of transnational corporations are rooted not only in the performance of those companies but of the Governments which are their hosts.

It is true that the misconduct of certain transnational corporations on certain occasions can be documented. It is no less true that the misconduct of certain Governments on certain occasions towards transnational corporations can be documented. There are many, many cases in which governments have behaved arbitrarily towards multinational corporations whose entry and activities they have invited or permitted. I do not suggest that such governmental behavior is universal. But it is not uncommon.

To take an outstanding instance of what, at any rate in some cases, may have amounted to a series of forced sales, in the 1970s a vast system of concession contracts constructed over decades at great risk and with immense investment was bought out (in some cases, nationalized) by the Governments concerned for a fraction of value, related to the book value of physical investment. Nothing was paid for the concession rights themselves. While these transfers of the 1970s – surely one of the most massive transfers of wealth in history – generally were made in legal form, it cannot be maintained that they were transfers for full value.

One often hears of the great power of the modern multinational enterprise. It is pointed out that the annual cash flow, even the annual profits, of some of the great multinationals may exceed that of some smaller national Governments. It is suggested that such large multinational enterprises can, and do, push around the smaller Governments, exploit them for the sake of their own profits.

Closer to the truth is that a Government, however small and weak, has powers at its disposal that a foreign corporation, however strong, lacks. In a confrontation between a foreign corporation and a State, the Government of the State almost always seems to win. It may have been different in the days of gunboat diplomacy, when transnational corporations were in their infancy. But how many instances of gunboat diplomacy successfully exerted on behalf of an investor can one recall since World War II, or even World War I? How many times have these powerful multinational corporations been able to override the will of a sovereign State? How many times have the Governments of which such corporations are the nationals effectively brought their power to bear on behalf of those corporations?

In short, the problem is not solely one of subjecting transnational corporations to social discipline but also of subjecting Governments to legal and political discipline – to the discipline of the rule of law and the application of sound policy. Governments have not only rights but responsibilities. In their relations to multinational corporations, their responsibilities have not always been recognized and exercised.

As to whether, as Ambassador Pinto in his paper suggested, few companies have paid attention to the creation of enduring and mutually beneficial relationships with the Governments of countries in which they operate, I can again speak only impressionistically and out of my own limited experience, largely deriving from oil operations.

My own impression is that some of the international oil companies did an immense amount for the countries in which they operated, contributing mightily to their transformation into countries which today have not only oil but other industries, whose populations, elements of which benefited from training by the multinationals and education abroad fostered by them, today are literate, skilled, healthy, productive, and in command of their own destinies in ways in which they were not before the advent of the foreign corporation. Far from multinational corporations serving as proxies of neo-colonialism, these corporations have played a paramount role in liberating these countries from economic torpor. If such performance has not led to the creation of enduring relationships – sometimes it has – any fault may not lie entirely with the corporations concerned.

Now I wish to turn to another aspect of Ambassador Pinto's survey and analysis: bilateral investment treaties, a subject which Mr. Lauterpacht also embraces.

Ambassador Pinto notes their salient provisions, and observes that, despite their value, host countries may maintain an ambivalence towards transnational corporations which surrounds the conclusion of those treaties. He remarks that, while some authorities regard the provisions of such treaties as State practice of a quality that generates rules of law out of clauses "which are so often included as to justify the proposition that they have become part of international custom," on another view these principles of bilateral investment treaties can be no more than important elements of a synthesis which must incorporate certain other elements, namely, elements of social discipline to be adopted by and presumably applied to such enterprises. He submits that these principles of social discipline are generated by "another kind of State practice," the support for them manifested by States in the negotiation of codes of conduct relating to multinationals in several international fora. Ambassador Pinto then runs through the experience of the United Nations in its resolutions on permanent sovereignty over natural resources, the Declaration on the Establishment of the New International Economic Order, the Charter of Economic Rights and Duties of States, and, particularly, the drafting of a Code of Conduct under the auspices of the United Nations Commission on Transnational Corporations, a process which is as yet incomplete, and he refers to the experience of the Organization for Economic Cooperation and Development (OECD) as well.

I wish to address myself to two points: first, do the clauses of some 300 bilateral investment treaties evidence State practice which may give rise to customary international law? Second, do the positions taken by governments in the negotiation of pertinent United Nations resolutions evidence State practice which may give rise to customary international law? Let me begin with the second.

In United Nations fora the last thirty years, the Group of Seventy-Seven developing countries often have united with the States of the East to take positions which asserted *vis-à-vis* transnational corporations national sovereignty unrestrained by international law. If one recalls the Charter of Economic Rights and Duties of States, one finds asserted, for example, the right to "nationalize, expropriate or transfer ownership of foreign property," taking into account only the law of the acting State but not international law, and providing only for "appropriate" compensation in accordance with national law. The industrialized democracies did not accept this formulation, and voted against or abstained in respect of it.

It is clear that such a provision of a resolution of the General Assembly of the United Nations, in itself a recommendatory resolution, cannot possibly reflect what is accepted as customary international law, since the major capital-exporting States viewed it not only as not reflective but *contra legem*.

Are the positions which States took respecting this and other provisions of the Charter of Economic Rights and Duties of States evidence of State practice? What States say, and how they vote, in the United Nations, may be expressive in some instances of considered State policy; in other instances it may simply express bloc voting. But is it State practice? Can what States say in the United Nations General Assembly be equated with what they do outside it?

Where, in a process of codification of international law, questions are put to States to which they respond after an examination of State policy and practice, particularly their own, weight is to be attached to the answers given. Illustrations are the Bases of Discussion prepared for The Hague Codification Conference held under the auspices of the League of Nations and the replies to questionnaires circulated among States on behalf of the International Law Commission. That process is not the same as that which led to the adoption of the Declaration and Program of Action on the New International Economic Order or the Charter of Economic Rights and Duties of States. Perhaps the very extended process of the negotiation of a United Nations Code of Conduct relating to transnational corporations conduces to more considered and less emotive expressions of the views of the States concerned.

In any event, in the belief that what States do is more significant that what they say or even what they say they do, clauses contained in some 300 bilateral investment treaties surely are a more reliable guide to what States see as their real interests. They are a more reliable guide to what States see as the applicable international legal principles, for such clauses are contained in legal instruments having binding force under international law which are designed to govern and do govern actual investments.

And it is extraordinary to see that, whereas the States of the developing world and the East vote against the applicability of international law to the treatment of transnational corporations when they vote in United Nations organs, they subscribe to its application or to a more refined description of its substance in carefully negotiated treaties which are duly ratified and brought into force.

Let me give a few illustrations. The bilateral investment treaties entered into by the United States with developing countries, including indeed what are or were "People's Republics" both in the developing world and in Eastern Europe, contain such provisions as: "Investment shall at all times be accorded fair and equitable treatment, shall enjoy full protection and security and shall in no case be accorded treatment less than that required by international law. Neither Party shall in any way impair by arbitrary and discriminatory measures the management, operation, ... enjoyment, acquisition ... or disposal of investments. Each Party shall observe any obligation it may have entered into with regard to investments ... Investments shall not be expropriated or nationalized either directly or indirectly through measures tantamount to expropriation or nationalization ... except ... upon payment of prompt, adequate and effective ... compensation ... equivalent to the fair market value of the expropriated investment immediately before expropriatory action was taken." These treaties further contain provision for international arbitration of investment disputes.

A recent treaty between Australia and China contains similar provisions for fair and equitable treatment of investments and provides that expropriatory and like measures may only be taken "against reasonable compensation" computed on the basis of the market value of the investment.[1] An even more recent treaty between France and the Soviet Union provides that investments of investors of either party in the territory of the other shall enjoy "full and complete protection and security," that "each Contracting Party shall respect any commitment it has made to an investor from the other ..." and that no expropriatory measures shall be taken contrary to such commitments and that any such measures "shall be accompanied by the payment of prompt and adequate compensation ... equivalent to the value of the investment."[2]

Are such provisions illustrative of State practice which gives rise to rules of customary international law?

They certainly are illustrative of State practice, much more certainly than the confrontational or negotiating positions taken in United Nations debates. But does such practice give rise to or reflect rules of international law?

A classic question in international law is whether a treaty provision reflects customary international law or varies it. There is no certain answer to that question. When a constant provision is found in a multiplicity of treaties, it is possible that it demonstrates the will of the States concerned uniformly to depart from, or at least clarify, what otherwise would be the content of customary international law; but it is likelier that such a concordance of treaty provisions reflects, or will in time come to reflect, what the view of States is as to what existing international law requires.

Nevertheless, in the case of treatment of foreign investment, I believe that the views of States and the practice of States remain too divided to conclude that such treaty provisions of themselves as yet demonstrate the existence of current rules of customary international law. When Mr. Lauterpacht says that it is idle to pretend that the position in customary international law is other than uncertain in this sphere, he is right.

---

[1] *International Legal Materials* (1989), Vol. 28, p. 123.   [2] *Ibid.* (1990), Vol. 29, p. 320.

But I will say that I believe these bilateral investment treaty provisions much more faithfully illustrate the trend of the law, the way in which the law is developing, than do the pertinent United Nations resolutions. These provisions not only indicate what States the world over, developed and developing, East as well as West, see as the governing legal principles, indisputably between the parties to these treaties, but arguably *erga omnes*; they also respond to economic realities. As for a Code of Conduct respecting transnational corporations being negotiated under United Nations auspices, judgment must be reserved until the code is complete and until it is seen what measure of genuine support it attracts.

Time has not permitted me to comment on the environmental questions which Ambassador Pinto has addressed. I would just observe that, once again, the problem is not only the behavior or misbehavior of transnational corporations but of governments as well, as the catastrophic fouling of the environment in Eastern Europe by governmental enterprises illustrates.

As for Ambassador Pinto's proposal that transnational corporations should be invited to participate directly in the negotiation of new international legal rules on technological topics on which they have special expertise, it is a creative and challenging idea, which merits every consideration.

Finally, permit me to make a few comments on Mr. Lauterpacht's paper. The first is that I do not believe – and in this I seem to differ with Mr. Lauterpacht – that the judgment of the Chamber of the International Court of Justice in the *ELSI* case raises doubt about the standing of a State to extend diplomatic protection to an investment made by a corporation of its nationality in a company of the nationality of the State in which the investment is made. It is true that it was argued in the *ELSI* case that the Treaty of Friendship, Commerce, and Navigation between the USA and Italy was essentially irrelevant to the claims of the USA, since the measures taken by Italy directly affected not a US corporation but an Italian corporation, ELSI, whose shares had been bought by a US corporation, Raytheon. But the chamber certainly did not accept this argument, even if one of its members did in some measure.

Second, Mr. Lauterpacht is right to emphasize that a critical issue in matters of the evaluation of expropriated enterprises is whether account should be taken only of the value of the physical assets or whether the revenue or profit-earning capacity of such assets shall also be appraised. The failure to give any weight whatsoever to vast assets of precisely this latter kind is why I find the sellout arrangements of the 1970s to which I alluded earlier so questionable. I agree with Mr. Lauterpacht that standards such as net book value or updated book value generally are not appropriate to an objective process of value determination.

PART V

Aggression under, Compliance with, and Development of International Law

ଏ୨

29

The Legal Effect of Resolutions and Codes of Conduct of the United Nations

cↄ

The Contending Positions

The topic of the impact of resolutions of the United Nations General Assembly on the principles of customary international law has been a subject of controversy for some years. This lecture reconsiders that question in the light of recent material, including current work of the Institute of International Law and the American Law Institute. It will look particularly at relevant holdings in four international arbitral awards. And it will touch upon the subject of the influence of Codes of Conduct on international law, one of the many topics on which that distinguished scholar, Professor Pieter Sanders, has shed light.

The parameters of the question can be summarized as follows. On one side of the debate are those who emphasize that, under the Charter of the United Nations, the General Assembly lacks legislative powers. It does have certain internal and financial powers whose exercise creates legal obligations. Thus when the General Assembly elects the Secretary-General or a Member of the Security Council, or when it apportions the expenses of the Organization, Members are legally bound. But, putting resolutions on such subjects aside, it is plain that not a phrase of the Charter suggests that the General Assembly is empowered to enact or alter international law. It has the broadest authority to adopt recommendations, and those recommendations may embrace legal as well as other matters. But they remain recommendations, which States are legally free to adopt or disclaim. As Judge Sir Hersch Lauterpacht put it, "the paramount rule" of the Charter is that "the General Assembly has no legal power to legislate or bind its Members by way of recommendations ..."[1]

First published in *Forum Internationale* (October 1985). Reprinted by permission of Kluwer Academic Publishers.

[1] *South-West Africa–Voting Procedure, Advisory Opinion of June 7th, 1955: ICJ Reports 1955*, Separate Opinion of Judge Sir Hersch Lauterpacht, pp. 90, 116.

This is clear not only by the terms of the Charter, but by a consideration of its *travaux préparatoires*. At the San Francisco Conference on International Organization, only one State voted for a proposal that would have permitted the General Assembly to enact rules of international law that would become binding for the Members of the Organization once they had been approved by a majority vote in the Security Council.[2] What the terms and the *travaux* of the Charter do not support can scarcely be implied.

Those who deny that the General Assembly's resolutions affect the content of customary international law also observe that States Members often vote for much with which they actually do not agree. They may go along with a "consensus" to which they consent only in form and not in substance. Their Delegates may vote without instructions or be loosely instructed; they may vote in accordance with group dictates rather than as an expression of what their Government believes that the law requires. The Members of the General Assembly generally vote in response to political, not legal, considerations. Their intention normally is not to affect the law but to make the point which the resolution makes. "The issue often is one of image rather than international law; States will vote a given way repeatedly not because they consider that their reiterated votes are evidence of a practice accepted as law but because it is politically unpopular to vote otherwise."[3]

The United Nations General Assembly is a forum in which States can express their views, but what they do is more important than what they say, and especially more important than what they say in the General Assembly – not only because the General Assembly is not authorized to legislate but, as Professor Arangio-Ruiz tellingly sums it up, because its Members don't "mean it."[4] That is to say, General Assembly Members often do not meaningfully support what a resolution says and almost always do not mean that a resolution shall make international law. Indeed, as a comprehensive and searching report recently submitted to the Institute of International Law by Professor Krzysztof Skubiszewski observes, in referring to the practical effect of the non-binding nature of the Assembly's resolutions: "These instruments have often secured the required majority or general consensus and could, consequently, be adopted 'precisely because' – as Sir Gerald Fitzmaurice put it – 'they were not binding in law'. The records of discussion in the United

---

[2] *Documents of the United Nations Conference on International Organization*, Vol. 9, pp. 70, 316.

[3] S.M. Schwebel, "The Effect of Resolutions of the United Nations General Assembly on Customary International Law," *Proceedings of the 73rd Annual Meeting of the American Society of International Law* (1979), pp. 301, 302.

[4] G. Arangio-Ruiz, "The Normative Role of the General Assembly of the United Nations and the Declaration of Principles of Friendly Relations," *Recueil des Cours 1972-III* (1974), pp. 431, 457.

Nations abound in examples."[5] It should be recalled that Sir Gerald Fitzmaurice spoke not only with his exceptional authority as a judge and scholar, but, as the Legal Adviser of the Foreign Office for many years, as an analyst who had an intimate knowledge of how and why the General Assembly actually operates and how and why Governments instruct (or fail to instruct) their representatives in the General Assembly.

Moreover, those who discount the effect of General Assembly resolutions point out that some States – including some of the Permanent Members of the Security Council – have officially and emphatically maintained in recent years that resolutions of the General Assembly which treat questions of customary international law, even if adopted without dissent, are no more than recommendatory – or, exceptionally, declaratory of what international law is. How exceptionally is illustrated by the following statement of the Department of State:

> General Assembly resolutions are regarded as recommendations to Member States of the United Nations. To the extent, which is exceptional, that such resolutions are meant to be declaratory of international law, are adopted with the support of all members, and are observed by the practice of States, such resolutions are evidence of customary international law on a particular subject matter."[6]

It is clear that these are substantial conditions. The statement speaks of resolutions which are "declaratory" of international law, which may be read to exclude resolutions which are frankly lawmaking rather than declaring. Such resolutions must be adopted with the support of "all members," not simply with the support of a very large majority or with the support of the major groups. And such resolutions must be "observed" in State practice, though it is not specified how universally. If these conditions are met, then such resolutions are "evidence" of customary international law.

On the other side of the controversy are those who acknowledge that the United Nations Charter accords the General Assembly no authority to enact or alter international law. Yet, in practice, some of its resolutions – including some not interpreting Charter principles – have effects in and on international law (and they cite resolutions of the General Assembly which have been widely recognized to be declaratory of international law on subjects such as the Nuremberg principles and outer space); and this practice, they maintain, this broad construction of the General Assembly's powers, is now established. What States say, formally and consistently, may give rise to

---

[5] K. Skubiszewski, "The elaboration of general multilateral conventions and of non-contractual instruments having a normative function or objective," *Annuaire de l'Institut de Droit International* (1985), Vol. 61–I, p. 41.

[6] *Digest of United States Practice in International Law* (1975), p. 85.

expectations of what the law is. The International Court of Justice itself has given a certain, if indeterminate, legal weight to a few resolutions of the General Assembly in the development of law of the United Nations Charter regarding non-self-governing territories.[7] The General Assembly affords States a medium for the concentrated and accelerated expression of their views which did not exist when customary international law only grew disparately and unevenly through the bilateral interactions of States. In the very least, General Assembly resolutions may authoritatively find what the law is, and such resolutions, declaratory of international law, can have an important effect in crystallizing and even progressively developing international law. Thus General Assembly resolution 3232 (XXIX) of November 12, 1974 contains this provision:

> *Recognizing* that the development of international law may be reflected, *inter alia*, by declarations and resolutions of the General Assembly which may to that extent be taken into consideration by the International Court of Justice.[8]

That resolution was adopted by the General Assembly by consensus.

Yet the circumstances of the adoption of the foregoing paragraph of a General Assembly resolution illustrate the frailty of consensus in the General Assembly as an indication of *ipinio juris*. As Professor Skubiszewski rightly recalls:

> Nonetheless several Governments voiced their opposition to, or doubts on, this paragraph. Some of them declared that had there been a separate vote on it, they would not have supported it.[9]

The paragraph is found in a resolution which concluded an uninspiring review by the General Assembly of the role of the International Court of Justice, a review initiated by States who wished to increase recourse to the Court. Many States resisted that objective, and were prepared ultimately at most to accept a rather anodyne resolution. But some of them said to those who wished the Court to play a larger role, unless you accept the quoted paragraph, there will be no resolution on the Court at all. In view of this condition, the paragraph was included. What is its worth, in that circum-

---

[7] *Legal Consequences for States of the Continued Presence of South Africa in Namibia (South-West Africa) Notwithstanding Security Council resolution 276 (1970), Advisory Opinion, ICJ Reports 1971*, pp. 16, 31–32; *Western Sahara, Advisory Opinion, ICJ Reports 1975*, pp. 12, 31–33. Subsequently, the Court found the General Assembly's "Declaration on Principles of International Law concerning Friendly Relations" (resolution 2625 XXV) to constitute an expression of *opinio juris* as to the existence of a principle of customary international law on the non-use of force. It also found the General Assembly's Definition of Aggression (resolution 3314 XXIX) reflective of customary international law. *Military and Paramilitary Activities in and against Nicaragua, ICJ Reports 1986*, pp. 100, 103.

[8] Resolution 3232 (XXIX), preamble.   [9] "General Multilateral Conventions," p. 98.

stance, and having regard to the reservations expressed by States about it at the time of its adoption? How much genuine weight does it lend to the position that the development of international law may be reflected by declarations and resolutions of the General Assembly? Even the terms of the paragraph itself actually are non-committal: it says no more than that the development of international law "may" be reflected by such declarations and resolutions, which of course imports as well that the development of international law may not be so reflected. That element of equivocation was critical to acceptance of the paragraph by States who were anxious to have a review of the role of the Court concluded with a resolution, and a resolution which, however mild, was positive.

In describing the weight attached by the International Court of Justice to resolutions of the General Assembly, I used the word "indeterminate." The following quotation from the study now before the Institute of International Law indicates why:

> The Court was rather cautious in the choice of language when it referred to the Assembly resolutions bearing on inter-State relations and on rights and duties of States; besides, such references were until now not too frequent. In the *Namibia Case* the Court saw in resolution 1514 (XV) an "important stage" in the development of international law regarding territories under colonial régime, *viz.* in the application of the principles of self-determination to all of them and the expansion of the concept of the sacred trust. The Court did not explicitly link this resolution to a source of law, though it spoke of "the subsequent development of law, through the Charter of the United Nations and by way of customary law". Judge Jiménez de Aréchaga thinks that "it is clear from the context of the Opinion that this reference to customary law is meant to include resolution 1514 (XV) of the General Assembly". In the *Western Sahara Case* the Court explained the right of self-determination of peoples by citing resolutions 1514 (XV) and 2625 (XX), yet in conclusion it described them as "the basic principles governing the decolonization policy of the General Assembly". This phrase seems to place the resolutions on the plane of policies rather than establishing a more direct connection between them and a source of law.[10]

Moreover, it may be said that, in the *Namibia* and *Western Sahara* Opinions, the Court was taking account of General Assembly resolutions interpreting what the Court found to be the Charter principle of self-determination. There is relatively little dispute about whether United Nations organs may interpret Charter provisions and principles. Thus one of the conclusions found in Professor Skubiszewski's report reads:

---

[10] *Ibid.*, pp. 68–69.

74. A standard of conduct set forth in a resolution can be used in aid of treaty interpretation.

75. A unanimous resolution which interprets a provision of the United Nations Charter constitutes an authoritative (authentic, binding) interpretation of the Charter if by their votes all the United Nations Members intended to, and did, accept it as such.[11]

But there is, as indicated, very considerable dispute over the authority of the General Assembly to adopt resolutions which lay down general and abstract rules of conduct binding upon States.

Consideration in the Institut de Droit International

The larger conclusions reached by Professor Skubiszewski, with the benefit of a distinguished committee of the Institute, which, however, is not unanimous in its views, are more far reaching. It would unduly extend this paper to set out, still less analyze, the ninety conclusions which he reaches.[12] To be relatively brief, his essential conclusions are these. As to the elaboration of normative resolutions, the General Assembly has no competence to enact general international law; nevertheless, States may declare, develop, and make law by way of resolutions. In the least, resolutions may reveal and express contemporary tendencies of development of general international law. If a resolution lays down a rule that is contrary to international law, it can lead to the loss by the relevant provisions of international law of their general or universal nature and can constitute the beginning of change in existing law. An agreement expressed by consensus can constitute a stage in the elaboration of new law. The normal majority voting of the General Assembly is insufficient; it must be replaced by a negotiated arrangement. In assessing the value of unanimity, it is necessary to take into account the number and nature of abstentions and those reservations which detract from the rules as approved. A State's approval of the resolution cannot be taken at face value; there must be a law-stating or law-creating intention. Relevant majorities must be representative, displaying no geopolitical gaps and including the main legal systems. The resolution does not limit the freedom of opposing and abstaining States, and States may make such reservations to a resolution as they wish.

---

[11] *Ibid.*, p. 239.

[12] *Ibid.*, pp. 229–241. In 1987, the Institute adopted a resolution stating that "some resolutions" of the General Assembly have "a normative role." It further stated that the conclusions of the Commission of which Professor Skubiszewski was Rapporteur merited "thorough study" and appended the twenty-six conclusions of the Commission. *Annuaire de l'Institut de Droit International* (1987), Vol. 62–II, pp. 274–288.

In respect of resolutions constituting evidence of law, Professor Skubi-szewski concludes that normally the political manner in which the General Assembly functions does not allow for the proper assessment of the state of the law. Nonetheless, intergovernmental negotiations in the General Assembly can lead to the adoption of resolutions which constitute evidence of customary international law or its ingredients: custom-creating practice and/or *opinio juris*. To be declaratory of law, the object of the resolution must be to state law. Where the Assembly affirms rules applied in State practice or judicial decisions, such affirmation, if unanimous or nearly so, becomes evidence of universal acceptance of the rules as law. A State's approval of a resolution is not by itself conclusive of the fact that a State already participates in a practice that conforms to the resolution. Evidence of law supplied by the resolution is rebuttable. In particular, contrary practice cancels the evident-iary effect of the resolution which states the existence of *opinio juris*. Unanim-ity behind the resolution creates a presumption that the resolution contains an exact statement of law. Consensus creates weaker evidence than unanimity. A majority vote of a law–declaring resolution produces its effects only for those voting in favor. But a representative majority may give a resolution a status similar to one adopted by unanimity.

Professor Skubiszewski further concludes, in respect of resolutions contri-buting to the emergence of customary rules, that resolutions can accelerate the formation of custom. Rules so proclaimed can initiate, influence, or determine State conduct and thereby generate State practice. Where practice is in progress, resolutions can contribute to its consolidation. But resolutions themselves do not constitute State practice. Repetition of the rule in other resolutions is not State practice. If not followed by practice, repetition loses its significance in the law-creating process. It may then become proof of non–compliance. Acceptance by States of the legal nature of a rule en-gendered in their practice can find expression in a resolution. The resolution is made obligatory by unequivocal State acceptance. In sum, resolutions may be a means for deducing rules from international law, for articulating such rules, and for clarifying their content. States which approved the resolution are barred from challenging the lawfulness of the conduct conforming to it.

Permit me in a few minutes to give some inferential indication of my reaction to this subtle and searching draft which is now before the Institute – a report of whose scope and depth only an impression can be given in this lecture. But first let me add to this new body of scholarly codification the *Foreign Relations Law of the United States (Revised)*. It treats resolutions of the General Assembly not as a source of international law but, in narrowly confined circumstances, as evidence of international law, in these terms:

Declaratory resolutions of international organizations. States often pronounce their views on points of international law, sometimes jointly through resolutions of international organizations that undertake to declare what the law is on a particular question, usually as a matter of general customary law. International organizations generally have no authority to make law, and their determinations of law ordinarily have no special weight, but their declaratory pronouncements provide some evidence of what the states voting for it regard the law to be. The evidentiary value of such resolutions is variable. Resolutions of universal international organizations, if not controversial and if adopted by consensus or virtual unanimity, are given substantial weight.[13]

In my view, the Institute is very close to the mark. If General Assembly resolutions may be evidence in some circumstances of international law, that evidentiary value is variable, and, in some cases, may be low.

Pertinent Holdings in Four Arbitral Awards

Let us now introduce the holdings in four rather recent arbitral awards, of which the drafts of the two Institutes take account.

In his 1977 Award on the Merits in the case of *Texaco Overseas Petroleum Company (Topco) and California Asiatic Oil Company v. The Government of the Libyan Arab Republic,* the Sole Arbitrator, Professor René-Jean Dupuy, addressed, among other questions, "the place which resolutions by the General Assembly of the United Nations could occupy" in "the content of positive law."[14] He recalled that, under the United Nations Charter, the General Assembly issues only recommendations. Yet he concluded that "it is impossible to deny that the United Nations' activities have had a significant influence on the content of contemporary international law."[15] In appraising "the legal validity" of certain United Nations resolutions, Professor Dupuy found it appropriate to examine the voting conditions and the provisions concerned. With respect to one such resolution, resolution 1803 (XVII) on "Permanent Sovereignty over Natural Resources," he noted that it was adopted by a majority which included "not only all geographical areas but also all economic systems," particularly the market economy States and developing countries.[16] That contrasted with the majorities which adopted

---

[13] American Law Institute, *Restatement of the Law, Foreign Relations Law of the United States (Revised),* Volume 1, Section 103, Commentary, p. 37.

[14] *International Law Reports* (1979), Vol. 53, pp. 420, 484; *Yearbook Commercial Arbitration* (1979), 4, p. 177.

[15] *Ibid.,* p. 487.

[16] It was not accurate to conclude that "all economic systems" supported the resolution, since it was adopted by a vote of eighty-seven (nearly all developing and Western States) to two (France and South Africa), the Soviet Union and like-minded States abstaining, together with Ghana and Burma. The Soviet Union pressed fundamental amendments to the resolution which were defeated.

another resolution on that subject, resolution 3171 (XXVIII), as well as resolution 3201 (S-VI), the "Declaration on the Establishment of a New International Economic Order" and resolution 3281 (XXIX), the "Charter of Economic Rights and Duties of States." Dupuy noted that the most important Western countries did not support these three resolutions. Dupuy held that "the absence of any binding force of the resolutions of the General Assembly of the United Nations implies that such resolutions must be accepted by the members of the United Nations in order to be legally binding."[17] He held that:

> It appears essential to this Tribunal to distinguish between those provisions of a resolution stating the existence of a right on which the generality of the States has expressed agreement and those provisions introducing new principles which were rejected by certain representative groups of States and having nothing more than a *de lege ferenda* value only in the eyes of the States which have adopted them; as far as the others are concerned, the rejection of these same principles implies that they considered them being *contra legem*. With respect to the former, which proclaim rules recognized by the community of nations, they do not create a custom but confirm one by formulating it and specifying its scope.[18]

Resolution 1803 (XVII) – which recognizes that a State's taking of foreign assets must be in accordance with international law – accordingly is declaratory of customary international law, while the other resolutions cited – which subject such takings to national law only – are not declaratory of international law. Professor Dupuy further observed that his conclusions were supported by State practice, which is not in conformity with the contention that the treatment of foreign property is exclusively governed by domestic legislation and courts.

A few months after the delivery of Professor Dupuy's award, a second Sole Arbitrator (like Dupuy, appointed by the President of the International Court of Justice), Dr. Sobhi Mahmassani, reached relatively summary conclusions consistent with those of Dupuy. In *Libyan American Oil Company (LIAMCO) v. Government of the Libyan Arab Republic* (1977), Dr. Mahmassani referred to the relevant passage of texts of certain General Assembly resolutions. He noted that the claimant observed that resolution 1803 (XVII) provided for respect for foreign investment agreements, and that this provision was in the contemplation of the parties when they entered into the contract at issue in the case, but that, as for the Charter of Economic Rights and Duties of States, "it does not represent a consensus of nations and cannot

---

[17] *International Law Reports* (1979), Vol. 53, p. 491.   [18] *Ibid.*

be invoked as a source of international law."[19] Dr. Mahmassani concluded that:

> The said resolutions, if not a unanimous source of law, are evidence of the recent dominant trend of international opinion concerning the sovereign right of States over their natural resources, and that the said right is always subject to the respect for contractual agreements and to the obligation of compensation.[20]

It does not appear that Dr. Mahmassani equated "the recent dominant trend of international opinion" with the content of international law. Nor does it appear that he saw this emergent dominant opinion as sufficient to deprive existing customary international law of the *opinio juris* which is an essential element of customary international law.

Two additional international arbitral awards are in point. In an award on jurisdiction given in 1982 by an *ad hoc* Arbitral Tribunal composed of Professor Pierre Lalive, President, and Professors Berthold Goldman and Jacques Robert, in proceedings between *Framatome and others v. Atomic Energy Organization of Iran*, the defendant invoked certain resolutions of the United Nations General Assembly subsequent to resolution 1803 (XVII), including those on permanent sovereignty over natural resources and the Charter of Economic Rights and Duties of States. The Arbitral Tribunal held:

> The first of these texts is relevant to the present case, although it relates to nationalizations, since it concerns the exercise of sovereignty, in a different manner, certainly, but "comparable" and analogous. The second text authorizes each State to regulate foreign investments within the limits of its national jurisdiction and to exercise over them its authority in conformity with its laws and regulations, and in conformity with its national priorities and objectives. The two texts invoked thus have the common feature of submitting to the sole national appreciation of the interested State, to the exclusive jurisdiction of its legislation and Tribunals, disputed questions concerning not only nationalizations but, in a general manner, the exercise by the State of its full and permanent sovereignty over all its riches, natural resources and economic activities.
>
> The resolutions invoked by the defendant cannot, for many independent reasons, lead to a conclusion of invalidity in relation to the international obligation to arbitrate assumed ... in the Contract in dispute, a contract concluded on the instructions and with the agreement of the Government ..., and moreover ratified and confirmed by it in the inter-State agreements.
>
> First, it has not been alleged by the Defendant that the said resolutions are part of international positive law and must overrule, as *jus cogens*, the undertakings freely made by the parties to the present arbitration. Such a theory, if it had been

---

[19] *International Law Reports* (1982), Vol. 62, pp. 140, 189; *Yearbook Commercial Arbitration* (1981), 6, pp. 89, 101.

[20] *Ibid.*

argued, would have been rejected; the General Assembly of the United Nations can only, in principle, issue "recommendations" which are not of a binding character, according to Article 10 of the Charter of the United Nations, an organization of which Iran is a member. However, a certain legal validity may today be recognized in relation to certain of the United Nations resolutions in well-defined conditions, in other words essentially to the extent that these resolutions are accepted by the majority of the member States of the organisation (appertaining to different groups of States) and that they have a declaratory character and not a creative character . . .

Furthermore, in conformity with the thorough analysis of the problem made in the TOPCO Award by the Sole Arbitrator, Professor René-Jean Dupuy, it may be observed that the Charter of Economic Rights and Duties of States expressly mentions, among the fundamental elements of international economic relations, the principle of "performance in good faith of international obligations."[21]

It will be observed that this Arbitral Tribunal adopted Professor Dupuy's reasoning, holding that "a certain legal validity" may be attributed to certain United Nations resolutions only "in well-defined conditions, in other words essentially to the extent that these resolutions are accepted by the majority of the member States of the Organization (appertaining to different groups of States) and that they also have a declaratory and not a creative character."[22]

Also in 1982, another distinguished international Arbitral Tribunal, composed of Professor Paul Reuter, as President, and Professor Hamed Sultan and Sir Gerald Fitzmaurice, *In the Matter of an Arbitration between the Government of the State of Kuwait and the American Independent Oil Company (Aminoil)*, held:

(2) Equally on the public international law plane it has been claimed that permanent sovereignty over natural resources has become an imperative rule of *jus cogens* prohibiting States from affording, by contract or by treaty, guarantees of any kind against the exercise of the public authority in regard to all matters relating to natural riches. This contention lacks all foundation. Even if the Assembly resolution 1803 (XVII) adopted in 1962, is to be regarded, by reason of the circumstances of its adoption, as reflecting the then state of international law, such is not the case with subsequent resolutions which have not had the same degree of authority. Even if some of their provisions can be regarded as codifying rules that reflect international practice, it would not be possible from this to deduce the existence of a rule of international law prohibiting a State from undertaking not to proceed to a nationalization during a limited period of time.[23]

---

[21] The Award of April 30, 1982 is published, in French, in *Journal du Droit International* (1984), 3, p. 58; it is preceded by a commentary by Professor Bruno Oppetit. The English text quoted in this paper is taken from a translation found in the *Yearbook Commercial Arbitration* (1983), 8, pp. 94, 114, published under the title *Company Z and Others (Republic of Xanadu) v. State Organization ABC (Republic of Utopia)*.

[22] *Ibid.*

[23] *International Law Reports* (1984), Vol. 66, pp. 518, 587–588; *Yearbook Commercial Arbitration* (1984), 9, pp. 71, 82.

It will be noted that this Arbitral Tribunal equally follows Dupuy in attributing to resolution 1803 (XVII) declaratory value; "reflecting the then state of international law" – while it holds that later resolutions "have not had the same degree of authority." At a further point in its award, the Tribunal contrasts resolution 1803 (XVII), which it (incorrectly) describes as having received a unanimous vote in the General Assembly, as codifying "positive principles,"[24] whereas resolutions subsequent to it, "none of which obtained unanimous acceptance, and some of which, such as the Charter of the Economic Rights and Duties of States, have been the subject of divergent interpretations,"[25] apparently largely did not reflect existing international law.

Some Conclusions

What conclusions may be drawn, particularly from these arbitral awards, when read against the background of the insistence of some major Powers that the General Assembly can adopt resolutions treating questions of customary international law which are no more than recommendatory, and when considered in the light of the reality that States rarely "mean it" – that so often they feel able to vote for a resolution precisely because they do not see it as binding? They appear to be these:

(a) The United Nations Charter does not endow the General Assembly with the authority to enact or alter international law.

(b) Subsequent practice of the States Members of the United Nations in implementation of the Charter is inconsistent, and not so consistent as to accord the General Assembly an authority to affect international law which the Charter's text does not accord.

(c) Nevertheless, certain resolutions of the General Assembly – viewed as expressions of the assembled States of the world community rather than as acts within the constitutional or acquired authority of a quasi-legislative body – which treat questions of international law which are not the subject of principles found in the United Nations Charter may be recognized to be declaratory, though not creative, of international law, provided that they are:

(i) adopted with the support of all assembled States, or, at any rate, of all the groups of States represented in the General Assembly, including major States that are not members of a group, such as the United States of America and China;

[24] *Ibid.*, p. 601.   [25] *Ibid.*, p. 602.

510

(*ii*) adopted with the intent of declaring the law (an intent which the resolution can state); and

(*iii*) in accordance with State practice;

(*d*) Resolutions of the General Assembly which go beyond the declaratory to the law-creating (or destroying) are without effect upon the content of customary international law (a principle which is not vitiated by the fact that the line between what is declaratory and creative may at times be indistinct).

It would follow from these conclusions that, if a resolution of the General Assembly, even if adopted by more than a two-thirds majority which regards the resolution as re-stating international law, is not supported by all groups in the General Assembly, and by the Permanent Members of the Security Council which are not members of groups, it cannot, by definition, be "declaratory" of international law. To be declaratory is to be reflective of the perceptions and practice of the international community as a whole; if the mirror is broken, its reflection cannot be unbroken. Not only is virtual unanimity or, in the least, the purposeful support of all groups and Great Powers, required; above all, conformity with the practice of States is required, if what is declared to be the existing law is to be an accurate declaration of what actually exists. The General Assembly, not being endowed with legislative powers, cannot make or unmake the law simply by saying so (even unanimously and repeatedly). The States which come together in the General Assembly can only declare the law when they exceptionally mean to declare it and when they do so in conformity with the practice of States which underlies the law.

Now if we look at the particular resolutions which are the particular impetus for controversy over the scope of the law-making authority of the General Assembly, we are struck by two facts. First, unanimity or even the support of all groups in some leading instances is lacking. If there is consensus, as, for example, with respect to the resolutions adopted at a Special Session of the General Assembly on the establishment of a or the New International Economic Order, it is, or may be, a false consensus – false in the sense that a cascade of reservations made at the time of adoption of those resolutions, and a torrent of indifference or opposition which has been manifested since, demonstrates that support, still less *opinio juris*, is absent. Those resolutions and subsequent repeated invocation of them so well illustrate the stricture of the report to the Institute of International Law that repetition of resolutions in the face of contrary practice is proof of non-compliance. They also illustrate the fact that, if resolutions are bludgeoned through the General

Assembly by a majority which rides roughshod over a minority, if the majority dictates rather than negotiates, the results will not meet the majority's intentions to reshape principles and provisions of international law.

The second striking fact is that general, supportive, practice is lacking. Some of the resolutions which are most vigorously proclaimed to declare the law are in fact not sustained by State practice. Thus those resolutions cannot be and are not valid and effective indicia of the law. Not only are they not declaratory of it; they are not evidence of it.

Contrasting Codes of Conduct

Let me finally say a few words about Codes of Conduct. The United Nations for many years has been trying to draft a Code of Conduct for transnational corporations: a Code which, like the few other such Codes, would not be binding, which would not be meant to be declaratory of international law or creative of international law. It has not succeeded in doing so, for a very creditable reason: States do not, at least yet, agree on the content of critical provisions of the Code. If they do not agree, there is much to be said for their not pretending to agree.

However, the General Assembly did succeed in adopting a Set of Multilaterally Agreed Equitable Principles and Rules for the Control of Restrictive Business Practices.[26] Those principles and rules are expressly recommendatory. Nevertheless, as Professor Sanders has pointed out, the Code contains a section dealing with its implementation. So do the Guidelines by the OECD for multinational enterprises.

In the former Code, there is provision for an Intergovernmental Group of Experts, which provides a forum for multilateral consultations, discussions, and exchange of views between States on matters related to the Set of Principles and Rules. The Group is expressly denied the authority to pass judgment on the conduct of individual Governments or enterprises.

At the same time, as Professor Sanders demonstrates, such codes can have a genuine impact on the behavior of States and enterprises. They may operate in law by transformation into national law. They may operate through the pressure of publicity. "The least one may conclude," Professor Sanders writes, "is, that even a legally non-binding Code may have con-

---

[26] See General Assembly resolution 35/63, as well as "The Set of Multilaterally Agreed Equitable Principles and Rules for the Control of Restrictive Business Practices," United Nations doc. A/C.2/35/6. They expressly provide that the Principles and Rules "take the form of recommendations" (p. 4).

sequences. A Code, once established, constitutes a factor which cannot be neglected."[27]

This is particularly the case because such Codes as have been adopted, in the United Nations, the ILO, and the OECD, have been the object of sustained and meticulous negotiation which has achieved genuine consensus. Professor Sanders does not view the norm-setting provisions of the Codes as constituting customary international law, though they could evolve into a general practice accepted as law. Citing examples of international commercial arbitration, Professor Sanders observes:

> The question therefore arises whether norm-setting standards in a Code, reflecting international consensus could not be considered as forming part of the body of *lex mercatoria* as far as they reflect international customs or generally accepted principles of law. Under these conditions a provision of the Code might, in spite of the Code being legally non-binding, nevertheless have legal effects.[28]

And he concludes that code provisions may come to form – through expectations to which they give rise – part of the body of the *lex mercatoria* with which multinational corporations would have to comply.

It may well be that, particularly in the area of interactions between States and other entities, a more promising route to international progress than resolutions of the General Assembly which purport to make or unmake international law are Codes of Conduct which are not meant to be and are not legally binding, which are carefully negotiated in a spirit of the sovereign equality of States, which take account of the real status, rights, and interests of other actors on the international scene, and which contain provisions for implementation which are restrained and practical. It may be better to weave the fabric of a stronger international law thread by thread than to strain it by the forced introduction of synthetic fabrics.

---

[27] Pieter Sanders, "Codes of Conduct and Sources of Law," *Le Droit des Relations Économiques Internationales, Etudes offertes à Berthold Goldman* (1982), p. 293.

[28] *Ibid.*, p. 297.

30

The United Nations and the Challenge of a Changing International Law

୧୨

Our theme is the legal accommodation of contending systems. The principal forum for such accommodation is the United Nations. Whether the United Nations is *more* than a forum for international accommodation is in fact one of the main subjects of dispute among contending systems. The dispute over the function of the United Nations is important in itself, and as an indicator of the approach of States to the development of international law. Let us measure contending systems against their attitude towards international organization, with this caveat: that the systems are not systematic. It is plain that, if one speaks of a "Western" approach to the United Nations, or an "unaligned" approach, or the approach of the less developed countries, or even a Communist approach, one speaks in general terms which admit of exceptions.

By the way, I use the word "Communist" advisedly. I note that the advance program of this distinguished Society, in its panel on "The Status of Competing Claims to Use Outer Space," had these entries: Professor Taubenfeld: "An American Viewpoint"; Signor Fiorio: "A Small-Country Viewpoint" (from San Marino); and "Speaker to be announced: A Socialist Viewpoint." Who was that to be? Not Norman Thomas, since we already have an American viewpoint. Harold Wilson perhaps? Gunnar Myrdal? Or Paul-Henri Spaak? Or could it be that the use of the word "Socialist" was a euphemism, as it is in the present title of the address, "Some Comments on the Socialist Position"? Recalling the homage that is paid to virtue by what is not virtuous, perhaps we should take comfort in the practice of the Communists calling themselves Socialists. At any rate, while I may have to pull some punches this evening, I boldly propose to call Communists "Communists."

An element of the Communist approach to the United Nations is what Dag Hammarskjöld called "the conference concept." In the introduction to his last Annual Report, the Secretary-General put it this way:

First published in *Proceedings of the American Society of International Law* (1963).

Certain Members conceive of the Organization as a static conference machinery for resolving conflicts of interests and ideologies with a view to peaceful co-existence, within the Charter, to be served by a Secretariat which is to be regarded not as fully internationalized but as representing within its ranks those very interests and ideologies.

Hammarskjöld contrasted with what clearly was and is the Communist approach the view of other Members:

Other Members have made it clear that they conceive of the Organization primarily as a dynamic instrument of Governments through which they ... should seek such reconciliation but through which they should also try to develop forms of executive action, undertaken on behalf of all Members, and aiming at forestalling conflicts and resolving them, ... in a spirit of objectivity and in implementation of the principles and purposes of the Charter.

These other Members take the conference concept "only as a starting point, envisaging the possibility of continued growth to increasingly effective forms of active international cooperation, adapted to experience" and served by a genuinely international Secretariat which is responsible to the Organization alone.

Now a vital fact is that what Hammarskjöld describes as the "executive concept" of the United Nations is a concept that is shared among the Western Powers and the unaligned, among the more developed and less developed countries. There are few facts of more importance to the future potential, as well as the present-day effectiveness, of international law.

The significance of that fact is that the bulk of what is loosely termed the "free world" is following a policy and practice which is progressively developing international law through the development of international organization. The policy is not coherent, the practice is not pervasive, the progress is not steady. But the trend is there. It can hardly be denied that, for the most part, the United States has given its strong support to the "executive concept" of the United Nations and that the great majority of the smaller countries of the world have as well. The Congo is a case in point. The Security Council adopted decisions of a far-reaching character, decisions which carry the force of law, or, at least, such force as international law possesses. Those decisions, of course, bind not only the Members of the Council, but all Members of the Organization, if not non-Members. The General Assembly, for its part, adopted binding decisions for the financing of the Organization's operations in the Congo, and various recommendations which the Security Council rendered binding by incorporation by reference in its own resolutions. The Secretary-General was entrusted with large powers which he implemented with vigor, and, on the whole, with success. The outcome of the enterprise is as yet unsettled. Aspects of it are disquieting: for example, the poor response of the membership in meeting its financial obligations flowing from the Congo effort. Yet it is clear that the Congo represents a progressive development in the powers of international organization: that it is an innovation in collective intervention which obviated the necessity of application of collective security. Moreover, it represents a victory in the preservation, as well as the development, of the powers accorded the Organization by the Charter, for it marked the rejection of the Soviet attempt to destroy the international character of the Secretariat.

Now granting that, by and large, the free world stands together in developing the law of international organization, is it split apart in its appreciation of the remainder of international law? In particular, do the less developed countries tend to view much of customary international law as colonialist and obsolete, as a Western creation which does not, or at least should not, bind those who often had little and in many cases nothing to do with its creation?

There is unquestionably sentiment of this kind. There is even some thought of this kind, though more sentiment than thought. As a rule, questioning of whether the newer States should be bound by the rules and institutions of the international community to which they have acceded is on a high level of generality. When one comes to specifics, one finds that the newer States, and the less developed countries, some of which are not "new," do not offer a great deal which illustrates such vague feelings of discomfort as they may have or are alleged to have. It is all very well to say that that Western creature, international law, is colonialist and obsolete, but, when one takes a closer look at the body of international law, there is less certainty about what in the Western legacy one should discard and what in another tradition one should add. We can all do without letters of marque and reprisal, and without a regime of capitulations. In fact, we do do without them. Now what else? Someone is certain to say: the minimum standard in international law, particularly as it applies to the treatment of foreign property; surely here we have an area in which the less developed countries challenge the rule of customary international law, and with some precision.

For the most part that is true. What is equally true, however, is that, in this area as in others, the less developed countries approach international law with a pragmatic self-interest (which does not characterize their approach alone). Consider the resolution which the United Nations General Assembly adopted at its last session on the subject of "Permanent Sovereignty over Natural Resources." Having its source in one of their favorite themes, self-determination, the resolution incants another favorite theme of the less developed countries – sovereignty. The real issue posed by the resolution, however, is not whether nations have sovereignty over the resources within their jurisdiction – obviously they do – but how that sovereignty shall be exercised. The Communist bloc maintained, in the words of the Delegate of Hungary, that the State "was the sole judge in the matter and could brook no outside interference whatsoever in the exercise of its sovereignty." Essentially, its view was that there is no international law governing the treatment of foreign property. The Western Members naturally took a contrary stand. What did the less developed countries do? Joining with the West, they adopted, by a vote of eighty-seven in favor, two opposed and twelve abstentions, a resolution which, the Delegate of Bulgaria complained, comprised "a charter of foreign investment." The resolution provides that, where foreign property is taken, the owner "shall" be paid "appropriate compensation" – a standard which the United States Delegation defined as prompt, adequate, and effective compensation. The resolution further provides that: "Foreign investment agreements freely entered into by, or between, sovereign States shall be observed in good faith," thus placing the authority of the General Assembly behind the view that contracts between States and foreign investors are made to be upheld.

Now it could be true, as Professor Oliver Lissitzyn suggests in his perceptive paper on "International Law in a Divided World," that this happy result stemmed largely from "fear of offending States that extend economic . . . assistance," and from the desire to achieve the largest possible majority for an affirmation of permanent sovereignty over natural resources, "rather than solicitude for the existing norms of international law." If this be the case, this shows that the less developed countries, while not responding to existing international norms for their own sake, nevertheless uphold them because, in this case at any rate, they believe that their content makes sense – sense for their self-interest in attracting foreign capital. Such an enlightened sense of the national interest is no mean basis for a progressive and meaningful international law. Presumably it was an aspect of what gave birth to the rule of the minimum standard in the first place.

Differences between the approach to international law of the less developed countries and of the West and Japan should not be minimized. But neither should they be exaggerated. Customary international law is largely Western in origin. But much of it, such as the law of diplomatic immunities, springs not from a specifically Western tradition but from the necessities of a law regulating States. Other elements of it, such as the minimum standard in the treatment of aliens, have close connections with the rule of law and respect for human rights – elements of the Western tradition of which every man may be proud and which have, or should have, universal appeal. As the States of the world join together in the continuing United Nations process of codification and progressive development of international law, newer as well as older States should be afforded a sense of participation in the refinement and growth of international law which should conduce to its relatively universal acceptance and application.

What of the Soviet bloc? Its attitude towards the United Nations is straightforward in its backwardness. It takes a profoundly restrictive view of the Charter, of the powers of United Nations organs, of the effect of United Nations resolutions. As a rule, it accentuates national sovereignty and depreciates international responsibility. Not only is its approach to the Charter conservative; it is reactionary, for it would destroy the Charter's farthest advance towards internationalism, which is found in Article 100's provision for "the exclusively international character of the responsibilities of the Secretary-General and the staff," and substitute the notorious troika.

At the same time, Soviet policy is not so rigid as to exclude a more expansive interpretation of the Organization's authority, when on occasion Moscow judges the exercise of that authority will promote Soviet interests. Cases in point are the Soviet support of a broad view of the Secretary-General's powers at a time when Moscow apparently entertained misplaced hopes about Trygve Lie; its support of the Security Council's undertaking extensive responsibilities of a kind not expressly foreseen by the Charter in the case of the Trieste Statute; and its support, at various stages, of the plan for the partition of Palestine, and of United Nations action in Suez and the Congo.

Moreover, Soviet jurists display a touching paternalism towards the United Nations Charter. It is Korovin who has discovered that the origins of the United Nations are to be traced to the Soviet–Polish Declaration of Friendship and Mutual Aid, concluded in Moscow on December 4, 1941. It is he who asserts that, at San Francisco,

> it was due to the Soviet Government that the most progressive provisions [of the Charter] were introduced: sovereign equality of States, the right of self-determination, human rights and fundamental freedoms ... the development of colonies "towards self-Government or independence" ... not to mention the red thread, running through the entire United Nations Charter, of the principles of peaceful co-existence.

And what of the Soviet approach to international law more generally? With a view towards finding out, I read a book published under the auspices of the Soviet Academy of Sciences, written by a collegium of Soviet scholars,

entitled *International Law: A Textbook for Use in Law Schools.* Its title might
better have read: "International Law, Chiefly as Misinterpreted and Misapplied by the USSR." The book is interesting. It rings all the changes about
peaceful coexistence, sovereignty, unequal treaties, and so forth. It contains a
large dose of Russian nationalism and of Communist parochialism. I had not
realized that the pre-Revolutionary contribution of Russia to international
law was so substantial. I had not begun to realize that the post-Revolutionary
contribution of the Soviet Union to international law was so paramount. If I
may sum up the impression with which the book leaves me, I would say that
it attempts to demonstrate that a great progressive international lawyer of the
twentieth century was not Lauterpacht but Lenin.

Now the Soviet Union does not place itself wholly outside the reach of
international law. It acknowledges the universally valid character of much of
it, while leaving itself free to interpret its contents freely, as, for example, by
its doctrine of "unequal treaties." Not only is the Soviet Union a member of
certain international organizations; it conducts itself in some respects in
routine accordance with much of international law, such as diplomatic
immunities. Where the sanction of reciprocity may be brought into play, the
Soviet Union tends to comply with international law. More important
principles of international law, and the ones it most loudly proclaims, it
honors in the breach: for example, non-intervention (as in Hungary), non-
aggression (as in Finland); and, assuming it to be a principle of international
law, self-determination (as in the Baltic countries). Its scorn for international
adjudication is well known.

However, we have peaceful coexistence. "Peaceful coexistence," the Soviet
Branch of the International Law Association assures us, "is a qualitatively
new and higher stage in the development of interstate relations." "Naturally," it points out, "international law could not remain aloof from the
triumphant march of this idea which is so vitally essential to the nations." Of
what does this new revelation consist? Of this, says the Soviet Branch:

> There is no longer any right to war, but each State possesses the right to peace.
> This is the major content of the principle of peaceful co-existence in the frame-
> work of present-day international law.

To my mind, this "qualitatively new and higher stage" in international
law, which, mind you, is the contribution of no less a personage than Lenin,
ranks with Korovin's discovery of the origins of the United Nations Charter.

Of course, one may say that if, as Communist spokesmen themselves often
indicate, peaceful coexistence is no more than a phrase which sums up the
essence of the Charter, albeit passively, it is harmless enough. Obviously all of

us hope that the nations of the world will exist in peace. If the Communists –
or rather, some Communists – concede that much, we should welcome it.
We should indeed, while at the same time recognizing the content of the
concept of peaceful coexistence as it is authoritatively expounded, not in the
United Nations, but, for example, before the Moscow Conference of Representatives of Communist and Workers Parties on January 6, 1961, by N.S.
Khrushchev:

> Peaceful coexistence helps to develop the forces of progress, the forces struggling
> for socialism, and in capitalist countries it facilitates the activities of Communist
> Parties and other progressive organizations of the working class. It facilitates the
> struggle that the people wage against aggressive military blocs, against foreign
> military bases. It helps the national liberation movement to gain successes. Thus,
> the policy of peaceful coexistence, as regards its social content, is a form of intense
> economic, political, and ideological struggle of the proletariat against the
> aggressive forces of imperialism in the international arena.

All this is not to say that such present degree of communication and
understanding as we have with the Communist world should not be encouraged and developed. To the extent that the Communist world, or part of it, is
willing to cooperate in the construction of a more effective, and genuinely
universal, international law, we should of course cooperate with it. Our true
mutual interest in a more meaningful international law need not be elaborated. Nor can hope for better things be abandoned. As Professor Lasswell
reminds us:

> The doctrines of any political system are open to changes of many kinds,
> particularly in the intensity with which they are held and the specific interpreta-
> tions to which they give rise. Considering the sobering realities of the world
> picture, it is well within the range of possibility that totalitarian leaders will come
> to believe ... that the common peace is to be preferred to common disaster, and
> that the conditions of at least minimum public order can be achieved at bearable
> cost.

31

What Weight to Conquest?

☙

In his admirable address of December 9, 1969, on the situation in the Middle East, Secretary of State William P. Rogers took two positions of particular international legal interest, one implicit and the other explicit.[1] Secretary Rogers called upon the Arab States and Israel to establish "a state of peace . . . instead of the state of belligerency, which has characterized relations for over 20 years." Applying this and other elements of the American approach to the United Arab Republic and Israel, the Secretary of State suggested that, "in the context of peace and agreement [between the UAR and Israel] on specific security safeguards, withdrawal of Israeli forces from Egyptian territory would be required."[2]

Secretary Rogers accordingly inferred that, in the absence of such peace and agreement, withdrawal of Israeli forces from Egyptian territory would not be required. That is to say, he appeared to uphold the legality of continued Israeli occupation of Arab territory pending "the establishment of a state of peace between the parties instead of the state of belligerency."[3] In this Secretary Rogers is on sound ground. That ground may well be based on appreciation of the fact that Israel's action in 1967 was defensive, and on the theory that, since the danger in response to which defensive action was taken remains, occupation – though not annexation – is justified, pending a peace settlement. But Mr. Rogers's conclusion may be simply a pragmatic judgment (indeed, certain other Permanent Members of the Security Council, which are not likely to share the foregoing legal perception, are not now pressing for Israeli withdrawal except as an element of a settlement).

More questionable, however, is the Secretary of State's explicit conclusion on a key question of the law and politics of the Middle East dispute: that "any changes in the pre-existing [1949 armistice] lines should not reflect the weight

First published in *American Journal of International Law* (1970), 64.
[1] The text is published in full in *New York Times*, December 11, 1969, p. 16.   [2] *Ibid.*   [3] *Ibid.*

of conquest and should be confined to insubstantial alterations required for mutual security. We do not support expansionism." Secretary Rogers referred approvingly in this regard to the Security Council's resolution of November 1967, which,

> *Emphasizing* the inadmissibility of the acquisition of territory by war[4] and the need to work for a just and lasting peace in which every State in the area can live in security,
>
> *Emphasizing further* that all Member States in their acceptance of the Charter of the United Nations have undertaken a commitment to act in accordance with Article 2 of the Charter,
>
> 1. Affirms that the fulfilment of Charter principles requires the establishment of a just and lasting peace in the Middle East which should include the application of both the following principles:
>   (*i*) Withdrawal of Israeli armed forces from territories occupied in the recent conflict;[5]
>   (*ii*) Termination of all claims or states of belligerency and respect for and acknowledgement of the sovereignty, territorial integrity and political independence of every State in the area and their right to live in peace within secure and recognized boundaries free from threats or acts of force; . . ."[6]

It is submitted that the Secretary's conclusion is open to question on two grounds: first, that it fails to distinguish between aggressive conquest and defensive conquest; second, that it fails to distinguish between the taking of territory which the prior holder held lawfully and that which it held unlawfully. These contentions share common ground.

As a general principle of international law, as that law has been reformed

---

[4] The resolution's use of the word "war" is of interest. The June 1967 hostilities were not marked by a declaration of war. Certain Arab States have regarded themselves at war with Israel – or, at any rate, in a state of belligerency – since 1948, a questionable position under the law of the Charter. In view of the defeat in the United Nations organs of resolutions holding Israel to have been the aggressor in 1967, presumably the use of the word "war" was not meant to indicate that Israel's action was not in exercise of self-defense. It may be added that territory would not in any event be acquired by war, but, if at all, by the force of treaties of peace.

[5] It should be noted that the resolution does not specify "all territories" or "the territories" but "territories." The subparagraph immediately following is, by way of contrast, more comprehensively cast, specifying "all claims or states of belligerency."

[6] Resolution 242 (1967) of November 22, 1967; 62 *AJIL* 482 (1968). President Johnson, in an address of September 10, 1968, declared:

> We are not the ones to say where other nations should draw the lines between them that will assure each the greatest security. It is clear, however, that a return to the situation of June 4, 1967, will not bring peace. There must be secure and there must be recognized borders . . .
>
> At the same time, it should be equally clear that boundaries cannot and should not reflect the weight of conquest. Each change must have a reason which each side, in honest negotiation, can accept as part of a just compromise. (59 Department of State Bulletin 348 [1968])

since the League, particularly by the Charter, it is both vital and correct to say that there shall be no weight to conquest, that the acquisition of territory by war is inadmissible.[7] But that principle must be read in particular cases together with other general principles, among them the still more general principle of which it is an application, namely, that no legal right shall spring from a wrong, and the Charter principle that the Members of the United Nations shall refrain in their international relations from the threat or use of force against the territorial integrity or political independence of any State. So read, the distinctions between aggressive conquest and defensive conquest, between the taking of territory legally held and the taking of territory illegally held, become no less vital and correct than the central principle itself.

Those distinctions may be summarized as follows: (*a*) a State acting in lawful exercise of its right of self-defense may seize and occupy foreign territory as long as such seizure and occupation are necessary to its self-defense; (*b*) as a condition of its withdrawal from such territory, that State may require the institution of security measures reasonably designed to ensure that that territory shall not again be used to mount a threat or use of force against it of such a nature as to justify exercise of self-defense; (*c*) where the prior holder of territory had seized that territory unlawfully, the State which subsequently takes that territory in the lawful exercise of self-defense has, against that prior holder, better title.

The facts of the June 1967 "Six Day War" demonstrate that Israel reacted defensively against the threat and use of force against her by her Arab neighbors. This is indicated by the fact that Israel responded to Egypt's prior closure of the Straits of Tiran, its proclamation of a blockade of the Israeli port of Eilat, and the manifest threat of the UAR's use of force inherent in its massing of troops in Sinai, coupled with its ejection of UNEF. It is indicated by the fact that, upon Israeli responsive action against the UAR, Jordan initiated hostilities against Israel. It is suggested as well by the fact that, despite the most intense efforts by the Arab States and their supporters, led by the Premier of the Soviet Union, to gain condemnation of Israel as an aggressor by the hospitable organs of the United Nations, those efforts were decisively defeated. The conclusion to which these facts lead is that the Israeli conquest of Arab and Arab-held territory was defensive rather than aggressive conquest.

The facts of the 1948 hostilities between the Arab invaders of Palestine and the nascent State of Israel further demonstrate that Egypt's seizure of the Gaza Strip, and Jordan's seizure and subsequent annexation of the West Bank and

---

[7] See, however, Kelsen (2nd ed. by Tucker), *Principles of International Law* (1967), pp. 420–433.

the old city of Jerusalem, were unlawful. Israel was proclaimed to be an independent State within the boundaries allotted to her by the General Assembly's partition resolution. The Arabs of Palestine and of neighboring Arab States rejected that resolution. But that rejection was no warrant for the invasion by those Arab States of Palestine, whether of territory allotted to Israel, to the projected, stillborn Arab State or to the projected, internationalized city of Jerusalem. It was no warrant for attack by the armed forces of neighboring Arab States upon the Jews of Palestine, whether they resided within or without Israel. But that attack did justify Israeli defensive measures, both within and, as necessary, without the boundaries allotted her by the partition plan (as in the new city of Jerusalem). It follows that the Egyptian occupation of Gaza, and the Jordanian annexation of the West Bank and Jerusalem, could not vest in Egypt and Jordan lawful, indefinite control, whether as occupying Power or sovereign: *ex injuria jus non oritur.*

If the foregoing conclusions that (*a*) Israeli action in 1967 was defensive and (*b*) Arab action in 1948, being aggressive, was inadequate to legalize Egyptian and Jordanian taking of Palestinian territory, are correct, what follows?

It follows that the application of the doctrine of according no weight to conquest requires modification in double measure. In the first place, having regard to the consideration that, as between Israel, acting defensively in 1948 and 1967, on the one hand, and her Arab neighbors, acting aggressively in 1948 and 1967, on the other, Israel has better title in the territory of what was Palestine, including the whole of Jerusalem, than do Jordan and Egypt (the UAR indeed has, unlike Jordan, not asserted sovereign title), it follows that modifications of the 1949 armistice lines among those States within former Palestinian territory are lawful (if not necessarily desirable), whether those modifications are, in Secretary Rogers's words, "insubstantial alterations required for mutual security" or more substantial alterations – such as recognition of Israeli sovereignty over the whole of Jerusalem.[8] In the second place, as regards territory bordering Palestine, and under unquestioned Arab sovereignty in 1949 and thereafter, such as Sinai and the Golan Heights, it follows not that no weight shall be given to conquest, but that such weight shall be given to defensive action as is reasonably required to ensure that such Arab territory will not again be used for aggressive purposes against Israel. For example – and this appears to be envisaged both by the Secretary of State's address and the resolution of the Security Council – free navigation through the Straits of Tiran shall be effectively guaranteed and demilitarized zones shall be established.

---

[8] It should be added that the armistice agreements of 1949 expressly preserved the territorial claims of all parties and did not purport to establish definitive boundaries between them.

The foregoing analysis accords not only with the terms of the United Nations Charter, notably Article 2, paragraph 4, and Article 51, but law and practice as they have developed since the Charter's conclusion. In point of practice, it is instructive to recall that the Republic of Korea and indeed the United Nations itself have given considerable weight to conquest in Korea, to the extent of that substantial territory north of the 38th parallel from which the aggressor was driven and remains excluded – a territory which, if the full will of the United Nations had prevailed, would have been much larger (indeed, perhaps the whole of North Korea). In point of law, provisions of the Vienna Convention on the Law of Treaties are pertinent. Article 52 provides that: "A treaty is void if its conclusion has been procured by the threat or use of force in violation of the principles of international law embodied in the Charter of the United Nations" – a provision which clearly does not debar conclusion of a treaty where force has been applied, as in self-defense, in accordance with the Charter. And Article 75 provides that: "The provisions of the present Convention are without prejudice to any obligation in relation to a treaty which may arise for an aggressor State in consequence of measures taken in conformity with the Charter of the United Nations with reference to that State's aggression."

The state of the law has been correctly summarized by Elihu Lauterpacht, who points out that

> territorial change cannot properly take place as a result of the *unlawful* use of force. But to omit the word "unlawful" is to change the substantive content of the rule and to turn an important safeguard of legal principle into an aggressor's charter. For if force can never be used to effect lawful territory change, then, if territory has once changed hands as a result of the unlawful use of force, the illegitimacy of the position thus established is sterilized by the prohibition upon the use of force to restore the lawful sovereign. This cannot be regarded as reasonable or correct.[9]

---

[9] Elihu Lauterpacht, *Jerusalem and the Holy Places*, Anglo-Israel Association, Pamphlet No. 19 (1968), p. 52.

32

The Brezhnev Doctrine Repealed and Peaceful Coexistence Enacted

❧

One of the more striking provisions of the declaration of "Basic Principles of Mutual Relations"[1] between the United States and the Soviet Union, agreed upon in Moscow on May 29, 1972 by President Nixon and Mr. Brezhnev, is a paragraph that appears to repeal the "Brezhnev Doctrine." Even if one assumes that the declaration does not really mean what it clearly says, this provision is intriguing.

It will be recalled that, when the Soviet Union and other selected parties to the Warsaw Pact invaded Czechoslovakia in 1968, they initially claimed to have been invited in by Czechoslovak authorities. This fabricated claim was rejected in Prague by the Czechoslovak Parliament and in the United Nations Security Council by the Foreign Minister of Czechoslovakia. It took a few years before even the Prague Government installed by Moscow could bring itself publicly to support that claim.

Accordingly, the Soviet Government apparently felt driven to provide an alternative legal basis for invading Czechoslovakia (as Dr. Kissinger is reported to have noted in Moscow, the Soviet Union attaches high importance to juridical considerations). Mr. Brezhnev himself took on this not inconsiderable burden in an address in Warsaw in November 1968, the substance of which came to be known in the West as the "Brezhnev Doctrine."

Mr. Brezhnev declared that:

> The forces of imperialism and reaction seek to deprive the people now of this, now of that socialist country of their sovereign right they have gained to insure ... the well-being and happiness of the broad mass of the working people ... And when the internal and external forces hostile to socialism seek to revert the development of any socialist country toward the restoration of the capitalist order,

First published in *American Journal of International Law* (1972), 66.
[1] *Department of State Bulletin*(1972), 66, p. 898. Reprinted in *American Journal of International Law* (1972), 66, pp. 920–922; also in *International Legal Materials* (1972), 11, p. 756.

when a threat to the cause of socialism in that country, a threat to the security of the socialist community as a whole, emerges, this is no longer only a problem of the people of that country but also a common problem ... for all socialist States.

"It goes without saying," Mr. Brezhnev continued, "that such an action as military aid to a fraternal country to cut short the threat to the socialist order is an extraordinary enforced step, it can be sparked off only by direct actions of the enemies of socialism inside the country and beyond its boundaries, actions creating a threat to the common interests of the camp of socialism."[2]

Mr. Brezhnev thus maintained that, when the Soviet Union decides that what it sees as "socialism" in what it defines as a "socialist" country is threatened by what it deems to be counter-revolution, it and the "socialist camp" are entitled to defend what he called "socialist sovereignty" by "military aid to a fraternal country" – i.e., military intervention.

In earlier days of Khrushchev's preaching of peaceful coexistence, the Soviet Union had made it plain that mere peaceful coexistence did not suffice for relations among the socialist group, which were governed by the principles of "socialist internationalism." But it is believed that the Soviet Union had not expressly asserted that it reserved the right to ensure that once a State was socialist, it must always remain so.

In view of the provisions of the United Nations Charter, this claim of Brezhnev was of course a claim for a quite special right in world affairs – the right to intervene by force to prevent the people of a "socialist" State from exercising their right of self-determination. This, despite the categorical and comprehensive injunction of the United Nations Charter that: "All Members shall refrain in their international relations from the threat or use of force against the territorial integrity or political independence of any State."[3]

Now the eleventh paragraph of the Moscow declaration of basic principles has this to say about claims of special rights: "The USA and the USSR make no claim for themselves and would not recognize the claims of anyone else to any special rights or advantages in world affairs. They recognize the sovereign equality of all States."[4]

---

[2] Speech by Leonid Brezhnev, General Secretary of the Communist Party of the USSR, at the Fifth Congress of the Polish United Workers' Party, Warsaw, November 12, 1968, as quoted in "Czechoslovakia and the Brezhnev Doctrine," prepared for the Sub-Committee on National Security and International Operations of the Committee on Government Operations of the United States Senate, 91st Congress, 1st Session 22–23 (1969). See also the statement in *Pravda* of April 7, 1969: "Socialism and sovereignty are indivisible. Marxists–Leninists believe that when a threat arises to the revolutionary achievements of a people in any country, and thereby to its sovereignty as a socialist country ... then the socialist States' international duty is to do everything to suppress this threat" (*ibid.*, p. 8).

[3] Article 2, paragraph 4.

[4] See also the third paragraph of the declaration in which the parties pledge to "seek to promote conditions in which all countries will live in peace and security and will not be subject to outside interference in their

Accordingly, the Soviet Union seems to have renounced the Brezhnev Doctrine – the more so since it is altogether incompatible with the "sovereign equality" of one socialist (or any other kind of) State, such as Czechoslovakia, with another, such as the Soviet Union.

At the same time, Moscow may with equal reason treat this declaration as a renunciation by the United States of the Monroe Doctrine. However, the Monroe Doctrine has in any event long been superseded by the Charter of the Organization of American States, not to speak of the United Nations Charter. But, if the "aspiration" Dr. Kissinger voiced in Moscow that both parties will live up to the declaration is realized, presumably the United States will refrain from future interventions, Dominican Republic style. It may be that the Moscow declaration has accordingly been appreciatively read not only in Yugoslavia and Romania but in various Latin American capitals. To the people of Czechoslovakia, it must appear to be another heartbreaking manifestation of Great Power cynicism.

The Moscow declaration would have been startling in another respect, had it not been anticipated by the communiqué issued in Peking. As did the Peking communiqué, so does the Moscow declaration assert that there is no alternative to conducting mutual relations "on the basis of peaceful co-existence." It declares that: "Differences in ideology and in the social systems of the USA and the USSR are not obstacles to the bilateral development of normal relations based on the principles of sovereignty, equality, non-interference in internal affairs and mutual advantage."[5]

This seems harmless enough, until one recalls that, for years, and until President Nixon's Peking journey, the Government of the United States fled from endorsement of the term and the principles of "peaceful co-existence." Why? Not because the term and the principles of themselves are objectionable – in fact, they neither consequentially add to nor detract from the United Nations Charter – but because the Soviet Union had regularly, emphatically, and propagandistically given to these words a special meaning. A few quotations from official and authoritative Soviet sources may be, as Mr. Gromyko is fond of putting it, "instructive."

Peaceful coexistence, while debarring "the unleashing of a thermo-nuclear world war,"[6] is "an integral part of the revolutionary struggle against

internal affairs." "Basic Principles of Mutual Relations between the United States of America and the Union of Soviet Socialist Republics," cited note 1 above, see *American Journal of International Law* (1972), 66, p. 921.

[5] *Ibid.*

[6] *Pravda* Editorial Article of November 1, 1964, on Soviet Goals and Policies quoted in Ramundo, *Peaceful Co-existence, International Law in the Building of Communism* (1967), p. 112.

imperialism."[7] Thus, "Revolutionary national-liberation wars, like class struggle in any capitalist country, do not clash with coexistence and can be brought to success only under peaceful coexistence."[8]

As Brezhnev himself put it at the Twenty-Third Congress of the Communist Party in 1966: "There can be no peaceful coexistence where matters concern the internal processes of the class and national liberation struggle in the capitalist countries or in colonies. Peaceful coexistence is not applicable to the relations between oppressors and oppressed, between colonialists and the victims of colonial oppression."[9]

In view of statements such as these, the United States and the majority of other Members steadfastly refused in the United Nations to agree to Soviet attempts to codify the principles of peaceful coexistence as being equivalent to the fundamental principles of the United Nations Charter. And, in view of statements such as these, one cannot help but wonder why the President of the United States and his advisers have decided that, in this respect, the US Government and so many other Governments were so wrong for so many years. It may be that embracing the principles of peaceful coexistence really does add to the very great achievements of the President's summitry, but, if so, it would be instructive to find out how.

---

[7] Open Letter of the Central Committee of the Communist Party, quoted in Ramundo, *Peaceful Co-existence*, at 113.

[8] "Lenin's Behest: Peaceful Co-existence," *International Affairs* (1962), 4, as quoted in Ramundo, *Peaceful Co-existence*, at 116.

[9] Quoted in Ramundo, *Peaceful Co-existence*, at 116.

33

Aggression, Intervention, and Self-Defense in Modern International law

ℭℑ

I

Introduction

These lectures will deal with the problems of aggression, intervention, and self-defense in modern international law in the context of the question of defining aggression. In the course of analyzing the definition of aggression, aspects of intervention and of self-defense will necessarily be considered.

The use of armed force in international relations is probably the most profound of the problems which confront mankind. Accordingly, the question of what uses of force are aggressive inevitably is of paramount importance. This is recognized on all sides. Yet the possibility, the desirability, the practicality, the efficacy, of defining aggression has provoked and provokes extreme controversy.

The problem of the definition of aggression goes back at least to 1923. The arguments then advanced in the early days of the League of Nations have continued to recur in United Nations debates as recently as March 1972. However, the same States have not always made the same arguments. The principal proponent of a definition of aggression over the years has been the Soviet Union – a fact which, for more than one reason, has not promoted the adoption of a definition. But, at times (as in 1923 and 1945), representatives of the Soviet Government have opposed adoption of any definition. The principal opponents of a definition of aggression over the years have been the United Kingdom and the United States. But, in 1945, at the Nuremberg Trials, the United States favored adopting a definition, and, in 1968, it took an unenthusiastic lead, together with the United Kingdom and four other States, in advancing a definition in the United Nations.

Lectures at The Hague Academy of International Law; first published in *Receuil des Cours – 1972 II* (1973), 136. Leiden, A. W. Sijthoff.

In these many years of recurrent efforts, repeated attempts to reach general agreement on a definition of aggression have failed. That is to say, no definition has as yet attracted the wide acceptance of the world community. However, the United Nations today appears closer to a generally accepted definition than it or the League of Nations ever was. It is especially notable that, at this juncture, nearly all States have officially declared themselves in favor of some definition or, at any rate, in favor of the principle of a definition. There is a great difference between the principle of a definition and the principles of a definition. And some States clearly see greater virtue in having a definition than others do. Nevertheless, this agreement in principle is a strikingly new development of the last four years.

Can Aggression Be Defined?

Aggression can of course be defined. The question is not whether a definition is possible, but whether a definition is desirable. A number of definitions have been submitted to League and United Nations organs over the years. Some definitions have been adopted in transient treaties to which a restricted number of States are or were parties. So clearly a definition can be devised which is or was acceptable to at least some States. And it is not impossible that, within the next year or two, the United Nations may actually succeed in adopting a definition acceptable to the community of States. But if it does, it would remain to be seen how valuable such a definition would really be.

Yet it should be noted that at times certain States, international organs, and distinguished scholars have maintained that a definition of aggression is not possible. Thus the League of Nations Permanent Advisory Commission held in 1923 that, under the conditions of modern warfare, "it would seem impossible to decide, even in theory, what constitutes a case of aggression."[1] As a successor League body more moderately put it:

> The real act of aggression may lie not so much in orders given to its troops by one of the parties as in the attitude which it adopts in the negotiations concerning the subjects of dispute. Indeed, it might be that the real aggression lies in the political policy pursued by one of the parties toward the other ... It is clear, therefore, that no simple definition of aggression can be drawn up, and that no simple test of when an act of aggression has actually taken place can be devised. It is therefore clearly necessary to leave the Council [of the League] complete discretion in the matter, merely indicating that ... various factors ... may provide the elements of a just decision.[2]

[1] As quoted in the *Yearbook of the International Law Commission of the United Nations* (1951), 3, p. 61.
[2] Report of the Special Committee of the League of Nations Temporary Mixed Commission, as quoted *ibid*, p. 64.

At the San Francisco Conference on International Organization, the drafters of the United Nations Charter similarly declined to define aggression. They rejected a proposal to include in the Charter a list of eventualities – of acts of aggression – in response to which action by the Security Council would have been automatic, a proposal which was to have been coupled with acknowledgment of the Council's residual power to determine other cases in which it should intervene. The majority decided that a preliminary definition of aggression went beyond the possibilities of the San Francisco Conference and the purposes of the Charter. "The progress of the technique of modern warfare," it was concluded, "renders very difficult the definition of all cases of aggression ... the list of such cases being necessarily incomplete, the Council would have a tendency to consider of less importance the acts not mentioned therein; these omissions would encourage the aggressor to distort the definition or might delay action by the Council. Furthermore, in the other cases [which were] listed, automatic action by the Council might bring about a premature application of enforcement measures." Accordingly, the Committee of the San Francisco Conference concerned "decided ... to leave to the Security Council the entire decision as to what constitutes a threat to the peace, breach of the peace, or an act of aggression."[3] This decision was in accord with the Dumbarton Oaks proposals of the United States, the United Kingdom, the Soviet Union, and China, and was accepted by the Conference as a whole.

Nevertheless, in 1950, the Soviet Union proposed to the United Nations that it adopt a definition of aggression. That proposal was referred to the International Law Commission. It in turn appointed a distinguished rapporteur, Mr. Spiropoulos. He submitted a report which concluded that aggression is a "natural notion," a "concept *per se*, which is inherent to any human mind and which, as a *primary notion*, is not *susceptible of definition*."[4]

There were, to be sure, objective criteria of aggression. One was violence; another was complicity in violence. But, Mr. Spiropoulos held:

> As regards both direct and indirect aggression, it cannot be said in advance what *degree* of violence or complicity must exist in order that one may consider itself (sic) in the presence of "aggression under international law". An answer to this question can only be given in each concrete case in conjunction with *all* constitutive elements of the concept of aggression.[5]

A second objective criterion of aggression, Mr. Spiropoulos submitted, was which party acted first. But he added – turning to a subjective criterion –

---

[3] *Documents of the United Nations Conference on International Organization*, 1945, Vol. 12, p. 505.
[4] *Yearbook of the International Law Commission of the United Nations* (1951), 2, p. 68.
[5] *Ibid.*

the mere fact that a State acted first does not, *per se*, constitute aggression as long as its behavior was not due to an aggressive intention. In the light of considerations such as these, Mr. Spiropoulos concluded that "the notion of aggression is a notion *per se*" which, "by its very essence, is not susceptible of definition."[6]

The Undesirability of a Definition of Aggression

Others have held that a definition, if not impossible, is certainly undesirable, perhaps even dangerous. The reasons advanced over the years, by many States and scholars in various fora, may be summarized as follows:

1. The determination of aggression rests on the facts and motives of the particular case. As Sir Gerald Fitzmaurice, now judge of the International Court of Justice, put it,

   > one and the same act may be aggression or may be the reverse if committed from different motives and in different circumstances ... An enumerated definition could ... do little more than list a number of acts which are fairly obvious cases of *aggression, if committed without adequate justification* ... The whole problem is to determine when certain acts are justified and, therefore, are not aggressive, and when they are not justified, and therefore, are aggressive ... This determination ... cannot be achieved by *a priori* rules laid down in advance.[7]

2. Not much better is a general definition, of which the following is an excellent example:

   > Aggression is the threat or use of force by a State or Government against another State, in any manner, whatever the weapons employed and whether openly or otherwise, for any reason or for any purpose other than individual or collective self-defense or in pursuance of a decision or recommendation by a competent organ of the United Nations.[8]

   This definition, prepared but rejected by the International Law Commission of the United Nations, like other general definitions of aggression, necessarily uses terms which themselves are of uncertain meaning. For

---

[6] *Ibid.*, p. 69. Judge Charles De Visscher maintains: "Aggression, in the present state of international relations, is not a concept that can be enclosed in any legal definition whatever; the finding that it has occurred in any concrete case involves political and military judgments and a subjective weighing of motives that make this in each instance a strictly individual manner." (*Theory and Reality in Public International Law*, 2nd edn [1968] as translated by P.E. Corbett, p. 303). For a similar view, developed fully and brilliantly, see Stone, *Aggression and World Order* (1958), *passim*.

[7] Fitzmaurice, "The Definition of Aggression," *International & Comparative Law Quarterly* (1952), p. 140.

[8] *Yearbook of the United Nations* (1951), p. 833.

example, what is "individual or collective self-defense"? What is "a decision or recommendation by a competent organ of the United Nations"? Concepts such as "self-defense" and "competent organ" of the United Nations are in themselves complex and controversial. Accordingly, such a definition is in need of defining; it provides a solution which is transparent rather than real.

3. Admittedly no definition can be automatic in effect. It is widely assumed that the Security Council would apply a definition in the light of its appreciation of the facts of the particular case. This is now agreed alike by the proponents and opponents of a definition of aggression, though formerly the principal proponents of a definition avidly sought automaticity. But if this is so – if, particularly, the Council is free to add fresh acts *ad hoc* to discount enumerated acts in view of the facts of the case – then what is the use of a definition? For example, if a definition, such as some definitions do, purported to list the acts which, if committed first, are necessarily aggressive, and at the same time permitted the Security Council in particular cases to add other acts as constituting aggression to that list, then could not an aggressive State justify its action on the argument that it was acting in self-defense against the sort of aggressive act which the Security Council could choose to add to the list?[9]

4. Moreover,

> an incomplete list would be extremely dangerous because it would almost inevitably imply that other acts not listed did not constitute aggression. States would thus be encouraged to commit the acts not listed, because, prima facie at any rate, they would not be regarded as acts of aggression. In addition, the existence of an incomplete list would show potential aggressors how to accomplish their aims without actually being branded as aggressors, for they would keep their acts within the precise letter of the definition and then claim that they were technically justified.[10]

5. This last contention is close to maintaining – as did a British Foreign Secretary – that a definition would be a "trap for the innocent" and a "signpost for the guilty."[11] With the definition in view, the cunning aggressor would so arrange things as to avoid the reach of the definition while entrapping its victim in it. The innocent, peace-loving State would tend to fall into the trap. As Sir Gerald Fitzmaurice put it: "Major

---

[9] See Pompe, *Aggressive War: An International Crime* (1953), pp. 91–92, and Blix, *Sovereignty, Aggression and Neutrality* (1970), p. 36.

[10] Sir Gerald Fitzmaurice, as quoted in the *Report by the Secretary-General [of the United Nations on the Question of Defining Aggression]*, General Assembly, *Official Records*: Seventh Session, Annexes, Agenda item 54, United Nations doc. of October 3, 1952, A/2211, p. 57.

[11] Sir Austen Chamberlain to the House of Commons on November 24, 1927, as quoted *ibid.*

aggressors acted from military and political motives and would not be discouraged by a definition of aggression. The Egyptian representative," he said, "thought such a definition would make them reflect by showing them the consequences of their acts. Mr. Fitzmaurice did not think that a possible aggressor would have scruples of that kind; his main concern would be to know whether he had any chance of succeeding, for in case of victory, he would have nothing to fear from the consequences of his acts. The most a definition could do would be to induce him to modify the technique of his aggression so as to appear in the right in public opinion in his country."[12]

6. The lack of definition of aggression had never been felt in the history of the League of Nations or the United Nations, apart, arguably, from what was seen as the need for a definition if an international criminal court having jurisdiction over acts of aggression were to be created. As to the latter point, the International Military Tribunal at Nuremberg had operated successfully without a definition. Absence of a definition had not, for example, prevented the Council of the League from condemning Italian aggression in the Italo–Ethiopian war and Soviet aggression in the Soviet–Finnish war; it had not prevented the United Nations from condemnation of the Democratic Republic of Korea and the People's Republic of China for aggression in the Korean case.

7. There are times when the interests of peace, the cessation of hostilities will not be served by denomination of the aggressor. A definition could introduce an undesirable rigidity and automaticity into the processes of international organization.

Arguments in Favor of a Definition of Aggression

The arguments in favor of a definition are essentially these:

1. States would know what acts are aggressive, and hence unlawful and to be avoided. They accordingly would be less prone to commit aggression.

2. Knowing what aggression is by reason of its having been satisfactorily defined, States would not only not slip into its commission; they also would recognize its commission by others and be able to react accordingly. They would know when they could, and when they could not, act in legitimate self-defense. They would know when they should, and should not, apply sanctions, and to whom.

---

[12] *Official Records of the General Assembly*, Sixth Session, Sixth Committee, 292nd meeting, para. 45, quoted in *ibid*, p. 56.

3. A definition would assist the Security Council in making a determination of aggression; and, in view of it, the Council would be the less likely to excuse an act of aggression on political grounds. If a body such as the Security Council has complete freedom of action in its determination of an act of aggression, it is liable to take arbitrary action, responsive to political rather than legal considerations. A generally accepted definition would provide a measure of security against arbitrary determinations, especially for smaller States.

4. When charges of aggression are made, international public opinion flounders. An agreed definition would assist public appreciation of the facts, and reinforce the law with public understanding.

5. Adoption of a definition would not deprive States of the freedom of appreciation of the merits of a particular situation. No definition acts automatically. There would necessarily be an element of judgment on the part of the Security Council and of States in applying the elements of the definition to the case before it.[13] But a definition would give the Security Council and individual States valuable guidance in reacting appropriately to the international use of armed force.

6. The Nuremberg trials established that those who plan and direct aggressive war are liable to individual, criminal punishment. Yet it is contrary to the general principles of law to try persons – if not to adjudge States – for undefined crimes. If an international criminal court is to be established, if a Code of Offences Against the Peace and Security of Mankind is to be enacted, the crime of aggression must be defined.

Accommodation of Conflicting Views in the United Nations

These conflicting considerations were advanced with much spirit both in the debates of the League of Nations and, until recently, the United Nations. Despite them, however, the United Nations since 1969 has moved within striking distance of agreement upon the terms of a definition of aggression.

The primary reason for this progress – if it be progress – seems to be that both the traditional proponents and opponents of a definition now see less importance in a definition of the type currently proposed than formerly was the case. This perception, in turn, may be rooted largely in agreement that a

---

[13] See Lauterpacht, *Oppenheim's International Law* (1952), 7th edn., Vol. 2, p. 189, note 2, and McDougal and Feliciano, *Law and Minimum World Public Order* (1961), pp. 151–155. See also, for a recent summation of considerations favoring adoption of a definition, Ferencz, "Defining Aggression: Where It Stands and Where It's Going," *American Journal of International Law* (1972), 66, pp. 506–508.

definition will serve merely to guide the Security Council and individual States.

A definition will not be embodied in a treaty. It will be a resolution of the General Assembly of the United Nations, presumably declaratory of international law, but not lawmaking. But apart from its genus, its particular characteristics will be suggestive rather than imperative.

Thus, the three major draft definitions of aggression now before the United Nations Special Committee on the Question of Defining Aggression recognize the supervening powers of the Security Council. The draft proposal of the USSR recalls the Security Council's powers under Article 39 of the Charter, and specifies acts which, if committed first, shall be acts of armed aggression, "without prejudice to the functions and powers of the Security Council."[14] The Thirteen-Power draft of certain small and middle powers likewise recalls Article 39, and also sets out acts which, when committed first, shall constitute acts of aggression, "without prejudice to the powers and duties of the Security Council."[15] And the Six-Power draft definition proposed by Australia, Canada, Italy, Japan, the United Kingdom, and the United States also recalls Article 39, and affirms that "aggression" is a term to be applied by the Security Council "when appropriate" in the exercise of its primary responsibility for the maintenance of international peace and security under Article 24 and its functions under Article 39.[16]

Moreover, the Six-Power draft specifies that, "although the question of whether an act of aggression has been committed must be considered in the light of all the circumstances of each particular case, a generally accepted definition of aggression may nevertheless provide guidance for such consideration."[17] The Thirteen-Power draft considers that, "although the question whether aggression has occurred must be determined in the circumstances of each particular case, it is nevertheless appropriate to facilitate that task by formulating certain principles for such determination."[18] The Soviet draft submits that, "although the question whether an act of aggression has been committed must be considered in the light of all the circumstances in each particular case, it is nevertheless appropriate to formulate basic principles as guidance for such determination."[19]

From these provisions, three points emerge: first, automaticity is abandoned. The idea that a definition will be mechanistically applied to certain acts, and that inevitable conclusions will follow, is gone. The particular circumstances of each case must be brought to bear in determining whether

---

[14] *Report of the Special Committee on the Question of Aggression, General Assembly, Official Records: Twenty-Seventh Session, Supplement No. 19 (A/8719), p. 8.*

[15] *Ibid.*, p. 10.   [16] *Ibid.*, p. 11.   [17] *Ibid.*   [18] *Ibid.*, p. 9.   [19] *Ibid.*, p. 7.

or not there has been an act of aggression. This represents a vital retreat by the principal proponents over the years of a definition of aggression.

Second, it is acknowledged on all sides that, under the régime of the United Nations Charter, it is the Security Council which shall determine the existence of an act of aggression in the light of the particular facts of the case. Inherent in this acknowledgement is the liberty of the Security Council to choose not to make a finding of aggression. The essential discretion of the Security Council is thus recognized. As that discretion is the larger, so is the importance of a definition of aggression the smaller. This too represents a marked retreat from the contentions of the traditional advocates of a definition.

Third, such definition as may be adopted will not bind the Security Council but explicitly serve as "guidance" to it. The Council will be guided but not controlled. This also lessens both the importance and the contentiousness of a definition of aggression.

Depreciation of the Importance of a Definition of Aggression

For those who have doubted the utility of a definition of aggression, this is all to the good. The complexity of a judgment that an act of aggression has occurred hopefully will be met by consideration of all of the circumstances of each particular case. The authority with which the Security Council was endowed at San Francisco to determine an act of aggression will be unimpaired. But, from the viewpoint of advocates of a definition of aggression, it should be recognized that the developments just traced reintroduce much of the element of uncertainty which a definition was supposed to dispel.

It is submitted that, on balance, this depreciation of the paramountcy of a definition of aggression is both the better part of wisdom and of the United Nations Charter. It makes sense to draft a definition which expressly recognizes that, inevitably, the facts of the particular case are critical; that judgment must be applied to the appreciation of those facts, a judgment which can be informed by, but not controlled by, a definition; and that, under the concept of the Charter, it is the Security Council which is primarily entrusted with the exercise of that judgment.

It makes equal sense to draft a definition with its purpose in view, that is to say, to guide the Security Council, rather than to bind a tribunal adjudging the guilt or innocence of an individual charged with a criminal act of aggression. The case for a definition which a tribunal would apply may be much stronger than the case for a definition to be applied by the Security

Council. But it is doubtful that the same definition would serve both purposes.

Importance of a Definition in the League of Nations Context

The importance of the discretionary authority of the Security Council emerges the more clearly when the situation under the Charter is contrasted with that which obtained under the Covenant of the League of Nations.

Under the Covenant of the League, the Members undertook "to respect and preserve as against external aggression the territorial integrity and existing political independence of all Members of the League." Article 10 of the Covenant further provided that: "In case of any such aggression or in case of any threat or danger of such aggression the Council shall advise upon the means by which this obligation" was to have been fulfilled. Article 16 of the Covenant placed a duty upon the individual Members of the League immediately to apply economic sanctions against a State which resorted to war in disregard of its covenants. The decision of the individual Members of the League to apply economic sanctions to the Covenant-breaker was, in principle, not conditional upon any prior decision of the Council of the League. And the Council – which was not charged with the task of determining an act of aggression – was not to decide upon the means of fulfilling the obligation to preserve League Members as against external aggression, but was charged only with advising on those means. It had the authority to recommend but not to decide.

Accordingly, when aggression occurred, the obligation of Members of the League to apply immediate, responsive sanctions arose automatically. Each Member itself carried the burden of deciding whether or not aggression had taken place.

Thus it was thought particularly important that the criteria for determining the legality or illegality of resort to war should not be open to differing legal interpretations.[20] Presumably the Members of the League needed to know what aggression was in order to know when and as against whom they were to apply sanctions.

These considerations were among those which gave the question of the

---

[20] See Blix, *Sovereignty*, pp. 30–31, and Waldock, "The Regulation of the Use of Force by Individual States in International Law," *Recueil des Cours*, 1952–II, pp. 481–484. An excellent survey of the treatment of the question of defining aggression by the League and the United Nations is contained in the previously cited *Report by the Secretary-General [of the United Nations on the Question of Defining Aggression]*, United Nations doc. A/2211. Broms, *The Definition of Aggression in the United Nations* (1968) provides a useful summary and analysis of League and United Nations consideration of the problem through 1968. Another able treatment is found in Brownlie, *International Law and the Use of Force by States* (1963), pp. 66–107, 361–383.

definition of aggression the emphasis it received in the League. Nevertheless, it should be recalled that some Members of the League gave proposals to define aggression an unenthusiastic response which the most negative of United Nations debates has never surpassed. In League days, Great Britain undoubtedly won the highest marks for a persistent and profound lack of enthusiasm for a definition. Yet, in 1923, it was not Britain but the Soviet Union which submitted the following observations on the League's Draft Treaty of Mutual Assistance:

> The Soviet Government denies the possibility of determining in the case of every international conflict which State is the aggressor and which is the victim. There are, of course, cases in which a State attacks another without provocation, and the Soviet Government is prepared, in its conventions with other Governments, to undertake, in particular cases, to oppose attacks of this kind undertaken without due cause. But in the present international situation, it is impossible in most cases to say which party is the aggressor. Neither the entry into foreign territory nor the scale of war preparations can be regarded as satisfactory criteria. Hostilities generally break out after a series of mutual aggressive acts of the most varied character. For example, when the Japanese torpedo boats attacked the Russian Fleet at Port Arthur in 1904, it was clearly an act of aggression from a technical point of view, but, politically speaking, it was an act caused by the aggressive policy of the Czarist Government towards Japan, who, in order to forestall the danger, struck the first blow at her adversary. Nevertheless, Japan cannot be regarded as the victim, as the collision between the two States was not merely the result of the aggressive acts of the Czarist Government but also of the imperialist policy of the Japanese Government towards the peoples of China and Korea.[21]

Indeed, "It may be said that until 1933 there was general acceptance of the concept of flexible criteria of aggression to be evaluated by the body qualified to determine the aggressor; it was in 1933, at the Disarmament Conference, that the concept of a precise definition of aggression excluding the use of force and rejecting the idea of provocation took shape and was put forward. Then, and in subsequent years, it was seen that there was a sharp division of opinion with regard to the two opposing concepts."[22]

Lesser Importance of a Definition in the United Nations

Nevertheless, if the League Covenant admitted such a diversity of view as to the need for a definition of aggression, the Charter of the United Nations presents an *a fortiori* case. This is true for three reasons.

[21] Doc. A/2211, see note 20, p. 26.
[22] The quotation is taken from the foregoing report of the Secretary-General of the United Nations, United Nations doc. A/2211, p. 24.

First, the United Nations Charter does not oblige its Members individually to appraise the actions of other States, to decide for themselves whether such States have committed aggression, and to react. Rather, under the régime of the Charter, this process of decision-making is centralized. Under Article 24, paragraph 1, United Nations Members "confer on the Security Council primary responsibility for the maintenance of international peace and security, and agree that in carrying out its duties under this responsibility the Security Council acts on their behalf." By the terms of Article 25, "The Members of the United Nations agree to accept and carry out the decisions of the Security Council in accordance with the present Charter." Under Article 39, it is the Security Council which shall determine the existence of an act of aggression. Thus, the decision lies with the Council, which may bind all Members of the Organization to act in response to it.

Second, despite the imperative tenor of Article 39 – the Security Council "shall" determine the existence of an act of aggression – it is understood that the Council is free to decide or not to decide upon the existence of an act of aggression. As it was definitively put by the report adopted at the San Francisco Conference, it was resolved to adhere to the text drawn up at Dumbarton Oaks and "to leave to the Council the entire decision as to what constitutes a threat to the peace, a breach of the peace, or an act of aggression."[23] If the Council is accordingly entirely free to decide what constitutes an act of aggression, it necessarily is free to decide whether, in a given case, what has occurred is an act of aggression. This is particularly true in circumstances where the drafters of the Charter refused to incorporate in it a definition of what acts are acts of aggression.

Third, the régime of the United Nations Charter requires a definition of aggression less than arguably did the régime of the League Covenant because the Security Council can determine not only the existence of an act of aggression, but the existence of any threat to the peace or breach of the peace.

As the Legal Adviser of the Swedish Ministry for Foreign Affairs, Hans Blix, has concluded, because of the Security Council's authority to find either (*a*) a threat to the peace or (*b*) a breach of the peace or (*c*) an act of aggression,

> The Security Council is thus, like a policeman, given wide discretion to intervene to restore order. If the situation confronting the Council is deemed by the Council to fall into any of these three categories, it is authorized to make recommendations or to decide upon sanctions. There can hardly be any doubt that the broadest of these categories is a threat to the peace. It encompasses the two others. Thus, if the members of the Council were convinced that a situation constituted a threat to the peace but were divided as to whether it amounted to a breach of the peace or act of

<hr />

[23] *Ibid.*, p. 40.

aggression, no terminological choice would actually be needed, as in either case the Council would be entitled to act. Thus, in order to function, the Council hardly needs any detailed definition of breaches of the peace or acts of aggression. Nor has it, so far, needed any definition of the category threat to the peace, if, indeed, one were at all feasible.[24]

In practice, holdings of aggression by United Nations organs have been very rare. The United Nations typically exerts its efforts towards bringing about a cease-fire once hostilities have erupted. It has not normally found it necessary or helpful to that process to designate the aggressor, if there is one.

Nevertheless, the present state of affairs is that it has been generally agreed, without much passion or conviction, that a satisfactory definition of aggression should provide the Security Council with useful guidance in the performance of its functions. When, as is not unusual, the Security Council fails to perform its functions, because of the exercise of the veto power or otherwise, a definition of aggression should provide the General Assembly and individual Members of the Organization with like guidance. And, in the time before it may be possible or politic for the Security Council to act, a definition of aggression may perhaps provide States with some sense of what acts they may legitimately take in exercise of their inherent right of self-defense. It is not seriously thought that a definition will prevent a State determined to embark on aggression from doing so; there are, indeed, flagrant cases of aggression – such, for example, as those of Hitler – where policies and practices were followed which were meant, and were sometimes proclaimed, to be aggressive.

Perhaps the most compelling reason for a definition of aggression would be its usefulness in criminal prosecutions of those charged with a "war of aggression," which the General Assembly of the United Nations has recently declared constitutes "a crime against the peace, for which there is responsibility under international law."[25]

Establishment of an international criminal court to try offences against the peace and security of mankind under an International Criminal Code has been deferred by the United Nations pending adoption of a definition of

---

[24] Blix, *Sovereignty*, p. 32. In support, see Stone, *Aggression*, pp. 22–23. For a contrasting view, see McDougal and Feliciano, *Public Order*, pp. 155–160. The distinguished authors maintain that the findings of a threat to the peace or breach of the peace also import characterization of coercion as permissible or impermissible. They are of the view that the clarification of "the community policies at stake in this most fundamental of all problems" cannot be escaped by "the replacement of 'aggression' with some other nonemotive words of the same level of abstraction" (at pp. 158, 159).

[25] Declaration on Principles of International Law concerning Friendly Relations and Cooperation among States in accordance with the Charter of the United Nations, General Assembly resolution 2625 (XXV).

aggression[26] – though lack of such a definition is hardly the only barrier to the creation and functioning of such a court.

II

Various Types of Approach to the Definition of Aggression

The history of the endeavor to define aggression has seen various approaches. Those approaches will now be illustrated, but not extensively analyzed, not least because both the literature and the lectures of this Academy have amply set out the history of the problem.[27]

A Procedural Definition

One approach is known as the "procedural" approach: that State is the aggressor which fails to abide by the procedures for peaceful settlement of disputes specified in a treaty. In the days of the League of Nations, this approach had considerable support, to which the terms of the Covenant conduced. The aggressor would be the State which failed to do within prescribed time-limits what the Covenant specified and the League Council recommended. The League Covenant did not designate the Covenant-breaking State expressly as the aggressor. But League Members agreed that they would not resort to war with a Member of the League which complied with an arbitral award or decision of the Permanent Court of International Justice concerning a dispute between Members of the League;[28] they further agreed that they would not go to war with any party to a dispute which complied with the recommendations of the report of the Council of the League.[29]

If any Member of the League resorted to war in disregard of Covenants such as these, it was provided that that should *ipso facto* be deemed an act of war against all other Members of the League, who undertook immediately to apply specified economic sanctions to the Covenant-breaker.[30]

The thrust of all this clearly was to treat the treaty-breaker – the State that

---

[26] See United Nations doc. A/2211; Stone, *Aggression*; Broms, *Definition*; Brownlie, *Use of Force*; Waldock, "Regulation"; Zourek, "La définition de l'agression et le droit international. Développements récents de la question," *Recueil des Cours, 1957–II*, pp. 759–860; and Komarnicki, "La définition de l'agresseur dans le droit international moderne," *Recueil des Cours 1949–II*, pp. 5–110.

[27] See United Nations doc. A/2211; Stone, *Aggression*; Broms, *Definition*; Brownlie, *Use of Force*; Waldock, "Regulation"; Zourek, "La définition de l'agression et le droit international. Développpments récents de la question," *Recueil des Cours, 1957–II*, pp. 759–860; and Komarnicki, "La définition de l'agresseur dans de droit international moderne," *Recueil des Cours 1949–II*, pp. 5–110.

[28] Article 13, paragraph 4.   [29] Article 15, paragraph 6.   [30] Article 16, paragraph 1.

failed to abide by the various procedures set out in the Covenant – as the aggressor. Nevertheless, the League vigorously pursued the question of the substantive definition of aggression. While some States were content with a procedural definition, others were not, one reason being that the procedural and substantive obligations of the Covenant were not watertight. The use of force was not comprehensively regulated; and even resort to war was not absolutely prohibited. The League Council might fail to reach a report which was unanimously agreed to by the members of the Council other than the disputant States, with the result that no report would be adopted. In that case, the Members of the League reserved to themselves the right to take such action as they considered "necessary for the maintenance of right and justice."[31]

The Charter of the United Nations may similarly be said to embody a procedural approach to the definition of aggression, or, rather, the designation of the aggressor.

Article 1, paragraph 1 of the Charter provides that the first purpose of the United Nations is to maintain international peace and security, and, to that end, to take effective collective measures for the suppression of acts of aggression.

Article 2, paragraph 3 provides that all Members shall settle their international disputes by peaceful means in such a manner that international peace and security, and justice, are not endangered. Article 2, paragraph 4 provides that all Members shall refrain in their international relations from the threat or use of force against the territorial integrity or political independence of any State, or in any other manner inconsistent with the purposes of the United Nations. Article 2, paragraph 5 provides that all Members shall give the United Nations every assistance in any action it takes in accordance with the Charter, and shall refrain from giving assistance to any State against which the United Nations is taking preventive or enforcement action.

By the terms of Article 24, the Members confer on the Security Council primary responsibility for the maintenance of international peace and security, and agree that in carrying out its duties under this responsibility the Security Council acts on their behalf. Under Article 25, the Members agree to accept and carry out the decisions of the Security Council in accordance with the Charter. Under Article 33, the parties to any dispute likely to endanger the peace shall seek a solution by various peaceful means; and the Security Council may call upon them to do so. Under Articles 36 and 37, the Security Council may recommend appropriate methods of adjustment or

---

[31] Article 15, paragraphs 6 and 7. See, with regard to a procedural definition of aggression, United Nations doc. A/2211, p. 73.

terms of settlement. Under Article 39, it shall determine the existence of an act of aggression. Furthermore, under Article 40, in order to prevent an aggravation of the situation, the Council may call upon the parties to comply with provisional measures. The Council "shall duly take account of failure to comply with such provisional measures." And the Security Council, pursuant to Articles 41 and 42, may impose economic and military sanctions. The action to carry out the decisions of the Security Council in this sphere shall be taken by all Members of the United Nations or some, as the Council determines; they shall be carried out directly by Members of the United Nations and through agencies of which they are members.

While none of these provisions, standing alone, provides for a procedural definition of aggression, cumulatively they lay the foundation for a procedural determination of aggression. For example, it would not be difficult, as a matter of principle, for the United Nations to resolve that States failing to comply with the provisional measures indicated by the Security Council shall be deemed aggressive.

Probably the closest approach in the United Nations to a procedural definition of aggression is represented by General Assembly resolution 378 (V), entitled, "Duties of States in the event of the outbreak of hostilities," adopted at that notable General Assembly in 1950 when the resolutions on "Uniting for peace"[32] and "Peace through deeds"[33] were also adopted. The resolution merits extended quotation:

> *The General Assembly,*
>
> *Reaffirming* the Principles embodied in the Charter, which require that the force of arms shall not be resorted to except in the common interest, and shall not be used against the territorial integrity or political independence of any State,
>
> *Desiring* to create a further obstacle to the outbreak of war, even after hostilities have started, and to facilitate the cessation of the hostilities by the action of the parties themselves, thus contributing to the peaceful settlement of disputes,
>
> 1. Recommends:
>   (a) That if a State becomes engaged in armed conflict with another State or States, it takes all steps practicable in the circumstances and compatible with the right of self-defence to bring the armed conflict to an end at the earliest possible moment;
>   (b) In particular, that such State shall immediately, and in any case not later than 24 hours after the outbreak of the hostilities, make a public statement wherein it will proclaim its readiness, provided that the States with which it is in conflict will do the same, to discontinue all military operations and withdraw all its military forces which have invaded the territory or territorial water of another State or crossed a demarcation line, either on

---

[32] Resolution 377 (V). [33] Resolution 380 (V).

terms agreed by the parties to the conflict or under conditions to be indicated to the parties by the appropriate organs of the United Nations;

(c) That such State immediately notify the Secretary-General, for communication to the Security Council and to the Members of the United Nations, of the statement made in accordance with the preceding subparagraph and of the circumstances in which the conflict has arisen;

(d) That such State, in its notification to the Secretary-General, invite the appropriate organs of the United Nations to dispatch the Peace Observation Commission to the area in which the conflict has arisen, if the Commission is not already functioning there;

(e) That the conduct of the States concerned in relation to the matters covered by the foregoing recommendations be taken into account in any determination of responsibility for the breach of the peace or act of aggression in the case under consideration and in all other relevant proceedings before the appropriate organs of the United Nations;

2. Determines that the provisions of the present resolution in no way impair the rights and obligations of States under the Charter of the United Nations nor the decisions or recommendations of the Security Council, the General Assembly or any other competent organ of the United Nations.

It should be noted that, by a second section of this same resolution, the General Assembly decided to refer the draft definition of aggression submitted to it in 1950 by the Soviet Union to the International Law Commission.

Subparagraph (e) of this resolution is of particular interest. If a State or States in conflict do not declare their readiness to discontinue military operations and withdraw all their military forces, when their opponents do so declare, then that conduct – according to this recommendation of the General Assembly – shall be "taken into account" in any determination of responsibility for an act of aggression in the case.

While, however, this is an approach towards a procedural definition of aggression, clearly it is not a realization of the concept. For the culpable conduct does not result in a determination of aggression; rather, that conduct shall merely be "taken into account" by appropriate organs of the United Nations. Moreover, the rights and obligations of the Security Council, the General Assembly, or other competent United Nations organs are in no way impaired – that is to say, the Council retains its essential discretion.

More than this, the whole history of United Nations consideration of the question of defining aggression demonstrates that a procedural definition is not deemed to be adequate by the membership at large. And in fact, at the very session of the General Assembly in which the foregoing resolution was adopted, that on "Peace through deeds" also was adopted, a resolution which contains an important substantive definition of elements of aggression.

A General Definition

A second approach is that of the general definition. An exemplar has already been quoted:

> Aggression is the threat or use of force by a State or Government against another State, in any manner, whatever the weapons employed and whether openly or otherwise, for any reason or for any purpose other than individual or collective self-defence or in pursuance of a decision or recommendation by a competent organ of the United Nations.[34]

A definition of this kind has its advantages. It is short if not simple. It wisely limits itself to force – to the threat or use of force. That force may be applied in any manner, indirectly as well as directly. The weapons used are not relevant: "whatever the weapons employed." They may be applied overtly or covertly – a recognition that much aggression, particularly since the rise of modern totalitarianism, is undertaken by secret and subversive means. The threat or use of force constitutes aggression whatever its reason or purpose – an important and contentious point that apparently would eliminate the element of "aggressive intention" from the definition of aggression; any reason or purpose, that is, except (a) individual or collective self-defense or (b) in pursuance of a decision or recommendation by a competent organ of the United Nations.

These exceptions are both broad and, it is submitted, correct. But they pose two salient difficulties. The first is that, in the absence of a definition of individual or collective self-defense or other specifications which have the effect of delimiting the exercise of self-defense, the definition defines little. For, broadly construed, self-defense may permit a very wide range of actions; so wide that a definition which, without more, sets up self-defense as the legitimate use of force which, when otherwise exercised, is aggressive, really adds little to what the United Nations Charter provides. Some would say that this is just as well, on constitutional as well as political grounds. A definition should not vary the Charter or introduce undesirable limitations on the defensive use of force. The draft definitions of aggression now before the United Nations endeavor to deal with this problem in distinctive ways. That which is closest to the foregoing general definition is the Six-Power draft. The farthest is that of the Thirteen Powers. That of the Soviet Union falls in between – distinctions to be elaborated when we turn to these drafts.

The second notable difficulty posed by this general definition is the legitimization of a threat or use of force effected in pursuance of a decision or recommendation by a competent organ of the United Nations. This proviso

---

[34] *Yearbook of the United Nations* (1951), p. 833.

547

clearly is not limited to action by the Security Council. By implication, it embraces the General Assembly as well. This is, of course, a point of high interest, for, in accordance with a clause such as this, the use of force by States against another pursuant to a recommendation of the General Assembly would not be aggressive – a proviso which may be found disquieting by certain States of special unpopularity in this world, because, for example, of racial, colonial, or other policies. In their tradition of support of the General Assembly's residual authority in the sphere of the maintenance of international peace and security, it is the Six Powers, the "West," which reproduce a provision of this kind in their draft definition. Equally true to tradition, the Soviet Union would debar the General Assembly from adopting recommendations in this sphere, and would not exempt from its definition of aggression action taken in pursuance of such recommendations. What is not at all traditional is the fact that the Thirteen-Power draft would jettison the authority of the General Assembly in regard to the maintenance of international peace and security, which otherwise small and middle Powers have largely upheld.

At any rate, the course of United Nations consideration of the question of defining aggression demonstrates that a general definition is not acceptable; most Members want a good deal more.

An Enumerative Definition

Accordingly, in both the League of Nations and the United Nations, enumerative definitions have received more extended consideration.

The most famous of such definitions is that which the Soviet Union submitted to the Disarmament Conference in 1933. It merits extensive quotation:

1. The aggressor in an international conflict shall be considered that State which is the first to take any of the following actions:

    (a) Declaration of war against another State;
    (b) The invasion by its armed forces of the territory of another State without declaration of war;
    (c) Bombarding the territory of another State by its land, naval or air forces or knowingly attacking the naval or air forces of another State;
    (d) The landing in, or introduction within the frontiers of, another State of land, naval or air forces without the permission of the Government of such a State, or the infringement of the conditions of such permission, particularly as regards the duration of sojourn or extension of area;
    (e) The establishment of a naval blockade of the coast or ports of another State.

2. No considerations whatsoever of a political, strategical, or economic nature, including the desire to exploit natural riches or to obtain any sort of advantages or privileges on the territory of another State, no references to considerable

capital investments or other special interests in a given State, or to the alleged absence of certain attributes of State organization in the case of a given country, shall be accepted as justification of aggression as defined in Clause 1.

In particular, justification for attack cannot be based upon:

A. The international situation in a given State, as, for instance:

(a) Political, economic or cultural backwardness of a given country;
(b) Alleged mal-administration;
(c) Possible danger to life or property of foreign residents;
(d) Revolutionary or counter-revolutionary movements, civil war, disorders or strikes;
(e) The establishment or maintenance in any State of any political, economic or social order.

B. Any acts, laws or regulations of a given State, as, for instance:

(a) The infringement of international agreements;
(b) The infringement of the commercial, concessional or other economic rights or interests of a given State or its citizens;
(c) The rupture of diplomatic or economic relations;
(d) Economic or financial boycott;
(e) Repudiation of debts;
(f) Non-admission or limitation of immigration, or restriction of rights or privileges of foreign residents;
(g) The infringement of the privileges of official representatives of other States;
(h) The refusal to allow armed forces transit to the territory of a third State;
(i) Religious or anti-religious measures;
(j) Frontier incidents.

3. In the case of the mobilization or concentration of armed forces to a considerable extent in the vicinity of its frontiers, the State which such activities threaten may have recourse to diplomatic or other means for the peaceful solution of international controversies. It may at the same time take steps of a military nature, analogous to those described above, without, however, crossing the frontier.[35]

The Soviet draft was referred to a Committee under the chairmanship of Mr. Nicolas Politis. That Committee drew up an Act relating to the Definition of the Aggressor, which followed the Soviet draft in substantial measure. Its essential thrust is that the aggressor is the State which first employs force outside its territory. The Politis proposal added to the acts which, when committed first, constitute aggression:

Provision of support to armed bands formed on its territory which have invaded the territory of another State, or refusal, notwithstanding the request of the invaded State, to take in its own territory all the measures in its power to deprive those bands of all assistance or protection.[36]

[35] United Nations doc. A/2211. pp. 34–35.   [36] *Ibid.*, p. 35.

549

And otherwise the Politis report moderated and rearranged the passages of the Soviet draft concerning excuses or justifications for aggression.

Both the Soviet draft of 1933 and the Politis revision are enumerative definitions in a pure form, that is to say, they purport to set out an exhaustive list of the acts which are to be deemed aggressive. That has provoked the criticism referred to earlier, that States with aggression in mind would be tempted to tailor their plans to avoid the proscribed measures and to employ measures which the list imprudently (or designedly) omits. It should be noted that the draft definition of aggression currently submitted by the Soviet Union to the United Nations endeavors to meet this criticism, insofar as it can be met, by including the provision, in operative paragraph 3, that:

> In addition to the acts listed above, other acts by States may be deemed to constitute an act of aggression if in each specific instance they are declared to be such by a decision of the Security Council.

There were and are a good many other objections to a definition of the Soviet–Politis type, a type which advances a precise definition of aggression and rejects the idea of provocation. Since the bulk of those objections related to the draft definition which the Soviet Union now maintains in the United Nations, those criticisms will be reserved for discussion of that draft.

A proper respect for historical fact suggests, however, that one criticism which has been aired in the United Nations – and which has undoubtedly affected the climate of consideration of the question – be mentioned at this point. The Soviet Union in 1933 concluded two conventions, which reproduce almost word for word the Politis definition of aggression, with Afghanistan, Czechoslovakia, Estonia, Finland, Iran, Latvia, Poland, Rumania, Turkey, and Yugoslavia. Of these ten States, five have since been invaded by the Soviet Union; substantial portions of the territory of four of them have been incorporated into the Soviet Union; two have been annexed *in toto* by the USSR and no longer exist as independent States; one has been the object of territorial claims; another has barely escaped dismemberment when Soviet troops overstayed their permission to remain on its territory; another has been subjected at times to serious threats, and there is evidence that the Soviet Union sought to overthrow its Government; indeed, only one of the ten States with which the Soviet Union contracted in 1933 appears to have been spared from the very types of aggression which the Soviet definition interdicted.[37]

---

[37] See in this regard the terms of the resolution of the Assembly of the League of Nations of December 14, 1939, expelling the Soviet Union from the League because of what it denominated Soviet aggression against Finland. The Assembly referred in this connection to the Convention for the Definition of

A Combined Definition

It has been thought that the disadvantages of a general definition and of an enumerative definition, respectively, may be overcome or mitigated by a definition which combines a general with an enumerative definition. The three definitions currently under United Nations consideration are combined definitions. They contain a general statement of what constitutes aggression together with specific illustrations and limitations; and they either expressly or impliedly authorize the Security Council to add other cases of aggression to those specifically enumerated. There appears to be every likelihood that, if agreement on a definition is reached in the United Nations, it will be a combined definition. In that event, since the list of acts it sets out will not be exhaustive, the definition will necessarily not be and will not purport to be conclusive.

Case-Law Definition

A final approach has been denominated a "case-law" definition.[38] That is aggression which the qualified majority of competent international organs designates to be aggression, as, for example, in the cases of the Italian attack on Ethiopia, the Soviet attack on Finland, and the attacks by North Korea and the People's Republic of China on the Republic of Korea and United Nations forces defending it. "With precedent being added to precedent, the underlying concepts should gradually become perceptible, for, as the Rumanian statesman and lawyer, Nicolas Titulesco, stated: 'Every time a State has been declared an aggressor, a definition has been applied and it has been upheld that the facts corresponded to that definition'."[39]

Such an approach is congenial both to the common lawyer and to the international lawyer, related as it is to the processes both of creation of the common law and of customary international law.[40] But a problem with this approach is that it is so infrequently invoked. It is plain that the actual cases of aggression far outrun the enunciation of aggression or the designation of the aggressor by international organs. This is for more than one reason. The international community may well find that restoration of peace will be hindered rather than helped in a given case by an assignment of aggression. Or it may find the facts and the law so mixed, the equities so apportioned or uncertain, that a holding of aggression seems unjustified. Or it may shrink

---

Aggression of July 3, 1933, noting transgression by the USSR of its precise terms. As quoted in United Nations doc. A/2211, p. 38.

[38] See Blix, *Sovereignty*, pp. 35–36.   [39] *Ibid.*, p. 36.

[40] See, in this regard, Hazard, "Why Try Again to Define Aggression?," *American Journal of International Law* (1968), 62, pp. 701–710.

from adjudging a Great Power to be an aggressor, whatever the law and the equities involved. Or a Great Power may arbitrarily exercise its veto on its own behalf or that of an associated State. Or, when international organs do act, they may do so with manifest bias impelled by the threat of invocation of the veto or the action of a mechanical majority, or both. Holdings of aggression have been so rare that the experience of the last fifty-nine years indicates that, if a case-law approach is to be adopted, a definition of aggression will be long deferred. Some would say that, in view of the manner in which the Security Council and the General Assembly have for the most part functioned in recent years, that is just as well.

III

Problems Posed by Current United Nations Drafts

The problems posed by the draft definitions of aggression currently under consideration by the United Nations Special Committee on the Question of Defining Aggression are multiple.[41] The more salient problems will now be considered.

By What Majority Must a Definition Be Adopted?

A preliminary question is, by what kind of majority need the General Assembly adopt a definition for it to have authority in international law, or, more precisely, to render authoritative guidance to the Security Council?

It is assumed in the United Nations that a definition which will emerge, if one does, will be adopted by the General Assembly as a resolution of that body. There are of course alternative ways of proceeding. For example, a text might be adopted by the Special Committee, or, more, the General Assembly, which would be opened for signature and ratification as a treaty. As noted, definitions of aggression have been incorporated in more than one treaty.[42] A treaty would bind only those States which would ratify it; and failing virtually universal acceptance, it would not be an instrument well calculated to furnish authoritative guidance to the Security Council. Or the Security Council – the organ principally concerned – might adopt a resolution containing a definition (perhaps one earlier adopted by the General Assembly).

---

[41] These drafts, which are reproduced in Annex I (pp. 7–12) of the Report of the Special Committee for 1972, *Official Records of the General Assembly: Twenty-seventh Session*, Supplement No. 19 (A/8719), are printed as an annex to this chapter.

[42] See doc. A/2211, pp. 49 ff.

But the modality which appears to be accepted is that of a resolution of the General Assembly which will not make the law but declare it. By what majority need that resolution be adopted?

It might at first blush be thought that a resolution defining aggression would require a vote of two-thirds of the General Assembly for adoption, since Article 18, paragraph 2 of the Charter provides that decisions of the General Assembly on "important questions" shall be made by a two-thirds majority of the Members present and voting, and since "recommendations with respect to the maintenance of international peace and security" – as a definition of aggression would be – are specified as among such important questions. Clearly adoption of a definition of aggression would require no less than a vote of two-thirds. But would such a vote suffice?

It is submitted that it would not. For a resolution defining aggression would not, as noted, make the law, a competence which, generally speaking, the General Assembly lacks. Rather, it would be declaratory of international law: it would state what international law is. This being so, that resolution, to be authoritative, would require essential unanimity of support in the General Assembly, including the support of the Permanent Members of the Security Council.

It has been urged to the contrary in the United Nations that to require essential unanimity is to set up a requirement which the Charter itself does not lay down, and that, to require the support – or, minimally, the abstention from voting – of the five Permanent Members of the Security Council is to extend the veto from matters of security to matters of the progressive development of international law.

While these contentions have their point, it is submitted that the view which is both legally sound and politically viable is that which requires essential unanimity. For what the United Nations is endeavoring to do is to draft a definition of aggression which, when adopted by the General Assembly, will be an authoritative reflection of the views held by the international community as a whole. Since the General Assembly lacks broad lawmaking authority, it can authoritatively act in this sphere – apart from opening a treaty for signature – by a law-declaring resolution. Such a resolution, such a declaration, will have legal weight only if it is accurate. That is to say, if the General Assembly declares that the law is such-and-such because the States of the world, as represented in the General Assembly, in fact recognize the law to be such-and-such, then, as a matter of fact, that representation must be true if that statement of the purported law is to be meaningful. If it is false, the General Assembly stultifies itself.

Thus, in this case, should the General Assembly adopt a resolution which purports to be declaratory of international legal principles, and should, for example, the sponsors of the Six-Power draft vote against that resolution, that resolution would, by definition, be legally crippled. It could not be a correct statement of principles to be taken as guidance by United Nations organs and States. For six States, representing among them a significant portion of the world's power, of economic vitality, political leadership, military strength, and legal tradition, would be saying that the guiding principles are otherwise; that the statement that they are such-and-such is in fact untrue. That would make that statement untrue; it cannot be an authoritative rendering of the pertinent legal principles if that rendering lacks the assent of those States. This would be equally true if the resolution were opposed by other consequential elements of the General Assembly's membership.

Moreover, in this case, the fact that the resolution would be opposed by two Permanent Members of the Security Council would make it an *a fortiori* case. It is simply frivolous to look to a definition of aggression to guide the Security Council above all when certain Permanent Members of the Council make it clear from the outset that they will not take guidance from a resolution which they regard as an erroneous rendering of the pertinent legal principles.[43]

What Effect Will a Definition Have on the Security Council?

Assuming that a definition is adopted by virtual unanimity by the General Assembly, what effect will it have on the Security Council? Will it be binding on the Council or will the Council, by the terms of the definition or otherwise, retain its essential discretion?

It is clear that the draft definitions now before the United Nations Special Committee indicate or assume that the Security Council will retain its essential discretion; the definition is designed to provide guidance rather than direction to the Council and to States. This is well advised, particularly in view of two provisions of the Charter: that of Article 39, providing that the Security Council shall determine the existence of an act of aggression (a proviso which must be read in the light of the discussion at San Francisco on the question of defining aggression); and Article 51, which recognizes the inherent right of individual or collective self-defense of Members until the

---

[43] See the statement of Stephen M. Schwebel, United States Representative to the Special Committee on the Question of Defining Aggression, July 22, 1970, Press Release USIS, Geneva, pp. 10–11. See also, Schwebel, "Law Making in the United Nations," *Federal Law Review* of the Australian National University (1970), Vol. 4, No. 1, pp. 118–119.

Security Council has taken the measures necessary to maintain international peace and security.

It is not possible to predict what effect, if any, a definition of aggression, if adopted, actually will have on the functioning of the Security Council. As has been noted, in practice the Security Council has been responsive to factors other than, or, at any rate, additional to, legal considerations. In particular, whether because of the operation of the veto or otherwise, it has sometimes acted arbitrarily, if not in its very infrequent express enunciations of aggression, then in its more frequent implied designations of the aggressor.

What Acts Shall a Definition of Aggression Embrace?

One of the most contentious areas of debate over the definition of aggression concerns the acts which a definition shall embrace. There appear to be two principal, interwoven problems: is aggression confined to the use of armed force? In any event, does it include the use of such force by indirect as well as direct means? Linked with these questions is the United Nations view of what constitutes unlawful intervention. There is also the lesser problem of whether a definition of aggression shall enumerate certain of its consequences.

Is aggression confined to the use of armed force?

The Charter of the United Nations is understandably preoccupied with the regulation of the use of armed force in international relations. Thus its Preamble recites that the peoples of the United Nations are determined to ensure, by the acceptance of principles and the institution of methods, that "armed force shall not be used, save in the common interest." The first purpose of the United Nations is to maintain international peace and security, and to that end to take effective collective measures for the suppression of acts of aggression. Article 2, paragraph 4 of the Charter governs the threat or use of force in international relations. Article 44 speaks of a Security Council decision "to use force" in terms which make it clear that that term refers to armed force. That provision is found in the Chapter of the Charter concerning action of the Security Council with respect to threats to the peace, breaches of the peace, and acts of aggression. And Article 51 provides that nothing in the Charter shall impair the inherent right of individual or collective self-defense "if an armed attack occurs against a Member of the United Nations." These provisions, and their *travaux préparatoires*, apparently have led the Six Powers to treat aggression under the United Nations Charter as necessarily involving the use of armed force. Other Members, such as Egypt, have at times taken a like approach.[44]

---

[44] United Nations doc. A/2211, p. 74.

The Soviet Union and the Thirteen Powers also now limit their definitions of aggression to armed force, but for other reasons. They view aggression actually as having connotations wider than the use of armed force. But they choose to limit the definitions currently being drafted by the United Nations Special Committee to "armed aggression." They see "armed aggression" as the "most serious and dangerous form of aggression" and accordingly believe it proper to concentrate on its definition at this stage.

This substantially agreed conclusion, even if springing from different roots, has had the effect of putting aside an issue which was debated at an earlier stage of United Nations consideration of the definition of aggression: whether aggression embraces acts other than those involving armed force.

In 1952, Bolivia maintained that a form of aggression was economic aggression. A definition then submitted stated that: "Also to be considered an act of aggression shall be ... unilateral action to deprive a State of economic resources derived from the fair practice of international trade."[45] Some years later, an enactment of another Government denominated the withdrawal by the United States of that Government's option to sell sugar on the United States market at preferential prices to be an act of aggression. Ideological aggression was another form of aggression complained of in the 1952 debates[46] and, on a subsequent occasion, when a Caribbean Government maintained that release of a film of a novel unfavorable to its régime constituted ideological aggression.

The 1952 Report of the Secretary-General on the definition of aggression incisively summarizes criticism of the concept of economic aggression as follows:

> The concept of economic aggression appears particularly liable to extend the concept of aggression almost indefinitely. The acts in question not only do not involve the use of force, but are usually carried out by a State by virtue of its sovereignty or discretionary power. Where there are no commitments a State is free to fix its customs tariffs and to limit or prohibit exports and imports. If it concludes a commercial treaty with another State, superior political, economic and financial strength may of course give it an advantage over the weaker party; but that applies to every treaty, and it is difficult to see how such inequalities, which arise from differences in situation, can be evened out short of changing the

---

[45] United Nations doc. A/2211, p. 74.

[46] *Ibid.* At the San Francisco Conference and subsequently, various States have submitted definitions or attributions of aggression embracing economic aggression, ideological aggression, subversion, inundation with unarmed men, and other phenomena. *Ibid.*, pp. 71–74. General Assembly resolution 2625 (XXV), in interpreting Article 2, paragraph 4 of the Charter, provides: "In accordance with the purposes and principles of the United Nations, States have a duty to refrain from propaganda for wars of aggression."

entire structure of international society and transferring powers inherent in States to international organs.[47]

Yet the scope of what is in effect treated, if not always described, as aggression continues to pose great practical problems. The measures involving the use of force undertaken by the United States Government with the authorization of the Organization of American States in 1962 during the Cuban Missile Crisis were not in response to a use of armed force by the Soviet Union or Cuba. More recently, a State has apparently claimed that the influx of millions of largely unarmed refugees from a neighboring State was tantamount to aggression by the State whose policies forced the refugees to flee.[48] To take another recent example, the Vice-President of the International Court of Justice has denominated the continued presence of South Africa in Namibia "as aggression."[49] It should be added that, were the United Nations to apply a "procedural" definition of aggression, it would then be open to a finding of aggression even where armed force had not come into play.

In any event, though the issue has for the time being been placed aside in United Nations debates, it is by no means a simple one. It has been pointed out by perceptive commentators that the problem is really that of the intensity of coercion mounted by one State against another; and that, while armed force will normally be the most intense form of coercion, and the only form justifying armed response, other forms of coercion, such as economic coercion, could be so intense that, if they were unlawfully applied, they could amount to aggression. They accordingly would justify invocation of the powers of the Security Council to deal with acts of aggression, and might be argued to justify the use of force in self-defense as well.[50] The exceptional use of such responsive force, to be lawful, would have to be "necessary" and "proportional" to the coercion to which it is a response.

What is "intervention" in the view of the United Nations?

Before pursuing the question of whether or not all modalities of the employment of force may constitute aggression, it may at this point be useful to

---

[47] United Nations doc. A/1211, p. 74.

[48] See Tucker, "Reprisals and Self-Defense: The Customary Law," *American Journal of International Law* (1972), Vol. 66, pp. 588–589, and the remarks of the United Kingdom Delegate quoted in United Nations doc. A/2211, p. 72, para. 423.

[49] See the Separate Opinion of Vice-President Ammoun, in the advisory proceedings on *The Legal Consequences for States of the Continued Presence of South Africa in Namibia (South West Africa)*, *ICJ Reports 1971*, pp. 89–95. See also General Assembly resolution A/2372 (XXII) and Security Council resolution 269 (1969): the Council described continued South African occupation of Namibia as "an aggressive encroachment on the authority of the United Nations."

[50] See McDougal and Feliciano, *Public Order*, pp. 194–202; Bowett, *Self-Defence in International Law* (1958), p. 24; Tucker, "Reprisals," pp. 588–589 and 594.

557

consider what the scope of "intervention" is, as seen in the United Nations – if not as practiced, then as preached.

The rhetoric of the United Nations is most fully set out in the General Assembly's "Declaration on the Inadmissibility of Intervention in the Domestic Affairs of States and the Protection of Their Independence and Sovereignty" of 1965.[51] That Declaration expresses the deep concern of the General Assembly at the increasing threat to universal peace "due to armed intervention and other direct or indirect forms of interference threatening the sovereign personality and the political independence of States." It considers "that armed intervention is synonymous with aggression" – an important holding requiring comment. It further considers that "direct intervention, subversion and all forms of indirect intervention ... constitute a violation of the Charter of the United Nations." In the light of these and other considerations, the General Assembly solemnly declared:

1. No State has the right to intervene, directly or indirectly, for any reason whatever, in the internal or external affairs of any other State. Consequently, armed intervention and all other forms of interference or attempted threats against the personality of the State or against its political, economic and cultural elements, are condemned.

2. No State may use or encourage the use of economic, political or any other type of measures to coerce another State in order to obtain from it the subordination of the exercise of its sovereign rights or to secure from it advantages of any kind. Also, no State shall organize, assist, foment, finance, incite or tolerate subversive, terrorist or armed activities directed towards the violent overthrow of the régime of another State, or interfere in civil strife in another State.

3. The use of force to deprive peoples of their national identity constitutes a violation of their inalienable rights and of the principle of non-intervention.

4. The strict observance of these obligations is an essential condition to ensure that nations live together in peace with one another, since the practice of any form of intervention not only violates the spirit and letter of the Charter of the United Nations but also leads to the creation of situations which threaten international peace and security.

---

[51] General Assembly resolution 2131 (XX). This resolution was adopted by the vote of 109 to 0, with 1 abstention (the United Kingdom). In explaining his favorable vote, the representative of the United States characterized the resolution "as a political Declaration with a vital political message, not as a declaration or elaboration of the law governing non-intervention" (*Official Records of the General Assembly*, Twentieth Session, First Committee, Verbatim Record of the 143rd meeting, A/C.1/PV.1422, p. 12). However, much of the substance of resolution 2131 (XX) is repeated in the General Assembly's "Declaration on Principles of International Law concerning Friendly Relations and Co-operation among States in Accordance with the Charter of the United Nations," resolution 2625 (XXV), which was adopted by acclamation and accepted by the General Assembly as declaratory of international law.

Other resolutions of the General Assembly that call for support of insurgents in Southern Africa are difficult to reconcile with resolution 2131 (XX). See, e.g., resolutions 2107 (XX), 2151 (XXI), and 2465 (XXIII). See also the discussion below of resolution 2625 (XXV).

5. Every State has an inalienable right to choose its political, economic, social and cultural systems, without interference in any form by another State.

6. All States shall respect the right of self-determination and independence of peoples and nations, to be freely exercised without any foreign pressure, and with absolute respect for human rights and fundamental freedoms. Consequently, all States shall contribute to the complete elimination of racial discrimination and colonialism in all its forms and manifestations.

The far-reaching character of this interdiction of intervention is clear. Not only is armed intervention condemned as aggression, "all other forms of interference or attempted threats against the personality of the State or against its political, economic and cultural elements" are also condemned, though not as aggression. It may be doubted whether so sweeping an interdiction comports with the realities and current necessities of contemporary international life. Does this mean, for example, that devaluation by one State of its currency is condemned, because that threatens an economic element of another State – and devaluation may certainly threaten the exports of other States?

No State, the Declaration continues, may use any measures to coerce another State to secure advantages of any kind. Does this mean that a State acts unlawfully in severing diplomatic relations with another State in order to exert pressure upon that other State to alter policies offensive to it?

The Declaration further asserts that the practice of "any form of intervention" not only violates the spirit and letter of the Charter of the United Nations but may threaten international peace. Yet it defines intervention in such broad terms that, were those terms to be interpreted literally, it might be wondered if much of customary diplomatic intercourse would remain lawful. As Messrs. McDougal and Feliciano have pointed out, "a certain degree of coercion is inevitable in States' day-to-day interactions for values. Fundamental community policy does not seek to reach and prohibit this coercion" – at any rate, it did not before the adoption of the Assembly's Declaration – "as indeed it cannot without attempting to impose moral perfection, not to mention social stagnation, on humanity."[52]

An attempt to impose moral perfection is precisely what is suggested in the Declaration's assertion that all States shall respect the right of self-determination and independence of peoples and nations "to be freely exercised without any foreign pressure, and with absolute respect for human rights and fundamental freedoms." To obviate "any" foreign pressure is to do a great

---

[52] McDougal and Feliciano, *Public Order*, p. 197. Views of similar substance were advanced by the United Kingdom and the United States at the First Session in Mexico City in 1964 of the United Nations Special Committee on Principles of International Law concerning Friendly Relations and Co-operation among States.

deal, since the mere existence of powerful foreign States may give rise to a degree of pressure upon other States. To speak of "absolute respect" for human rights and fundamental freedoms is to speak of that which exists nowhere; rights and freedoms obviously are necessarily relative, the rights and freedoms of some necessarily affecting those of others, and requiring consequent accommodation.

The appropriate course may be to take these extreme asseverations no more seriously than the Members of the United Nations demonstrate by their actions that they do, while accenting the more plausible elements of the United Nations definition of intervention. The condemnation of subversive, terrorist, or armed activities directed towards the violent overthrow of the régime of another State is sound, as are provisions debarring the use of force to deprive peoples of their national identity and asserting the inalienable right of States to choose their own political, economic, social, and cultural systems, "without interference in any form by another State." That latter provision, of course, has been flagrantly violated since 1965, not least by one of the most articulate proponents of the Declaration.

For purposes of the definition of aggression, in any event, these conclusions emerge:

1. The General Assembly has placed on record that "armed intervention is synonymous with aggression." Presumably, the phrase "armed intervention" is not synonymous with armed attack, but is suggestive of something distinct. The distinct element which the phrase "armed intervention" seems to import is armed and unlawful action within the territory or jurisdiction of another State which does not constitute an armed attack upon that State. History has known a number of cases. What many see as an outstanding example of such armed intervention took place in 1965 in the Dominican Republic, an event which appears to have been a major stimulus to the adoption by the General Assembly of its Declaration.
2. There are other forms of intervention – indeed, perhaps innumerable other forms – which also are unlawful, but which are not "synonymous with aggression." They are not synonymous because they are not armed.

Does aggression embrace the use of armed force by indirect means?
This brings us to what is probably the most vexed issue now before the United Nations in its endeavor to define aggression: does a sound definition of aggression necessarily embrace the use of armed force by indirect means?

The use of force by indirect means is to be distinguished from forms of aggression or alleged aggression not involving the use of armed force, such as economic or ideological aggression. "The characteristic of indirect aggression appears to be that the aggressor State, without itself committing hostile acts as a State, operates through third parties who are either foreigners or nationals seemingly acting on their own initiative."[53] A distinct if often allied concept is covert, as contrasted with overt, armed aggression. This is aggression directly carried out by the aggressor by acts which are concealed – for example, invasion of another State by the aggressor's troops who do not wear uniforms and who infiltrate over the border rather than publicly drive across it.

The draft definitions of aggression now before the United Nations divide sharply over the issues of the treatment to be given to indirect aggression and the response which may lawfully be made to it.

The Soviet draft and the Six-Power draft both interdict indirect aggression. The Soviet draft describes "armed aggression" as "the most serious and dangerous form of aggression" – importing its support of the concept that there are forms of aggression in addition to armed aggression – and would confine a definition at this stage to armed aggression; and it proceeds to define "Armed aggression (direct or indirect)." Among the enumerations of acts of armed aggression which the Soviet draft definition sets out is: "The use by a State of armed force by sending armed bands, mercenaries, terrorists or saboteurs to the territory of another State and engagement in other forms of subversive activity involving the use of armed force with the aim of promoting an internal upheaval in another State or a reversal of policy in favor of the aggressor." This, the Soviet draft specifies, "shall be considered an act of indirect aggression."

The Six-Power draft provides that: "The term 'aggression' is applicable . . . to the use of force in international relations, overt or covert, direct or indirect, by a State against the territorial integrity or political independence of any other State, or in any other manner inconsistent with the purposes of the United Nations." It specifies that the use of force which "may" constitute aggression includes the foregoing uses effected by such means as:

(6) Organizing, supporting or directing armed bands or irregular or volunteer forces that make incursions or infiltrate into another State;

(7) Organizing, supporting or directing violent civil strife or acts of terrorism in another State; or

(8) Organizing, supporting or directing subversive activities aimed at the violent overthrow of the Government of another State.

[53] The quotation is from the frequently cited *Report of the Secretary-General*, United Nations doc. A/2211, p. 56. Aggression not involving the use of armed force can equally be mounted by indirect as well as direct means. See the discussion in McDougal and Feliciano, *Public Order*, which describes as "indirect aggression" exercises of coercion emphasizing political or ideological instruments, with military instruments "in a muted and background role" (pp. 190 ff.).

In vivid contrast to these two draft definitions, that advanced by the Thirteen Powers takes a very different approach. It initially equates "armed attack" with "armed aggression" and then, like the Soviet draft, states that, at this stage, it is this form of aggression which should be defined. But, unlike the Soviet and Six-Power drafts, the Thirteen-Power draft, in its general clause, does not define aggression to include indirect as well as direct uses of force. It speaks only of "the use of armed force by a State against another State." Its list of acts of aggression is conspicuous by its failure to include acts of force effected by indirect means. And that these omissions are deliberate is confirmed by a separate provision, not included among acts of aggression, specifying:

> 7. When a State is a victim in its own territory of subversive and/or terrorist acts by irregular, volunteer or armed bands organized or supported by another State, it may take all reasonable and adequate steps to safeguard its existence and its institutions, without having recourse to the right of individual or collective self-defence against the other State under Article 51 of the Charter.[54]

That provision is to be read as complementary to an anterior specification that: "The inherent right of individual or collective self-defence of a State can be exercised only in the case of the occurrence of armed attack (armed aggression) by another State."

It is submitted that these provisions of the Thirteen-Power draft have scant basis in the United Nations Charter, in customary international law, in the practice of States, and in the expectations of States. The considerations which lead to these conclusions are several.

A paramount consideration is that the Charter of the United Nations makes no distinction between direct and indirect uses of force.

> The Charter speaks in Article 2, paragraph 4, of "the use of force" in international relations; it does not differentiate among the various kinds of illegal force, ascribing degrees of illegality according to the nature of the techniques of force employed. Articles 1 and 39 of the Charter speak of "aggression"; similarly, they altogether fail to differentiate among kinds of aggressions on the basis of the methods of violence which a particular aggressor may favor. There is simply no provision in the Charter, from start to finish, which suggests that a State can in any way escape or ameliorate the Charter's condemnation of illegal acts of force against another State by a judicious selection of means to its illegal ends.[55]

[54] All quotations of the draft definitions currently before the United Nations are taken from United Nations doc. A/8719, pp. 7–12. For an interpretation of these definitions which appears to find a closer correspondence on indirect aggression between the USSR and the Thirteen Powers than does this writer, see Ferencz, "Defining Aggression," p. 499. See also, Chkhikvadze and Bogdanov, "Who Is Hindering Progress in the Definition of Aggression?," *International Affairs* (October 1971), p. 26.

[55] Statement by John Lawrence Hargrove, United States Representative to the Special Committee on the Question of Defining Aggression, March 25, 1969, Press Release USUN-32 (69), p. 5. See also Broms, *Definitions*, pp. 152–153.

A second consideration is that the history of the last fifty years demonstrates that much of the violence that has afflicted the world has been of the very type which the Thirteen-Power draft would exempt from a definition of aggression: the exercise of force by one State upon another by methods other than open invasion across a frontier by a uniformed army. The most pervasive forms of modern aggression tend to be indirect ones.

A third consideration is that the General Assembly has more than once denominated as aggression the use of force by indirect as well as direct means. Thus, in its resolution entitled "Peace through deeds," the Assembly condemned the intervention of a State in the internal affairs of another State for the purpose of changing its legally established Government by the threat or use of force and solemnly reaffirmed that: "Whatever the weapons used, any aggression, whether committed openly, or by fomenting civil strife in the interest of a foreign Power, or otherwise, is the gravest of crimes against peace and security throughout the world."[56] Again, the General Assembly, in the Declaration on Non-Intervention just discussed, equated armed intervention with aggression, but it did not equate it with armed attack. The import of this distinction arguably is that armed intervention which is other than an armed attack may constitute aggression, just as armed attack may; that is to say, the use of force by indirect means (which armed intervention certainly includes) may be aggressive, just as may be the use of force by direct means. Furthermore, the General Assembly, in its landmark Declaration on Principles of International Law concerning Friendly Relations and Cooperation among States holds, in interpreting Article 2, paragraph 4 of the Charter, that:

> Every State has the duty to refrain from organizing or encouraging the organization of irregular forces or armed bands, including mercenaries, for incursion into the territory of another State.
>
> Every State has the duty to refrain from organizing, instigating, assisting or participating in acts of civil strife or terrorist acts in another State or acquiescing in organized activities within its territory directed towards the commission of such acts, when the acts referred to in the present paragraph involve a threat or use of force.[57]

And, in interpreting the duty of non-intervention, the Assembly in this resolution further held:

> No State or group of States has the right to intervene, directly or indirectly, for any reason whatever, in the internal or external affairs of any other State. Consequently, armed intervention and all other forms of interference or

---

[56] Resolution 380 (V).   [57] Resolution 2625 (XXV).

attempted threats against the personality of the State or against its political, economic and cultural elements, are in violation of international law.

No State may use or encourage the use of economic, political or any other type of measures to coerce another State in order to obtain from it the subordination of the exercise of its sovereign rights and to secure from it advantages of any kind. Also, no State shall organize, assist, foment, finance, incite or tolerate subversive, terrorist or armed activities directed towards the violent overthrow of the régime of another State, or interfere in civil strife in another State.[58]

There is no suggestion in this resolution that these acts are less than aggressive, while acts of the same substance and effect, but involving the direct rather than the indirect use of force, are aggressive.

In this regard, it should be recalled that the International Law Commission of the United Nations has taken the position that "a definition of aggression should cover not only force used openly by one State against another, but also indirect forms of aggression such as the fomenting of civil strife by one State in another, the arming by a State of organized bands for offensive purposes directed against another State, and the sending of 'volunteers' to engage in hostilities against another State."[59] The Report of the Secretary-General says of this statement: "It will be noticed that the examples quoted refer to cases involving the complicity of a State in violent activities directed against another State."[60]

It should be noted that the Inter-American Treaty of Reciprocal Assistance provides that:

If the inviolability or the integrity of the territory or the sovereignty or political independence of any American State should be affected by an aggression which is not an armed attack ... the Organ of Consultation shall meet immediately in order to agree on the measures which must be taken in case of aggression to assist the victim of aggression.[61]

The Treaty thus squarely recognized "aggression which is not an armed attack." In view of this provision of a treaty binding upon all of the Latin American States, there is room for puzzlement at the preclusive equation between armed attack and armed aggression which the Thirteen-Power draft definition contains – a definition co-sponsored by a number of States of South and Central America.

As noted earlier, the General Assembly, including all its American

---

[58] *Ibid.*

[59] As quoted in A/2211, p. 72. The International Law Commission thus recognized that: "Aggression in the modern world is achieved through indirect and concealed uses of force" (Waldock, "Regulation," p. 510).

[60] *Ibid.* See also pp. 63–65 and 71–73.

[61] Article 6 of the Treaty of September 2, 1947, *Treaties and Other International Acts Series (TIAS), p. 1838.*

members, has agreed that armed intervention is synonymous with aggression. Armed intervention, then, is one form of aggression. Another is armed attack, which the Thirteen-Power draft maintains equates with armed aggression. Aggression accordingly embraces at least armed attack and armed intervention. By the terms of the Inter-American Treaty of Reciprocal Assistance, there is a form of aggression "which is not an armed attack." It, presumably, is either armed intervention, or aggression by means not involving armed force, or both. If the Treaty may be understood to refer to armed intervention, it can only reasonably be understood to embrace the use of force by indirect means, since such indirection frequently is a characteristic of armed intervention. And if the Treaty refers to aggression by means not involving use of force – as it may – it surely also refers to aggression involving the use of force by indirect means insofar as it covers armed intervention.

The problem of to what responsive measures of coercion States which are the victims of aggressive uses of force exerted by indirect means may lawfully resort will be discussed at a later point. But it should now be emphasized that a number of influential States have expressed the view that aggression by indirect means presents a greater danger to national and international security these days than does aggression by direct means. Accordingly, a definition which either ignores "indirect aggression" or degrades the measures which may be taken in response to it appears to have little chance of universal acceptance. At the same time, if a definition of aggression is to be confined to the use of armed force (whether by direct or indirect means), it is important that the elements of "indirect aggression" specified actually entail the use of armed force.[62]

Are the legal consequences of aggression to be addressed in a definition?
The Soviet draft definition of aggression provides that: "No territorial gains or special advantages resulting from armed aggression shall be recognized." It further specifies that: "Armed aggression shall be an international crime against peace entailing the political and material responsibility of States and the criminal responsibility of the persons guilty of this crime." The Thirteen-Power draft contains similar provisions.

These specifications of legal consequences flowing from acts of aggression have not met with substantive opposition in United Nations debates. A number of States, however, question their inclusion, on the ground that the consequences of aggression do not logically comprise its definition. In their

---

[62] See in this regard, Pompe, *Aggressive War*, p. 111.

view, the task is to draft a definition of aggression, not to prepare a catalog of the results of aggression which, moreover, emphasizes certain results and excludes others. The latest round of negotiations in the United Nations suggest that a compromise of these views, inclining towards the position of the Soviet Union and the Thirteen Powers, may be found.[63]

IV

Problems Posed by Current United Nations Drafts (continued)

Is the Aggressor the State Which First Commits Specified Acts (the "Principle of Priority")?

The cornerstone of the definition of aggression which Maxim Litvinov submitted on behalf of the Soviet Union to the Disarmament Conference in 1933, of the definition which the Committee chaired by Nicolas Politis drew up that same year, of the definitions submitted to the United Nations at various stages by the USSR and more lately by the Thirteen Powers, is the principle of priority: the aggressor is the State which first employs force outside its territory. Mr. Politis put it this way:

> It is clearly specified that the State which will be recognized as the aggressor is the first State which commits one of the acts of aggression. Thus, if the armed forces of one State invade the territory of another State, the latter State may declare war on the invading State or invade its territory in turn, without itself being regarded as an aggressor. The chronological order of the facts is decisive here.

He added:

> Emphasis should be placed on the word "first". It might very well be that, in the complicated circumstances of an international dispute, there might at one time or another have been committed by either party certain acts coming within the scope of the definition ... The only way of having a clear view in so complicated a situation and so being able to apportion the responsibilities and finally to determine the aggressor was to observe the chronological order of events – namely, to ascertain who had been the first to begin to commit one of the forbidden acts – since, once it was proved that one of the parties had been the first to commit one of those acts, the attitude of the other party would immediately be seen to be that of legitimate defence and, by that fact alone, should be excluded from the concept of aggression.[64]

---

[63] See United Nations doc. A/8719, p. 14; but note also p. 17.
[64] These quotations are found in United Nations doc. A/2211, pp. 60, 75.

Thus, in the Litvinov–Politis concept which finds a somewhat less categorical expression in two draft definitions of aggression currently before the United Nations, the principle of priority is critical. It draws the line between permissible self-defense and prohibited preventive war.[65]

The principle of priority is plausible. It seems reasonable that the State which first uses force should be deemed the aggressor and that the victim of that use should be permitted to act in self-defense. The principle of priority in fact does make sense – when it is applied in a sensible manner. When, however, it is invested with the determinative force with which the Litvinov–Politis approach would invest it, it is a principle which presents profound dangers. These dangers are essentially two. One is the assumption of simplicity in establishing who did what to whom first. The second is the specification of acts which shall, if committed first, be of decisive effect in determining the identity of the aggressor. In both cases, the complexity of international law and life is underestimated.

Consider what is often thought to be the easiest type of case: invasion across a frontier by uniformed armies which drive forward with great force and success. Surely, it might be thought, the essential facts of such a case are not difficult to establish; the State which acted first is plain to see.

Putting aside for the moment questions of justifiable provocation and legitimate apprehension of imminent attack, and concentrating solely on the question, is a major assault across an international frontier easily established, it is instructive to recall the history and the controversy which has surrounded the most notable such instance since World War II.

In the case of the attack upon the Republic of Korea by North Korea in 1950, the Secretary-General of the United Nations and the Security Council were authoritatively informed by a United Nations Commission which happened to be in Korea when hostilities broke out that the attack was in fact launched by North Korea. The rapid advance of North Korean forces southward lent weight to that finding. It was generally accepted by the community of States. Nevertheless, to this day, certain Members of the United Nations maintain officially and vigorously that it was the Republic of Korea which attacked rather than the Republic of Korea which was the victim of attack. The issue is not seriously in doubt, but, if United Nations Observers had not been on the scene, it might well be.

Other examples, such as the entry of forces of the Arab States on to the territory of what had been Palestine in 1948, the penetration of the territory of Arab States by forces of Israel in 1956 and 1967, and the measures taken by

---

[65] See Stone, *Aggression*, p. 70. At pp. 69–72, Stone sweepingly attacks the concept of priority. McDougal and Feliciano take a decidedly less critical view, *Public Order*, pp. 168–171.

forces of India against Pakistani forces in what is now Bangladesh in 1971, are less enlightening in this regard, since all these cases better illustrate the second central problem: that of determining which act is the decisive act determinative of aggression, and which acts are responsive, legitimate acts. But it is submitted that the Korean case is instructive, not least in the circumstance that it is the principal proponent of the principle of priority which refuses to accept the clearest application of that principle that has arisen since World War II.

The genuine difficulties that may arise in applying that principle in cases where the facts are not so clear, and not so authoritatively established by international authority, are obvious. Sir Gerald Fitzmaurice has remarked on one type of case: "When you get a war involving a group of States, you get a chain of events in which it is very difficult to say which action comes first, and vis-à-vis of whom."[66] It may of course be replied that, normally, and in most cases, it is not difficult to establish who attacked first, despite the customary contradictory claims of the parties to the conflict. But, even if this is granted, it hardly supports investing the principle of priority with inexorable and unvarying authority in all cases.

Much more difficult still are the problems inherent in affording decisive effect to certain acts when they are committed first, without regard to the surrounding circumstances. Consider the difficulties of applying the principle of priority in a situation like that of the "blockade" of Berlin in 1948. Would the determinative, first act of aggression have been the blockade itself? The airlift? An attempt by a British armored car to drive through barriers in East Germany? The use of force to frustrate that attempt?

The Soviet observations of 1923 stating that the entry of troops into foreign territory is not a satisfactory criterion of aggression has been quoted above.[67] At that time, a League of Nations Committee elaborated on that theme in these terms:

> The passage of the frontier by the troops of another country does not always mean that the latter country is the aggressor. Particularly in the case of small States, the object of such action may be to establish an initial position which shall be as advantageous as possible for the defending country, and to do so before the adversary has had time to mass his superior forces. A military offensive of as rapid a character as possible may therefore be a means, and perhaps the only means, whereby the weaker party can defend himself against the stronger. It is also conceivable that a small nation might be compelled to make use of its air forces in

---

[66] Fitzmaurice, "Definition of Aggression," p. 140.
[67] It is set out in United Nations doc. A/2211, p. 69.

order to forestall the superior forces of the enemy and take what advantage was possible for such action.[68]

This League Committee thus maintained that, in certain, presumably exceptional, cases, anticipatory self-defense is justified. Support for that viewpoint was voiced by a representative of the United States when he declared:

> The USSR draft resolution ... provided that "that State shall be declared the attacker which first commits" certain acts, one of which was "the carrying out of a deliberate attack on the ships or aircraft" of another State. He wondered whether under that wording the United States of America would have been considered an aggressor if it had received prior notice of the attack on Pearl Harbour and had destroyed the enemy forces entrusted with that operation. Such a definition might require a State to let itself be attacked before it could defend itself.
>
> The USSR draft resolution ... defined the aggressor as the one who was the "first" to commit such actions. In his view that definition was illusory, for the word "first" was not defined, nor were the expressions which followed it. To ask a State to wait so as not to be the "first" to attack might give the enemy a great tactical advantage.[69]

In that same debate, the representative of Belgium replied to the representative of Poland as follows:

> The Polish representative had taken the Belgian delegation to task for having defended an argument which might permit a "preventive" war. But the representative of Poland had actually contended that, when his country was invaded from the east and the west in 1939, it had been the victim of aggression only on the part of Germany; the entry of the Russian armies into Poland had been a "preventive" measure which had saved Poland from being completely occupied by the Nazi troops. There was an obvious contradiction in that argument.[70]

Sir Humphrey Waldock has made a further point: the principle of priority merits the less application when the real probability of collective security effectively assisting the victim of attack is slender.

> The definition [of the USSR] would be a complete "trap for the innocent" until there is much greater certainty that the forces of the international community will instantaneously spring to the aid of a threatened State, if attack occurs. The Emperor of Abyssinia lost important military advantages going to great lengths to avoid being the first to strike against one of the most calculated and obvious aggressions in history.[71]

Moreover, the dangers of the application of the principle of priority are more acute in a nuclear age, when the victim of an attack can be destroyed, or suffer unbearable casualties, at the first strike. With the refinement of the

---

[68] *Ibid.*   [69] *Ibid.*, p. 70.   [70] *Ibid.*   [71] "Regulation," p. 484.

569

complexities of modern warfare, the obsolescence of rigid reliance on the principle of priority is ever greater.[72]

Quite apart from these determinative deficiencies, the principle of priority does not take account of frontier incidents. For example, the current Soviet draft provides that, among the acts which shall be considered an act of armed aggression if committed by a State first is "firing at the territory and population of another State." Presumably, then, when the border guards of an Eastern European State recently pursued a civilian on to the territory of Austria, firing at him and Austrian territory in the process, they were guilty of an act of aggression.

The implausibility of that conclusion might perhaps be met by adding to the criterion of first use of force the factor of aggressive intent. But neither the Soviet nor the Thirteen-Power draft include that factor, a matter to be more fully considered shortly.

Or it might be said that the discretion to be accorded the Security Council would allow it to discount frontier incidents.[73] Implying a *de minimis* clause in the definition might also deal with frontier incidents. Possibilities such as these merit consideration. Nevertheless, the risks of reliance on the principle of priority are further illustrated by the difficulties which it has in grappling with frontier incidents.

The point comes to this, that there is no substitute for judgment in the light of the facts of the case. It is not possible – or at least not always possible – reasonably to confine a determination of aggression "to the occurrence of a precisely defined act, at a particular moment, in insulation from the broader context of the relations of the States concerned."[74]

But that is not to say priority in the performance of certain acts should not be given weight by the Security Council, the General Assembly, and States in exercising the judgment they should bring to bear on the facts of a particular case. The initial commission of an act which is presumptively aggressive is an important circumstance among those circumstances in the light of which, in each particular case, a decision must be made. The principle of priority may be reasonably employed to set up a rebuttable presumption of aggression; it

---

[72] As O'Connell puts it: "In certain situations, to await the launching of a controlled projectile from a potentially hostile contact before exercising the right of self-defence may well be to lose the capacity of self-defence, for whoever employs his weapon first may have a pre-emptive advantage which can prove decisive." (O'Connell, "International Law and Contemporary Naval Operations," *British Year Book of International Law* [1970], p. 25). But see Farer, "Law and War," in Black and Falk (eds.), *The Future of the International Legal Order*, Vol. 3: *Conflict Management* (1971), pp. 30–42, 63–64.

[73] See the *Report of the Special Committee on the Question of Aggression*, United Nations doc. A/8719, p. 15. See also p. 14.

[74] Stone, *Aggression*, p. 71.

may not be reasonably employed to afford a determinative holding of aggression.

This indeed appears to be the direction in which United Nations discussions are moving.[75]

Must There Be Aggressive Intent to Constitute Aggression?

A notable difference in approach among the three draft definitions of aggression currently under consideration by the United Nations is that the Six-Power draft contains the element of "aggressive intent" whereas the Soviet and Thirteen-Power draft definitions do not. Paragraph IV, sub-paragraph A of the Six-Power draft provides that the uses of force which may constitute aggression include, "but are not necessarily limited to," a use of force in international relations by a State against the territorial integrity or political independence of any other State, or in any other manner inconsistent with the purposes of the United Nations, in order to do specified things, including the compendious object of inflicting harm or obtaining concessions of any sort.

The criticisms that have been directed to this provision are multiple. First, it has been claimed that if, in order for there to be a finding of aggression, an intent to realize an aggressive object must be shown, the burden of proof would be placed on the victim; the victim of aggression would have to prove that the apparent aggressor has aggressive intent, and meanwhile it would be helpless. Second, proof of aggressive intention – of that subjective fact – would often be impossible, or very difficult, to establish. Third, it is unthinkable that, if various acts, like the invasion of foreign territory, were committed, intention to commit aggression must also be established if there is to be a finding of aggression; commission of the acts, such as invasion, is enough. A benevolent intent coupled with commission of these acts would not suffice to absolve the actor from a charge of aggression.

The Six Powers have not dismissed this criticism but responded as follows. Under the Charter, the actual or alleged victim of aggression need not wait until the Security Council has established an act of aggression, including the intent of the actor to commit aggression, before it can defend itself; the Charter clearly provides that, until the Security Council has taken the measures necessary to maintain international peace and security, a State may exercise its inherent right of self-defense if an armed attack occurs against it. The claim that proof of objective facts such as invasion is easy and proof of

---

[75] See United Nations doc. 8719, pp. 16, 18, 21 and 22. See also Falk, "Quincy Wright: On Legal Tests of Aggressive War," *American Journal of International Law* (1972), 66, pp. 565–567.

subjective facts such as intent to invade is difficult is open to argument. Proof of objective facts is not necessarily easy; witness contemporary disputes over the most essential facts, such as whose army crossed a border first, or who infiltrated over a border when. Proof of intent may be more difficult still. But in certain cases, such as the invasion of the Republic of Korea, aggressive intent may be presumed from the force and eloquence of the ascertained facts. Equally, there can be cases where absence of intent can be assumed from the known facts. For example, an unarmed missile launched from the territory of State A lands on the territory of its friendly neighbor, State B. Relations between the two States are excellent; the missile carried no warhead; it lands in an uninhabited and unimportant stretch of territory. These are easy cases at the two extremes. But cannot cases in between these extremes occur in which the establishment of aggressive intent would be vital to the establishment of an act of aggression?[76]

The Six Powers further point out that, under the United Nations Charter, an illicit use of force may constitute a threat to the peace or breach of the peace without amounting to aggression. Frontier incidents are a salient illustration of this fact. Such an incident may certainly constitute a breach of the peace but, since it is not normally meant to be aggressive, it is not normally accounted as aggression. Now, if the reference in Article 39 of the Charter to an "act of aggression" is to have any meaning, it cannot be synonymous with a "threat to the peace" or "breach of the peace." In distinguishing between an act of aggression and other illicit uses of force, it is necessary that some identifiable criterion be found. They maintain that the element of intent is the only criterion which has been suggested in the fifty years in which the problem has been considered which offers a basis for making such a distinction. Moreover, if a "war of aggression constitutes a crime against the peace, for which there is responsibility under international law,"[77] it is difficult to divorce that responsibility from aggressive intent. Under the general principles of law recognized by civilized nations, intent and responsibility – at any rate, intent and the criminal responsibility which would attach to individuals – are inextricably tied together.

In the latest round of negotiations, the Six Powers have suggested that it would be sufficient if "due regard" were paid to the factors of intent they list, as well as to which State acted first.[78] It may well be that this suggestion contains the makings of a suitable compromise on these issues.

---

[76] See the statement of the United States Representative of July 22, 1970 (note 43), pp. 7–9.
[77] General Assembly resolution 2625 (XXV).
[78] United Nations doc. A/8719, p. 16.

Is Aggression Confined to States?

A lesser question which has embroiled the United States Special Committee on the Question of Defining Aggression is whether aggression may be perpetrated by, or upon, States alone, or by or upon entities whose statehood is challenged.

The Six-Power draft definition provides: "Any act which would constitute aggression by or against a State likewise constitutes aggression when committed by a State or other political entity delimited by international boundaries or internationally agreed lines of demarcation against any State or other political entity so delimited and not subject to its authority."

Other Members of the Committee have opposed such a provision on the grounds that the United Nations Charter refers to States, not other entities; that only States can be the victims of aggression or, presumably, its perpetrators; and that the importation of the concept of so-called "non-State entities" would be confusing and even dangerous.

However, it should be noted that the Charter speaks of "the suppression of acts of aggression" and of "an act of aggression." It does not specify "acts of aggression by States." When the Charter does speak of a State in this connection, it is of an enemy State in the very special clause which is Article 53. It is of course true that Article 2, paragraph 4 of the Charter provides that "All Members" shall refrain in their international relations from the threat or use of force against the territorial integrity and political independence of "any State." It does not speak of Members and States not recognized to be such – naturally enough. But it would be a pedantic literalism to maintain that, accordingly, an entity whose statehood is disputed is excluded from the reach of Article 2, paragraph 4. In fact, all Members of the United Nations, in a healthy rejection of undue literalism, have read "All Members" to mean "All States" in Article 2, paragraph 4.[79] There is nothing to prevent them, and everything to impel them, to interpret States as embracing entities whose statehood is disputed.

The argument that only States can be the victims or perpetrators of aggression does not withstand analysis. If an entity now situated in Africa, not recognized by any State to be a State, but under a régime actually exercising governmental authority, however unlawfully, were tomorrow to attack one of its African neighbors, would it be said that this cannot be aggression because the aggressor is not a State? If an entity which sought to break away from an African State in the course of its rebellion attacked a neighboring State sympathetic to the cause of the central Government, would it be said

---

[79] See General Assembly resolution 2625 (XXV): "Every State has the duty to refrain in its international relations from the threat or use of force."

573

that that was not aggression because the aggressor was not generally recognized, or recognized by the victim, to be a State? If a State in the Middle East, a Member of the United Nations which is widely recognized as a State, were to attack its neighbors which have not recognized it as a State, would those neighbors be estopped from alleging aggression because of their non-recognition? If a European State part of the territory of a former European State were to attack a neighboring entity which it and most other States do not yet recognize to be a State in pursuance of the so-called "revanchist" ambitions it is alleged to harbor, would it be claimed that the victim has no ground for complaint because it is a "non-State entity"?

It is difficult to see why use of the concept of non-State entities would be confusing. On the contrary, it is clarifying, for it introduces helpful precision. Far from being dangerous, it would rather be dangerous to suggest that entities whose statehood is in dispute are not covered by a definition of aggression. This is vividly demonstrated by the history of the postwar years. The two largest armed conflicts of the time have involved violation of internationally agreed lines of demarcation – and there has been no lack of charges of aggression in those conflicts. Other actual and potential conflicts have involved entities not recognized as States by all concerned, sometimes, by any concerned. To exclude this kind of conflict is to ignore both history and current events.[80]

At the most recent Session of the United Nations Special Committee, it was provisionally agreed by an informal negotiating group that: "In this definition, the term 'State' is used without prejudice to questions of recognition or to whether a State is a member of the United Nations and includes the concept of a 'group of States'."[81] It accordingly appears that the question of non-State entities is one which may be readily resolved.

V

Problems Posed by Current United Nations Drafts (continued)

What Are the Permissible Uses of Force Not Constituting Aggression Under the United Nations Charter?

We come now to the problem which, together with the question of "indirect aggression" to which it is linked, constitutes perhaps the profoundest

[80] See the statement of the United States Representative of July 22, 1970 (note 43), pp. 5–6. See also McDougal and Feliciano, *Public Order*, pp. 220–222. It should be noted that General Assembly resolution 2625 (XXV) provides that States have "the duty to refrain from the threat or use of force to violate international lines of demarcation, such as armistice lines."

[81] United Nations doc. A/8719, p. 15.

problem of the definition of aggression: the uses of force which are permissible under the régime of the Charter of the United Nations and which, accordingly, do not constitute aggression.

Three such uses of force are generally agreed – but in such general terms as to subsume vital differences of view. Action by the United Nations in pursuance of its mandate to take effective collective measures for the suppression of acts of aggression; action by regional organizations, under specified conditions; and action in individual and collective self-defence, are universally acknowledged to be legitimate. But there is bitter dispute over which organ or organs of the United Nations may take such measures; under what conditions regional organizations may act; and over the scope of individual and collective self-defense.

Moreover, at least two other uses of force are alleged to be permitted by the Charter, but these allegations have not attracted universal acceptance, even in general terms. One is the claim that "wars of liberation" or "anticolonial" wars are legitimate; the other is the claim that "military aid to a fraternal country to cut short the threat to socialist order" – or democratic order – is legitimate.

These agreed and alleged permissible uses of force will now be considered in turn.

Action by United Nations organs

The Six-Power draft definition provides that: "The use of force in the exercise of the inherent right of individual or collective self-defence, or pursuant to decisions of or authorization by competent United Nations organs or regional organizations consistent with the Charter of the United Nations, does not constitute aggression." This succinct statement provides a useful focus for an analysis of the question of permissible uses of force.

As readily appears, the Six-Power draft does not specify which United Nations organs are "competent." By way of contrast, the draft definition advanced by the Thirteen Powers does: its operative paragraph 2 confines the use of armed force which is not aggressive to individual or collective self-defense "or when undertaken by or under the authority of the Security Council." The draft of the Soviet Union provides that: "Nothing in the foregoing shall prevent the use of armed force in accordance with the Charter of the United Nations, including its use by dependent peoples in order to exercise their inherent right of self-determination in accordance with General Assembly resolution 1514 (XV)." It nevertheless is clear that the Soviet position coincides on this point with that which the Thirteen-Power draft expresses, for that has long been the Soviet view. Indeed a recent Soviet elaboration of its position maintains that: "Only the Security Council has the right to use force on behalf of the United Nations to maintain or restore international peace."[82]

This is not the place to set out the conflicting arguments over the competence of the General Assembly which have raged for so long between the Soviet Union, like-minded, and one or two other States, on the one hand, and the United Nations majority, on the other. It should suffice now to recall that the International Court of Justice, in its advisory proceedings on *Certain Expenses of the United Nations (Article 17, Paragraph 2, of the Charter)*,[83] noted that the responsibility conferred on the Security Council is "primary," not exclusive; that the Charter makes it abundantly clear that the General Assembly also is to be concerned with international peace and security; and that the functions and powers conferred by the Charter on the General Assembly are not confined to discussion, consideration, the initiation of studies, and the making of recommendations. The Court in particular held that the General Assembly is empowered, by means of recommendations to States or the Security Council or both, to organize peacekeeping operations, at the request, or with the consent, of the States concerned. There is a sphere of action under the Charter which is solely within the province of the Security Council, but it is restricted to enforcement action, a phrase which the Court appears to equate with what is stated by the title of Chapter VII of the Charter, namely "Action with respect to threats to the peace, breaches of the peace, and acts of aggression." Only the Security Council may order coercive action, but the General Assembly may make both general and specific recommendations, and take specific as well as general measures, relating to the maintenance and restoration of international peace.

There may be room for questioning whether this opinion of the International Court of Justice upholds the full scope of the authority which the General Assembly's resolution on "Uniting for peace" sought to find in the General Assembly. For by that resolution, the Assembly resolved "that if the Security Council, because of the lack of unanimity of the permanent members, fails to exercise its primary responsibility for the maintenance of international peace and security in any case where there appears to be a threat to the peace, breach of the peace, or act of aggression, the General Assembly shall consider the matter immediately with a view to making appropriate recommendations to Members for collective measures, including in the case of a breach of the peace or act of aggression the use of armed force when

---

[82] *Ibid.*, p. 20.   [83] *ICJ Reports 1962*, p. 151.

necessary, to maintain or restore international peace and security."[84] The Court's opinion is not definitive in this regard; it directly deals with peace-keeping operations, not with coercive operations. Yet it may arguably be open to the construction that, in its view, the General Assembly is restricted to the recommendation of measures which are not coercive -- to measures which are those of "peacekeeping" rather than of "collective security." In any event, the Court indisputably holds that the General Assembly may recommend and take peacekeeping measures, that is, that it may use armed force in international relations in certain ways.

This holding of the Court, and, *a fortiori*, the terms of the General Assembly's resolution on "Uniting for Peace," squarely conflict with a definition of aggression which would limit the use of armed force consonant with the Charter to self-defense and to the authority or action of the Security Council.[85] That the Soviet Union should maintain its traditional position on this issue is no cause for surprise. That thirteen small and middle Powers, many of which on earlier occasions have upheld, both in principle and practice, the authority of the General Assembly in this sphere, should now seek so to cut back the General Assembly's powers, is both puzzling and remarkable.

The failure of the General Assembly to uphold its financial authority in 1964 and 1965 in the crisis over the application of Article 19 of the Charter in large measure resulted from the unwillingness of many small and middle Powers to defend the powers of the Assembly, the only United Nations principal organ in which they are all represented. That failure constituted a grave setback for the cause of international law, of international organization, and of the security of the small and middle Powers who above all require a vital United Nations. In that case, two Great Powers took the lead in asserting the authority of the General Assembly which too many smaller Powers deserted. In the case of the definition of aggression, once again those two Great Powers are found affirming an authority of the General Assembly which a number of (possibly unrepresentative) smaller Powers deny. One may wonder how long these two Great Powers will continue to uphold a position which, whatever its legal and political merits, may present certain dangers for their security interests, if smaller Powers who most benefit by that position demonstrate such inconsistent support for it. At any rate, for the

---

[84] General Assembly resolution 377 (V).

[85] The International Law Commission, in its Draft Code of Offences against the Peace and Security of Mankind, similarly excepted from the definition of aggression the use of armed force "in pursuance of a decision or recommendation by a competent organ of the United Nations" (United Nations doc. A/2211, p. 45).

purposes of the definition of aggression, it is clear that, in the short run, the differences over the authority of the General Assembly which have surfaced in that debate cannot be resolved. They can only be avoided by the use of general language which does not specify which United Nations organs are those entitled to use or authorize the use of force.

Action by regional organizations

The dispute over action by regional organizations presents certain parallels. Again, there is a history of broad construction of the authority of regional organizations in which smaller Powers took a leading role, a number of which, however, in the debates on aggression, now take a narrow construction.

The Six-Power draft would provide for the use of force pursuant to decisions of or authorization by regional organizations consistent with the Charter of the United Nations. This is general language, designed, to be sure, to preserve rather than preclude positions, but designed as well to avoid rather than provoke disputes.

The Thirteen-Power draft is more particular and provocative. "Enforcement action or any use of armed force by regional arrangements or agencies may only be resorted to if there is a decision to that effect by the Security Council acting under Article 53 of the Charter." The Soviet draft prudently says nothing more specific than: "Nothing in the foregoing shall prevent the use of armed force in accordance with the Charter of the United Nations." Insofar as it has felt obliged to particularize, the Soviet Union has proposed: "Enforcement actions under regional arrangements or by regional agencies, consistent with the purposes and principles of the United Nations, may be taken only in accordance with Article 53 of the United Nations."[86]

Article 53 substantially provides: "The Security Council shall, where appropriate, utilize ... regional arrangements or agencies for enforcement action under its authority. But no enforcement action shall be taken under regional arrangements or by regional agencies without the authorization of the Security Council."

The Thirteen-Power draft thus presumes to rewrite Article 53 of the Charter, first by its insertion of the proviso that not only enforcement action but "any use of armed force" by regional agencies is governed by Article 53, and second by its specifying that such expanded uses of force may only be resorted to "if there is a decision to that effect by the Security Council." The purpose of these forthright revisions is clear: to reverse the position ex-

---

[86] United Nations doc. A/8719, p. 21.

pounded by the United States, with the support of the generality of its fellow members of the Organization of American States, that the action authorized by the OAS in the Cuban Missile Crisis was lawful because, among other considerations, (*a*) it was not enforcement action requiring authorization by the Security Council since enforcement action as used in the United Nations Charter and United Nations practice refers to binding, coercive measures while the measures recommended by the OAS in that crisis were not binding; and (*b*) the fact that the Security Council did not enjoin those measures may in any event be interpreted as authorization of them, authorization which can be *post facto* as well as anterior.[87]

There is ample room for difference of view on the validity of these constructions. Once again, however, what is clear is that a definition of aggression does not present a viable vehicle for resolving that difference. If a definition of aggression is to attract universal support, it will necessarily have to bury, rather than exhume and exacerbate, disputes over the extent of the authority of regional organizations and of the Security Council.

Action in individual or collective self-defense

Both the Soviet and the Six-Power drafts deal with individual or collective self-defense in general terms designed to avoid controversy over the scope of these concepts. Such modest elaboration as they have indulged in remains on a plane of generality.[88] The Thirteen-Power draft, however, specifies that: "The inherent right of individual or collective self-defence of a State can be exercised only in case of the occurrence of armed attack (armed aggression) by another State in accordance with Article 51 of the Charter." It further provides that nothing in the provision just quoted "shall be construed as entitling the State exercising a right of individual or collective self-defence . . . to take any measures not reasonably proportionate to the armed attack against it." And it finally prescribes that, "when a State is a victim in its own territory of subversive and/or terrorist acts by irregular volunteer or armed bands organized or supported by another State, it may take all reasonable and adequate steps to safeguard its existence and its institutions, without having recourse to the right of self-defence against the other State under Article 51 of the Charter."

These specifications of the Thirteen-Power draft pose the following critical questions:

[87] See Chayes, "Law and the Quarantine of Cuba," *Foreign Affairs* (1963), 41, p. 550; Chayes, "The Legal Case for US Action on Cuba," *Department of State Bulletin* (1962), 47, p. 763; and Meeker, "Defensive Quarantine and the Law," *American Journal of International Law* (1963), 57, p. 515.

[88] See United Nations doc. A/8719, pp. 20, 19.

May the inherent right of individual or collective self-defense be exercised only when an armed attack has occurred or, on the contrary, is the exercise of anticipatory self-defense in appropriate circumstances lawful?

May the inherent right of individual or collective self-defense be exercised in response to the use of armed force exercised by indirect means as well as direct means?

Must measures taken in self-defense be proportionate to the acts to which they are responsive?

The further question of whether the right of self-defense may be employed against acts of alleged aggression which do not involve the use of armed force will not be considered, in the light of the general assent in the United Nations to consider within the scope of aggression only acts of armed force.

Article 51 of the Charter provides:

> Nothing in the present Charter shall impair the inherent right of individual or collective self-defence if an armed attack occurs against a Member of the United Nations, until the Security Council has taken the measures necessary to maintain international peace and security. Measures taken by Members in the exercise of this right of self-defence shall be immediately reported to the Security Council and shall not in any way affect the authority and responsibility of the Security Council under the present Charter to take at any time such action as it deems necessary in order to maintain or restore international peace and security.

A substantial number of States and a distinguished range of scholars[89] interpret Article 51 to mean that the inherent right of individual or collective self-defense may be exercised under the Charter only "if an armed attack occurs against a Member of the United Nations." Such an interpretation would render anticipatory self-defense unlawful, however imminent and grave the danger of aggression, and that indeed is a professed aim of the Thirteen Powers as well as some other United Nations Members. But other States – who offset those of differing views by weight if not number – interpret Article 51 in another sense, as do other distinguished scholars.[90]

The contentions of those who read Article 51 to preclude preventive action, to preclude anticipatory self-defense, are that the "ordinary meaning" of the phraseology of Article 51 so indicated; that the discussions at San

---

[89] Among them, Kelsen, *The Law of the United Nations* (1950), pp. 269, 787–789; Jessup, *A Modern Law of Nations* (1948), pp. 165–168; Wright, "The Prevention of Aggression," *American Journal of International Law* (1956), 50, p. 529; Pompe, *Aggressive War*, pp. 98, 100; and Brownlie, "The Use of Force in Self-Defence," *British Year Book of International Law* (1961), 27, pp. 232–247, as well as his work earlier cited note 20, pp. 275–278.

[90] Among them, Bowett, *Self-Defence*, pp. 182–199; McDougal and Feliciano, *Public Order*, pp. 231–241; and Waldock, "Regulation," pp. 500–501.

Francisco assumed that any permission for the unilateral use of force would be exceptional, and that accordingly the exception set out in Article 51 should be narrowly construed; that the particular provisions of Article 51 were meant to restrict and did restrict the right of self-defense enjoyed by States under customary international law; and that, if the Charter is to be interpreted effectively, resort to the unilateral use of force must be closely confined.

Those who maintain that Article 51 does not bar anticipatory self-defense respond that, while the "ordinary meaning" of the provision that self-defense may be exercised "if an armed attack occurs" does suggest the sense of "only if" an armed attack occurs, this is not the sole possible or plausible meaning. Article 51 does not in terms say that self-defense may be exercised only if an armed attack occurs;[91] there is room for more than one interpretation of what it does say. Dr. Bowett maintains that the reasoning of those who read Article 51 as debarring anticipatory self-defense is that "because Article 51 says nothing in the Charter forbids or prevents self-defense against an armed attack, it must therefore follow that self-defense is valid only against an armed attack – a complete *non sequitur.*"[92] They point out that anticipatory self-defense was accepted in customary international law, not only in the nineteenth century as exemplified by the *Caroline,*[93] but in the twentieth century when the International Military Tribunal for the Far East held that the Netherlands, being apprised of the imminence of Japanese armed attack, had declared war against Japan in self-defense.[94] Relinquishment or restriction of a right of a State in international law – a right, moreover, described as "inherent" – is not to be presumed; the rights formerly belonging to Member States under customary international law continue except insofar as obligations inconsistent with those rights are assumed under the Charter. At the San Francisco Conference, the Committee which drew up the fundamental relevant norm – that of Article 2, paragraph 4, of the Charter – held that under it "the use of arms in legitimate self-defence remains admitted and unimpaired."[95] The purpose of Article 51 was not to restrict the right of self-defense but to ensure that regional organizations could act in self-defense under the Charter despite the operation of the veto. Moreover, that Article

---

[91] McDougal and Feliciano, *Public Order,* p. 237, note 261. (The distinguished authors also assail "ordinary meaning," as a satisfactory canon of treaty interpretation, at p. 234.) But see Farer, "Law and War"; and Henkin, "Force, Intervention and Neutrality in Contemporary International Law," *Proceedings of the American Society of International Law,* 1963, pp. 150–151, 168–169.

[92] Bowett, *Self-Defence,* p. 188.   [93] Moore, *Digest of International Law* (1906), 7, p. 919.

[94] *Judgment of the International Military Tribunal for the Far East, 1948,* pp. 994–995; McDougal and Feliciano, *Public Order,* pp. 231–232.

[95] United Nations Conference on International Organization, *Documents,* Vol. VI, p. 459.

51 cannot reasonably be interpreted as debarring action against a threat of armed attack is indicated by the terms of Article 2, paragraph 4, which enjoins "the threat or use of force in international relations."

As indicated earlier in quotations which have been given, some Members of the United Nations have maintained that, in certain circumstances, anticipatory self-defense may be justified. It is of interest in this regard to recall that, in 1946, the United Nations Atomic Energy Commission observed that: "In consideration of the problem of violation of the terms of the treaty or convention, it should also be borne in mind that a violation might be of so grave a character as to give rise to the inherent right of self-defence recognized in Article 51."[96] That is to say, it contemplated the exercise of self-defense in the absence of an armed attack. A more pointed and dramatic demonstration of United Nations practice is more recent: the June 1967 War. There Israel (despite initial claims to the contrary) appears initially to have attacked Egypt. The United Nations decisively rejected, both in the Security Council and the General Assembly, the most vigorous efforts to condemn Israel as the aggressor, in circumstances which suggest that many Members saw Israel's action as an exercise of legitimate, anticipatory self-defense.[97]

Perhaps the most compelling argument against reading Article 51 to debar anticipatory self-defense whatever the circumstances is that, in an age of missiles and nuclear weapons, it is an interpretation that does not comport with reality. Since a first strike can inflict appalling and perhaps decisive destruction, a State which is about to be the victim of such an attack cannot be expected to await it before acting in self-defense – if not self-preservation. At the same time, especially in this atomic age, the dangers of the exercise, not to speak of the abuse, of anticipatory self-defense – an exercise which is initially subjective – are profound.[98]

These conflicting views are substantial; there is weight on both sides. It is in any event once again clear that the grave and contentious issues surrounding the legitimacy of anticipatory self-defense will not be settled in the course of the drafting of a definition of aggression. If there is to be a generally agreed

---

[96] As quoted in Bowett, *Self-Defence*, p. 189.

[97] This precedent is complicated by the fact that, before the Israeli attack, President Nasser had proclaimed that passage of Israeli ships would not be permitted through the Straits of Tiran, a proclamation that was widely seen as tantamount to a blockade of Eilat. If the principle of priority in its absolute form were to have been applied in that instance, it would have entitled Israel to treat that blockade as an act of aggression to which it might lawfully respond in self-defence. For a comparison of the distinctive reactions of the United Nations to the 1956 and 1967 attacks upon Egypt, see Farer, "Law and War," pp. 64–66.

[98] See Farer's stimulating analysis, "Law and War" pp. 36–42.

definition, it will have to avoid rather than confront the scope of self-defense in this respect as in others.

Similar considerations apply to the endeavor by the Thirteen Powers to debar action in self-defense by States which are victims of subversive or terrorist acts, or both, by irregular, volunteer, or armed bands organized and supported by another State. The Thirteen Powers apparently do not construe such activities as tantamount to armed attack; they see these acts as acts of indirect rather than direct aggression; accordingly, they maintain that self-defense in response to them is unjustified.

There are two fundamental difficulties with this approach. The first is that it takes a restrictive view of the Charter which the Charter hardly requires. The second is that it conflicts with the requirements of national and international security.

Under the Charter, if armed personnel invade the territory of another State, the right of that State to defend itself does not depend on the obtrusiveness with which the invasion was carried out, or the candor which the aggressor evidenced in acknowledging his responsibility for the invasion. It is legally irrelevant whether the invasion is committed by regulars or irregulars, whether they were volunteers or draftees, whether they were highly organized as armed troops or less organized as armed bands. There is nothing in the Charter which suggests otherwise. The Charter proscribes the threat or use of armed force, without specifying the means by which that force is exerted. Even if, *arguendo*, one construes Article 51 as confining the exercise of self-defense to response to armed attack, subversive or terrorist acts carried out by irregular, volunteer, or armed bands with the organization and support of a foreign State comprehend forms of armed attack.

Moreover, the magnitude of the danger to be defended against has no necessary relationship to the openness or stealth of aggression. As the history of the Charter era painfully illustrates, the most serious threat to national well-being can be mounted by aggression which is not in the form of direct and open armed attack. It was not for nothing that the General Assembly of the United Nations has resolved, in resolution 380 (V), that, "whatever the weapons used, any aggression, whether committed openly, or by fomenting civil strife in the interest of a foreign Power, or otherwise, is the gravest of all crimes against peace and security throughout the world."

The fear that apparently motivates this proposal of the Thirteen Powers is that, if self-defense against indirect or covert measures of force were to be acknowledged as permissible, such self-defense would allow taking of measures which would not be proportionate to those to which they are a response. State A organizes and equips a few hundred irregulars on the territory of State B which invade State C; should State C be entitled to strike with all its air force at the territory of State A? The Thirteen Powers say no, and in this they are right; such a massive air strike would appear to be disproportionate. But it does not follow that State C lawfully cannot take defensive measures against State A. It lawfully can act in self-defense insofar as the customary rules of necessity and proportionality permit.

The Thirteen Powers rightly specify the rule of proportionality to govern response to an armed attack (a phrase whose scope they appear to confine to open and direct attack). They do not indicate why the same rule of proportionality is not sufficient to govern response to the illicit use of armed force which is covert or indirect.[99]

"Wars of liberation" and "anti-colonial wars"

The delicate subject of "wars of liberation" and "anti-colonial wars" is hardly approached in the draft definitions of aggression now under consideration in the United Nations – wisely enough. The only hints are to be found, in the Soviet draft, in the preambular clause that: "The use of force to deprive dependent peoples of the exercise of their inherent right to self-determination ... is contrary to the Charter of the United Nations" and in the final, operative clause, which provides that: "Nothing in the foregoing shall prevent the use of armed force in accordance with the Charter of the United Nations, including its use by dependent peoples in order to exercise their inherent right of self-determination in accordance with General Assembly resolution 1514 (XV)." The Thirteen-Power draft, for its part, guardedly submits, in its final paragraph, that: "None of the preceding paragraphs may be interpreted as limiting the scope of the Charter's provisions concerning the right of peoples to self-determination, sovereignty and territorial integrity." The Six Powers maintain that these provisions are unnecessary, since nothing in their draft, at any rate, does impair the provisions of the Charter which concern the exercise of self-determination. They submit that it is for the authors of the Soviet and Thirteen-Power drafts to say whether, absent the saving clauses their drafts contain, their drafts would impair the principle of self-determination.

The issue is accordingly not very squarely or provocatively posed in the context of defining aggression. It has been confronted somewhat more directly in the General Assembly's "Declaration on Principles of International Law concerning Friendly Relations and Co-operation among States," however; and, of course, views elsewhere have been expressed about "wars of

---

[99] See the statement by the United States Representative of March 25, 1969 (note 55), and McDougal and Feliciano, *Public Order*, pp. 241–244.

liberation" and "anti-colonial" wars which have not attracted like unanimity.

The "Friendly Relations" Declaration is the subject of detailed consideration by two other lecturers at this session of the Academy and accordingly
will not be fully discussed here. But attention should be drawn to the salient
relevant provisions. The Declaration's elaboration of the principle of equal
rights and self-determination of peoples expresses the view that: "Subjection
of peoples to alien subjugation, domination and exploitation . . . is contrary to
the Charter." It provides that: "Every State has the duty to refrain from any
forcible action which deprives peoples . . . of their right to self-determination
and freedom and independence. In their actions against, and resistance to,
such forcible action in pursuit of the exercise of their right to self-determination, such peoples are entitled to seek and to receive support in accordance
with the purposes and principles of the Charter."[100] The Declaration's
elaboration of Article 2, paragraph 4 of the Charter has a provision conforming to the foregoing. That portion of the Declaration concludes: "Nothing in
the foregoing paragraphs shall be construed as enlarging or diminishing in
any way the scope of the provisions of the Charter concerning cases in which
the use of force is lawful."[101]

The Charter does not of course inhibit the right of revolution any more
than does customary international law. Any people, colonial or otherwise,
may revolt without transgressing international law. These provisions of the
"Friendly Relations" Declaration – which the Declaration pronounces to be
principles which "constitute basic principles of international law" – are
accordingly consonant to this extent with the facts of international law and
life. What is a progressive development of international law is the holding
that every State has the duty to refrain from any forcible action which
deprives peoples of their right to self-determination and freedom and
independence. The General Assembly would thereby seem to have held that a
colonial Power, and indeed any State not "possessed of a Government
representing the whole people belonging to the territory without distinction
as to race, creed or colour," may not use force to deprive peoples of freedom
and independence. Presumably, then, it is not lawful for a colonial Power to
suppress anti-colonial revolution. Nor is it legal for a State to take forcible
action against elements of its population set apart by race, religion, or color

---

[100] General Assembly resolution 2625 (XXV).

[101] *Ibid.* It should be noted that some Members of the Special Committee on Principles of International
Law concerning Friendly Relations and Co-operation among States made far more radical proposals
in respect of "self-defence against colonial domination" which were not accepted by the Committee or
the General Assembly.

which deprives such peoples of their freedom and independence – a provision which has occasion for implementation in more than one part of the world.

What is even more controversial and less clear is the provision that, in their actions against and resistance to forcible action by a colonial or non-representative Government, peoples are entitled to seek and receive support in accordance with the purposes and principles of the Charter. This provision appears to derogate, or could be interpreted as derogating, from the traditional rule of international law that foreign States are not entitled to render support to insurgents. That rule is under pervasive attack, both in doctrine and practice.[102] These provisions of the "Friendly Relations" Declaration may make a contribution to its revision.

It is important to note that the Declaration provides that the peoples concerned are entitled to seek and receive support "in accordance with the purposes and principles of the Charter." Those purposes and principles emphasize above all the maintenance of international peace and security and the settlement of disputes by peaceful means in conformity with the principles of justice and international law. It is accordingly submitted that support given by foreign States to insurgents in accordance with the Declaration should not include armed support. This conclusion is reinforced by the Declaration's provision that nothing in it "shall be construed as enlarging or diminishing in any way the scope of the provisions of the Charter concerning cases in which the use of force is lawful."[103]

It will be recalled that the applicability of the Charter's restrictions on the use of force to colonial situations was debated with much vigor in the case of the forcible absorption by India of Goa in 1961. India maintained that colonialism constituted permanent aggression, to which it could lawfully react; Portugal maintained that she had been the sovereign of Goa in the eyes of international law for hundreds of years and remained so. The majority of the Security Council rejected India's claims, but the view of the majority was frustrated by the veto. India continues to hold Goa, a fact which does not seem to be actively contested, or perhaps contested at all, by other States any more, with the possible exception of Portugal.

---

[102] See, for example, Falk (ed.), *The International Law of Civil War* (1971); Falk, "Janus Tormented: the International Law of Internal War," in Rosenau (ed.), *International Aspects of Civil Strife* (1964), pp. 185 ff.; Falk (ed.), *The Vietnam War and International Law*, Vols. I (1968), II (1969) and III (1972); Farer, "Law and War," pp. 42–52, and Franck, "Who Killed Article 2 (4)? Or: Changing Norms Governing the Use of Force by States," *American Journal of International Law* (1970) 64, pp. 809 ff. For an especially useful and balanced survey, see also Higgins, "Internal War and International Law," in Black and Falk, *Future*, pp. 81 ff.

[103] It may be said to be further reinforced by the rejection, in the course of preparing the Declaration, of proposals designed to legitimize armed support of "self-defence against colonial domination."

Whatever the ambiguity of that precedent, it is clear that "wars of liberation" have been invoked to justify sins committed or desired, as, for example, the obviously unlawful measures pursued against Malaysia in 1964. The veto in that case once again stultified the Security Council. Any definition of aggression which can attract universal support cannot give support to so controversial and partisan a doctrine, a doctrine which is so capable of subjective molding to promote particular political ends which may have much, little, or nothing to do with advancement of the purposes and principles of the United Nations Charter.

Military aid responsive to threats to socialist or democratic order
A final alleged exception to Charter norms governing the use of force is what the General Secretary of the Communist Party of the USSR has called "military aid to a fraternal country to cut short the threat to socialist order."[104] Parallels between this claim, asserted shortly after the invasion of Czechoslovakia in 1968 by the Soviet Union and selected members of the Warsaw Pact, and justifications advanced by the United States Government after its intervention in the Dominican Republic in 1965, have been drawn.[105]

Mr. Brezhnev declared that, when forces hostile to socialism seek "to revert the development of any socialist country toward the restoration of capitalist order ... a threat to the security of the socialist community as a whole, emerges" justifying "military aid to a fraternal country to cut short the threat to the socialist order."[106]

This claim of the Soviet Union was of course a claim for a quite special right in world affairs – the right to intervene by force to prevent the people of a "socialist" State from exercising its right of self-determination. Clearly the "Brezhnev Doctrine" has no basis in the United Nations Charter, and cannot, in a definition of aggression, provide anything but an example of aggression.

It is interesting to note that the "Declaration of Basic Principles of Mutual Relations" between the United States and the USSR agreed upon in

---

[104] Speech by Leonid Brezhnev of November 12, 1968, quoted in "Czechoslovakia and the Brezhnev Doctrine," Subcommittee on National Security and International Operations, Committee on Government Operations, United States Senate, 1969, p. 23.

[105] See Franck, "Article 2(4)," pp. 834–835, and Farer, "Law and War," pp. 56–62.

[106] See the extended quotations set out in the source noted in note 22 above, as well as in Schwebel, "The Brezhnev Doctrine Repealed and Peaceful Co-existence Enacted," *American Journal of International Law* (1972), 66, p. 816.

It should be noted that, in the case of the invasion of Czechoslovakia in 1968, the Soviet Union invoked the justification of anticipatory self-defense which otherwise it has regularly denounced.

Moscow on May 29, 1972 by Mr. Brezhnev and President Nixon has this to say about claims of special rights: "The USA and the USSR make no claim for themselves and would not recognize the claims of anyone else to any special rights or advantages in world affairs. They recognize the sovereign equality of all States."[107] If this declaration is to be taken seriously, it constitutes a renunciation of the "Brezhnev Doctrine" – the more so since it is altogether incompatible with the sovereign equality of States. Equally, it constitutes a renunciation by the United States of any special rights of intervention in the Western Hemisphere, as, for example, in application of the Monroe Doctrine or in pursuance of more recent licence for intervention which aspects of the Dominican precedent of 1965 might be thought to afford.

What is more likely is that the Moscow declaration of May 1972 constitutes one more demonstration that there is a profound difference between what States preach and what they practice in respect of the use of force in international relations. Whether a definition of aggression will materially affect that lamentable situation is open to the gravest doubt.

DRAFT PROPOSALS BEFORE THE SPECIAL COMMITTEE

A. Draft proposal submitted by the Union of Soviet Socialist Republics (A/AC.134L.12)

The General Assembly,

Basing itself on the fact that one of the fundamental purposes of the United Nations is to maintain international peace and security and to take effective collective measures for the prevention and removal of threats to the peace, and for the suppression of acts of aggression or other breaches of the peace,

Noting that according to the principles of international law the planning, preparation, initiation or waging of an aggressive war is a most serious international crime,

Bearing in mind that the use of force to deprive dependent peoples of the exercise of their inherent right to self-determination in accordance with General Assembly resolution 1514 (XV) of 14 December 1960 is a denial of fundamental human rights, is contrary to the Charter of the United Nations and hinders the development of cooperation and the establishment of peace throughout the world,

Considering that the use of force by a State to encroach upon the social and political achievements of the peoples of other States is incompatible with the principle of the peaceful coexistence of States with different social systems,

Recalling also that Article 39 of the Charter states that the Security Council shall determine the existence of any threat to the peace, breach of the peace or act of aggression and shall decide what measures shall be taken in accordance with Articles 41 and 42 to maintain or restore international peace and security,

Believing that, although the question whether an act of aggression has been committed must

---

[107] *New York Times*, May 30, 1972, p. 18. In the Declaration, the parties pledge to "seek to promote conditions in which all countries will live in peace and security and will not be subject to outside interference in their internal affairs."

be considered in the light of all the circumstances in each particular case, it is nevertheless appropriate to formulate basic principles as guidance for such determination,

Convinced that the adoption of a definition of aggression would have a restraining influence on a potential aggressor, would simplify the determination of acts of aggression and the implementation of measures to stop them and would also facilitate the rendering of assistance to the victim of aggression and the protection of his lawful rights and interests,

Considering also that armed aggression is the most serious and dangerous form of aggression, being fraught, in the conditions created by the existence of nuclear weapons, with the threat of a new world conflict with all its catastrophic consequences and that this form of aggression should be defined at the present stage,

Declares that:

1. Armed aggression (direct or indirect) is the use by a State, *first*, of armed force against another State contrary to the purposes, principles and provisions of the Charter of the United Nations.

2. In accordance with and without prejudice to the functions and powers of the Security Council:

   A. Declaration of war by one State, *first*, against another State shall be considered an act of armed aggression,

   B. Any of the following acts, if committed by a State *first*, even without a declaration of war, shall be considered an act of armed aggression:

   (*a*) The use of nuclear, bacteriological or chemical weapons or any other weapons of mass destruction;

   (*b*) Bombardment of or firing at the territory and population of another State or an attack on its land, sea or air forces;

   (*c*) Invasion or attack by the armed forces of a State against the territory of another State, military occupation or annexation of the territory of another State or part thereof, or the blockade of coasts or ports.

   C. The use by a State of armed force by sending armed bands, mercenaries, terrorists or saboteurs to the territory of another State and engagement in other forms of subversive activity involving the use of armed force with the aim of promoting an internal upheaval in another State or a reversal of policy in favour of the aggressor shall be considered an act of indirect aggression.

3. In addition to the acts listed above, other acts by States may be deemed to constitute an act of aggression if in each specific instance they are declared to be such by a decision of the Security Council.

4. No territorial gains or special advantages resulting from armed aggression shall be recognized.

5. Armed aggression shall be an international crime against peace entailing the political and material responsibility of States and the criminal responsibility of the persons guilty of this crime.

6. Nothing in the foregoing shall prevent the use of armed force in accordance with the Charter of the United Nations, including its use by dependent peoples in order to exercise their inherent right of self-determination in accordance with General Assembly resolution 1514 (XV).

B. Draft proposal submitted by Colombia, Cyprus, Ecuador, Ghana, Guyana, Haiti, Iran, Madagascar, Mexico, Spain, Uganda, Uruguay and Yugoslavia (A/AC/134/L.16 and Adds. 1 and 2)

The General Assembly,

Basing itself on the fact that one of the fundamental purposes of the United Nations is to maintain international peace and security and to take effective collective measures for the prevention and removal of threats to the peace, and for the suppression of acts of aggression or other breaches of the peace,

Convinced that armed attack (armed aggression) is the most serious and dangerous form of aggression and that it is proper at this stage to proceed to a definition of this form of aggression,

Further convinced that the adoption of a definition of aggression would serve to discourage possible aggressors and would facilitate the determination of acts of aggression,

Bearing in mind also the powers and duties of the Security Council, embodied in Article 39 of the Charter of the United Nations, to determine the existence of any threat to the peace, breach of the peace, or act of aggression, and to decide the measures to be taken in accordance with Articles 41 and 42, to maintain or restore international peace and security,

Considering that, although the question whether aggression has occurred must be determined in the circumstances of each particular case, it is nevertheless appropriate to facilitate that task by formulating certain principles for such determination,

Reaffirming further the duty of States under the Charter of the United Nations to settle their international disputes by pacific methods in order not to endanger international peace, security and justice,

Convinced that no considerations of whatever nature, save as stipulated in operative paragraph 3 hereof, may provide an excuse for the use of force by one State against another State,

Declares that:

1. In the performance of its function to maintain international peace and security, the United Nations only has competence to use force in conformity with the Charter;
2. For the purpose of this definition, aggression is the use of armed force by a State against another State, including its territorial waters or air space, or in any way affecting the territorial integrity, sovereignty or political independence of such State, save under the provisions of paragraph 3 hereof or when undertaken by or under the authority of the Security Council;
3. The inherent right of individual or collective self-defence of a State can be exercised only in case of the occurrence of armed attack (armed aggression) by another State in accordance with Article 51 of the Charter;
4. Enforcement action or any use of armed force by regional arrangements or agencies may only be resorted to if there is decision to that effect by the Security Council acting under Article 53 of the Charter;
5. In accordance with the foregoing and without prejudice to the powers and duties of the Security Council, as provided in the Charter, any of the following acts when committed by a State *first* against another State in violation of the Charter shall constitute acts of aggression:
   (*a*) Declaration of war by one State against another State;
   (*b*) The invasion or attack by the armed forces of a State, against the territories of another State, or any military occupation, however temporary, or any forcible annexation of the territory of another State or part thereof;
   (*c*) Bombardment by the armed forces of a State against the territory of another State, or the use of any weapons, particularly weapons of mass destruction, by a State against the territory of another State;
   (*d*) The blockade of the coasts or ports of a State by the armed forces of another State;
6. Nothing in paragraph 3 above shall be construed as entitling the State exercising a right

of individual or collective self-defence, in accordance with Article 51 of the Charter, to take any measures not reasonably proportionate to the armed attack against it;

7. When a State is a victim in its own territory of subversive and/or terrorist acts by irregular, volunteer or armed bands organized or supported by another State, it may take all reasonable and adequate steps to safeguard its existence and its institutions, without having recourse to the right of individual or collective self-defence against the other State under Article 51 of the Charter;

8. The territory of a State is inviolable and may not be the object, even temporarily, of military occupation or of other measures of force taken by another State on any grounds whatever, and that such territorial acquisitions obtained by force shall not be recognized;

9. Armed aggression, as defined herein, and the acts enumerated above, shall constitute crimes against international peace, giving rise to international responsibility;

10. None of the preceding paragraphs may be interpreted as limiting the scope of the Charter's provisions concerning the right of peoples to self-determination, sovereignty and territorial integrity.

c. Draft proposal submitted by Australia, Canada, Italy, Japan, the United Kingdom of Great Britain and Northern Ireland and the United States of America (A/AC/134/L.17 and Adds. 1 and 2)

The General Assembly,

Conscious that a primary purpose of the United Nations is to maintain international peace and security, and, to that end, to take effective collective measures for the prevention and removal of threats to the peace, and for the suppression of acts of aggression or other breaches of the peace,

Recalling that Article 39 of the Charter of the United Nations provides that the Security Council shall determine the existence of any threat to the peace, breach of the peace, or act of aggression and shall make recommendations, or decide what measures shall be taken in accordance with Articles 41 and 42, to maintain or restore international peace and security,

Reaffirming that all States shall settle their international disputes by peaceful means in such a manner that international peace and security, and justice, are not endangered,

Believing that, although the question of whether an act of aggression has been committed must be considered in the light of all the circumstances of each particular case, a generally accepted definition of aggression may nevertheless provide guidance for such consideration,

Being of the view that such a definition of aggression may accordingly facilitate the processes of the United Nations and encourage States to fulfil in good faith their obligations under the Charter of the United Nations,

Adopts the following definition:

I. Under the Charter of the United Nations, "aggression" is a term to be applied by the Security Council when appropriate in the exercise of its primary responsibility for the maintenance of international peace and security under Article 24 and its functions under Article 39.

II. The term "aggression" is applicable, without prejudice to a finding of threat to the peace or breach of the peace, to the use of force in international relations, overt or covert, direct or indirect, by a State against the territorial integrity or political independence of any other State, or in any other manner inconsistent with the purposes of the United Nations. Any act which would constitute aggression by or against a State likewise constitutes aggression when committed by a State or other

591

political entity delimited by international boundaries or internationally agreed lines of demarcation against any State or other political entity so delimited and not subject to its authority.

III. The use of force in the exercise of the inherent right of individual or collective self-defence, or pursuant to decisions of or authorization by competent United Nations organs or regional organizations consistent with the Charter of the United Nations, does not constitute aggression.

IV. The uses of force which may constitute aggression include, but are not necessarily limited to, a use of force by a State as described in paragraph II

A. In order to:

(1) Diminish the territory or alter the boundaries of another State;

(2) Alter internationally agreed lines of demarcation;

(3) Disrupt or interfere with the conduct of the affairs of another State;

(4) Secure changes in the Government of another State; or

(5) Inflict harm or obtain concessions of any sort;

B. By such means as:

(1) Invasion by its armed forces of territory under the jurisdiction of another State;

(2) Use of its armed forces in another State in violation of the fundamental conditions of permission for their presence, or maintaining them there beyond the termination of permission;

(3) Bombardment by its armed forces of territory under the jurisdiction of another State;

(4) Inflicting physical destruction on another State through the use of other forms of armed force;

(5) Carrying out deliberate attacks on the armed forces, ships or aircraft of another State;

(6) Organizing, supporting or directing armed bands or irregular or volunteer forces that make incursions or infiltrate into another State;

(7) Organizing, supporting or directing violent civil strife or acts of terrorism in another State; or

(8) Organizing, supporting or directing subversive activities aimed at the violent overthrow of the Government of another State.

34

Address and Commentary

ℰℛ

Address

Ambassador and Mrs. Dyess, distinguished guests, it is a pleasure and honour to join in welcoming you to this reception in honour of Grotius and to welcome those who have come together in a Commemorative Colloquium in celebration of the 400th birthday of Grotius.

I wish to join forces with the Ambassador in thanking Dr. Voskuil and his colleagues of the Asser Institute, and the Grotiana Foundation, for their initiative in the organization of the Colloquium. May I also thank their colleagues in the United States who have taken a notable initiative, or series of initiatives, through the medium of the Committee to Commemorate the 400th Birthday of Hugo Grotius. Particular thanks are due to Mrs. Ruth Steinkraus Cohen, Chairman of the United Nations Association of Connecticut, who has taken the lead in the United States in organizing and directing that energetic Committee. We are delighted that she is here, as indeed she should be, and that her most distinguished collaborator in this and a thousand other good causes, Professor Myres McDougal, is with us as well. We genuinely regret that Judge Philip Jessup was not able to join both them and us.

We have heard a number of splendid and learned speeches about Grotius over the last few days, which praise and appraise that great genius and his seminal contributions to international law. I shall accordingly confine these remarks to recalling the influence which Grotius has had in the United States, a topic of special topicality not least because of the place of this reception.

In 1899, at the First Hague Peace Conference, an extraordinary ceremony took place on the Fourth of July.

In Delft, in the church that we have today visited, the whole of the Peace Conference came together for the dedication by the Chairman of the United States Delegation, Ambassador Andrew White, of a wreath in memory of

First published in *International Law and the Grotian Heritage; A Commemorative Colloquium*, T.M.C. Asser Instituut (1985), The Hague, Asser Institute.

Grotius. Ambassador White made a remarkable speech on that occasion. Allow me to quote a few passages from it, for they give an indication of the standing of Grotius in the perceptions of those who took the first modern steps that led, among other things, to the establishment of the World Court and its location in The Hague.

Of The Hague Peace Conference itself, Ambassador White said that: "For the first time in human history there are now assembled delegates with a common purpose, from all nations." That conference, he said, "has for its sole purpose, a further evolution of the principles which Grotius, first of all men, developed thoroughly and stated effectively."

Of Grotius's most notable book, Ambassador White declared that: "Of all works not claiming divine inspiration, that book ... has proved the greatest blessing to humanity" in its promotion of peace and in highlighting the horrors of war. The debt all nations owe to Grotius was particularly great in the United States: "Perhaps in no other country," White said, "has his thought penetrated more deeply and influence more strongly." White proceeded to give concrete examples of Grotius's influence, from Lieber's Code of Conduct for armies in the field, to the absence of reprisals by the United States against the Confederacy. He praised Grotius for elucidating not only what the practice of States was but what it ought to be. The first seeds of arbitration in modern thought were planted by Grotius. Arbitration was a field in which the United States together with Great Britain, had taken the lead, and which was of central concern to The Hague Peace Conference. After all this and a great deal more, Ambassador White on behalf of the people of the United States placed a tribute on Grotius's tomb with the inscription:

> To the Memory of Hugo Grotius
> In Reverence and Gratitude
> From the United States of America
> On the Occasion of the International Peace Conference
> at The Hague
> July 4th 1899

Let me give a second example of the influence of Grotius on American thought and American policies. You will recall that critical juncture in the history of civilization when Great Britain stood alone against Nazi Germany. It was then the declared policy of the Government of the United States to extend to Britain all aid "short of war." At the same time, it was the declared policy of the United States to avoid entry into the war as a belligerent. These policies were declared by some distinguished American international lawyers of the day to be irreconcilable. It was asserted that, for example, international law prohibited the United States from exchanging old destroyers for bases. The then Attorney General of the United States, Robert Jackson, took counsel with a most distinguished international lawyer who later came to serve as a judge of the International Court of Justice, the then Professor H. Lauterpacht. And he produced a speech in justification of the policy of extending all aid short of war to Britain which relied on Grotius.

Attorney General Jackson recalled that it was Henry Adams who complained that Grotius was educated in one century and was living in another. He observed that all of us, even some of our international lawyers, suffer the same dislocation of ideas. "The difference is that Henry Adams recognized it." "Some of our scholarship," Jackson observed, "has not caught up with this century which, by its League of Nations Covenant with sanctions against aggressors, the Kellogg–Briand Pact for renunciation of war … has swept away the nineteenth-century basis for contending that all wars are alike … this adoption in our time of a discriminating attitude towards warring States is really a return to earlier and more healthy precepts." And Jackson cited the earlier distinction between just and unjust wars and the legal duty of States to discriminate against a State engaged in an unjust war – in a war undertaken without a cause recognized by international law. That duty, he said, "was voiced by Grotius, the father of modern international law … There was, in his view, no duty of impartial treatment when one of the belligerents had resorted to war in violation of international law." Writing in 1625, he said: "It is the duty of neutrals to do nothing which may strengthen the side which has the worse cause, or which may impede the motions of him who is carrying on a just war." And from this authority and more modern authorities Jackson built his cogent defense of the American policy of aiding Britain to defeat the most appalling aggressor of our age.

Lauterpacht later came to write one of his characteristically surpassing articles about Grotius, "The Grotian Tradition in International Law," on the 300th anniversary of his death. That article is a model of balance and insight in its appreciation of Grotius. He concludes with a summary of the principal features of the Grotian tradition in international law, which, by way of my conclusion, I would like to quote:

> They are: the subjection of the totality of international relations to the rule of law; the acceptance of the law of nature as an independent source of international law; the affirmation of the social nature of man as the basis of the law of nature; the recognition of the essential identity of States and individuals; the rejection of

reason of State; the distinction between just and unjust war; the doctrine of qualified neutrality; the binding force of promises; the fundamental rights and freedoms of the individual; the idea of peace; and the tradition of idealism and progress.[1]

Lauterpacht added that some of these elements of the Grotian tradition have now become part of positive law; others are still an aspiration. The inspiration to reach for Grotius's aspirations remains with this gathering, and let us hope with others the world over.

Commentary

Professor McDougal, friends: my comment is not directed to the trenchant paper of Professor Röling, but rather to those of earlier distinguished speakers this morning.

I would agree that the Grotian tradition in international law embraces the affirmation of the social nature of man, the subjection of the totality of international relations to the rule of law, and I see Grotius's exposition of idealism and progress as being in the tradition of international law. Distinguished speakers this morning have, I think, summarized those strands of the Grotian tradition in the word "interdependence" which is, in a measure, a reality today and even more an ideal and one to which I think we can all subscribe. But interdependence is a very general term. The question remains, "interdependence on what terms"? Two of our speakers, in their excellent papers, have invoked the New International Economic Order and the Charter of Economic Rights and Duties of States as Grotian examples of progressive development of interdependence. That is where I venture to differ, because I see those documents as very mixed, containing progressive elements, but regressive elements as well. The resolutions on the New International Economic Order were forced through the General Assembly in a lamentable atmosphere. They were not negotiated solutions but a partisan set of demands. Some forty States at once rose to express their reservations to resolutions which contain elements which, in my submission, are not acceptable. For example, their endorsement of cartels and condemnation of efforts of States to resist cartels is, in my view, unacceptable if the New International Economic Order is to be viewed as anything more than a one-sided "wishlist." As for the Charter of Economic Rights and Duties of States, it is not international law, and happily so, for in some respects it is sound, but in other respects, quite nationalistic and unsound. I subscribe to interdependence no

---

[1] H. Lauterpacht, "The Grotian Tradition in International Law," *British Year Book of International Law* (1947), 23, p. 51.

less than others but suggest that its content must be scrutinized and that uncritical invocations of the New International Economic Order, the Charter of Economic Rights and Duties of States and so on, are open to attack even when cast in Grotian terms.

35

The Compliance Process and the Future of International Law

☙

The subject allotted to me by the convokers of this convocation is as difficult a subject as is known to the indisciplines of international law and relations. If the US dollar had not so depreciated, it might be termed "the sixty-four dollar question." Or, to sustain the materialistic metaphor which characterizes our society, compliance might be described as the "bottom line" in the accounting of international law.

It is obvious enough that international law is a meaningful force in the affairs of men only to the extent that men and their instruments comply with that law. Nevertheless, among international lawyers there is a certain tendency to avoid grappling with problems of compliance. Compliance sometimes appears to be assumed, or it may be treated as a problem more of politics than law. Or it is affirmed that compliance is predominant and that indeed the record of compliance with international law compares favorably with that of the domestic law of States. One way or another, the need for the international lawyer to confront the awful truths of noncompliance may be reasoned away. But diplomats, politicians, political scientists, the press, and others who handle, mishandle, manhandle, or merely interpret international relations do not fall victim to the error of discounting the importance of compliance with international law. They tend to fall into still more fundamental error. They overlook the importance of international law itself. Citing actual or alleged noncompliance with international law, they may conclude that international law does not exist, or is not "law," or at any rate does not govern the really important things that States do.

In these remarks, I shall not seek to evaluate with any specificity the extent to which States do and do not comply with international law. But I shall address the classic question of why States and other subjects of international law do comply with international law, to the extent that they do. And since

First published in *Proceedings of the American Society of International Law* (1981).

that extent clearly is not sufficient, I shall also take up the question of what may be done to improve the processes of compliance. Such prescriptions will inevitably be somewhat futuristic, and thus I shall be brought into compliance with my subject, "The Compliance Process and the Future of International Law."

Since this 75th Anniversary Convocation inherently invokes the origins of the Society, I take as my initial text the pertinent words of Elihu Root, spoken if not at the Society's first, then its second, Annual Meeting. Mr. Root could not be accused of speaking simply in the idealistic capacity of one of his capacities, namely, as President of the Society. For he also then was serving as Secretary of State. Moreover, his familiarity with the real world presumably was enhanced by service about that time as Secretary of War. Admittedly he was also to serve as the US member of the Committee of Jurists which drafted the Statute of the Permanent Court of International Justice, but that enterprise of 1920 cannot fairly be held to impeach the hardheadedness of his insights of 1908.

Before turning to the topic of his speech, "The sanction of international law," Mr. Root observed that the year which had passed since the first Annual Meeting of the Society furnished abundant proof that "it is no academic subject which we are studying, and that it is no dead language in which we speak." During that short year the Second Hague Conference had made "what may fairly be declared the greatest single advance ever made at one time in the development and acceptance of rules of international law for the Government of national conduct." Eleven of the resultant conventions had been approved by the Senate. The establishment of a general system "under which there may be impartial judgment upon the application of the rules of international law to international conduct has been advanced" by ratification of US Treaties of Arbitration with eight countries. The five Central American States had established, after "temperate and kindly discussion" in Washington, a permanent court to settle disputes among them. And the Society, in the short period of its existence, without much advertising, had expanded until there were 900 members on the rolls.[1]

Against this heartening background, Mr. Root referred initially to the striking apparent difference between municipal and international law. The domestic lawyer aims to secure a judicial judgment to be enforced by the entire power of the State over litigants subject to its jurisdiction and control. Before him lies a clear, definite conclusion of the controversy, and for the finality and effectiveness of that conclusion the sheriff and the policeman

---

[1] *Proceedings of the American Society of International Law* (1908), pp. 13–14.

stand always as guarantors in the last resort. But the international lawyer has apparently no objective point to which he can address his arguments, except the sense of justice of the opposing party. In the vast majority of practical questions arising under the rules of international law, there does not appear to be on the surface any reason why either party should yield against its own interest to the arguments of the other side. This apparent absence of sanction for the enforcement of the rules of international law has led great authority to deny that those rules are entitled to be called law at all.

Yet, Mr. Root continued, all the Foreign Offices of the civilized world are continually discussing with each other questions of international law, "cheerfully and hopefully marshaling facts ... presenting arguments designed to show that the rules of international law require such and such ... And in countless cases nations are yielding to such arguments and shaping their conduct against their own apparent interests ... in obedience to the rules which are shown to be applicable."[2] Why?

Root's answer is that it is a mistake to assume that the sanction which secures obedience to any law consists exclusively or chiefly of the penalties imposed by the law for its violation. Men generally refrain from crime not through fear of imprisonment but because they are unwilling to incur in the community in which they live the public condemnation which would follow a repudiation of the standard of conduct prescribed by that community for its members. The force of law is in the public opinion that prescribes it. The practical considerations which determine success or failure in life reinforce the impulse toward conformity. It is these considerations rather than the threat of the sheriff that lead men to keep their contracts. It is only for the occasional nonconformist that the policeman is kept in reserve; if the nonconformists were not occasional, the policeman would have no effect.

Root maintained that the rules of international law are enforced by the same kind of sanction, less certain and peremptory, but continually increasing in effectiveness. He refers to "a decent respect to the opinions of mankind." As the isolation of nations breaks down, a community of nations is gradually emerging, in which standards of conduct are being established, and a worldwide public opinion is holding nations to conformity with those standards. "There is no civilized country now which is not sensitive to this general opinion, none that is willing to subject itself to the discredit of standing brutally on its power to deny to other countries the benefit of recognized rules of right conduct."[3] The deference which a State shows to international public opinion is in due proportion to a nation's degree of civilization. States

[2] *Ibid.*, pp. 15–16.   [3] *Ibid.*, p. 18.

appreciate that nonconformity to the standard of nations means condemnation and isolation. They appreciate that it is better for every nation to secure the protection of the law by complying with it than to forfeit the law's benefits by ignoring it. The nation that has with it the moral force of the world's approval is strong.

Thus, Root concludes, the real sanction which enforces international law is the injury which inevitably follows nonconformity to public opinion. Moreover, for the occasional violent and persistent international lawbreaker, there stands behind discussion the ultimate possibility of war, as the sheriff and policeman await the occasional domestic lawbreaker. Of course, public opinion can be brought to bear upon only comparatively simple questions and clearly ascertained rights; hence the importance of arbitration and the importance of informing public opinion.

Whether Elihu Root would have spoken so optimistically in 1981 as he did in 1908 is open to question. Certainly those who have lived through the aggression and genocide of this century cannot have like confidence that some States will not subject themselves to the discredit of standing brutally on their power. Even Root's comments on the domestic effectiveness of law today seem somewhat out of date in this crime-ridden city; what he gently calls "non-conformists" are more than occasional.

Yet I have quoted Root at this length not simply out of respectful remembrance of things past in the Society's history, but because of the pertinence of his insights to present problems. In significant measure, States do comply with international law for the reasons he assigns: because States generally do feel impelled to conform to standards which are widely accepted and which are inculcated into their public opinion and leadership; because normally they wish to avoid condemnation by and isolation from other States, particularly as it may be manifested in economic as well as psychic losses; and because usually they appreciate the mutuality of the law's benefits. States understand and count upon reciprocity of obligation and of performance, both in treaty relations and in the application of customary international law. They see that it is in their self-interest to do so. Reciprocity is the norm. It is the cement that holds the structure of international law together, if not invariably then usually.

It may be added that the reasons why Governments comply with the law domestically – why, for example, the US Government complies with judgments of the Court of Claims when there is no sheriff to compel it to do so – are not very different. Governments do not respond to the law domestically because of the evils which superior authority will impose upon them if they do not. There is no superior authority. They respond because they see that it is in their interest to respond.[4] They see that they have a greater interest in the lawful disposition of disputes than they do in imposing their will arbitrarily in every dispute. Yet this enlightened perception unfortunately is not regularly replicated on the international scene. Democratic and legally responsive Governments habitually are willing to submit their legal disputes with citizens and aliens to domestic courts, and are quite prepared to lose. They recognize that if they won all the cases, there would be no courts. But internationally these same Governments are habitually unwilling to lose. The first question a Government asks when international adjudication is considered is, will we win? If the answer is only "possibly," adjudication is normally rejected and claims of the Court's jurisdiction are resisted. Their larger interest in the promotion of the judicial settlement of international disputes is sacrificed to the perception of their immediate interests.

For more reasons than that, Root's fundamentally sound analysis is not sufficient to meet the demands of today and tomorrow for a more effective international law. In the remainder of these remarks, I shall accordingly try to set out salient ways and means by which the compliance processes of international law are being or may be strengthened.

One way is in fact indicated by Root in his reference to arbitration. Before the law can be enforced, it must be established. That is a particular problem in international law. If State A is in dispute with State B as to what the law is, and if each State takes an opposing position, it is premature to speak of enforcing the law: what the law is must first be settled. In a domestic context, courts can and do establish the law. Internationally, courts can but too often do not, essentially because they do not enjoy the compulsory jurisidiction routinely exercised by national courts.

This is not to suggest that the sole way in which the law can be established is by the processes of international adjudication and arbitration.[5] But it is the best way – provided, at any rate, that the judgments of the International Court of Justice and the awards of Arbitral Tribunals are complied with. To the extent that they are not, and to the extent that they are not enforced, a gap arises between authority and effectiveness. It is not clear that the interests of international law are served by emphasizing a conjunction between the authority to declare the law and impotence to enforce it. The remedy is not to submit fewer cases to international adjudication, but to take all feasible steps to enforce international judgments. Enforcement of judgments of the International Court of Justice is a community responsibility, as the terms of Article 94 of the United Nations Charter import. But, in the first place it is

---

[4] See Fisher, "Bringing Law to Bear on Governments," *Harvard Law Review* (1961),74, p. 1130.

[5] See R. Falk, *The Status of Law in International Society* (1970), pp. 332–334.

the responsibility of the State in whose favor the Court has ruled to have recourse to the Security Council. Yet we have seen in the last year a most striking example of the failure to take the most obvious, still less all feasible, steps to enforce one of the most extraordinary judgments ever rendered by the International Court of Justice.

States in the ordinary yet important run of their affairs generally observe international law. And the record of observance of the judgments of the World Court and of Arbitral Tribunals is quite good – though not good enough. But contemporary history provides painful exceptions to the predominant rule of compliance with international obligations. When those exceptions entail, as some do, the illegal use of force internationally, the whole structure of international law and life may be endangered. Controlling the use of force is the most vital test of any legal system. International law does not yet meet that test. The daily headlines so demonstrate. For this reason alone, the problem of sanctions to enforce the law must be confronted. And for this reason above all, ways and means of enhancing compliance with international law, those that involve inducements as well as penalties, demand continuing consideration. The nurturing of the processes of international compliance is of paramount importance not only because particular violations of the law may be of great, even devastating importance. It is important because expectations are the vitals of the law. "The life of the law is not logic but experience." If experience demonstrates that States may safely violate international law, its credibility suffers. States will not expect compliance by others and be the less conscientious about their own. Correspondingly, observance of the law, and enforcement of the law, will generate expectations of future compliance and will thus enhance the present effectiveness of international law.

What then is being done or can be done to enhance compliance with international law? Time does not permit me to be comprehensive even if there were more answers; but let me try to recall some primary ones.

Perhaps the most encouraging sphere of activity is in what has been called "cooperative international law."[6] States increasingly cooperate in an immense and intense range of endeavors, largely through the medium of international organizations such as the ILO, the World Bank, the International Monetary Fund, and the International Civil Aviation Organization. They materially advance their interests through these organizations. But if they fail to meet the standards of cooperative behavior which the constitutions of these organizations prescribe or their practice maintains, then they

---

[6] W. Friedmann, *The Changing Structure of International Law* (1964), pp. 88–95.

face the penalty of non-participation. They may lose the benefits of co-operation. Thus a State may refrain from defaulting on a loan of the World Bank – or may refrain from uncompensated expropriation of foreign invest-ments – in the realization that otherwise its eligibility for future loans of the Bank will suffer. A State will conform to the air navigation rules and standards of the International Civil Aviation Organization to avoid being excluded from the benefits of international air travel. These examples could be multiplied. The United Nations Specialized Agencies are established by treaty. They are creatures of and creators of international law. As States habitually cooperate in the Specialized Agencies and like institutions, as they come increasingly to rely on cooperative institutional arrangements, the impulse to abide by the law, their perceived interest in abiding by the law, should continue to grow – with beneficial effects beyond the immediate sphere of the organizations and subjects concerned.

International organizations play still another role in promoting compliance with international law, "the mobilization of shame."[7] The ILO has a distin-guished record of achievement in this vein. Its organized and expert scrutiny of the record of the performance of Governments in meeting their treaty obligations respecting labor standards unquestionably has a marked effect on how States behave – on how they comply with the specialized body of law which the ILO has done so much to establish.[8] Similarly, in the sphere of human rights at large, bodies such as the Inter-American Commission of Human Rights have done a great deal to bring law to bear on Governments through processes of fact-finding and influencing public and governmental opinion.

The European Community has exceptional ways and means of its own to induce compliance with the Treaty of Rome. I do not feel able to appraise that record beyond voicing the impression that the sense of community which supports the measure of integration which the European Community manifests also supports a high, though not uniform, degree of compliance.

The emphasis which is increasingly and rightly placed on multilateral means for enhancing national compliance with international law does not suggest that unilateral action is obsolete. On the contrary, particularly as long as so much of international intercourse remains in bilateral channels, possi-bilities of unilateral enforcement must be fully exploited.

One medium for the national application of international law is national courts. National courts should increasingly apply international law, as they often have, not only to their Governments and others incontestably subject to

[7] See S. Schwebel (ed.), *The Effectiveness of International Decisions* (1971), pp. 434–436, 447–456, 493–494.
[8] Valticos, "The International Labor Organization," in Schwebel, *International Decisions*, pp. 134–155.

their jurisdiction; they should also increasingly apply international law to foreign Governments. To the extent that that implies cutting back on sovereign immunity and cutting out the act-of-State doctrine, that is to be welcomed. Moreover, the enforcement of international judicial and arbitral judgments by national courts and other national authorities should be vigorously pursued. The increasing interdependence of the world economy furnishes opportunities for enforcement – such as the freezing of assets – which should be seized upon as circumstances may warrant. It is in the interest of enlightened Governments and their judicial and administrative instrumentalities to lend their weight to the enforcement of international obligations and judgments rather than to their avoidance.

A traditional means of enforcing international law which may be due for a revival is the use of reprisals. It is accepted that where State A materially violates a treaty with State B, State B may reciprocally withhold performance or even denounce the treaty. But where State A has violated the legal rights of State B, State B may in some circumstances go beyond that to take retaliatory action against State A which, but for the prior illegal act of State A, would be unlawful.

In its current codification of the law of State responsibility, the International Law Commission has recently given striking endorsement to the continued legality of proportionate reprisals which do not entail the use of armed force.[9] And the vitality of resort to reprisals was upheld in 1978 in the *Case Concerning the Air Services Agreement of 27 March 1946 (United States v. France).*[10]

Clearly there are dangers in recourse to reprisals. But the dangers of riskless violation of international law are greater. In the present parlous state of international relations, Governments cannot be expected to forgo resort to reprisals that do not involve the use of armed force. Indeed, they should explore the possibilities of widening their reach and sharpening their bite by including among the number of States that exercise reprisals not only the State immediately injured by the breach of international law but other States which, while not directly affected, have an interest in the maintenance of the integrity of the pertinent rule of international law. An informal coalition of the law abiding should be prepared first of all jointly to take measures of lawful adverse response to clear and grave violations of international law. For example, the lawbreaker can be quarantined by measures of trade restriction or diplomatic ostracism – measures which a State is free to adopt or not to

---

[9] United Nations General Assembly, *Official Records*, Thirty-Fourth Session, Supplement No. 10 (A/34/10), *Report of the International Law Commission on the Work of its Thirty-First Session*, pp. 311–328.
[10] *International Law Reports*, Vol. 54, pp. 337–341.

adopt. But where such measures are insufficient, then that informal coalition of law-abiding States should jointly exercise measures of reprisal against the law-breaking State. For example, where State A abets the perpetration of acts of international terrorism and hijacking, States B, C, and D might combine to cut off air travel with State A even if one or more of them are parties to valid treaties with State A providing for the maintenance of air services. The breach of such treaties would be unlawful but for the prior unlawful acts of State A in abetting terrorist activity.

Measures such as these, if imaginatively and persistently pursued, can do a great deal to bring about wider compliance with international law. But they will not of themselves be sufficient to deal with the gravest dangers to the integrity of international law and life – the use and threat of use of aggressive armed force. To the extent that measures such as those described build the law habit, enmesh States in a web of regularized intercourse, and deter them from violating less critical but still important elements of international law, to this extent these measures should also inhibit a State's resort to international aggression. But until the international community builds that much greater sense of community which is necessary to support a central enforcement authority capable of compelling States to observe international law, truly effective multilateral sanctions will remain elusive.

While the Security Council is not generally empowered to employ sanctions to maintain international law – or arguably is not – it clearly is authorized and obligated to support international law at its weakest point, in the maintenance of international peace and security. In practice, the Security Council has made significant contributions to keeping or restoring the peace, but its practice also demonstrates the gravest failures of omission and commission. To put the point more precisely, the record of the Members of the United Nations in the sphere of the Organization's supreme concern is dismal. No one, at least to my knowledge, appears to have the answer to this most profound problem of international law and relations: effectively holding States to their obligations to refrain in their international relations from the threat or use of force. While the fundamental prescriptions of the United Nations Charter appear to have a certain indeterminate but positive influence, a third and perhaps final World War seems to have been so far avoided more by the imperatives of a balance of international terror and of restraint, than by the influence of international law. Lesser wars are fought in the shadow of muscle-bound Great Powers, sometimes noticed and foreshortened by the United Nations, sometimes not.

The prescription for survival, then, appears to be this: maintenance of a sufficient balance of power to deter the outbreak of nuclear catastrophe and meanwhile intensive cultivation of ways and means of strengthening compliance with international law. The hope is that there thus will be a longer run, and that in the course of it, much stronger international institutions supported by a much deeper sense of international community will gradually develop. If and when that day comes, satisfactory sanctions with which to support a truly effective international law should become as practicable as today they are necessary.

36

Government Legal Advising in the Field of Foreign Affairs

❧

International law is largely the creation of Governments. In that creative process, those who render legal advice to Governments play a critical part. The forces which shape international law, like the forces which shape international affairs, are many and complex. But what is singular and clear is that those who advise Governments on what international law is and should be exert a particular, perhaps at times a paramount, influence on the formation of international law.

This paper will consider, first, of what Government legal advising in the field of foreign affairs consists (or should consist) and, second, organizational patterns which Governments have evolved to provide them with such legal advice. In so doing, it will draw on the illuminating book on *Legal Advisers and Foreign Affairs* which was published for the *American Society of International Law* following upon a conference of legal advisers and scholars from twelve countries and certain international organizations, which took place at Princeton in 1963.[1]

The Content of Government Legal Advising in the Field of Foreign Affairs

The governmental Legal Adviser on foreign affairs – whether he be the Legal Adviser of the Foreign Ministry, the Attorney General or other personage – has a subtle and multiple job. He plays, or should play, several roles, among them, the following:

(a) Enunciator of "the law." When a problem arises on which he is asked or volunteers an opinion, he will inform his principal what the law on the

---

First published by the Nigerian Institute of International Affairs and the Carnegie Endowment for International Peace, *African Conference Proceedings* (1967).
[1] Merillat (ed.), *Legal Advisers and Foreign Affairs* (1964).

point is. If there is a relatively clear and well-established rule, he will say so. But – as was repeatedly pointed out at the Princeton conference[2] – too often in international law there is no clear rule. As the late Judge Lauterpacht elsewhere remarked, "How could it be otherwise in a society in which judicial settlement is sporadic, in which there is no legislative activity in the accepted sense and in which custom is slow of growth and controversial in interpretation and application?"[3]

(b) Accordingly, "Where customary norms and treaty obligations offer no clear answer, or where norms have been widely challenged by other nations, there is an opportunity to contribute to the establishment of new norms, and in the process the legal adviser may point out that, however much an *ad hoc* decision may seem to satisfy some immediate national interest, it may offer an uncomfortable precedent for the future, taking a longer view of the national interest."[4] Thus, in this common case, the Legal Adviser acts – to the extent his Government receives and follows his advice – not merely (as in case (*a*)) as a contributor to that State practice which confirms and may in some measure shade an established rule of law, but as a shaper of the law in the fullest sense. Here the Legal Adviser's policy preferences are most clearly exposed. If those preferences are enlightened, if they are responsive to higher human values and the facts of international interdependence as well as to the practicalities of the national interest, the Legal Adviser – always to the extent his Government is persuaded to follow his advice – can have the most influential positive impact on the "progressive development of International Law."

(c) Both as enunciator of "the law" and adviser of what the law ought to be, the Legal Adviser acts (or should act) as the conscience of the Foreign Ministry. The diplomat is habituated to the short view, to the small step, to avoiding and postponing rather than confronting issues, to minimizing or disposing of the immediate problem rather than to shaping the principles it poses. The diplomat inclines – in two phrases of Washington jargon – towards "keeping all the options open" in dealing with those characteristically complex problems he inelegantly describes as "a can of worms." The foreign affairs Legal Adviser cannot be immune to the tempo and tone of the Foreign Ministry. He must operate in this milieu of indecision and indirection, appreciating, moreover, its merit of minimizing international disputes while letting time pass. And, in fact, at least

---

[2] Merillat, *Legal Advisers*, pp. 16–18.
[3] Lauterpacht, "Codification and Development of International Law," *American Journal of International Law* (1955), 49, pp. 16–43, at p. 19.
[4] Merillat, *Legal Advisers*, p. 16.

if he is integrated in the Foreign Ministry, he himself will tend to deal rapidly with a succession of problems, more minor than major – so much so that he may easily fall into a pattern of improvisation which neglects considerations of principle (not to speak of legal scholarship).

If, however, the Legal Adviser performs as he ideally should perform, if he brings to bear a scholarly grasp – and a critical appraisal – of the pertinent precedents and principles as well as a dedication to the promotion of a better world order, he can complement the diplomat's preoccupation with the immediate problem with an enlightened concern for considerations of legal principle and international progress. He can inform the pervasive preoccupation with "the national interest" with a measure of concern for the international interest. This is not, of course, to suggest that diplomats are unconcerned about the international interest or legal advisers unconcerned about the national interest. But, in a world where sensitivity to the international interest – of which international law is (or should be) the crystallized expression – is inadequate, the Legal Adviser has or should have a special perception of it.

(d) The Legal Adviser acts not only as the conscience of the Foreign Ministry; he is its advocate, if not apologist, as well. Indeed, it might be said that he is customarily its advocate and occasionally its conscience.

The Legal Adviser may be in the position of advocating a policy which comports with international law as he perceives it. Given the amenable state of much of international law, this is not difficult. Most diplomatic notes of legal aspect, most public statements in explanation of governmental decisions, most arguments before international tribunals, most speeches to organs of international organizations, presumably are expressions of this position. It is in the nature of the lawyer to believe in his client's case. This natural tendency is enhanced when the lawyer is not independent of his client. When the client is his own Government, question may be raised about the purity of the independence of almost any lawyer; and, when that lawyer is in his Government's service – particularly when he is "house counsel" of the Ministry of Foreign Affairs – the tendency towards being convinced by one's own advocacy is the stronger still.

(e) Among the defects of the foregoing comments on the role of the foreign affairs Legal Adviser may be an undue impression of dramatic policy combat. While the Legal Adviser may often be locked in bureaucratic struggle, the policy issue involved – if there is one – may not be large. Moreover, much of the Legal Adviser's time (especially if the term "legal adviser" is understood to embrace his professional staff) may be spent on more bloodless, though not unimportant, pursuits: the drafting of treaties and action pursuant to them, points of diplomatic privileges and immunities, the consideration and occasional espousal of international claims, questions of nationality, administrative problems of the Foreign Ministry and Foreign Service, and so forth.

(*f*) Whether on large questions or small, the role of the Legal Adviser may be purely advisory or it may be "operational." The Legal Adviser's office may content itself with passing upon, with "clearing" the legal content of cables or memoranda drafted by another office; or, where the problem has a legal aspect – and so many problems have some legal aspect, immediate or implied – it may itself draft the document and seek the clearance of other offices. "Action," and hence responsibility for drafting the documentation, will tend to go to the Legal Adviser on problems primarily of legal content. Whether he will have "action" on others depends on the traditions of the Ministry and the personalities involved.

(*g*) The "operational" role of the Legal Adviser is particularly marked in the expanding arenas of international organization. In the Sixth (Legal) Committee of the United Nations General Assembly, Legal Advisers or their representatives usually sit not as advisers to the Delegate but as Delegates; and this equally applies to the conferences of plenipotentiaries which occasionally meet to draft treaties in pursuance of the work of the International Law Commission or other bodies of the United Nations system. In the other committees and organs of the United Nations, the role of the Legal Adviser is more advisory than operational; and it might be said that in too many of these committees and organs, that advisory role is unduly muted. As Oscar Schachter,[5] Rosalyn Higgins,[6] and others have pointed out, the contribution of United Nations bodies to the shaping of international law is often underestimated, even by the Legal Advisers of Foreign Ministries.

The Organization of Government Legal Advising in the Field of Foreign Affairs

The foregoing discussion may reflect service in a large legal office of a Foreign Ministry of a State whose international responsibilities are great. A consideration of the various types of organization of legal services in a number of countries may bring more comprehensive perspective to bear.

There appear to be essentially three distinct patterns of organization in use.

---

[5] See his comments in Merillat, *Legal Advisers*, pp. 159–162.
[6] *The Development of International Law Through the Political Organs of the United Nations* (1963).

They are (1) a permanent legal service which forms an autonomous section of the Ministry of Foreign Affairs; (2) a legal service which is more closely integrated into the Foreign Ministry in the sense that its members rotate on diplomatic assignment; and (3) a legal service which is external to the Foreign Ministry and lodged in that section of the Government which generally advises the Government on legal matters. Each of these arrangements has its advantages and disadvantages.

A Permanent Legal Service within the Foreign Ministry

The United States, the United Kingdom, and the Netherlands, among others, follow this system, with certain variations.

In the Department of State, some sixty lawyers, headed by the Legal Adviser and three Deputy Legal Advisers, form a Bureau which has co-ordinate status with the other Bureaus of the Department. The Legal Adviser has the rank of the Director of a Bureau, i.e., Assistant Secretary of State. His Office is divided among a dozen Assistant Legal Advisers and their staffs, who service a particular geographical or functional Bureau of the Department (African Affairs, United Nations Affairs, Economic Affairs, etc.). There are a few Assistant Legal Advisers who do not have Bureau "clients," for example, the Assistant Legal Advisers for Treaties and for Claims. While the Assistant Legal Advisers work under the ultimate supervision and responsibility of the Legal Adviser, for the most part they deal directly with the Bureaus they advise, taking part in the staff meetings of their principal officers and submitting their views directly to the Bureaus. Where matters of larger consequence are concerned, particularly where questions are to go up to the Secretary of State and the Under-Secretaries for decision, the Legal Adviser and the Deputy Legal Advisers will be involved.

The professional staff of the Office of the Legal Adviser are all lawyers, usually in civil rather than foreign service reserve status. They are not liable to posting abroad in a diplomatic capacity unless they seek to be temporarily detached from the Office for such assignments (as a few younger lawyers have been encouraged to do). Virtually all legal advice is concentrated in Washington. In recent years, a few exceptions have grown up, Legal Advisers – who operate under the authority of the local Chief of Mission – having been placed in Geneva and shortly to be placed in New York and Brussels, to deal with problems of international organization at those centers.[7]

Arrangements for legal advice in the British Foreign Office are similar,

---

[7] See the discussion by Professor Metzger in Merillat, *Legal Advisers*, pp. 153–158; Bilder, "The Office of the Legal Adviser: The State Department Lawyer and Foreign Affairs," *American Journal of International Law* (1962), 56, pp. 633–684, and Merillat at pp. 6–8, 19–22, 26–30.

there being, however, no Legal Department or Office of the Legal Adviser as such, but rather a Legal Adviser, a Deputy Legal Adviser, and some dozen Legal Counsellors and Assistant Legal Advisers responsible to the Legal Adviser for their work. Each of these officers has his own Foreign Office "clients," geographical or functional, and his relationship with them is close and direct. Nevertheless, the operational and policy-making involvements of the British Legal Advisers appear to be less marked than those of their American counterparts – just as the functions of the English lawyer in private practice are less policy oriented than those of the American lawyer.

British Legal Advisers serve in a legal capacity at the United Nations and a few other posts. They form a special cadre within the Foreign Service, and are not liable to non-legal assignments. The Legal Adviser is directly responsible to the British Foreign Secretary, just as the Department of State's Legal Adviser is directly responsible to the Secretary of State; neither is under the authority of the Attorney-General or other principal legal officer of the Government.[8]

In the Netherlands, the Legal Adviser has a similar responsibility. He is assisted by a small group of civil servants (in 1963, they numbered four). They are not formally divided by function, though there are practical tendencies towards specialization. "Though in principle the Office of the Legal Adviser is 'passive' in the sense that it only gives advice when asked, practice is often different."[9]

A Legal Service within the Foreign Ministry Whose Members Rotate on Diplomatic Assignment

Among the countries that follow this system are Argentina, Canada, Colombia, Japan, Mexico, the Philippines, and the United Arab Republic.

The Legal Offices of Ministries of Foreign Affairs of countries such as these are staffed largely or exclusively by career diplomats who are legally trained. After a tour of duty in the Legal Office, they are customarily posted abroad in non-legal capacities, just as other diplomatic officers are.

It is estimated that, in Japan, one-third of the career diplomats serve at one time or another in the Legal Office (the "Treaties Bureau").[10] Those with particular interest in and talent for international law may serve more than one legal tour.

In Canada, nearly a quarter of the Foreign Service are qualified lawyers or

---

[8] See Dr. Clive Parry's paper in Merillat, *Legal Advisers*, pp. 101–152, and Merillat at pp. 6–8, 19–22, 26.

[9] Professor W. Riphagen, General Counsellor and Legal Adviser of the Netherlands Ministry of Foreign Affairs, in Merillat, *Legal Advisers*, pp. 79–83, at p. 80.

[10] *Ibid.*, p. 2, and the paper by Professor Yuichi Takano therein, at pp. 54–66.

have law degrees, and the bulk of the Legal Division is recruited from these career diplomats, who in due time rotate to non-legal work. However, a small proportion of the staff of the Legal Division is composed of specialists in international law who do not rotate "so as to ensure the essential continuity and expertise in particular subjects."[11]

In the United Arab Republic, the Department of Legal Affairs and Treaties is composed of officers who alternate between that department and UAR diplomatic missions abroad. Those officers have not only training in national and international law, but postgraduate international legal studies or service in permanent missions to international organizations.[12]

In Mexico, the legal advising function is distributed among several of the Bureaus of the Ministry of Foreign Affairs, and staffed by career diplomats.

Integration with Other Governmental Legal Services

Among the countries which lodge legal advising in the sphere of foreign affairs in that Ministry which has general responsibility for rendering legal advice to the Government are Nigeria and Malaysia. The United Arab Republic followed this procedure until 1960.

In Nigeria, the Federal Ministry of Justice is responsible for the legal work of the Government. Among its Divisions are an Industrial and Mercantile Law Division and a Public International Law and Comparative Law Division. Both Divisions, and particularly the latter, render international legal advice to the Ministries of Foreign Affairs and Commonwealth Relations. Their officers are not situated within the Ministry of Foreign Affairs; rather, that Ministry will address a communication to the Solicitor-General of the Federation setting out the facts and requesting legal advice on specific points. Law officers are often included in Nigerian negotiating teams which participate in negotiations with foreign countries or international organizations.[13]

Legal Advice by Other Ministries with Restricted Areas of Foreign Concern

Quite apart from the question of whether international legal advice is centered in the Foreign Ministry or the Ministry of Justice or *Conseil d'Etat*, it is clear that a multiplicity of Ministries have functions which bear upon foreign affairs, in their legal as well as other aspects. In the United States, the Departments of Justice, Treasury, Defense, Commerce, Agriculture, and Labor, and a number of independent regulatory commissions, such as the

---

[11] Deputy Under-Secretary of State and Legal Adviser Marcel Cadieux, *ibid*, pp. 33–43, at p. 34.
[12] Legal Adviser Abdullah El-Erian, *ibid*, pp. 98–100.
[13] Deputy Solicitor General S.D. Adebiyi, *ibid*, pp. 84–89.

Atomic Energy Commission, have important international legal responsibilities, and experienced legal advisers to handle them. This phenomenon is duplicated in varying degree in many countries, and has perhaps reached its peak in the States members of the European communities, where dealing with counterparts in other States members has become the daily work of many Ministries.[14] The result is a need for coordination among Government Departments by the Ministry of the Government having paramount responsibility in the sphere of international legal advice. Concentration of all international legal advice in the Ministry of Foreign Affairs or elsewhere does not seem to be practical; the diversity of international relations has grown too large.[15]

Advantages and Disadvantages of the Differing Forms of Organization

The advantages and disadvantages of the three principal patterns of organization may be summarized as follows:

Integration with other Government legal services of advice in the sphere of foreign affairs tends to assure professional legal competence and a high degree of autonomy and independence. Moreover, coordination of Government-wide concern with international legal problems is facilitated by centering international legal advice in the Ministry which is the principal legal adviser to the Government as a whole.

The disadvantages of this system are, first, that the Legal Adviser who is not physically and bureaucratically part of the Foreign Ministry is not likely to be as frequently, fully, and intimately consulted as he might be; second, if he is consulted, it will tend to be on the "law," not "policy"; and third, he is not so likely to acquire that familiarity with the substance of foreign affairs which both lends reality and insight to his advice and enhances his status among his diplomatic clients.

A legal service within the Foreign Ministry whose members rotate on diplomatic assignment has the advantage of immersing its members in the substance of the Ministry's work. They thereby acquire a familiarity with its problems and procedures and personnel which is likely to enhance the receptivity of their legal advice, and may facilitate their influential involvement in policy making. A Legal Adviser who has served as a diplomat and will again serve as one is more readily accepted by other diplomats as one of their own. His advice may be treated as less intrusive than would be advice rendered by a Legal Section composed of lawyers who do not serve abroad and who may be regarded by some Foreign Service personnel as remote from diplomatic

---

[14] Merillat, *Legal Advisers*, pp. 9–13.   [15] Metzger, *ibid*, at pp. 155–158.

realities. Moreover, in small Foreign Offices, there may be considerable advantage in being able to draw on legal as well as non-legal officers for postings abroad. Further, rotation of legal officers within the diplomatic service affords such officers greater opportunities for promotion – at least at the peak of the service – than they otherwise might have. While there is but one chief Legal Adviser, there are many Ambassadors. Lastly, rotation has the advantage of dispensing a knowledge of and sensitivity to international law among diplomatic personnel.

The disadvantages of this system are several. First, diplomats who serve occasionally as lawyers are not as likely as career lawyers are to acquire that depth of knowledge of and commitment to international law which is desirable if a Government is to be professionally advised. Second, continuity in legal services is prejudiced. Those who become expert in a particular legal speciality or case may be posted abroad when their expertise is needed at home. Third, much of the value of the career lawyer in the Ministry of Foreign Affairs is his cumulative experience. This experience is not only of great legal value; it often is of substantial political value. A lawyer who, for some years, is counsel for a geographical Bureau or Legal Adviser on international organizations, will come to acquire a knowledge, to build up a memory bank in his particular sphere which Foreign Service officers, often freshly assigned to that sphere after service in another, cannot begin to match. This knowledge enhances both his legal and political impact. Fourth, the independence of the lawyer who has served and will serve again as a diplomat in advising a client who has been and will be his immediate employer may be more difficult to sustain than in the case of the professional international lawyer, working in an autonomous section, with its own procedures for bureaucratic protection and promotion. Fifth, the occasional lawyer may tend, to the extent he serves as a lawyer, to concentrate on public international law, to the detriment of his competence in other kinds of law which may affect foreign affairs, such as national law and conflicts of law.

A permanent legal service within the Foreign Ministry has the advantage of continuity and high professional competence of a specialized character. It provides a kind of "in-service training" which is invaluable. It equally conduces towards independence of viewpoint, and bureaucratic support by the Legal Adviser of his associates in the advancement of their independent views. Service over a period of years for the same clients makes the lawyer at home both in the law and the politics of the sphere of his responsibility, and affords him personal associations of great utility. While there may be a certain distrust in some diplomatic quarters of the advice of the professional lawyer – especially when that advice is not solicited – this distrust may often be dissipated by arrangements for bureaucratic coordination and, more, by the play of personalities. A further advantage of this system, which perhaps is peculiar to the United States, is that the professional international lawyer, working as a lawyer in the Office of the Legal Adviser, retains his legal credentials. He often has the option of transferring from that office to another legal office of the Government, or to the private practice of law, or to law teaching. These options tend to enhance the independence and vigor of his participation in the Department's policy-making processes. They also enhance the ability of the Office of the Legal Adviser to recruit first-class personnel.

The disadvantages of this system are, first, that the members of a permanent legal service may be regarded by diplomatic decision-makers as technicians who are to abstain from policy-oriented functions; second, that lack of diplomatic experience may conduce towards a certain lack of realism in their advice; and third, that, if there is no opportunity for members of the legal service to move into and be promoted upwards within the diplomatic service, limitation of career opportunities within the Legal Office may promote an undesirable rate of turnover in personnel – especially of those who are most competent and thus most easily able to take up other opportunities.

It would be presumptuous to suggest which of these three systems invariably is the best. For one thing, these three do not exhaust possible variations. Sweden, for example, has a system of legal advice which is not easily confined to any of these categories. Moreover, as conditions evidently vary among countries, so will the most suitable system. It may be worth pointing out, however, that there appears to be an increasing trend towards marrying elements of the various approaches. For example, the Office of the Legal Adviser of the Department of State has taken steps to encourage some of its younger officers to serve a tour in a diplomatic category; it has posted Legal Advisers to three centers of international organization; many of its members acquire extensive diplomatic experience through participation in bilateral and multilateral negotiations; and it has supported proposals that would enable legal officers to transfer more easily to diplomatic service. Other countries, which rely principally on the rotational system, have moderated its disadvantages by retaining a small core of permanent professional personnel in the Foreign Ministry. It may well be that, for smaller countries, there is special merit in combining a rotational system with a Permanent Legal Adviser and Deputy Legal Adviser who are resident in the Foreign Ministry.

PUBLICATIONS OF STEPHEN M. SCHWEBEL

$\wp$

BOOKS

The Secretary-General of the United Nations: His Political Powers and Practice (Cambridge MA: Harvard University Press, 1952).

The Effectiveness of International Decisions (ed.) (Leiden: Sijthoff, 1971).

International Arbitration: Three Salient Problems (Cambridge: Grotius Publications Limited, 1987).

OTHER PUBLICATIONS

"Impasse on the Atom," *The Harvard Advocate* (April 1947), 130.

Testimony on Ratification of the North Atlantic Treaty, *Hearings before the Committee on Foreign Relations*, United States Senate, Eighty-First Congress, First Session (1949).

Testimony on Revision of the United Nations Charter, *Hearings before a Subcommittee of the Committee on Foreign Relations*, United States Senate, Eighty-First Congress, Second Session (1950).

"The Origins and Development of Article 99 of the Charter," *British Year Book of International Law 1951* (1952), 28.

"The International Character of the Secretariat of the United Nations," *British Year Book of International Law 1953* (1954), 30.

"Secretary-General and Secretariat," *Charter Review Conference* (Commission to Study the Organization of Peace, New York: 1955).

"A United Nations 'Guard' and a United Nations 'Legion'," a staff paper prepared for the Carnegie Endowment for International Peace, 1957 (printed in William R. Frye, *A United Nations Peace Force* [1957]).

Report of the Committee on Nationalization of Property of the American Branch of the International Law Association, *Proceedings and Committee Reports of the American Branch of the International Law Association*, 1957–1958.

"Trygve Lie," *Encyclopedia Britannica* (1959).

"International Protection of Contractual Arrangements," *Proceedingsof the American Society of International Law* (1959).

"The Alsing Case," *International and Comparative Law Quarterly* (April 1959), 8, 2.

Testimony on the Compulsory Jurisdiction of the International Court of Justice, *Hearings before the Committee on Foreign Relations*, United States Senate, Eighty-Sixth Congress, Second Session (1960).

"Financial Problems of the United Nations," *Proceedings and Committee Reports of the American Branch of the International Law Association* (1961–1962).

"Written Statement Submitted by the Government of the United States of America," *ICJ Pleadings, Certain Expenses of the United Nations*, 1962.

"The Story of the UN's Declaration on Permanent Sovereignty over Natural Resources," *American Bar Association Journal* (May 1963).

"The United Nations and the Challenge of a Changing International Law," *Proceedings of the American Society of International Law* (1963).

"Article 19 of the Charter of the United Nations: Memorandum of Law," reprinted in *American Journal of International Law* (July 1964), 58, 3.

"Speculations on Specific Performance of a Contract between a State and Foreign National," Southwestern Legal Foundation, *The Rights and Duties of Private Investors Abroad* (1965).

"Some Little-Known Cases on Concessions" (with J. Gillis Wetter), *British Year Book of International Law 1964* (1966), 40.

"Arbitration and the Exhaustion of Local Remedies" (with J. Gillis Wetter), *American Journal of International Law* (July 1966), 60, 3.

"Government Legal Advising in the Field of Foreign Affairs," Nigerian Institute of International Affairs and the Carnegie Endowment for International Peace, *African Conference Proceedings* (1967).

"Law Making in the United Nations," *Australian National University Federal Law Review* (1970), 4, 1.

"What Weight to Conquest?," *American Journal of International Law* (April 1970), 64, 2.

"International Law in the Middle East," *New York Times*, June 20, 1970.

"The United States Assaults the ILO," *American Journal of International Law* (January 1971), 65, 1.

Testimony on Limiting US Contributions to the United Nations, *Hearings before the Subcommittee on International Organizations and Movements*, Committee on Foreign Affairs, United States House of Representatives, Ninety-Second Congress, First Session (1971).

"Admitting China to the UN: What is US Strategy?," *Washington Post*, August 23, 1971.

"Peking's Effect on the UN: Some Speculations," *Washington Post*, August 29, 1971.

"Selecting a New Secretary-General for the UN," *Washington Post*, September 13, 1971.

"What Should the UN Do About the Mini-States?," *Washington Post*, September 26, 1971.

"United States Nears Front Ranks of Treaty-Breakers," *Washington Post*, October 19, 1971.

"A Chrome-Plated Treaty Violation," *Washington Post*, November 19, 1971.

"A Solution for Sinai," *New York Times*, November 22, 1971.

"The Choice of the New UN Secretary-General," *Washington Post*, December 23, 1971.

"Is the 'Recognition' of Governments Obsolete?," *Washington Post*, February 23, 1972.

"Congress v. International Law," *Washington Post*, May 25, 1972.

"Foreign Policy and the Government Legal Adviser," *Georgia Journal of International & Comparative Law* (1972), 2, 2.

"The Brezhnev Doctrine Repealed and Peaceful Co-Existence Enacted," *American Journal of International Law* (October 1972), 66, 5.

"The Mobilization of Shame," *VISTA* (February 1972).

"Waiting for Jarring," *VISTA* (July–August 1972).

"The American Assembly Looks at the UN," *VISTA* (September–October 1972).

"What To Do Now in the Middle East," *Proceedings and Committee Reports of the American Branch of the International Law Association* (1971–1972).

"On Preventing the Export of Terrorism," *VISTA* (November 1972).

"Who Shall Control the Seas, and for What Purposes?," *Washington Post*, November 8, 1972.

"The Double Standard on Racism in Africa," *Louisville Courier-Journal Times*, December 10, 1972.

"Aggression, Intervention and Self-Defense in Modern International Law," lectures at the Hague Academy of International Law, *Receuil des Cours*, Volume 136 (II), 1972.

"Mini-States and a More Effective United Nations," *American Journal of International Law* (January 1973), 67, 1.

"Chile, Confiscation and the Law," *Washington Post*, February 3, 1973.

"A Takeover of Kuwait?," *Washington Post*, June 26, 1973.

Testimony on Strengthening the International Court of Justice, *Hearings before the Committee on Foreign Relations*, United States Senate, Ninety-Third Congress, First Session (1973).

"A Mixed Review for International Law," *VISTA* (October 1973).

"Defining Aggression," *SAIS* [School of Advanced International Studies] *Review* (Fall, 1973).

"Entente Cordiale: Divergence and Accommodation," *Proceedings of the American Society of International Law* (1974).

"Comments," in Robert R. Bowie, *Suez 1966: International Crises and the Role of Law* (1974).

"The Effect of Resolutions of the United Nations General Assembly on Customary

International Law," *Proceedings of the American Society of International Law* (1979).

"First Report on the Law of the Non-Navigational Uses of International Watercourses," *Yearbook of the International Law Commission 1979*, Volume 2, Part I.

"The Thirty-First Session of the International Law Commission," *American Journal of International Law* (October 1979), 73, 4.

"Confrontation, Consensus and Codification in International Law," *Proceedings and Committee Reports of the American Branch of the International Law Association* (1979–1980).

"Second Report on the Law of the Non-Navigational Uses of International Watercourses," *Yearbook of the International Law Commission 1980*, Volume 2, Part I.

"Responses to Crises in Iran and Afghanistan," *Proceedings of the Annual Meeting of the American Society of International Law* (1980).

"The ICJ Decisions and Other Public International Law Issues," *The Iran Crisis and International Law, Proceedings of the John Bassett Moore Society of International Law* (University of Virginia, 1980).

"The Thirty-Second Session of the International Law Commission," *American Journal of International Law* (October 1980).

Oral Statements by Mr. Schwebel, *ICJ Pleadings, Interpretation of the Agreement of 25 March 1951 between the WHO and Egypt*, 1981, pp. 230, 290.

"United Nations Secretary-General," in Bernhardt (ed.) *Encyclopedia of Public International Law*, Volume V (1981).

"The Compliance Process and the Future of International Law," *Proceedings of the American Society of International Law* (1981).

"Richard R. Baxter," *Proceedings of the American Society of International Law* (1981), p. 225.

Argument of Mr. Schwebel, *ICJ Pleadings, United States Diplomatic and Consular Staff in Tehran*, 1982, p. 274.

"Dedication: Judge Richard R. Baxter," *American University Law Review* (1982), 31, 4.

"Third Report on the Law of the Non-Navigational Uses of International Watercourses," *Yearbook of the International Law Commission 1982*, Volume 2, Part I.

"New Life for the World Court," *Virginia Journal of International Law* (1983), 23, 3.

"The Unused Potential of the International Court of Justice," *Nigerian Forum* (June 1983).

"Widening the Advisory Jurisdiction of the International Court of Justice Without Amending Its Statute," *Catholic University Law Review* (1984), 33, 2.

"Authorizing the Secretary-General of the United Nations to Request Advisory Opinions of the International Court of Justice," *Essays in Honour of Judge Manfred Lachs* (1984).

"Authorizing the Secretary-General of the United Nations to Request Advisory Opinions of the International Court of Justice," *American Journal of International Law* (1984), 78, 4.

"Preface," Leo Gross, *Essays on International Law and Organization* (1984).

"Address" and "Commentary," *International Law and the Grotian Heritage*, T.M.C. Asser Institute, The Hague (1985).

"The Legal Effect of Resolutions and Codes of Conduct of the United Nations," *Forum Internationale* (October 1985).

"Reflections on the Role of the International Court of Justice," *Washington Law Review* (1986), 61.

"United Nations Resolutions, Recent Arbitral Awards and Customary International Law," *Realism in Law Making: Festschrift for Willem Riphagen* (1986).

"Philip C. Jessup," *American Journal of International Law* (1986), 80, 4.

"Some Aspects of International Law in Arbitration between States and Aliens," Southwestern Legal Foundation, *Symposium, Private Investors Abroad: Problems and Solutions* (1986).

"The Docket of the World Court," *Harvard Law Record* (November 1986).

"Public Policy and Arbitral Procedure" (with Susan Lahne), International Council for Commercial Arbitration, *Congress Series* No. 3 (1986).

"On Whether the Breach by a State of a Contract with an Alien is a Breach of International Law," *International Law at the Time of its Codification: Essays in Honour of Roberto Ago* (1987).

"*Ad Hoc* Chambers of the International Court of Justice," *American Journal of International Law* (1987), 81, 4.

"Preliminary Rulings by the International Court of Justice at the Instance of National Courts," *Mededelingen van de Nederlandse Vereniging voor Internationaal Recht* (October 1987), 95.

"Preliminary Rulings by the International Court of Justice at the Instance of National Courts," *Virginia Journal of International Law* (1988), 28, 2.

"Chambers of the International Court of Justice Formed for Particular Cases," Y. Dinstein (ed.), M. Tabory (assoc. ed.), *International Law at a Time of Perplexity: Essays in Honour of Shabtai Rosenne* (1989).

"Arbitration and the Exhaustion of Local Remedies Revisited," *The International Lawyer* (1989), 23, 4.

"Relations between the International Court of Justice and the United Nations," *Merkouris* (Utrecht, 1989), 4.

"Herbert W. Briggs, 1900–1990," *American Journal of International Law* (1990), 84, 2.

"The Prospects for International Arbitration: Inter-State Disputes," A.H.A. Soons (ed.), *International Arbitration: Past and Prospects* (1990).

"The Docket and Decision-making Process of the International Court of Justice," *Suffolk Transnational Law Journal* (Spring 1990), 13, 2.

Commentary on "Social Discipline and the Multinational Enterprise" and "Security of Investment Abroad," International Bar Association, Section on Energy & Natural Resources Law, *Energy Law '90* (1991).

"Relations between the International Court of Justice and the United Nations,"

Prosper Weil et al. (eds.), *Le Droit International au Service de la Paix, de la Justice et du Développement, Mélanges Michel Virally* (1991).

"Remarks on the Role of the Legal Adviser of the US State Department," *European Journal of International Law* (1991), 2, 1.

"Indirect Aggression in the International Court," Address to the USSR–USA Conference of Scholars of the American Society of International Law and the Carnegie Endowment for International Peace, published in Damrosch and Scheffer (eds.), *International Law and the New World Order* (1991).

"Three Cases of Fact-Finding by the International Court of Justice," Richard B. Lillich (ed.), *Fact-Finding before International Tribunals* (1991).

"Preventing Delay or Disruption of Arbitration: Practice of Public International Law Tribunals," International Council for Commercial Arbitration, *Congress Series* No. 5 (1991).

"F.A. Mann, 1907–1991," *American Journal of International Law* (1992), 86, 1.

"Human Rights in the World Court," *Vanderbilt Journal of Transnational Law* (Winter 1992).

"Human Rights in the World Court," R.S. Pathak and R.P. Dhokalia (eds.), *International Law in Transition, Essays in Memory of Judge Nagendra Singh* (1992).

"Role of the International Court of Justice in a Changing United Nations Collective Security Context," *Contemporary International Law Issues: Sharing Pan-European and American Perspectives* (1992).

"Was the Capacity to Request an Advisory Opinion Wider in the Permanent Court of International Justice than it is in the International Court of Justice?," *British Year Book of International Law 1991* (1992), 62.

"The Majority Vote of an International Arbitral Tribunal," C. Dominicé, R. Patry, and C. Reymond (eds.), *Recueil en hommage à Pierre Lalive* (1993) (reprinted in the *American Journal of International Arbitration 1991* [1993], 2, 4).

"Concluding Observations on the Special Issue on International Arbitration," *Leiden Journal of International Law* (1993).

"Manfred Lachs, 1914–1993," *American Journal of International Law* (1993), 87, 3.

"Goldberg Variations," M. Rama-Montaldo (ed.), *Liber Amicorum: Estudios en homenaje a los 75 años del Profesor Eduardo Jiménez de Aréchaga* (1994).

JUDICIAL OPINIONS

Separate or dissenting opinions appear in:

Case Concerning the Continental Shelf (Tunisia/Libyan Arab Jamahiriya), Application by Malta for Permission to Intervene, Judgment, ICJ Reports 1981, page 35.

Continental Shelf (Tunisia/Libyan Arab Jamahiriya), Judgment, ICJ Reports 1982, page 99.

Application for Review of Judgement No. 273 of the United Nations Administrative Tribunal, Advisory Opinion, ICJ Reports 1982, page 454.

Continental Shelf (Libyan Arab Jamahiriya/Malta), Application by Italy for Permission to Intervene, Judgment, ICJ Reports 1984, page 131.

Military and Paramilitary Activities in and against Nicaragua (Nicaragua v. United States of America), Request for Provisional Measures, Order, ICJ Reports 1984, page 190.

Military and Paramilitary Activities in and against Nicaragua (Nicaragua v. United States of America), Declaration of Intervention of the Republic of El Salvador, ICJ Reports 1984, Order, page 223.

Delimitation of the Maritime Boundary in the Gulf of Maine Area, Judgment, ICJ Reports 1984, page 353.

Military and Paramilitary Activities in and against Nicaragua (Nicaragua v. United States of America), Jurisdiction and Admissibility, Judgment, ICJ Reports 1984, page 558.

Continental Shelf (Libyan Arab Jamahiriya/Malta), Judgment, ICJ Reports 1985, page 172.

Application for Revision and Interpretation of the Judgment of 24 February 1982 in the Case Concerning the Continental Shelf (Tunisia/Libyan Arab Jamahiriya) (Tunisia v. Libyan Arab Jamahiriya), Judgment, ICJ Reports 1985, page 246.

Military and Paramilitary Activities in and against Nicaragua (Nicaragua v. United States of America), Merits, Judgment, ICJ Reports 1986, page 259.

Application for Review of Judgement No. 333 of the United Nations Administrative Tribunal, Advisory Opinion, ICJ Reports 1987, page 110.

Applicability of the Obligation to Arbitrate under Section 21 of the United Nations Headquarters Agreement of 26 June 1947, Order, ICJ Reports 1988, page 6.

Applicability of the Obligation to Arbitrate under Section 21 of the United Nations Headquarters Agreement of 26 June 1947, Advisory Opinion, ICJ Reports 1988, page 42.

Case Concerning Border and Transborder Armed Actions (Nicaragua v. Honduras), Jurisdiction and Admissibility, Judgment, ICJ Reports 1988, page 126.

Case Concerning Elettronica Sicula S.p.A. (ELSI), Judgment, ICJ Reports 1989, page 94.

Case Concerning the Aerial Incident of 3 July 1988 (Islamic Republic of Iran v. United States of America), Order of 13 December 1989, ICJ Reports 1989, page 136.

Certain Phosphate Lands in Nauru (Nauru v. Australia), Preliminary Objections, Judgment, ICJ Reports 1992, page 329.

Case Concerning Maritime Delimitation in the Area between Greenland and Jan Mayen (Denmark v. Norway), Judgment, ICJ Reports 1993, page 38.

BOOKS REVIEWED

Jiménez de Aréchaga, *Voting and the Handling of Disputes in the Security Council;* Yale Law Journal (1954), 63.

Haviland, *The Political Role of the General Assembly;* Yale Law Journal (1954), 63.

United Nations, *Repertory of Practice of United Nations Organs;* Yale Law Journal (1956), 65.

Goodrich, *The United Nations;* American Journal of International Law (1960), 54.

Higgins, *The Development of International Law by the Political Organs of the United Nations;* Yale Law Journal (1966), 75.

Barros, *Betrayal from Within: Joseph Avenol, Secretary-General of the League of Nations, 1933–1940; American Journal of International Law* (1971), 65.

Moore, *The Arab–Israeli Conflict; Virginia Journal of International Law* (1975–1976), 16.

Barros, *Office Without Power: Secretary-General Sir Eric Drummond, 1919–1933; American Journal of International Law* (1980), 74.

Barros, *Trygve Lie and the Cold War; American Journal of International Law* (January 1991), 85.

INDEX

Printed in the United Kingdom
by Lightning Source UK Ltd.
131014UK00001BA/4/P